P. G. WODEHOUSE

Nothing But Wodehouse

EDITED BY

OGDEN NASH

G·C·P

Garden City Publishing Company, Inc.
Garden City, New York

FOREWORD

To inhabit *the same world as Mr. Wodehouse is a high privilege; to inhabit the same volume, even as doorkeeper, is perilous. Not because people may make comparisons, for who is there to compare to him? Every schoolboy knows that no one can hold a candle to P. G. Wodehouse, and not for lack of effort either. The woods are full of ambitious candleholders, but none of them has yet come within scorching distance of the Old Master.*

No, the peril lies in the certainty of going down in history as the man who left out of the Wodehouse Omnibus this tale of Jeeves, and that tale of Stanley Featherstonehaugh Ukridge, such and such a Mulliner feat, and such and such a whopper of the Oldest Member. There are horrid omissions in even this monumental tome, and to you who mourn them, I can only say that this heart breaks with yours, and ask you to consider for a moment the difficulties of the editor who is delegated to select the best from the work of an author who seems always to be at his best.

"Others abide our question. Thou art free." Thus Arnold summarized the Elizabethan Wodehouse, and so our own Wodehouse summarized London's gilded youth's opinion of Archibald Mulliner's imitation of a hen laying an egg. So, too, we might summarize Mr. Wodehouse himself, if we cared to summarize Mr. Wodehouse. Me, I prefer to read him.

OGDEN NASH.

CONTENTS

vii

CONTENTS

CONTENTS

INTRODUCTION

THE WORK of *P. G. Wodehouse needs no intro-duction.*

O. N.

JEEVES

PRESENTING *once more Jeeves, the one and only gentleman's gentleman; and Bertie Wooster, his gilded charge; together with several ingenious stratagems employed by Jeeves on those occasions when Aunt was calling to Aunt like mastodons bellowing across primeval swamps.*

JEEVES EXERTS
THE OLD CEREBELLUM

"MORNING, Jeeves," I said.

"Good morning, sir," said Jeeves.

He put the good old cup of tea softly on the table by my bed, and I took a refreshing sip. Just right, as usual. Not too hot, not too sweet, not to weak, not too strong, not too much milk, and not a drop spilled in the saucer. A most amazing cove, Jeeves. So dashed competent in every respect. I've said it before, and I'll say it again. I mean to say, take just one small instance. Every other valet I've ever had used to barge into my room in the morning while I was still asleep, causing much misery: but Jeeves seems to know when I'm awake by a sort of telepathy. He always floats in with the cup exactly two minutes after I come to iife. Makes a deuce of a lot of difference to a fellow's day.

"How's the weather, Jeeves?"

"Exceptionally clement, sir."

"Anything in the papers?"

"Some slight friction threatening in the Balkans, sir. Otherwise, nothing."

9

"I say, Jeeves, a man I met at the club last night told me to put my shirt on Privateer for the two o'clock race this afternoon. How about it?"

"I should not advocate it, sir. The stable is not sanguine."

That was enough for me. Jeeves knows. How, I couldn't say, but he knows. There was a time when I would laugh lightly, and go ahead, and lose my little all against his advice, but not now.

"Talking of shirts," I said, "have those mauve ones I ordered arrived yet?"

"Yes, sir. I sent them back."

"Sent them back?"

"Yes, sir. They would not have become you."

Well, I must say I'd thought fairly highly of those shirtings, but I bowed to superior knowledge. Weak? I don't know. Most fellows, no doubt, are all for having their valets confine their activities to creasing trousers and what not without trying to run the home; but it's different with Jeeves. Right from the first day he came to me, I have looked on him as a sort of guide, philosopher, and friend.

"Mr. Little rang up on the telephone a few moments ago, sir. I informed him that you were not yet awake."

"Did he leave a message?"

"No, sir. He mentioned that he had a matter of importance to discuss with you, but confided no details."

"Oh, well, I expect I shall be seeing him at the club."

"No doubt, sir."

I wasn't what you might call in a fever of impatience. Bingo Little is a chap I was at school with, and we see a lot of each other still. He's the nephew of old Mortimer Little, who retired from business recently with a goodish pile. (You've probably heard of Little's Liniment—It Limbers Up the Legs.) Bingo biffs about London on a pretty comfortable allowance given him by his uncle, and leads on the whole a fairly unclouded life. It wasn't likely that anything which he described as a matter of importance would turn out to be really so frightfully important. I took it that he had discovered some new brand of cigarette which he wanted me to try, or something like that, and didn't spoil my breakfast by worrying.

After breakfast I lit a cigarette and went to the open window to inspect the day. It certainly was one of the best and brightest.

"Jeeves," I said.

"Sir?" said Jeeves. He had been clearing away the breakfast things, but at the sound of the young master's voice cheesed it courteously.

"You were absolutely right about the weather. It is a juicy morning."

"Decidedly, sir."

"Spring and all that."

"Yes, sir."

"In the spring, Jeeves, a livelier iris gleams upon the burnished dove."

"So I have been informed, sir."

"Right ho! Then bring me my whangee, my yellowest shoes, and the old green Homburg. I'm going into the Park to do pastoral dances."

I don't know if you know that sort of feeling you get on these days round about the end of April and the beginning of May, when the sky's a light blue, with cotton-wool clouds, and there's a bit of a breeze blowing from the west? Kind of uplifted feeling. Romantic, if you know what I mean. I'm not much of a ladies' man, but on this particular morning it seemed to me that what I really wanted was some charming girl to buzz up and ask me to save her from assassins or something. So that it was a bit of an anti-climax when I merely ran into young Bingo Little, looking perfectly foul in a crimson satin tie decorated with horseshoes.

"Hallo, Bertie," said Bingo.

"My God, man!" I gargled. "The cravat! The gent's neckwear! Why? For what reason?"

"Oh, the tie?" He blushed. "I—er—I was given it."

He seemed embarrassed, so I dropped the subject. We toddled along a bit, and sat down on a couple of chairs by the Serpentine.

"Jeeves tells me you want to talk to me about something," I said.

"Eh?" said Bingo, with a start. "Oh yes, yes. Yes."

I waited for him to unleash the topic of the day, but he didn't seem to want to get going. Conversation languished. He stared straight ahead of him in a glassy sort of manner.

"I say, Bertie," he said, after a pause of about an hour and a quarter.

"Hallo!"

"Do you like the name Mabel?"

"No."

"No?"

"No."

"You don't think there's a kind of music in the word, like the wind rustling gently through the tree-tops?"

"No."

He seemed disappointed for a moment; then cheered up.

"Of course, you wouldn't. You always were a fat-headed worm without any soul, weren't you?"

"Just as you say. Who is she? Tell me all."

For I realised now that poor old Bingo was going through it once again. Ever since I have known him—and we were at school together—he has been perpetually falling in love with someone, generally in the spring, which seems to act on him like magic. At school he had the finest collection of actresses' photographs of anyone of his time; and at Oxford his romantic nature was a byword.

"You'd better come along and meet her at lunch," he said, looking at his watch.

"A ripe suggestion," I said. "Where are you meeting her? At the Ritz?"

"Near the Ritz."

He was geographically accurate. About fifty yards east of the Ritz there is one of those blighted tea-and-bun shops you see dotted about all over London, and into this, if you'll believe me, young Bingo dived like a homing rabbit; and before I had time to say a word we were wedged in at a table, on the brink of a silent pool of coffee left there by an early luncher.

I'm bound to say I couldn't quite follow the development of the scenario. Bingo, while not absolutely rolling in the stuff, has always had a fair amount of the ready. Apart from what he got from his uncle, I knew that he had finished up the jumping season well on the right side of the ledger. Why, then, was he lunching the girl at this God-forsaken eatery? It couldn't be because he was hard up.

Just then the waitress arrived. Rather a pretty girl.

"Aren't we going to wait——?" I started to say to Bingo, thinking it somewhat thick that, in addition to asking a girl to lunch with him in a place like this, he should fling himself on the foodstuffs before she turned up, when I caught sight of his face, and stopped.

The man was goggling. His entire map was suffused with a rich blush. He looked like the Soul's Awakening done in pink.

"Hallo, Mabel!" he said, with a sort of gulp.

"Hallo!" said the girl.

"Mabel," said Bingo, "this is Bertie Wooster, a pal of mine."

"Pleased to meet you," she said. "Nice morning."

"Fine," I said.

"You see I'm wearing the tie," said Bingo.

"It suits you beautiful," said the girl.

Personally, if anyone had told me that a tie like

that suited me, I should have risen and struck them
on the mazzard, regardless of their age and sex; but
poor old Bingo simply got all flustered with gratification, and smirked in the most gruesome manner.

"Well, what's it going to be to-day?" asked the girl,
introducing the business touch into the conversation.

Bingo studied the menu devoutly.

"I'll have a cup of cocoa, cold veal and ham pie,
slice of fruit cake, and a macaroon. Same for you,
Bertie?"

I gazed at the man, revolted. That he could have
been a pal of mine all these years and think me capable
of insulting the old tum with this sort of stuff cut me
to the quick.

"Or how about a bit of hot steak-pudding, with a
sparkling limado to wash it down?" said Bingo.

You know, the way love can change a fellow is really
frightful to contemplate. This chappie before me,
who spoke in that absolutely careless way of macaroons
and limado, was the man I had seen in happier days
telling the head-waiter at Claridge's exactly how he
wanted the *chef* to prepare the *sole frite au gourmet
aux champignons,* and saying he would jolly well
sling it back if it wasn't just right. Ghastly! Ghastly!

A roll and butter and a small coffee seemed the only
things on the list that hadn't been specially prepared
by the nastier-minded members of the Borgia family
for people they had a particular grudge against, so I
chose them, and Mabel hopped it.

"Well?" said Bingo rapturously.

I took it that he wanted my opinion of the female poisoner who had just left us.

"Very nice," I said.

He seemed dissatisfied.

"You don't think she's the most wonderful girl you ever saw?" he said wistfully.

"Oh, absolutely!" I said, to appease the blighter. "Where did you meet her?"

"At a subscription dance at Camberwell."

"What on earth were you doing at a subscription dance at Camberwell?"

"Your man Jeeves asked me if I would buy a couple of tickets. It was in aid of some charity or other."

"Jeeves? I didn't know he went in for that sort of thing."

"Well, I suppose he has to relax a bit every now and then. Anyway, he was there, swinging a dashed efficient shoe. I hadn't meant to go at first, but I turned up for a lark. Oh, Bertie, think what I might have missed!"

"What might you have missed?" I asked, the old lemon being slightly clouded.

"Mabel, you chump. If I hadn't gone I shouldn't have met Mabel."

"Oh, ah!"

At this point Bingo fell into a species of trance, and only came out of it to wrap himself round the pie and macaroon.

"Bertie," he said, "I want your advice."

"Carry on."

"At least, not your advice, because that wouldn't

be much good to anybody. I mean, you're a pretty consummate old ass, aren't you? Not that I want to hurt your feelings, of course."

"No, no, I see that."

"What I wish you would do is to put the whole thing to that fellow Jeeves of yours, and see what he suggests. You've often told me that he has helped other pals of yours out of messes. From what you tell me, he's by way of being the brains of the family."

"He's never let me down yet."

"Then put my case to him."

"What case?"

"My problem."

"What problem?"

"Why, you poor fish, my uncle, of course. What do you think my uncle's going to say to all this? If I sprang it on him cold, he'd tie himself in knots or the hearthrug."

"One of these emotional johnnies, eh?"

"Somehow or other his mind has got to be prepared to receive the news. But how?"

"Ah!"

"That's a lot of help, that 'ah'! You see, I'm pretty well dependent on the old boy. If he cut off my allowance, I should be very much in the soup. So you put the whole binge to Jeeves and see if he can't scare up a happy ending somehow. Tell him my future is in his hands, and that, if the wedding bells ring out, he can rely on me, even unto half my kingdom. Well, call it ten quid. Jeeves would exert himself with ten quid on the horizon, what?"

"Undoubtedly," I said.

I wasn't in the least surprised at Bingo wanting to lug Jeeves into his private affairs like this. It was the first thing I would have thought of doing myself if I had been in any hole of any description. As I have frequently had occasion to observe, he is a bird of the ripest intellect, full of bright ideas. If anybody could fix things for poor old Bingo, he could.

I stated the case to him that night after dinner.

"Jeeves."

"Sir?"

"Are you busy just now?"

"No, sir."

"I mean, not doing anything in particular?"

"No, sir. It is my practice at this hour to read some improving book; but, if you desire my services, this can easily be postponed, or, indeed, abandoned altogether."

"Well, I want your advice. It's about Mr. Little."

"Young Mr. Little, sir, or the elder Mr. Little, his uncle, who lives in Pounceby Gardens?"

Jeeves seemed to know everything. Most amazing thing. I'd been pally with Bingo practically all my life, and yet I didn't remember ever having heard that his uncle lived anywhere in particular.

"How did you know he lived in Pounceby Gardens?" I said.

"I am on terms of some intimacy with the elder Mr. Little's cook, sir. In fact, there is an understanding."

I'm bound to say that this gave me a bit of a start.

Somehow I'd never thought of Jeeves going in for that sort of thing.

"Do you mean you're engaged?"

"It may be said to amount to that, sir."

"Well, well!"

"She is a remarkably excellent cook, sir," said Jeeves, as though he felt called on to give some explanation. "What was it you wished to ask me about Mr. Little?"

I sprang the details on him.

"And that's how the matter stands, Jeeves," I said. "I think we ought to rally round a trifle and help poor old Bingo put the thing through. Tell me about old Mr. Little. What sort of a chap is he?"

"A somewhat curious character, sir. Since retiring from business he has become a great recluse, and now devotes himself almost entirely to the pleasures of the table."

"Greedy hog, you mean?"

"I would not, perhaps, take the liberty of describing him in precisely those terms, sir. He is what is usually called a gourmet. Very particular about what he eats, and for that reason sets a high value on Miss Watson's services."

"The cook?"

"Yes, sir."

"Well, it looks to me as though our best plan would be to shoot young Bingo in on him after dinner one night. Melting mood, I mean to say, and all that."

"The difficulty is, sir, that at the moment Mr. Little is on a diet, owing to an attack of gout."

"Things begin to look wobbly."

"No, sir, I fancy that the elder Mr. Little's misfortune may be turned to the younger Mr. Little's advantage. I was speaking only the other day to Mr. Little's valet, and he was telling me that it has become his principal duty to read to Mr. Little in the evenings. If I were in your place, sir, I should send young Mr. Little to read to his uncle."

"Nephew's devotion, you mean? Old man touched by kindly action, what?"

"Partly that, sir. But I would rely more on young Mr. Little's choice of literature."

"That's no good. Jolly old Bingo has a kind face, but when it comes to literature he stops at the *Sporting Times.*"

"That difficulty may be overcome. I would be happy to select books for Mr. Little to read. Perhaps I might explain my idea further?"

"I can't say I quite grasp it yet."

"The method which I advocate is what, I believe, the advertisers call Direct Suggestion, sir, consisting as it does of driving an idea home by constant repetition. You may have had experience of the system?"

"You mean they keep on telling you that some soap or other is the best, and after a bit you come under the influence and charge round the corner and buy a cake?"

"Exactly, sir. The same method was the basis of all the most valuable propaganda during the recent war. I see no reason why it should not be adopted to bring about the desired result with regard to the subject's views on class distinctions. If young Mr. Little were to read day after day to his uncle a series of narratives in which marriage with young persons of an inferior social status was held up as both feasible and admirable, I fancy it would prepare the elder Mr. Little's mind for the reception of the information that his nephew wishes to marry a waitress in a tea-shop."

"*Are* there any books of that sort nowadays? The only ones I ever see mentioned in the papers are about married couples who find life grey, and can't stick each other at any price."

"Yes, sir, there are a great many, neglected by the reviewers but widely read. You have never encountered 'All for Love," by Rosie M. Banks?"

"No."

"Nor 'A Red, Red Summer Rose,' by the same author?"

"No."

"I have an aunt, sir, who owns an almost complete set of Rosie M. Banks'. I could easily borrow as many volumes as young Mr. Little might require. They make very light, attractive reading."

"Well, it's worth trying."

"I should certainly recommend the scheme, sir."

"All right, then. Toddle round to your aunt's to-morrow and grab a couple of the fruitiest. We can but have a dash at it."

"Precisely, sir."

NO WEDDING BELLS FOR BINGO

BINGO reported three days later that Rosie M. Banks was the goods and beyond a question the stuff to give the troops. Old Little had jibbed somewhat at first at the proposed change of literary diet, he not being much of a lad for fiction and having stuck hitherto exclusively to the heavier monthly reviews; but Bingo had got chapter one of "All for Love" past his guard before he knew what was happening, and after that there was nothing to it. Since then they had finished "A Red, Red Summer Rose," "Madcap Myrtle" and "Only a Factory Girl," and were halfway through "The Courtship of Lord Strathmorlick."

Bingo told me all this in a husky voice over an egg beaten up in sherry. The only blot on the thing from his point of view was that it wasn't doing a bit of good to the old vocal cords, which were beginning to show signs of cracking under the strain. He had been looking his symptoms up in a medical dictionary, and he thought he had got "clergyman's throat." But against this you had to set the fact that he was making an undoubted hit in the right quarter, and also that after the evening's reading he always stayed on to dinner; and, from what he told me, the dinners turned out by old Little's cook had to be tasted to be believed. There were tears in the old blighter's eyes as he got on the subject of the clear soup. I suppose to a fellow who for weeks had been tackling macaroons and limado it must have been like Heaven.

Old Little wasn't able to give any practical assistance at these banquets, but Bingo said that he came to the table and had his whack of arrowroot, and sniffed the dishes, and told stories of *entrées* he had had in the past, and sketched out scenarios of what he was going to do to the bill of fare in the future, when the doctor put him in shape; so I suppose he enjoyed himself, too, in a way. Anyhow, things seemed to be buzzing along quite satisfactorily, and Bingo said he had got an idea which, he thought, was going to clinch the thing. He wouldn't tell me what it was, but he said it was a pippin.

"We make progress, Jeeves," I said.

"That is very satisfactory, sir."

"Mr. Little tells me that when he came to the big scene in 'Only a Factory Girl,' his uncle gulped like a stricken bull-pup."

"Indeed, sir?"

"Where Lord Claude takes the girl in his arms, you know, and says——"

"I am familiar with the passage, sir. It is distinctly moving. It was a great favourite of my aunt's."

"I think we're on the right track."

"It would seem so, sir."

"In fact, this looks like being another of your successes. I've always said, and I always shall say, that for sheer brain, Jeeves, you stand alone. All the other great thinkers of the age are simply in the crowd, watching you go by."

"Thank you very much, sir. I endeavour to give satisfaction."

About a week after this, Bingo blew in with the news that his uncle's gout had ceased to trouble him, and that on the morrow he would be back at the old stand working away with knife and fork as before.

"And, by the way," said Bingo, "he wants you to 'unch with him to-morrow."

"Me? Why me? He doesn't know I exist."

"Oh, yes, he does. I've told him about you."

"What have you told him?"

"Oh, various things. Anyhow, he wants to meet you. And take my tip, laddie—you go! I should think lunch to-morrow would be something special."

I don't know why it was, but even then it struck me that there was something dashed odd—almost sinister, if you know what I mean—about young Bingo's manner. The old egg had the air of one who has something up his sleeve.

"There is more in this than meets the eye," I said. "Why should your uncle ask a fellow to lunch whom he's never seen?"

"My dear old fathead, haven't I just said that I've been telling him all about you—that you're my best pal—at school together, and all that sort of thing?"

"But even then—and another thing. Why are you so dashed keen on my going?"

Bingo hesitated for a moment.

"Well, I told you I'd got an idea. This is it. I want you to spring the news on him. I haven't the nerve myself."

"What! I'm hanged if I do!"

"And you call yourself a pal of mine!"

"Yes, I know; but there are limits."

"Bertie," said Bingo reproachfully, "I saved your life once."

"When?"

"Didn't I? It must have been some other fellow, then. Well, anyway, we were boys together and all that. You can't let me down."

"Oh, all right," I said. "But, when you say you haven't nerve enough for any dashed thing in the world, you misjudge yourself. A fellow who——"

"Cheerio!" said young Bingo. "One-thirty to-morrow. Don't be late."

* * * * *

I'm bound to say that the more I contemplated the binge, the less I liked it. It was all very well for Bingo to say that I was slated for a magnificent lunch; but what good is the best possible lunch to a fellow if he is slung out into the street on his ear during the soup course? However, the word of a Wooster is his bond and all that sort of rot, so at one-thirty next day I tottered up the steps of No. 16, Pounceby Gardens, and punched the bell. And half a minute later I was up in the drawing-room, shaking hands with the fattest man I have ever seen in my life.

The motto of the Little family was evidently "variety." Young Bingo is long and thin and hasn't

had a superfluous ounce on him since we first met;
but the uncle restored the average and a bit over. The
hand which grasped mine wrapped it round and
enfolded it till I began to wonder if I'd ever get it out
without excavating machinery.

"Mr. Wooster, I am gratified—I am proud—I am
honoured."

It seemed to me that young Bingo must have boosted
me to some purpose.

"Oh, ah!" I said.

He stepped back a bit, still hanging on to the good
right hand.

"You are very young to have accomplished so
much!"

I couldn't follow the train of thought. The family,
especially my Aunt Agatha, who has savaged me incessantly from childhood up, have always rather made
a point of the fact that mine is a wasted life, and that,
since I won the prize at my first school for the best
collection of wild flowers made during the summer
holidays, I haven't done a dam' thing to land me on
the nation's scro'l of fame. I was wondering if he
couldn't have got me mixed up with someone else,
when the telephone-bell rang outside in the hall, and
the maid came in to say that I was wanted. I buzzed
down, and found it was young Bingo.

"Hallo!" said young Bingo. "So you've got there?
Good man! I knew I could rely on you. I say, old
crumpet, did my uncle seem pleased to see you?"

"Absolutely all over me. I can't make it out."

"Oh, that's all right. I just rang up to explain.

The fact is, old man, I know you won't mind, but I told him that you were the author of those books I've been reading to him."

"What!"

"Yes, I said that 'Rosie M. Banks' was your pen-name, and you didn't want it generally known, because you were a modest, retiring sort of chap. He'll listen to you now. Absolutely hang on your words. A brightish idea, what? I doubt if Jeeves in person could have thought up a better one than that. Well, pitch it strong, old lad, and keep steadily before you the fact that I must have my allowance raised. I can't possibly marry on what I've got now. If this film is to end with the slow fade-out on the embrace, at least double is indicated. Well, that's that. Cheerio!"

And he rang off. At that moment the gong sounded, and the genial host came tumbling downstairs like the delivery of a ton of coals.

*   *   *   *   *

I always look back to that lunch with a sort of aching regret. It was the lunch of a lifetime, and I wasn't in a fit state to appreciate it. Subconsciously, if you know what I mean, I could see it was pretty special, but I had got the wind up to such a frightful extent over the ghastly situation in which young Bingo had landed me that its deeper meaning never really penetrated. Most of the time I might have been eating sawdust for all the good it did me.

Old Little struck the literary note right from the start.

"My nephew has probably told you that I have been

making a close study of your books of late?" he began.

"Yes. He did mention it. How—er—how did you like the bally things?"

He gazed reverently at me.

"Mr. Wooster, I am not ashamed to say that the tears came into my eyes as I listened to them. It amazes me that a man as young as you can have been able to plumb human nature so surely to its depths; to play with so unerring a hand on the quivering heart-strings of your reader; to write novels so true, so human, so moving, so vital!"

"Oh, it's just a knack," I said.

The good old persp. was bedewing my forehead by this time in a pretty lavish manner. I don't know when I've been so rattled.

"Do you find the room a trifle warm?"

"Oh, no, no, rather not. Just right."

"Then it's the pepper. If my cook has a fault—which I am not prepared to admit—it is that she is inclined to stress the pepper a trifle in her made dishes. By the way, do you like her cooking?"

I was so relieved that we had got off the subject of my literary output that I shouted approval in a ringing baritone.

"I am delighted to hear it, Mr. Wooster. I may be prejudiced, but to my mind that woman is a genius."

"Absolutely!" I said.

"She has been with me seven years, and in all that time I have not known her guilty of a single lapse from the highest standard. Except once, in the winter of 1917, when a purist might have condemned a certain mayonnaise of hers as lacking in creaminess. But one must make allowances. There had been several air-raids about that time, and no doubt the poor woman was shaken. But nothing is perfect in this world, Mr. Wooster, and I have had my cross to bear. For seven years I have lived in constant apprehension lest some evilly-disposed person might lure her from my employment. To my certain knowledge she has received offers, lucrative offers, to accept service elsewhere. You may judge of my dismay, Mr. Wooster, when only this morning the bolt fell. She gave notice!"

"Good Lord!"

"Your consternation does credit, if I may say so, to the heart of the author of 'A Red, Red Summer Rose.' But I am thankful to say the worst has not happened. The matter has been adjusted. Jane is not leaving me."

"Good egg!"

"Good egg, indeed—though the expression is not familiar to me. I do not remember having come across it in your books. And, speaking of your books, may I say that what has impressed me about them even more than the moving poignancy of the actual narrative, is your philosophy of life. If there were more men like you, Mr. Wooster, London would be a better place."

This was dead opposite to my Aunt Agatha's philosophy of life, she having always rather given me to understand that it is the presence in it of chappies like me that makes London more or less of a plague spot; but I let it go.

"Let me tell you, Mr. Wooster, that I appreciate your splendid defiance of the outworn fetishes of a purblind social system. I appreciate it! *You* are big enough to see that rank is but the guinea stamp and that, in the magnificent words of Lord Bletchmore in 'Only a Factory Girl,' 'Be her origin ne'er so humble, a good woman is the equal of the finest lady on earth!'"

I sat up.

"I say! Do you think that?"

"I do, Mr. Wooster. I am ashamed to say that there was a time when I was like other men, a slave to the idiotic convention which we call Class Distinction. But, since I read your books——"

I might have known it. Jeeves had done it again.

"You think it's all right for a chappie in what you might call a certain social position to marry a girl of what you might describe as the lower classes?"

"Most assuredly I do, Mr. Wooster."

I took a deep breath, and slipped him the good news.

"Young Bingo—your nephew, you know—wants to marry a waitress," I said.

"I honour him for it," said old Little.

"You don't object?"

"On the contrary."

I took another deep breath and shifted to the sordid side of the business.

"I hope you won't think I'm butting in, don't you know," I said, "but—er—well, how about it?"

"I fear I do not quite follow you."

"Well, I mean to say, his allowance and all that. The money you're good enough to give him. He was rather hoping that you might see your way to jerking up the total a bit."

Old Little shook his head regretfully.

"I fear that can hardly be managed. You see, a man in my position is compelled to save every penny. I will gladly continue my nephew's existing allowance, but beyond that I cannot go. It would not be fair to my wife."

"What! But you're not married?"

"Not yet. But I propose to enter upon that holy state almost immediately. The lady who for years has cooked so well for me honoured me by accepting my hand this very morning." A cold gleam of triumph came into his eye. "Now let 'em try to get her away from me!" he muttered, defiantly.

   * * * * *

"Young Mr. Little has been trying frequently during the afternoon to reach you on the telephone, sir," said Jeeves that night, when I got home.

"I'll bet he has," I said. I had sent poor old Bingo an outline of the situation by messenger-boy shortly after lunch.

"He seemed a trifle agitated."

"I don't wonder. Jeeves," I said, "so brace up and bite the bullet. I'm afraid I've bad news for you."

"That scheme of yours—reading those books to old Mr. Little and all that—has blown out a fuse."

"They did not soften him?"

"They did. That's the whole bally trouble. Jeeves,

I'm sorry to say that *fiancée* of yours—Miss Watson, you know—the cook, you know—well, the long and the short of it is that she's chosen riches instead of honest worth, if you know what I mean."

"Sir?"

"She's handed you the mitten and gone and got engaged to old Mr. Little!"

"Indeed, sir?"

"You don't seem much upset."

"That fact is, sir, I had anticipated some such outcome."

I stared at him. "Then what on earth did you suggest the scheme for?"

"To tell you the truth, sir, I was not wholly averse from a severance of my relations with Miss Watson. In fact, I greatly desired it. I respect Miss Watson exceedingly, but I have seen for a long time that we were not suited. Now, the *other* young person with whom I have an understanding——"

"Great Scott, Jeeves! There isn't another?"

"Yes, sir."

"How long has this been going on?"

"For some weeks, sir. I was greatly attracted by her when I first met her at a subscription dance at Camberwell."

"My sainted aunt! Not——"

Jeeves inclined his head gravely.

"Yes, sir. By an odd coincidence it is the same young person that young Mr. Little—— I have placed the cigarettes on the small table. Good night, sir."

INTRODUCING
CLAUDE AND EUSTACE

THE blow fell precisely at one forty-five (summer time). Spenser, Aunt Agatha's butler, was offering me the fried potatoes at the moment, and such was my emotion that I lofted six of them on to the sideboard with the spoon. Shaken to the core, if you know what I mean.

Mark you, I was in a pretty enfeebled condition already. I had been engaged to Honoria Glossop nearly two weeks, and during all that time not a day had passed without her putting in some heavy work in the direction of what Aunt Agatha had called "moulding" me. I had read solid literature till my eyes bubbled; we had legged it together through miles of picture-galleries; and I had been compelled to undergo classical concerts to an extent you would hardly believe. All in all, therefore, I was in no fit state to receive shocks, especially shocks like this. Honoria had lugged me round to lunch at Aunt Agatha's, and I had just been saying to myself, "Death, where is thy jolly old sting?" when she hove the bomb.

"Bertie," she said, suddenly, as if she had just remembered it, "what is the name of that man of yours —your valet?"

"Eh? Oh, Jeeves."

"I think he's a bad influence for you," said Honoria. "When we are married, you must get rid of Jeeves."

It was at this point that I jerked the spoon and sent six of the best and crispest sailing on to the sideboard, with Spenser gambolling after them like a dignified old retriever.

"Get rid of Jeeves!" I gasped.

"Yes. I don't like him."

"*I* don't like him," said Aunt Agatha.

"But I can't. I mean—why, I couldn't carry on for a day without Jeeves."

"You will have to," said Honoria. "I don't like him at all."

"*I* don't like him at all," said Aunt Agatha. "I never did."

Ghastly, what? I'd always had an idea that marriage was a bit of a wash-out, but I'd never dreamed that it demanded such frightful sacrifices from a fellow. I passed the rest of the meal in a sort of stupor.

The scheme had been, if I remember, that after lunch I should go off and caddy for Honoria on a shopping tour down Regent Street; but when she got up and started collecting me and the rest of her things, Aunt Agatha stopped her.

"You run along, dear," she said. "I want to say a few words to Bertie."

So Honoria legged it, and Aunt Agatha drew up her chair and started in.

"Bertie," she said, "dear Honoria does not know it, but a little difficulty has arisen about your marriage."

"By Jove! not really?" I said, hope starting to dawn.

"Oh, it's nothing at all, of course. It is only a little exasperating. The fact is, Sir Roderick is being rather troublesome."

"Thinks I'm not a good bet? Wants to scratch the fixture? Well, perhaps he's right."

"Pray do not be so absurd, Bertie. It is nothing so serious as that. But the nature of Sir Roderick's profession unfortunately makes him—over-cautious."

I didn't get it.

"Over-cautious?"

"Yes. I suppose it is inevitable. A nerve specialist with his extensive practice can hardly help taking a rather warped view of humanity."

I got what she was driving at now. Sir Roderick Glossop, Honoria's father, is always called a nerve specialist, because it sounds better, but everybody knows that he's really a sort of janitor to the looney-bin. I mean to say, when your uncle the Duke begins to feel the strain a bit and you find him in the blue drawing-room sticking straws in his hair, old Glossop 's the first person you send for. He toddles round, gives the patient the once-over, talks about over-excited nervous systems, and recommends complete rest and seclusion and all that sort of thing. Practically every posh family in the country has called him in at one time or another, and I suppose that, being in that position—I mean constantly having to sit on people's heads while their nearest and dearest phone to the asylum to send round the wagon—does tend to make a chappie take what you might call a warped view of humanity.

"You mean he thinks I may be a looney, and he doesn't want a looney son-in-law?" I said.

Aunt Agatha seemed rather peeved than otherwise at my ready intelligence.

"Of course, he does not think anything so ridiculous. I told you he was simply exceedingly cautious. He wants to satisfy himself that you are perfectly normal." Here she paused, for Spenser had come in with the coffee. When he had gone, she went on: "He appears to have got hold of some extraordinary story about your having pushed his son Oswald into the lake at Ditteredge Hall. Incredible, of course. Even you would hardly do a thing like that."

"Well, I did sort of lean against him, you know, and he shot off the bridge."

"Oswald definitely accuses you of having pushed him into the water. That has disturbed Sir Roderick, and unfortunately it has caused him to make inquiries, and he has heard about your poor Uncle Henry."

She eyed me with a good deal of solemnity, and I took a grave sip of coffee. We were peeping into the family cupboard and having a look at the good old skeleton. My late Uncle Henry, you see, was by way of being the blot on the Wooster escutcheon. An extremely decent chappie personally, and one who had always endeared himself to me by tipping me with considerable lavishness when I was at school; but there's no doubt he did at times do rather rummy things, notably keeping eleven pet rabbits in his bedroom; and I suppose a purist might have considered him more or less off his onion. In fact, to be perfectly frank, he wound up his career, happy to the last and completely surrounded by rabbits, in some sort of a home.

"It is very absurd, of course," continued Aunt Agatha. "If any of the family had inherited poor Henry's eccentricity—and it was nothing more—it would have been Claude and Eustace, and there could not be two brighter boys."

Claude and Eustice were twins, and had been kids at school with me in my last summer term. Casting my mind back, it seemed to me that "bright" just about described them. The whole of that term, as I remembered it, had been spent in getting them out of a series of frightul rows.

"Look how well they are doing at Oxford. Your Aunt Emily had a letter from Claude only the other day saying that they hoped to be elected shortly to a very important college club, called The Seekers."

"Seekers?" I couldn't recall any club of the name in my time at Oxford. "What do they seek?"

"Claude did not say. Truth or knowledge, I should imagine. It is evidently a very desirable club to belong to, for Claude added that Lord Rainsby, the Earl of Datchet's son, was one of his fellow-candidates. However, we are wandering from the point, which is that Sir Roderick wants to have a quiet talk with you quite alone. Now I rely on you, Bertie, to be—I won't say intelligent, but at least sensible. Don't giggle nervously: try to keep that horrible glassy expression out of your eyes: don't yawn or fidget; and remember that Sir Roderick is the president of the West London branch of the anti-gambling league, so please do not talk about horse-racing. He will lunch with you at your flat to-morrow at one-thirty. Please remember that he drinks no wine, strongly disapproves of smoking, and can only eat the simplest food, owing to an impaired digestion. Do not offer him coffee, for he considers it the root of half the nerve-trouble in the world."

"I should think a dog-biscuit and a glass of water would about meet the case, what?"

"Bertie!"

"Oh, all right. Merely persiflage."

"Now it is precisely that sort of idiotic remark that would be calculated to arouse Sir Roderick's worst suspicions. Do please try to refrain from any misguided flippancy when you are with him. He is a very serious-minded man . . . Are you going? Well, please remember all I have said. I rely on you, and, if anything goes wrong, I shall never forgive you."

"Right-o!" I said.

And so home, with a jolly day to look forward to.

*   *   *   *   *

I breakfasted pretty late next morning and went for a stroll afterwards. It seemed to me that anything I could do to clear the old lemon ought to be done, and a bit of fresh air generally relieves that rather foggy feeling that comes over a fellow early in the day. I had taken a stroll in the park, and got back as far as Hyde Park Corner, when some blighter sloshed me between the shoulder-blades. It was young Eustace, my cousin. He was arm-in-arm with two other fellows, the one on the outside being my cousin Claude and the one in the middle a pink-faced chappie with light hair and an apologetic sort of look.

"Bertie, old egg!" said young Eustace affably.

"Hallo!" I said, not frightfully chirpily.

"Fancy running into you, the one man in London who can support us in the style we are accustomed to! By the way, you've never met old Dog-Face, have you? Dog-Face, this is my cousin Bertie. Lord Rainsby— Mr. Wooster. We've just been round to your flat, Bertie. Bitterly disappointed that you were out, but were hospitably entertained by old Jeeves. That man's a corker, Bertie. Stick to him."

"What are you doing in London?" I asked.

"Oh, buzzing round. We're just up for the day. Flying visit, strictly unofficial. We oil back on the three-ten. And now, touching that lunch you very decently volunteered to stand us, which shall it be? Ritz? Savoy? Carlton? Or, if you're a member of Ciro's or the Embassy, that would do just as well."

"I can't give you lunch. I've got an engagement myself. And, by Jove," I said, taking a look at my watch, "I'm late." I hailed a taxi. "Sorry."

"As man to man, then," said Eustace, "lend us a fiver."

I hadn't time to stop and argue. I unbelted the fiver and hopped into the cab. It was twenty to two when I got to the flat. I bounded into the sitting-room, but it was empty.

Jeeves shimmied in.

"Sir Roderick has not yet arrived, sir."

"Good egg!" I said. "I thought I should find him

smashing up the furniture." My experience is that the less you want a fellow, the more punctual he's bound to be, and I had had a vision of the old lad pacing the rug in my sitting-room, saying, "He cometh not!" and generally hotting up. "Is everything in order?"

"I fancy you will find the arrangements quite satisfactory, sir."

"What are you giving us?"

"Cold consommé, a cutlet, and a savoury, sir. With lemon-squash, iced."

"Well, I don't see how that can hurt him. Don't go getting carried away by the excitement of the thing and start bringing in coffee."

"No, sir."

"And don't let your eyes get glassy, because, if you do, you're apt to find yourself in a padded cell before you know where you are."

"Very good, sir."

There was a ring at the bell.

"Stand by, Jeeves," I said. "We're off!"

SIR RODERICK COMES TO LUNCH

I HAD met Sir Roderick Glossop before, of course, but only when I was with Honoria; and there is something about Honoria which makes almost anybody you meet in the same room seem sort of under-sized and trivial by comparison. I had never realised till this moment what an extraordinarily formidable old bird he was. He had a pair of shaggy eyebrows which gave his eyes a piercing look which was not at all the sort of thing a fellow wanted to encounter on an empty stomach. He was fairly tall and fairly broad, and he had the most enormous head, with practically no hair on it, which made it seem bigger and much more like the dome of St. Paul's. I suppose he must have taken about a nine or something in hats. Shows what a rotten thing it is to let your brain develop too much.

"What ho! What ho! What ho!" I said, trying to strike the genial note, and then had a sudden feeling that that was just the sort of thing I had been warned not to say. Dashed difficult it is to start things going properly on an occasion like this. A fellow living in a London flat is so handicapped. I mean to say, if I had been the young squire greeting the visitor in the country, I could have said, "Welcome to Meadowsweet Hall!" or something zippy like that. It sounds silly to say "Welcome to Number 6A, Crichton Mansions, Berkeley Street, W."

"I am afraid I am a little late," he said, as we sat down. "I was detained at my club by Lord Alastair Hungerford, the Duke of Ramfurline's son. His Grace, he informed me, had exhibited a renewal of the symptoms which have been causing the family so much concern. I could not leave him immediately. Hence my unpunctuality, which I trust has not discommoded you."

"Oh, not at all. So the Duke is off his rocker, what?"

"The expression which you use is not precisely the one I should have employed myself with reference to the head of perhaps the noblest family in England, but there is no doubt that cerebral excitement does, as you suggest, exist in no small degree." He sighed as well as he could with his mouth full of cutlet. "A profession like mine is a great strain, a great strain."

"Must be."

"Sometimes I am appalled at what I see around me." He stopped suddenly and sort of stiffened. "Do you keep a cat, Mr. Wooster?"

"Eh? What? Cat? No, no cat."

"I was conscious of a distinct impression that I had heard a cat mewing either in the room or very near to where we are sitting."

"Probably a taxi or something in the street."

"I fear I do not follow you."

"I mean to say, taxis squawk, you know. Rather like cats in a sort of way."

"I had not observed the resemblance," he said, rather coldly.

"Have some lemon-squash," I said. The conversation seemed to be getting rather difficult.

"Thank you. Half a glassful, if I may." The hell-brew appeared to buck him up, for he resumed in a slightly more pally manner. "I have a particular dislike for cats. But I was saying—— Oh, yes. Sometimes I am positively appalled at what I see around me. It is not only the cases which come under my professional notice, painful as many of those are. It is what I see as I go about London. Sometimes it seems to me that the whole world is mentally unbalanced. This very morning, for example, a most singular and distressing occurrence took place as I was driving from my house to the club. The day being clement, I had instructed my chauffeur to open my landaulette, and I was leaning back, deriving no little pleasure from the sunshine, when our progress was arrested in the middle of the thoroughfare by one of those blocks in the traffic which are inevitable in so congested a system as that of London."

I suppose I had been letting my mind wander a bit, for when he stopped and took a sip of lemon-squash I had a feeling that I was listening to a lecture and was expected to say something.

"Hear, hear!" I said.

"I beg your pardon?"

"Nothing, nothing. You were saying——"

"The vehicles proceeding in the opposite direction had also been temporarily arrested, but after a moment they were permitted to proceed. I had fallen into a meditation, when suddenly the most extraordinary thing took place. My hat was snatched abruptly from my head! And as I looked back I perceived it being waved in a kind of feverish triumph from the interior of a taxicab, which, even as I looked, disappeared through a gap in the traffic and was lost to sight."

I didn't laugh, but I distinctly heard a couple of my floating ribs part from their moorings under the strain.

"Must have been meant for a practical joke," I said. "What?"

This suggestion didn't seem to please the old boy.

"I trust," he said, "I am not deficient in an appreciation of the humorous, but I confess that I am at a loss to detect anything akin to pleasantry in the outrage. The action was beyond all question that of a mentally unbalanced subject. These mental lesions may express themselves in almost any form. The Duke of Ramfurline, to whom I had occasion to allude just now, is under the impression—this is in the strictest confidence —that he is a canary; and his seizure to-day, which so perturbed Lord Alastair, was due to the fact that a careless footman had neglected to bring him his morning lump of sugar. Cases are common, again, of men waylaying women and cutting off portions of their hair. It is from a branch of this latter form of mania that I should be disposed to imagine that my assailant was suffering. I can only trust that he will be placed under proper control before he—— Mr. Wooster, there *is* a cat close at hand! It is *not* in the street! The mewing appears to come from the adjoining room."

This time I had to admit there was no doubt about it. There was a distinct sound of mewing coming from the next room. I punched the bell for Jeeves, who drifted in and stood waiting with an air of respectful devotion.

"Sir?"

"Oh, Jeeves," I said. "Cats! What about it? Are there any cats in the flat?"

"Only the three in your bedroom, sir."

"What!"

"Cats in his bedroom!" I heard Sir Roderick whisper in a kind of stricken way, and his eyes hit me amidships like a couple of bullets.

"What do you mean," I said, "only the three in my bedroom?"

"The black one, the tabby and the small lemon-coloured animal, sir."

"What on earth?——"

I charged round the table in the direction of the door. Unfortunately, Sir Roderick had just decided to edge in that direction himself, with the result that we collided in the doorway with a good deal of force, and staggered out into the hall together. He came smartly out of the clinch and grabbed an umbrella from the rack.

"Stand back!" he shouted, waving it overhead. "Stand back, sir! I am armed!"

It seemed to me that the moment had come to be soothing.

"Awfully sorry I barged into you," I said.

"Wouldn't have had it happen for worlds. I was just dashing out to have a look into things."

He appeared a trifle reassured, and lowered the umbrella. But just then the most frightful shindy started in the bedroom. It sounded as though all the cats in London, assisted by delegates from outlying suburbs, had got together to settle their differences once for all. A sort of augmented orchestra of cats.

"This noise is unendurable," yelled Sir Roderick. "I cannot hear myself speak."

"I fancy, sir," said Jeeves respectfully, "that the animals may have become somewhat exhilarated as the result of having discovered the fish under Mr. Wooster's bed."

The old boy tottered.

"Fish! Did I hear you rightly?"

"Sir?"

"Did you say that there was a fish under Mr. Wooster's bed?"

"Yes, sir."

Sir Roderick gave a low moan, and reached for his hat and stick.

"You aren't going?" I said.

"Mr. Wooster, I *am* going! I prefer to spend my leisure time in less eccentric society."

"But I say. Here, I must come with you. I'm sure the whole business can be explained. Jeeves, my hat."

Jeeves rallied round. I took the hat from him and shoved it on my head.

"Good heavens!"

Beastly shock it was! The bally thing had absolutely engulfed me, if you know what I mean. Even as I was putting it on I got a sort of impression that it was a trifle roomy; and no sooner had I let go of it than it settled down over my ears like a kind of extinguisher.

"I say! This isn't my hat!"

"It is *my* hat!" said Sir Roderick in about the coldest, nastiest voice I'd ever heard. "The hat which was stolen from me this morning as I drove in my car."

"But——"

I suppose Napoleon or somebody like that would have been equal to the situation, but I'm bound to say it was too much for me. I just stood there goggling in a sort of coma, while the old boy lifted the hat off me and turned to Jeeves.

"I should be glad, my man," he said, "if you would accompany me a few yards down the street. I wish to ask you some questions."

"Very good, sir."

"Here, but, I say——!" I began, but he left me standing. He stalked out, followed by Jeeves. And at that moment the row in the bedroom started again, louder than ever.

I was about fed up with the whole thing. I mean, cats in your bedroom—a bit thick, what? I didn't know how the dickens they had got in, but I was jolly well resolved that they weren't going to stay picknicking there any longer. I flung open the door. I got a momentary flash of about a hundred and fifteen cats of all sizes and colours scrapping in the middle of the room, and then they all shot past me with a rush and out of the front door; and all that was left of the mob-scene was the head of a whacking big fish, lying on the carpet and staring up at me in a rather austere sort of way, as if it wanted a written explanation and apology.

There was something about the thing's expression that absolutely chilled me, and I withdrew on tiptoe and shut the door. And, as I did so, I bumped into someone.

"Oh, sorry!" he said.

I spun round. It was the pink-faced chappie, Lord Something or other, the fellow I had met with Claude and Eustace.

"I say," he said apologetically, "awfully sorry to bother you, but those weren't my cats I met just now legging it downstairs, were they? They looked like my cats."

"They came out of my bedroom."

"Then they *were* my cats!" he said sadly. "Oh, dash it!"

"Did you put cats in my bedroom?"

"Your man, what's-his-name, did. He rather decently said I could keep them there till my train went. I'd just come to fetch them. And now they've gone! Oh, well, it can't be helped, I suppose. I'll take the hat and the fish, anyway."

I was beginning to dislike this chappie.

"Did you put that bally fish there, too?"

"No, that was Eustace's. The hat was Claude's."

I sank limply into a chair.

"I say, you couldn't explain this, could you?" I said
The chappie gazed at me in mild surprise.

"Why, don't you know all about it? I say!" He
blushed profusely. "Why, if you don't know about it,
I shouldn't wonder if the whole thing didn't seem
rummy to you."

"Rummy is the word."

"It was for The Seekers, you know."

"The Seekers?"

"Rather a blood club, you know, up at Oxford,
which your cousins and I are rather keen on getting
into. You have to pinch something, you know, to get
elected. Some sort of a souvenir, you know. A policeman's helmet, you know, or a door-knocker or something, you know. The room's decorated with the
things at the annual dinner, and everybody makes
speeches and all that sort of thing. Rather jolly!
Well, we wanted rather to make a sort of special effort
and do the thing in style, if you understand, so we
came up to London to see if we couldn't pick up something here that would be a bit out of the ordinary. And
we had the most amazing luck right from the start.
Your cousin Claude managed to collect a quite decent
top-hat out of a passing car, and your Cousin Eustace
got away with a really goodish salmon or something
from Harrods, and I snaffled three excellent cats all in
the first hour. We were fearfully braced, I can tell you.
And then the difficulty was to know where to park the
things till our train went. You look so beastly conspicuous, you know, tooling about London with a fish
and a lot of cats. And then Eustace remembered you,

and we all came on here in a cab. You were out, but your man said it would be all right. When we met you, you were in such a hurry that we hadn't time to explain. Well, I think I'll be taking the hat, if you don't mind."

"It's gone."

"Gone?"

"The fellow you pinched it from happened to be the man who was lunching here. He took it away with him."

"Oh, I say! Poor old Claude will be upset. Well, how about the goodish salmon or something?"

"Would you care to view the remains?" He seemed all broken up when he saw the wreckage.

"I doubt if the committee would accept that," he said sadly. "There isn't a frightful lot of it left, what?"

"The cats ate the rest."

He sighed deeply.

"No cats, no fish, no hat. We've had all our trouble for nothing. I do call that hard! And on top of that —I say, I hate to ask you, but you couldn't lend me a tenner, could you?"

"A tenner? What for?"

"Well, the fact is, I've got to pop round and bail Claude and Eustace out. They've been arrested."

"Arrested!"

"Yes. You see, what with the excitement of collaring the hat and the salmon or something, added to the fact that we had rather a festive lunch, they got a bit above themselves, poor chaps, and tried to pinch a motor-lorry. Silly, of course, because I don't see how they could have got the thing to Oxford and shown it to the committee. Still, there wasn't any reasoning with them, and when the driver started making a fuss, there was a bit of a mix-up, and Claude and Eustace are more or less languishing in Vine Street police-station till I pop round and bail them out. So if you could manage a tenner—Oh, thanks, that's fearfully good of you. It would have been too bad to leave them there, what? I mean, they're both such frightfully good chaps, you know. Everybody likes them up at the 'Varsity. They're fearfully popular."

"I bet they are!" I said.

*   *   *   *   *

When Jeeves came back, I was waiting for him on the mat. I wanted speech with the blighter.

"Well?" I said.

"Sir Roderick asked me a number of questions, sir, respecting your habits and mode of life, to which I replied guardedly."

"I don't care about that. What I want to know is why you didn't explain the whole thing to him right at the start? A word from you would have put everything clear."

"Yes, sir."

"Now he's gone off thinking me a looney."

"I should not be surprised, from his conversation with me, sir, if some such idea had not entered his head."

I was just starting in to speak, when the telephone bell rang. Jeeves answered it.

"No, madam, Mr. Wooster is not in. No, madam, I do not know when he will return. No, madam, he left no message. Yes, madam, I will inform him." He put back the receiver. "Mrs. Gregson, sir."

Aunt Agatha! I had been expecting it. Ever since the luncheon-party had blown out a fuse, her shadow had been hanging over me, so to speak.

"Does she know? Already?"

"I gather that Sir Roderick has been speaking to her on the telephone, sir, and——"

"No wedding bells for me, what?"

Jeeves coughed.

"Mrs. Gregson did not actually confide in me, sir, but I fancy that some such thing may have occurred. She seemed decidedly agitated, sir."

It's a rummy thing, but I'd been so snootered by the old boy and the cats and the fish and the hat and the pink-faced chappie and all the rest of it that the bright side simply hadn't occurred to me till now. By Jove, it was like a bally weight rolling off my chest! I gave a yelp of pure relief.

"Jeeves!" I said, "I believe you worked the whole thing!"

"Sir?"

"I believe you had the jolly old situation in hand right from the start."

"Well, sir, Spenser, Mrs. Gregson's butler, who inadvertently chanced to overhear something of your conversation when you were lunching at the house, did mention certain of the details to me; and I confess that, though it may be a liberty to say so, I entertained hopes that something might occur to prevent the match. I doubt if the young lady was entirely suitable to you, sir."

"And she would have shot you out on your ear five minutes after the ceremony."

"Yes, sir. Spenser informed me that she had expressed some such intention. Mrs. Gregson wishes you to call upon her immediately, sir."

"She does, eh? What do you advise, Jeeves?"

"I think a trip abroad might prove enjoyable, sir." I shook my head. "She'd come after me."

"Not if you went far enough afield, sir. There are excellent boats leaving every Wednesday and Saturday for New York."

"Jeeves," I said, "you are right, as always. Book the tickets."

THE GREAT SERMON HANDICAP

AFTER Goodwood's over, I generally find that I
get a bit restless. I'm not much of a lad for the
birds and the trees and the great open spaces as a rule,
but there's no doubt that London's not at its best in
August, and rather tends to give me the pip and make
me think of popping down into the country till things
have bucked up a trifle. London, about a couple of
weeks after that spectacular finish of young Bingo's
which I've just been telling you about, was empty and
smelled of burning asphalt. All my pals were away,
most of the theatres were shut, and they were taking
up Piccadilly in large spadefuls.

It was most infernally hot. As I sat in the old flat
one night trying to muster up energy enough to go to
bed, I felt I couldn't stand it much longer: and when
Jeeves came in with the tissue-restorers on a tray I
put the thing to him squarely.

"Jeeves," I said, wiping the brow and gasping like
a stranded goldfish, "it's beastly hot."

"The weather *is* oppressive, sir."

"Not all the soda, Jeeves."

"No, sir."

"I think we've had about enough of the metrop. for

the time being, and require a change.   Shift-ho, I think, Jeeves, what?"

"Just as you say, sir.   There is a letter on the tray, sir."

"By Jove, Jeeves, that was practically poetry. Rhymed, did you notice?"   I opened the letter.   "I say, this is rather extraordinary."

"Sir?"

"You know Twing Hall?"

"Yes, sir."

"Well, Mr. Little is there."

"Indeed, sir?"

"Absolutely in the flesh.   He's had to take another of those tutoring jobs."

After that fearful mix-up at Goodwood, when young Bingo Little, a broken man, had touched me for a tenner and whizzed silently off into the unknown, I had been all over the place, asking mutual friends if they had heard anything of him, but nobody had.   And all the time he had been at Twing Hall.   Rummy. And I'll tell you why it was rummy.   Twing Hall belongs to old Lord Wickhammersley, a great pal of my guv'nor's when he was alive, and I have a standing invitation to pop down there when I like.   I generally put in a week or two some time in the summer, and I was thinking of going there before I read the letter.

"And, what's more, Jeeves, my cousin Claude, and my cousin Eustace—you remember them?"

"Very vividly, sir."

"Well, they're down there, too, reading for some exam. or other with the vicar.   I used to read with him myself at one time. He's known far and wide as a pretty hot coach for those of fairly feeble intellect. Well, when I tell you he got *me* through Smalls, you'll gather that he's a bit of a hummer. I call this most extraordinary."

I read the letter again. It was from Eustace. Claude and Eustace are twins, and more or less generally admitted to be the curse of the human race.

The Vicarage,
Twing, Glos.

DEAR BERTIE—Do you want to make a bit of money? I hear you had a bad Goodwood, so you probably do. Well, come down here quick and get in on the biggest sporting event of the season. I'll explain when I see you, but you can take it from me it's all right.

Claude and I are with a reading-party at old Heppenstall's. There are nine of us, not counting your pal Bingo Little, who is tutoring the kid up at the Hall.

Don't miss this golden opportunity, which may never occur again. Come and join us.

Yours,
EUSTACE.

I handed this to Jeeves. He studied it thoughtfully.

"What do you make of it? A rummy communication, what?"

"Very high-spirited young gentlemen, sir, Mr. Claude and Mr. Eustace. Up to some game, I should be disposed to imagine."

"Yes. But what game, do you think?"

"It is impossible to say, sir. Did you observe that the letter continues over the page?"

"Eh, what?" I grabbed the thing. This was what was on the other side of the last page:

SERMON HANDICAP
RUNNERS AND BETTING
PROBABLE STARTERS.

Rev. Joseph Tucker (Badgwick), scratch.
Rev. Leonard Starkie (Stapleton), Scratch.
Rev. Alexander Jones (Upper Bingley), receives three minutes.
Rev. W. Dix (Little Clickton-in-the-Wold), receives five minutes.
Rev. Francis Heppenstall (Twing), receives eight minutes.
Rev. Cuthbert Dibble (Boustead Parva), receives nine minutes.
Rev. Orlo Hough (Boustead Magna), receives nine minutes.
Rev. J. J. Roberts (Fale-by-the-Water), receives ten minutes.
Rev. G. Hayward (Lower Bingley), receives twelve minutes.
Rev. James Bates (Gandle-by-the-Hill), receives fifteen minutes.

(The above have arrived.)

Prices.—5-2, Tucker, Starkie; 3-1, Jones; 9-2, Dix; 6-1, Heppenstall, Dibble, Hough; 100-8, any other.

It baffled me.

"Do you understand it, Jeeves?"

"No, sir."

"Well, I think we ought to have a look into it, anyway, what?"

"Undoubtedly, sir."

"Right-o, then. Pack our spare dickey and a toothbrush in a neat brown-paper parcel, send a wire to Lord Wickhammersley to say we're coming, and buy two tickets on the five-ten at Paddington to-morrow."

*   *   *   *   *

The five-ten was late as usual, and everybody was dressing for dinner when I arrived at the Hall. It was only by getting into my evening things in record time and taking the stairs to the dining-room in a couple of bounds that I managed to dead-heat with the soup. I slid into the vacant chair, and found that I was sitting next to old Wickhammersley's youngest daughter, Cynthia.

"Oh, hallo, old thing," I said.

Great pals we've always been. In fact, there was a time when I had an idea I was in love with Cynthia. However, it blew over. A dashed pretty and lively and attractive girl, mind you, but full of ideals and all that. I may be wronging her, but I have an idea that she's the sort of girl who would want a fellow to carve out a career and what not. I know I've heard her speak favourably of Napoleon. So what with one thing and another the jolly old frenzy sort of petered out, and now we're just pals. I think she's a topper, and she thinks me next door to a looney, so everything's nice and matey.

"Well, Bertie, so you've arrived?"

"Oh, yes, I've arrived. Yes, here I am. I say, I seem to have plunged into the middle of quite a young dinner-party. Who are all these coves?"

"Oh, just people from round about. You know most of them. You remember Colonel Willis, and the Spencers——"

"Of course, yes. And there's old Heppenstall. Who's the other clergyman next to Mrs. Spencer?"

"Mr. Hayward, from Lower Bingley."

"What an amazing lot of clergymen there are round here. Why, there's another, next to Mrs. Willis."

"That's Mr. Bates, Mr. Heppenstall's nephew. He's an assistant-master at Eton. He's down here during the summer holidays, acting as locum tenens for Mr Spettigue, the rector of Gandle-by-the-Hill."

"I thought I knew his face. He was in his fourth year at Oxford when I was a fresher. Rather a blood. Got his rowing-blue and all that." I took another look round the table, and spotted young Bingo. "Ah, there he is," I said. "There's the old egg."

"There's who?"

"Young Bingo Little. Great pal of mine. He's tutoring your brother, you know."

"Good gracious! Is he a friend of yours?"

"Rather! Known him all my life."

"Then tell me, Bertie, is he at all weak in the head?"

"Weak in the head?"

"I don't mean simply because he's a friend of yours. But he's so strange in his manner."

"How do you mean?"

"Well, he keeps looking at me so oddly."

"Oddly? How? Give an imitation."

"I can't in front of all these people."

"Yes, you can. I'll hold my napkin up."

"All right, then. Quick. There!"

Considering that she had only about a second and a half to do it in, I must say it was a jolly fine exhibition. She opened her mouth and eyes pretty wide and let her jaw drop sideways, and managed to look so like a dyspeptic calf that I recognised the symptoms immediately.

"Oh, that's all right," I said. "No need to be alarmed. He's simply in love with you."

"In love with me. Don't be absurd."

"My dear old thing, you don't know young Bingo.
He can fall in love with *anybody*."

"Thank you!"

"Oh, I didn't mean it that way, you know. I don't
wonder at his taking to you. Why, I was in love
with you myself once."

"Once? Ah! And all that remains now are the cold
ashes? This isn't one of your tactful evenings,
Bertie."

"Well, my dear sweet thing, dash it all, considering
that you gave me the bird and nearly laughed yourself
into a permanent state of hiccoughs when I asked
you——"

"Oh, I'm not reproaching you. No doubt there
were faults on both sides. He's very good-looking,
isn't he?"

"Good-looking? Bingo? Bingo good-looking?
No, I say, come now, really!"

"I mean, compared with some people," said Cynthia.

Some time after this, Lady Wickhammersley gave
the signal for the females of the species to leg it, and
they duly stampeded. I didn't get a chance of talking
to young Bingo when they'd gone, and later, in the
drawing-room, he didn't show up. I found him eventually in his room, lying on the bed with his feet on
the rail, smoking a toofah. There was a notebook on
the counterpane beside him.

"Hallo, old scream," I said.

"Hallo, Bertie," he replied, in what seemed to me
rather a moody, distrait sort of manner.

"Rummy finding you down here. I take it your

uncle cut off your allowance after that Goodwood binge and you had to take this tutoring job to keep the wolf from the door?"

"Correct," said young Bingo tersely.

"Well, you might have let your pals know where you were."

He frowned darkly.

"I didn't want them to know where I was. I wanted to creep away and hide myself. I've been through a bad time, Bertie, these last weeks. The sun ceased to shine——"

"That's curious. We've had gorgeous weather in London."

"The birds ceased to sing——"

"What birds?"

"What the devil does it matter what birds?" said young Bingo, with some asperity. "Any birds. The birds round about here. You don't expect me to specify them by their pet names, do you? I tell you, Bertie, it hit me hard at first, very hard."

"What hit you?" I simply couldn't follow the blighter.

"Charlotte's calculated callousness."

"Oh, ah!" I've seen poor old Bingo through so many unsuccessful love-affairs that I'd almost forgotten there was a girl mixed up with that Goodwood business. Of course! Charlotte Corday Rowbotham. And she had given him the raspberry, I remembered, and gone off with Comrade Butt.

"I went through torments. Recently, however, I've —er—bucked up a bit. Tell me, Bertie, what are you doing down here? I didn't know you knew these people."

"Me? Why, I've known them since I was a kid."

Young Bingo put his feet down with a thud.

"Do you mean to say you've known Lady Cynthia all that time?"

"Rather! She can't have been seven when I met her first."

"Good Lord!" said young Bingo. He looked at me for the first time as though I amounted to something, and swallowed a mouthful of smoke the wrong way. "I love that girl, Bertie," he went on, when he'd finished coughing.

"Yes. Nice girl, of course."

He eyed me with pretty deep loathing.

"Don't speak of her in that horrible casual way. She's an angel. An angel! Was she talking about me at all at dinner, Bertie?"

"Oh, yes."

"What did she say?"

"I remember one thing. She said she thought you good-looking."

Young Bingo closed his eyes in a sort of ecstasy. Then he picked up the notebook.

"Pop off now, old man, there's a good chap," he said, in a hushed, far-away voice. "I've got a bit of writing to do."

"Writing?"

"Poetry, if you must know. I wish the dickens," said young Bingo, not without some bitterness, "she had been christened something except Cynthia. There isn't a dam' word in the language it rhymes with. Ye gods, how I could have spread myself if she had only been called Jane!"

* * * * *

Bright and early next morning, as I lay in bed blinking at the sunlight on the dressing-table and wondering when Jeeves was going to show up with a cup of tea, a heavy weight descended on my toes, and the voice of young Bingo polluted the air. The blighter had apparently risen with the lark.

"Leave me," I said, "I would be alone. I can't see anybody till I've had my tea."

"When Cynthia smiles," said young Bingo, "the skies are blue; the world takes on a roseate hue: birds in the garden trill and sing, and Joy is king of everything, when Cynthia smiles." He coughed, changing gears. "When Cynthia frowns——"

"What the devil are you talking about?"

"I'm reading you my poem. The one I wrote to Cynthia last night. I'll go on, shall I?"

"No!"

"No?"

"No. I haven't had my tea."

At this moment Jeeves came in with the good old beverage, and I sprang on it with a glad cry. After a couple of sips things looked a bit brighter. Even young Bingo didn't offend the eye to quite such an extent. By the time I'd finished the first cup I was a new man, so much so that I not only permitted but encouraged the poor fish to read the rest of the bally thing, and even went so far as to criticise the scansion of the fourth line of the fifth verse. We were still arguing the point when the door burst open and in blew Claude and Eustace. One of the things which discourage me about rural life is the frightful earliness with which events begin to break loose. I've stayed at places in the country where they've jerked me out of the dreamless at about six-thirty to go for a jolly swim in the lake. At Twing, thank heaven, they know me, and let me breakfast in bed

The twins seemed pleased to see me.

"Good old Bertie!" said Claude.

"Stout fellow!" said Eustace. "The Rev. told us you had arrived. I thought that letter of mine would fetch you."

"You can always bank on Bertie," said Claude. "A sportsman to the finger-tips. Well, has Bingo told you about it?"

"Not a word. He's been——"

"We've been talking," said Bingo hastily, "of other matters."

Claude pinched the last slice of thin bread-and-butter, and Eustace poured himself out a cup of tea.

"It's like this, Bertie," said Eustace, settling down cosily. "As I told you in my letter, there are nine of us marooned in this desert spot, reading with old Heppenstall. Well, of course, nothing is jollier than sweating up the Classics when it's a hundred in the shade, but there does come a time when you begin to feel the need of a little relaxation; and, by Jove, there are absolutely no facilities for relaxation in this place whatever. And then Steggles got this idea. Steggles is one of our reading-party, and, between ourselves, rather a worm as a general thing. Still, you have to give him credit for getting this idea."

"What idea?"

"Well, you know how many parsons there are round about here. There are about a dozen hamlets within a radius of six miles, and each hamlet has a church and each church has a parson and each parson preaches a sermon every Sunday. To-morrow week—Sunday the twenty-third—we're running off the great Sermon Handicap. Steggles is making the book. Each parson is to be clocked by a reliable steward of the course and the one that preaches the longest sermon wins. Did you study the race-card I sent you?"

"I couldn't understand what it was all about."

"Why, you chump, it gives the handicaps and the current odds on each starter. I've got another one here, in case you've lost yours. Take a careful look at it. It gives you the thing in a nutshell. Jeeves, old son, do you want a sporting flutter?"

"Sir?" said Jeeves, who had just meandered in with my breakfast.

Claude explained the scheme. Amazing the way Jeeves grasped it right off. But he merely smiled in a paternal sort of way.

"Thank you, sir, I think not."

"Well, you're with us, Bertie, aren't you?" said Claude, sneaking a roll and a slice of bacon. "Have you studied that card? Well, tell me, does anything strike you about it?"

"Of course it did. It had struck me the moment I looked at it."

"Why, it's a sitter for old Heppenstall," I said. "He's got the event sewed up in a parcel. There isn't a parson in the land who could give him eight minutes. Your pal Steggles must be an ass, giving him a handicap like that. Why, in the days when I was with him, old Heppenstall never used to preach under half an hour, and there was one sermon of his on Brotherly Love which lasted forty-five minutes if it lasted a second. Has he lost his vim lately, or what is it?"

"Not a bit of it," said Eustace. "Tell him what happened, Claude."

"Why," said Claude, "the first Sunday we were here, we all went to Twing church, and old Heppenstall preached a sermon that was well under twenty minutes. This is what happened. Steggles didn't notice it, and the Rev. didn't notice it himself, but Eustace and I both spotteo that he had dropped a chunk of at least half a dozen pages out of his sermon-case as he was walking up to the pulpit. He sort of flickered when he got to the gap in the manuscript, but carried on all right, and Steggles went away with the impression that twenty minutes or a bit under was his usual form. The next Sunday we heard Tucker and Starkie, and they both went well over the thirty-five minutes, so Steggles arranged the handicapping as you see on the card. You must come into this, Bertie. You see, the trouble is that I haven't a bean, and Eustace hasn't a bean, and Bingo Little hasn't a bean, so you'll have to finance the syndicate. Don't weaken! It's just putting money in all our pockets. Well, we'll have to be getting back now. Think the thing over, and phone me later in the day. And, if you let us down, Bertie, may a cousin's curse—— Come on, Claude, old thing."

The more I studied the scheme, the better it looked.

"How about it, Jeeves?" I said.

Jeeves smiled gently and drifted out.

"Jeeves has no sporting blood," said Bingo.

"Well, I have. I'm coming into this. Claude's quite right. It's like finding money by the wayside."

"Good man!" said Bingo. "Now I can see daylight. Say I have a tenner on Heppenstall, and cop; that'll give me a bit in hand to back Pink Pill with in the two o'clock at Gatwick the week after next: cop on that, put the pile on Musk-Rat for the one-thirty at Lewes, and there I am with a nice little sum to take to Alexandra Park on September the tenth, when I've got a tip straight from the stable."

It sounded like a bit out of "Smiles's Self-Help."

"And then," said young Bingo, "I'll be in a position to go to my uncle and beard him in his lair somewhat. He's quite a bit of a snob, you know, and when he hears that I'm going to marry the daughter of an earl——"

"I say, old man," I couldn't help saying, "aren't you looking ahead rather far?"

"Oh, that's all right. It's true nothing's actually settled yet, but she practically told me the other day she was fond of me."

"What!"

"Well, she said that the sort of man she liked was the self-reliant, manly man with strength, good looks, character, ambition, and initiative."

"Leave me, laddie," I said. "Leave me to my fried egg."

*   *   *   *   *

Directly I'd got up I went to the phone, snatched Eustace away from his morning's work, and instructed him to put a tenner on the Twing flier at current odds for each of the syndicate; and after lunch Eustace rang me up to say that he had done business at a snappy seven-to-one, the odds having lengthened owing to a rumour in knowledgable circles that the Rev. was subject to hay-fever, and was taking big chances strolling in the paddock behind the Vicarage in the early mornings. And it was dashed lucky, I thought next day, that we had managed to get the money on in time, for on the Sunday morning old Heppenstall fairly took the bit between his teeth and gave us thirty-six solid minutes on Certain Popular Superstitions. I was sitting next to Steggles in the pew, and I saw him blench visibly. He was a little, rat-faced fellow, with shifty eyes and a suspicious nature. The first thing he did when we emerged into the open air was to announce, formally, that anyone who fancied the Rev. could now be accommodated at fifteen-to-eight on, and he added, in a rather nasty manner, that if he had his way, this sort of in-and-out running would be brought to the attention of the Jockey Club, but that he supposed that there was nothing to be done about it. This ruinous price checked the punters at once, and there was little money in sight. And so matters stood till just after lunch on Tuesday afternoon, when, as I was strolling up and down in front of the house with a cigarette, Claude and Eustace came bursting up the drive on bicycles, dripping with momentous news.

"Bertie," said Claude, deeply agitated, "unless we take immediate action and do a bit of quick thinking, we're in the cart."

"What's the matter?"

"G. Hayward's the matter," said Eustace morosely. "The Lower Bingley starter."

"We never even considered him," said Claude. "Somehow or other, he got overlooked. It's always the way. Steggles overlooked him. We all overlooked him. But Eustace and I happened by the merest fluke to be riding through Lower Bingley this morning, and there was a wedding on at the church, and it suddenly struck us that it wouldn't be a bad move to get a line on G. Hayward's form, in case he might be a dark horse."

"And it was jolly lucky we did," said Eustace. "He delivered an address of twenty-six minutes by Claude's stop-watch. At a village wedding, mark you! What'll he do when he really extends himself!"

"There's only one thing to be done, Bertie," said Claude. "You must spring some more funds, so that we can hedge on Hayward and save ourselves."

"But——"

"Well, it's the only way out."

"But I say, you know, I hate the idea of all that money we put on Heppenstall being chucked away."

"What else can you suggest? You don't suppose the Rev. can give this absolute marvel a handicap and win, do you?"

"I've got it!" I said.

"What?"

"I see a way by which we can make it safe for our nominee. I'll pop over this afternoon, and ask him as a personal favour to preach that sermon of his on Brotherly Love on Sunday."

Claude and Eustace looked at each other, like those chappies in the poem, with a wild surmise.

"It's a scheme," said Claude.

"A jolly brainy scheme," said Eustace. "I didn't think you had it in you, Bertie."

"But even so," said Claude, "fizzer as that sermon no doubt is, will it be good enough in the face of a four-minute handicap?"

"Rather!" I said. "When I told you it lasted forty-five minutes, I was probably understating it. I should call it—from my recollection of the thing—nearer fifty."

"Then carry on," said Claude.

I toddled over in the evening and fixed the thing up. Old Heppenstall was most decent about the whole affair. He seemed pleased and touched that I should have remembered the sermon all these years, and said he had once or twice had an idea of preaching it again, only it had seemed to him, on reflection, that it was perhaps a trifle long for a rustic congregation.

"And in these restless times, my dear Wooster," he said, "I fear that brevity in the pulpit is becoming more and more desiderated by even the bucolic church-goer, who one might have supposed would be less afflicted with the spirit of hurry and impatience than his metropolitan brother. I have had many arguments on the subject with my nephew, young Bates, who is taking my old friend Spettigue's cure over at Gandle-by-the-Hill. His view is that a sermon nowadays should be a bright, brisk, straight-from-the-shoulder address, never lasting more than ten or twelve minutes."

"Long?" I said. "Why, my goodness! you don't call that Brotherly Love sermon of yours *long,* do you?"

"It takes fully fifty minutes to deliver."

"Surely not?"

"Your incredulity, my dear Wooster, is extremely flattering—far more flattering, of course, than I deserve. Nevertheless, the facts are as I have stated. You are sure that I would not be well advised to make certain excisions and eliminations? You do not think it would be a good thing to cut, to prune? I might, for example, delete the rather exhaustive excursus into the family life of the early Assyrians?"

"Don't touch a word of it, or you'll spoil the whole thing," I said earnestly.

"I am delighted to hear you say so, and I shall preach the sermon without fail next Sunday morning."

*   *   *   *   *

What I have always said, and what I always shall say, is, that this ante-post betting is a mistake, an error, and a mug's game. You never can tell what's going to happen. If fellows would only stick to the good old S.P. there would be fewer young men go wrong. I'd hardly finished my breakfast on the Saturday morning when Jeeves came to my bedside to say that Eustace wanted me on the telephone.

"Good Lord, Jeeves, what's the matter, do you think?"

I'm bound to say I was beginning to get a bit jumpy by this time.

"Mr. Eustace did not confide in me, sir."

"Has he got the wind up?"

"Somewhat vertically, sir, to judge by his voice."

"Do you know what I think, Jeeves? Something's gone wrong with the favourite."

"Which is the favourite, sir?"

"Mr. Heppenstall. He's gone to odds on. He was intending to preach a sermon on Brotherly Love which would have brought him home by lengths. I wonder if anything's happened to him."

"You could ascertain, sir, by speaking to Mr. Eustace on the telephone. He is holding the wire."

"By Jove, yes!"

I shoved on a dressing-gown and flew downstairs like a mighty, rushing wind. The moment I heard Eustace's voice I knew we were in for it. It had a croak of agony in it.

"Bertie?"

"Here I am."

"Deuce of a time you've been. Bertie, we're sunk. The favourite's blown up."

"No!"

"Yes. Coughing in his stable all last night."

"What!"

"Absolutely! Hay-fever."

"Oh, my sainted aunt!"

"The doctor is with him now, and it's only a question of minutes before he's officially scratched. That means the curate will show up at the post instead, and he's no good at all. He is being offered at a hundred-to-six, but no takers. What shall we do?"

I had to grapple with the thing for a moment in silence.

"Eustace."

"Hallo?"

"What can you get on G. Hayward?"

"Only four-to-one now. I think there's been a leak, and Steggles has heard something. The odds shortened late last night in a significant manner."

"Well, four-to-one will clear us. Put another fiver all round on G. Hayward for the syndicate. That'll bring us out on the right side of the ledger."

"If he wins."

"What do you mean? I thought you considered him a cert, bar Heppenstall."

"I'm beginning to wonder," said Eustace gloomily, "if there's such a thing as a cert. in this world. I'm told the Rev. Joseph Tucker did an extraordinary fine trial gallop at a mothers' meeting over at Badgwick yesterday. However, it seems our only chance So-long."

Not being one of the official stewards, I had my choice of churches next morning, and naturally I didn't hesitate. The only drawback to going to Lower Bingley was that it was ten miles away, which meant an early start, but I borrowed a bicycle from one of the grooms and tooled off. I had only Eustace's word for it that G. Hayward was such a stayer, and it might have been that he had showed too flattering form at that wedding where the twins had heard him preach; but any misgivings I may have had disappeared the moment he got into the pulpit. Eustace had been right. The man was a trier. He was a tall, rangy-looking greybeard, and he went off from the start with a nice, easy action, pausing and clearing his throat at the end of each sentence, and it wasn't five minutes before I realised that here was the winner. His habit of stopping dead and looking round the church at intervals was worth minutes to us, and in the home stretch we gained no little advantage owing to his dropping his pince-nez and having to grope for them. At the twenty-minute mark he had merely settled down. Twenty-five minutes saw him going strong. And when he finally finished with a good burst, the clock showed thirty-five minutes fourteen seconds. With the handicap which he had been given, this seemed to me to make the event easy for him, and it was with much bonhomie and goodwill to all men that I hopped on to the old bike and started back to the Hall for lunch.

Bingo was talking on the phone when I arrived.

"Fine! Splendid! Topping!" he was saying. "Eh? Oh, we needn't worry about him. Right-o, I'll tell Bertie." He hung up the receiver and caught sight of me. "Oh, hallo, Bertie; I was just talking to Eustace. It's all right, old man. The report from Lower Bingley has just got in. G. Hayward romps home."

"I knew he would. I've just come from there."

"Oh, were you there? I went to Badgwick. Tucker ran a splendid race, but the handicap was too much for him. Starkie had a sore throat and was nowhere. Roberts, of Fale-by-the-Water, ran third. Good old G. Hayward!" said Bingo affectionately, and we strolled out on to the terrace.

"Are all the returns in, then?" I asked.

"All except Gandle-by-the-Hill. But we needn't worry about Bates. He never had a chance. By the way, poor old Jeeves loses his tenner. Silly ass!"

"Jeeves? How do you mean?"

"He came to me this morning, just after you had left, and asked me to put a tenner on Bates for him. I told him he was a chump and begged him not to throw his money away, but he would do it."

"I beg your pardon, sir. This note arrived for you just after you had left the house this morning."

Jeeves had materialised from nowhere, and was standing at my elbow.

"Eh? What? Note?"

"The Reverend Mr. Heppenstall's butler brought it

over from the Vicarage, sir. It came too late to be delivered to you at the moment."

Young Bingo was talking to Jeeves like a father on the subject of betting against the form-book. The yell I gave made him bite his tongue in the middle of a sentence.

"What the dickens is the matter?" he asked, not a little peeved.

"We're dished! Listen to this!"

I read him the note:

> The Vicarage,
> Twing, Glos.

MY DEAR WOOSTER,—As you may have heard, circumstances over which I have no control will prevent my preaching the sermon on Brotherly Love for which you made such a flattering request. I am unwilling, however, that you shall be disappointed, so, if you will attend divine service at Gandle-by-the-Hill this morning, you will hear my sermon preached by young Bates, my nephew. I have lent him the manuscript at his urgent desire, for, between ourselves, there are wheels within wheels. My nephew is one of the candidates for the headmastership of a well-known public school, and the choice has narrowed down between him and one rival.

Late yesterday evening James received private information that the head of the Board of Governors of the school proposed to sit under him this Sunday in order to judge of the merits of his preaching, a most important item in swaying the Board's choice. I acceded to his plea that I lend him my sermon on Brotherly Love, of which, like you, he apparently retains a vivid recollection. It would have been too late for him to compose a sermon of suitable length in place of the brief address which—mistakenly, in my opinion—he had designed to deliver to his rustic flock, and I wished to help the boy.

Trusting that his preaching of the sermon will supply you with as pleasant memories as you say you have of mine, I remain,

> Cordially yours,
> F. HEPPENSTALL.

P.S.—The hay-fever has rendered my eyes unpleasantly weak for the time being, so I am dictating this letter to my butler, Brookfield, who will convey it to you.

I don't know when I've experienced a more massive silence than the one that followed my reading of this cheery epistle. Young Bingo gulped once or twice, and practically every known emotion came and went on his face. Jeeves coughed one soft, low, gentle cough like a sheep with a blade of grass stuck in its throat, and then stood gazing serenely at the landscape. Finally young Bingo spoke.

"Great Scott!" he whispered hoarsely. "An S.P. job!"

"I believe that is the technical term, sir," said Jeeves.

"So you had inside information, dash it!" said young Bingo.

"Why, yes, sir," said Jeeves. "Brookfield happened to mention the contents of the note to me when he brought it. We are old friends."

Bingo registered grief, anguish, rage, despair and resentment.

"Well, all I can say," he cried, "is that it's a bit thick! Preaching another man's sermon! Do you call that honest? Do you call that playing the game?"

"Well, my dear old thing," I said, "be fair. It's quite within the rules. Clergymen do it all the time. They aren't expected always to make up the sermons they preach."

Jeeves coughed again, and fixed me with an expressionless eye.

"And in the present case, sir, if I may be permitted to take the liberty of making the observation, I think we should make allowances. We should remember that the securing of this headmastership meant everything to the young couple."

"Young couple! What young couple?"

"The Reverend James Bates, sir, and Lady Cynthia. I am informed by her ladyship's maid that they have been engaged to be married for some weeks—provisionally, so to speak; and his lordship made his consent conditional on Mr. Bates securing a really important and remunerative position."

Young Bingo turned a light green.

"Engaged to be married!"

"Yes, sir."

There was a silence.

"I think I'll go for a walk," said Bingo.

"But, my dear old thing," I said, "it's just lunch-time. The gong will be going any minute now."

"I don't want any lunch!" said Bingo.

THE PURITY OF THE TURF

AFTER that, life at Twing jogged along pretty peacefully for a bit. Twing is one of those places where there isn't a frightful lot to do nor any very hectic excitement to look forward to. In fact, the only event of any importance on the horizon, as far as I could ascertain, was the annual village school treat. One simply filled in the time by loafing about the grounds, playing a bit of tennis, and avoiding young Bingo as far as was humanly possible.

This last was a very necessary move if you wanted a happy life, for the Cynthia affair had jarred the unfortunate mutt to such an extent that he was always waylaying one and decanting his anguished soul. And when, one morning, he blew into my bedroom while I was toying with a bit of breakfast, I decided to take a firm line from the start. I could stand having him moaning all over me after dinner, and even after lunch; but at breakfast, no. We Woosters are amiability itself, but there is a limit.

"Now look here, old friend," I said. "I know your bally heart is broken and all that, and at some future time I shall be delighted to hear all about it, but——"

"I didn't come to talk about that.'

"No? Good egg!"

"The past," said young Bingo, "is dead. Let us say no more about it."

"Right-o!"

"I have been wounded to the very depths of my soul, but don't speak about it."

"I won't."

"Ignore it. Forget it."

"Absolutely!"

I hadn't seen him so dashed reasonable for days.

"What I came to see you about this morning, Bertie," he said, fishing a sheet of paper out of his pocket, "was to ask if you would care to come in on another little flutter."

If there is one thing we Woosters are simply dripping with, it is sporting blood. I bolted the rest of my sausage, and sat up and took notice.

"Proceed," I said. "You interest me strangely, old bird."

Bingo laid the paper on the bed.

"On Monday week," he said, "you may or may not know, the annual village school treat takes place. Lord Wickhammersley lends the Hall grounds for the purpose. There will be games, and a conjurer, and coker-nut shies, and tea in a tent. And also sports."

"I know. Cynthia was telling me."

Young Bingo winced.

"Would you mind not mentioning that name? I am not made of marble."

"Sorry!"

"Well, as I was saying, this jamboree is slated for Monday week. The question is, Are we on?"

"How do you mean, 'Are we on'?"

"I am referring to the sports. Steggles did so well out of the Sermon Handicap that he has decided to make a book on these sports. Punters can be accommodated at ante-post odds or starting price, according to their preference. I think we ought to look into it," said young Bingo.

I pressed the bell.

"I'll consult Jeeves. I don't touch any sporting proposition without his advice. Jeeves," I said, as he drifted in, "rally round."

"Sir?"

"Stand by. We want your advice."

"Very good, sir."

"State your case, Bingo."

Bingo stated his case.

"What about it, Jeeves?" I said. "Do we go in?"

Jeeves pondered to some extent.

"I am inclined to favour the idea, sir."

That was good enough for me. "Right," I said. "Then we will form a syndicate and bust the Ring. I supply the money, you supply the brains, and Bingo— what do you supply, Bingo?"

"If you will carry me, and let me settle up later," said young Bingo, "I think I can put you in the way of winning a parcel on the Mothers' Sack Race."

"All right. We will put you down as Inside Information. Now, what are the events?"

* * * * *

Bingo reached for his paper and consulted it.

"Girls' Under Fourteen Fifty-Yard Dash seems to open the proceedings."

"Anything to say about that, Jeeves?"

"No, sir. I have no information."

"What's the next?"

"Boys' and Girls' Mixed Animal Potato Race, All Ages."

This was a new one to me. I had never heard of it at any of the big meetings.

"What's that?"

"Rather sporting," said young Bingo. "The competitors enter in couples, each couple being assigned an animal cry and a potato. For instance, let's suppose that you and Jeeves entered. Jeeves would stand at a fixed point holding a potato. You would have your head in a sack, and you would grope about trying to find Jeeves and making a noise like a cat; Jeeves also making a noise like a cat. Other competitors would be making noises like cows and pigs and dogs, and so on, and groping about for *their* potato-holders, who would also be making noises like cows and pigs and dogs and so on——"

I stopped the poor fish.

"Jolly if you're fond of animals," I said, "but on the whole——"

"Precisely, sir," said Jeeves. "I wouldn't touch it."

"Too open, what?"

"Exactly, sir. Very hard to estimate form."

"Carry on, Bingo. Where do we go from there?"

"Mothers' Sack Race."

"Ah! that's better. This is where you know something."

"A gift for Mrs. Penworthy, the tobacconist's wife," said Bingo confidently. "I was in at her shop yesterday, buying cigarettes, and she told me she had won three times at fairs in Worcestershire. She only moved to these parts a short time ago, so nobody knows about her. She promised me she would keep herself dark, and I think we could get a good price."

"Risk a tenner each way, Jeeves, what?"

"I think so, sir."

"Girls' Open Egg and Spoon Race," read Bingo. "How about that?"

"I doubt if it would be worth while to invest, sir," said Jeeves. "I am told it is a certainty for last year's winner, Sarah Mills, who will doubtless start an odds-on favourite."

"Good, is she?"

"They tell me in the village that she carries a beautiful egg, sir."

"Then there's the Obstacle Race," said Bingo. "Risky, in my opinion. Like betting on the Grand National. Fathers' Hat-Trimming Contest—another speculative event. That's all, except for the Choir Boys' Hundred Yards Handicap, for a pewter mug presented by the vicar—open to all whose voices have not broken before the second Sunday in Epiphany. Willie Chambers won last year, in a canter, receiving fifteen yards. This time he will probably be handicapped out of the race. I don't know what to advise."

"If I might make a suggestion, sir."

I eyed Jeeves with interest. I don't know that I'd ever seen him look so nearly excited.

"You've got something up your sleeve?"

"I have, sir."

"Red-hot?"

"That precisely describes it, sir. I think I may confidently assert that we have the winner of the Choir Boys' Handicap under this very roof, sir. Harold, the page-boy."

"Page-boy? Do you mean the tubby little chap in buttons one sees bobbing about here and there? Why, dash it, Jeeves, nobody has a greater respect for your knowledge of form than I have, but I'm hanged if I can see Harold catching the judge's eye. He's practically circular, and every time I've seen him he's been leaning up against something, half asleep."

"He receives thirty yards, sir, and could win from scratch. The boy is a flier."

"How do you know?"

Jeeves coughed, and there was a dreamy look in his eye.

"I was as much astonished as yourself, sir, when I first became aware of the lad's capabilities. I happened to pursue him one morning with the intention of fetching him a clip on the side of the head——"

"Great Scott, Jeeves! You!"

"Yes, sir. The boy is of an outspoken disposition, and had made an opprobrious remark respecting my personal appearance."

"What did he say about your appearance?"

"I have forgotten, sir," said Jeeves, with a touch of austerity. "But it was opprobrious. I endeavoured to correct him, but he outdistanced me by yards and made good his escape."

"But, I say, Jeeves, this is sensational. And yet— if he's such a sprinter, why hasn't anybody in the village found it out? Surely he plays with the other boys?"

"No, sir. As his lordship's page-boy, Harold does not mix with the village lads."

"Bit of a snob, what?"

"He is somewhat acutely alive to the existence of class distinctions, sir."

"You're absolutely certain he's such a wonder?" said Bingo. "I mean, it wouldn't do to plunge unless you're sure."

"If you desire to ascertain the boy's form by personal inspection, sir, it will be a simple matter to arrange a secret trial."

"I'm bound to say I should feel easiet in my mind,' I said.

"Then if I may take a shilling from the money on your dressing-table——"

"What for?"

"I propose to bribe the lad to speak slightingly of the second footman's sprint, sir. Charles is somewhat sensitive on the point, and should undoubtedly make the lad extend himself. If you will be at the first floor passage-window, overlooking the back-door, in half an hour's time——"

I don't know when I've dressed in such a hurry.

As a rule, I'm what you might call a slow and careful dresser: I like to linger over the tie and see that the trousers are just so; but this morning I was all worked up. I just shoved on my things anyhow, and joined Bingo at the window with a quarter of an hour to spare.

The passage-window looked down on to a broad sort of paved courtyard, which ended after about twenty yards in an archway through a high wall. Beyond this archway you got on to a strip of the drive, which curved round for another thirty yards or so, till it was lost behind a thick shrubbery. I put myself in the stripling's place and thought what steps I would take with a second footman after me. There was only one thing to do—leg it for the shrubbery and take cover; which meant that at least fifty yards would have to be covered—an excellent test. If good old Harold could fight off the second footman's challenge long enough to allow him to reach the bushes, there wasn't a choir-boy in England who could give him thirty yards in the hundred. I waited, all of a twitter, for what seemed hours, and then suddenly there was a confused noise without, and something round and blue and buttony shot through the back-door and buzzed for the archway like a mustang. And about two seconds later out came the second footman, going his hardest.

There was nothing to it. Absolutely nothing. The field never had a chance. Long before the footman reached the half-way mark, Harold was in the bushes, throwing stones. I came away from the window thrilled to the marrow; and when I met Jeeves on the stairs I was so moved that I nearly grasped his hand.

"Jeeves," I said, "no discussion! The Wooster shirt goes on this boy!"

"Very good, sir," said Jeeves.

*　　　*　　　*　　　*　　　*

The worst of these country meetings is that you can't plunge as heavily as you would like when you get a good thing, because it alarms the Ring. Steggles, though pimpled, was, as I have indicated, no chump, and if I had invested all I wanted to he would have put two and two together. I managed to get a good solid bet down for the syndicate, however, though it did make him look thoughtful. I heard in the next few days that he had been making searching inquiries in the village concerning Harold; but nobody could tell him anything, and eventually he came to the conclusion, I suppose, that I must be having a long shot on the strength of that thirty-yards start. Public opinion wavered between Jimmy Goode, receiving ten yards, at seven-to-two, and Alexander Bartlett, with six yards start, at eleven-to-four. Willie Chambers, scratch, was offered to the public at two-to-one, but found no takers.

We were taking no chances on the big event, and directly we had got our money on at a nice hundred-to-twelve Harold was put into strict training. It was a wearing business, and I can understand now why most of the big trainers are grim, silent men, who look as though they had suffered. The kid wanted constant watching. It was no good talking to him about honour and glory and how proud his mother would be when he wrote and told her he had won a real cup—the moment blighted Harold discovered that training meant knocking off pastry, taking exercise, and keeping away from the cigarettes, he was all against it, and it was only by unceasing vigilance that we managed to keep him in any shape at all. It was the diet that was the stumbling-block. As far as exercise went, we could generally arrange for a sharp dash every morning with the assistance of the second footman. It ran into money, of course, but that couldn't be helped. Still, when a kid has simply to wait till the butler's back is turned to have the run of the pantry, and has only to nip into the smoking-room to collect a handful of the best Turkish, training becomes a rocky job. We could only hope that on the day his natural stamina would pull him through.

And then one evening young Bingo came back from the links with a disturbing story. He had been in the habit of giving Harold mild exercise in the afternoons by taking him out as a caddie.

At first he seemed to think it humorous, the poor chump! He bubbled over with merry mirth as he began his tale.

"I say, rather funny this afternoon," he said. "You ought to have seen Steggles's face!"

"Seen Steggles's face? What for?"

"When he saw young Harold sprint, I mean."

I was filled with a grim foreboding of an awful doom.

"Good heavens! You didn't let Harold sprint in front of Steggles?"

Young Bingo's jaw dropped.

"I never thought of that," he said, gloomily. "I wasn't my fault. I was playing a round with Steggles and after we'd finished we went into the club-house for a drink, leaving Harold with the clubs outside. In about five minutes we came out, and there was the kid on the gravel practising swings with Steggles's driver and a stone. When he saw us coming, the kid dropped the club and was over the horizon like a streak. Steggles was absolutely dumbfounded. And I must say it was a revelation even to me. The kid certainly gave of his best. Of course, it's a nuisance in a way; but I don't see, on second thoughts," said Bingo, brightening up, "what it matters. We're on at a good price. We've nothing to lose by the kid's form becoming known. I take it he will start odds-on, but that doesn't affect us."

I looked at Jeeves. Jeeves looked at me.

"It affects us all right if he doesn't start at all."

"Precisely, sir."

"What do you mean?" asked Bingo.

"If you ask me," I said, "I think Steggles will try to nobble him before the race."

"Good Lord! I never thought of that." Bingo blenched. "You don't think he would really do it?"

"I think he would have a jolly good try. Steggles is a bad man. From now on, Jeeves, we must watch Harold like hawks."

"Undoubtedly, sir."

"Ceaseless vigilance, what?"

"Precisely, sir."

"You wouldn't care to sleep in his room, Jeeves?"

"No, sir, I should not."

"No, nor would I, if it comes to that. But dash it all," I said, "we're letting ourselves get rattled! We're losing our nerve. This won't do. How can Steggles possibly get at Harold, even if he wants to?"

There was no cheering young Bingo up. He's one of those birds who simply leap at the morbid view, if you give them half a chance.

"There are all sorts of ways of nobbling favourites," he said, in a sort of death-bed voice. "You ought to read some of these racing novels. In 'Pipped on the Post,' Lord Jasper Mauleverer as near as a toucher outed Bonny Betsy by bribing the head lad to slip a cobra into her stable the night before the Derby!"

"What are the chances of a cobra biting Harold, Jeeves?"

"Slight, I should imagine, sir. And in such an event, knowing the boy as intimately as I do, my anxiety would be entirely for the snake."

"Still, unceasing vigilance, Jeeves."

"Most certainly, sir."

*   *   *   *   *

I must say I got a bit fed with young Bingo in the next few days. It's all very well for a fellow with a big winner in his stable to exercise proper care, but in my opinion Bingo overdid it. The blighter's mind appeared to be absolutely saturated with racing fiction; and in stories of that kind, as far as I could make out, no horse is ever allowed to start in a race without at least a dozen attempts to put it out of action. He stuck to Harold like a plaster. Never let the unfortunate kid out of his sight. Of course, it meant a lot to the poor old egg if he could collect on this race, because it would give him enough money to chuck his tutoring job and get back to London; but all the same, he needn't have woken me up at three in the morning twice running—once to tell me we ought to cook Harold's food ourselves to prevent doping: the other time to say that he had heard mysterious noises in the shrubbery. But he reached the limit, in my opinion, when he insisted on my going to evening service on Sunday, the day before the sports.

"Why on earth?" I said, never being much of a lad for evensong.

"Well, I can't go myself. I shan't be here. I've got to go to London to-day with young Egbert." Egbert was Lord Wickhammersley's son, the one Bingo was tutoring. "He's going for a visit down in Kent, and I've got to see him off at Charing Cross. It's an infernal nuisance. I shan't be back till Monday afternoon. In fact, I shall miss most of the sports, I expect. Everything, therefore, depends on you Bertie."

"But why should either of us go to evening service?"

"Ass! Harold sings in the choir, doesn't he?"

"What about it? I can't stop him dislocating his neck over a high note, if that's what you're afraid of."

"Fool! Steggles sings in the choir, too. There may be dirty work after the service."

"What absolute rot!"

"Is it?" said young Bingo. "Well, let me tell you that in 'Jenny, the Girl Jocky,' the villain kidnapped the boy who was to ride the favourite the night before the big race, and he was the only one who understood and could control the horse, and if the heroine hadn't dressed up in riding things and——"

"Oh, all right, all right. But, if there's any danger, it seems to me the simplest thing would be for Harold not to turn out on Sunday evening."

"He must turn out. You seem to think the infernal kid is a monument of rectitude, beloved by all. He's got the shakiest reputation of any kid in the village. His name is as near being mud as it can jolly well stick. He's played hookey from the choir so often that the vicar told him, if one more thing happened, he would fire him out. Nice chumps we should look if he was scratched the night before the race!"

Well, of course, that being so, there was nothing for it but to toddle along.

There's something about evening service in a country church that makes a fellow feel drowsy and peaceful. Sort of end-of-a-perfect-day feeling. Old Heppenstall was up in the pulpit, and he has a kind of regular, bleating delivery that assists thought. They had left the door open, and the air was full of a mixed scent of trees and honeysuckle and mildew and villagers' Sunday clothes. As far as the eye could reach, you could see farmers propped up in restful attitudes, breathing heavily; and the children in the congregation who had fidgeted during the earlier part of the proceedings were now lying back in a surfeited sort of coma. The last rays of the setting sun shone through the stained-glass windows, birds were twittering in the trees, the women's dresses crackled gently in the still-ness. Peaceful. That's what I'm driving at. I felt peaceful. Everybody felt peaceful. And that is why the explosion, when it came, sounded like the end of all things.

I call it an explosion, because that was what it seemed like when it broke loose. One moment a dreamy hush was all over the place, broken only by old Heppenstall talking about our duty to our neigh-bours; and then, suddenly, a sort of piercing, shriek-ing squeal that got you right between the eyes and ran all the way down your spine and out at the soles of the feet.

"EE-ee-ee-ee-ee! Oo-ee! Ee-ee-ee-ee!"

It sounded like about six hundred pigs having their tails twisted simultaneously, but it was simply the kid Harold, who appeared to be having some species of fit. He was jumping up and down and slapping at the back of his neck. And about every other second he would take a deep breath and give out another of the squeals.

Well, I mean, you can't do that sort of thing in the middle of the sermon during evening service with-out exciting remark. The congregation came out of its trance with a jerk, and climbed on the pews to get a better view. Old Heppenstall stopped in the middle of a sentence and spun round. And a couple of vergers with great presence of mind bounded up the aisle like leopards, collected Harold, still squealing, and marched him out. They disappeared into the vestry, and I grabbed my hat and legged it round to the stage-door, full of apprehension and what not. I couldn't think what the deuce could have happened, but somewhere dimly behind the proceedings there seemed to me to lurk the hand of the blighter Steggles.

*   *   *   *   *

By the time I got there and managed to get someone to open the door, which was locked, the service seemed to be over. Old Heppenstall was standing in the middle of a crowd of choir-boys and vergers and sextons and what not, putting the wretched Harold through it with no little vim. I had come in at the tail-end of what must have been a fairly fruity oration.

"Wretched boy! How dare you——"

"I got a sensitive skin!"

"This is no time to talk about your skin——"

"Somebody put a beetle down my back!"

"Absurd!"

"I felt it wriggling——"

"Nonsense!"

"Sounds pretty thin, doesn't it?" said someone at my side.

It was Steggles, dash him. Clad in a snowy surplice or cassock, or whatever they call it, and wearing an expression of grave concern, the blighter had the cold, cynical crust to look me in the eyeball without a blink.

"Did you put a beetle down his neck?" I cried.

"Me!" said Steggles. "Me!"

Old Heppenstall was putting on the black cap.

"I do not credit a word of your story, wretched boy!

I have warned you before, and now the time has come to act. You cease from this moment to be a member of my choir. Go, miserable child!"

Steggles plucked at my sleeve.

"In that case," he said, "those bets, you know—I'm afraid you lose your money, dear old boy. It's a pity you didn't put it on S.P. I always think S.P.'s the only safe way."

I gave him one look. Not a bit of good, of course.

"And they talk about the Purity of the Turf!" I said. And I meant it to sting, by Jove!

*   *   *   *   *

Jeeves received the news bravely, but I think the man was a bit rattled beneath the surface.

"An ingenious young gentleman, Mr. Steggles, sir."

"A bally swindler, you mean."

"Perhaps that would be a more exact description. However, these things will happen on the Turf, and it is useless to complain."

"I wish I had your sunny disposition, Jeeves!"

Jeeves bowed.

"We now rely, then, it would seem, sir, almost entirely on Mrs. Penworthy. Should she justify Mr. Little's encomiums and show real class in the Mothers' Sack Race, our gains will just balance our losses."

"Yes; but that's not much consolation when you've been looking forward to a big win."

"It is just possible that we may still find ourselves on the right side of the ledger after all, sir. Before Mr. Little left, I persuaded him to invest a small sum for the syndicate of which you were kind enough to make me a member, sir, on the Girls' Egg and Spoon Race."

"On Sarah Mills?"

"No, sir. On a long-priced outsider. Little Prudence Baxter, sir, the child of his lordship's head gardener. Her father assures me she has a very steady hand. She is accustomed to bring him his mug of beer from the cottage each afternoon, and he informs me she has never spilled a drop."

Well, that sounded as though young Prudence's control was good. But how about speed? With seasoned performers like Sarah Mills entered, the thing practically amounted to a classic race, and in these big events you must have speed.

"I am aware that it is what is termed a long shot, sir. Still, I thought it judicious."

"You backed her for a place, too, of course?"

"Yes, sir. Each way."

"Well, I suppose it's all right. I've never known you make a bloomer, yet."

"Thank you very much, sir."

*   *   *   *   *

I'm bound to say that, as a general rule, my idea of a large afternoon would be to keep as far away from a village school-treat as possible. A sticky business. But with such grave issues toward, if you know what I mean, I sank my prejudices on this occasion and rolled up. I found the proceedings about as scaly as I had expected. It was a warm day, and the hall grounds were a dense, practically liquid mass of peasantry. Kids seethed to and fro. One of them, a small girl of sorts, grabbed my hand and hung on to it as I clove my way through the jam to where the Mothers' Sack Race was to finish. We hadn't been introduced, but she seemed to think I would do as well as anyone else to talk to about the rag-doll she had won in the Lucky Dip, and she rather spread herself on the topic.

"I'm going to call it Gertrude," she said. "And I shall undress it every night and put it to bed, and wake it up in the morning and dress it, and put it to bed at night, and wake it up next morning and dress it——"

"I say, old thing," I said, "I don't want to hurry you and all that, but you couldn't condense it a bit, could you? I'm rather anxious to see the finish of this race. The Wooster fortunes are by way of hanging on it."

"I'm going to run in a race soon," she said, shelving the doll for the nonce and descending to ordinary chit-chat.

"Yes?" I said. Distrait, if you know what I mean, and trying to peer through the chinks in the crowd. "What race is that?"

"Egg'n Spoon."

"No, really? Are you Sarah Mills?"

"Na-ow!" Registering scorn. "I'm Prudence Baxter."

Naturally this put our relations on a different footing. I gazed at her with considerable interest. One of the stable. I must say she didn't look much of a flier. She was short and round. Bit out of condition, I thought.

"I say," I said, "that being so, you mustn't dash

about in the hot sun and take the edge off yourself.
You must conserve your energies, old friend. Sit down
here in the shade.

"Don't want to sit down."

"Well, take it easy, anyhow."

The kid flitted to another topic like a butterfly hovering from flower to flower.

"I'm a good girl," she said.

"I bet you are. I hope you're a good egg-and-spoon
racer, too."

"Harold's a bad boy. Harold squealed in church
and isn't allowed to come to the treat. I'm glad," continued this ornament of her sex, wrinkling her nose
virtuously, "because he's a bad boy. He pulled my
hair Friday. Harold isn't coming to the treat! Harold
isn't coming to the treat! Harold isn't coming to the
treat!" she chanted, making a regular song of it.

"Don't rub it in, my dear old gardener's daughter,"
I pleaded. "You don't know it, but you've hit on
rather a painful subject."

"Ah, Wooster, my dear fellow! So you have made
friends with this little lady?"

It was old Heppenstall, beaming pretty profusely.
Life and soul of the party.

"I am delighted, my dear Wooster," he went on,
"quite delighted at the way you young men are throwing yourselves into the spirit of this little festivity of
ours."

"Oh, yes?" I said.

"Oh, yes! Even Rupert Steggles. I must confess

that my opinion of Rupert Steggles has materially altered for the better this afternoon."

Mine hadn't. But I didn't say so.

"I have always considered Rupert Steggles, between ourselves, a rather self-centred youth, by no means the kind who would put himself out to further the enjoyment of his fellows. And yet twice within the last half-hour I have observed him escorting Mrs. Penworthy, our worthy tobacconist's wife, to the refreshment-tent."

I left him standing. I shook off the clutching hand of the Baxter kid and hared it rapidly to the spot where the Mothers' Sack Race was just finishing. I had a horrid presentiment that there had been more dirty work at the cross-roads. The first person I ran into was young Bingo. I grabbed him by the arm.

"Who won?"

"I don't know. I didn't notice." There was bitterness in the chappie's voice. "It wasn't Mrs. Penworthy, dash her! Bertie, that hound Steggles is nothing more nor less than one of our leading snakes. I don't know how he heard about her, but he must have got on to it that she was dangerous. Do you know what he did? He lured that miserable woman into the refreshment-tent five minutes before the race, and brought her out so weighed down with cake and tea that she blew up in the first twenty yards. Just rolled over and lay there! Well, thank goodness, we still have Harold!"

I gaped at the poor chump.

"Harold! Haven't you heard?"

"Heard?" Bingo turned a delicate green. "Heard what? I haven't heard anything. I only arrived five minutes ago. Came here straight from the station. What has has happened? Tell me!"

I slipped him the information. He stared at me for a moment in a ghastly sort of way, then with a hollow groan tottered away and was lost in the crowd. A nasty knock, poor chap. I didn't blame him for being upset.

They were clearing the decks now for the Egg and Spoon Race, and I thought I might as well stay where I was and watch the finish. Not that I had much hope. Young Prudence was a good conversationalist, but she didn't seem to me to be the build for a winner.

As far as I could see through the mob, they got off to a good start. A short, red-haired child was making the running with a freckled blonde second, and Sarah Mills lying up an easy third. Our nominee was straggling along with the field, well behind the leaders. It was not hard even as early as this to spot the winner. There was a grace, a practised precision, in the way Sarah Mills held her spoon that told its own story. She was cutting out a good pace, but her egg didn't even wobble. A natural egg-and-spooner, if ever there was one.

Class will tell. Thirty yards from the tape, the red-haired kid tripped over her feet and shot her egg on to the turf. The freckled blonde fought gamely, but she had run herself out half-way down the straight, and Sarah Mills came past and home on a tight rein by several lengths, a popular winner. The blonde was second. A sniffing female in blue gingham beat a pie-faced kid in pink for the place-money, and Prudence Baxter, Jeeves's long shot, was either fifth or sixth, I couldn't see which.

And then I was carried along with the crowd to where old Heppenstall was going to present the prizes. I found myself standing next to the man Steggles.

"Hallo, old chap!" he said, very bright and cheery. "You've had a bad day, I'm afraid."

I looked at him with silent scorn. Lost on the blighter, of course.

"It's not been a good meeting for any of the big punters," he went on. "Poor old Bingo Little went down badly over that Egg and Spoon Race."

I hadn't been meaning to chat with the fellow, but I was startled.

"How do you mean badly?" I said. "We—he only had a small bet on."

"I don't know what you call small. He had thirty quid each way on the Baxter kid."

The landscape reeled before me.

"What!"

"Thirty quid at ten to one. I thought he must have heard something, but apparently not. The race went by the form-book all right."

I was trying to do sums in my head. I was just in the middle of working out the syndicate's losses when old Heppenstall's voice came sort of faintly to me out of the distance. He had been pretty fatherly and debonair when ladling out the prizes for the other events, but now he had suddenly grown all pained and grieved. He peered sorrowful at the multitude.

*   *   *   *   *

"With regard to the Girls' Egg and Spoon Race, which has just concluded," he said, "I have a painful duty to perform. Circumstances have arisen which it is impossible to ignore. It is not too much to say that I am stunned."

He gave the populace about five seconds to wonder why he was stunned, then went on.

"Three years ago, as you are aware, I was compelled to expunge from the list of events at this annual festival the Fathers' Quarter-Mile, owing to reports coming to my ears of wagers taken and given on the result at the village inn and a strong suspicion that on at least one occasion the race had actually been sold by the speediest runner. That unfortunate occurrence shook my faith in human nature, I admit—but still there was one event at least which I confidently expected to remain untainted by the miasma of professionalism. I allude to the Girls' Egg and Spoon Race. It seems, alas, that I was too sanguine."

He stopped again, and wrestled with his feelings.

"I will not weary you with the unpleasant details. I will merely say that before the race was run a stranger in our midst, the manservant of one of the guests at the Hall—I will not specify with more particularity—approached several of the competitors and presented each of them with five shillings on condition that they—er—finished. A belated sense of remorse has led him to confess to me what he did, but it is too late. The evil is accomplished, and retribution must take its course. It is no time for half-measures. I must be firm. I rule that Sarah Mills, Jane Parker, Bessie Clay, and Rosie Jukes, the first four to pass the winning-post, have forfeited their amateur status and are disqualified, and this handsome work-bag, presented by Lord Wickhammersley, goes, in consequence, to Prudence Baxter. Prudence, step forward!"

JEEVES
AND THE YULETIDE SPIRIT

Jeeves and the Yuletide Spirit

THE letter arrived on the morning of the sixteenth. I was pushing a bit of breakfast into the Wooster face at the moment; and, feeling fairly well fortified with coffee and kippers, I decided to break the news to Jeeves without delay. As Shakespeare says, if you're going to do a thing you might just as well pop right at it and get it over. The man would be disappointed, of course, and possibly even chagrined; but, dash it all, a spot of disappointment here and there does a fellow good. Makes him realize that life is stern and life is earnest.

"Oh, Jeeves," I said.

"Sir?"

"We have here a communication from Lady Wickham. She has written inviting me to Skeldings for the festivities. So will you see about bunging the necessaries together? We repair thither on the twenty-third. We shall be there some little time, I expect."

There was a pause. I could feel he was directing a frosty gaze at me, but I dug into the marmalade and refused to meet it.

"I thought I understood you to say, sir, that you proposed to visit Monte Carlo immediately after Christmas."

"I know. But that's all off. Plans changed."

63

At this point the telephone bell rang, tiding over nicely what had threatened to be an awkward moment. Jeeves unhooked the receiver.

"Yes? . . . Yes, madam. . . . Very good, madam. Here is Mr. Wooster." He handed me the instrument. "Mrs. Spenser Gregson, sir."

You know, every now and then I can't help feeling that Jeeves is losing his grip. In his prime it would have been with him the work of a moment to have told my aunt Agatha that I was not at home. I gave him one of those reproachful glances, and took the machine.

"Hullo?" I said. "Yes? Yes? Yes? Bertie speaking. Hullo? Hullo? Hullo?"

"Don't keep on saying Hullo," yipped the old relative, in her customary curt manner. "You're not a parrot. Sometimes I wish you were, because then you might have a little sense."

Quite the wrong sort of tone to adopt toward a fellow in the early morning, of course, but what can one do?

"Bertie, Lady Wickham tells me she has invited you to Skeldings for Christmas. Are you going?"

"Rather!"

"Well, mind you behave yourself. Lady Wickham is an old friend of mine."

"I shall naturally endeavour, Aunt Agatha," I replied stiffly, "to conduct myself in a manner befitting an English gentleman paying a visit——"

"What did you say? Speak up. I can't hear."

"I said, 'Right ho.' "

"Oh? Well, mind you do. And there's another reason why I particularly wish you to be as little of an imbecile as you can manage while at Skeldings. Sir Roderick Glossop will be there."

"What!"

"Don't bellow like that."

"Did you say Sir Roderick Glossop?"

"I did."

"You don't mean Tuppy Glossop?"

"I mean Sir Roderick Glossop. Which was my reason for saying Sir Roderick Glossop. Now, Bertie, I want you to listen to me attentively. Are you there?"

"Yes. Still here."

"Well, then, listen. I have at last succeeded, after incredible difficulty and in face of all the evidence, in almost persuading Sir Roderick that you are not actually insane. He is prepared to suspend judgment until he has seen you once more. On your behaviour at Skeldings, therefore——"

But I had hung up the receiver. Shaken. That's what I was. S. to the core.

This Glossop was a formidable old bird with a bald head and outsize eyebrows, by profession a loony-doctor. How it happened, I couldn't tell you to this day, but I once got engaged to his daughter Honoria, a ghastly dynamic exhibit who read Nietzsche and had a laugh like waves breaking on a stern and rock-bound coast. The fixture was scratched, owing to events occurring which convinced the old boy that I was off my napper; and since then he has always had my name at the top of his list of Loonies I Have Lunched With.

"Jeeves," I said, all of a twitter, "do you know what? Sir Roderick Glossop is going to be at Lady Wickham's."

"Very good, sir. If you have finished breakfast I will clear away."

Cold and haughty. No sympathy. None of the rallying-around spirit which one likes to see. As I had anticipated, Jeeves had been looking forward to a little flutter at the tables. We Woosters can wear the mask. I ignored his lack of decent feeling.

"Do so, Jeeves," I said proudly.

Going down to Skeldings in the car on the afternoon of the twenty-third, Jeeves was aloof and reserved. And before dinner on the first night of my visit he put the studs in my dress shirt in what I can only call a marked manner. The whole thing was extremely painful, and it seemed to me, as I lay in bed on the morning of the twenty-fourth, that the only step to take was to put the whole facts of the case before him and trust to his native good sense to effect an understanding.

My hostess, Lady Wickham, was a beaky female built far too closely on the lines of my aunt Agatha for comfort; but she had seemed matey enough on my arrival. Her daughter Roberta had welcomed me with a warmth which, I'm bound to say, had set the old heartstrings fluttering a bit. And Sir Roderick, in the brief moment we had had together, had said, "Ha, young man!"——not particularly chummily, but he said it; and my view was that it practically amounted to the lion lying down with the lamb.

So, all in all, life at this juncture seemed pretty well

all to the mustard, and I decided to tell Jeeves exactly how matters stood.

"Jeeves," I said, as he appeared with the steaming.
"Sir?"

"I'm afraid scratching that Monte Carlo trip has
been a bit of a jar for you, Jeeves."

"Not at all, sir."

"Oh, yes, it has. The heart was set on wintering
in the world's good old plague spot, I know. I saw
your eye light up when I said we were due for a visit
there. You snorted a bit and your fingers twitched. I
know, I know. And now that there has been a change
of programme, the iron has entered into your soul."

"Not at all, sir."

"Oh, yes, it has. I've seen it. Very well, then. What
I wish to impress upon you, Jeeves, is that it was
through no light and airy caprice that I accepted this
invitation to Lady Wickham's. I have been angling
for it for weeks, prompted by many considerations. It
was imperative that I should come to Skeldings for
Christmas, Jeeves, because I knew that young Tuppy
Glossop was going to be here."

"Sir Roderick Glossop, sir?"

"His nephew. You may have observed hanging
about the place a fellow with light hair and a Chesh-
ire-cat grin. That is Tuppy, and I have been anxious
for some time to get to grips with him. The Wooster
honour is involved."

I took a sip of tea, for the mere memory of my
wrongs had shaken me.

"In spite of the fact that young Tuppy is the
nephew of Sir Roderick Glossop, at whose hands,

Jeeves, as you are aware, I have suffered much, I fraternized with him freely. I said to myself that a man is not to be blamed for his relations, and that I should hate to have my pals hold my aunt Agatha, for instance, against me. Broad-minded, Jeeves, I think?"

"Extremely, sir."

"Well, then, as I say, I sought this Tuppy out, Jeeves, and hobnobbed; and what do you think he did?"

"I could not say, sir."

"I will tell you. One night, after dinner at the Drones' Club, he bet me I wouldn't swing myself across the swimming bath by the ropes and rings. I took him on, and was buzzing along in great style until I came to the last ring. And then I found that this fiend in human shape had looped it back against the rail, thus leaving me hanging in the void with no means of getting ashore to my home and loved ones.

"There was nothing for it but to drop into the water. And what I maintain, Jeeves, is that, if I can't get back at him somehow at Skeldings—with all the vast resources which a country house affords at my disposal—I am not the man I was."

"I see, sir."

"And now, Jeeves, we come to the most important reason why I had to spend Christmas at Skeldings. Jeeves," I said, diving into the old cup once more for a moment and bringing myself out wreathed in blushes, "the fact of the matter is, I'm in love."

"Indeed, sir?"

"You've seen Miss Roberta Wickham?"

"Yes, sir."

"Very well, then."

There was a pause while I let it sink in.

"During your stay here, Jeeves," I said, "you will, no doubt, be thrown a good deal together with Miss Wickham's maid. On such occasions pitch it strong."

"Sir?"

"You know what I mean. Tell her I'm rather a good chap. Mention my hidden depths. These things get round. A boost is never wasted, Jeeves."

"Very good, sir. But——"

"But what?"

"Well, sir——"

"Carry on, Jeeves. We are always glad to hear from you, always."

"What I was about to remark, if you will excuse me, sir, was that I would scarcely have thought Miss Wickham a suitable——"

"Jeeves," I said coldly, "what is your kick against Miss Wickham?"

"Oh, really, sir!"

"Jeeves, I insist. This is a time for plain speaking. You have beefed about Miss Wickham. I wish to know why."

"It merely crossed my mind, sir, that for a gentleman of your description Miss Wickham is not a suitable mate."

"What do you mean by 'a gentleman of my description'?"

"I beg your pardon, sir. The expression escaped me inadvertently. I was about to observe, sir, that, though Miss Wickham is a charming young lady——"

"There, Jeeves, you spoke an imperial quart. What eyes!"

"Yes, sir."

"What hair!"

"Very true, sir."

"And what *espièglerie*—if that's the word I want.'

"The exact word, sir."

"All right, then. Carry on."

"I grant Miss Wickham the possession of all these desirable qualities, sir. Nevertheless, considered as a matrimonial prospect for a gentleman of your description, I cannot look upon her as suitable. In my opinion, Miss Wickham lacks seriousness, sir. She is too volatile and frivolous. To qualify as Miss Wickham's husband, a gentleman would need to possess a commanding personality and considerable strength of character."

"Exactly!"

"I would always hesitate to recommend as a life's companion a young lady with such a vivid shade of red hair. Red hair, sir, is dangerous."

I eyed the blighter squarely.

"Jeeves," I said, "you're talking rot."

"Very good, sir."

"Absolute drivel."

"Very good, sir."

"Pure mashed potatoes."

"Very good, sir."

"Very good, sir—I mean very good, Jeeves; that will be all," I said.

And I drank a modicum of tea with a good deal of hauteur.

It isn't often that I find myself able to prove Jeeves in the wrong; but by dinner time that night I was in a position to do so, and I did it without delay.

"Touching on that matter we were touching on, Jeeves," I said, coming in from the bath and tackling him as he studded the shirt, "I should be glad if you would give me your careful attention for a moment. I warn you that what I am about to say is going to make you look pretty silly."

"Indeed, sir?"

"Yes, Jeeves. Pretty dashed silly it's going to make you look. This morning, if I remember rightly, you stated that Miss Wickham was volatile, frivolous, and lacking in seriousness. Am I correct?"

"Quite correct, sir."

"Then what I have to tell you may cause you to alter that opinion. I went for a walk with Miss Wickham this afternoon; and, as we walked I told her about what young Tuppy Glossop did to me in the swimming bath at the Drones'. She hung upon my words, Jeeves, and was full of sympathy."

"Indeed, sir?"

"Dripping with it. And that's not all. Almost before I had finished she was suggesting the ripest, fruitiest, brainiest scheme for bringing young Tuppy's gray hairs in sorrow to the grave that anyone could possibly imagine."

"That is very gratifying, sir."

" 'Gratifying' is the word. It appears that at the school where Miss Wickham was educated, Jeeves, it used to become necessary from time to time for the right-thinking element to slip it across certain of the baser sort. Do you know what they did, Jeeves?"

"No, sir."

"They took a long stick, Jeeves, and—follow me closely here—they tied a darning needle to the end of it. Then, at dead of night, it appears, they sneaked into the party of the second part's cubicle and shoved the needle through the bedclothes and punctured her hot-water bottle.

"Girls are much subtler in these matters than boys, Jeeves. At my old school one would occasionally heave a jug of water over another bloke during the night watches, but we never thought of effecting the same result in this particularly neat and scientific manner.

"Well, Jeeves, that was the scheme which Miss Wickham suggested I should work on young Tuppy, and that is the girl you call frivolous and lacking in seriousness. Any girl who can think up a wheeze like that is my idea of a helpmate.

"I shall be glad, Jeeves, if by the time I come to bed to-night you have waiting for me in this room a stout stick with a good sharp darning needle attached."

"Well, sir——"

I raised my hand.

"Jeeves," I said, "not another word. Stick, one, and needle, darning, good, sharp, one, without fail, in this room at eleven-thirty to-night."

"Very good, sir."

"Have you any idea where young Tuppy sleeps?"

"I could ascertain, sir."

"Do so, Jeeves."

In a few minutes he was back with the necessary informash.

"Mr. Glossop is established in the Moat Room, sir."

"Where's that?"

"The second door on the floor below, sir."

"Right ho, Jeeves. Are the studs in my shirt?"

"Yes, sir."

"And the links also?"

"Yes, sir."

"Then push me into it."

The task to which I had set myself was one that involved hardship and discomfort, for it meant sitting up till well into the small hours, and then padding down a cold corridor. But I did not shrink from it. After all, there is a lot to be said for family tradition. We Woosters did our bit in the Crusades.

It being Christmas Eve, there was, as I had foreseen, a good deal of revelry and what not; so that it wasn't till past one that I got to my room. Allowing for everything, it didn't seem that it was going to be safe to start my little expedition till half-past two at the earliest; and I'm bound to say that it was only the utmost resolution that kept me from snuggling into the sheets and calling it a day. I'm not much of a lad now for late hours.

However, by half-past two everything appeared to be quiet. I shook off the mists of sleep, grabbed the good old stick and needle, and was off along the corridor. And presently, pausing outside the Moat Room,

I turned the handle, found the door wasn't locked, and went in.

At first, when I had beetled in, the room had seemed as black as a coal cellar; but after a bit things began to lighten. The curtains weren't quite drawn over the window, and I could see a trifle of the scenery here and there.

The bed was opposite the window, with the head against the wall and the end where the feet were jutting out toward where I stood, thus rendering it possible, after one had sown the seed, so to speak, to make a quick get-away.

There only remained now the rather tricky problem of locating the old hot-water bottle. I mean to say, the one thing you can't do if you want to carry a job like this through with secrecy and dispatch is to stand at the end of a fellow's bed, jabbing at random.

I was a good deal cheered, at this juncture, to hear a fruity snore from the direction of the pillows. Reason told me that a bloke who could snore like that wasn't going to be awakened by a trifle. I edged forward and ran a hand in a gingerly sort of way over the coverlet. A moment later I had found the bulge. I steered the good old darning needle on to it, gripped the stick, and shoved. Then, pulling out the weapon, I sidled toward the door, and in an another moment would have been outside, buzzing for home and the good night's rest, when suddenly there was a crash that sent my spine shooting up through the top of my head, and the contents of the bed sat up like a jack-in-the-box and said:

"Who's that?"

It just shows how your most careful strategic moves can be the very ones that dish your campaign. In order to facilitate the orderly retreat according to plan, I had left the door open, and the beastly thing had slammed like a bomb.

But I wasn't giving much thought to the causes of the explosion. What was disturbing me was the discovery that, whoever else the bloke in the bed might be, he was not young Tuppy. Tuppy has one of those high, squeaky voices that sound like the tenor of the village choir failing to hit a high note. This one was something in between the last trump and a tiger calling for breakfast after being on a diet for a day or two. It was the sort of nasty, rasping voice you hear shouting "Fore!" when you're one of a slow foursome on the links and are holding up a couple of retired colonels.

I did not linger. Getting swiftly off the mark, I dived for the door handle, and was off and away, banging the door behind me. I may be a chump in many ways, as my aunt Agatha will freely attest, but I know when and when not to be among those present.

And I was just about to do the stretch of corridor leading to the stairs in a split second under the record time for the course, when something brought me up with a sudden jerk. An irresistible force was holding me straining at leash, as it were.

You know, sometimes it seems to me as if Fate were going out of its way to such an extent to snooter you that you wonder if it's worth while to struggle. The night being a trifle chillier than the dickens, I had donned for this expedition a dressing gown. It was the tail of this infernal garment that had caught in the door and pipped me at the eleventh hour.

The next moment the door had opened, light was streaming through it, and the bloke with the voice had grabbed me by the arm.

It was Sir Roderick Glossop.

For about three and a quarter seconds, or possibly more, we just stood there, drinking each other in, so to speak, the old boy still attached with a limpetlike grip to my elbow. If I hadn't been in a dressing gown and he in pink pajamas with a blue stripe, and if he hadn't been glaring quite so much as if he were shortly going to commit a murder, the tableau would have looked rather like one of those advertisements you see in the magazines, where the experienced elder is patting the young man's arm and saying to him: "My boy, if you subscribe to the Mutt-Jeff Correspondence School of Oswego, Kansas, as I did, you may some day, like me, become Third Assistant Vice President of the Schenectady Consolidated Nail File and Eyebrow Tweezer Corporation."

"You!" said Sir Roderick finally. And in this connection I want to state that it's all rot to say you can't hiss a word that hasn't an *s* in it. The way he pushed out that "You!" sounded like an angry cobra.

By rights, I suppose, at this point I ought to have said something. The best I could manage, however, was a faint, soft, bleating sound.

"Come in here," he said, lugging me into the room. "We don't want to wake the whole house. Now," he said, depositing me on the carpet and closing the door, and doing a bit of eyebrow work, "kindly inform me what is this latest manifestation of insanity?"

It seemed to me that a light and cheery laugh might help. So I had a pop at one.

"Don't gibber!" said my genial host. And I'm bound to admit that the light and cheery hadn't come out quite as I'd intended.

I pulled myself together with a strong effort.

"Awfully sorry about all this," I said in a hearty sort of voice. "The fact is, I thought you were Tuppy."

"Kindly refrain from inflicting your idiotic slang on me. What do you mean by the adjective 'tuppy'?"

"It isn't so much an adjective, don't you know. More of a noun, I should think, if you examine it squarely. What I mean to say is, I thought you were your nephew."

"You thought I was my nephew? Why should I be my nephew?"

"What I'm driving at is, I thought this was his room."

"My nephew and I changed rooms. I have a great dislike for sleeping on an upper floor. I am nervous about fire."

For the first time since this interview had started I braced up a trifle. I lost that sense of being a toad under the harrow which had been cramping my style up till now. I even went so far as to eye this pink-pajamaed poltroon with a good deal of contempt and loathing. Just because he had this craven fear of fire and this selfish preference for letting Tuppy be cooked instead of himself, should the emergency occur, my nicely reasoned plans had gone up the spout. I gave him a look, and I think I may even have snorted a bit.

"I should have thought that your manservant would have informed you," said Sir Roderick, "that we contemplated making this change. I met him shortly before luncheon and told him to tell you."

This extraordinary statement staggered me. That Jeeves had been aware all along that this old crumb would occupy the bed which I was proposing to prod with darning needles and had let me rush upon my doof without a word of warning was almost beyond belief. You might say I was aghast. Yes, practically aghast.

"You told Jeeves that you were going to sleep in this room?" I gasped.

"I did. I was aware that you and my nephew were on terms of intimacy, and I wished to spare myself the possibility of a visit from you. I confess that it never occurred to me that such a visit was to be anticipated at three o'clock in the morning. What the devil do you mean," he barked, suddenly hotting up, "by prowling about the house at this hour? And what is that thing in your hand?"

I looked down, and found that I was still grasping the stick. I give you my honest word that, what with the maelstrom of emotions into which his revelation about Jeeves had cast me, the discovery came as an absolute surprise.

"This?" I said. "Oh, yes."

"What do you mean, 'Oh, yes'? What is it?"

"Well, it's a long story."

"We have the night before us."

"It's this way: I will ask you to picture me some weeks ago, perfectly peaceful and inoffensive, after dinner at the Drones', smoking a thoughtful cigarette and——"

I broke off. The man wasn't listening. He was goggling in a rapt sort of way at the end of the bed, from which there had now begun to drip on to the carpet a series of drops.

"Good heavens!"

"——thoughtful cigarette and chatting pleasantly of this and that——"

I broke off again. He had lifted the sheets and was gazing at the corpse of the hot-water bottle.

"Did you do this?" he said in a low, strangled sort of voice.

"Er—yes. As a matter of fact, yes. I was just going to tell you——"

"And your aunt tried to persuade me that you were not insane!"

"I'm not. Absolutely not. If you'll just let me explain——"

"I will do nothing of the kind."

"It all began——"

"Silence!"

"Right ho."

He did some deep-breathing exercises.

"My bed is drenched!"

"The way it all began——"

"Be quiet!" He heaved somewhat for a while. "You wretched, miserable idiot," he said, "kindly inform me which bedroom you are supposed to be occupying."

"It's on the floor above. The Clock Room."

"Thank you. I will find it."

"Eh?"

He gave me the eyebrow.

"I propose," he said, "to pass the remainder of the night in your room, where, I presume, there is a bed in a condition to be slept in. You may bestow yourself as comfortably as you can here. I will wish you good-night."

He buzzed off, leaving me flat.

Well, we Woosters are old campaigners. We can take the rough with the smooth. But to say that I liked the prospect now before me would be paltering with the truth. One glance at the bed told me that any idea of sleeping there was out. A goldfish could have done it, but not Bertram. After a bit of a look round I decided that the best chance of getting any night's rest was to doze as well as I could in the armchair. I pinched a couple of pillows off the bed, shoved the hearthrug over my knees, and sat down and started counting sheep.

But it wasn't any good. The old lemon was sizzling much too much to admit of anything in the nature of slumber. This hideous revelation of the blackness of Jeeves's treachery kept coming back to me every time I nearly succeeded in dropping off. I was just wondering if I would ever get to sleep again in this world when a voice at my elbow said, "Good-morning, sir," and I sat up with a jerk.

I could have sworn I hadn't so much as dozed off for even a minute; but apparently I had. For the curtains were drawn back and daylight was coming in through the window, and there was Jeeves with a cup of tea on a tray.

"Merry Christmas, sir!"

I reached out a feeble hand for the restoring brew. I swallowed a mouthful or two, and felt a little better. I was aching in every limb, and the dome felt like lead; but I was now able to think with a certain amount of clearness, and I fixed the man with a stony eye and prepared to let him have it.

"You think so, do you?" I said. "Much, let me tell you, depends on what you mean by the adjective 'merry.' If, moreover, you suppose that it is going to be merry for you, correct that impression. Jeeves," I said, taking another half oz. of tea and speaking in a cold, measured voice, "I wish to ask you one question. Did you or did you not know that Sir Roderick Glossop was sleeping in this room last night?"

"Yes, sir."

"You admit it!"

"Yes, sir."

"And you didn't tell me!"

"No, sir. I thought it would be more judicious not to do so."

"Jeeves——"

"If you will allow me to explain, sir."

"Explain!"

"I was aware that my silence might lead to something in the nature of an embarrassing contretemps. sir——"

"You thought that, did you?"

"Yes, sir."

"You were a good guesser," I said, sucking down further bohea.

"But it seemed to me, sir, that whatever might occur was all for the best."

I would have put in a crisp word or two here, but he carried on without giving me the opp.

"I thought that possibly, on reflection, sir, your views being what they are, you would prefer your relations with Sir Roderick Glossop and his family to be distant rather than cordial."

"My views? What do you mean, 'my views'?"

"As regards a matrimonial alliance with Miss Honoria Glossop, sir."

Something like an electric shock seemed to zip through me. The man had opened up a new line of thought. I suddenly saw what he was driving at, and realized all in a flash that I had been wronging this faithful fellow. All the while I supposed he had been landing me in the soup he had really been steering me away from it.

It was like those stories one used to read as a kid, about the traveller going along on a dark night, and his dog grabs him by the leg of his trousers, and he says, "Down, sir! What are you doing, Rover?" And the dog hangs on, and he gets rather hot under the collar and curses a bit, but the dog won't let him go, and then suddenly the moon shines through the clouds and he finds he's been standing on the edge of a precipice and one more step would have—well, anyway, you get the idea. And what I'm driving at is that much the same thing seemed to be happening now.

I give you my honest word, it had never struck me till this moment that my aunt Agatha had been scheming to get me in right with Sir Roderick so that I should eventually be received back into the fold, if you see what I mean, and subsequently pushed off on Honoria.

"My God, Jeeves!" I said, paling.

"Precisely, sir."

"You think there was a risk?"

"I do, sir. A very grave risk."

A disturbing thought struck me.

"But, Jeeves, on calm reflection, won't Sir Roderick have gathered by now that my objective was young Tuppy, and that puncturing his hot-water bottle was just one of those things that occur when the Yuletide spirit is abroad—one of those things that have to be overlooked and taken with the indulgent smile and the fatherly shake of the head? What I mean is, he'll realize that I wasn't trying to snooter him, and then all the good work will have been wasted."

"No, sir. I fancy not. That might possibly have been Sir Roderick's mental reaction, had it not been for the second incident."

"The second incident?"

"During the night, sir, while Sir Roderick was occupying your bed, somebody entered the room, pierced his hot-water bottle with some sharp instrument, and vanished in the darkness."

I could make nothing of this.

"What! Do you think I walked in my sleep?"

"No, sir. It was young Mr. Glossop who did it. I encountered him this morning, sir, shortly before I came here. He was in cheerful spirits, and inquired of me how you were feeling about the incident—not being aware that his victim had been Sir Roderick."

"But, Jeeves, what an amazing coincidence!"

"Sir?"

"Why, young Tuppy getting exactly the same idea as I did. Or, rather, as Miss Wickham did. You can't say that's not a miracle."

"Not altogether, sir. It appears that he received the suggestion from her."

"From Miss Wickham?"

"Yes, sir."

"You mean to say that, after she had put me up to the scheme of puncturing Tuppy's hot-water bottle, she went off and tipped Tuppy off to puncturing mine?"

"Precisely, sir. She is a young lady with a keen sense of humour, sir."

I sat there—you might say, stunned. When I thought how near I had come to offering the Wooster heart and hand to a girl capable of double-crossing a strong man's honest love like that, I shivered.

"Are you cold, sir?"

"No, Jeeves. Just shuddering."

"The occurrence, if I may take the liberty of saying so, sir, will perhaps lend colour to the view which I put forward yesterday that Miss Wickham, though in many respects a charming young lady——"

I raised the hand.

"Say no more, Jeeves," I replied. "Love is dead." I brooded for a while.

"You've seen Sir Roderick this morning?"

"Yes, sir."

"How did he seem?"

"A trifle feverish, sir."

"Feverish?"

"A little emotional, sir. He expressed a strong desire to meet you, sir."

"What would you advise?"

"If you were to slip out by the back entrance, sir, it would be possible for you to make your way across the field without being observed and reach the village, where you could hire an automobile to take you to London. I could bring on your effects later in your own car."

"But London, Jeeves? Is any man safe? My aunt Agatha is in London."

"Yes, sir."

"Well, then?"

He regarded me for a moment with a fathomless eye.

"I think the best plan, sir, would be for you to leave England, which is not pleasant at this time of the year, for some little while. I would not take the liberty of dictating your movements, sir, but, as you already have accommodation engaged on the Blue Train for Monte Carlo for the day after to-morrow———"

"But you cancelled the booking?"

"No, sir."

"I told you to."

"Yes, sir. It was remiss of me, but the matter slipped my mind."

"Oh?"

"Yes, sir."

"All right, Jeeves. Monte Carlo, ho, then."

"Very good, sir."

"It's lucky, as things have turned out, that you forgot to cancel that booking."

"Very fortunate indeed, sir. If you will wait here, sir, I will return to your room and procure a suit of clothes."

JEEVES AND THE SONG OF SONGS

Jeeves and the Song of Songs

Aɴᴏᴛʜᴇʀ day dawned all hot and fresh and, in pursuance of my unswerving policy at that time, I was singing "Sonny Boy" in my bath, when Jeeves's voice filtered through the woodwork.

"I beg your pardon, sir."

I had just got to that bit about the angels being lonely, where you need every ounce of concentration in order to make the spectacular finish, but I signed off courteously.

"Yes, Jeeves? Say on."

"Mr. Glossop, sir."

"What about him?"

"He is in the sitting room, sir."

"Young Tuppy Glossop?"

"Yes, sir," Jeeves answered in his monosyllabic way.

"You say that he is in the sitting room?" I asked.

"Yes, sir."

"Desiring speech with me?"

"Yes, sir."

"H'm!"

"Sir?"

"I only said 'H'm.'"

And I'll tell you why I said "H'm." It was because the man's story had interested me strangely. And I'll tell you why the man's story had interested me strangely. Owing to a certain episode that had oc-curred one night at the Drones' Club, there had sprung up recently a coolness, as you might describe it, between this Glossop and myself. The news, there-fore, that he was visiting me at my flat, especially at an hour when he must have known that I would be in my bath and consequently in a strong strategic posi-tion to heave a wet sponge at him, surprised me con-siderably.

I hopped out with some briskness and, slipping a couple of towels about the torso, made for the sitting room. I found young Tuppy at the piano, playing "Sonny Boy" with one finger.

"What ho!" I said, not without hauteur.

"Oh, hullo, Bertie," said Tuppy. "I say, Bertie, I want to see you about something important."

It seemed to me that the bloke was embarrassed. He had moved to the mantelpiece, and now he broke a vase in a constrained way.

"The fact is, Bertie, I'm engaged."

"Engaged?"

"Engaged," said young Tuppy, coyly dropping a photograph frame upon the fender. "Practically, that is."

"Practically?"

"Yes. You'll like her, Bertie. Her name is Cora Bellinger. She's studying for opera. Wonderful voice she has. Also dark, flashing eyes and a great soul."

"How do you mean, 'practically'?"

"Well, it's this way. Before ordering the trousseau there is one little point she wants cleared up. You see, what with her great soul and all that, she has a rather serious outlook on life, and the one thing she absolutely bars is anything in the shape of hearty humour. You know, practical joking and so forth.

"She said if she thought I was a practical joker she would never speak to me again. And unfortunately she appears to have heard about that little affair at the Drones'. . . . I expect you have forgotten all about that, Bertie?"

"I have not!"

"No, no, not forgotten exactly. What I mean is, nobody laughs more heartily at the recollection than you. And what I want you to do, old man, is to seize an early opportunity of taking Cora aside and categorically denying that there is any truth in the story. My happiness, Bertie, is in your hands, if you know what I mean."

Well, of course, if he put it like that, what could I do? We Woosters have our code.

"Oh, all right," I said, but far from brightly.

"Splendid fellow!"

"When do I meet this blighted female?" I asked.

"Don't call her 'this blighted female,' Bertie, old man. I have planned all that out. I will bring her around here to-day for a spot of lunch."

"What!"

"At one-thirty. Right. Good. Fine. Thanks. I knew I could rely on you."

He pushed off, and I turned to Jeeves, who had shimmered in with the morning meal.

"Lunch for three to-day, Jeeves," I said.

"Very good, sir."

"You know, Jeeves, it's a bit thick. You remember

my telling you about what Mr. Glossop did to me that night at the Drones'?"

"Yes, sir."

"For months I have been cherishing dreams of a hideous vengeance. And now, so far from crushing him into the dust, I've got to fill him and fiancée with rich food, and generally rally round and be the good angel."

"Life is like that, sir."

"True, Jeeves. What have we here?" I asked, inspecting the tray.

"Kippered herrings, sir."

"And I shouldn't wonder," I said, for I was in thoughtful mood, "if even herrings haven't troubles of their own."

"Quite possibly, sir."

"I mean, apart from getting kippered."

"Yes, sir."

"And so it goes on, Jeeves, so it goes on."

I can't say I saw exactly eye to eye with young Tuppy in his admiration for the Bellinger female. Delivered on the mat at one-twenty-five, she proved to be an upstanding light-heavyweight of some thirty summers with a commanding eye and a square chin which I, personally, would have steered clear of.

She seemed to me a good deal like what Cleopatra would have been after going in too freely for the starches and cereals. I don't know why it is, but women who have anything to do with opera, even if they're only studying for it, always appear to run to surplus poundage.

Tuppy, however, was obviously all for her. His whole demeanour, both before and during luncheon, was that of one striving to be worthy of a noble soul. When Jeeves offered him a cocktail he practically recoiled as from a serpent. It was terrible to see the change which love had effected in the man. The spectacle put me off my food.

At half-past two the Bellinger left to go to a singing lesson. Tuppy trotted after her to the door, bleating and frisking a goodish bit, and then came back and looked at me in a marked manner.

"Well, Bertie?"

"Well, what?"

"I mean, isn't she?"

"Oh, rather," I said, humouring the poor fish.

"Wonderful eyes?"

"Oh, rather."

"Wonderful figure?"

"Oh, quite."

"Wonderful voice?"

Here I was able to intone the response with a little more heartiness. The Bellinger, at Tuppy's request, had sung us a few songs before digging in at the trough, and nobody could have denied that her pipes were in great shape. The plaster was still falling from the ceiling.

"Terrific," I said.

Tuppy sighed, and, having helped himself to about four inches of whisky and one of soda, took a deep, refreshing draft.

"Ah!" he said. "I needed that."

"Why didn't you have it at lunch?"

"Well, it's this way," said Tuppy. "I have not actually ascertained what Cora's opinions are on the subject of the taking of slight snorts from time to time, but I thought it more prudent to lay off. The view I took was that laying off would seem to indicate the serious mind. It is touch and go, as you might say, at the moment, and the smallest thing may turn the scale."

"What beats me is how on earth you expect to make her think you've got a mind at all—let alone a serious one."

"Well, I have my own methods, Bertie, old man."

"I bet they're rotten, Tuppy."

"You do, do you?" said Tuppy warmly. "Well, let me tell you, my lad, that that's exactly what they're anything but. I am handling this affair with consummate generalship. Do you remember Beefy Bingham who was at Oxford with us?"

"I ran into him only the other day. He's a parson now."

"Yes. Down in the East End. Well, he runs a lads' club for the local toughs—you know the sort of thing —cocoa and backgammon in the reading room and occasional clean, bright entertainments in the Oddfellows' Hall; and I've been helping him. I don't suppose I've passed an evening away from the backgammon board for weeks.

"Cora is extremely pleased. I've got her to promise to sing on Tuesday at Beefy's next clean, bright entertainment."

"You have?"

"I absolutely have. And now mark my devilish ingenuity, Bertie. I'm going to sing, too."

"Why do you suppose that's going to get you anywhere?"

"Because the way I intend to sing the song I intend to sing will prove to her that there are great deeps in my nature, whose existence she has not suspected. She will see that rough, unlettered audience wiping the tears out of its bally eyes and she will say to herself, 'What ho! The old egg really has a soul!'

"For it is not one of your mouldy comic songs, Bertie. No low buffoonery of that sort for me. It is all about angels being lonely and what not."

I uttered a sharp cry. "You can't mean you're going to sing 'Sonny Boy'?"

"I jolly well do."

I was shocked. Yes, dash it, I was shocked. You see, I held strong views on "Sonny Boy." I considered it a song only to be attempted by a few of the elect in the privacy of the bathroom. And the thought of its being murdered in open Oddfellows' Hall by a bloke who could treat a pal as young Tuppy had treated me that night at the Drones' sickened me. Yes, sickened me.

I hadn't time, however, to express my horror and disgust, for at this juncture Jeeves came in.

"Mrs. Travers has just rung up on the telephone, sir. She desired me to say that she will be calling to see you in a few minutes."

"Contents noted, Jeeves," I said. "Now listen, Tuppy——" I began.

I stopped. The fellow wasn't there.

"Mr. Glossop has left, sir."

"Left? How can he have left? He was sitting there."

"That is the front door closing now, sir."

"But what made him shoot off like that?"

"Possibly Mr. Glossop did not wish to meet Mrs. Travers, sir."

"Why not?"

"I could not say, sir. But undoubtedly at the mention of Mrs. Travers's name he rose very swiftly.

"Strange, Jeeves."

"Yes, sir."

I turned to a subject of more moment.

"Jeeves," I said, "Mr. Glossop proposes to sing 'Sonny Boy' at an entertainment down in the East End next Tuesday before an audience consisting mainly of costermongers, with a sprinkling of whelk-stall owners, purveyors of blood oranges, and minor pugilists."

"Indeed, sir?"

"Make a note to remind me to be there. He will infallibly get the bird, and I want to witness his downfall."

"Very good, sir."

"And when Mrs. Travers arrives I shall be in the sitting room."

Those who know Bertram Wooster best are aware that in his journey through life he is impeded and generally snookered by about as scaly a collection of aunts as was ever assembled. But there is one exception to the general ghastliness—viz. my aunt Dahlia. She married old Tom Travers the year Bluebottle won the Cambridgeshire, and is one of the best. It is always a pleasure to me to chat with her, and it was with a courtly geniality that I rose to receive her as she sailed over the threshold at about two-fifty-five.

She seemed somewhat perturbed, and plunged into the agenda without delay. Aunt Dahlia is one of those big, hearty women. She used to go in a lot for hunting, and she generally speaks as if she had just sighted a fox on a hillside half a mile away.

"Bertie," she cried, in the manner of one encouraging a platoon of hounds to renewed efforts, "I want your help."

"And you shall have it, Aunt Dahlia," I replied suavely. "I can honestly say that there is no one to whom I would more readily do a good turn, no one to whom I am more delighted to be——"

"Less of it," she begged; "less of it. You know that friend of yours, young Glossop?"

"He's just been lunching here."

"He has, has he? Well, I wish you'd poisoned his soup."

"We didn't have soup. And when you describe him as a 'friend of mine,' I wouldn't quite say the term absolutely squared with the facts. Some time ago, one night when we had been dining together at the Drones'——"

At this point Aunt Dahlia—a little brusquely, it seemed to me—said that she would rather wait for the story of my life till she could get it in book form. I could see now that she was definitely not her usual sunny self, so I shelved my personal grievances and asked what was biting her.

"It's that young hound Glossop," she said.

"What's he been doing?"

"Breaking Angela's heart."

(Angela. Daughter of above. My cousin. Quite a good egg.)

"What!"

"I say he's—breaking—Angela's—*heart!*"

"You say he's breaking Angela's heart?"

She begged me to suspend the vaudeville cross-talk stuff.

"How's he doing that?" I asked.

"With his neglect. With his low, callous, double-crossing duplicity."

" 'Duplicity' is the word, Aunt Dahlia," I said. "In treating of young Tuppy Glossop, it springs naturally to the lips. Let me tell you what he did to me one night at the Drones'. We had finished dinner——"

"Ever since the beginning of the season, up to about three weeks ago, he was all over Angela. The sort of thing which, when I was a girl, we should have described as courting."

"Or wooing?"

"Wooing or courting, whichever you like."

"Whichever *you* like, Aunt Dahlia," I said courteously.

"Well, anyway, he haunted the house, lapped up daily lunches, took her out dancing half the night, and so on, till naturally the poor kid, who's quite off her oats about him, took it for granted that it was only a question of time before he suggested that they should feed for life out of the same crib. And now he's gone and dropped her like a hot brick, and I hear he's infatuated with some girl he met at a Chelsea tea party —a girl named—now, what was it?"

"Cora Bellinger."

"How do you know?"

"She was lunching here to-day."

"He brought her?"

"Yes."

"What's she like?"

"Pretty massive. In shape, a bit on the lines of the Albert Hall."

"Did he seem very fond of her?"

"Couldn't take his eyes off the chassis."

"The modern young man," said Aunt Dahlia, "is a pot of poison and wants a nurse to lead him by the hand and some strong attendant to kick him regularly at intervals of a quarter of an hour."

I tried to point out the silver lining.

"If you ask me, Aunt Dahlia," I said, "I think Angela is well out of it. This Glossop is a tough baby. One of London's toughest. I was trying to tell you just now what he did to me one night at the Drones'.

"First, having got me in sporting mood with a bottle of the ripest, he bet me that I wouldn't swing myself across the swimming pool by the ropes and rings. I knew I could do it on my head, so I took him on, exulting in the fun, so to speak. And when I'd done half the trip, and was going strong, I found he had looped the last rope back against the rail, leaving me no alternative but to drop into the depths and swim ashore in correct evening costume."

"He did?"

"He certainly did. It was months ago, and I haven't got really dry yet. You wouldn't want your daughter to marry a man capable of a thing like that!"

"On the contrary, you restore my faith in the young hound. I see that there must be lots of good in him, after all. And I want this Bellinger business broken up, Bertie."

"How?"

"I don't care how. Any way you please."

"But what can I do?"

"Do? Why, put the whole thing before your man Jeeves. Jeeves will find a way. One of the most capable fellers I ever met. Put the thing squarely up to Jeeves and let Nature take its course."

"There may be something in what you say, Aunt Dahlia," I said thoughtfully.

"Of course there is," said Aunt Dahlia. "A little thing like this will be child's play to Jeeves. Get him working on it right away, and I'll look in to-morrow to hear the result."

With which, she biffed off, and I summoned Jeeves to the presence.

"Jeeves," I said, "you have heard all?"

"Yes, sir."

"I thought you would. Aunt Dahlia has what you might call a carrying voice. Has it ever occurred to you that, if all other sources of income failed, she could make a good living calling the cattle home across the sands of Dee?"

"I had not considered the point, sir, but no doubt you are right."

"Well, how do we go? What is your reaction? I think we should do our best to help and assist."

"Yes, sir."

"I am fond of Aunt Dahlia, and I am fond of Angela. Fond of them both, if you get my drift. What the misguided girl finds to attract her in young Tuppy, I cannot say, Jeeves, and you cannot say. But apparently she loves the man—which shows it can be done, a thing I wouldn't have believed myself—and is pining away like———"

"Patience on a monument, sir."

"Like Patience, as you very shrewdly remark, on a monument. So we must cluster round. Bend your brain to the problem, Jeeves. It is one that will tax you to the uttermost."

Aunt Dahlia blew in on the morrow, and I rang the bell for Jeeves. He appeared, looking brainier than one could have believed possible—sheer intellect shining from every feature—and I could see at once that the engine had been turning over.

"Speak, Jeeves," I said.

"Very good, sir."

"You have brooded?"

"Yes, sir."

"With what success?"

"I have a plan, sir, which I fancy may produce satisfactory results."

"Let's have it," said Aunt Dahlia.

"In affairs of this description, madam, the first essential is to study the psychology of the individual."

"The what?"

"The psychology, madam."

"He means the psychology," I said.

"Oh, ah," said Aunt Dahlia.

"And by psychology, Jeeves," I went on, to help the thing along, "you imply——?"

"The natures and dispositions of the principals in the matter, sir."

"You mean, what they're like?"

"Precisely, sir."

"Does he talk like this when you're alone, Bertie?" asked Aunt Dahlia.

"Sometimes. Occasionally. And on the other hand, sometimes not. Proceed, Jeeves."

"Well, sir, if I may say so, the thing that struck me most forcibly about Miss Bellinger when she was under my observation was that hers was a somewhat imperious nature. I could envisage Miss Bellinger applauding success. I could not so easily see her pitying and sympathizing with failure.

"Possibly you will recall, sir, her attitude when Mr. Glossop endeavoured to light her cigarette with his automatic lighter? I thought I detected a certain impatience at his inability to produce the necessary flame."

"True, Jeeves. She ticked him off."

"Precisely, sir."

"Let me get this straight," said Aunt Dahlia. "You think if he goes on trying to light her cigarette with his automatic lighter long enough, she will eventually get fed up and hand him the mitten?"

"I merely mentioned the episode, madam, as an indication of Miss Bellinger's somewhat ruthless nature."

"Ruthless," I said, "is right. The Bellinger is hard-boiled. Those eyes. That chin. I could read them. A vicious specimen, if ever there was one."

"Precisely, sir. I think, therefore, that, should Miss Bellinger be a witness of Mr. Glossop's appearing to disadvantage in public, she would cease to entertain affection for him. In the event, for instance, of his failing to entertain the audience on Tuesday with his singing———"

I saw daylight.

"By Jove, Jeeves! You mean if he gets the bird all will be off?"

"I shall be greatly surprised if such is not the case, sir."

I shook my head.

"We cannot leave this thing to chance, Jeeves. Young Tuppy singing 'Sonny Boy' is the likeliest prospect for the bird that I can think of—but no . . . You see for yourself that we must do more than simply trust to luck."

"We need not trust to luck, sir. I would suggest that you approach your friend Mr. Bingham and volunteer your services at his forthcoming entertainment. It could readily be arranged to have you sing immediately before Mr. Glossop. I fancy, sir, that if Mr. Glossop were to sing 'Sonny Boy' directly after you had sung 'Sonny Boy' the audience would respond satisfactorily. By the time Mr. Glossop began to sing they would have lost their taste for that particular song and would express their feelings warmly."

"Jeeves," said Aunt Dahlia, "you're a marvel!"

"Thank you, madam."

"Jeeves," I said, "you're an ass!"

"What do you mean, he's an 'ass'?" said Aunt Dahlia hotly. "I think it's the greatest scheme I ever heard."

"Me sing 'Sonny Boy' at Beefy Bingham's clean, bright entertainment? I can see myself!"

"You sing it daily in your bath, sir. Mr. Wooster," said Jeeves, turning to Aunt Dahlia, "has a pleasant, light barytone."

"I bet he has," said Aunt Dahlia.

I checked the man with one of my looks.

"Between singing 'Sonny Boy' in one's bath, Jeeves, and singing it before a hall full of assorted blood-orange merchants and their young, there is a substantial difference."

"Bertie," said Aunt Dahlia, "you'll sing, and like it!"

"I will not."

"Bertie!"

"Nothing will induce——"

"Bertie," said Aunt Dahlia firmly, "you will sing 'Sonny Boy' on Tuesday, the third *prox.,* or may an aunt's curse——"

"I won't!"

"Think of Angela!"

"Dash Angela!"

"Bertie!"

"No; I mean, hang it all!"

"You won't?"

"No, I won't."

"That is your last word, is it?"

"It is. Once and for all, Aunt Dahlia, nothing will induce me to let out so much as a single note."

And so that afternoon I sent a prepaid wire to Beefy Bingham, offering my services in the cause, and by nightfall the thing was fixed up. I was billed to perform next but one after the intermission. Following me, came Tuppy. And immediately after him, Miss Cora Bellinger, the well-known operatic soprano.

How these things happen, I couldn't say. The chivalry of the Woosters, I suppose.

"Jeeves," I said that evening, and I said it coldly, "I shall be glad if you will pop round to the nearest music shop and procure me a copy of 'Sonny Boy.' It will now be necessary for me to learn both verse and refrain. Of the trouble and nervous strain which this will involve, I say nothing."

"Very good, sir."

"But this I do say——"

"I had better be starting immediately, sir, or the shop will be closed."

"Ha!" I said.

And I meant it to sting.

Although I had steeled myself to the ordeal before me and had set out full of the calm, quiet courage which makes men do desperate deeds with proud, set faces, I must admit that there was a moment, just after I had entered the Oddfellows' Hall at Bermondsey East and run an eye over the assembled pleasure seekers, when it needed all the bulldog pluck of the Woosters to keep me from calling it a day and taking a cab back to civilization.

The clean, bright entertainment was in full swing

when I arrived, and somebody who looked as if he might be the local undertaker was reciting "Gunga Din." And the audience, though not actually chiyiking in the full technical sense of the term, had a grim look which I didn't like at all.

As I scanned the multitude it seemed to me that they were for the nonce suspending judgment. Did you ever tap on the door of one of those New York speakeasy places and see the grille snap back and a Face appear? There is one long, silent moment when its eyes are fixed on yours and all your past life seems to rise up before you. Then you say that you are a friend of Mr. Zinzinheimer and he told you they would treat you right if you mentioned his name, and the strain relaxes.

Well, these costermongers and whelk stallers appeared to me to be looking just like that Face. Start something, they seemed to say, and they would know what to do about it. And I couldn't help feeling that my singing "Sonny Boy" would come, in their opinion, under the head of Starting Something.

"A nice, full house, sir," said a voice at my elbow.

It was Jeeves, watching the proceedings with an indulgent eye.

"You here, Jeeves?" I said coldly.

"Yes, sir. I have been present since the commencement."

"Oh?" I said. "Any casualties yet?"

"Sir?"

"You know what I mean, Jeeves," I said sternly, "and don't pretend you don't. Anybody got the bird yet?"

"Oh, no, sir."

"I shall be the first, you think?"

"No, sir, I see no reason to expect such a misfortune. I anticipate that you will be well received."

A sudden thought struck me. "And you think everything will go according to plan?"

"Yes, sir."

"Well, I don't," I said. "I've spotted a flaw in your beastly scheme."

"A flaw, sir?"

"Yes. Do you suppose for a moment that when Mr. Glossop hears me singing that dashed song he'll come calmly on a minute after me and sing it, too? Use your intelligence, Jeeves. He will perceive the chasm in his path and pause in time. He will back out and refuse to go on at all."

"Mr. Glossop will not hear you sing, sir. At my advice he has stepped across the road to the Jug and Bottle, an establishment immediately opposite the hall, and he intends to remain there until it is time for him to appear on the platform."

"Oh!" I said.

"If I might suggest it, sir, there is another house named the Goat and Grapes only a short distance down the street. I think it might be a judicious move——"

"If I were to put a bit of custom in their way?"

"It would ease the nervous strain of waiting, sir."

I had not been feeling any too pleased with the man for having let me in for this ghastly binge, but at these words I'm bound to say my austerity softened a trifle. He was undoubtedly right.

He had studied the psychology of the individual, if you see what I mean, and it had not led him astray. A quiet ten minutes at the Goat and Grapes was exactly what my system required. To buzz off there and inhale a couple of swift whisky-and-sodas was with Bertram Wooster the work of a moment.

The treatment worked like magic. What they had put into the stuff, besides vitriol, I could not have said; but it completely altered my outlook on life. That curious, gulpy feeling passed. I was no longer conscious of the sagging sensation at the knees. The limbs ceased to quiver gently, the tongue became loosened in its socket, and the backbone stiffened.

Pausing merely to order and swallow another of the same, I bade the barmaid a cheery good-night, nodded affably to one or two fellows in the bar whose faces I liked, and came prancing back to the hall, ready for anything.

And shortly afterward I was on the platform with about a million bulging eyes goggling up at me. There was a rummy sort of buzzing in my ears, and then through the buzzing I heard the sound of a piano starting to tinkle; and, commending my soul to God, I took a good long breath and charged in.

Well, it was a close thing. If ever my grandchildren cluster about my knee and want to know what I did in the Great War, I shall say, "Never mind about the Great War. Ask me about the time I sang 'Sonny Boy' at the Oddfellows' Hall at Bermondsey East."

The whole incident is a bit blurred, but I seem to recollect a kind of murmur as I hit the refrain. I thought at the time it was an attempt on the part of the many-headed to join in the chorus, and at the moment it rather encouraged me.

I passed the thing over the larynx with all the vim at my disposal, hit the high note, and off gracefully into the wings. I didn't come on again to take a bow. I just receded and oiled round to where Jeeves awaited me among the standees at the back.

"Well, Jeeves," I said, anchoring myself at his side and brushing the honest perspiration from the brow. "They didn't rush the platform."

"No, sir."

"But you can spread it about that that's the last time I perform outside my bath. My swan song, Jeeves. Anybody who wants to hear me in future must present himself at the bathroom door and shove his ear against the keyhole. I may be wrong, but it seemed to me that toward the end they were hotting up a trifle. The bird was hovering in the air. I could hear the beating of its wings."

"I did detect a certain restlessness, sir, in the audience. I fancy they had lost their taste for that particular melody. I should have informed you earlier, sir, that the song had already been sung twice before you arrived."

"What!"

"Yes, sir. Once by a lady and once by a gentleman. It is a very popular song, sir."

I gaped at the man. That, with this knowledge, he could calmly have allowed the young master to step straight into the jaws of death, so to speak, paralyzed me. It seemed to show that the old feudal spirit had passed away altogether. I was about to give him my

views on the matter in no uncertain fashion, when I
was stopped by the spectacle of young Tuppy lurching
onto the platform.

Young Tuppy had the unmistakable air of a man
who has recently been round to the Jug and Bottle. A
few cheery cries of welcome, presumably from some
of his backgammon-playing pals who felt that blood
was thicker than water, had the effect of causing the
genial smile on his face to widen till it nearly met at
the back.

He was plainly feeling about as good as a man can
feel and still remain on his feet. He waved a kindly
hand to his supporters and bowed in a regal sort of
manner, rather like an Eastern monarch acknowledg-
ing the plaudits of the mob.

Then the female at the piano struck up the opening
bars of "Sonny Boy," and Tuppy swelled like a balloon, clasped his hands together, rolled his eyes up at
the ceiling in a manner denoting Soul, and began.

I think the populace was too stunned for the moment to take immediate steps. It may seem incredible,
but I give you my word that young Tuppy got right
through the verse without so much as a murmur. Then
they seemed to pull themselves together.

A costermonger roused is a terrible thing. I have
never seen the proletariat really stirred before, and
I'm bound to say it rather awed me. I mean, it gave
you some idea of what it must have been like during
the French Revolution.

From every corner of the hall there proceeded
simultaneously the sort of noise you hear at one of
those East End boxing places when the referee dis-

qualifies the popular favourite and makes the quick dash for life. And then they passed beyond mere words and began to introduce the vegetable motif.

I don't know why, but somehow I had got it into my head that the first thing thrown at Tuppy would be a potato. One gets these fancies. It was, however, as a matter of fact, a banana, and I saw in an instant that the choice had been made by wiser heads than mine. These blokes who have grown up from childhood in the knowledge of how to treat a dramatic entertainment that doesn't please them are aware by a sort of instinct just what is best to do, and the moment I saw that banana splash on Tuppy's shirt front I realized how infinitely more effective and artistic it was than any potato could have been.

Not that the potato school of thought had not also its supporters. As the proceedings warmed up I noticed several intelligent-looking fellows who threw nothing else.

The effect on young Tuppy was rather remarkable. His eyes bulged and his hair seemed to stand up, and yet his mouth went on opening and shutting, and you could see that in a dazed, automatic way he was still singing "Sonny Boy."

Then, coming out of his trance, he began to pull for the shore with some rapidity. The last seen of him, he was beating a tomato to the exit by a short head.

Presently the tumult and the shouting died. I turned to Jeeves.

"Painful, Jeeves," I said. "But what would you?"

"Yes, sir."

"The surgeon's knife what?"

"Precisely, sir."

"Well, with this happening beneath her eyes, I think that we may definitely consider the Glossop-Bellinger romance off."

"Yes, sir."

At this point old Beefy Bingham came out upon the platform.

I supposed that he was about to rebuke his flock for the recent expression of feeling. But such was not the case. No doubt he was accustomed by now to the wholesome give-and-take of these clean, bright entertainments and had ceased to think it worth while to make any comment when there was a certain liveliness.

"Ladies and gentlemen," said old Beefy. "The next item on the program was to have been songs by Miss Cora Bellinger, the well-known operatic soprano. I have just received a telephone message from Miss Bellinger, saying that her car has broken down. She is, however, on her way here in a cab and will arrive shortly. Meanwhile, our friend Mr. Enoch Simpson will recite 'The Charge of the Light Brigade.'"

I clutched at Jeeves. "Jeeves! You heard?"

"Yes, sir."

"She wasn't here!"

"No, sir."

"She saw nothing of Tuppy's Waterloo."

"No, sir."

"The whole bally scheme has blown a fuse."

"Yes, sir."

"Come, Jeeves," I said, and those standing by wondered, no doubt, what had caused that clean-cut face to grow so pale and set. "I have been subjected to a nervous strain unparalleled since the days of the early martyrs. I have lost pounds in weight and permanently injured my entire system. I have gone through an ordeal which will make me wake up screaming in the night for months to come. And all for nothing. Let us go."

"If you have no objection, sir, I would like to witness the remainder of the entertainment."

"Suit yourself, Jeeves," I said moodily. "Personally, my heart is dead and I am going to look in at the Goat and Grapes for another of their cyanide specials and then home."

It must have been about half-past ten, and I was in the old sitting room sombrely sucking down a more or less final restorative, when the front doorbell rang, and there on the mat was young Tuppy. He looked like a man who has passed through some great experience and stood face to face with his soul. He had the beginnings of a black eye.

"Oh, hullo, Bertie," said young Tuppy.

He came in and hovered about the mantelpiece, as if he were looking for things to fiddle with and break.

"I've just been singing at Beefy Bingham's entertainment," he said after a pause. "You weren't there, by any chance?"

"Oh, no," I said. "How did you go?"

"Like a breeze," said young Tuppy. "Held them spellbound."

"Knocked 'em, eh?"

"Cold," said young Tuppy. "Not a dry eye."

And this, mark you, a man who had had a good up-bringing and had, no doubt, spent years at his mother's knee being taught to tell the truth.

"I suppose Miss Bellinger is pleased?" I said.

"Oh, yes. Delighted."

"So now everything's all right?"

"Oh, quite." Tuppy paused. "On the other hand, Bertie——"

"Yes?"

"Well, I've been thinking things over. Somehow, I don't believe Miss Bellinger is the mate for me, after all."

"What!"

"No, I don't."

"What makes you think that?"

"Oh, I don't know. These things sort of flash on you. I respect Miss Bellinger, Bertie. I admire her. But—er—well, I can't help feeling now that a sweet, gentle girl—er—like your cousin Angela, Bertie—would—er—in fact—— Well, what I came round for was to ask if you would phone Angela and find out how she reacts to the idea of coming out with me to-night to the Berkeley for a bit of supper and a spot of dancing."

"Go ahead. There's the phone."

"No; I'd rather you asked her, Bertie. What with one thing and another, if you paved the way—— You see, there's just a chance that she may be—I mean, you know how misunderstandings occur—and—— Well, what I'm driving at, Bertie, old man, is that I'd rather you surged round and did a bit of paving, if you don't mind."

I went to the phone and called up Angela.

"She says come right round," I said.

"Tell her," said Tuppy, in a devout sort of voice, "that I will be with her in something under a couple of ticks."

He had barely biffed when I heard a click in the keyhole and a soft padding in the passage without.

"Jeeves," I called.

"Sir," said Jeeves, manifesting himself.

"Jeeves, a remarkably rummy thing has happened. Mr. Glossop has just been here. He tells me all is off between him and Miss Bellinger."

"Yes, sir."

"You don't seem surprised."

"No, sir. I confess I had anticipated some such eventuality."

"Eh? What gave you that idea?"

"It came to me, sir, when I observed Miss Bellinger strike Mr. Glossop in the eye."

"Strike him!"

"Yes, sir."

"In the eye?"

"The right eye, sir."

I clutched the brow. "What on earth made her do that?"

"I fancy she was a little upset, sir, at the reception accorded her singing."

"Great Scott! Don't tell me she got the bird, too?"

"Yes, sir."

"But why? She's got a red-hot voice."

"Yes, sir. But I think the audience resented her choice of a song."

"Jeeves!" Reason was beginning to do a bit of tottering on its throne. "You aren't going to stand there and tell me that Miss Bellinger sang 'Sonny Boy,' too!"

"Yes, sir. And—mistakenly, in my opinion— brought a large doll onto the platform to sing it to. The audience affected to mistake it for a ventriloquist's dummy, and there was some little disturbance."

"But Jeeves, what a coincidence!"

"Not altogether, sir. I ventured to take the liberty of accosting Miss Bellinger on her arrival at the hall and recalling myself to her recollection. I then said that Mr. Glossop had asked me to request her that as a particular favour to him—the song being a favourite of his—she would sing 'Sonny Boy.'

"And when she found that you and Mr. Glossop had also sung the song immediately before her, I rather fancy that she supposed that she had been made the victim of a practical pleasantry by Mr. Glossop. Will there be anything further, sir?"

"No, thanks."

"Good-night, sir."

"Good-night, Jeeves," I said reverently.

JEEVES
AND THE LOVE THAT PURIFIES

Jeeves and the Love That Purifies

THERE is a ghastly moment in the year, generally about the beginning of August, when Jeeves insists on taking a holiday, the slacker, and legs it off to some seaside resort for a couple of weeks, leaving me stranded. This moment had now arrived, and we were discussing what was to be done with the young master.

"I had gathered the impression, sir," said Jeeves, "that you were proposing to accept Mr. Sipperley's invitation to join him at his Hampshire residence."

I laughed. One of those bitter, rasping ones.

"Correct, Jeeves. I was. But mercifully I was enabled to discover young Sippy's foul plot in time. Do you know what?"

"No, sir."

"My spies informed me that Sippy's fiancée, Miss Moon, was to be there. Also his fiancée's mother, Mrs. Moon, and his fiancée's small brother, Master Moon. You see the hideous treachery lurking behind the invitation?

"Obviously, my job was to be the task of keeping Mrs. Moon and little Sebastian Moon interested and amused while Sippy and his blighted girl went off for the day, roaming the pleasant woodlands and talking of this and that. I doubt if anyone has ever had a narrower escape. You remember little Sebastian?"

"Yes, sir."

"His goggle-eyes? His golden curls?"

"Yes, sir."

"I don't know why it is, but I've never been able to bear with fortitude anything in the shape of a kid with golden curls. Confronted with one, I feel the urge to step on him or drop things on him from a height."

"Many strong natures are affected in the same way, sir."

"So no *chez* Sippy for me. Was that the front door bell ringing?"

"Yes, sir."

"Somebody stands without?"

"Yes, sir."

"Better go and see who it is."

"Yes, sir."

He oozed off, to return a moment later bearing a telegram. I opened it, and a soft smile played about the lips.

"Amazing how often things happen as if on a cue, Jeeves. This is from Aunt Dahlia, inviting me down to her place in Worcestershire."

"Most satisfactory, sir."

"Yes. How I came to overlook her when searching for a haven, I can't think. The ideal home from home. Picturesque surroundings, company's own water, and the best cook in England. You have not forgotten Anatole?"

"No, sir."

"And above all, Jeeves, at Aunt Dahlia's there should be an almost total shortage of blasted kids. True, there is her son Bonzo, who, I take it, will be

home for the holidays, but I don't mind Bonzo. Buzz
off and send a wire, accepting."

"Yes, sir."

"And then shove a few necessaries together, including golf clubs and tennis racket."

"Very good, sir. I am glad that matters have been
so happily adjusted."

I think I have mentioned before that my aunt
Dahlia stands alone in the grim regiment of my aunts
as a real sort and a chirpy sportsman. She is the one,
if you remember, who married old Tom Travers and,
with the assistance of Jeeves, lured Mrs. Bingo Little's French cook, Anatole, into her own employment.

To visit her is always a pleasure. She generally has
some cheery birds staying with her, and there is none
of that rot about getting up for breakfast which one is
so sadly apt to find at country houses.

It was, accordingly, with unalloyed lightness of
heart that I edged the two-seater into the garage at
Brinkley Court, Worc., and strolled round to the
house by way of the shrubbery and the tennis lawn, to
report arrival. I had just got across the lawn when a
head poked itself out of the smoking-room window
and beamed at me in an amiable sort of way.

"Ah, Mr. Wooster," it said.

"What ho," I replied, not to be outdone in the courtesies.

It had taken me a couple of seconds to place this
head. I now perceived that it belonged to a rather
moth-eaten septuagenarian of the name of Anstruther, an old friend of Aunt Dahlia's late father.

I had met him at her house in London once or twice. An agreeable cove, but somewhat given to nervous breakdowns.

"Just arrived?" he asked, beaming as before.

"This minute," I said, also beaming.

"I fancy you will find our good hostess in the drawing room."

"Right," I said, and after a bit more beaming to and fro I pushed on.

Aunt Dahlia was in the drawing room, and welcomed me with gratifying enthusiasm. She beamed, too. It was one of those big days for beamers.

"Hullo, ugly," she said. "So here you are. Thank heaven you were able to come."

It was the right tone, and one I should be glad to hear in others of the family circle, notably my aunt Agatha.

"Always a pleasure to enjoy your hosp., Aunt Dahlia," I said cordially. "I anticipate a delightful and restful visit. I see you've got Mr. Anstruther staying here. Anybody else?"

"Do you know Lord Snettisham?" Aunt Dahlia asked.

"I've met him, racing," I answered.

"He's here, and Lady Snettisham."

"And Bonzo, of course?"

"Yes. And Thomas."

"Uncle Thomas?"

"No, he's in Scotland. Your cousin Thomas."

"You don't mean Aunt Agatha's loathly son?"

"Of course I do. How many cousin Thomases do

you think you've got, fathead? Agatha has gone to Homburg and planted the child on me."

I was visibly agitated.

"But Aunt Dahlia! Do you realize what you've taken on? Have you an inkling of the scourge you've introduced into your home? In the society of young Thos., strong men quail. He is England's premier fiend in human shape. There is no devilry beyond his scope."

"That's what I always gathered from the form book," agreed the relative. "But just now, curse him, he's behaving like something out of a Sunday-school story. You see, poor old Mr. Anstruther is very frail these days, and when he found he was in a house containing two small boys he acted promptly. He offered a prize of five pounds to whichever behaved best during his stay.

"The consequence is that, ever since, Thomas has had large white wings sprouting out of his shoulders." A shadow seemed to pass across her face. She appeared embittered. "Mercenary little brute!" she said. "I never saw such a sickeningly well-behaved kid in my life. It's enough to make one despair of human nature."

I couldn't follow her. "But isn't that all to the good?" I asked.

"No, it's not."

"I can't see why. Surely a smug, oily Thos. about the house is better than a Thos. raging hither and thither and being a menace to society? Stands to reason."

"It doesn't stand to anything of the kind. You see, Bertie, this Good Conduct prize has made things a bit complex. There are wheels within wheels. The thing stirred Jane Snettisham's sporting blood to such an extent that she insisted on having a bet with me on the result."

A great light shone upon me. I got what she was driving at.

"Ah!" I said. "Now I follow. Now I see. Now I comprehend. She's betting on Thos., is she?"

"Yes. And naturally, knowing him, I thought the thing was in the bag."

"Of course."

"I couldn't see myself losing. Heaven knows I have no illusions about my darling Bonzo. Bonzo is, and has been from birth, a pest. But to bet that he would nose out Thomas in a Good Conduct contest seemed to me simply money for jam."

"Absolutely."

"When it comes to devilry, Bonzo is just a good, ordinary selling plater, whereas Thomas is a classic yearling."

"Exactly. I don't see that you have any cause to worry. Thos. can't last. He's bound to crack."

"Yes. But before that the mischief may be done."

"Mischief?"

"Yes. There is dirty work afoot, Bertie," said Aunt Dahlia gravely. "When I booked this bet I reckoned without the hideous blackness of the Snettisham soul. Only yesterday it came to my knowledge that Jack Snettisham had been urging Bonzo to climb on the roof and boo down Mr. Anstruther's chimney."

"No!"

"Yes. Mr. Anstruther is very frail, poor old fellow, and it would have frightened him into a fit. On coming out of which, his first action would have been to disqualify Bonzo and declare Thomas the winner by default."

"But Bonzo did not boo?"

"No," said Aunt Dahlia, and a mother's pride rang in her voice. "He firmly refused to boo. Mercifully, he is in love at the moment, and it has quite altered his nature. He scorned the tempter."

"In love? With whom?"

"Lillian Gish. We had an old film of hers at the Bijou Dream in the village a week ago, and Bonzo saw her for the first time. He came out with a pale, set face, and ever since has been trying to lead a finer, better life. So the peril was averted."

"That's good."

"Yes. But now it's my turn. You don't suppose I am going to take a thing like that lying down, do you? Treat me right, and I am fairness itself; but if there is going to be any of this nobbling of starters they'll jolly well find I can play that game, too.

"If this Good Conduct contest is to be run on rough lines I can do my bit as well as anyone. Far too much hangs on the issue for me to handicap myself by remembering the lessons I learned at my mother's knee."

"Lot of money involved?"

"Much more than mere money. I've bet Anatole against Jane Snettisham's kitchenmaid."

"Great Scott! Uncle Thomas will have something to say if he comes back and finds Anatole gone."

"And won't he say it!"

"Pretty long odds. I mean, Anatole is famed far and wide as a hash-slinger without peer."

"Well, Jane Snettisham's kitchenmaid is not to be sneezed at. She is very hot stuff, they tell me, and good kitchenmaids nowadays are about as rare as original Holbeins. Besides, I had to give her a shade the better of the odds. She stood out for it.

"Well, anyway, to get back to what I was saying, if the opposition are going to place temptations in Bonzo's path, they shall jolly well be placed in Thomas's path, too, and plenty of them. So ring for Jeeves and let him get his brain working."

"But I haven't brought Jeeves."

"You haven't brought Jeeves?"

"No. He always takes his holiday at this time of year. He's down at Bognor for the shrimping."

Aunt Dahlia registered deep concern. "Then send for him at once! What earthly use do you suppose you are without Jeeves, you poor ditherer?"

I drew myself up a trifle—in fact, if I recollect rightly, to my full height. Nobody has a greater respect for Jeeves than I have, but the Wooster pride was stung.

"Jeeves isn't the only one with brains," I said coolly. "Leave this thing to me, Aunt Dahlia. By dinner time to-night I shall hope to have a fully matured scheme to submit for your approval. If I can't thoroughly encompass this Thos., I'll eat my hat."

"About all you'll get to eat if Anatole leaves," said

Aunt Dahlia, in a manner which I did not like to see.

I was brooding pretty tensely as I left the presence.
I have always had a suspicion that Aunt Dahlia, while
invariably matey and bonhomous and seeming to take
pleasure in my society, has a lower opinion of my intelligence than I quite like. Too often it is her practice
to address me as fathead, and if I put forward any
little thought or idea or fancy in her hearing it is apt
to be greeted with the affectionate but jarring guffaw.

In our interview she had hinted quite plainly that
she considered me negligible in a crisis which, like the
present one, called for initiative and resource. It was
my intention to show her how greatly she had under-
estimated me.

To let you see the sort of fellow I really am, I got
a ripe, excellent idea before I had gone halfway down
the corridor. I examined it for the space of one and
a half cigarettes, and could see no flaw in it, provided
—I say, provided old Mr. Anstruther's notion of
what constituted bad conduct squared with mine.

The great thing on these occasions, as Jeeves will
tell you, is to get a toe hold on the psychology of the
individual. Study the individual, and you will bring
home the bacon.

Now, I had been studying young Thos. for years,
and I knew his psychology from caviar to nuts. He is
one of those kids who never let the sun go down on
their wrath, if you know what I mean. I mean to say,
do something to annoy or offend or upset this juvenile
thug and he will proceed at the earliest possible opp.
to wreak a hideous vengeance upon you.

Only the previous summer, for instance, it having

been drawn to his attention that the man had reported him for smoking, he had marooned a cabinet minister on an island in the lake at Aunt Agatha's place in Hertfordshire—in the rain, mark you, and with no company but that of one of the nastiest-minded swans I have ever encountered. Well, I mean!

So now it seemed to me that a few well-chosen taunts, or gibes, directed at his more sensitive points, must infallibly induce in this Thos. a frame of mind which would lead to his working sensational violence upon me. And if you wonder some that I was willing to sacrifice myself to this frightful extent in order to do Aunt Dahlia a bit of good, I can only say that we Woosters are like that.

The one point that seemed to me to want a spot of cleaning up was this—viz.: Would old Mr. Anstruther consider an outrage perpetrated on the person of Bertram Wooster a crime sufficiently black to cause him to rule Thos. out of the race? Or would he just give a senile chuckle and mumble something about boys being boys? Because, if the latter, the thing was off. I decided to have a word with the old boy to make sure.

He was still in the smoking room, looking very frail over the morning's *Times*. I got to the point at once.

"What ho, Mr. Anstruther!" I said.

"I don't like the way the American market is shaping," he said. "I don't like this strong bear movement."

"No?" I said. "Well, be that as it may, about this Good Conduct prize of yours."

"Ah, yes?"

"I don't quite understand how you are doing the judging."

"No? It is very simple. I have a system of daily marks. At the beginning of each day I accord the two lads twenty marks apiece. These are subjected to withdrawal either in small or large quantities according to the magnitude of the offense. To take a simple example, shouting outside my bedroom in the early morning would involve a loss of three marks; whistling two. The penalty for a more serious lapse would be correspondingly greater. Before retiring to rest at night I record the day's marks in my little book. Simple, but, I think, ingenious, Mr. Wooster?"

"Absolutely."

"So far the result has been extremely gratifying. Neither of the little fellows has lost a single mark."

"I see," I said. "Great work. And how do you react to what I might call general moral turpitude?"

"I beg your pardon?"

"Well, I mean when the thing doesn't affect you personally. Suppose one of them did something to me, for instance—set a booby trap or something? Or, shall we say, put a toad in my bed?"

He seemed shocked at the very idea. "I would certainly in such circumstances deprive the culprit of a full ten marks."

"Only ten?"

"Fifteen, then."

"Twenty is a nice round number."

"Well, possibly even twenty. I have a peculiar horror of practical joking."

"Me, too."

"You will not fail to advise me, Mr. Wooster, should such an outrage occur?"

"You shall have the news before anyone," I assured him.

And so out into the garden, ranging to and fro in quest of young Thos. I knew where I was now. Bertram's feet were on solid ground.

I found him in the summer house, reading an improving book.

"Hullo," he said, smiling a saintlike smile.

This scourge of humanity was a chunky kid whom a too-indulgent public had allowed to infest the country for a matter of thirteen years. His nose was snub, his eyes green, his general aspect that of one studying to be a gangster. I had never liked his looks much, and with a saintlike smile added they became ghastly to a degree.

I ran over in my mind a few assorted taunts. "Well, young Thos.," I said. "So there you are. You're getting as fat as a pig."

It seemed as good an opening as any other. Experience had taught me that if there was a subject on which he was unlikely to accept persiflage in a spirit of amused geniality it was this matter of his bulging tum.

On the last occasion when I made a remark of this nature, he had replied to me, child though he was, in terms which I should have been proud to have in my own vocabulary. But now, though a sort of wistful gleam did flit for a moment into his eyes, he merely smiled in a more saintlike manner.

"Yes, I think I have been putting on a little weight,"

he said gently. "I must try to get a lot of exercise while I'm here. Won't you sit down, Bertie?" he asked, rising. "You must be tired after your journey. I'll get you a cushion. Have you cigarettes? And matches? I could bring you some from the smoking room."

It is not too much to say that I felt baffled. In spite of what Aunt Dahlia had told me, I don't think that until this moment I had really believed there could have been anything in the nature of a sensational change in this young plug-ugly's attitude toward his fellows. But now, hearing him talk as if he were a combination of Boy Scout and delivery wagon, I felt baffled. However, I stuck at it in the old bulldog way.

"Are you still at that rotten kids' school of yours?" I asked.

He might have been proof against gibes at his *embonpoint*, but it seemed to me incredible that he could have sold himself for gold so completely as to lie down under taunts directed at his school. I was wrong. The money lust held him in its grip. He merely shook his head.

"I left this term. I'm going to Cheltenham next term."

"They wear mortar boards there, don't they?"

"Yes."

"With pink tassels?"

"Yes."

"What a priceless ass you'll look!" I said, but without much hope. And I laughed heartily.

"I expect I shall," he said, and laughed still more heartily.

"Mortar boards!"

"Ha, ha!"

"Pink tassels!"

"Ha, ha!"

I gave the thing up. "Well, teuf-teuf," I said moodily, and withdrew.

A couple of days later I realized that the virus had gone even deeper than I had thought. The kid was irremediably sordid.

It was old Mr. Anstruther who sprang the bad news.

"Oh, Mr. Wooster," he said, meeting me on the stairs. "You were good enough to express an interest in this little prize for Good Conduct which I am offering."

"Oh, ah?"

"I explained to you my system of marking, I believe. Well, this morning I was impelled to vary it somewhat. The circumstances seemed to me to demand it. I happened to encounter our hostess's nephew, the boy Thomas, returning to the house, his aspect somewhat weary, it appeared to me, and travel-stained.

"I inquired of him where he had been that early hour—it was not yet breakfast time—and he replied that he had heard you mention overnight a regret that you had omitted to order the *Sporting Times* to be sent to you before leaving London, and he had walked all the way to the railway station, a distance of more than three miles, to procure it for you."

The old boy swam before my eyes. He looked like

two old Mr. Anstruthers, both flickering at the edges. "What!"

"I can understand your emotion, Mr. Wooster," said the old boy. "I can appreciate it. It is indeed rarely that one encounters such unselfish kindliness in a lad of his age. So genuinely touched was I by his goodness of heart that I have deviated from my original system and awarded the little fellow a bonus of fifteen marks."

"Fifteen!"

"On second thoughts, I shall make it twenty. That, as you yourself suggested, is a nice round number."

He doddered away, and I bounded off to find Aunt Dahlia.

"Aunt Dahlia," I said, "matters have taken a sinister turn."

"You bet your Sunday spats they have," agreed Aunt Dahlia emphatically. "Do you know what happened just now? That crook Snettisham offered Bonzo ten shillings if he would burst a paper bag behind Mr. Anstruther's chair at breakfast.

"Thank heaven, the love of a good woman triumphed again. My sweet Bonzo merely looked at him and walked away in a marked manner. But it just shows you what we are up against."

"We are up against worse than that, Aunt Dahlia," I said. And I told her what had happened.

She was stunned. Aghast, you might call it. "*Thomas* did that?"

"Thos. in person."

"Walked six miles to get you a paper?"

"Six miles and a bit."

"The young hound!"

"A blighter, beyond question."

"Good heavens, Bertie, do you realize that he may go on doing these Acts of Kindness daily—perhaps twice a day? Is there no way of stopping him?"

"None that I can think of. No, Aunt Dahlia, I must confess it. Bertram is baffled. There is only one thing to do. We must send for Jeeves."

"And about time," said the relative churlishly. "He ought to have been here from the start. Wire him this morning."

There is good stuff in Jeeves. His heart is in the right place. The acid test does not find him wanting. Many men in his position, summoned back by telegram in the middle of their annual vacation, might have cut up rough a bit. But not Jeeves. On the following afternoon in he blew, looking fit, and I gave him the scenario without delay.

"So there you have it, Jeeves," I said, having sketched out the facts. "The problem is one that will exercise your intelligence to the utmost. Rest now, and to-night, after a light repast, get down to it.

"Is there any particular stimulating food or beverage you would like for dinner? Anything that you feel would give the old brain just that extra fillip? If so, name it."

"Thank you very much, sir, but I have already hit upon a plan which should, I fancy, prove effective."

I gazed at the man with reverent awe. "Already?"

"Yes, sir."

"Not *already?*"

"Yes, sir."

"Something to do with the psychology of the individual?"

"Precisely, sir."

I shook my head, a bit discouraged. Doubts had begun to creep in.

"Well, spring it, Jeeves," I said. "But I have not much hope. Having only just arrived, you cannot possibly be aware of the frightful change that has taken place in young Thos. You are probably building on your knowledge of him, when last seen. Useless, Jeeves. Stirred by the prospects of getting his hooks on five of the best, this blighted boy has become so dashed virtuous that his armour seems to contain no chink.

"I mocked at his waistline and sneered at his school and he merely smiled in a pale, dying-duck sort of way. Well, that'll show you. However, let us hear what you have to suggest."

"It occurred to me, sir, that the most judicious plan would be for you to request Mrs. Travers to invite Master Sebastian Moon here for a short visit."

I shook the onion again. The scheme sounded to me like pure apple sauce.

"What earthly good would that do?" I asked, not without a touch of asperity.

"He has golden curls, sir."

"What of it?"

"The strongest natures are sometimes not proof against long golden curls."

Well it was a thought, of course. But I can't say I was leaping about to any great extent. It might be that the sight of Sebastian Moon would break down Thos.'s iron self-control to the extent of causing him to inflict mayhem on the person, but I wasn't any too hopeful.

"It may be so, Jeeves."

"I do not think I am too sanguine, sir. You must remember that Master Moon, apart from his curls, has a personality which is not uniformly pleasing. He is apt to express himself with a breezy candour which I fancy Master Thomas might feel inclined to resent in one some years his junior."

I had had a feeling all along that there was a flaw somewhere, and now it seemed to me that I had spotted it.

"But Jeeves. Granted that little Sebastian is the pot of poison you indicate, why won't he act just as forcibly on young Bonzo as on Thos.? Pretty silly we should look if our nominee started putting it across him. Never forget that already Bonzo is twenty marks down and falling back in the betting."

"I do not anticipate any such contingency, sir. He is in love, and love is a very powerful restraining influence at the age of thirteen."

"H'm," I mused. "Well, we can but try, Jeeves."

"Yes, sir."

"I'll get Aunt Dahlia to write to Sippy to-night."

I'm bound to say that the spectacle of little Sebastian when he arrived two days later did much to remove pessimism from my outlook. If ever there was a kid whose whole appearance seemed to call aloud to any right-minded boy to lure him into a quiet spot and inflict violence upon him, that kid was undeniably Sebastian Moon. He reminded me strongly of Little Lord Fauntleroy.

I marked young Thos.'s demeanour closely at the moment of their meeting and, unless I was much mistaken, there came into his eyes the sort of look which would come into those of an Indian chief—Chingachcook, let us say, or Sitting Bull—just before he started reaching for his scalping knife. He had the air of one who is about ready to begin.

True, his manner as he shook hands was guarded. Only a keen observer could have detected that he was stirred to his depths. But I had seen, and I summoned Jeeves forthwith.

"Jeeves," I said, "if I appeared to think poorly of that scheme of yours, I now withdraw my remarks. I believe you have found the way. I was noticing Thos. at the moment of impact. His eyes had a strange gleam."

"Indeed, sir?"

"He shifted uneasily on his feet and his ears wiggled. He had, in short, the appearance of a boy who was holding himself in with an effort almost too great for his frail body."

"Yes, sir?"

"Yes, Jeeves. I received a distinct impression of something being on the point of exploding. To-morrow I shall ask Aunt Dahlia to take the two warts for a country ramble, to lose them in some sequestered spot, and to leave the rest to Nature."

"It is a good idea, sir."

"It is more than a good idea, Jeeves," I said. "It is a pip."

You know, the older I get the more firmly do I become convinced that there is no such thing as a pip in existence. Again and again have I seen the apparently sure thing go *phut,* and now it is rarely indeed that Bertram Wooster can be lured from his aloof skepticism.

Fellows come sidling up to him at the Drones' and elsewhere, urging him to invest on some horse that can't lose even if it gets struck by lightning at the starting point, but Bertram Wooster shakes his head. He has seen too much of life to be certain of anything.

If anyone had told me that my cousin Thos., left alone for an extended period of time with a kid of the outstanding foulness of Sebastian Moon, would not only refrain from cutting off his curls with a pocket-knife and chasing him across country into a muddy pond, but would actually return home carrying the ghastly kid on his back because he had got a blister on his foot, I would have laughed scornfully. I knew Thos. I knew his work. I had seen him in action. And I was convinced that not even the prospect of collecting five pounds would give him pause.

And yet, what happened? In the quiet evenfall, when the little birds were singing their sweetest and all Nature seemed to whisper of hope and happiness, the blow fell. I was chatting with old Mr. Anstruther on the terrace when suddenly round a bend in the drive the two kids hove in view. Sebastian, seated on Thos.'s back, his hat off and his golden curls floating on the breeze, was singing a comic song, and Thos., bowed down by the burden but carrying on gamely, was trudging along, smiling that bally saint-like smile of his.

He parked the kid on the front steps and came across to us.

"Sebastian got a nail in his shoe," he said in a virtuous voice. "It hurt him to walk, so I gave him a piggy-back."

I heard old Mr. Anstruther draw in his breath sharply.

"All the way home?"

"Yes, sir."

"In this hot sunshine?"

"Yes, sir."

"But was he not very heavy?"

"He was a little, sir," said Thos., uncorking the saintlike once more. "But it would have hurt him awfully to walk."

I pushed off. I had had enough. If ever a septuagenarian looked on the point of handing out another bonus, that septuagenarian was old Mr. Anstruther. I withdrew, and found Jeeves in my bedroom.

He pursed the lips a bit on hearing the news. "Serious, sir."

"Very serious, Jeeves."

"I had feared this, sir."

"Had you? I hadn't. I was convinced Thos. would massacre young Sebastian. I banked on it. It just shows what the greed for money will do. This is a commercial age, Jeeves. When I was a boy I would cheerfully have forfeited five quid in order to deal faithfully with a kid like Sebastian. I would have considered it money well spent."

"You are mistaken, sir, in your estimate of the motives actuating Master Thomas. It was not a mere desire to win five pounds that caused him to curb his natural impulses. I have ascertained the true reason for his change of heart, sir."

I felt fogged. "Not religion, Jeeves?"

"No, sir. Love."

"Love?"

"Yes, sir. The young gentleman confided in me during a brief conversation in the hall shortly after luncheon. We had been speaking for a while on neutral subjects, when he suddenly turned a deeper shade of pink and after some slight hesitation inquired of me if I did not think Miss Greta Garbo the most beautiful woman at present in existence."

I clutched the brow. "Jeeves! Don't tell me Thos. is in love with Greta Garbo?"

"Yes, sir. Unfortunately such is the case. He gave me to understand that it had been coming on for some time, and her last picture settled the issue. His voice shook with an emotion which it was impossible to misread. I gathered from his observations, sir, that he proposes to spend the rest of his life trying to make himself worthy of her."

It was a knock-out. This was the end.

"This is the end, Jeeves," I said. "Bonzo must be a good forty marks behind by now. Only some sensational outrage upon the public weal on the part of young Thos. could have enabled him to wipe out the lead. And of that there is now, apparently, no chance."

"The eventuality does appear remote, sir."

I brooded. "Uncle Thomas will have a fit when he comes back and finds Anatole gone."

"Yes, sir."

"Aunt Dahlia will drain the bitter cup to the dregs."

"Yes, sir."

"And speaking from a purely selfish point of view, the finest cooking I have ever bitten will pass out of my life forever, unless the Snettishams invite me in some night to take potluck. And that eventuality is also remote."

"Yes, sir."

"Then the only thing I can do is square the shoulders and face the inevitable."

"Yes, sir."

"Like some aristocrat of the French Revolution popping into the tumbrel, what? The brave smile. The stiff upper lip."

"Yes, sir."

"Right ho, then. Is the shirt studded?"

"Yes, sir."

"The tie chosen?"

"Yes, sir."

"The collar and evening underwear all in order?"

"Yes, sir."

"Then I'll have a bath and be with you in two ticks."

It is all very well to talk about the brave smile and

the stiff upper lip, but my experience—and I dare say others have found the same—is that they are a dashed sight easier to talk about than actually to fix on the face. For the next few days, I'm bound to admit, I found myself, in spite of every effort, registering gloom pretty consistently. For, as if to make things tougher, Anatole at this juncture suddenly developed a cooking streak which put all his previous efforts in the shade.

Night after night we sat at the dinner table, the food melting in our mouths, and Aunt Dahlia would look at me and I would look at Aunt Dahlia, and the male Snettisham would ask the female Snettisham in a ghastly, gloating sort of way if she had ever tasted such cooking and the female Snettisham would smirk at the male Snettisham and say she never had in all her puff, and I would look at Aunt Dahlia and Aunt Dahlia would look at me and our eyes would be full of unshed tears, if you know what I mean.

And all the time old Mr. Anstruther's visit was drawing to a close.

And then, on the very last afternoon of his stay, the thing happened.

It was one of those warm, drowsy, peaceful after-noons. I was up in my bedroom getting off a spot of correspondence, and from where I sat I looked down on the shady lawn fringed with its gay flower beds. There was a bird or two hopping about, a butterfly or so fluttering to and fro, and an assortment of bees buzzing hither and thither. In a garden chair sat old Mr. Anstruther, getting his eight hours.

It was a sight which, had I had less on my mind,

would no doubt have soothed the old soul a bit. The only blot on the landscape was Lady Snettisham, walking about and probably sketching out future menus, curse her.

And so for a time everything carried on. The birds hopped, the butterflies fluttered, the bees buzzed, and old Mr. Anstruther snored—all in accordance with the programme. And I worked through a letter to my tailor to the point where I proposed to say something pretty strong about the way the right sleeve of my last coat bagged.

There was a tap on the door, and Jeeves entered, bringing the second post. I laid the letters listlessly beside me.

"Well, Jeeves," I said sombrely.

"Sir?"

"Mr. Anstruther leaves to-morrow."

"Yes, sir."

I gazed down at the sleeping septuagenarian. "In my young days, Jeeves," I said, "however much I might have been in love, I could never have resisted the spectacle of an old gentleman asleep like that. I would have done *something* to him, no matter what the cost."

"Indeed, sir?"

"Yes. Probably with a pea shooter. But the modern boy is degenerate. He has lost his vim. I suppose Thos. is indoors, showing Sebastian his stamp album or something. Ha!" I said, and I said it rather nastily.

"I fancy Master Thomas and Master Sebastian are playing in the stable yard, sir. I encountered Master Sebastian not long back and he informed me he was on his way thither."

"The motion pictures, Jeeves," I said, "are the curse of the age. But for them, if Thos. had found himself alone in a stable yard with a kid like Sebastian——"

I broke off. From some point to the southwest, out of my line of vision, there had proceeded a piercing squeal.

It cut through the air like a knife, and old Mr. Anstruther started as if it had run into the fleshy part of his leg. And the next moment Sebastian appeared, going well and followed by Thos., who was going even better.

In spite of the fact that he was hampered in his movements by a large stable bucket which he bore in his right hand, Thos. was running a great race. He had almost come up with Sebastian, when the latter, with great presence of mind, dodged behind Mr. Anstruther, and there for a moment the matter rested.

But only for a moment. Thos., for some reason plainly stirred to the depths of his being, moved adroitly to one side, and, poising the bucket for an instant, discharged its contents. And Mr. Anstruther received, as far as I could gather from a distance, the entire consignment. In one second he had become the wettest man in Worcestershire.

"Jeeves!" I cried.

"Yes, indeed, sir," said Jeeves, and seemed to me to put the whole thing in a nutshell.

Down below, things were hotting up nicely. Old Mr. Anstruther may have been frail, but he undoubtedly had his moments. I have rarely seen a man of his years conduct himself with such a lissom abandon. There was a stick lying beside the chair, and with this in hand he went into action like a two-year-old. A moment later, he and Thos. had passed out of the picture round the house, Thos. cutting out a rare pace but, judging from the sounds of anguish, not good enough to distance the field.

The tumult and the shouting died; and after gazing for a while with considerable satisfaction at the Snettisham, who was standing there with a sandbagged look watching her nominee pass right out of the betting, I turned to Jeeves. I felt quietly triumphant. It is not often that I score off him, but now I had scored in no uncertain manner.

"You see, Jeeves," I said, "I was right and you were wrong. Blood will tell. Once a Thos., always a Thos. Can the leopard change his spots or the Ethiopian his what not? What was that thing they used to teach us at school about expelling Nature?"

"You may expel Nature with a pitchfork, sir, but she will always return? In the original Latin——"

"Never mind about the original Latin. The point is that I told you Thos. could not resist those curls, and he couldn't. You would have it that he could."

"I do not fancy it was the curls that caused the upheaval, sir. I think Master Sebastian had been speaking disparagingly of Miss Garbo."

"Eh? Why should he do that?"

"I suggested that he should do so, sir, not long ago when I encountered him on his way to the stable yard. It was a move which he was very willing to make, as he informed me that in his opinion Miss Garbo was definitely inferior both in beauty and talent to Miss Clara Bow."

I sank into a chair. The Wooster system can stand just so much.

"Jeeves!"

"Sir?"

"You tell me that Sebastian Moon, a stripling of such tender years that he can go about the place with long curls without causing mob violence, is in love with Clara Bow?"

"And has been for some little time, he gave me to understand, sir."

"Jeeves, this Younger Generation is hot stuff."

"Yes, sir."

"Were you like that in your day?"

"No, sir."

"Nor I, Jeeves. At the age of fourteen I once wrote to Marie Lloyd for her autograph, but apart from that my private life could bear the strictest investigation. However, that is not the point. The point is, Jeeves, that once more I must pay you a marked tribute."

"Thank you very much, sir."

"Once more, like the great man you are, you have stepped forward and spread sweetness and light in no uncertain measure."

"I am glad to have given satisfaction, sir. Would you be requiring my services any further?"

"You mean you wish to return to Bognor and its shrimps? Do so, Jeeves, and stay there another fortnight, if you wish. And may success attend your net."

"Thank you very much, sir."

I eyed the man fixedly. His head stuck out at the back and his eyes sparkled with the light of pure intelligence. "I pity the shrimp that tries to pit its feeble cunning against you, Jeeves," I said.

And I meant it.

JEEVES AND THE OLD SCHOOL CHUM

Jeeves and the Old School Chum

I<small>N THE</small> autumn of the year in which Yorkshire Pudding won the Manchester November Handicap, the fortunes of my old pal Richard ("Bingo") Little seemed to have reached their—what's the word I want? He was, to all appearances, absolutely on plush.

He ate well, slept well, was happily married; and, his uncle Wilberforce having at last handed in his dinner pail, respected by all, had come into possession of a large income and a fine old place in the country about thirty miles from Norwich. Buzzing down there for a brief visit, I came away convinced that if ever a bird was sitting on top of the world that bird was Bingo.

I had to come away because the family were shooting me off to Harrogate to chaperon my uncle George, whose liver had been giving him the elbow again. But as we sat pushing down the morning meal on the day of my departure, I readily agreed to play a return date as soon as ever I could fight my way back to civilization.

"Come in time for the Lakenham races," urged young Bingo. He took aboard a second dollop of sausages and bacon, for he had always been a good trencherman and the country air seemed to improve his appetite. "We're going to motor over with a luncheon basket and more or less revel."

I was just about to say that I would make a point of it, when Mrs. Bingo, who was opening letters behind the coffee apparatus, suddenly uttered a pleased yowl.

"Oh, sweetie-lambkin!" she cried.

Mrs. B., if you remember, before her marriage was the celebrated female novelist, Rosie M. Banks, and it is in some such ghastly fashion that she habitually addresses the other half of the sketch. She had got that way, I take it, from a lifetime of writing for the masses.

Bingo doesn't seem to mind. I suppose, seeing that the little woman is the author of such outstanding bilge as *Mervyn Keene, Clubman* and *Only a Factory Girl,* he is thankful it isn't anything worse.

"Oh, sweetie-lambkin, isn't that lovely?"

"What?"

"Laura Pyke wants to come here."

"Who?"

"You must have heard me speak of Laura Pyke. She was my dearest friend at school. I simply worshiped her. She always had such a wonderful mind. She wants us to put her up for a week or two."

"Right ho. Bung her in."

"You're sure you don't mind?"

"Of course not. Any pal of yours——"

"Darling!" said Mrs. Bingo, blowing him a kiss.

"Angel!" said Bingo, going on with the sausages.

All very charming, in fact. Pleasant domestic scene.

I mean. Cheery give-and-take in the home and all that.
I said as much to Jeeves as we drove off.

"In these days of unrest, Jeeves," I said, "with
wives yearning to fulfill themselves and husbands
slipping round the corner to do what they shouldn't,
and the home, generally speaking, in the melting pot,
as it were, it is nice to find a thoroughly united
couple."

"Decidedly agreeable, sir."

"I allude to the Bingos—Mr. and Mrs. What was
it the poet said of couples like the Bingeese?"

"Two minds with but a single thought, two hearts
that beat as one, sir."

"A dashed good description, Jeeves."

"It has, I believe, given uniform satisfaction, sir."

And yet if I had only known, what I had been listening to that A. M. was the first faint rumble of the coming storm. Unseen, in the background, Fate was
quietly slipping the lead into the boxing glove.

I managed to give Uncle George a miss at a fairly
early date and, leaving him wallowing in the waters,
sent a wire to the Bingos announcing my return. It
was a longish drive and I fetched up at my destina-
tion only just in time to dress for dinner. I had done
a quick dash into the soup-and-fish and was feeling
pretty good at the prospect of a cocktail and the well-
cooked, when the door opened and Bingo appeared.

"Hello, Bertie," he said. "Ah, Jeeves."

He spoke in one of those toneless voices; and,
catching Jeeves's eye as I adjusted the old cravat, I
exchanged a questioning glance with it. From its ex-

pression I gathered that the same thing had struck him that had struck me: viz., that our host, the young squire, was none too chirpy. The brow was furrowed, the eye lacked that hearty sparkle, and the general bearing and demeanour were those of a body discovered after being several days in the water.

"Anything up, Bingo?" I asked, with the natural anxiety of a boyhood friend. "You have a mouldy look. Are you sickening for some sort of plague?"

"I've got it."

"Got what?"

"The plague."

"What do you mean?"

"She's on the premises now," said Bingo, and laughed in an unpleasant, hacking manner, as if he were missing on one tonsil.

I couldn't follow him. The old egg seemed to me to speak in riddles.

"You seem to me, old egg," I said, "to speak in riddles. Don't you think he speaks in riddles, Jeeves?"

"Yes, sir."

"I'm talking about the Pyke," said Bingo.

"What pike?"

"Laura Pyke. Don't you remember?"

"Oh, ah. Of course. The school chum. The seminary crony. Is she still here?"

"Yes, and looks like staying forever. Rosie's absolutely potty about her. Hangs on her lips."

"The glamour of the old days still persists, eh?"

"I should say it does," said young Bingo. "This business of schoolgirl friendship beats me. 'Hypnotic' is the only word. I can't understand it. Men aren't like that. You and I were at school together, Bertie, but my gosh, I don't look on you as a sort of master mind."

"You don't?"

"I don't treat your lightest utterance as a pearl of wisdom.'

"Why not?"

"Yet Rosie does with this Pyke. In the hands of the Pyke she is mere putty. If you want to see what was once a first-class Garden of Eden becoming utterly ruined as a desirable residence by the machinations of a Serpent, take a look round this place."

"Why, what's the trouble?"

"Laura Pyke," said young Bingo with intense bitterness, "is a food crank, curse her. She says we all eat too much and eat it too quickly and, anyway, ought not to be eating it at all but living on parsnips and similar muck. And Rosie, instead of telling the woman not to be a fathead, gazes at her in wide-eyed admiration, taking it in through the pores.

"The result is that the cuisine of this house has been shot to pieces, and I am starving on my feet. Well, when I tell you that it's weeks since a beefsteak pudding raised its head in the home, you'll understand what I mean."

At this point the gong went. Bingo listened with a moody frown.

"I don't know why they still bang that confounded thing," he said. "There's nothing to bang it for. By the way, Bertie, would you like a cocktail?"

"I would."

"Well, you won't get one. We don't have cocktails

any more. The girl friend says they corrode the stomachic tissues."

I was appalled. I had had no idea that the evil had spread as far as this.

"No cocktails!"

"No. And you'll be dashed lucky if it isn't a vegetarian dinner."

"Bingo," I cried, deeply moved, "you must act! You must assert yourself. You must put your foot down. You must take a strong stand. You must be master in the home."

He looked at me. A long, strange look. "You aren't married, are you, Bertie?"

"You know I'm not."

"I should have guessed it, anyway. Come on."

Well, the dinner wasn't absolutely vegetarian, but when you had said that you had said everything. It was sparse, meagre, not at all the jolly, chunky repast for which the old tum was standing up and clamouring after its long motor ride. And what there was of it was turned to ashes in the mouth by the conversation of Miss Laura Pyke.

In happier circs., and if I had not been informed in advance of the warped nature of her soul, I might have been favourably impressed by this female at the moment of our meeting. She was really rather a good-looking girl, a bit strong in the face but nevertheless quite reasonably attractive. But had she been a thing of radiant beauty she never could have clicked with Bertram Wooster. Her conversation was of a kind which would have queered Helen of Troy with any right-thinking man.

During dinner she talked all the time, and it did not take me long to see why the iron had entered into Bingo's soul. Practically all she said was about food and Bingo's tendency to shovel it down in excessive quantities, thereby handing the lemon to his stomachic tissues.

She didn't seem particularly interested in my stomachic tissues, rather giving the impression that if Bertram burst it would be all right with her. It was on young Bingo that she concentrated as the brand to be saved from the burning.

Gazing at him like a high priestess at the favourite, though erring, disciple, she told him all the things that were happening to his inside because he would insist on eating stuff lacking in fat-soluble vitamins. She spoke freely of proteins, carbohydrates, and the physiological requirements of the average individual.

She was not a girl who believed in mincing words, and a racy little anecdote she told about a man who refused to eat prunes had the effect of causing me to be a non-starter for the last two courses.

"Jeeves," I said, on reaching the sleeping chamber that night, "I don't like the look of things."

"No, sir?"

"No, Jeeves, I do not. I view the situation with concern. Things are worse than I thought they were. Mr. Little's remarks before dinner may have given you the impression that the Pyke merely lectured on food reform in a general sort of way. Such, I now find, is not the case. By way of illustrating her theme, she points to Mr. Little as the awful example. She criticizes him, Jeeves."

"Indeed, sir?"

"Yes. Openly. Keeps telling him he eats too much, drinks too much, and gobbles his food. I wish you could have heard a comparison she drew between him and the late Mr. Gladstone, considering them in the capacity of food chewers. It left young Bingo very much with the short end of the stick. And the sinister thing is that Mrs. Bingo approves. Are wives often like that? Welcoming criticism of the lord and master, I mean?"

"They are generally open to suggestions with regard to the improvement of their husbands, sir."

"That is why married men are wan, what?"

"Yes, sir."

I had the foresight to send the man downstairs for biscuits. I bit a representative specimen thoughtfully.

"Do you know what I think, Jeeves?"

"No, sir."

"I think Mr. Little doesn't realize the full extent of the peril which threatens his domestic happiness. I'm beginning to understand this business of matrimony. I'm beginning to see how the thing works. Would you care to hear how I figure it out, Jeeves?"

"Extremely, sir."

"Well, it's like this. Take a couple of birds. These birds get married, and for a while all is gas and gaiters. The female regards her mate as about the best thing that ever came a girl's way. He is her king, if you know what I mean. She looks up to him and respects him. Joy, as you might say, reigns supreme. Eh?"

"Very true, sir."

"Then gradually, by degrees—little by little, if I may use the expression—disillusionment sets in. She sees him eating a poached egg, and the glamour starts to fade. She watches him mangling a chop, and it continues to fade. And so on and so on, if you follow me, and so forth."

"I follow you perfectly, sir."

"But mark this, Jeeves. This is the point. Here we approach the nub. Usually it is all right, because, as I say, the disillusionment comes gradually and the female has time to adjust herself. But in the case of young Bingo, owing to the indecent outspokenness of the Pyke, it's coming in a rush.

"Absolutely in a flash, without previous preparation, Mrs. Bingo is having Bingo presented to her as a sort of human boa constrictor full of unpleasantly jumbled interior organs. The picture which the Pyke is building up for her in her mind is that of one of those men you see in restaurants with three chins, bulging eyes, and the veins starting out on the forehead. A little more of this, and love must wither."

"You think so, sir?"

"I'm sure of it. No affection can stand the strain. Twice during dinner to-night the Pyke said things about young Bingo's intestinal canal which I shouldn't have thought would have been possible in mixed company even in this lax post-war era.

"Well, you see what I mean. You can't go on knocking a man's intestinal canal indefinitely without causing his wife to stop and ponder The danger, as I see

it, is that after a bit more of this Mrs. Little will decide that tinkering is no use and that the only thing to
do is to scrap Bingo and get a newer model."

"Most disturbing, sir."

"Something must be done, Jeeves. You must act.
Unless you can find some way of getting this Pyke out
of the woodwork, and that right speedily, the home's
number is up. You see, what makes matters worse is
that Mrs. Bingo is romantic. Women like her, who
consider the day ill spent if they have not churned out
five thousand words of super-fatted fiction, are apt
even at the best of times to yearn a trifle. The ink gets
into their heads.

"I mean to say, I shouldn't wonder if right from the
start Mrs. Bingo hasn't had a sort of sneaking regret
that Bingo isn't one of those strong, curt, empire-
building kind of Englishmen she puts into her books,
with sad, unfathomable eyes, lean, sensitive hands,
and riding boots. You see what I mean?"

"Precisely, sir. You imply that Miss Pyke's criticisms will have been instrumental in moving the hitherto unformulated dissatisfaction from the subconscious to the conscious mind."

"Once again, Jeeves?" I said, trying to grab it off
the bat, but missing it by several yards.

He repeated the dose.

"Well, I dare say you're right," I said. "Anyway,
the point is, P.M.G. Pyke must go. How do you propose to set about it?"

"I fear I have nothing to suggest at the moment,
sir."

"Come, come, Jeeves!"

"I fear not, sir. Possibly after I have seen the lady——"

"You mean, you want to study the psychology of the individual and what not?"

"Precisely, sir."

"Well, I don't know how you're going to do it. After all, I mean, you can hardly cluster round the dinner table and drink in the Pyke's small talk."

"There is that difficulty, sir."

"Your best chance, it seems to me, will be when we go to the Lakenham races on Thursday. We shall feed out of a luncheon basket in God's air, and there's nothing to stop you hanging about and passing the sandwiches. Prick the ears and be at your most observant then is my advice."

"Very good, sir."

"Very good, Jeeves. And, meanwhile, dash downstairs and see if you can dig up another installment of these biscuits. I need them sorely."

The morning of the Lakenham races dawned bright and juicy. A casual observer would have said that God was in His heaven and all was right with the world. It was one of those days you sometimes get latish in the autumn when the sun beams, the birds toot, and there is bracing tang in the air that sends the blood beetling briskly through the veins.

Personally, however, I wasn't any too keen on the bracing tang. It made me feel so exceptionally fit that almost immediately after breakfast I found myself beginning to wonder what there would be for luncheon. And the thought of what there probably

would be for luncheon, if the Pyke's influence made
itself felt, lowered my spirits considerably. I feared
the worst.

"I fear the worst, Jeeves," I said. "Last night at
dinner Miss Pyke threw out the remark that the
carrot was the best of all vegetables, having an astonishing effect on the blood and beautifying the complexion. Now, I am all for anything that bucks up the
Wooster blood. Also, I would like to give the natives
a treat by letting them take a look at my rosy, glowing cheeks. But not at the expense of lunching on raw
carrots.

"To avoid any rannygazoo, therefore, I think it
will be best if you add a bit for the young master to
your personal packet of sandwiches. I don't want to
be caught short."

"Very good, sir."

At this point young Bingo came up. I hadn't seen
him look so jaunty for days.

"I've just been superintending the packing of the
lunch basket, Bertie," he said. "I stood over the butler
and saw that there was no nonsense."

"All pretty sound?" I asked, relieved.

"All indubitably sound."

"No carrots?"

"No carrots," said young Bingo. "There's ham
sandwiches," he proceeded, a strange, soft light in his
eyes, "and tongue sandwiches and potted-meat sandwiches and game sandwiches and hard-boiled eggs and
lobster and a cold chicken and sardines and a cake and
a couple of bottles of Bollinger and some old
brandy——"

"It has the right ring," I said. "And if we want a bite to eat after that, of course we can go to the pub."

"What pub?"

"Isn't there a pub on the course?"

"There's not a pub for miles. That's why I was so particularly careful that there should be no funny work about the basket. The common, where these races are held, is a desert without an oasis. Practically a death trap. I met a fellow the other day who told me he got there last year and unpacked his basket and found that the champagne had burst and, together with the salad dressing, had soaked into the ham, which in its turn had got mixed up with the Gorgonzola cheese, forming a sort of paste. He had had rather a bumpy bit of road to travel over."

"What did he do?"

"Oh, he ate the mixture. It was the only course. But he said he could still taste it sometimes, even now."

In ordinary circs., I can't say I should have been any too braced at the news that we were going to split up for the journey in the following order: Bingo and Mrs. Bingo in their car and the Pyke in mine, with Jeeves sitting behind in the dickey. But, things being as they were, the arrangement had its points. It meant that Jeeves would be able to study the back of the Pyke's head and draw his deductions, while I could engage her in conversation and let him see what manner of female she was.

I started, accordingly, directly we had rolled off, and all through the journey until we fetched up at the course she gave of her best. It was with considerable satisfaction that I parked the car beside a tree and hopped out.

"You were listening, Jeeves?" I said.

"Yes, sir."

"A tough baby?"

"Undeniably, sir."

Bingo and Mrs. Bingo came up.

"The first race won't be for half an hour," said Bingo. "We'd better lunch now. Fish the basket out, Jeeves, would you mind?"

"Sir?"

"The luncheon basket," said Bingo in a devout voice, licking his lips slightly.

"The basket is not in Mr. Wooster's car, sir."

"What!"

"I assumed that you were bringing it in your own, sir."

I have never seen the sunshine fade out of anybody's face as quickly as it did out of Bingo's. He uttered a cry.

"Rosie!"

"Yes, sweetie-pie?"

"The bunch! The lasket!"

"What, darling?"

"The luncheon basket!"

"What about it, precious?"

"It's been left behind!"

"Oh, has it?" said Mrs. Bingo.

I confess she had never fallen lower in my estimation. I had always known her as a woman with as healthy an appreciation of her meals as any of my acquaintance. A few years previously, when my aunt

Dahlia had stolen her French cook, Anatole, she had called Aunt Dahlia some names in my presence which had impressed me profoundly.

Yet now, when informed that she was marooned on a bally prairie without bite or sup, all she could find to say was, "Oh, has it?" I had never fully realized before the extent to which she had allowed herself to be dominated by the deleterious influence of the Pyke.

The Pyke, for her part, touched an even lower level.

"It is just as well," she said, and her voice seemed to cut Bingo like a knife. "Luncheon is a meal better omitted. If taken, it should consist merely of a few muscatels, bananas, and grated carrots. It is a well-known fact . . ."

And she went on to speak at some length of the gastric juices in a vein far from suited to any gathering at which gentlemen were present.

"So, you see, darling," said Mrs. Bingo, "you will really feel ever so much better and brighter for not having eaten a lot of indigestible food. It is much the best thing that could have happened."

Bingo gave her a long, lingering look. "I see," he said. "Well, if you will excuse me, I'll go off somewhere where I can cheer without exciting comment."

I perceived Jeeves withdrawing in a meaning manner, and I followed him, hoping for the best. My trust was not misplaced. He had brought enough sandwiches for two. In fact, enough for three. I whistled to Bingo, and he came slinking up, and we restored the tissues in a makeshift sort of way behind a hedge.

Then Bingo went off to interview bookies about the first race, and Jeeves gave a cough.

"Swallowed a crumb the wrong way?" I said.

"No, sir, I thank you. It is merely that I desired to express a hope that I had not been guilty of taking a liberty, sir."

"How?"

"In removing the luncheon basket from the car before we started, sir."

I quivered like an aspen. I stared at the man. Aghast. Shocked to the core.

"You, Jeeves?" I said, and I should rather think Cæsar spoke in the same sort of voice on finding Brutus puncturing him with a sharp instrument. "You mean to tell me it was you who deliberately, if that's the word I want——?"

"Yes, sir. It seemed to me the most judicious course to pursue. It would not have been prudent, in my opinion, to have allowed Mrs. Little, in her present frame of mind, to witness Mr. Little eating a meal on the scale which he outlined in his remarks this morning."

I saw his point.

"True, Jeeves," I said thoughtfully. "I see what you mean. If young Bingo has a fault, it is that, when in the society of a sandwich, he is apt to get a bit rough. I've picnicked with him before, many a time and oft, and his method of approach to the ordinary tongue or ham sandwich rather resembles that of the lion, the king of beasts, tucking into an antelope. Add lobster and cold chicken, and I admit the spectacle might have been something of a jar for the little

woman. Still . . . All the same . . . Nevertheless . . ."

"And there is another aspect of the matter, sir."

"What's that?"

"A day spent without nourishment in the keen
autumnal air may induce in Mrs. Little a frame of
mind not altogether in sympathy with Miss Pyke's
view on diet."

"You mean, hunger will gnaw and she'll be apt to
bite at the Pyke when she talks about how jolly it is
for the gastric juices to get a day off?"

"Exactly, sir."

I shook the head. I hated to damp the man's enthusiasm, but it had to be done.

"Abandon the idea, Jeeves," I said. "I fear you
have not studied the sex as I have. Missing her lunch
means little or nothing to the female of the species.
The feminine attitude toward lunch is notoriously
airy and casual.

"Where you have made your bloomer is in confusing lunch with tea. Hell, it is well known, has no fury
like a woman who wants her tea and can't get it. At
such times the most amiable of the sex become mere
bombs which a spark may ignite. But lunch, Jeeves,
no. I should have thought you would have known that
—a bird of your established intelligence."

"No doubt you are right, sir."

"If you could somehow arrange for Mrs. Little to
miss her tea . . . But these are idle dreams, Jeeves.
By tea time she will be back at the old home, in the
midst of plenty. It only takes an hour to do the trip.
The last race is over shortly after four. By five o'clock

Mrs. Little will have her feet tucked under the table and will be revelling in buttered toast. I am sorry, Jeeves, but your scheme was a washout from the start. No earthly. A dud."

"I appreciate the point you have raised, sir. What you say is extremely true."

"Unfortunately. Well, there it is. The only thing to do seems to be to get back to the course and try to skin a bookie or two and forget."

Well, the long day wore on, so to speak. I can't say I enjoyed myself much. I was distrait, if you know what I mean. Preoccupied. From time to time assorted clusters of spavined local horses clumped down the course with farmers on top of them, but I watched them with a languid eye. To get into the spirit of one of these rural meetings, it is essential that the subject have a good fat luncheon inside him. Subtract the luncheon, and what ensues? Ennui.

Not once but many times during the afternoon I found myself thinking hard thoughts about Jeeves. The man seemed to me to be losing his grip. A child could have told him that that footling scheme of his would not get him anywhere.

I mean to say, when you reflect that the average woman considers she has lunched luxuriously if she swallows a couple of macaroons, half a chocolate éclair, and a raspberry vinegar, is she going to be peevish because you do her out of a midday sandwich? Of course not. Perfectly ridiculous. Too silly for words. All that Jeeves had accomplished by his bally trying to be clever was to give me a feeling as if foxes were gnawing my vitals and a strong desire for home.

It was a relief, therefore, when, as the shades of evening were beginning to fall, Mrs. Bingo announced her intention of calling it a day and shifting.

"Would you mind very much missing the last race, Mr. Wooster?" she asked.

"I am all for it," I replied cordially. "The last race means little or nothing in my life. Besides, I am a shilling and sixpence ahead of the game, and the time to stop is when you're winning."

"Laura and I thought we would go home. I feel I should like an early cup of tea. Bingo says he will stay on. So I thought you could drive our car, and he would follow later in yours, with Jeeves."

"Right ho."

"You know the way?"

"Oh, yes. Main road to that turning by the pond, and then across country."

"I can direct you from there."

I sent Jeeves to fetch the car, and presently we were bowling off in good shape. The short afternoon had turned into a rather chilly, misty sort of evening, the kind of evening that sends a fellow's thoughts straying off in the direction of hot Scotch and water with a spot of lemon in it. I put the foot firmly on the accelerator, and we did the five or six miles of main road in quick time.

Turning eastward at the pond, I had to go a bit slower, for we had struck a wildish stretch of country where the going wasn't so good. I don't know any part of England where you feel so off the map as on the byroads of Norfolk. Occasionally we would meet a cow or two, but otherwise we had the world pretty much to ourselves.

I began to think about that drink again, and the more I thought the better it looked. It's rummy how people differ in this matter of selecting the beverage that is to touch the spot. It's what Jeeves would call the "psychology of the individual."

Some fellows in my position might have voted for a tankard of ale, and the Pyke's idea of a refreshing snort was, as I knew from what she had told me on the journey out, a cupful of tepid pip-and-peel water, or, failing that, what she called the "fruit liquor." You make this, apparently, by soaking raisins in cold water and adding the juice of a melon. After which, I suppose, you invite some old friends in and have an orgy, burying the bodies in the morning.

Personally, I had no doubts. I never wavered. Hot Scotch and water was the stuff for me—stressing the Scotch, if you know what I mean, and going fairly easy on the H2O. I seemed to see the beaker smiling at me across the misty fields, beckoning me on, as it were, and saying, "Courage, Bertram! It will not be long now!" And with renewed energy I bunged the old foot down on the accelerator and tried to send the needle up to sixty.

Instead of which, if you follow my drift, the bally thing flickered for a moment to thirty-five, and then gave the business up as a bad job. Quite suddenly and unexpectedly, no one more surprised than myself, the car let out a faint gurgle like a sick moose and stopped in its tracks. And there we were, somewhere in Norfolk, with darkness coming on and a cold wind that smelled of guano and dead mangel-wurzels playing about the spinal column.

The back-seat drivers gave tongue. "What's the matter? What has happened? Why don't you go on? What are you stopping for?"

I explained. "I'm not stopping. It's the car."

"Why has the car stopped?"

"Ah!" I said, with a manly frankness that became me well. "There you have me."

You see, I'm one of those birds who drive a lot but don't know the first thing about the works. The policy I pursue is to get aboard, prod the self-starter, and leave the rest to Nature. If anything goes wrong I scream for an A. A. scout. It's a system that answers admirably as a rule, but on the present occasion it blew a fuse owing to the fact that there wasn't an A. A. scout within miles.

I explained as much to the fair cargo and received in return a "Pshaw" from the Pyke that nearly lifted the top of my head off. What with having a covey of female relations who have regarded me from child-hood as about ten degrees short of a half-wit, I have become rather a connoisseur of "Pshaws," and the Pyke's seemed to me well up in Class A, possessing much of the timbre and *brio* of my aunt Agatha's.

"Perhaps I can find out what the trouble is," she said, becoming calmer. "I understand cars."

She got out and began peering into the thing's vitals. I thought for a moment of suggesting that its gastric juices might have taken a turn for the worse owing to lack of fat-soluble vitamins, but decided on the whole not. I'm a pretty close observer, and it didn't seem to me that she was in the mood.

And yet, as a matter of fact, I should have been about right, at that. For after fiddling with the engine for a while in a discontented sort of way the female was suddenly struck with an idea. She tested it, and it was proved correct. There was not a drop in the tank. No gas. In other words, a complete lack of fat-soluble vitamins. What it amounted to was that the job now before us was to get the old bus home purely by will power.

Feeling that, from whatever angle they regarded the regrettable occurrence, they could hardly blame me, I braced up a trifle—in fact, to the extent of a hearty "Well, well, well!"

"No gas," I said. "Fancy that."

"But Bingo said he was going to fill the tank this morning," said Mrs. Bingo.

"I suppose he forgot," said the Pyke. "He would!"

"What do you mean by that?" said Mrs. Bingo, and I noted in her voice a touch of what-is-it.

"I mean he is just the sort of man who would forget to fill the tank," replied the Pyke, who also appeared somewhat moved.

"I should be very much obliged, Laura," said Mrs. Bingo, doing the loyal-little-woman stuff, "if you would refrain from criticizing my husband."

"Pshaw!" said the Pyke.

"And don't say 'Pshaw'!" said Mrs. Bingo.

"I shall say whatever I please," said the Pyke.

"Ladies, ladies!" I said. "Ladies, ladies, ladies!"

It was rash. Looking back, I can see that. One of the first lessons life teaches us is that on these occasions of back-chat between the delicately nurtured a man should retire into the offing, curl up in a ball, and imitate the prudent tactics of the opossum, which, when danger is in the air, pretends to be dead, frequently going to the length of hanging out crape and instructing its friends to stay round and say what a pity it all is. The only result of my dash at the soothing intervention was that the Pyke turned on me like a wounded leopardess.

"Well!" she said. "Aren't you proposing to do anything, Mr. Wooster?"

"What can I do?"

"There's a house over there. I should have thought it would be well within even your powers to go and borrow a can of gasoline."

I looked. There was a house. And one of the lower windows was lighted, indicating to the trained mind the presence of a taxpayer.

"A very sound and brainy scheme," I said ingratiatingly. "I will first honk a little on the horn to show we're here, and then rapid action."

I honked, with the most gratifying results. Almost immediately a human form appeared in the window. It seemed to be waving its arms in a matey and welcoming sort of way. Stimulated and encouraged, I hastened to the front door and gave it a breezy bang with the knocker. Things, I felt, were moving.

The first bang produced no result. I had just lifted the knocker for the encore, when it was wrenched out of my hand. The door flew open. and there stood a bloke with an expression of strained anguish on his face. A bloke with a secret sorrow.

I was sorry he had troubles, of course, but, having some of my own, I came right down to the agenda without delay.

"I say——" I began.

The bloke's hair was standing up in a kind of tousled mass, and at this juncture he ran a hand through it. And for the first time I noted that his eyes had a hostile gleam.

"Was that you making that infernal noise?" he asked.

"Er—yes," I said. "I did honk."

"Honk once more—just once," said the bloke, speaking in a low, strangled voice, "and I'll shred you up into little bits with my bare hands. My wife's gone out for the evening and after hours of ceaseless toil I've at last managed to get the baby to sleep, and you come along making that hideous din with your confounded horn. What do you mean by it, blast you?"

"Er——"

"Well, that's how matters stand," said the bloke, summing up. "One more toot—just one single solitary suggestion of the faintest shadow or suspicion of anything remotely approaching a toot—and may the Lord have mercy on your soul."

"What I want," I said, "is gasoline."

"What you'll get," said the bloke, "is a thick ear."

And closing the door with the delicate caution of one brushing flies off a sleeping Venus, he passed out of my life.

Women as a sex are always apt to be a trifle down

on the defeated warrior. Returning to the car, I was not well received. The impression seemed to be that Bertram had not acquitted himself in a fashion worthy of his crusading ancestors.

I did my best to smooth matters over, but you know how it is. When you've broken down on a chilly autumn evening miles from anywhere and have missed luncheon and look like missing tea as well, mere charm of manner can never be a really satisfactory substitute for a can of the juice.

Things got so noticeably unpleasant, in fact, that after a while, mumbling something about getting help, I sidled off down the road. And by Jove, I hadn't gone half a mile before I saw lights in the distance and there, in the middle of this forsaken desert, was a car.

I stood in the road and whooped as I had never whooped before.

"Hi!" I shouted. "I say! Hi! Half a minute! Hi! Ho! Hi! Just a second, if you don't mind."

The car reached me and slowed up. A voice spoke.

"Is that you, Bertie?"

"Hullo, Bingo! Is that you? I say, Bingo, we've broken down."

Bingo hopped out. "Give us five minutes, Jeeves," he said, "and then drive slowly on."

"Very good, sir."

Bingo joined me.

"We aren't going to walk, are we?" I asked. "Where's the sense?"

"Yes, walk, laddie," said Bingo, "and warily

withal. I want to make sure of something. Bertie, how were things when you left? Hotting up?"

"A trifle."

"You observed symptoms of a row, a quarrel, a parting of brass rags between Rosie and the Pyke?"

"There did seem a certain liveliness."

"Tell me."

I related what had occurred. He listened intently.

"Bertie," he said as we walked along, "you are present at a crisis in your old friend's life. It may be that this vigil in a broken-down car will cause Rosie to see what you'd have thought she ought to have seen years ago: viz., that the Pyke is entirely unfit for human consumption and must be cast into outer darkness where there is wailing and gnashing of teeth.

"I am not betting on it, but stranger things have happened. Rosie is the sweetest girl in the world, but, like all women, she gets edgy toward tea time. And to-day, having missed lunch—— Hark!"

He grabbed my arm, and we paused. Tense. Agog. From down the road came the sound of voices, and a mere instant was enough to tell us that it was Mrs. Bingo and the Pyke talking things over.

I had never listened in on a real, genuine female row before, and I'm bound to say it was pretty impressive. During my absence matters appeared to have developed on rather a spacious scale. They had reached the stage now where the combatants had begun to dig into the past and rake up old scores.

Mrs. Bingo was saying that the Pyke would never have got into the hockey team at St. Adela's if she hadn't flattered and fawned upon the captain in a way that it made Mrs. Bingo, even after all these years, sick to think of. The Pyke replied that she had refrained from mentioning it until now, having always felt it better to let bygones be bygones, but that if Mrs. Bingo supposed her to be unaware that Mrs. Bingo had won the Scripture prize by taking a list of the Kings of Judah into the examination room, tucked into her middy blouse, Mrs. Bingo was vastly mistaken.

Furthermore, the Pyke proceeded, Mrs. Bingo was also labouring under an error if she imagined that the Pyke proposed to remain a night longer under her roof. It had been in a moment of weakness, a moment of mistaken kindliness, supposing her to be lonely and in need of intellectual society, that the Pyke had decided to pay her a visit at all.

Her intention now was, if ever Providence sent them aid and enabled her to get out of this beastly car and back to her trunks, to pack those trunks and leave by the next train, even if that train was a milk train, stopping at every station. Indeed, rather than endure another night at Mrs. Bingo's, the Pyke was quite willing to walk to London.

To this, Mrs. Bingo's reply was long and eloquent, and touched on the fact that in her last term at St. Adela's a girl named Simpson had told her (Mrs. Bingo) that a girl named Waddesley had told her (the Simpson) that the Pyke, while pretending to be a friend of hers (the Bingo's), had told her (the Waddesley) that she (the Bingo) couldn't eat strawberries and cream without coming out in spots, and, in addition, had spoken in the most catty manner about the shape of her nose. It could all have been condensed, however, into the words "Right ho."

It was when the Pyke had begun to say that she had never had such a hearty laugh in her life as when she read the scene in Mrs. Bingo's last novel where the heroine's little boy dies of croup that we felt it best to call the meeting to order before bloodshed set in. Jeeves had come up in the car, and Bingo, removing a can of gasoline from the dickey, placed it in the shadows at the side of the road. Then we hopped on and made the spectacular entry.

"Hullo, hullo, hullo!" said Bingo brightly. "Bertie tells me you've had a breakdown."

"Oh, Bingo!" cried Mrs. Bingo, wifely love trilling in every syllable. "Thank goodness you've come!"

"Now, perhaps," said the Pyke, "I can get home and do my packing. If Mr. Wooster will allow me to use his car his man can drive me back to the house in time to catch the six-fifteen."

"You aren't leaving us?" said Bingo.

"I am," said the Pyke.

"Too bad," said Bingo.

She climbed in beside Jeeves and they popped off. There was a short silence after they had gone. It was too dark to see her, but I could feel Mrs. Bingo struggling between love of her mate and the natural urge to say something crisp about his forgetting to fill the gasoline tank that morning. Eventually Nature took its course.

"I must say, sweetie-pie," she said, "it was a little careless of you to leave the tank almost empty when we started to-day. You promised me you would fill it, darling."

"But I did fill it, darling."

"But darling, it's empty."

"It can't be, darling."

"Laura said it was."

"The woman's an ass," said Bingo. "There's plenty of gas. What's wrong is probably that the sprockets aren't running true with the differential gear. It happens that way sometimes. I'll fix it in a second. But I don't want you to sit freezing out here while I'm doing it. Why not go to that house over there and ask them if you can't come in and sit down for ten minutes? They might give you a cup of tea, too."

A soft moan escaped Mrs. Bingo. "Tea!" I heard her whisper.

I had to bust Bingo's daydream.

"I'm sorry, old man," I said, "but I fear the old English hospitality which you outline is off. That house is inhabited by a sort of bandit. As unfriendly a bird as I ever met. His wife's out and he's just got the baby to sleep, and this has darkened his outlook. Tap even lightly on his front door and you take your life into your hands."

"Nonsense," said Bingo. "Come along."

He banged the knocker, and produced an immediate response.

"Hell!" said the Bandit, appearing as if out of a trap.

"I say," said young Bingo, "I'm just fixing our car outside. Would you object to my wife coming in out of the cold for a few minutes?"

"Yes," said the Bandit, "I would."

"And you might give her a cup of tea."

"I won't," said the Bandit.

"You won't?"

"No. And for heaven's sake don't talk so loud. I know that baby. A whisper sometimes does it."

"Let us get this straight," said Bingo. "You refuse to give my wife tea?"

"Yes."

"You would see a woman starve?"

"Yes."

"Well, you jolly well aren't going to," said young Bingo. "Unless you go straight to your kitchen, put the kettle on, and start slicing bread for buttered toast, I'll yell and wake the baby."

The Bandit turned ashen. "You wouldn't do that?"

"I would."

"Have you no heart?"

"No."

"No human feeling?"

"No."

The Bandit turned to Mrs. Bingo. You could see his spirit was broken.

"Do your shoes squeak?" he asked humbly.

"No."

"Then come on in."

"Thank you," said Mrs. Bingo.

She turned for an instant to Bingo, and there was a look in her eyes that one of those damsels in distress might have given the knight as he shot his cuffs and turned away from the dead dragon. It was a look of adoration, of almost reverent respect. Just the sort of look, in fact, that a husband likes to see.

"Darling!" she said.

"Darling!" said Bingo.

"Angel!" said Mrs. Bingo.

"Precious!" said Bingo. "Come along, Bertie, let's get at that car."

He was silent till he had fetched the can of gasoline and filled the tank and screwed the cap on again. Then he drew a deep breath.

"Bertie," he said, "I am ashamed to admit it, but occasionally in the course of a lengthy acquaintance there have been moments when I have temporarily lost faith in Jeeves."

"My dear chap!" I said, shocked.

"Yes, Bertie, there have. Sometimes my belief in him has wabbled. I have said to myself, 'Has he the old speed, the ancient vim?' I shall never say it again. From now on, childlike trust. It was his idea, Bertie, that if a couple of women headed for tea suddenly found the cup snatched from their lips, so to speak, they would turn and rend each other. Observe the result."

"But dash it, Jeeves couldn't have known that the car would break down."

"On the contrary. He let all the gasoline out of the tank when you sent him to fetch the machine—all except just enough to carry it well into the wilds beyond the reach of human aid. He foresaw what would happen. I tell you, Bertie, Jeeves stands alone."

"Absolutely."

"He's a marvel."

"A wonder."

"A wizard."

"A stout fellow," I agreed. "Full of fat-soluble vitamins."

"The exact expression," said young Bingo. "And now let's go and tell Rosie the car is fixed, and then home to the tankard of ale."

"Not the tankard of ale, old man," I said firmly. "The hot Scotch and water with a spot of lemon in it."

"You're absolutely right," said Bingo. "What a flair you have in these matters, Bertie. Hot Scotch and water it is."

THE INDIAN SUMMER OF AN UNCLE

The Indian Summer of an Uncle

Ask anyone at the Drones', and they will tell you that Bertram Wooster is a fellow whom it is dashed difficult to deceive. Old Lynx-Eye is about what it amounts to. I observe and deduce. I weigh the evidence and draw my conclusions. And that is why Uncle George had not been in my midst more than about two minutes before I, so to speak, saw all. To my trained eye the thing stuck out a mile.

And yet it seemed so dashed absurd. Consider the facts, if you know what I mean.

I mean to say, for years, right back to the time when I first went to Eton, this bulging relative had been one of the recognized eyesores of London. He was fat then, and day by day in every way has been getting fatter ever since, till now tailors measure him just for the sake of the exercise. He is what they call a prominent London clubman—one of those birds in tight morning coats and gray toppers whom you see toddling along St. James's Street on fine afternoons, puffing a bit as they make the grade. Slip a ferret into any good club between Piccadilly and Pall Mall, and you would start half a dozen Uncle Georges.

He spends his time lunching and dining at the Buffers' and, between meals, sucking down spots in the smoking room and talking about the lining of his stomach to anyone who will listen. About twice a year

his liver lodges a formal protest and he goes off to
Harrogate or Carlsbad to get planed down. Then
back again and on with the programme. The last
bloke in the world, in short, who you would think
would ever fall a victim to the divine pash. And yet,
if you will believe me, that was absolutely the strength
of it.

This old pestilence blew in on me one morning at
about the hour of the after-breakfast cigarette.

"Oh, Bertie," he said.

"Hullo?"

"You know those ties you've been wearing. Where
did you get them?"

"Blucher's, in the Burlington Arcade."

"Thanks."

He walked across to the mirror and stood in front
of it, gazing at himself in an earnest manner.

"Smut on your nose?" I asked courteously.

Then I suddenly perceived that he was wearing a
sort of horrible simper, and I confess it chilled the
blood to no little extent. Uncle George, with face in
repose, is hard enough on the eye. Simpering, he goes
right above the odds.

"Ha!" he said.

He heaved a long sigh, and turned away. Not too
soon, for the mirror was on the point of cracking.

"I'm not so old," he said, in a musing sort of voice.

"So old as what?"

"Properly considered, I'm in my prime. Besides,
what a young and inexperienced girl needs is a man
of weight and years to lean on. The sturdy oak, not
the sapling."

It was at this point that, as I said above, I saw all.

"Great Scott, Uncle George!" I said. "You aren't thinking of getting married?"

"Who isn't?" he said.

"You aren't," I said.

"Yes, I am. Why not?"

"Oh, well . . ."

"Marriage is an honourable state."

"Oh, absolutely."

"It might make you a better man, Bertie."

"Who says so?"

"I say so. Marriage might turn you from a frivolous young scallywag into—er—a non-scallywag. Yes, confound you, I *am* thinking of getting married, and if Agatha comes sticking her oar in I'll—I'll—well, I shall know what to do about it."

He excited on the big line, and I rang the bell for Jeeves. The situation seemed to me one that called for a cozy talk.

"Jeeves," I said.

"Sir?"

"You know my uncle George?"

"Yes, sir. His lordship has been familiar to me for some years."

"I don't mean do you know my uncle George. I mean do you know what my uncle George is thinking of doing?"

"Contracting a matrimonial alliance, sir."

"Good Lord! Did he tell you?"

"No, sir. Oddly enough, I chance to be acquainted with the other party in the matter."

"The girl?"

"The young person, yes, sir. It was from her aunt, with whom she resides, that I received the information that his lordship was contemplating matrimony."

"Who is she?"

"A Miss Platt, sir. Miss Rhoda Platt. Of Wistaria Lodge, Kitchener Road, East Dulwich."

"Young?"

"Yes, sir."

"The old fathead!"

"Yes, sir. The expression is one which I would, of course, not have ventured to employ myself, but I confess to thinking his lordship somewhat ill advised. One must remember, however, that it is not unusual to find gentlemen of a certain age yielding to what might be described as a 'sentimental urge.' They appear to experience what I may term a sort of 'Indian summer,' a kind of temporarily renewed youth. The phenomenon is particularly noticeable, I am given to understand, in the United States of America among the wealthier inhabitants of the city of Pittsburgh. It is notorious, I am told, that sooner or later, unless restrained, they always endeavour to marry chorus girls. Why this should be so, I am at a loss to say, but . . ."

I saw that this was going to take some time. I tuned out.

"From something in Uncle George's manner, Jeeves, as he referred to my aunt Agatha's probable reception of the news, I gather that this Miss Platt is not of the *noblesse*."

"No, sir. She is a waitress at his lordship's club."

"My God! The proletariat!"

"The lower middle classes, sir."

"Well, yes, by stretching it a bit, perhaps. Still, you know what I mean."

"Yes, sir."

"Rummy thing, Jeeves," I said thoughtfully, "this modern tendency to marry waitresses. If you remember, before he settled down young Bingo Little was repeatedly trying to do it."

"Yes, sir."

"Odd!"

"Yes, sir."

"Still, there it is, of course. The point to be considered now is, What will Aunt Agatha do about this? You know her, Jeeves. She is not like me. I'm broadminded. If Uncle George wants to marry waitresses, let him, say I. I hold that the rank is but the penny stamp——"

"Guinea stamp, sir."

"All right, guinea stamp. Though I don't believe there is such a thing. I shouldn't have thought they came higher than five bob. Well, as I was saying, I maintain that the rank is but the guinea stamp and a girl's a girl for all that."

"'For *a*' that,' sir. The poet Burns wrote in the North British dialect."

"Well, 'a' that,' then, if you prefer it."

"I have no preference in the matter, sir. It is simply that the poet Burns——"

"Never mind about the poet Burns."

"No, sir."

"Forget the poet Burns."

"Very good, sir."

"Expunge the poet Burns from your mind."

"I will do so immediately, sir."

"What we have to consider is not the poet Burns but the aunt Agatha. She will kick, Jeeves."

"Very probably, sir."

"And, what's worse, she will lug me into the mess. There is only one thing to be done. Pack the tooth-brush and let us escape while we may, leaving no address."

"Very good, sir."

At this moment the bell rang.

"Ha!" I said. "Someone at the door."

"Yes, sir."

"Probably Uncle George back again. I'll answer it. You go and get ahead with the packing."

"Very good, sir."

I sauntered along the passage, whistling carelessly, and there on the mat was Aunt Agatha. Herself. Not a picture.

A nasty jar.

"Oh, hullo!" I said, it seeming but little good to tell her I was out of town and not expected back for some weeks.

"I wish to speak to you, Bertie," said the Family Curse. "I am greatly upset."

She legged it into the sitting room and volplaned into a chair. I followed, thinking wistfully of Jeeves packing in the bedroom. That suitcase would not be needed now. I knew what she must have come about.

"I've just seen Uncle George," I said, giving her a lead.

"So have I," said Aunt Agatha, shivering in a marked manner. "He called on me while I was still in bed to inform me of his intention of marrying some impossible girl from South Norwood."

"East Dulwich, the cognoscenti inform me."

"Well, East Dulwich, then. It is the same thing. But who told you?"

"Jeeves."

"And how, pray, does Jeeves come to know all about it?"

"There are very few things in this world, Aunt Agatha," I said gravely, "that Jeeves doesn't know all about. He's met the girl."

"Who is she?"

"One of the waitresses at the Buffers."

I had expected this to register, and it did. The relative let out a screech rather like the Cornish Express going through a junction.

"I take it from your manner, Aunt Agatha," I said, "that you want this thing stopped."

"Of course it must be stopped."

"Then there is but one policy to pursue. Let me ring for Jeeves and ask his advice."

Aunt Agatha stiffened visibly. Very much the *grande dame* of the old régime.

"Are you seriously suggesting that we should discuss this intimate family matter with your manservant?"

"Absolutely. Jeeves will find the way."

"I have always known that you were an imbecile, Bertie," said the flesh and blood, now down at about three degrees Fahrenheit, "but I did suppose that yor had some proper feeling, some pride, some respect for your position."

"Well, you know what the poet Burns says."

She squelched me with a glance.

"Obviously the only thing to do," she said, "is to offer this girl money."

"Money?"

"Certainly. It will not be the first time your uncle has made such a course necessary."

We sat for a bit, brooding. The family always sits brooding when the subject of Uncle George's early romance comes up. I was too young to be actually in on it at the time, but I've had the details frequently from many sources, including Uncle George. Let him get even the slightest bit pickled, and he will tell you the whole story, sometimes twice in an evening. It was a barmaid at the Criterion, just before he came into the title. Her name was Maudie and he loved her dearly, but the family would have none of it. They dug down into the sock and paid her off. Just one of those human-interest stories, if you know what I mean.

I wasn't so sold on this money-offering scheme.

"Well, just as you like, of course," I said, "but you're taking an awful chance. I mean, whenever people do it in novels and plays they always get the dickens of a welt. The girl gets the sympathy of the audience every time. She just draws herself up and looks at them with clear, steady eyes, causing them to feel not a little cheesy. If I were you, I would sit tight and let Nature take its course."

"I don't understand you."

"Well, consider for a moment what Uncle George looks like. No Greta Garbo, believe me. I should simply let the girl go on looking at him. Take it from me, Aunt Agatha, I've studied human nature and I don't believe there's a female in the world who could see Uncle George fairly often in those waistcoats he wears without feeling that it was due to her better self to give him the gate. Besides, this girl sees him at meal times, and Uncle George with his head down among the foodstuffs is a spectacle which——"

"If it is not troubling you too much, Bertie, I should be greatly obliged if you would stop drivelling."

"Just as you say. All the same, I think you're going to find it dashed embarrassing, offering this girl money."

"I am not proposing to do so. *You* will undertake the negotiations."

"Me?"

"Certainly. I should think a hundred pounds would be ample. But I will give you a blank check, and you are at liberty to fill it in for a higher sum if it becomes necessary. The essential point is that, cost what it may, your uncle must be released from this entanglement."

"So you're going to shove this off on me?"

"It is quite time you did something for the family."

"And when she draws herself up and looks at me with clear, steady eyes, what do I do for an encore?"

"There is no need to discuss the matter any further. You can get down to East Dulwich in half an hour. There is a frequent service of trains. I will remain here to await your report."

"But, listen!"

"Bertie, you will go and see this woman immediately."

"Yes, but dash it!"

"Bertie!"

I threw in the towel.

"Oh, right ho, if you say so."

"I do say so."

"Oh, well, in that case, right ho."

I don't know if you have ever tooled off to East Dulwich to offer a strange female a hundred smackers to release your uncle George. In case you haven't, I may tell you that there are plenty of things that are lots better fun. I didn't feel any too good driving to the station. I didn't feel any too good in the train. And I didn't feel any too good as I walked to Kitchener Road. But the moment when I felt least good was when I had actually pressed the front doorbell and a rather grubby-looking maid had let me in and shown me down a passage and into a room with pink paper on the walls, a piano in the corner, and a lot of photographs on the mantelpiece.

Barring a dentist's waiting room, which it rather resembles, there isn't anything that quells the spirit much more than one of these suburban parlours. They are extremely apt to have stuffed birds in glass cases standing about on small tables, and if there is one thing which gives the man of sensibility that sinking feeling it is the cold, accusing eye of a ptarmigan, or

whatever it may be that has had its interior organs
removed and sawdust substituted.

There were three of these cases in the parlour
of Wistaria Lodge, so that, wherever you looked,
you were sure to connect. Two were singletons, the
third a family group, consisting of a father bullfinch,
a mother bullfinch, and little Master Bullfinch, the
last named of whom wore an expression that was
definitely that of a thug and did more to damp my
joie de vivre than all the rest of them put together.

I had moved to the window and was examining
the aspidistra in order to avoid this creature's gaze,
when I heard the door open and, turning, found myself confronted by something which, since it could
hardly be the girl, I took to be the aunt.

"Oh, good-morning," I said.

The words came out rather roopily, for I was feeling a bit on the stunned side. I mean to say, the room
being so small and this exhibit so large, I had got that
feeling of wanting air. There are some people who
don't seem to be intended to be seen close to, and this
aunt was one of them. Billowy curves, if you know
what I mean. I should think that in her day she must
have been a very handsome girl, though even then on
the substantial side. By the time she came into my life
she had taken on a good deal of excess weight. She
looked like a photograph of an opera singer of the
'eighties. Also the orange hair and the magenta dress.

However, she was a friendly soul. She seemed glad
to see Bertram. She smiled broadly.

"So here you are at last!" she said.

I couldn't make anything of this.

"Eh?"

"But I don't think you had better see my niece just yet. She's just having a nap."

"Oh, in that case . . ."

"Seems a pity to wake her, doesn't it?"

"Oh, absolutely," I said, relieved.

"When you get the influenza you don't sleep at night, and then if you doze off in the morning, well, it seems a pity to wake someone, doesn't it?"

"Miss Platt has influenza?"

"That's what we think it is. But, of course, you'll be able to say. But we needn't waste time. Since you're here, you can be taking a look at my knee."

"Your knee?"

I am all for knees at their proper time and, as you might say, in their proper place, but somehow this didn't seem the moment. However, she carried on according to plan.

"What do you think of that knee?" she asked, lifting the seven veils.

Well, of course, one has to be polite.

"Terrific!" I said.

"You wouldn't believe how it hurts me sometimes."

"Really?"

"A sort of shooting pain. It just comes and goes. And I'll tell you a funny thing."

"What's that?" I said, feeling I could do with a good laugh.

"Lately I've been having the same pain just here, at the end of the spine."

"You don't mean it!"

"I do. Like red-hot needles. I wish you'd have a look at it."

"At your spine?"

"Yes."

I shook my head. Nobody is fonder of a bit of fun than myself, and I am all for Bohemian camaraderie and making a party go, and all that. But there is a line, and we Woosters know when to draw it.

"It can't be done," I said austerely. "Not spines. Knees, yes. Spines, no," I said.

She seemed surprised.

"Well," she said, "you're a funny sort of doctor, I must say."

I'm pretty quick, as I said before, and I began to see that something in the nature of an understanding must have arisen.

"Doctor?"

"Well, you call yourself a doctor, don't you?"

"Did you think I was a doctor?"

"Aren't you a doctor?"

"No. Not a doctor."

We had got it straightened out. The scales had fallen from our eyes. We knew where we were.

I had suspected that she was a genial soul. She now endorsed this view. I don't think I have ever heard a woman laugh so heartily.

"Well, that's the best thing!" she said, borrowing my handkerchief to wipe her eyes. "Did you ever! But if you aren't the doctor, who are you?"

"Wooster's the name. I came to see Miss Platt."

"What about?"

This was the moment, of course, when I should have come out with the check and sprung the big effort. But somehow I couldn't make it. You know how it is. Offering people money to release your uncle is a scaly enough job at best, and when the atmosphere's not right the shot simply isn't on the board.

"Oh, just came to see her, you know." I had rather a bright idea. "My uncle heard she was seedy, don't you know, and asked me to look in and make inquiries," I said.

"Your uncle?"

"Lord Yaxley."

"Oh! So you are Lord Yaxley's nephew?"

"That's right. I suppose he's always popping in and out here, what?"

"No. I've never met him."

"You haven't?"

"No. Rhoda talks a lot about him, of course, but for some reason she's never so much as asked him to look in for a cup of tea."

I began to see that this Rhoda knew her business. If I'd been a girl with someone wanting to marry me and knew that there was an exhibit like this aunt hanging around the home, I, too, should have thought twice about inviting him to call until the ceremony was over and he had actually signed on the dotted line. I mean to say, a thoroughly good soul—heart of gold beyond a doubt—but not the sort of thing you wanted to spring on Romeo before the time was ripe.

"I suppose you were all very surprised when you heard about it?" she said.

"'Surprised' is right."

"Of course, nothing is definitely settled yet."

"You don't mean that? I thought . . ."

"Oh, no. She's thinking it over."

"I see."

"Of course, she feels it's a great compliment. But then sometimes she wonders if he isn't too old."

"My aunt Agatha has rather the same idea."

"Of course, a title *is* a title."

"Yes, there's that. What do you think about it yourself?"

"Oh, it doesn't matter what I think. There's no doing anything with girls these days, is there?"

"Not much."

"What I often say is, I wonder what girls are coming to. Still, there it is."

"Absolutely."

There didn't seem much reason why the conversation shouldn't go on for ever. She had the air of a woman who has settled down for the day. But at this point the maid came in and said the doctor had arrived.

I got up.

"I'll be tooling off, then."

"If you must."

"I think I'd better."

"Well, pip pip."

"Toodle-oo," I said, and out into the fresh air.

Knowing what was waiting for me at home, I would have preferred to go to the club and spend the rest of the day there. But the thing had to be faced.

"Well?" said Aunt Agatha, as I trickled into the sitting room.

"Well, yes and no," I replied.

"What do you mean? Did she refuse the money?"

"Not exactly."

"She accepted it?"

"Well, there, again, not precisely."

I explained what had happened. I wasn't expecting her to be any too frightfully pleased, and it's as well that I wasn't, because she wasn't. In fact, as the story unfolded, her comments became fruitier and fruitier, and when I had finished she uttered an exclamation that nearly broke a window. It sounded something like "Gor!"—as if she had started to say "Gorblimey!" and had remembered her ancient lineage just in time.

"I'm sorry," I said. "And can a man say more? I lost my nerve. The old morale suddenly turned blue on me. It's the sort of thing that might have happened to anyone."

"I never heard of anything so spineless in my life."

I shivered, like a warrior whose old wound hurts him.

"I'd be most awfully obliged, Aunt Agatha," I said, "if you would not use that word 'spine.' It awakens memories."

The door opened. Jeeves appeared.

"Sir?"

"Yes, Jeeves?"

"I thought you called, sir."

"No, Jeeves."

"Very good, sir."

There are moments when, even under the eye of Aunt Agatha, I can take the firm line. And now, see-

ing Jeeves standing there with the light of intelligence simply fizzing in every feature, I suddenly felt
how perfectly footling it was to give this preëminent
source of balm and comfort the go-by simply because
Aunt Agatha had prejudices against discussing family affairs with the staff. It might make her say "Gor!"
again, but I decided to do as we ought to have done
right from the start—put the case in his hands.

"Jeeves," I said, "this matter of Uncle George."

"Yes, sir."

"You know the circs."

"Yes, sir."

"You know what we want."

"Yes, sir."

"Then advise us. And make it snappy. Think on
your feet."

I heard Aunt Agatha rumble like a volcano just
before it starts to set about the neighbours, but I did
not wilt. I had seen the sparkle in Jeeves's eye which
indicated that an idea was on the way.

"I understand that you have been visiting the
young person's home, sir?"

"Just got back."

"Then you no doubt encountered the young person's aunt?"

"Jeeves, I encountered nothing else but."

"Then the suggestion which I am about to make
will, I feel sure, appeal to you, sir. I would recommend that you confronted his lordship with this
woman. It has always been her intention to continue
residing with her niece after the latter's marriage.
Should he meet her, this reflection might give his

lordship pause. As you are aware, sir, she is a kind-hearted woman, but definitely of the people."

"Jeeves, you are right! Apart from anything else, that orange hair!"

"Exactly, sir."

"Not to mention the magenta dress."

"Precisely, sir."

"I'll ask her to lunch to-morrow, to meet him. You see," I said to Aunt Agatha, who was still fermenting in the background, "a ripe suggestion first crack out of the box. Did I or did I not tell you——"

"That will do, Jeeves," said Aunt Agatha.

"Very good, madam."

For some minutes after he had gone Aunt Agatha strayed from the point a bit, confining her remarks to what she thought of a Wooster who could lower the prestige of the clan by allowing menials to get above themselves. Then she returned to what you might call the "main issue."

"Bertie," she said, "you will go and see this girl again to-morrow, and this time you will do as I told you."

"But, dash it! With this excellent alternative scheme, based firmly on the psychology of the individual——"

"That is quite enough, Bertie. You heard what I said. I am going. Good-bye."

She buzzed off, little knowing of what stuff Bertram Wooster was made. The door had hardly closed before I was shouting for Jeeves.

"Jeeves," I said, "the recent aunt will have none of your excellent alternative scheme, but none the less

I propose to go through with it unswervingly. I consider it a ball of fire. Can you get hold of this female and bring here here for lunch to-morrow?"

"Yes, sir."

"Good. Meanwhile, I will be phoning Uncle George. We will do Aunt Agatha good despite herself. What is it the poet says, Jeeves?"

"The poet Burns, sir?"

"Not the poet Burns. Some other poet. About doing good by stealth."

"These little acts of unremembered kindness, sir?"

"That's it in a nutshell, Jeeves."

"I suppose doing good by stealth" ought to give one a glow, but I can't say I found myself exactly looking forward to the binge in prospect. Uncle George by himself is a mouldy enough luncheon companion, being extremely apt to collar the conversation and confine it to a description of his symptoms, he being one of those birds who can never be brought to believe that the general public isn't agog to hear about the lining of his stomach. Add the aunt, and you have a little gathering which might well dismay the stoutest. The moment I woke I felt conscious of some impending doom, and the cloud, if you know what I mean, grew darker all the morning. By the time Jeeves came in with the cocktails I was feeling pretty low.

"For two pins, Jeeves," I said, "I would turn the whole thing up and leg it to the Drones'."

"I can readily imagine that this will prove something of an ordeal, sir."

"How did you get to know these people, Jeeves?"

"It was through a young fellow of my acquaintance, sir, Colonel Mainwaring-Smith's personal gentleman's gentleman. He and the young person had an understanding at the time, and he desired me to accompany him to Wistaria Lodge and meet her."

"They were engaged?"

"Not precisely engaged, sir. An understanding."

"What did they quarrel about?"

"They did not quarrel, sir. When his lordship began to pay his addresses the young person, naturally flattered, began to waver between love and ambition. But even now she has not formally rescinded the understanding."

"Then, if your scheme works and Uncle George edges out, it will do your pal a bit of good?"

"Yes, sir, Smethurst—his name is Smethurst—would consider it a consummation devoutly to be wished."

An unseen hand without tootled on the bell, and I braced myself to play the host. The binge was on.

"Mrs. Wilberforce, sir," announced Jeeves.

"And how I'm to keep a straight face with you standing behind my chair and saying 'Madam, can I tempt you with a potato?' is more than I know," said the aunt, sailing in, looking larger and pinker and matier than ever. "I know him, you know," she said, jerking a thumb after Jeeves. "He's been round and taken tea with us."

"So he told me."

She gave the sitting room the once-over.

"You've got a nice place here," she said, "though

i like more pink about. It's so cheerful. What's that you've got there? Cocktails?"

"Martini with a spot of absinthe," I said, beginning to pour.

She gave a girlish squeal.

"Don't you try to make me drink that stuff! Do you know what would happen if I touched one of those things? I'd be racked with pain. What they do to the lining of your stomach!"

"Oh, I don't know."

"I do. If you had been a barmaid as long as I was you'd know, too."

"Oh—er—were you a barmaid?"

"For years, when I was younger than I am. At the Criterion."

I dropped the shaker.

"There!" she said, pointing the moral. "That's through drinking that stuff. Makes your hand wobble. What I always used to say to the boys was: 'Port, if you like. Port's wholesome. I appreciate a drop of port myself. But these new-fangled messes from America, no.' But they would never listen to me."

I was eyeing her warily. Of course, there must have been thousands of barmaids at the Criterion in its time, but still it gave one a bit of a start. It was years ago that Uncle George's dash at a mésalliance had occurred—long before he came into the title—but the Wooster clan still quivered at the name of the Criterion.

"Er—when you were at the Cri.," I said, "did you ever happen to run into a fellow of my name?"

"I've forgotten what it is. I'm always silly about names."

"Wooster."

"Wooster! When you were there yesterday I thought you said 'Foster.' Wooster! Did I run into a fellow named Wooster? Well! Why, George Wooster and me—Piggy, I used to call him—were going off to the registrar's, only his family heard of it and interfered. They offered me a lot of money to give him up, and, like a silly girl, I let them persuade me. If I've wondered once what became of him, I've wondered a thousand times. Is he a relation of yours?"

"Excuse me," I said. "I just want a word with Jeeves." I legged it for the pantry.

"Jeeves!"

"Sir?"

"Do you know what's happened?"

"No, sir."

"This female——"

"Sir?"

"She's Uncle George's barmaid!"

"Sir?"

"Oh, dash it, you must have heard of Uncle George's barmaid. You know all the family history. The barmaid he wanted to marry years ago."

"Ah, yes, sir."

"She's the only woman he ever loved. He's told me so a million times. Every time he gets to the second liqueur he always becomes maudlin about this female. What a dashed bit of bad luck! The first thing we know the call of the past will be echoing in his heart. I can feel it, Jeeves. She's just his sort. The first thing she did when she came in was to start talking about the lining of her stomach. You see the hideous significance of that, Jeeves? The lining of his stomach is Uncle George's favourite topic of conversation. It means that he and she are kindred souls. This woman and he will be like . . ."

"Deep calling to deep, sir?"

"Exactly."

"Most disturbing, sir."

"What's to be done?"

"I could not say, sir."

"I'll tell you what I'm going to do—phone him and say the lunch is off."

"Scarcely feasible, sir. I fancy that is his lordship at the door now."

And so it was. Jeeves let him in, and I followed him as he navigated down the passage to the sitting room. There was a stunned silence as he went in, and then a couple of the startled yelps you hear when old buddies get together after long separation.

"Piggy!"

"Maudie!"

"Well, I never!"

"Well, I'm dashed!"

"Did you ever!"

"Well, bless my soul!"

"Fancy you being Lord Yaxley!"

"Came into the title soon after we parted."

"Just to think!"

"You could have knocked me down with a feather!"

I hung about in the offing, now on this leg, now on

that. For all the notice they took of me, I might just as well have been the late Bertram Wooster, disembodied.

"Maudie, you don't look a day older, dash it!"

"Nor do you, Piggy."

"How have you been all these years?"

"Pretty well. The lining of my stomach isn't all it should be."

"Good Gad! You don't say so? I have trouble with the lining of *my* stomach."

"It's a sort of heavy feeling after meals."

"*I* get a sort of heavy feeling after meals. What are you trying for it?"

"I've been taking Perkins' Digestine."

"My dear girl, no use! No use at all. Tried it myself for years, and got no relief. Now, if you really want something that is some good . . ."

I slid away. The last I saw of them, Uncle George was down beside her on the Chesterfield, buzzing hard.

"Jeeves," I said, tottering into the pantry.

"Sir?"

"There will only be two for lunch. Count me out. If they notice I'm not there tell them I was called away by an urgent phone message. The situation has got beyond Bertram, Jeeves. You will find me at the Drones'."

"Very good, sir."

It was latish in the evening when one of the waiters came to me as I played a distrait game of snooker pool and informed me that Aunt Agatha was on the phone.

"Bertie!"

"Hullo?"

I was amazed to note that her voice was that of an aunt who feels that things are breaking right. It had the birdlike trill.

"Bertie, have you that check I gave you?"

"Yes."

"Then tear it up. It will not be needed."

"Eh?"

"I say it will not be needed. Your uncle has been speaking to me on the telephone. He is not going to marry that girl."

"Not?"

"No. Apparently he has been thinking it over and sees how unsuitable it would have been. But what is astonishing is that he *is* going to be married!"

"He is?"

"Yes, to an old friend of his, a Mrs. Wilberforce. A woman of a sensible age, he gave me to understand. I wonder which Wilberforces that would be. There are two main branches of the family—the Essex Wilberforces and the Cumberland Wilberforces. I believe there is also a cadet branch somewhere in Shropshire."

"And one in East Dulwich," I said.

"What did you say?"

"Nothing," I said. "Nothing."

I hung up. Then back to the old flat, feeling a trifle sandbagged.

"Well, Jeeves," I said, and there was censure in the eyes. "So I gather everything is nicely settled?"

"Yes, sir. His lordship formally announced the

engagement between the sweets and cheese courses, sir."

"He did, did he?"

"Yes, sir."

I eyed the man sternly.

"You do not appear to be aware of it, Jeeves," I said, in a cold, level voice, "but this binge has depreciated your stock very considerably. I have always been accustomed to look upon you as a counsellor without equal. I have, so to speak, hung upon your lips. And now see what you have done. All this is the direct consequence of your scheme, based on the psychology of the individual. I should have thought, Jeeves, that, knowing the woman—meeting her socially, as you might say, over the afternoon cup of tea —you might have ascertained that she was Uncle George's barmaid."

"I did, sir."

"What!"

"I was aware of the fact, sir."

"Then you must have known what would happen if she came to lunch and met him."

"Yes, sir."

"Well, I'm dashed!"

"If I might explain, sir. The young man Smethurst, who is greatly attached to the young person, is an intimate friend of mine. He applied to me some little while back in the hope that I might be able to do something to insure that the young person followed the dictates of her heart and refrained from permitting herself to be lured by gold and the glamour of his lordship's position. There will now be no obstacle to their union."

"I see. Little acts of unremembered kindness, what?"

"Precisely, sir."

"And how about Uncle George? You've landed him pretty nicely in the cart."

"No, sir, if I may take the liberty of opposing your view. I fancy that Mrs. Wilberforce should make an ideal mate for his lordship. If there was a defect in his lordship's mode of life, it was that he was a little unduly attached to the pleasures of the table."

"Ate like a pig, you mean?"

"I would not have ventured to put it in quite that way, sir, but the expression does meet the facts of the case. He was also inclined to drink rather more than his medical adviser would have approved of. Elderly bachelors who are wealthy and without occupation tend somewhat frequently to fall into this error, sir. The future Lady Yaxley will check this. Indeed, I overheard her ladyship saying as much as I brought in the fish. She was commenting on a certain puffiness of the face which had been absent in his lordship's appearance in the earlier days of their acquaintanceship, and she observed that his lordship needed looking after. I fancy, sir, that you will find the union will turn out an extremely satisfactory one."

It was—what's the word I want—it was plausible, of course, but still I shook the onion.

"But, Jeeves!"

"Sir?"

"She *is,* as you remarked not long ago, definitely

of the people." He looked at me in a reproachful sort of way.

"Sturdy lower-middle-class stock, sir."

"H'm!"

"Sir?"

"I said 'H'm!' Jeeves."

"Besides, sir, remember what the poet Tennyson said. Kind hearts are more than coronets."

"And which of us is going to tell Aunt Agatha that?"

"If I might make the suggestion, sir, I would advise that we omit to communicate with Mrs. Spenser Gregson in any way. I have your suitcase practically packed. It would be a matter of but a few minutes to bring the car round from the garage . . ."

"And off over the horizon to where men are men?"

"Precisely, sir."

"Jeeves," I said, "I'm not sure that even now I can altogether see eye to eye with you regarding your recent activities. You think you have scattered light and sweetness on every side. I am not so sure. However, with this latest suggestion you have rung the bell. I examine it narrowly and I find no flaw in it. It is the goods. I'll get the car at once."

"Very good, sir."

"Remember what the poet Shakespeare said, Jeeves."

"What was that, sir?"

"Exit hurriedly, pursued by a bear. You'll find it in one of his plays. I remember drawing a picture of it on the side of the page, when I was at school."

HE RATHER ENJOYED IT

PRESENTING *that invincible idealist,*
Stanley Featherstonehaugh Ukridge.
   "Fortunately I had given him a false name."
   "Why?"
   "Just an ordinary business precaution," ex-
plained Ukridge.

UKRIDGE'S DOG COLLEGE

"LADDIE," said Stanley Featherstonehaugh Ukridge, that much-enduring man, helping himself to my tobacco and slipping the pouch absently into his pocket, "listen to me, you son of Belial."

"What?" I said, retrieving the pouch.

"Do you want to make an enormous fortune?"

"I do."

"Then write my biography. Bung it down on paper, and we'll split the proceeds. I've been making a pretty close study of your stuff lately, old horse, and it's all wrong. The trouble with you is that you don't plumb the well-springs of human nature and all that. You just think up some rotten yarn about some-dam-thing-or-other and shove it down. Now, if you tackled my life, you'd have something worth writing about. Pots of money in it, my boy—English serial rights and American serial rights and book rights, and dramatic rights and movie rights—well, you can take it from

11

me that, at a conservative estimate, we should clean up at least fifty thousand pounds apiece."

"As much as that?"

"Fully that. And listen, laddie, I'll tell you what. You're a good chap and we've been pals for years, so I'll let you have my share of the English serial rights for a hundred pounds down."

"What makes you think I've got a hundred pounds?"

"Well, then, I'll make it my share of the English *and* American serial rights for fifty."

"Your collar's come off its stud."

"How about my complete share of the whole dashed outfit for twenty-five?"

"Not for me, thanks."

"Then I'll tell you what, old horse," said Ukridge, inspired. "Just lend me half a crown to be going on with."

*   *   *   *   *

If the leading incidents of S. F. Ukridge's disreputable career are to be given to the public—and not, as some might suggest, decently hushed up—I suppose I am the man to write them. Ukridge and I had been intimate since the days of school. Together we sported on the green, and when he was expelled no one missed him more than I. An unfortunate business, this expulsion. Ukridge's generous spirit, ever ill-attuned to school rules, caused him eventually to break the solemnest of them all by sneaking out at night to try his skill at the coco-nut-shies of the local village fair; and his foresight in putting on scarlet whiskers and a false nose for the expedition was completely neutralised by the fact that he absent-mindedly wore his school cap throughout the entire proceedings. He left the next morning, regretted by all.

After this there was a hiatus of some years in our friendship. I was at Cambridge, absorbing culture, and Ukridge, as far as I could gather from his rare letters and the reports of mutual acquaintances, flitting about the world like a snipe. Somebody met him in New York, just off a cattle-ship. Somebody else saw him in Buenos Ayres. Somebody, again, spoke sadly of having been pounced on by him at Monte Carlo and touched for a fiver. It was not until I settled down in London that he came back into my life. We met in Piccadilly one day, and resumed our relations where they had been broken off. Old associations are strong, and the fact that he was about my build and so could wear my socks and shirts drew us very close together.

Then he disappeared again, and it was a month or more before I got news of him.

It was George Tupper who brought the news. George was head of the school in my last year, and he has fulfilled exactly the impeccable promise of those early days. He is in the Foreign Office, doing well and much respected. He has an earnest, pulpy heart and takes other people's troubles very seriously. Often he had mourned to me like a father over Ukridge's erratic progress through life, and now, as he spoke, he seemed to be filled with a solemn joy, as over a reformed prodigal.

"Have you heard about Ukridge?" said George

Tupper. "He has settled down at last. Gone to live with an aunt of his who owns one of those big houses on Wimbledon Common. A very rich woman. I am delighted. It will be the making of the old chap."

I suppose he was right in a way, but to me this tame subsidence into companionship with a rich aunt in Wimbledon seemed somehow an indecent, almost a tragic, end to a colourful career like that of S. F. Ukridge. And when I met the man a week later my heart grew heavier still.

It was in Oxford Street at the hour when women come up from the suburbs to shop; and he was standing among the dogs and commissionaires outside Selfridge's. His arms were full of parcels, his face was set in a mask of wan discomfort, and he was so beautifully dressed that for an instant I did not recognise him. Everything which the Correct Man wears was assembled on his person, from the silk hat to the patent-leather boots; and, as he confided to me in the first minute, he was suffering the tortures of the damned. The boots pinched him, the hat hurt his forehead, and the collar was worse than the hat and boots combined.

"She makes me wear them," he said, moodily, jerking his head towards the interior of the store and uttering a sharp howl as the movement caused the collar to gouge his neck.

"Still," I said, trying to turn his mind to happier things, "you must be having a great time. George Tupper tells me that your aunt is rich. I suppose you're living off the fat of the land."

"The browsing and sluicing are good," admitted Ukridge. "But it's a wearing life, laddie. A wearing life, old horse."

"Why don't you come and see me sometimes?"

"I'm not allowed out at night."

"Well, shall I come and see you?"

A look of poignant alarm shot out from under the silk hat.

"Don't dream of it, laddie," said Ukridge, earnestly. "Don't dream of it. You're a good chap—my best pal and all that sort of thing—but the fact is, my standing in the home's none too solid even now, and one sight of you would knock my prestige into hash. Aunt Julia would think you worldly."

"I'm not worldly."

"Well, you look worldly. You wear a squash hat and a soft collar. If you don't mind my suggesting it, old horse, I think, if I were you, I'd pop off now before she comes out. Good-bye, laddie."

"Ichabod!" I murmured sadly to myself as I passed on down Oxford Street. "Ichabod!"

I should have had more faith. I should have known my Ukridge better. I should have realised that a London suburb could no more imprison that great man permanently than Elba did Napoleon.

One afternoon, as I let myself into the house in Ebury Street of which I rented at that time the bedroom and sitting-room on the first floor, I came upon Bowles, my landlord, standing in listening attitude at the foot of the stairs.

"Good afternoon, sir," said Bowles. "A gentleman

is waiting to see you. I fancy I heard him calling me a moment ago."

"Who is he?"

"A Mr. Ukridge, sir. He——"

A vast voice boomed out from above.

"Bowles, old horse!"

Bowles, like all other proprietors of furnished apart-
ments in the southwestern district of London, was
an ex-butler, and about him, as about all ex-butlers,
there clung like a garment an aura of dignified superi-
ority which had never failed to crush my spirit. He
was a man of portly aspect, with a bald head and
prominent eyes of a lightish green—eyes that seemed
to weigh me dispassionately and find me wanting.
"H'm!" they seemed to say. "Young—very young.
And not at all what I have been accustomed to in
the best places." To hear this dignitary addressed—
and in a shout at that—as "old horse" affected me
with much the same sense of imminent chaos as would
afflict a devout young curate if he saw his bishop
slapped on the back. The shock, therefore, when he
responded not merely mildly but with what almost
amounted to camaraderie was numbing.

"Sir?" cooed Bowles.

"Bring me six bones and a corkscrew."

"Very good, sir."

Bowles retired, and I bounded upstairs and flung
open the door of my sitting-room.

"Great Scott!" I said, blankly.

The place was a sea of Pekingese dogs. Later investigation reduced their number to six, but in that

first moment there seemed to be hundreds. Goggling eyes met mine wherever I looked. The room was a forest of waving tails. With his back against the mantelpiece, smoking placidly, stood Ukridge.

"Hallo, laddie!" he said, with a genial wave of the hand, as if to make me free of the place. "You're just in time. I've got to dash off and catch a train in a quarter of an hour. Stop it, you mutts!" he bellowed, and the six Pekingese, who had been barking steadily since my arrival, stopped in mid-yap, and were still. Ukridge's personality seemed to exercise a magnetism over the animal kingdom, from ex-butlers to Pekes, which bordered on the uncanny. "I'm off to Sheep's Cray, in Kent. Taken a cottage there."

"Are you going to live there?"

"Yes."

"But what about your aunt?"

"Oh, I've left her. Life is stern and life is earnest, and if I mean to make a fortune I've got to bustle about and not stay cooped up in a place like Wimbledon."

"Something in that."

"Besides which, she told me the very sight of me made her sick and she never wanted to see me again."

I might have guessed, directly I saw him, that some upheaval had taken place. The sumptuous raiment which had made him such a treat to the eye at our last meeting was gone, and he was back in his pre-Wimbledon costume, which was, as the advertisements say, distinctly individual. Over grey flannel trousers, a golf coat, and a brown sweater he wore like a royal robe a bright yellow mackintosh. His collar had broken free from its stud and showed a couple of inches of bare neck. His hair was disordered, and his masterful nose was topped by a pair of steel-rimmed pince-nez cunningly attached to his flapping ears with ginger-beer wire. His whole appearance spelled revolt.

Bowles manifested himself with a plateful of bones.

"That's right. Chuck 'em down on the floor."

"Very good, sir."

"I like that fellow," said Ukridge, as the door closed. "We had a dashed interesting talk before you came in. Did you know he had a cousin on the music-halls?"

"He hasn't confided in me much."

"He's promised me an introduction to him later on. May be useful to be in touch with a man who knows the ropes. You see, laddie, I've hit on the most amazing scheme." He swept his arm round dramatically, overturning a plaster cast of the Infant Samuel at Prayer. "All right, all right, you can mend it with glue or something, and, anyway, you're probably better without it. Yessir, I've hit on a great scheme. The idea of a thousand years."

"What's that?"

"I'm going to train dogs."

"Train dogs?"

"For the music-hall stage. Dog acts, you know. Performing dogs. Pots of money in it. I start in a modest way with these six. When I've taught 'em a few tricks, I sell them to a fellow in the profession for a large sum and buy twelve more. I train those, sell 'em for a large sum, and with the money buy twenty-four more. I train those——"

"Here, wait a minute." My head was beginning to swim. I had a vision of England paved with Pekingese dogs, all doing tricks. "How do you know you'll be able to sell them?"

"Of course I shall. The demand's enormous. Supply can't cope with it. At a conservative estimate I should think I ought to scoop in four or five thousand pounds the first year. That, of course, is before the business really starts to expand."

"I see."

"When I get going properly, with a dozen assistants under me and an organised establishment, I shall begin to touch the big money. What I'm aiming at is a sort of Dogs' College out in the country somewhere. Big place with a lot of ground. Regular classes and a set curriculum. Large staff, each member of it with so many dogs under his care, me looking on and superintending. Why, once the thing starts moving it'll run itself, and all I shall have to do will be to sit back and endorse the cheques. It isn't as if I would have to confine my operations to England. The demand for performing dogs is universal throughout the civilised world. America wants performing dogs. Australia wants performing dogs. Africa could do with a few, I've no doubt. My aim, laddie, is gradually to get a monopoly of the trade. I want everybody who needs a performing dog of any description to come automatically to me. And I'll tell you what, laddie.

If you like to put up a bit of capital, I'll let you in on the ground floor."

"No, thanks."

"All right. Have it your own way. Only don't forget that there was a fellow who put nine hundred dollars into the Ford Car business when it was starting and he collected a cool forty million. I say, is that clock right? Great Scott! I'll be missing my train. Help me mobilise these dashed animals."

Five minutes later, accompanied by the six Pekingese and bearing about him a pound of my tobacco, three pairs of my socks, and the remains of a bottle of whisky, Ukridge departed in a taxi-cab for Charing Cross Station to begin his life-work.

Perhaps six weeks passed, six quiet Ukridgeless weeks, and then one morning I received an agitated telegram. Indeed, it was not so much a telegram as a cry of anguish. In every word of it there breathed the tortured spirit of a great man who has battled in vain against overwhelming odds. It was the sort of telegram which Job might have sent off after a lengthy session with Bildad the Shuhite:—

"Come here immediately, laddie. Life and death matter, old horse. Desperate situation. Don't fail me."

It stirred me like a bugle, I caught the next train.

The White Cottage, Sheep's Cray—destined, presumably, to become in future years an historic spot and a Mecca for dog-loving pilgrims—was a small and battered building standing near the main road to Lon-

don at some distance from the village. I found it
without difficulty, for Ukridge seemed to have achieved
a certain celebrity in the neighbourhood; but to effect
an entry was a harder task. I rapped for a full minute
without result, then shouted; and I was about to conclude that Ukridge was not at home when the door
suddenly opened. As I was just giving a final bang
at the moment, I entered the house in a manner reminiscent of one of the Ballet Russe practising a new
and difficult step.

"Sorry, old horse," said Ukridge. "Wouldn't have
kept you waiting if I'd known who it was. Thought
you were Gooch, the grocer—goods supplied to the
value of six pounds three and a penny."

"I see."

"He keeps hounding me for his beastly money,"
said Ukridge, bitterly, as he led the way into the sitting-room. "It's a little hard. Upon my Sam it's a
little hard. I come down here to inaugurate a vast
business and do the natives a bit of good by establishing a growing industry in their midst, and the first
thing you know they turn round and bite the
hand that was going to feed them. I've been hampered
and rattled by these blood-suckers ever since I got here.
A little trust, a little sympathy, a little of the good old
give-and-take spirit—that was all I asked. And what
happened? They wanted a bit on account! Kept
bothering me for a bit on account, I'll trouble you, just
when I needed all my thoughts and all my energy
and ever ounce of concentration at my command for
my extraordinarily difficult and delicate work. *I*

couldn't give them a bit on account. Later on, if they
had only exercised reasonable patience, I would no
doubt have been in a position to settle their infernal
bills fifty times over. But the time was not ripe. I
reasoned with the men. I said, 'Here am I, a busy
man, trying hard to educate six Pekingese dogs for
the music-hall stage, and you come distracting my attention and impairing my efficiency by babbling about
a bit on account. It isn't the pull-together spirit,' I
said. 'It isn't the spirit that wins to wealth. These
narrow petty-cash ideas can never make for success.'
But no, they couldn't see it. They started calling here
at all hours and waylaying me in the public highways
till life became an absolute curse. And now what do
you think has happened?"

"What?"

"The dogs."

"Got distemper?"

"No. Worse. My landlord's pinched them as security for his infernal rent! Sneaked the stock. Tied
up the assets. Crippled the business at the very outset. Have you ever in your life heard of anything so
dastardly? I know I agreed to pay the damned rent
weekly and I'm about six weeks behind, but, my gosh!
surely a man with a huge enterprise on his hands isn't
supposed to have to worry about these trifles when he's
occupied with the most delicate—— Well, I put all
that to old Nickerson, but a fat lot of good it did. So
then I wired to you."

"Ah!" I said, and there was a brief and pregnant
pause.

"I thought," said Ukridge, meditatively, "that you might be able to suggest somebody I could touch."

He spoke in a detached and almost casual way, but his eye was gleaming at me significantly, and I avoided it with a sense of guilt. My finances at the moment were in their customary unsettled condition—rather more so, in fact, than usual, owing to unsatisfactory speculations at Kempton Park on the previous Saturday; and it seemed to me that, if ever there was a time for passing the buck, this was it. I mused tensely. It was an occasion for quick thinking.

"George Tupper!" I cried, on the crest of a brain-wave.

"George Tupper?" echoed Ukridge, radiantly, his gloom melting like fog before the sun. "The very man, by Gad! It's a most amazing thing, but I never thought of him. George Tupper, of course! Big-hearted George, the old school-chum. He'll do it like a shot and won't miss the money. These Foreign Office blokes have always got a spare tenner or two tucked away in the old sock. They pinch it out of the public funds. Rush back to town, laddie, with all speed, get hold of Tuppy, lush him up, and bite his ear for twenty quid. Now is the time for all good men to come to the aid of the party."

I had been convinced that George Tupper would not fail us, nor did he. He parted without a murmur— even with enthusiasm. The consignment was one that might have been made to order for him. As a boy, George used to write sentimental poetry for the school magazine, and now he is the sort of man who is al-

ways starting subscription lists and getting up me-
morials and presentations. He listened to my story
with the serious official air which these Foreign Office
fellows put on when they are deciding whether to declare war on Switzerland or send a firm note to San
Marino, and was reaching for his cheque-book before
I had been speaking two minutes. Ukridge's sad case
seemed to move him deeply.

"Too bad," said George. "So he is training dogs,
is he? Well, it seems very unfair that, if he has at
last settled down to real work, he should be hampered
by financial difficulties at the outset. We ought to do
something practical for him. After all, a loan of
twenty pounds cannot relieve the situation permanently."

"I think you're a bit optimistic if you're looking on
it as a loan."

"What Ukridge needs is capital."

"He thinks that, too. So does Gooch, the grocer."

"Capital," repeated George Tupper, firmly, as if
he were reasoning with the plenipotentiary of some
Great Power. "Every venture requires capital at
first." He frowned thoughtfully. "Where can we
obtain capital for Ukridge?"

"Rob a bank."

George Tupper's face cleared.

"I have it!" he said. "I will go straight over to
Wimbledon to-night and approach his aunt."

"Aren't you forgetting that Ukridge is about as
popular with her as a cold welsh rabbit?"

"There may be a temporary estrangement, but if

I tell her the facts and impress upon her that Ukridge
is really making a genuine effort to earn a living——"

"Well, try if you like. But she will probably set
the parrot on to you."

"It will have to be done diplomatically, of course.
It might be as well if you did not tell Ukridge what
I propose to do. I do not wish to arouse hopes which
may not be fulfilled."

A blaze of yellow on the platform of Sheep's Cray
Station next morning informed me that Ukridge had
come to meet my train. The sun poured down from a
cloudless sky, but it took more than sunshine to make
Stanley Featherstonehaugh Ukridge discard his mackintosh. He looked like an animated blob of mustard.

When the train rolled in, he was standing in solitary
grandeur trying to light his pipe, but as I got out I
perceived that he had been joined by a sad-looking
man, who, from the rapid and earnest manner in
which he talked and the vehemence of his gesticula-
tions, appeared to be ventilating some theme on which
he felt deeply. Ukridge was looking warm and harassed, and, as I approached, I could hear his voice
booming in reply.

"My dear sir, my dear old horse, do be reasonable,
do try to cultivate the big, broad flexible outlook——"

He saw me and broke away—not unwillingly; and,
gripping my arm, drew me off along the platform.
The sad-looking man followed irresolutely.

"Have you got the stuff, laddie?" enquired Ukridge,
in a tense whisper. "Have you got it?"

"Yes, here it is."

"Put it back, put it back!" moaned Ukridge in agony, as I felt in my pocket. "Do you know who that was I was talking to? Gooch, the grocer!"

"Goods supplied to the value of six pounds three and a penny?"

"Absolutely!"

"Well, now's your chance. Fling him a purse of gold. That'll make him look silly."

"My dear old horse, I can't afford to go about the place squandering my cash simply in order to make grocers look silly. That money is earmarked for Nickerson, my landlord."

"Oh! I say, I think the six pounds three and a penny bird is following us."

"Then for goodness' sake, laddie, let's get a move on! If that man knew we had twenty quid on us, our lives wouldn't be safe. He'd make one spring."

He hurried me out of the station and led the way up a shady lane that wound off through the fields, slinking furtively "like one that on a lonesome road doth walk in fear and dread, and having once looked back walks on and turns no more his head, because he knows a frightful fiend doth close behind him tread." As a matter of fact, the frightful fiend had given up the pursuit after the first few steps, and a moment later I drew this fact to Ukridge's attention, for it was not the sort of day on which to break walking records unnecessarily.

He halted, relieved, and mopped his spacious brow with a handkerchief which I recognised as having once been my property.

"Thank goodness we've shaken him off," he said. "Not a bad chap in his way, I believe—a good husband and father, I'm told, and sings in the church choir. But no vision. That's what he lacks, old horse—vision. He can't understand that all vast industrial enterprises have been built upon a system of liberal and cheerful credit. Won't realise that credit is the life-blood of commerce. Without credit commerce has no elasticity. And if commerce has no elasticity what dam' good is it?"

"I don't know."

"Nor does anybody else. Well, now that he's gone, you can give me that money. Did Tuppy cough up cheerfully?"

"Blithely."

"I knew it," said Ukridge, deeply moved, "I knew it. A good fellow. One of the best. I've always liked Tuppy. A man you can rely on. Some day, when I get going on a big scale, he shall have this back a thousandfold. I'm glad you brought small notes."

"Why?"

"I want to scatter 'em about on the table in front of this Nickerson blighter."

"Is this where he lives?"

We had come to a red-roofed house, set back from the road amidst trees. Ukridge wielded the knocker forcefully.

"Tell Mr. Nickerson," he said to the maid, "that Mr. Ukridge has called and would like a word."

About the demeanour of the man who presently entered the room into which we had been shown there

was that subtle but well-marked something which
stamps your creditor the world over. Mr. Nickerson
was a man of medium height, almost completely surrounded by whiskers, and through the shrubbery he
gazed at Ukridge with frozen eyes, shooting out waves
of deleterious animal magnetism. You could see at a
glance that he was not fond of Ukridge. Take him
for all in all, Mr. Nickerson looked like one of the less
amiable prophets of the Old Testament about to interview the captive monarch of the Amalekites.

"Well?" he said, and I have never heard the word
spoken in a more forbidding manner.

"I've come about the rent."

"Ah!" said Mr. Nickerson, guardedly.

"To pay it," said Ukridge.

"To pay it!" ejaculated Mr. Nickerson, incredulously.

"Here!" said Ukridge, and with a superb gesture
flung money on the table.

I understood now why the massive-minded man
had wanted the small notes. They made a brave display. There was a light breeze blowing in through
the open window, and so musical a rustling did it set
up as it played about the heaped-up wealth that Mr.
Nickerson's austerity seemed to vanish like breath off
a razor-blade. For a moment a dazed look came into
his eyes and he swayed slightly; then, as he started
to gather up the money, he took on the benevolent
air of a bishop blessing pilgrims. As far as Mr. Nickerson was concerned, the sun was up.

"Why, thank you, Mr. Ukridge, I'm sure," he said.

"Thank you very much. No hard feelings, I trust?"

"Not on my side, old horse," responded Ukridge, affably. "Business is business."

"Exactly."

"Well, I may as well take those dogs now," said Ukridge, helping himself to a cigar from a box which he had just discovered on the mantelpiece and putting a couple more in his pocket in the friendliest way. "The sooner they're back with me the better. They've lost a day's education as it is."

"Why, certainly, Mr. Ukridge; certainly. They are in the shed at the bottom of the garden. I will get them for you at once."

He retreated through the door, babbling ingratiatingly.

"Amazing how fond these blokes are of money," sighed Ukridge. "It's a thing I don't like to see. Sordid, I call it. That blighter's eyes were gleaming, positively gleaming, laddie, as he scooped up the stuff. Good cigars these," he added, pocketing three more.

There was a faltering footstep outside, and Mr. Nickerson re-entered the room. The man appeared to have something on his mind. A glassy look was in his whisker-bordered eyes, and his mouth, though it was not easy to see it through the jungle, seemed to me to be sagging mournfully. He resembled a minor prophet who has been hit behind the ear with a stuffed eel-skin.

"Mr. Ukridge!"

"Hallo?"

"The—the little dogs!"

"Well?"

"The little dogs!"

"What about them?"

"They have gone!"

"Gone?"

"Run away!"

"Run away? How the devil could they run away?"

"There seems to have been a loose board at the back of the shed. The little dogs must have wriggled through. There is no trace of them to be found."

Ukridge flung up his arms despairingly. He swelled like a captive balloon. His pince-nez rocked on his nose, his mackintosh flapped menacingly, and his collar sprang off its stud. He brought his fist down with a crash on the table.

"Upon my Sam!"

"I am extremely sorry——"

"Upon my Sam!" cried Ukridge. "It's hard. It's pretty hard. I come down here to inaugurate a great business which would eventually have brought trade and prosperity to the whole neighbourhood, and I have hardly had time to turn round and attend to the preliminary details of the enterprise when this man comes and sneaks my dogs. And now he tells me with a light laugh——"

"Mr. Ukridge, I assure you——"

"Tells me with a light laugh that they've gone. Gone! Gone where? Why, dash it, they may be all over the county. A fat chance I've got of ever seeing them again. Six valuable Pekingese, already educated practically to the stage where they could have been sold at an enormous profit——"

Mr. Nickerson was fumbling guiltily, and now he produced from his pocket a crumpled wad of notes, which he thrust agitatedly upon Ukridge, who waved them away with loathing.

"This gentleman," boomed Ukridge, indicating me with a sweeping gesture, "happens to be a lawyer. It is extremely lucky that he chanced to come down to-day to pay me a visit. Have you followed the proceedings closely?"

I said I had followed them very closely.

"Is it your opinion that an action will lie?"

I said it seemed highly probable, and this expert ruling appeared to put the final touch on Mr. Nickerson's collapse. Almost tearfully he urged the notes on Ukridge.

"What's this?" said Ukridge, loftily.

"I—I thought, Mr. Ukridge, that, if it were agreeable to you, you might consent to take your money back, and—and consider the episode closed."

Ukridge turned to me with raised eyebrows.

"Ha!" he cried. "Ha, ha!"

"Ha, ha!" I chorused, dutifully.

"He thinks that he can close the episode by giving me my money back. Isn't that rich?"

"Fruity," I agreed.

"Those dogs were worth hundreds of pounds, and he thinks he can square me with a rotten twenty. Would you have believed it if you hadn't heard it with your own ears, old horse?"

"Never!"

"I'll tell you what I'll do," said Ukridge, after thought. "I'll take this money." Mr. Nickerson thanked him. "And there are one or two trifling accounts which want settling with some of the local tradesmen. You will square those——"

"Certainly, Mr. Ukridge, certainly."

"And after that—well, I'll have to think it over. If I decide to institute proceedings my lawyer will communicate with you in due course."

And we left the wretched man, cowering despicably behind his whiskers.

It seemed to me, as we passed down the tree-shaded lane and out into the white glare of the road, that Ukridge was bearing himself in his hour of disaster with a rather admirable fortitude. His stock-in-trade, the life-blood of his enterprise, was scattered all over Kent, probably never to return, and all that he had to show on the other side of the balance-sheet was the cancelling of a few weeks' back rent and the paying-off of Gooch, the grocer, and his friends. It was a situation which might well have crushed the spirit of an ordinary man, but Ukridge seemed by no means dejected. Jaunty, rather. His eyes shone behind their pince-nez and he whistled a rollicking air. When presently he began to sing, I felt it was time to create a diversion.

"What are you going to do?" I asked.

"Who, me?" said Ukridge, buoyantly. "Oh, I'm coming back to town on the next train. You don't mind hoofing it to the next station, do you? It's only

five miles. It might be a trifle risky to start from
Sheep's Cray."

"Why risky?"

"Because of the dogs, of course."

"Dogs?"

Ukridge hummed a gay strain.

"Oh, yes. I forgot to tell you about that. I've got
'em."

"What?"

"Yes. I went out late last night and pinched them
out of the shed." He chuckled amusedly. "Perfectly
simple. Only needed a clear, level head. I borrowed
a dead cat and tied a string to it, legged it to old
Nickerson's garden after dark, dug a board out of the
back of the shed, and shoved my head down and
chirruped. The dogs came trickling out, and I hared
off, towing old Colonel Cat on his string. Great run
while it lasted, laddie. Hounds picked up the scent
right away and started off in a bunch at fifty miles
an hour. Cat and I doing a steady fifty-five. Thought
every minute old Nickerson would hear and start
blazing away with a gun, but nothing happened. I led
the pack across country for a run of twenty minutes
without a check, parked the dogs in my sitting-room,
and so to bed. Took it out of me, by gosh! Not so
young as I was."

I was silent for a moment, conscious of a feeling
almost of reverence. This man was undoubtedly
spacious. There had always been something about
Ukridge that dulled the moral sense.

"Well," I said at length, "you've certainly got vision."

"Yes?" said Ukridge, gratified.

"*And* the big, broad, flexible outlook."

"Got to, laddie, nowadays. The foundation of a successful business career."

"And what's the next move?"

We were drawing near to the White Cottage. It stood and broiled in the sunlight, and I hoped that there might be something cool to drink inside it. The window of the sitting-room was open, and through it came the yapping of Pekingese.

"Oh, I shall find another cottage somewhere else," said Ukridge, eyeing his little home with a certain sentimentality. "That won't be hard. Lots of cottages all over the place. And then I shall buckle down to serious work. You'll be astounded at the progress I've made already. In a minute I'll show you what those dogs can do."

"They can bark all right."

"Yes. They seem excited about something. You know, laddie, I've had a great idea. When I saw you at your rooms my scheme was to specialise in performing dogs for the music-halls—what you might call professional dogs. But I've been thinking it over, and now I don't see why I shouldn't go in for developing amateur talent as well. Say you have a dog— Fido, the household pet—and you think it would brighten the home if he could do a few tricks from time to time. Well, you're a busy man, you haven't the time to give up to teaching him. So you just tie a label to his collar and ship him off for a month to the Ukridge Dog College, and back he comes, thoroughly educated. No trouble, no worry, easy terms. Upon my Sam, I'm not sure there isn't more money in the amateur branch than in the professional. I don't see why eventually dog owners shouldn't send their dogs to me as a regular thing, just as they send their sons to Eton and Winchester. My golly! this idea's beginning to develop. I'll tell you what—how would it be to issue special collars to all dogs which have graduated from my college? Something distinctive which everybody would recognise. See what I mean? Sort of badge of honour. Fellow with a dog entitled to wear the Ukridge collar would be in a position to look down on the bloke whose dog hadn't got one. Gradually it would get so that anybody in a decent social position would be ashamed to be seen out with a non-Ukridge dog. The thing would become a landslide. Dogs would pour in from all corners of the country. More work than I could handle. Have to start branches. The scheme's colossal. Millions in it, my boy! Millions!" He paused with his fingers on the handle of the front door. "Of course," he went on, "just at present it's no good blinking the fact that I'm hampered and handicapped by lack of funds and can only approach the thing on a small scale. What it amounts to, laddie, is that somehow or other I've got to get capital."

It seemed the moment to spring the glad news.

"I promised him I wouldn't mention it," I said, "for fear it might lead to disappointment, but as a matter of fact George Tupper is trying to raise some capital for you. I left him last night starting out to get it."

"George Tupper!"—Ukridge's eyes dimmed with a not unmanly emotion—"George Tupper! By Gad, that fellow is the salt of the earth. Good, loyal fellow! A true friend. A man you can rely on. Upon my Sam, if there were more fellows about like old Tuppy, there wouldn't be all this modern pessimism and unrest. Did he seem to have any idea where he could raise a bit of capital for me?"

"Yes. He went round to tell your aunt about your coming down here to train those Pekes, and—— What's the matter?"

A fearful change had come over Ukridge's jubilant front. His eyes bulged, his jaw sagged. With the addition of a few feet of grey whiskers he would have looked exactly like the recent Mr. Nickerson.

"My aunt?" he mumbled, swaying on the door-handle.

"Yes. What's the matter? He thought, if he told her all about it, she might relent and rally round."

The sigh of a gallant fighter at the end of his strength forced its way up from Ukridge's mackintosh-covered bosom.

"Of all the dashed, infernal, officious, meddling, muddling, fat-headed, interfering asses," he said, wanly, "George Tupper is the worst."

"What do you mean?"

"The man oughtn't to be at large. He's a public menace."

"But——"

"Those dogs *belong* to my aunt. I pinched them when she chucked me out!"

Inside the cottage the Pekingese were still yapping industriously.

"Upon my Sam," said Ukridge, "it's a little hard."

I think he would have said more, but at this point a voice spoke with a sudden and awful abruptness from the interior of the cottage. It was a woman's voice, a quiet, steely voice, a voice, it seemed to me, that suggested cold eyes, a beaky nose, and hair like gunmetal.

"Stanley!"

That was all it said, but it was enough. Ukridge's eye met mine in a wild surmise. He seemed to shrink into his mackintosh like a snail surprised while eating lettuce.

"Stanley."

"Yes, Aunt Julia?" quavered Ukridge.

"Come here. I wish to speak to you."

"Yes, Aunt Julia."

I sidled out into the road. Inside the cottage the yapping of the Pekingese had become quite hysterical. I found myself trotting, and then—though it was a warm day—running quite rapidly. I could have stayed if I had wanted to, but somehow I did not want to. Something seemed to tell me that on this holy domestic scene I should be an intruder.

What it was that gave me that impression I do not know—probably vision of the big, broad, flexible outlook.

UKRIDGE'S ACCIDENT SYNDICATE

HALF a minute, Laddie," said Ukridge. And, gripping my arm, he brought me to a halt on the outskirts of the little crowd which had collected about the church door.

It was a crowd such as may be seen any morning during the London mating-season outside any of the churches which nestle in the quiet squares between Hyde Park and the King's Road, Chelsea.

It consisted of five women of cook-like aspect, four nurse-maids, half a dozen men of the non-producing class who had torn themselves away for the moment from their normal task of propping up the wall of the Bunch of Grapes public-house on the corner, a costermonger with a barrow of vegetables, divers small boys, eleven dogs, and two or three purposeful-looking young fellows with cameras slung over their shoulders. It was plain that a wedding was in progress—and, arguing from the presence of the camera-men and the line of smart motor-cars along the kerb, a fairly fashionable wedding. What was not plain—to me—was why Ukridge, sternest of bachelors, had desired to add himself to the spectators.

"What," I enquired, "is the thought behind this? Why are we interrupting our walk to attend the obsequies of some perfect stranger?"

Ukridge did not reply for a moment. He seemed plunged in thought. Then he uttered a hollow, mirthless laugh—a dreadful sound like the last gargle of a dying moose.

"Perfect stranger, my number eleven foot!" he responded, in his coarse way. "Do you know who it is who's getting hitched up in there?"

"Who?"

"Teddy Weeks."

"Teddy Weeks? Teddy Weeks? Good Lord!" I exclaimed. "Not really?"

And five years rolled away.

It was at Barolini's Italian restaurant in Beak Street that Ukridge evolved his great scheme. Barolini's was a favourite resort of our little group of earnest strugglers in the days when the philanthropic restaurateurs of Soho used to supply four courses and coffee for a shilling and sixpence; and there were present that night, besides Ukridge and myself, the following men-about-town: Teddy Weeks, the actor, fresh from a six-weeks' tour with the Number Three "Only a Shop-Girl" Company; Victor Beamish, the artist, the man who drew that picture of the O-So-Eesi Piano-Player in the advertisement pages of the *Piccadilly Magazine;* Bertram Fox, author of *Ashes of Remorse*, and other unproduced motion-picture scenarios; and Robert Dunhill, who, being employed at a salary of eighty pounds per annum by the New Asiatic Bank, represented the sober, hard-headed commercial element. As usual, Teddy Weeks had collared the conversation, and was telling us once again how good he was and how hardly treated by a malignant fate.

There is no need to describe Teddy Weeks. Under another and a more euphonious name he has long since made his personal appearance dreadfully familiar to all who read the illustrated weekly papers. He was then, as now, a sickeningly handsome young man, possessing precisely the same melting eyes, mobile mouth, and corrugated hair so esteemed by the theatre-going public to-day. And yet, at this period of his career he was wasting himself on minor touring companies of the kind which open at Barrow-in-Furness and jump to Bootle for the second half of the week. He attributed this, as Ukridge was so apt to attribute his own difficulties, to lack of capital.

"I have everything," he said, querulously, emphasising his remarks with a coffee-spoon. "Looks, talent, personality, a beautiful speaking-voice—everything. All I need is a chance. And I can't get that because I have no clothes fit to wear. These managers are all the same, they never look below the surface, they never bother to find out if a man has genius. All they go by is his clothes. If I could afford to buy a couple of suits from a Cork Street tailor, if I could have my boots made to order by Moykoff instead of getting them ready-made and second-hand at Moses Brothers', if I could once contrive to own a decent hat, a really good pair of spats, and a gold cigarette-case, all at the same time, I could walk into any manager's office in

London and sign up for a West-end production to-morrow."

It was at this point that Freddie Lunt came in. Freddie, like Robert Dunhill, was a financial magnate in the making and an assiduous frequenter of Baro-lini's; and it suddenly occurred to us that a considerable time had passed since we had last seen him in the place. We enquired the reason for this aloofness.

"I've been in bed," said Freddie, "for over a fortnight."

The statement incurred Ukridge's stern disapproval. That great man made a practice of never rising before noon, and on one occasion, when a carelessly-thrown match had burned a hole in his only pair of trousers, had gone so far as to remain between the sheets for forty-eight hours; but sloth on so majestic a scale as this shocked him.

"Lazy young devil," he commented severely. "Letting the golden hours of youth slip by like that when you ought to have been bustling about and making a name for yourself."

Freddie protested himself wronged by the imputation.

"I had an accident," he explained. "Fell off my bicycle and sprained an ankle."

"Tough luck," was our verdict.

"Oh, I don't know," said Freddie. "It wasn't bad fun getting a rest. And of course there was the fiver."

"What fiver?"

"I got a fiver from the *Weekly Cyclist* for getting my ankle sprained."

"You—*what?*" cried Ukridge, profoundly stirred—as ever—by a tale of easy money. "Do you mean to sit there and tell me that some dashed paper paid you five quid simply because you sprained your ankle? Pull yourself together, old horse. Things like that don't happen."

"It's quite true."

"Can you show me the fiver?"

"No; because if I did you would try to borrow it."

Ukridge ignored this slur in dignified silence.

"Would they pay a fiver to *anyone* who sprained his ankle?" he asked, sticking to the main point.

"Yes. If he was a subscriber."

"I knew there was a catch in it," said Ukridge, moodily.

"Lot's of weekly papers are starting this wheeze," proceeded Freddie. "You pay a year's subscription and that entitles you to accident insurance."

We were interested. This was in the days before every daily paper in London was competing madly against its rivals in the matter of insurance and offering princely bribes to the citizens to make a fortune by breaking their necks. Nowadays papers are paying as high as two thousand pounds for a genuine corpse and five pounds a week for a mere dislocated spine; but at that time the idea was new and it had an attractive appeal.

"How many of these rags are doing this?" asked Ukridge. You could tell from the gleam in his eyes that that great brain was whirring like a dynamo. "As many as ten?"

"Yes, I should think so. Quite ten."

"Then a fellow who subscribed to them all and then sprained his ankle would get fifty quid?" said Ukridge, reasoning acutely.

"More if the injury was more serious," said Freddie, the expert. "They have a regular tariff. So much for a broken arm, so much for a broken leg, and so forth."

Ukridge's collar leaped off its stud and his pince-nez wobbled drunkenly as he turned to us.

"How much money can you blokes raise?" he demanded.

"What do you want it for?" asked Robert Dunhill, with a banker's caution.

"My dear old horse, can't you see? Why, my gosh, I've got the idea of the century. Upon my Sam, this is the giltest-edged scheme that was ever hatched. We'll get together enough money and take out a year's subscription for every one of these dashed papers."

"What's the good of that?" said Dunhill, coldly unenthusiastic.

They train bank clerks to stifle emotion, so that they will be able to refuse overdrafts when they become managers. "The odds are we should none of us have an accident of any kind, and then the money would be chucked away."

"Good heavens, ass," snorted Ukridge, "you don't suppose I'm suggesting that we should leave it to chance, do you? Listen! Here's the scheme. We take out subscriptions for all these papers, then we draw lots, and the fellow who gets the fatal card or whatever it is goes out and breaks his leg and draws the loot, and we split it up between us and live on it in luxury. It ought to run into hundreds of pounds."

A long silence followed. Then Dunhill spoke again. His was a solid rather than a nimble mind.

"Suppose he couldn't break his leg?"

"My gosh!" cried Ukridge, exasperated. "Here we are in the twentieth century, with every resource of modern civilisation at our disposal, with opportunities for getting our legs broken opening about us on every side—and you ask a silly question like that! Of course he could break his leg. Any ass can break a leg. It's a little hard! We're all infernally broke—personally, unless Freddie can lend me a bit of that fiver till Saturday, I'm going to have a difficult job of pulling through. We all need money like the dickens, and yet, when I point out this marvellous scheme for collecting a bit, instead of fawning on me for my ready intelligence you sit and make objections. It isn't the right spirit. It isn't the spirit that wins."

"If you're as hard up as that," objected Dunhill, "how are you going to put in your share of the pool?"

A pained, almost a stunned, look came into Ukridge's eyes. He gazed at Dunhill through his lop-sided pince-nez as one who speculates as to whether his hearing has deceived him.

"Me?" he cried. "Me? I like that! Upon my Sam, that's rich! Why, damme, if there's any justice in the world, if there's a spark of decency and good feeling in your bally bosoms, I should think you would let me in free for suggesting the idea. It's a little hard! I supply the brains and you want me to cough up cash as well. My gosh, I didn't expect this. This hurts me, by George! If anybody had told me that an old pal would——"

"Oh, all right," said Robert Dunhill. "All right, all right, all right. But I'll tell you one thing. If you draw the lot it'll be the happiest day of my life."

"I sha'n't," said Ukridge. "Something tells me that I sha'n't."

Nor did he. When, in a solemn silence broken only by the sound of a distant waiter quarrelling with the cook down a speaking-tube, we had completed the drawing, the man of destiny was Teddy Weeks.

I suppose that even in the springtime of Youth, when broken limbs seem a lighter matter than they become later in life, it can never be an unmixedly agreeable thing to have to go out into the public high-ways and try to make an accident happen to one. In such circumstances the reflection that you are thereby benefiting your friends brings but slight balm. To Teddy Weeks it appeared to bring no balm at all. That he was experiencing a certain disinclination to sacrifice himself for the public good became more and more evident as the days went by and found him still intact. Ukridge, when he called upon me to discuss the matter, was visibly perturbed. He sank into a chair beside the table at which I was beginning my modest morning meal, and, having drunk half my coffee, sighed deeply.

"Upon my Sam," he moaned, "it's a little disheartening. I strain my brain to think up schemes for getting us all a bit of money just at the moment when we are all needing it most, and when I hit on what is probably the simplest and yet ripest notion of our time, this blighter Weeks goes and lets me down by shirking his plain duty. It's just my luck that a fellow like that should have drawn the lot. And the worst of it is, laddie, that, now we've started with him, we've got to keep on. We can't possibly raise enough money to pay yearly subscriptions for anybody else. It's Weeks or nobody."

"I suppose we must give him time."

"That's what he says," grunted Ukridge morosely, helping himself to toast. "He says he doesn't know how to start about it. To listen to him, you'd think that going and having a trifling accident was the sort of delicate and intricate job that required years of study and special preparation. Why, a child of six could do it on his head at five minutes' notice. The man's so infernally particular. You make helpful suggestions, and instead of accepting them in a broad, reasonable spirit of co-operation he comes back at you every time with some frivolous objection. He's so dashed fastidious. When we were out last night, we came on a couple of navvies scrapping. Good hefty fellows, either of them capable of putting him in hospital for a month. I told him to jump in and start separating them, and he said no; it was a private dispute which was none of his business, and he didn't feel justified in interfering. Finicky, I call it. I tell you, laddie, this blighter is a broken reed. He has got cold feet. We did wrong to let him into the drawing at all. We might have known that a fellow like that would never give results. No conscience. No sense of esprit de corps. No notion of putting himself out to the most trifling extent for the benefit of the community. Haven't you any more marmalade, laddie?"

"I have not."

"Then I'll be going," said Ukridge, moodily. "I suppose," he added, pausing at the door, "you couldn't lend me five bob?"

"How did you guess?"

"Then I'll tell you what," said Ukridge, ever fair and reasonable; "you can stand me dinner to-night." He seemed cheered up for the moment by this happy compromise, but gloom descended on him again. His face clouded. "When I think," he said, "of all the money that's locked up in that poor faint-hearted fish, just waiting to be released, I could sob. Sob, laddie, like a little child. I never liked that man—he has a bad eye and waves his hair. Never trust a man who waves his hair, old horse."

Ukridge's pessimism was not confined to himself. By the end of a fortnight, nothing having happened to Teddy Weeks worse than a slight cold which he shook off in a couple of days, the general concensus of opinion among his apprehensive colleagues in the Syndicate was that the situation had become desperate. There were no signs whatever of any return on the vast capital which we had laid out, and meanwhile meals had to be bought, landladies paid, and a reasonable supply of tobacco acquired. It was a melancholy task in these circumstances to read one's paper of a morning.

All over the inhabited globe, so the well-informed sheet gave one to understand, every kind of accident was happening every day to practically everybody in existence except Teddy Weeks. Farmers in Minnesota were getting mixed up with reaping-machines, peasants in India were being bisected by crocodiles; iron girders from skyscrapers were falling hourly on the heads of citizens in every town from Philadelphia to San Francisco; and the only people who were not down with ptomaine poisoning were those who had walked over cliffs, driven motors into walls, tripped over manholes, or assumed on too slight evidence that the gun was not loaded. In a crippled world, it seemed, Teddy Weeks walked alone, whole and glowing with health. It was one of those grim, ironical, hopeless, grey, despairful situations which the Russian novelists love to write about, and I could not find it in me to blame Ukridge for taking direct action in this crisis. My only regret was that bad luck caused so excellent a plan to miscarry.

My first intimation that he had been trying to hurry matters on came when he and I were walking along the King's Road one evening, and he drew me into Markham Square, a dismal backwater where he had once had rooms.

"What's the idea?" I asked, for I disliked the place.

"Teddy Weeks lives here," said Ukridge. "In my

old rooms." I could not see that this lent any fascination to the place. Every day and in every way I was feeling sorrier and sorrier that I had been foolish enough to put money which I could ill spare into a venture which had all the earmarks of a wash-out, and my sentiments towards Teddy Weeks were cold and hostile.

"I want to enquire after him."

"Enquire after him? Why?"

"Well, the fact is, laddie, I have an idea that he has been bitten by a dog."

"What makes you think that?"

"Oh, I don't know," said Ukridge, dreamily. "I've just got the idea. You know how one gets ideas."

The mere contemplation of this beautiful event was so inspiring that for awhile it held me silent. In each of the ten journals in which we had invested dog-bites were specifically recommended as things which every subscriber ought to have. They came about half-way up the list of lucrative accidents, inferior to a broken rib or a fractured fibula, but better value than an in-growing toe-nail. I was gloating happily over the picture conjured up by Ukridge's words when an exclamation brought me back with a start to the realities of life. A revolting sight met my eyes. Down the street came ambling the familiar figure of Teddy Weeks, and one glance at his elegant person was enough to tell us that our hopes had been built on sand. Not even a toy Pomeranian had chewed this man.

"Hallo, you fellows!" said Teddy Weeks.

"Hallo!" we responded, dully.

"Can't stop," said Teddy Weeks. "I've got to fetch a doctor."

"A doctor?"

"Yes. Poor Victor Beamish. He's been bitten by a dog."

Ukridge and I exchanged weary glances. It seemed as if Fate was going out of its way to have sport with us. What was the good of a dog biting Victor Beamish? What was the good of a hundred dogs biting Victor Beamish? A dog-bitten Victor Beamish had no market value whatever.

"You know that fierce brute that belongs to my land-lady," said Teddy Weeks. "The one that always dashes out into the area and barks at people who come to the front door." I remembered. A large mongrel with wild eyes and flashing fangs, badly in need of a haircut. I had encountered it once in the street, when visiting Ukridge, and only the presence of the latter, who knew it well and to whom all dogs were as brothers, had saved me from the doom of Victor Beamish. "Somehow or other he got into my bed-room this evening. He was waiting there when I came home. I had brought Beamish back with me, and the animal pinned him by the leg the moment I opened the door."

"Why didn't he pin you?" asked Ukridge, aggrieved.

"What I can't make out," said Teddy Weeks, "is how on earth the brute came to be in my room. Some-body must have put him there. The whole thing is very mysterious."

"Why didn't he pin you?" demanded Ukridge again.

"Oh, I managed to climb on to the top of the ward-robe while he was biting Beamish," said Teddy Weeks. "And then the landlady came and took him away. But I can't stop here talking. I must go and get that doctor."

We gazed after him in silence as he tripped down the street. We noted the careful manner in which he paused at the corner to eye the traffic before cross-ing the road, the wary way in which he drew back to allow a truck to rattle past.

"You heard that?" said Ukridge, tensely. "He climbed on to the top of the wardrobe!"

"Yes."

"And you saw the way he dodged that excellent truck?"

"Yes."

"Something's got to be done," said Ukridge, firmly. "The man has got to be awakened to a sense of his responsibilities."

Next day a deputation waited on Teddy Weeks.

Ukridge was our spokesman, and he came to the point with admirable directness.

"How about it?" asked Ukridge.

"How about what?" replied Teddy Weeks, ner-vously, avoiding his accusing eye.

"When do we get action?"

"Oh, you mean that accident business?"

"Yes."

"I've been thinking about that," said Teddy Weeks.

Ukridge drew the mackintosh which he wore indoors and out of doors and in all weathers more closely around him. There was in the action something suggestive of a member of the Roman Senate about to denounce an enemy of the State. In just such a manner must Cicero have swished his toga as he took a deep breath preparatory to assailing Clodius. He toyed for a moment with the ginger-beer wire which held his pince-nez in place, and endeavoured without success to button his collar at the back. In moments of emotion Ukridge's collar always took on a sort of temperamental jumpiness which no stud could restrain.

"And about time you *were* thinking about it," he boomed, sternly.

We shifted appreciatively in our seats, all except Victor Beamish, who had declined a chair and was standing by the mantelpiece. "Upon my Sam, it's about time you were thinking about it. Do you realise that we've invested an enormous sum of money in you on the distinct understanding that we could rely on you to do your duty and get immediate results? Are we to be forced to the conclusion that you are so yellow and few in the pod as to want to evade your honourable obligations? We thought better of you, Weeks. Upon my Sam, we thought better of you. We took you for a two-fisted, enterprising, big-souled, one hundred-per-cent. he-man who would stand by his friends to the finish."

"Yes, but——"

"Any bloke with a sense of loyalty and an appreciation of what it meant to the rest of us would have rushed out and found some means of fulfilling his duty long ago. You don't even grasp at the oppor-

tunities that come your way. Only yesterday I saw
you draw back when a single step into the road would
have had a truck bumping into you."

"Well, it's not so easy to let a truck bump into you."

"Nonsense. It only requires a little ordinary resolution. Use your imagination, man. Try to think that
a child has fallen down in the street—a little golden-
haired child," said Ukridge, deeply affected. "And a
dashed great cab or something comes rolling up. The
kid's mother is standing on the pavement, helpless, her
hands clasped in agony. 'Dammit,' she cries, 'will no
one save my darling?' 'Yes, by George,' you shout, '*I*
will.' And out you jump and the thing's over in half
a second. I don't know what you're making such a
fuss about."

"Yes, but——" said Teddy Weeks.

"I'm told, what's more, it isn't a bit painful. A sort
of dull shock, that's all."

"Who told you that?"

"I forget. Someone."

"Well, you can tell him from me that he's an ass,"
said Teddy Weeks, with asperity.

"All right. If you object to being run over by a
truck there are lots of other ways. But, upon my
Sam, it's pretty hopeless suggesting them. You seem
to have no enterprise at all. Yesterday, after I went
to all the trouble to put a dog in your room, a dog
which would have done all the work for you—all that
you had to do was stand still and let him use his own
judgment—what happened? You climbed on to——"

Victor Beamish interrupted, speaking in a voice husky with emotion.

"Was it you who put that damned dog in the room?"

"Eh?" said Ukridge. "Why, yes. But we can have a good talk about all that later on," he proceeded, hastily. "The point at the moment is how the dickens we're going to persuade this poor worm to collect our insurance money for us. Why, damme, I should have thought you would have——"

"All I can say——" began Victor Beamish, heatedly.

"Yes, yes," said Ukridge; "some other time. Must stick to business now, laddie. I was saying," he resumed, "that I should have thought you would have been as keen as mustard to put the job through for your own sake. You're always beefing that you haven't any clothes to impress managers with. Think of all you can buy with your share of the swag once you have summoned up a little ordinary determination and seen the thing through. Think of the suits, the boots, the hats, the spats. You're always talking about your dashed career, and how all you need to land you in a West-end production is good clothes. Well, here's your chance to get them."

His eloquence was not wasted. A wistful look came into Teddy Weeks's eye, such a look as must have come into the eye of Moses on the summit of Pisgah. He breathed heavily. You could see that the man was mentally walking along Cork Street, weighing the merits of one famous tailor against another.

"I'll tell you what I'll do," he said, suddenly. "It's

no use asking me to put this thing through in cold blood. I simply can't do it. I haven't the nerve. But if you fellows will give me a dinner to-night with lots of champagne I think it will key me up to it."

A heavy silence fell upon the room. Champagne! The word was like a knell.

"How on earth are we going to afford champagne?" said Victor Beamish.

"Well, there it is," said Teddy Weeks. "Take it or leave it."

"Gentlemen," said Ukridge, "it would seem that the company requires more capital. How about it, old horses? Let's get together in a frank, business-like, cards-on-the-table spirit, and see what can be done. I can raise ten bob."

"What!" cried the entire assembled company, amazed. "How?"

"I'll pawn a banjo."

"You haven't got a banjo."

"No, but George Tupper has, and I know where he keeps it."

Started in this spirited way, the subscriptions came pouring in. I contributed a cigarette-case, Bertram Fox thought his landlady would let him owe for another week, Robert Dunhill had an uncle in Kensington who, he fancied, if tactfully approached, would be good for a quid, and Victor Beamish said that if the advertisement-manager of the O-So-Eesi Piano-Player was churlish enough to refuse an advance of five shillings against future work he misjudged him sadly. Within a few minutes, in short, the Lightning

Drive had produced the impressive total of two pounds six shillings, and we asked Teddy Weeks if he thought that he could get adequately keyed up within the limits of that sum.

"I'll try," said Teddy Weeks.

So, not unmindful of the fact that that excellent hostelry supplied champagne at eight shillings the quart bottle, we fixed the meeting for seven o'clock at Barolini's.

Considered as a social affair, Teddy Weeks's keying-up dinner was not a success. Almost from the start I think we all found it trying. It was not so much the fact that he was drinking deeply of Barolini's eight-shilling champagne while we, from lack of funds, were compelled to confine ourselves to meaner beverages; what really marred the pleasantness of the function was the extraordinary effect the stuff had on Teddy. What was actually in the champagne supplied to Barolini and purveyed by him to the public, such as were reckless enough to drink it, at eight shillings the bottle remains a secret between its maker and his Maker; but three glasses of it were enough to convert Teddy Weeks from a mild and rather oily young man into a truculent swashbuckler.

He quarrelled with us all. With the soup he was tilting at Victor Beamish's theories of Art; the fish found him ridiculing Bertram Fox's views on the future of the motion-picture; and by the time the leg of chicken with dandelion salad arrived—or, as some held, string salad—opinions varied on this point—the hell-brew had so wrought on him that he had begun to lecture Ukridge on his misspent life and was urging him in accents audible across the street to go out and get a job and thus acquire sufficient self-respect to enable him to look himself in the face in a mirror without wincing. Not, added Teddy Weeks with what we all thought uncalled-for offensiveness, that any amount of self-respect was likely to do that. Having said which, he called imperiously for another eight bobs'-worth.

We gazed at one another wanly. However excellent the end towards which all this was tending, there was no denying that it was hard to bear. But policy kept us silent. We recognised that this was Teddy Weeks's evening and that he must be humoured. Victor Beamish said meekly that Teddy had cleared up a lot of points which had been troubling him for a long time. Bertram Fox agreed that there was much in what Teddy had said about the future of the close-up. And even Ukridge, though his haughty soul was seared to its foundations by the latter's personal remarks, promised to take his homily to heart and act upon it at the earliest possible moment.

"You'd better!" said Teddy Weeks, belligerently, biting off the end of one of Barolini's cigars. "And there's another thing—don't let me hear of your coming and sneaking people's socks again."

"Very well, laddie," said Ukridge, humbly.

"If there is one person in the world that I despise," said Teddy, bending a red-eyed gaze on the offender, "it's a snock-seeker—a seek-snocker—a—well, you know what I mean."

We hastened to assure him that we knew what he meant and he relapsed into a lengthy stupor, from which he emerged three-quarters of an hour later to announce that he didn't know what he intended to do, but that he was going. We said that we were going too, and we paid the bill and did so.

Teddy Weeks's indignation on discovering us gathered about him upon the pavement outside the restaurant was intense, and he expressed it freely. Among other things, he said—which was not true—that he had a reputation to keep up in Soho.

"It's all right, Teddy, old horse," said Ukridge, soothingly. "We just thought you would like to have all your old pals round you when you did it."

"Did it? Did what?"

"Why, had the accident."

Teddy Weeks glared at him truculently. Then his mood seemed to change abruptly, and he burst into a loud and hearty laugh.

"Well, of all the silly ideas!" he cried, amusedly. "I'm not going to have an accident. You don't suppose I ever seriously intended to have an accident, do you? It was just my fun." Then, with another sudden change of mood, he seemed to become a victim to an acute unhappiness. He stroked Ukridge's arm affectionately, and a tear rolled down his cheek. "Just my fun," he repeated. "You don't mind my fun, do you?" he asked pleadingly. "You like my fun, don't you? All my fun. Never meant to have an accident at all. Just wanted dinner." The gay humour of it all overcame his sorrow once more. "Funniest thing ever heard," he said cordially. "Didn't want accident, wanted dinner. Dinner daxident, danner dixident," he added, driving home his point. "Well, good night all," he said, cheerily. And, stepping off the kerb on to a banana-skin, was instantly knocked ten feet by a passing lorry.

"Two ribs and an arm," said the doctor five minutes later, superintending the removal proceedings. "Gently with that stretcher."

It was two weeks before we were informed by the authorities of Charing Cross Hospital that the patient was in a condition to receive visitors. A whip-round secured the price of a basket of fruit, and Ukridge and I were deputed by the shareholders to deliver it with their compliments and kind enquiries.

"Hallo!" we said in a hushed, bedside manner when finally admitted to his presence.

"Sit down, gentlemen," replied the invalid.

I must confess even in that first moment to having experienced a slight feeling of surprise. It was not like Teddy Weeks to call us gentlemen. Ukridge, however, seemed to notice nothing amiss.

"Well, well, well," he said, buoyantly. "And how are you, laddie? We've brought you a few fragments of fruit."

"I am getting along capitally," replied Teddy Weeks, still in that odd precise way which had made his opening words strike me as curious. "And I should like to say that in my opinion England has reason to be proud of the alertness and enterprise of her great journals. The excellence of their reading-matter, the ingenuity of their various competitions, and, above all, the go-ahead spirit which has resulted in this accident insurance scheme are beyond praise. Have you got that down?" he enquired.

Ukridge and I looked at each other. We had been told that Teddy was practically normal again, but this sounded like delirium.

"Have we got that down, old horse?" asked Ukridge, gently.

Teddy Weeks seemed surprised.

"Aren't you reporters?"

"How do you mean, reporters?"

"I thought you had come from one of these weekly papers that have been paying me insurance money, to interview me," said Teddy Weeks.

Ukridge and I exchanged another glance. An uneasy glance this time. I think that already a grim foreboding had begun to cast its shadow over us.

"Surely you remember me, Teddy, old horse?" said Ukridge, anxiously.

Teddy Weeks knit his brow, concentrating painfully.

"Why, of course," he said at last. "You're Ukridge. aren't you?"

"That's right. Ukridge."

"Of course. Ukridge."

"Yes. Ukridge. Funny your forgetting me!"

"Yes," said Teddy Weeks. "It's the effect of the shock I got when that thing bowled me over. I must have been struck on the head, I suppose. It has had the effect of rendering my memory rather uncertain. The doctors here are very interested. They say it is a most unusual case. I can remember some things perfectly, but in some ways my memory is a complete blank."

"Oh, but I say, old horse," quavered Ukridge. "I suppose you haven't forgotten about that insurance, have you?"

"Oh, no, I remember that."

Ukridge breathed a relieved sigh.

"I was a subscriber to a number of weekly papers," went on Teddy Weeks. "They are paying me insurance money now."

"Yes, yes, old horse," cried Ukridge. "But what I mean is you remember the Syndicate, don't you?"

Teddy Weeks raised his eyebrows.

"Syndicate? What Syndicate?"

"Why, when we all got together and put up the money to pay for the subscriptions to these papers and drew lots, to choose which of us should go out and have an accident and collect the money. And you drew it, don't you remember?"

Utter astonishment, and a shocked astonishment at that, spread itself over Teddy Weeks's countenance. The man seemed outraged.

"I certainly remember nothing of the kind," he said, severely. "I cannot imagine myself for a moment consenting to become a party to what from your own account would appear to have been a criminal conspiracy to obtain money under false pretences from a number of weekly papers."

"But, laddie——"

"However," said Teddy Weeks, "if there is any

truth in this story, no doubt you have documentary evidence to support it."

Ukridge looked at me. I looked at Ukridge. There was a long silence.

"Shift-ho, old horse?" said Ukridge, sadly. "No use staying on here."

"No," I replied, with equal gloom. "May as well go."

"Glad to have seen you," said Teddy Weeks, "and thanks for the fruit."

The next time I saw the man he was coming out of a manager's office in the Haymarket. He had on a new Homburg hat of a delicate pearl grey, spats to match, and a new blue flannel suit, beautifully cut, with an invisible red twill. He was looking jubilant, and, as I passed him, he drew from his pocket a gold cigarette-case.

It was shortly after that, if you remember, that he made a big hit as the juvenile lead in that piece at the Apollo and started on his sensational career as a matinée idol.

Inside the church the organ had swelled into the familiar music of the Wedding March. A verger came out and opened the doors. The five cooks ceased their reminiscences of other and smarter weddings at which they had participated. The camera-men unshipped their cameras. The costermonger moved his barrow of vegetables a pace forward. A dishevelled and unshaven man at my side uttered a disapproving growl.

"Idle rich!" said the dishevelled man.

Out of the church came a beauteous being, leading attached to his arm another being, somewhat less beauteous.

There was no denying the spectacular effect of Teddy Weeks. He was handsomer than ever. His sleek hair, gorgeously waved, shone in the sun, his eyes were large and bright; his lissome frame, garbed in faultless morning-coat and trousers, was that of an Apollo. But his bride gave the impression that Teddy had married money. They paused in the doorway, and the camera-men became active and fussy.

"Have you got a shilling, laddie?" said Ukridge in a low, level voice.

"Why do you want a shilling?"

"Old horse," said Ukridge, tensely, "it is of the utmost vital importance that I have a shilling here and now."

I passed it over. Ukridge turned to the dishevelled man, and I perceived that he held in his hand a large rich tomato of juicy and over-ripe appearance.

"Would you like to earn a bob?" Ukridge said.

"Would I!" replied the dishevelled man.

Ukridge sank his voice to a hoarse whisper.

The camera-men had finished their preparations. Teddy Weeks, his head thrown back in that gallant way which has endeared him to so many female hearts, was exhibiting his celebrated teeth. The cooks, in undertones, were making adverse comments on the appearance of the bride.

"Now, please," said one of the camera-men.

Over the heads of the crowd, well and truly aimed,

whizzed a large juicy tomato. It burst like a shell full between Teddy Weeks's expressive eyes, obliterating them in scarlet ruin. It spattered Teddy Weeks's collar, it dripped on Teddy Weeks's morning-coat. And the dishevelled man turned abruptly and raced off down the street.

Ukridge grasped my arm. There was a look of deep content in his eyes.

"Shift-ho?" said Ukridge.

Arm-in-arm, we strolled off in the pleasant June sunshine.

FIRST AID FOR DORA

NEVER in the course of a long and intimate acquaintance having been shown any evidence to the contrary, I had always looked on Stanley Featherstonehaugh Ukridge, my boyhood chum, as a man ruggedly indifferent to the appeal of the opposite sex. I had assumed that, like so many financial giants, he had no time for dalliance with women—other and deeper matters, I supposed, keeping that great brain permanently occupied. It was a surprise, therefore, when, passing down Shaftesbury Avenue one Wednesday afternoon in June at the hour when matinée audiences were leaving the theatres, I came upon him assisting a girl in a white dress to mount an omnibus.

As far as this simple ceremony could be rendered impressive, Ukridge made it so. His manner was a blend of courtliness and devotion; and if his mackintosh had been a shade less yellow and his hat a trifle less disreputable, he would have looked just like Sir Walter Raleigh.

The bus moved on, Ukridge waved, and I proceeded to make enquiries. I felt that I was an interested party. There had been a distinctly "object-matrimony" look about the back of his neck, it seemed to me; and the prospect of having to support a Mrs. Ukridge and keep a flock of little Ukridges in socks and shirts perturbed me.

"Who was that?" I asked.

"Oh, hallo, laddie!" said Ukridge, turning. "Where did you spring from? If you had come a moment earlier, I'd have introduced you to Dora." The bus was lumbering out of sight into Piccadilly Circus, and the white figure on top turned and gave a final wave. "That was Dora Mason," said Ukridge, having flapped a large hand in reply. "She's my aunt's secretary-companion. I used to see a bit of her from time to time when I was living at Wimbledon. Old Tuppy gave me a couple of seats for that show at the Apollo, so I thought it would be a kindly act to ask her along. I'm sorry for that girl. Sorry for her, old horse."

"What's the matter with her?"

"Hers is a grey life. She has few pleasures. It's an act of charity to give her a little treat now and then. Think of it! Nothing to do all day but brush the Pekingese and type out my aunt's rotten novels."

"Does your aunt write novels?"

"The world's worst, laddie, the world's worst. She's been steeped to the gills in literature ever since I can remember. They've just made her president of the Pen and Ink Club. As a matter of fact, it was her novels that did me in when I lived with her. She used to send me to bed with the beastly things and ask me questions about them at breakfast. Absolutely without exaggeration, laddie, at breakfast. It was a dog's life, and I'm glad it's over. Flesh and blood couldn't stand the strain. Well, knowing my aunt, I don't mind telling you that my heart bleeds for poor little Dora. I know what a foul time she has, and I feel a better, finer man for having given her this passing gleam of sunshine. I wish I could have done more for her."

"Well, you might have stood her tea after the theatre."

"Not within the sphere of practical politics, laddie. Unless you can sneak out without paying, which is dashed difficult to do with these cashiers watching the door like weasels, tea even at an A B C shop punches the pocket-book pretty hard, and at the moment I'm down to the scrapings. But I'll tell you what, I don't mind joining you in a cup, if you were thinking of it."

"I wasn't."

"Come, come! A little more of the good old spirit of hospitality, old horse."

"Why do you wear that beastly mackintosh in mid-summer?"

"Don't evade the point, laddie. I can see at a glance that you need tea. You're looking pale and fagged."

"Doctors say that tea is bad for the nerves."

"Yes, possibly there's something in that. Then I'll tell you what," said Ukridge, never too proud to yield a point, "we'll make it a whisky-and-soda instead. Come along over to the Criterion."

It was a few days after this that the Derby was run, and a horse of the name of Gunga Din finished third. This did not interest the great bulk of the intelligentsia to any marked extent, the animal having started at a hundred to three, but it meant much to me, for I had drawn his name in the sweepstake at my club. After a monotonous series of blanks stretching back to the first year of my membership, this seemed to me the outstanding event of the century, and I celebrated my triumph by an informal dinner to a few friends. It was some small consolation to me later to remember that I had wanted to include Ukridge in the party, but failed to get hold of him. Dark hours were to follow, but at least Ukridge did not go through them bursting with my meat.

There is no form of spiritual exaltation so poignant as that which comes from winning even a third prize in a sweepstake. So tremendous was the moral uplift that, when eleven o'clock arrived, it seemed silly to sit talking in a club and still sillier to go to bed. I suggested spaciously that we should all go off and dress and resume the revels at my expense half an hour later at Mario's, where, it being an extension night, there would be music and dancing till three. We scattered in cabs to our various homes.

How seldom in this life do we receive any premonition of impending disaster. I hummed a gay air as I entered the house in Ebury Street where I lodged, and not even the usually quelling sight of Bowles, my landlord, in the hall as I came in could quench my bonhomie. Generally a meeting with Bowles had the effect on me which the interior of a cathedral has on the devout, but to-night I was superior to this weakness.

"Ah, Bowles," I cried, chummily, only just stopping myself from adding "Honest fellow!" "Hallo,

Bowles! I say, Bowles, I drew Gunga Din in the club sweep."

"Indeed, sir?"

"Yes. He came in third, you know."

"So I see by the evening paper, sir. I congratulate you."

"Thank you, Bowles, thank you."

"Mr. Ukridge called earlier in the evening, sir," said Bowles.

"Did he? Sorry I was out. I was trying to get hold of him. Did he want anything in particular?"

"Your dress-clothes, sir."

"My dress-clothes, eh?" I laughed genially. "Extraordinary fellow! You never know——" A ghastly thought smote me like a blow. A cold wind seemed to blow through the hall. "He didn't *get* them, did he?" I quavered.

"Why, yes, sir."

"Got my dress-clothes?" I muttered thickly, clutching for support at the hat-stand.

"He said it would be all right, sir," said Bowles, with that sickening tolerance which he always exhibited for all that Ukridge said or did. One of the leading mysteries of my life was my landlord's amazing attitude towards this hell-hound. He fawned on the man. A splendid fellow like myself had to go about in a state of hushed reverence towards Bowles, while a human blot like Ukridge could bellow at him over the banisters without the slightest rebuke. It was one of those things which make one laugh cynically when people talk about the equality of man.

"He got my dress-clothes?" I mumbled.

"Mr. Ukridge said that he knew you would be glad to let him have them, as you would not be requiring them to-night."

"But I do require them, damn it!" I shouted, lost to all proper feeling. Never before had I let fall an oath in Bowles's presence. "I'm giving half a dozen men supper at Mario's in a quarter of an hour."

Bowles clicked his tongue sympathetically.

"What am I going to do?"

"Perhaps if you would allow me to lend you mine, sir?"

"Yours?"

"I have a very nice suit. It was given to me by his lordship the late Earl of Oxted, in whose employment I was for many years. I fancy it would do very well on you, sir. His lordship was about your height, though perhaps a little slenderer. Shall I fetch it, sir? I have it in a trunk downstairs."

The obligations of hospitality are sacred. In fifteen minutes' time six jovial men would be assembled at Mario's, and what would they do, lacking a host? I nodded feebly.

"It's very kind of you," I managed to say.

"Not at all, sir. It is a pleasure."

If he was speaking the truth, I was glad of it. It is nice to think that the affair brought pleasure to some-one.

That the late Earl of Oxted had indeed been a somewhat slenderer man than myself became manifest to me from the first pulling on of the trousers.

Hitherto I had always admired the slim, small-boned type of aristocrat, but it was not long before I was wishing that Bowles had been in the employment of someone who had gone in a little more heartily for starchy foods. And I regretted, moreover, that the fashion of wearing a velvet collar on an evening coat, if it had to come in at all, had not lasted a few years longer. Dim as the light in my bedroom was, it was strong enough to make me wince as I looked in the mirror.

And I was aware of a curious odour.

"Isn't this room a trifle stuffy, Bowles?"

"No, sir. I think not."

"Don't you notice an odd smell?"

"No, sir. But I have a somewhat heavy cold. If you are ready, sir, I will call a cab."

Moth-balls! That was the scent I had detected. It swept upon me like a wave in the cab. It accompanied me like a fog all the way to Mario's, and burst out in its full fragrance when I entered the place and removed my overcoat. The cloak-room waiter sniffed in a startled way as he gave me my check, one or two people standing near hastened to remove themselves from my immediate neighbourhood, and my friends, when I joined them, expressed themselves with friend-like candour. With a solid unanimity they told me frankly that it was only the fact that I was paying for the supper that enabled them to tolerate my presence.

The leper-like feeling induced by this uncharitable attitude caused me after the conclusion of the meal to withdraw to the balcony to smoke in solitude. My guests were dancing merrily, but such pleasures were not for me. Besides, my velvet collar had already excited ribald comment, and I am a sensitive man. Crouched in a lonely corner of the balcony, surrounded by the outcasts who were not allowed on the lower floor because they were not dressed, I chewed a cigar and watched the revels with a jaundiced eye. The space reserved for dancing was crowded and couples either revolved warily or ruthlessly bumped a passage for themselves, using their partners as battering-rams. Prominent among the ruthless bumpers was a big man who was giving a realistic imitation of a steam-plough. He danced strongly and energetically, and when he struck the line, something had to give.

From the very first something about this man had seemed familiar; but owing to his peculiar crouching manner of dancing, which he seemed to have modelled on the ring-style of Mr. James J. Jeffries, it was not immediately that I was able to see his face. But presently, as the music stopped and he straightened himself to clap his hands for an encore, his foul features were revealed to me.

It was Ukridge. Ukridge, confound him, with my dress-clothes fitting him so perfectly and with such unwrinkled smoothness that he might have stepped straight out of one of Ouida's novels. Until that moment I had never fully realised the meaning of the expression "faultless evening dress." With a passionate cry I leaped from my seat, and, accompanied by a rich smell of camphor, bounded for the stairs.

Like Hamlet on a less impressive occasion, I wanted to slay this man when he was full of bread, with all his crimes, broad-blown, as flush as May, at drinking, swearing, or about some act that had no relish of salvation in it.

"But, laddie," said Ukridge, backed into a corner of the lobby apart from the throng, "be reasonable."

I cleansed my bosom of a good deal of that perilous stuff that weighs upon the heart.

"How could I guess that you would want the things? Look at it from my position, old horse. I knew you, laddie, a good true friend who would be delighted to lend a pal his dress-clothes any time when he didn't need them himself, and as you weren't there when I called, I couldn't ask you, so I naturally simply borrowed them. It was all just one of those little misunderstandings which can't be helped. And, as it luckily turns out, you had a spare suit, so everything was all right, after all."

"You don't think this poisonous fancy dress is mine, do you?"

"Isn't it?" said Ukridge, astonished.

"It belongs to Bowles. He lent it to me."

"And most extraordinarily well you look in it, laddie," said Ukridge. "Upon my Sam, you look like a duke or something."

"And smell like a second-hand clothes-store."

"Nonsense, my dear old son, nonsense. A mere faint suggestion of some rather pleasant antiseptic. Nothing more. I like it. It's invigorating. Honestly, old man, it's really remarkable what an air that suit gives you. Distinguished. That's the word I was searching for. You look distinguished. All the girls are saying so. When you came in just now to speak to me, I heard one of them whisper 'Who is it?' That shows you."

"More likely 'what is it?'"

"Ha, ha!" bellowed Ukridge, seeking to cajole me with sycophantic mirth. "Dashed good! Deuced good! Not 'Who is it?' but 'What is it?' It beats me how you think of these things. Golly, if I had a brain like yours—— But now, old son, if you don't mind, I really must be getting back to poor little Dora. She'll be wondering what has become of me."

The significance of these words had the effect of making me forget my just wrath for a moment.

"Are you here with that girl you took to the theatre the other afternoon?"

"Yes. I happened to win a trifle on the Derby, so I thought it would be a decent thing to ask her out for an evening's pleasure. Hers is a grey life."

"It must be, seeing you so much."

"A little personal, old horse," said Ukridge reprovingly. "A trifle bitter. But I know you don't mean it. Yours is a heart of gold really. If I've said that once, I've said it a hundred times. Always saying it. Rugged exterior but heart of gold. My very words. Well, good-bye for the present, laddie. I'll look in to-morrow and return these things. I'm sorry there was any misunderstanding about them, but it makes up for everything, doesn't it, to feel that you've helped brighten life for a poor little downtrodden thing who has few pleasures."

"Just one last word," I said. "One final remark."

"Yes?"

"I'm sitting in that corner of the balcony over there," I said. "I mention the fact so that you can look out for yourself. If you come dancing underneath there, I shall drop a plate on you. And if it kills you, so much the better. I'm a poor downtrodden little thing, and I have few pleasures."

Owing to a mawkish respect for the conventions, for which I reproach myself, I did not actually perform this service to humanity. With the exception of throwing a roll at him—which missed him but most fortunately hit the member of my supper-party who had sniffed with the most noticeable offensiveness at my camphorated costume—I took no punitive measures against Ukridge that night. But his demeanour, when he called at my rooms next day, could not have been more crushed if I had dropped a pound of lead on him. He strode into my sitting-room with the sombre tread of the man who in a conflict with Fate has received the loser's end. I had been passing in my mind a number of good snappy things to say to him, but his appearance touched me to such an extent that I held them in. To abuse this man would have been like dancing on a tomb.

"For Heaven's sake, what's the matter?" I asked. "You look like a toad under the harrow."

He sat down creakingly, and lit one of my cigars.

"Poor little Dora!"

"What about her?"

"She's got the push!"

"The push? From your aunt's, do you mean?"

"Yes."

"What for?"

Ukridge sighed heavily.

"Most unfortunate business, old horse, and largely my fault. I thought the whole thing was perfectly safe. You see, my aunt goes to bed at half-past ten every night, so it seemed to me that if Dora slipped out at eleven and left a window open behind her she could sneak back all right when we got home from Mario's. But what happened? Some dashed officious ass," said Ukridge, with honest wrath, "went and locked the damned window. I don't know who it was. I suspect the butler. He has a nasty habit of going round the place late at night and shutting things. Upon my Sam, it's a little hard! If only people would leave things alone and not go snooping about——"

"What happened?"

"Why, it was the scullery window which we'd left open, and when we got back at four o'clock this morning the infernal thing was shut as tight as an egg. Things looked pretty rocky, but Dora remembered that her bedroom window was always open, so we bucked up again for a bit. Her room's on the second floor, but I knew where there was a ladder, so I went and got it, and she was just hopping up as merry as dammit when somebody flashed a great beastly lantern on us, and there was a policeman, wanting to know what the game was. The whole trouble with the police force of London, laddie, the thing that makes them a hissing and a byword, is that they're snoopers to a man. Zeal, I suppose they call it. Why they can't attend to their own affairs is more than I can understand. Dozens of murders going on all the time, probably, all over Wimbledon, and all this bloke would do was stand and wiggle his infernal lantern and ask what the game was. Wouldn't be satisfied with a plain statement that it was all right. Insisted on rousing the house to have us identified."

Ukridge paused, a reminiscent look of pain on his expressive face.

"And then?" I said.

"We were," said Ukridge, briefly.

"What?"

"Identified. By my aunt. In a dressing-gown and a revolver. And the long and short of it is, old man, that poor little Dora has got the sack."

I could not find it in my heart to blame his aunt for what he evidently considered a high-handed and tyrannical outrage. If I were a maiden lady of regular views, I should relieve myself of the services of any secretary-companion who returned to roost only a few short hours in advance of the milk. But, as Ukridge plainly desired sympathy rather than an austere pronouncement on the relations of employer and employed, I threw him a couple of tuts, which seemed to soothe him a little. He turned to the practical side of the matter.

"What's to be done?"

"I don't see what you can do."

"But I must do something. I've lost the poor little thing her job, and I must try to get it back. It's a rotten sort of job, but it's her bread and butter. Do you think George Tupper would biff round and have a chat with my aunt, if I asked him?"

"I suppose he would. He's the best-hearted man in the world. But I doubt if he'll be able to do much."

"Nonsense, laddie," said Ukridge, his unconquerable optimism rising bravely from the depths. "I have the utmost confidence in old Tuppy. A man in a million. And he's such a dashed respectable sort of bloke that he might have her jumping through hoops and sham- ming dead before she knew what was happening to her. You never know. Yes, I'll try old Tuppy. I'll go and see him now."

"I should."

"Just lend me a trifle for a cab, old son, and I shall be able to get to the Foreign Office before one o'clock. I mean to say, even if nothing comes of it, I shall be able to get a lunch out of him. And I need refresh- ment, laddie, need it sorely. The whole business has shaken me very much."

It was three days after this that, stirred by a pleasant scent of bacon and coffee, I hurried my dressing and, proceeding to my sitting-room, found that Ukridge had dropped in to take breakfast with me, as was often his companionable practice. He seemed thoroughly cheerful again, and was plying knife and fork briskly like the good trencherman he was.

"Morning, old horse," he said agreeably.

"Good morning."

"Devilish good bacon, this. As good as I've ever bitten. Bowles is cooking you some more."

"That's nice. I'll have a cup of coffee, if you don't mind me making myself at home while I'm waiting." I started to open the letters by my plate, and became aware that my guest was eyeing me with a stare of intense penetration through his pince-nez, which were all crooked as usual. "What's the matter?"

"Matter?"

"Why," I said, "are you looking at me like a fish with lung-trouble?"

"Was I?" He took a sip of coffee with an over-done carelessness. "Matter of fact, old son, I was rather interested. I see you've a letter from my aunt."

"What?"

I had picked up the last envelope. It was addressed in a strong female hand, strange to me. I now tore it open. It was even as Ukridge had said. Dated the previous day and headed "Heath House, Wimbledon Common," the letter ran as follows:—

"DEAR SIR,—I shall be happy to see you if you will call at this address the day after to-morrow (Friday) at four-thirty.—Yours faithfully, JULIA UKRIDGE."

I could make nothing of this. My morning mail, whether pleasant or the reverse, whether bringing a bill from a tradesman or a cheque from an editor, had had till now the uniform quality of being plain, straightforward, and easy to understand; but this communication baffled me. How Ukridge's aunt had become aware of my existence, and why a call from me should ameliorate her lot, were problems beyond my unravelling, and I brooded over it as an Egyptologist might over some newly-discovered hieroglyphic.

"What does she say?" enquired Ukridge.

"She wants me to call at half-past four to-morrow afternoon."

"Splendid!" cried Ukridge. "I knew she would bite."

"What on earth are you talking about?"

Ukridge reached across the table and patted me affectionately on the shoulder. The movement involved the upsetting of a full cup of coffee, but I suppose he meant well. He sank back again in his chair and adjusted his pince-nez in order to get a better view of me. I seemed to fill him with honest joy, and he suddenly burst into a spirited eulogy, rather like some minstrel of old delivering an *ex-tempore* boost of his chieftain and employer.

"Laddie," said Ukridge, "if there's one thing about you that I've always admired it's your readiness to help a pal. One of the most admirable qualities a bloke can possess, and nobody has it to a greater extent than you. You're practically unique in that way. I've had men come up to me and ask me about you. 'What sort of a chap is he?' they say. 'One of the very best,' I reply. 'A fellow you can rely on. A man who would die rather than let you down. A bloke who would go through fire and water to do a pal a good turn. A bird with a heart of gold and a nature as true as steel.' "

"Yes, I'm a splendid fellow," I agreed, slightly perplexed by this panegyric. "Get on."

"I am getting on, old horse," said Ukridge, with faint reproach. "What I'm trying to say is that I knew you would be delighted to tackle this little job for me. It wasn't necessary to ask you. I *knew*."

A grim foreboding of an awful doom crept over me, as it had done so often before in my association with Ukridge.

"Will you kindly tell me what damned thing you've let me in for now?"

Ukridge deprecated my warmth with a wave of his fork. He spoke soothingly and with a winning persuasiveness. He practically cooed.

"It's nothing, laddie. Practically nothing. Just a simple little act of kindness which you will thank me for putting in your way. It's like this. As I ought to have foreseen from the first, that ass Tuppy proved a broken reed. In that matter of Dora, you know. Got no result whatever. He went to see my aunt the day before yesterday, and asked her to take Dora on again, and she gave him the miss-in-balk. I'm not surprised. I never had any confidence in Tuppy. It was a mistake ever sending him. It's no good trying frontal attack in a delicate business like this. What you need is strategy. You want to think what is the enemy's weak side and then attack him from that angle. Now, what is my aunt's weak side, laddie? Her weak side, what is it? Now think. Reflect, old horse."

"From the sound of her voice, the only time I ever got near her, I should say she hadn't one."

"That's where you make your error, old son. Butter her up about her beastly novels, and a child could
eat out of her hand. When Tuppy let me down I just
lit a pipe and had a good think. And then suddenly
I got it. I went to a pal of mine, a thorough sportsman—you don't know him. I must introduce you
some day—and he wrote my aunt a letter from you,
asking if you could come and interview her for
Woman's Sphere. It's a weekly paper, which I happen
to know she takes in regularly. Now, listen, laddie.
Don't interrupt for a moment. I want you to get
the devilish shrewdness of this. You go and interview her, and she's all over you. Tickled to death.
Of course, you'll have to do a good deal of Young
Disciple stuff, but you won't mind that. After you've
soft-soaped her till she's purring like a dynamo, you
get up to go. 'Well,' you say, 'this has been the
proudest occasion of my life, meeting one whose work
I have so long admired.' And she says, 'The pleasure
is mine, old horse.' And you slop over each other a
bit more. Then you say sort of casually, as if it had
just occurred to you, 'Oh, by the way, I believe my
cousin—or sister——' No, better make it cousin—
'I believe my cousin, Miss Dora Mason, is your secretary, isn't she?' 'She isn't any such dam' thing,' replies my aunt. 'I sacked her three days ago.' That's
your cue, laddie. Your face falls, you register concern,
you're frightfully cut up. You start in to ask her to
let Dora come back. And you're such pals by this time
that she can refuse you nothing. And there you are!
My dear old son, you can take it from me that if you

only keep your head and do the Young Disciple stuff properly the thing can't fail. It's an iron-clad scheme. There isn't a flaw in it."

"There is one."

"I think you're wrong. I've gone over the thing very carefully. What is it?"

"The flaw is that I'm not going anywhere near your infernal aunt. So you can trot back to your forger chum and tell him he's wasted a good sheet of letter-paper."

A pair of pince-nez tinkled into a plate. Two pained eyes blinked at me across the table. Stanley Featherstonehaugh Ukridge was wounded to the quick.

"You don't mean to say you're backing out?" he said, in a low, quivering voice.

"I never was in."

"Laddie," said Ukridge, weightily, resting an elbow on his last slice of bacon, "I want to ask you one question. Just one simple question. Have you ever let me down? Has there been one occasion in our long friendship when I have relied upon you and been deceived? Not one!"

"Everything's got to have a beginning. I'm starting now."

"But think of her. Dora! Poor little Dora. Think of poor little Dora."

"If this business teaches her to keep away from you, it will be a blessing in the end."

"But, laddie——"

I suppose there is some fatal weakness in my character, or else the brand of bacon which Bowles cooked possessed a peculiarly mellowing quality. All I know is that, after being adamant for a good ten minutes, I finished breakfast committed to a task from which my soul revolted. After all, as Ukridge said, it was rough on the girl. Chivalry is chivalry. We must strive to lend a helping hand as we go through this world of ours, and all that sort of thing. Four o'clock on the following afternoon found me entering a cab and giving the driver the address of Heath House, Wimbledon Common.

My emotions on entering Heath House were such as I would have felt had I been keeping a tryst with a dentist who by some strange freak happened also to be a duke. From the moment when a butler of super-Bowles dignity opened the door and, after regarding me with ill-concealed dislike, started to conduct me down a long hall, I was in the grip of both fear and humility. Heath House is one of the stately homes of Wimbledon; how beautiful they stand, as the poet says: and after the humble drabness of Ebury Street it frankly overawed me. Its keynote was an extreme neatness which seemed to sneer at my squashy collar and reproach my baggy trouser-leg. The farther I penetrated over the polished floor, the more vividly was it brought home to me that I was one of the submerged tenth and could have done with a hair-cut. I had not been aware when I left home that my hair was unusually long, but now I seemed to be festooned by a matted and offensive growth. A patch on my left shoe which had had a rather comfortable look in Ebury Street stood out like a blot on the landscape. No, I was not at my ease; and when I reflected that in a few moments I was to meet Ukridge's aunt, that legendary figure, face to face, a sort of wistful admiration filled me for the beauty of the nature of one who would go through all this to help a girl he had never even met. There was no doubt about it—the facts spoke for themselves—I was one of the finest fellows I had ever known. Nevertheless, there was no getting away from it, my trousers did bag at the knee.

"Mr. Corcoran," announced the butler, opening the drawing-room door. He spoke with just that intonation of voice that seemed to disclaim all responsibility. If I had an appointment, he intimated, it was his duty, however repulsive, to show me in; but, that done, he dissociated himself entirely from the whole affair.

There were two women and six Pekingese dogs in the room. The Pekes I had met before, during their brief undergraduate days at Ukridge's dog college, but they did not appear to recognise me. The occasion when they had lunched at my expense seemed to have passed from their minds. One by one they came up, sniffed, and then moved away as if my bouquet had disappointed them. They gave the impression that they saw eye to eye with the butler in his estimate of the young visitor. I was left to face the two women.

Of these—reading from right to left—one was a tall, angular, hawk-faced female with a stony eye. The other, to whom I gave but a passing glance at the moment, was small, and so it seemed to me, pleasant-looking. She had bright hair faintly powdered with grey, and mild eyes of a china blue. She reminded me of the better class of cat. I took her to be some casual caller who had looked in for a cup of tea. It was the hawk on whom I riveted my attention. She was looking at me with a piercing and unpleasant stare, and I thought how exactly she resembled the picture I had formed of her in my mind from Ukridge's conversation.

"Miss Ukridge?" I said, sliding on a rug towards her and feeling like some novice whose manager, against his personal wishes, has fixed him up with a match with the heavyweight champion.

"I am Miss Ukridge," said the other woman. "Miss Watterson, Mr. Corcoran."

It was a shock, but, the moment of surprise over, I began to feel something approaching mental comfort for the first time since I had entered this house of slippery rugs and supercilious butlers. Somehow I had got the impression from Ukridge that his aunt was a sort of stage aunt, all stiff satin and raised eyebrows. This half-portion with the mild blue eyes I felt that I could tackle. It passed my comprehension why Ukridge should ever have found her intimidating.

"I hope you will not mind if we have our little talk before Miss Watterson," she said with a charming smile. "She has come to arrange the details of the Pen and Ink Club dance which we are giving shortly. She will keep quite quiet and not interrupt. You don't mind?"

"Not at all, not at all," I said in my attractive way. It is not exaggerating to say that at this moment I felt debonair. "Not at all, not at all. Oh, not at all."

"Won't you sit down?"

"Thank you, thank you."

The hawk moved over to the window, leaving us to ourselves.

"Now we are quite cosy," said Ukridge's aunt.

"Yes, yes," I agreed. Dash it, I liked this woman.

"Tell me, Mr. Corcoran," said Ukridge's aunt, "are you on the staff of *Woman's Sphere?* It is one of my favourite papers. I read it every week."

"The outside staff."

"What do you mean by the outside staff?"

"Well, I don't actually work in the office, but the editor gives me occasional jobs."

"I see. Who is the editor now?"

I began to feel slightly less debonair. She was just making conversation, of course, to put me at my ease, but I wished she would stop asking me these questions. I searched desperately in my mind for a name —any name—but as usual on these occasions every name in the English language had passed from me.

"Of course. I remember now," said Ukridge's aunt, to my profound relief. "It's Mr. Jevons, isn't it? I met him one night at dinner."

"Jevons," I burbled. "That's right. Jevons."

"A tall man with a light moustache."

"Well, fairly tall," I said, judicially.

"And he sent you here to interview me?"

"Yes."

"Well, which of my novels do you wish me to talk about?"

I relaxed with a delightful sense of relief. I felt on solid ground at last. And then it suddenly came to me that Ukridge in his woollen-headed way had omitted to mention the name of a single one of this woman's books.

"Er—oh, all of them," I said hurriedly.

"I see. My general literary work."

"Exactly," I said. My feeling towards her now was one of positive affection.

She leaned back in her chair with her finger-tips together, a pretty look of meditation on her face.

"Do you think it would interest the readers of *Woman's Sphere* to know which novel of mine is my own favourite?"

"I am sure it would."

"Of course," said Ukridge's aunt, "it is not easy for an author to answer a question like that. You see, one has moods in which first one book and then another appeals to one."

"Quite," I replied. "Quite."

"Which of my books do *you* like best, Mr. Corcoran?"

There swept over me the trapped feeling one gets in nightmares. From six baskets the six Pekingese stared at me unwinkingly.

"Er—oh, all of them," I heard a croaking voice reply. My voice, presumably, though I did not recognise it.

"How delightful!" said Ukridge's aunt. "Now, I really do call that delightful. One or two of the critics have said that my work was uneven. It is so nice to meet someone who doesn't agree with them. Personally, I think my favourite is *The Heart of Adelaide.*"

I nodded my approval of this sound choice. The muscles which had humped themselves stiffly on my back began to crawl back into place again. I found it possible to breathe.

"Yes," I said, frowning thoughtfully, "I suppose *The Heart of Adelaide* is the best thing you have written. It has such human appeal," I added, playing it safe.

"Have you read it, Mr. Corcoran?"

"Oh, yes."

"And you really enjoyed it?"

"Tremendously."

"You don't think it is a fair criticism to say that it is a little broad in parts?"

"Most unfair." I began to see my way. I do not know why, but I had been assuming that her novels must be the sort you find in seaside libraries. Evidently they belonged to the other class of female novels, the sort which libraries ban. "Of course," I said, "it is written honestly, fearlessly, and shows life as it is. But broad? No, no!"

"That scene in the conservatory?"

"Best thing in the book," I said stoutly.

A pleased smile played about her mouth. Ukridge had been right. Praise her work, and a child could eat out of her hand. I found myself wishing that I had really read the thing, so that I could have gone into more detail and made her still happier.

"I'm so glad you like it," she said. "Really, it is most encouraging."

"Oh, no," I murmured modestly.

"Oh, but it is. Because I have only just started to write it, you see. I finished chapter one this morning."

She was still smiling so engagingly that for a moment the full horror of these words did not penetrate my consciousness.

"*The Heart of Adelaide* is my next novel. The scene in the conservatory, which you like so much, comes towards the middle of it. I was not expecting to reach it till about the end of next month. How odd that you should know all about it!"

I had got it now all right, and it was like sitting down on the empty space where there should have been a chair. Somehow the fact that she was so pleasant about it all served to deepen my discomfiture. In the course of an active life I have frequently felt a fool, but never such a fool as I felt then. The fearful woman had been playing with me, leading me on, watching me entangle myself like a fly on fly-paper. And suddenly I perceived that I had erred in thinking of her eyes as mild. A hard gleam had come into them. They were like a couple of blue gimlets. She looked like a cat that had caught a mouse, and it was revealed to me in one sickening age-long instant why Ukridge went in fear of her. There was that about her which would have intimidated the Sheik.

"It seems so odd, too," she tinkled on, "that you should have come to interview me for *Woman's Sphere*. Because they published an interview with me only the week before last. I thought it so strange that I rang up my friend Miss Watterson, who is the editress, and asked her if there had not been some mistake. And she said she had never heard of you. *Have* you ever heard of Mr. Corcoran, Muriel?"

"Never," said the hawk, fixing me with a revolted eye.

"How strange!" said Ukridge's aunt. "But then the whole thing is so strange. Oh, must you go, Mr. Corcoran?"

My mind was in a slightly chaotic condition, but on that one point it was crystal-clear. Yes, I must go. Through the door if I could find it—failing that, through the window. And anybody who tried to stop me would do well to have a care.

"You will remember me to Mr. Jevons when you see him, won't you?" said Ukridge's aunt.

I was fumbling at the handle.

"And, Mr. Corcoran." She was still smiling amiably, but there had come into her voice a note like that which it had had on a certain memorable occasion when summoning Ukridge to his doom from the unseen interior of his Sheep's Cray cottage. "Will you please tell my nephew Stanley that I should be glad if he would send no more of his friends to see me. Good afternoon."

I suppose that at some point in the proceedings my hostess must have rung a bell, for out in the passage

I found my old chum, the butler. With the uncanny telepathy of his species he appeared aware that I was leaving under what might be called a cloud, for his manner had taken on a warder-like grimness. His hand looked as if it was itching to grasp me by the shoulder, and when we reached the front door he eyed the pavement wistfully, as if thinking what a splendid spot it would be for me to hit with a thud.

"Nice day," I said, with the feverish instinct to babble which comes to strong men in their agony.

He scorned to reply, and as I tottered down the sunlit street I was conscious of his gaze following me.

"A very vicious specimen," I could fancy him saying. "And mainly due to my prudence and foresight that he hasn't got away with the spoons."

It was a warm afternoon, but to such an extent had the recent happenings churned up my emotions that I walked the whole way back to Ebury Street with a rapidity which caused more languid pedestrians to regard me with a pitying contempt. Reaching my sitting-room in an advanced state of solubility and fatigue, I found Ukridge stretched upon the sofa.

"Hallo, laddie!" said Ukridge, reaching out a hand for the cooling drink that lay on the floor beside him. "I was wondering when you would show up. I wanted to tell you that it won't be necessary for you to go and see my aunt after all. It appears that Dora has a hundred quid tucked away in a bank, and she's been offered a partnership by a woman she knows who runs one of these typewriting places. I advised her to close with it. So she's all right."

He quaffed deeply of the bowl and breathed a contented sigh.   There was a silence.

"When did you hear of this?" I asked at length.

"Yesterday afternoon," said Ukridge.   "I meant to pop round and tell you, but somehow it slipped my mind."

UKRIDGE SEES HER THROUGH

T HE girl from the typewriting and stenographic bureau had a quiet but speaking eye. At first it had registered nothing but enthusiasm and the desire to please. But now, rising from that formidable notebook, it met mine with a look of exasperated bewilderment. There was an expression of strained sweetness on her face, as of a good woman unjustly put upon. I could read what was in her mind as clearly as if she had been impolite enough to shout it. She thought me a fool. And as this made the thing unanimous, for I had been feeling exactly the same myself for the last quarter of an hour, I decided that the painful exhibition must now terminate.

It was Ukridge who had let me in for the thing. He had fired my imagination with the tales of authors who were able to turn out five thousand words a day by dictating their stuff to a stenographer instead of writing it; and though I felt at the time that he was merely trying to drum up trade for the typewriting bureau in which his young friend Dora Mason was now a partner, the lure of the idea had gripped me. Like all writers, I had a sturdy distaste for solid work, and this seemed to offer a pleasant way out, turning literary composition into a jolly tête-à-tête chat. It was only when those gleaming eyes looked eagerly into mine and that twitching pencil poised itself to record the lightest of my golden thoughts that I discovered what I was up against. For fifteen minutes I had been experiencing all the complex emotions of a nervous man who, suddenly called upon to make a public speech, realises too late that his brain has been withdrawn and replaced by a cheap cauliflower substitute: and I was through.

"I'm sorry," I said, "but I'm afraid it's not much use going on. I don't seem able to manage it."

Now that I had come frankly out into the open and admitted my idiocy, the girl's expression softened. She closed her notebook forgivingly.

"Lots of people can't," she said. "It's just a knack."

"Everything seems to go out of my head."

"I've often thought it must be very difficult to dictate."

Two minds with but a single thought, in fact. Her sweet reasonableness, combined with the relief that the thing was over, induced in me a desire to babble. One has the same feeling when the dentist lets one out of his chair.

"You're from the Norfolk Street Agency, aren't you?" I said. A silly question, seeing that I had expressly rung them up on the telephone and asked them to send somebody round; but I was still feeling the effects of the ether.

"Yes."

"That's in Norfolk Street, isn't it? I mean," I went on hurriedly, "I wonder if you know a Miss Mason there? Miss Dora Mason."

She seemed surprised.

"My name is Dora Mason," she said.

I was surprised, too. I had not supposed that partners in typewriting businesses stooped to going out on these errands. And I was conscious of a return of my former embarrassment, feeling—quite unreasonably, for I had only seen her once in my life, and then from a distance—that I ought to have remembered her.

"We were short-handed at the office," she explained, "so I came along. But how do you know my name?"

"I am a great friend of Ukridge's."

"Why, of course! I was wondering why your name was so familiar. I've heard him talk so much about you."

And after that we really did settle down to the cosy tête-à-tête of which I had had visions. She was a nice girl, the only noticeable flaw in her character being an absurd respect for Ukridge's intelligence and abilities. I, who had known that foe of the human race from boyhood up and was still writhing beneath the memory of the night when he had sneaked my dress clothes, could have corrected her estimate of him, but it seemed unkind to shatter her girlish dreams.

"He was wonderful about this typewriting business," she said. "It was such a splendid opportunity, and but for Mr. Ukridge I should have had to let it

slip. You see, they were asking two hundred pounds
for the partnership, and I only had a hundred. And
Mr. Ukridge insisted on putting up the rest of the
money. You see—I don't know if he told you—he
insisted that he ought to do something because he says
he lost me the position I had with his aunt. It wasn't
his fault at all, really, but he kept saying that if I
hadn't gone to that dance with him I shouldn't have
got back late and been dismissed. So——"

She was a rapid talker, and it was only now that I
was able to comment on the amazing statement which
she had made in the opening portion of her speech.
So stunning had been the effect of those few words
on me that I had hardly heard her subsequent remarks.

"Did you say that Ukridge insisted on finding the
rest?" I gasped.

"Yes. Wasn't it nice of him?"

"He gave you a hundred pounds? Ukridge!"

"Guaranteed it," said Miss Mason. "I arranged
to pay a hundred pounds down and the rest in sixty
days."

"But suppose the rest is not paid in sixty days?"

"Well, then I'm afraid I should lose my hundred.
But it will be, of course. Mr. Ukridge told me to have
no anxiety about that at all. Well, good-bye, Mr.
Corcoran. I must be going now. I'm sorry we didn't
get better results with the dictating. I should think it
must be very difficult to do till you get used to it."

Her cheerful smile as she went out struck me as one
of the most pathetic sights I had ever seen. Poor child,

bustling off so brightly when her whole future rested on Ukridge's ability to raise a hundred pounds! I presumed that he was relying on one of those Utopian schemes of his which were to bring him in thousands— "at a conservative estimate, laddie!"—and not for the first time in a friendship of years the reflection came to me that Ukridge ought to be in some sort of a home. A capital fellow in many respects, but not a man lightly to be allowed at large.

I was pursuing this train of thought when the banging of the front door, followed by a pounding of footsteps on the stairs and a confused noise without, announced his arrival.

"I say, laddie," said Ukridge, entering the room, as was his habit, like a northeasterly gale, "was that Dora Mason I saw going down the street? It looked like her back. Has she been here?"

"Yes. I asked her agency to send someone to take dictation, and she came."

Ukridge reached out for the tobacco jar, filled his pipe, replenished his pouch, sank comfortably on to the sofa, adjusted the cushions, and bestowed an approving glance upon me.

"Corky, my boy," said Ukridge, "what I like about you and the reason why I always maintain that you will be a great man one of these days is that you have vision. You have the big, broad, flexible outlook. You're not too proud to take advice. I say to you, 'Dictate your stuff, it'll pay you,' and, damme, you go straight off and do it. No arguing or shilly-shallying. You just go and do it. It's the spirit that wins to success. I like to see it. Dictating will add thousands a year to your income. I say it advisedly, laddie—thousands. And if you continue leading a steady and sober life and save your pennies, you'll be amazed at the way your capital will pile up. Money at five per cent. compound interest doubles itself every fourteen years. By the time you're forty——"

It seemed churlish to strike a jarring note after all these compliments, but it had to be done.

"Never mind about what's going to happen to me when I'm forty," I said. "What I want to know is what is all this I hear about you guaranteeing Miss Mason a hundred quid?"

"Ah, she told you? Yes," said Ukridge, airily, "I guaranteed it. Matter of conscience, old son. Man of honour, no alternative. You see, there's no getting away from it, it was my fault that she was sacked by my aunt. Got to see her through, laddie, got to see her through."

I goggled at the man.

"Look here," I said, "let's get this thing straight. A couple of days ago you touched me for five shillings and said it would save your life."

"It did, old man, it did."

"And now you're talking of scattering hundred quid about the place as if you were Rothschild. Do you smoke it or inject it with a hypodermic needle?"

There was pain in Ukridge's eyes as he sat up and gazed at me through the smoke.

"I don't like this tone, laddie," he said, reproachfully.

"Upon my Sam, it wounds me. It sounds as if you had lost faith in me, in my vision."

"Oh, I know you've got vision. And the big, broad, flexible outlook. Also snap, ginger, enterprise, and ears that stick out at right angles like the sails of a windmill. But that doesn't help me to understand where on earth you expect to get a hundred quid."

Ukridge smiled tolerantly.

"You don't suppose I would have guaranteed the money for poor little Dora unless I knew where to lay my hands on it, do you? If you ask me, Have I got the stuff at this precise moment? I candidly reply, No, I haven't. But it's fluttering on the horizon, laddie, fluttering on the horizon. I can hear the beating of its wings."

"Is Battling Billson going to fight someone and make your fortune again?"

Ukridge winced, and the look of pain flitted across his face once more.

"Don't mention that man's name to me, old horse," he begged. "Every time I think of him everything seems to go all black. No, the thing I have on hand now is a real solid business proposition. Gilt-edged, you might call it. I ran into a bloke the other day whom I used to know out in Canada."

"I didn't know you had ever been in Canada," I interrupted.

"Of course I've been in Canada. Go over there and ask the first fellow you meet if I was ever in Canada. Canada! I should say I had been in Canada. Why, when I left Canada, I was seen off on the steamer by

a couple of policemen. Well, I ran into this bloke in
Piccadilly. He was wandering up and down and looking rather lost. Couldn't make out what the deuce
he was doing over here, because, when I knew him,
he hadn't a cent. Well, it seems that he got fed up
with Canada and went over to America to try and make
his fortune. And, by Jove, he did, first crack out of the
box. Bought a bit of land about the size of a pocket-
handkerchief in Texas or Oklahoma or somewhere, and
one morning, when he was hoeing the soil or planting
turnips or something, out buzzed a whacking great
oil-well. Apparently that sort of thing's happening
every day out there. If I could get a bit of capital
together, I'm dashed if I wouldn't go to Texas myself.
Great open spaces where men are men, laddie—suit me
down to the ground. Well, we got talking, and he said
that he intended to settle in England. Came from
London as a kid, but couldn't stick it at any price now
because they had altered it so much. I told him the
thing for him to do was to buy a house in the country
with a decent bit of shooting, and he said, 'Well, how
do you buy a house in the country with a decent bit of
shooting?' and I said, 'Leave it entirely in my hands,
old horse. I'll see you're treated right.' So he told
me to go ahead, and I went to Farmingdons, the house-
agent blokes in Cavendish Square. Had a chat with
the manager. Very decent old bird with moth-eaten
whiskers. I said I'd got a millionaire looking for a
house in the country. 'Find him one, laddie,' I said,
'and we split the commish.' He said 'Right-o,' and
any day now I expect to hear that he's dug up some-

thing suitable. Well, you can see for yourself what that's going to mean. These house-agent fellows take it as a personal affront if a client gets away from them with anything except a collar-stud and the clothes he stands up in, and I'm in halves. Reason it out, my boy, reason it out."

"You're sure this man really has money?"

"Crawling with it, laddie. Hasn't found out yet there's anything smaller than a five-pound note in circulation. He took me to lunch, and when he tipped the waiter the man burst into tears and kissed him on both cheeks."

I am bound to admit that I felt easier in my mind, for it really did seem as though the fortunes of Miss Mason rested on firm ground. I had never supposed that Ukridge could be associated with so sound a scheme, and I said so. In fact, I rather overdid my approval, for it encouraged him to borrow another five shillings; and before he left we were in treaty over a further deal which was to entail my advancing him half a sovereign in one solid payment. Business breeds business.

For the next ten days I saw nothing of Ukridge. As he was in the habit of making these periodical disappearances, I did not worry unduly as to the whereabouts of my wandering boy, but I was conscious from time to time of a mild wonder as to what had become of him. The mystery was solved one night when I was walking through Pall Mall on my way home after a late session with an actor acquaintance who was going into vaudeville, and to whom I hoped—mistakenly, as it turned out—to sell a one-act play.

I say night, but it was nearly two in the morning. The streets were black and deserted, silence was everywhere, and all London slept except Ukridge and a friend of his whom I came upon standing outside Hardy's fishing tackle shop. That is to say, Ukridge was standing outside the shop. His friend was sitting on the pavement with his back against a lamp-post.

As far as I could see in the uncertain light, he was a man of middle age, rugged of aspect and grizzled about the temples. I was able to inspect his temples because —doubtless from the best motives—he was wearing his hat on his left foot. He was correctly clad in dress clothes, but his appearance was a little marred by a splash of mud across his shirt-front and the fact that at some point earlier in the evening he had either thrown away or been deprived of his tie. He gazed fixedly at the hat with a poached-egg-like stare. He was the only man I had ever seen who was smoking two cigars at the same time.

Ukridge greeted me with the warmth of a beleaguered garrison welcoming the relieving army.

"My dear old horse! Just the man I wanted!" he cried, as if he had picked me out of a number of competing applicants. "You can give me a hand with Hank, laddie."

"Is this Hank!" I enquired, glancing at the recumbent sportsman, who had now closed his eyes as if the spectacle of the hat had begun to pall.

"Yes. Hank Philbrick. This is the bloke I was

telling you about, the fellow who wants the house."

"He doesn't seem to want any house. He looks quite satisfied with the great open spaces."

"Poor old Hank's a bit under the weather," explained Ukridge, regarding his stricken friend with tolerant sympathy. "It takes him this way. The fact is, old man, it's a mistake for these blokes to come into money. They overdo things. The only thing Hank ever got to drink for the first fifty years of his life was water, with buttermilk as a treat on his birthday, and he's trying to make up for lost time. He's only just discovered that there are such things as liqueurs in the world, and he's making them rather a hobby. Says they're such a pretty colour. It wouldn't be so bad if he stuck to one at a time, but he likes making experiments. Mixes them, laddie. Orders the whole lot and blends them in a tankard. Well, I mean to say," said Ukridge reasonably, "you can't take more than five or six tankards of mixed benedictine, chartreuse, kummel, crème de menthe, and old brandy without feeling the strain a bit. Especially if you stoke up on champagne and burgundy."

A strong shudder ran through me at the thought. I gazed at the human cellar on the pavement with a feeling bordering on awe.

"Does he really?"

"Every night for the last two weeks. I've been with him most of the time. I'm the only pal he's got in London, and he likes to have me round."

"What plans have you for his future? His immediate future, I mean. Do we remove him somewhere or is he going to spend the night out here under the quiet stars?"

"I thought, if you would lend a hand, old man, we could get him to the Carlton. He's staying there."

"He won't be long, if he comes in in this state."

"Bless you, my dear old man, they don't mind. He tipped the night-porter twenty quid yesterday and asked me if I thought it was enough. Lend a hand, laddie. Let's go."

I lent a hand, and we went.

The effect which that nocturnal encounter had upon me was to cement the impression that in acting as agent for Mr. Philbrick in the purchase of a house Ukridge was on to a good thing. What little I had seen of Hank had convinced me that he was not the man to be finicky about price. He would pay whatever they asked him without hesitation. Ukridge would undoubtedly make enough out of his share of the commission to pay off Dora Mason's hundred without feeling it. Indeed, for the first time in his life he would probably be in possession of that bit of capital of which he was accustomed to speak so wistfully. I ceased, therefore, to worry about Miss Mason's future and concentrated myself on my own troubles.

They would probably have seemed to anyone else minor troubles, but nevertheless they were big enough to depress me. Two days after my meeting with Ukridge and Mr. Philbrick in Pall Mall I had received rather a disturbing letter.

There was a Society paper for which at that time I did occasional work and wished to do more; and the editor of this paper had sent me a ticket for the forth-coming dance of the Pen and Ink Club, with instructions to let him have a column and a half of bright descriptive matter. It was only after I had digested the pleasant reflection that here was a bit of badly needed cash dropping on me out of a clear sky that I realised why the words Pen and Ink Club seemed to have a familiar ring. It was the club of which Ukridge's aunt Julia was the popular and energetic president, and the thought of a second meeting with that uncomfortable woman filled me with a deep gloom. I had not forgotten—and probably would never forget—my encounter with her in her drawing-room at Wimbledon.

I was not in a financial position, however, to refuse editors their whims, so the thing had to be gone through; but the prospect damped me, and I was still brooding on it when a violent ring at the front-door bell broke in on my meditations. It was followed by the booming of Ukridge's voice enquiring if I were in. A moment later he had burst into the room. His eyes were wild, his pince-nez at an angle of forty-five, and his collar separated from its stud by a gap of several inches. His whole appearance clearly indicated some blow of fate, and I was not surprised when his first words revealed an aching heart.

"Hank Philbrick," said Ukridge without preamble, "is a son of Belial, a leper, and a worm."

"What's happened now?"

"He's let me down, the weak-minded Tishbite! Doesn't want that house in the country after all. My gosh, if Hank Philbrick is the sort of man Canada is producing nowadays, Heaven help the British Empire."

I shelved my petty troubles. They seemed insignificant beside this majestic tragedy.

"What made him change his mind?" I asked.

"The wobbling, vacillating hell-hound! I always had a feeling that there was something wrong with that man. He had a nasty, shifty eye. You'll bear me out, laddie, in that? Haven't I spoken to you a hundred times about his shifty eye?"

"Certainly. Why did he change his mind?"

"Didn't I always say he wasn't to be trusted?"

"Repeatedly. What made him change his mind?"

Ukridge laughed with a sharp bitterness that nearly cracked the window-pane. His collar leaped like a live thing. Ukridge's collar was always a sort of thermometer that registered the warmth of his feelings. Sometimes, when his temperature was normal, it would remain attached to its stud for minutes at a time; but the slightest touch of fever sent it jumping up, and the more he was moved the higher it jumped.

"When I knew Hank out in Canada," he said, "he had the constitution of an ox. Ostriches took his correspondence course in digestion. But directly he comes into a bit of money——— Laddie," said Ukridge earnestly, "when I'm a rich man, I want you to stand at my elbow and watch me very carefully. The moment you see signs of degeneration speak a warning word. Don't let me coddle myself. Don't let me get fussy about my health. Where was I? Oh yes. Directly this man comes into a bit of money he gets the idea that he's a sort of frigile, delicate flower."

"I shouldn't have thought so from what you were telling me the other night."

"What happened the other night was the cause of all the trouble. Naturally he woke up with a bit of a head."

"I can quite believe it."

"Yes, but my gosh, what's a head! In the old days he would have gone and worked it off by taking a dose of pain-killer and chopping down half-a-dozen trees. But now what happens? Having all this money, he wouldn't take a simple remedy like that. No, sir! He went to one of those Harley Street sharks who charge a couple of guineas for saying 'Well, how are we this morning?' A fatal move, laddie. Naturally, the shark was all over him. Tapped him here and prodded him there, said he was run down, and finally told him he ought to spend six months in a dry, sunny climate. Recommended Egypt. Egypt, I'll trouble you, for a bloke who lived fifty years thinking that it was a town in Illinois. Well, the long and the short of it is that he's gone off for six months, doesn't want a place in England, and I hope he gets bitten by a crocodile. And the lease all drawn out and ready to sign. Upon my Sam, it's a little hard. Sometimes I wonder whether it's worth while going on struggling."

A sombre silence fell upon us. Ukridge, sunk in gloomy reverie, fumbled absently at his collar stud. I smoked with a heavy heart.

"What will your friend Dora do now?" I said at length.

"That's what's worrying me," said Ukridge, lugubriously. "I've been trying to think of some other way of raising that hundred, but at the moment I don't mind confessing I am baffled. I can see no daylight."

Nor could I. His chance of raising a hundred pounds by any means short of breaking into the Mint seemed slight indeed.

"Odd the way things happen," I said. I gave him the editor's letter. "Look at that."

"What's this?"

"He's sending me to do an article on the Pen and Ink Club dance. If only I had never been to see your aunt——"

"And made a mess of it."

"I didn't make a mess of it. It just happened that——"

"All right, laddie, all right," said Ukridge, tonelessly. "Don't let's split straws. The fact remains, whether it's your fault or not, the thing was a complete frost. What were you saying?"

"I was saying that, if only I had never been to your aunt, I could have met her in a perfectly natural way at this dance."

"Done Young Disciple stuff," said Ukridge, seizing on the idea. "Rubbed in the fact that you could do her a bit of good by boosting her in the paper."

"And asked her to re-engage Miss Mason as her secretary."

Ukridge fiddled with the letter.

"You don't think even now——"

I was sorry for him and sorrier for Dora Mason, but on this point I was firm.

"No, I don't."

"But consider, laddie," urged Ukridge. "At this dance she may well be in malleable mood. The lights, the music, the laughter, the jollity."

"No," I said. "It can't be done. I can't back out of going to the affair, because if I did I'd never get any more work to do for this paper. But I'll tell you one thing. I mean to keep quite clear of your aunt. That's final. I dream of her in the night sometimes and wake up screaming. And in any case it wouldn't be any use my tackling her. She wouldn't listen to me. It's too late. You weren't there that afternoon at Wimbledon, but you can take it from me that I'm not one of her circle of friends."

"That's the way it always happens," sighed Ukridge. "Everything comes too late. Well, I'll be popping off. Lot of heavy thinking to do, laddie. Lot of heavy thinking."

And he left without borrowing even a cigar, a sure sign that his resilient spirit was crushed beyond recuperation.

The dance of the Pen and Ink Club was held, like so many functions of its kind, at the Lotus Rooms, Knightsbridge, that barrack-like building which seems to exist only for these sad affairs. The Pen and Ink evidently went in for quality in its membership rather than quantity; and the band, when I arrived, was giving out the peculiarly tinny sound which bands always produce in very large rooms that are only one-sixth part full. The air was chilly and desolate and a general melancholy seemed to prevail. The few couples dancing on the broad acres of floor appeared sombre and introspective, as if they were meditating on the body upstairs and realising that all flesh is as grass. Around the room on those gilt chairs which are only seen in subscription-dance halls weird beings were talking in undertones, probably about the trend of Scandinavian literature. In fact, the only bright spot on the whole gloomy business was that it occurred before the era of tortoise-shell-rimmed spectacles.

That curious grey hopelessness which always afflicts me when I am confronted with literary people in the bulk was not lightened by the reflection that at any moment I might encounter Miss Julia Ukridge. I moved warily about the room, keenly alert, like a cat that has wandered into a strange alley and sees in every shadow the potential hurler of a half-brick. I could envisage nothing but awkwardness and embarrassment springing from such a meeting. The lesson which I had drawn from my previous encounter with her was that happiness for me lay in keeping as far away from Miss Julia Ukridge as possible.

"Excuse me!"

My precautions had been in vain. She had sneaked up on me from behind.

"Good evening," I said.

It is never any good rehearsing these scenes in advance. They always turn out so differently. I had been assuming, when I slunk into this hall, that if I met this woman I should feel the same shrinking sense of guilt and inferiority which had proved so disintegrating at Wimbledon. I had omitted to make allowances for the fact that that painful episode had taken place on her own ground, and that right from the start my conscience had been far from clear. To-night the conditions were different.

"Are you a member of the Pen and Ink Club?" said Ukridge's aunt, frostily.

Her stony blue eyes were fixed on me with an expression that was not exactly loathing, but rather a cold and critical contempt. So might a fastidious cook look at a black-beetle in her kitchen.

"No," I replied, "I am not."

I felt bold and hostile. This woman gave me a pain in the neck, and I endeavoured to express as much in the language of the eyes.

"Then will you please tell me what you are doing here? This is a private dance."

One has one's moments. I felt much as I presume Battling Billson must have felt in his recent fight with Alf Todd, when he perceived his antagonist advancing upon him wide-open, inviting the knock-out punch.

"The editor of *Society* sent me a ticket. He wanted an article written about it."

If I was feeling like Mr. Billson, Ukridge's aunt must have felt very like Mr. Todd. I could see that she was shaken. In a flash I had changed from a black-beetle to a god-like creature, able, if conciliated, to do a bit of that log-rolling which is so dear to the heart of the female novelist. And she had not conciliated me. Of all sad words of tongue or pen, the saddest are these: It might have been. It is too much to say that her jaw fell, but certainly the agony of this black moment caused her lips to part in a sort of twisted despair. But there was good stuff in this woman. She rallied gamely.

"A Press ticket," she murmured.

"A Press ticket," I echoed.

"May I see it?"

"Certainly."

"Thank you."

"Not at all."

She passed on.

I resumed my inspection of the dancers with a lighter heart. In my present uplifted mood they did not appear so bad as they had a few minutes back. Some of them, quite a few of them, looked almost human. The floor was fuller now, and whether owing to my imagination or not, the atmosphere seemed to have taken on a certain cheeriness. The old suggestion of a funeral still lingered, but now it was possible to think of it as a less formal, rather jollier funeral. I began to be glad that I had come.

"Excuse me!"

I had thought that I was finished with this sort of thing for the evening, and I turned with a little impatience. It was a refined tenor voice that had addressed me, and it was a refined tenor-looking man whom I saw. He was young and fattish, with a Jovian coiffure and pince-nez attached to a black cord.

"Pardon me," said this young man, "but are you a member of the Pen and Ink Club?"

My momentary annoyance vanished, for it suddenly occurred to me that, looked at in the proper light, it was really extremely flattering, this staunch refusal on the part of these people to entertain the belief that I could be one of them. No doubt, I felt, they were taking up the position of the proprietor of a certain night-club, who, when sued for defamation of character by a young lady to whom he had refused admittance on the ground that she was not a fit person to associate with his members, explained to the court that he had meant it as a compliment.

"No, thank Heaven!" I replied.

"Then what——"

"Press ticket," I explained.

"Press ticket? What paper?"

"Society."

There was nothing of the Julia Ukridge spirit in this young man, no ingrained pride which kept him aloof and outwardly indifferent. He beamed like the rising sun. He grasped my arm and kneaded it. He gambolled about me like a young lamb in the springtime.

"My dear fellow!" he exclaimed, exuberantly, and clutched my arm more firmly, lest even now I might elude him. "My dear fellow, I really must apologise. I would not have questioned you, but there are some persons present who were not invited. I met a man only a moment ago who said that he had bought a ticket. Some absurd mistake. There were no tickets

for sale. I was about to question him further, but
he disappeared into the crowd and I have not seen him
since. This is a quite private dance, open only to
members of the club. Come with me, my dear fellow,
and I will give you a few particulars which you may
find of use for your article."

He led me resolutely into a small room off the floor,
closed the door to prevent escape, and, on the principle
on which you rub a cat's paws with butter to induce
it to settle down in a new home, began to fuss about
with whisky and cigarettes.

"Do, do sit down."

I sat down.

"First, about this club. The Pen and Ink Club is
the only really exclusive organisation of its kind in
London. We pride ourselves on the fact. We are to
the literary world what Brooks's and the Carlton are
to the social. Members are elected solely by invitation.
Election, in short, you understand, is in the nature of
an accolade. We have exactly one hundred members,
and we include only those writers who in our opinion
possess vision."

"And the big, broad, flexible outlook?"

"I beg your pardon?"

"Nothing."

"The names of most of those here to-night must be
very familiar to you."

"I know Miss Ukridge, the president," I said.

A faint, almost imperceptible shadow passed over the
stout young man's face. He removed his pince-nez

and polished them with a touch of disfavour.   There
was a rather flat note in his voice.

"Ah, yes," he said, "Julia Ukridge.   A dear soul,
but between ourselves, strictly between ourselves,
not a great deal of help in an executive capacity."

"No?"

"No.   In confidence, I do all the work.   I am the
club's secretary.   My name, by the way, is Charlton
Prout.   You may know it?"

He eyed me wistfully, and I felt that something
ought to be done about him.   He was much too sleek,
and he had no right to do his hair like that.

"Of course," I said.   "I have read all your books."

"Really?"

"'A Shriek in the Night.'   'Who Killed Jasper
Bossom?'—all of them."

He stiffened austerely.

"You must be confusing me with some other—ah
—writer," he said.   "My work is on somewhat different lines.   The reviewers usually describe the sort
of thing I do as Pastels in Prose.   My best-liked book,
I believe, is *Grey Myrtles*.   Dunstable's brought it out
last year.   It was exceedingly well received.   And I
do a good deal of critical work for the better class of
review."   He paused.   "If you think it would interest
your readers," he said, with a deprecating wave of the
hand, "I will send you a photograph.   Possibly your
editor would like to use it."

"I bet he would."

"A photograph somehow seems to—as it were—
set off an article of this kind."

"That," I replied, cordially, "is what it doesn't do nothing else but."

"And you won't forget *Grey Myrtles*. Well, if you have finished your cigarette, we might be returning to the ballroom. These people rather rely on me to keep things going, you know."

A burst of music greeted us as he opened the door, and even in that first moment I had an odd feeling that it sounded different. That tinny sound had gone from it. And as we debouched from behind a potted palm and came in sight of the floor, I realised why.

The floor was full. It was crammed, jammed, and overflowing. Where couples had moved as single spies, they were now in battalions. The place was alive with noise and laughter. These people might, as my companion had said, be relying on him to keep things going, but they seemed to have been getting along uncommonly well in his absence. I paused and surveyed the mob in astonishment. I could not make the man's figures balance.

"I thought you said the Pen and Ink Club had only a hundred members."

The secretary was fumbling for his glasses. He had an almost Ukridge-like knack of dropping his pince-nez in moments of emotion.

"It—it has," he stammered.

"Well, reading from left to right, I make it nearer seven hundred."

"I cannot understand it."

"Perhaps they have been having a new election and letting in some writers without vision," I suggested.

I was aware of Miss Ukridge bearing down upon us, bristling.

"Mr. Prout!"

The talented young author of *Grey Myrtles* leaped convulsively.

"Yes, Miss Ukridge?"

"Who are all these people?"

"I—I don't know," said the talented young man.

"You don't know! It's your business to know. You are the secretary of the club. I suggest that you find out as quickly as possible who they are and what they imagine they are doing here."

The goaded secretary had something of the air of a man leading a forlorn hope, and his ears had turned bright pink, but he went at it bravely. A serene-looking man with a light moustache and a made-up tie was passing, and he sprang upon him like a stoutish leopard.

"Excuse me, sir."

"Eh?"

"Will you kindly—would you mind—pardon me if I ask——"

"What are you doing here?" demanded Miss Ukridge, curtly, cutting in on his flounderings with a masterful impatience. "How do you come to be at this dance?"

The man seemed surprised.

"Who, me?" he said. "I came with the rest of 'em."

"What do you mean, the rest of them?"

"The members of the Warner's Stores Social and Outing Club."

"But this is the dance of the Pen and Ink Club," bleated Mr. Prout.

"Some mistake," said the other, confidently. "It's a bloomer of some kind. Here," he added, beckoning to a portly gentleman of middle age who was bustling by, "you'd better have a talk with our hon. sec. He'll know. Mr. Biggs, this gentleman seems to think there's been some mistake about this dance."

Mr. Biggs stopped, looked, and listened. Seen at close range, he had a forceful, determined air. I liked his looks.

"May I introduce Mr. Charlton Prout?" I said. "Author of *Grey Myrtles*. Mr. Prout," I went on, as this seemed to make little or no sensation, "is the secretary of the Pen and Ink Club."

"I'm the secretary of the Warner's Stores Social and Outing Club," said Mr. Biggs.

The two secretaries eyed each other warily, like two dogs.

"But what are you doing here?" moaned Mr. Prout, in a voice like the wind in the tree-tops. "This is a private dance."

"Nothing of the kind," said Mr. Biggs, resolutely. "I personally bought tickets for all my members."

"But there were no tickets for sale. The dance was for the exclusive——"

"It's perfectly evident that you have come to the wrong hall or chosen the wrong evening," snapped Miss Ukridge, abruptly superseding Mr. Prout in the supreme command. I did not blame her for feeling a little impatient. The secretary was handling the campaign very feebly.

The man behind the Warner's Stores Social and Outing Club cocked a polite but belligerent eye at this new enemy. I liked his looks more than ever. This was a man who would fight it out on these lines if it took all the summer.

"I have not the honour of this lady's acquaintance," he said, smoothly, but with a gradually reddening eye. The Biggses, that eye seemed to say, were loath to war upon women, but if the women asked for it they could be men of iron, ruthless. "Might I ask who this lady is?"

"This is our president."

"Happy to meet you, ma'am."

"Miss Ukridge," added Mr. Prout, completing the introduction.

The name appeared to strike a chord in Mr. Biggs. He bent forward and a gleam of triumph came into his eyes.

"Ukridge, did you say?"

"Miss Julia Ukridge."

"Then it's all right," said Mr. Biggs, briskly. "There's been no mistake. I bought our tickets from a gentleman named Ukridge. I got seven hundred at five bob apiece, reduction for taking a quantity and ten per cent. discount for cash. If Mr. Ukridge acted contrary to instructions, it's too late to remedy the matter now. You should have made it clear to him what you wanted him to do before he went and did it."

And with this extremely sound sentiment the honorary secretary of the Warner's Stores Social and Outing Club turned on the heel of his shining dancing-pump and was gone. And I, too, sauntered away. There seemed nothing to keep me. As I went, I looked over my shoulder. The author of *Grey Myrtles* appeared to be entering upon the opening stages of what promised to be a painful tête-à-tête. My heart bled for him. If ever a man was blameless Mr. Prout was, but the president of the Pen and Ink Club was not the woman to allow a trifle like that to stand in her way.

"Oh, it just came to me, laddie," said Stanley Featherstonehaugh Ukridge modestly, interviewed later by our representive. "You know me. One moment mind a blank, then—*bing!*—some dashed colossal idea. It was your showing me that ticket for the dance that set me thinking. And I happened to meet a bloke in a pub who worked in Warner's Stores. Nice fellow, with a fair amount of pimples. Told me their Social and Outing Club was working up for its semi-annual beano. One thing led to another, I got him to introduce me to the hon. sec., and we came to terms. I liked the man, laddie. Great treat to meet a bloke with a good, level business head. We settled the details in no time. Well, I don't mind telling you, Corky my boy, that at last for the first time in many years I begin to see my way clear. I've got a bit of capital now. After sending poor little Dora her hundred, I shall have at least fifty quid left over. Fifty quid! My dear old son, you may take it from me that there's no limit—absolutely no limit—to what I can accomplish with fifty o'goblins in my kick. From now on I see my way clear. My feet are on solid ground. The world, laddie, is my oyster. Nothing can stop me from making a colossal fortune. I'm not exaggerating, old horse—a colossal fortune. Why, by a year from now I calculate, at a conservative estimate——"

Our representative then withdrew.

NO WEDDING BELLS FOR HIM

TO Ukridge, as might be expected from one of his sunny optimism, the whole affair has long since come to present itself in the light of yet another proof of the way in which all things in this world of ours work together for good. In it, from start to finish, he sees the finger of Providence; and, when marshalling evidence to support his theory that a means of escape from the most formidable perils will always be vouchsafed to the righteous and deserving, this is the episode which he advances as Exhibit A.

The thing may be said to have had its beginning in the Haymarket one afternoon towards the middle of the summer. We had been lunching at my expense at the Pall Mall Restaurant, and as we came out a large and shiny car drew up beside the kerb, and the chauffeur, alighting, opened the bonnet and began to fiddle about in its interior with a pair of pliers. Had I been alone, a casual glance in passing would have contented me, but for Ukridge the spectacle of somebody else working always had an irresistible fascination, and, gripping my arm, he steered me up to assist him in giving the toiler moral support. About two minutes after he had started to breathe earnestly on the man's neck, the latter, seeming to become aware that what was tickling his back hair was not some wandering June zephyr, looked up with a certain petulance.

" 'Ere!" he said, protestingly. Then his annoyance gave place to something which—for a chauffeur—approached cordiality. " 'Ullo!" he observed.

"Why, hallo, Frederick," said Ukridge. "Didn't recognise you. Is this the new car?"

"Ah," nodded the chauffeur.

"Pal of mine," explained Ukridge to me in a brief aside. "Met him in a pub." London was congested with pals whom Ukridge had met in pubs. "What's the trouble?"

"Missing," said Frederick the chauffeur. "Soon 'ave her right."

His confidence in his skill was not misplaced. After a short interval he straightened himself, closed the bonnet, and wiped his hands.

"Nice day," he said.

"Terrific," agreed Ukridge. "Where are you off to?"

"Got to go to Addington. Pick up the guv'nor, playin' golf there." He seemed to hesitate for a moment, then the mellowing influence of the summer sunshine asserted itself. "Like a ride as far as East Croydon? Get a train back from there."

It was a handsome offer, and one which neither Ukridge nor myself felt disposed to decline. We climbed in, Frederick trod on the self-starter, and off we bowled, two gentlemen of fashion taking their afternoon airing. Speaking for myself, I felt tranquil and debonair, and I have no reason to suppose that Ukridge was otherwise. The deplorable incident which now occurred was thus rendered doubly distressing. We had stopped at the foot of the street to allow the north-bound traffic to pass, when our pleasant after-luncheon torpidity was shattered by a sudden and violent shout.

"Hi!"

That the shouter was addressing us there was no room for doubt. He was standing on the pavement not four feet away, glaring unmistakably into our costly tonneau—a stout, bearded man of middle age, unsuitably clad, considering the weather and the sartorial prejudices of Society, in a frock-coat and a bowler hat. "Hi! You!" he bellowed, to the scandal of all good passers-by.

Frederick the chauffeur, after one swift glance of god-like disdain out of the corner of his left eye, had ceased to interest himself in this undignified exhibition on the part of one of the lower orders, but I was surprised to observe that Ukridge was betraying all the discomposure of some wild thing taken in a trap. His face had turned crimson and assumed a bulbous expression, and he was staring straight ahead of him with a piteous effort to ignore what manifestly would not be ignored.

"I'd like a word with you," boomed the bearded one.

And then matters proceeded with a good deal of rapidity. The traffic had begun to move on now, and

as we moved with it, travelling with increasing speed,
the man appeared to realise that if 'twere done 'twere
well 'twere done quickly. He executed a cumbersome
leap and landed on our running-board; and Ukridge,
coming suddenly to life, put out a large flat hand and
pushed. The intruder dropped off, and the last I saw
of him he was standing in the middle of the road,
shaking his fist, in imminent danger of being run over
by a number three omnibus.

"Gosh!" sighed Ukridge, with some feverishness.

"What was it all about?" I enquired.

"Bloke I owe a bit of money to," explained Ukridge,
tersely.

"Ah!" I said, feeling that all had been made clear.
I had never before actually seen one of Ukridge's
creditors in action, but he had frequently given me to
understand that they lurked all over London like
leopards in the jungle, waiting to spring on him.
There were certain streets down which he would never
walk for fear of what might befall.

"Been trailing me like a bloodhound for two years,"
said Ukridge. "Keeps bobbing up when I don't expect him and turning my hair white to the roots."

I was willing to hear more, and even hinted as much,
but he relapsed into a moody silence. We were moving at a brisk clip into Clapham Common when the
second of the incidents occurred which were to make
this drive linger in the memory. Just as we came in
sight of the Common, a fool of a girl loomed up right
before our front wheels. She had been crossing the
road, and now, after the manner of her species, she

lost her head. She was a large, silly-looking girl, and she darted to and fro like a lunatic hen; and as Ukridge and I rose simultaneously from our seats, clutching each other in agony, she tripped over her feet and fell. But Frederick, master of his craft, had the situation well in hand. He made an inspired swerve, and when we stopped a moment later, the girl was picking herself up, dusty, but still in one piece.

These happenings affect different men in different ways. In Frederick's cold grey eye as he looked over his shoulder and backed the car there was only the weary scorn of a superman for the never-ending follies of a woollen-headed proletariat. I, on the other hand, had reacted in a gust of nervous profanity. And Ukridge, I perceived as I grew calmer, the affair had touched on his chivalrous side. All the time we were backing he was mumbling to himself, and he was out of the car, bleating apologies, almost before we had stopped.

"Awfully sorry. Might have killed you. Can't forgive myself."

The girl treated the affair in still another way. She giggled. And somehow that brainless laugh afflicted me more than anything that had gone before. It was not her fault, I suppose. This untimely mirth was merely due to disordered nerves. But I had taken a prejudice against her at first sight.

"I do hope," babbled Ukridge, "you aren't hurt? Do tell me you aren't hurt."

The girl giggled again. And she was at least twelve

pounds too heavy to be a giggler.   I wanted to pass on and forget her.

"No, reely, thanks."

"But shaken, what?"

"I did come down a fair old bang," chuckled this repellent female.

"I thought so. I was afraid so. Shaken. Ganglions vibrating. You must let me drive you home."

"Oh, it doesn't matter."

"I insist.   Positively I insist!"

" 'Ere!" said Frederick the chauffeur, in a low, compelling voice.

"Eh?"

"Got to get on to Addington."

"Yes, yes, yes," said Ukridge, with testy impatience, quite the seigneur resenting interference from an underling. "But there's plenty of time to drive this lady home. Can't you see she's shaken? Where can I take you?"

"It's only just round the corner in the next street. Balbriggan the name of the house is."

"Balbriggan, Frederick, in the next street," said Ukridge, in a tone that brooked no argument.

I suppose the spectacle of the daughter of the house rolling up to the front door in a Daimler is unusual in Peabody Road, Clapham Common. At any rate, we had hardly drawn up when Balbriggan began to exude its occupants in platoons. Father, mother, three small sisters, and a brace of brothers were on the steps in the first ten seconds. They surged down the garden path in a solid mass.

Ukridge was at his most spacious. Quickly establishing himself on the footing of a friend of the family, he took charge of the whole affair. Introductions sped to and fro, and in a few moving words he explained the situation, while I remained mute and insignificant in my corner and Frederick the chauffeur stared at his oil-gauge with a fathomless eye.

"Couldn't have forgiven myself, Mr. Price, if anything had happened to Miss Price. Fortunately my chauffeur is an excellent driver and swerved just in time. You showed great presence of mind, Frederick," said Ukridge, handsomely, "great presence of mind."

Frederick continued to gaze aloofly at his oil-gauge.

"What a lovely car, Mr. Ukridge!" said the mother of the family.

"Yes?" said Ukridge, airly. "Yes, quite a good old machine."

"Can you drive yourself?" asked the smaller of the two small brothers, reverently.

"Oh, yes. Yes. But I generally use Frederick for town work."

"Would you and your friend care to come in for a cup of tea?" said Mrs. Price.

I could see Ukridge hesitate. He had only recently finished an excellent lunch, but there was that about the offer of a free meal which never failed to touch a chord in him. At this point, however, Frederick spoke.

" 'Ere!" said Frederick.

"Eh?"

"Got to get on to Addington," said Frederick, firmly.

Ukridge started as one waked from a dream. I really believe he had succeeded in persuading himself that the car belonged to him.

"Of course, yes. I was forgetting. I have to be at Addington almost immediately. Promised to pick up some golfing friends. Some other time, eh?"

"Any time you're in the neighbourhood, Mr. Ukridge," said Mr. Price, beaming upon the popular pet.

"Thanks, thanks."

"Tell me, Mr. Ukridge," said Mrs. Price. "I've been wondering ever since you told me your name. It's such an unusual one. Are you any relation to the Miss Ukridge who writes books?"

"My aunt," beamed Ukridge.

"No, really? I do love her stories so. Tell me——"

Frederick, whom I could not sufficiently admire, here broke off what promised to be a lengthy literary discussion by treading on the self-starter, and we drove off in a flurry of good wishes and invitations. I rather fancy I heard Ukridge, as he leaned over the back of the car, promising to bring his aunt round to Sunday supper some time. He resumed his seat as we turned the corner and at once began to moralise.

"Always sow the good seed, laddie. Absolutely nothing to beat the good seed. Never lose the chance of establishing yourself. It is the secret of a successful life. Just a few genial words, you see, and here I am with a place I can always pop into for a bite when funds are low."

I was shocked at his sordid outlook, and said so. He rebuked me out of his larger wisdom.

"It's all very well to take that attitude, Corky my boy, but do you realise that a family like that has cold beef, baked potatoes, pickles, salad, blanc-mange, and some sort of cheese every Sunday night after divine service? There are moments in a man's life, laddie, when a spot of cold beef with blanc-mange to follow means more than words can tell."

It was about a week later that I happened to go to the British Museum to gather material for one of those brightly informative articles of mine which appeared from time to time in the weekly papers. I was wandering through the place, accumulating data, when I came upon Ukridge with a small boy attached to each hand. He seemed a trifle weary, and he welcomed me with something of the gratification of the shipwrecked mariner who sights a sail.

"Run along and improve your bally minds, you kids," he said to the children. "You'll find me here when you've finished."

"All right, Uncle Stanley," chorused the children. He winced a little. I had to give him credit for that.

"Those are the Price kids. From Clapham."

"I remember them."

"I'm taking them out for the day. Must repay hospitality, Corky my boy."

"Then you have really been inflicting yourself on those unfortunate people?"

"I have looked in from time to time," said Ukridge, with dignity.

"It's just over a week since you met them. How often have you looked in?"

"Couple of times, perhaps. Maybe three."

"To meals?"

"There was a bit of browsing going on," admitted Ukridge.

"And now you're Uncle Stanley!"

"Fine, warm-hearted people," said Ukridge, and it seemed to me that he spoke with a touch of defiance. "Made me one of the family right from the beginning. Of course, it cuts both ways. This afternoon, for instance, I got landed with those kids. But, all in all, taking the rough with the smooth, it has worked out distinctly on the right side of the ledger. I own I'm not over keen on the hymns after Sunday supper, but the supper, laddie, is undeniable. As good a bit of cold beef," said Ukridge, dreamily, "as I ever chewed."

"Greedy brute," I said, censoriously.

"Must keep body and soul together, old man. Of course, there are one or two things about the business that are a bit embarrassing. For instance, somehow or other they seem to have got the idea that that car we turned up in that day belongs to me, and the kids are always pestering me to take them for a ride. Fortunately I've managed to square Frederick, and he thinks he can arrange for a spin or two during the next few days. And then Mrs. Price keeps asking me to bring my aunt around for a cup of tea and a chat, and I haven't the heart to tell her that my aunt absolutely and finally disowned me the day after that business of the dance."

"You didn't tell me that."

"Didn't I? Oh, yes. I got a letter from her saying

that as far as she was concerned I had ceased to exist. I thought it showed a nasty, narrow spirit, but I can't say I was altogether surprised. Still, it makes it awkward when Mrs. Price wants to get matey with her. I've had to tell her that my aunt is a chronic invalid and never goes out, being practically bedridden. I find all this a bit wearing, laddie."

"I suppose so."

"You see," said Ukridge, "I dislike subterfuge."

There seemed no possibility of his beating this, so I left the man and resumed my researches.

After this I was out of town for a few weeks, taking my annual vacation. When I got back to Ebury Street, Bowles, my landlord, after complimenting me in a stately way on my sunburned appearance, informed me that George Tupper had called several times while I was away.

"Appeared remarkably anxious to see you, sir."

I was surprised at this. George Tupper was always glad—or seemed to be glad—to see an old school friend when I called upon him, but he rarely sought me out in my home.

"Did he say what he wanted?"

"No, sir. He left no message. He merely enquired as to the probable date of your return and expressed a desire that you would visit him as soon as convenient."

"I'd better go and see him now."

"It might be advisable, sir."

I found George Tupper at the Foreign Office, surrounded by important-looking papers.

"Here you are at last!" cried George, resentfully, it seemed to me. "I thought you were never coming back."

"I had a splendid time, thanks very much for asking," I replied. "Got the roses back to my cheeks."

George, who seemed far from his usual tranquil self, briefly cursed my cheeks and their roses.

"Look here," he said, urgently, "something's got to be done. Have you seen Ukridge yet?"

"Not yet. I thought I would look him up this evening."

"You'd better. Do you know what has happened? That poor ass has gone and got himself engaged to be married to a girl at Clapham!"

"What?"

"Engaged! Girl at Clapham! Clapham Common," added George Tupper, as if in his opinion that made the matter even worse.

"You're joking!"

"I'm not joking," said George peevishly. "Do I look as if I were joking? I met him in Battersea Park with her, and he introduced me. She reminded me," said George Tupper, shivering slightly, for that fearful evening had seared his soul deeply, "of that ghastly female in pink he brought with him the night I gave you two dinner at the Regent Grill—the one who talked at the top of her voice all the time about her aunt's stomach trouble."

Here I think he did Miss Price an injustice. She had struck me during our brief acquaintance as something of a blister, but I had never quite classed her with Battling Billson's Flossie.

"Well, what do you want me to do?" I asked, not, I think, unreasonably.

"You've got to think of some way of getting him out of it. I can't do anything. I'm busy all day."

"So am I busy."

"Busy my left foot!" said George Tupper, who in moments of strong emotion was apt to relapse into the phraseology of school days and express himself in a very un-Foreign Official manner. "About once a week you work up energy enough to write a rotten article for some rag of a paper on "Should Curates Kiss?" or some silly subject, and the rest of your time you loaf about with Ukridge. It is obviously your job to disentangle the poor idiot."

"But how do you know he wants to be disentangled? It seems to me you're jumping pretty readily to conclusions. It's all very well for you bloodless officials to sneer at the holy passion, but it's love, as I sometimes say, that makes the world go round. Ukridge probably feels that until now he never realised what true happiness could mean."

"Does he?" snorted George Tupper. "Well, he didn't look it when I met him. He looked like—well, do you remember when he went in for the heavy-weights at school and that chap in Seymour's house hit him in the wind in the first round? That's how he looked when he was introducing the girl to me."

I am bound to say the comparison impressed me. It is odd how these little incidents of one's boyhood linger in the memory. Across the years I could see Ukridge now, half doubled up, one gloved hand caressing his diaphragm, a stunned and horrified bewilderment in his eyes. If his bearing as an engaged man had reminded George Tupper of that occasion, it certainly did seem as if the time had come for his friends to rally round him.

"You seem to have taken on the job of acting as a sort of unofficial keeper to the man," said George. "You'll have to help him now."

"Well, I'll go and see him."

"The whole thing is too absurd," said George Tupper. "How can Ukridge get married to anyone! He hasn't a bob in the world."

"I'll point that out to him. He's probably overlooked it."

It was my custom when I visited Ukridge at his lodgings to stand underneath his window and bellow his name—upon which, if at home and receiving, he would lean out and drop me down his latchkey, thus avoiding troubling his landlady to come up from the basement to open the door. A very judicious proceeding, for his relations with that autocrat were usually in a somewhat strained condition. I bellowed now, and his head popped out.

"Hallo, laddie!"

It seemed to me, even at this long range, that there was something peculiar about his face, but it was not till I had climbed the stairs to his room that I was able to be certain. I then perceived that he had somehow managed to acquire a black eye, which, though past its first bloom, was still of an extraordinary richness.

"Great Scott!" I cried, staring at this decoration. "How and when?"

Ukridge drew at his pipe moodily.

"It's a long story," he said. "Do you remember some people named Price at Clapham——"

"You aren't going to tell me your fiancée has biffed you in the eye already?"

"Have you heard?" said Ukridge, surprised. "Who told you I was engaged?"

"George Tupper. I've just been seeing him."

"Oh, well, that saves a lot of explanation. Laddie," said Ukridge, solemnly, "let this be a warning to you. Never——"

I wanted facts, not moralisings.

"How did you get the eye?" I interrupted.

Ukridge blew out a cloud of smoke and his other eye glowed sombrely.

"That was Ernie Finch," he said, in a cold voice.

"Who is Ernie Finch? I've never heard of him."

"He's a sort of friend of the family, and as far as I can make out was going rather strong as regards Mabel till I came along. When we got engaged he was away, and no one apparently thought it worth while to tell him about it, and he came along one night and found me kissing her good-bye in the front garden. Observe how these things work out, Corky. The sight of him coming along suddenly gave Mabel a start, and she screamed; the fact that she screamed gave this man Finch a totally wrong angle on the situation; and this caused him, blast him, to rush up, yank off my glasses with one hand, and hit me with the other right in the eye. And before I could get at him the family were roused by Mabel's screeches and came out and separated us and explained that I was engaged to Mabel. Of course, when he heard that, the man apologised. And I wish you could have seen the beastly smirk he gave when he was doing it. Then there was a bit of a row and old Price forbade him the house. A fat lot of good that was? I've had to stay indoors ever since waiting for the colour-scheme to dim a bit."

"Of course," I urged, "one can't help being sorry for the chap in a way."

"*I* can," said Ukridge, emphatically. "I've reached the conclusion that there is not enough room in this world for Ernie Finch and myself, and I'm living in the hope of meeting him one of these nights down in a dark alley."

"You sneaked his girl," I pointed out.

"I don't want his beastly girl," said Ukridge, with ungallant heat.

"Then you really do want to get out of this thing?"

"Of course I want to get out of it."

"But, if you feel like that, how on earth did you ever let it happen?"

"I simply couldn't tell you, old horse," said Ukridge, frankly. "It's all a horrid blur. The whole affair was the most ghastly shock to me. It came absolutely out of a blue sky. I had never so much as suspected the possibility of such a thing. All I know is that we found ourselves alone in the drawing-room after Sunday supper, and all of a sudden the room became full of Prices of every description babbling blessings. And there I was!"

"But you must have given them something to go on."

"I was holding her hand. I admit that."

"Ah!"

"Well, my gosh, I don't see why there should have been such a fuss about that. What does a bit of hand-holding amount to? The whole thing, Corky, my boy, boils down to the question, Is any man safe? It's got so nowadays," said Ukridge, with a strong sense of injury, "that you've only to throw a girl a kindly word, and the next thing you know you're in the Lord Warden Hotel at Dover, picking the rice out of your hair."

"Well, you must own that you were asking for it. You rolled up in a new Daimler and put on enough dog for half a dozen millionaires. And you took the family for rides, didn't you?"

"Perhaps a couple of times."

"And talked about your aunt, I expect, and how rich she was?"

"I may have touched on my aunt occasionally."

"Well, naturally these people thought you were sent from heaven. The wealthy son-in-law." Ukridge projected himself from the depths sufficiently to muster up the beginnings of a faint smile of gratification at the description. Then his troubles swept him back again. "All you've got to do, if you want to get out of it, is to confess to them that you haven't a bob."

"But, laddie, that's the difficulty. It's a most unfor-

tunate thing, but, as it happens, I am on the eve of
making an immense fortune, and I'm afraid I hinted
as much to them from time to time."

"What do you mean?"

"Since I saw you last I've put all my money in a
bookmaker's business."

"How do you mean—all your money? Where did
you get any money?"

"You haven't forgotten the fifty quid I made selling
tickets for my aunt's dance? And I collected a bit
more here and there out of some judicious bets. So
there it is. The firm is in a small way at present, but
with the world full of mugs shoving and jostling one
another to back losers, the thing is a potential goldmine, and I'm a sleeping partner. It's no good my
trying to make these people believe I'm hard up. They
would simply laugh in my face and rush off and start
breach-of-promise actions. Upon my Sam, it's a little
hard! Just when I have my foot firmly planted on the
ladder of success, this has to happen." He brooded
in silence for awhile. "There's just one scheme that
occurred to me," he said at length. "Would you have
any objection to writing an anonymous letter?"

"What's the idea?"

"I was just thinking that, if you were to write them
an anonymous letter, accusing me of all sorts of
things—— Might say I was married already."

"Not a bit of good."

"Perhaps you're right," said Ukridge, gloomily, and
after a few minutes more of thoughtful silence I left

him.   I was standing on the front steps when I heard
him clattering down the stairs.

"Corky, old man!"

"Hallo?"

"I think I've got it," said Ukridge, joining me on
the steps.   "Came to me in a flash a second ago.   How
would it be if someone were to go down to Clapham
and pretend to be a detective making enquiries about
me?   Dashed sinister and mysterious, you know.   A
good deal of meaning nods and shakes of the head.
Give the impression that I was wanted for something or
other.   You get the idea?   You would ask a lot of
questions and take notes in a book——"

"How do you mean—*I* would?"

Ukridge looked at me in pained surprise.

"Surely, old horse, you wouldn't object to doing
a trifling service like this for an old friend?"

"I would, strongly.   And in any case, what would be
the use of my going?   They've seen me."

"Yes, but they wouldn't recognise you.   Yours,"
said Ukridge, ingratiatingly, "is an ordinary, meaning-
less sort of face.   Or one of those theatrical costumer
people would fit you out with a disguise——"

"No!" I said firmly.   "I'm willing to do anything
in reason to help you out of this mess, but I refuse to
wear false whiskers for you or anyone."

"All right then," said Ukridge, despondently; "in
that case, there's nothing to be——"

At this moment he disappeared.   It was so swiftly
done that he seemed to have been snatched up to
heaven.   Only the searching odour of his powerful

tobacco lingered to remind me that he had once been at my side, and only the slam of the front door told me where he had gone. I looked about, puzzled to account for this abrupt departure, and as I did so heard galloping footsteps and perceived a stout, bearded gentleman of middle age, clad in a frock-coat and a bowler hat. He was one of those men who, once seen, are not readily forgotten; and I recognised him at once. It was the creditor, the bloke Ukridge owed a bit of money to, the man who had tried to board our car in the Haymarket. Halting on the pavement below me, he removed the hat and dabbed at his forehead with a large coloured silk handkerchief.

"Was that Mr. Smallweed you were talking to?" he demanded, gustily. He was obviously touched in the wind.

"No," I replied, civilly. "No. Not Mr. Smallweed."

"You're lying to me, young man!" cried the creditor, his voice rising in a too-familiar shout. And at the words, as if they had been some magic spell, the street seemed suddenly to wake from slumber. It seethed with human life. Maids popped out of windows, areas disgorged landladies, the very stones seemed to belch forth excited spectators. I found myself the centre of attraction—and, for some reason which was beyond me, cast for the rôle of the villain of the drama. What I had actually done to the poor old man, nobody appeared to know; but the school of thought which held that I had picked his pocket and brutally assaulted him had the largest number of adherents, and there was a good deal of informal talk of lynching me. Fortunately a young man in a blue flannel suit, who had been one of the earliest arrivals on the scene, constituted himself a peacemaker.

"Come along, o' man," he said, soothingly, his arm weaving itself into that of the fermenting creditor. "You don't want to make yourself conspicuous, do you?"

"In there!" roared the creditor, pointing at the door.

The crowd seemed to recognise that there had been an error in its diagnosis. The prevalent opinion now was that I had kidnapped the man's daughter and was holding her prisoner behind that sinister door. The movement in favour of lynching me became almost universal.

"Now, now!" said the young man, whom I was beginning to like more every minute.

"I'll kick the door in!"

"Now, now! You don't want to go doing anything silly or foolish," pleaded the peacemaker. "There'll be a policeman along before you know where you are, and you'll look foolish if he finds you kicking up a silly row."

I must say that, if I had been in the bearded one's place and had had right so indisputably on my side, this argument would not have influenced me greatly, but I suppose respectable citizens with a reputation to lose have different views on the importance of colliding with the police, however right they may be. The creditor's violence began to ebb. He hesitated. He was plainly trying to approach the matter in the light of pure reason.

"You know where the fellow lives," argued the young man. "See what I mean? Meantersay, you can come and find him whenever you like."

This, too, sounded thin to me. But it appeared to convince the injured man. He allowed himself to be led away, and presently, the star having left the stage, the drama ceased to attract. The audience melted away. Windows closed, areas emptied themselves, and presently the street was given over once more to the cat lunching in the gutter and the coster hymning his Brussels sprouts.

A hoarse voice spoke through the letter-box.

"Has he gone, laddie?"

I put my mouth to the slit, and we talked together like Pyramus and Thisbe.

"Yes."

"You're sure?"

"Certain."

"He isn't lurking round the corner somewhere, waiting to pop out?"

"No. He's gone."

The door opened and an embittered Ukridge emerged.

"It's a little hard!" he said, querulously. "You would scarcely credit it, Corky, but all that fuss was about a measly one pound two and threepence for a rotten little clockwork man that broke the first time I wound it up. Absolutely the first time, old man! It's not as if it had been a tandem bicycle, an enlarging camera, a Kodak, and a magic lantern."

I could not follow him.

"Why should a clockwork man be a tandem bicycle and the rest of it?"

"It's like this," said Ukridge. "There was a bicycle and photograph shop down near where I lived a couple of years ago, and I happened to see a tandem bicycle there which I rather liked the look of. So I ordered it provisionally from this cove. Absolutely provisionally, you understand. Also an enlarging camera, a Kodak, and a magic lantern. The goods were to be delivered when I had made up my mind about them. Well, after about a week the fellow asks if there are any further particulars I want to learn before definitely buying the muck. I say I am considering the matter, and in the meantime will he be good enough to let me have that little clockwork man in his window which walks when wound up?"

"Well?"

"Well, damme," said Ukridge, aggrieved, "it didn't walk. It broke the first time I tried to wind it. Then a few weeks went by and this bloke started to make himself dashed unpleasant. Wanted me to pay him money! I reasoned with the blighter. I said: 'Now look here, my man, need we say any more about this? Really, I think you've come out of the thing extremely well. Which,' I said, 'would you rather be owed for? A clockwork man, or a tandem bicycle, an enlarging camera, a Kodak, and a magic lantern?' You'd think that would have been simple enough for the meanest intellect, but no, he continued to make a fuss, until finally I had to move out of the neighbourhood. Fortunately, I had given him a false name——"

"Why?"

"Just an ordinary business precaution," explained Ukridge.

"I see."

"I looked on the matter as closed. But ever since then he has been bounding out at me when I least expect him. Once, by Gad, he nearly nailed me in the middle of the Strand, and I had to leg it like a hare up Burleigh Street and through Covent Garden. I'd have been collared to a certainty, only he tripped over a basket of potatoes. It's persecution, damme, that's what it is—persecution!"

"Why don't you pay the man?" I suggested.

"Corky, old horse," said Ukridge, with evident disapproval of these fiscal methods, "talk sense. How can I pay the man? Apart from the fact that at this stage of my career it would be madness to start flinging money right and left, there's the principle of the thing!"

The immediate result of this disturbing episode was that Ukridge, packing his belongings in a small suitcase and reluctantly disgorging a week's rent in lieu of notice, softly and silently vanished away from his own lodgings and came to dwell in mine, to the acute gratification of Bowles, who greeted his arrival with a solemn joy and brooded over him at dinner the first night like a father over a long-lost son. I had often given him sanctuary before in his hour of need, and he settled down with the easy smoothness of an old campaigner. He was good enough to describe my little place as a home from home, and said that he had half a mind to stay on and end his declining years there.

I cannot say that this suggestion gave me the rapturous pleasure it seemed to give Bowles, who nearly dropped the potato dish in his emotion; but still I must say that on the whole the man was not an exacting guest. His practice of never rising before lunch-time ensured me those mornings of undisturbed solitude which are so necessary to the young writer if he is to give *Interesting Bits* of his best; and if I had work to do in the evenings he was always ready to toddle downstairs and smoke a pipe with Bowles, whom he seemed to find as congenial a companion as Bowles found him. His only defect, indeed, was the habit he had developed of looking in on me in my bedroom at all hours of the night to discuss some new scheme designed to relieve him of his honorable obligations to Miss Mabel Price, of Balbriggan, Peabody Road, Clapham Common. My outspoken remarks on this behaviour checked him for forty-eight hours, but at three o'clock on the Sunday morning that ended the first week of his visit light flashing out above my head told me that he was in again.

"I think, laddie," I heard a satisfied voice remark, as a heavy weight descended on my toes, "I think, laddie, that at last I have hit the bull's-eye and rung the bell. Hats off to Bowles, without whom I would never have got the idea. It was only when he told me the plot of that story he is reading that I began to see daylight. Listen, old man," said Ukridge, settling himself more comfortably on my feet, "and tell me if you don't think I am on to a good thing. About a couple of days before Lord Claude Tremaine was to marry Angela Bracebridge, the most beautiful girl in London——"

"What the devil are you talking about? And do you know what the time is?"

"Never mind the time, Corky my boy. To-morrow is the day of rest and you can sleep on till an advanced hour. I was telling you the plot of this Primrose Novelette thing that Bowles is reading."

"You haven't woken me up at three in the morning to tell me the plot of a rotten novelette!"

"You haven't been listening, old man," said Ukridge, with gentle reproach. "I was saying that it was this plot that gave me my big idea. To cut it fairly short, as you seem in a strange mood, this Lord Claude bloke, having had a rummy pain in his left side, went to see a doctor a couple of days before the wedding, and the doc. gave him the start of his young life by telling him that he had only six months to live. There's a lot more of it, of course, and in the end it turns out that the fool of a doctor was all wrong; but what I'm driving at is that this development absolutely put the bee on the wedding. Everybody sympathised with Claude and said it was out of the question that he could dream of getting married. So it suddenly occurred to me, laddie, that here was the scheme of a lifetime. I'm going to supper at Balbriggan to-morrow, and what I want you to do is simply to——"

"You can stop right there," I said, with emotion. "I know what you want me to do. You want me to come along with you, disguised in a top-hat and a stethoscope, and explain to these people that I am a

Harley Street specialist, and have been sounding you and have discovered that you are in the last stages of heart-disease."

"Nothing of the kind, old man, nothing of the kind. I wouldn't dream of asking you to do anything like that."

"Yes, you would, if you had happened to think of it."

"Well, as a matter of fact, since you mention it," said Ukridge, thoughtfully, "it wouldn't be a bad scheme. But if you don't feel like taking it on——"

"I don't."

"Well, then, all I want you to do is to come to Balbriggan at about nine. Supper will be over by then. No sense," said Ukridge, thoughtfully, "in missing supper. Come to Balbriggan at about nine, ask for me, and tell me in front of the gang that my aunt is dangerously ill."

"What's the sense in that?"

"You aren't showing that clear, keen intelligence of which I have often spoken so highly, Corky. Don't you see? The news is a terrible shock to me. It bowls me over. I clutch at my heart——"

"They'll see through it in a second."

"I ask for water——"

"Ah, that's a convincing touch. That'll make them realise you aren't yourself."

"And after awhile we leave. In fact, we leave as quickly as we jolly well can. You see what happens? I have established the fact that my heart is weak, and in a few days I write and say I've been looked over

and the wedding must unfortunately be off because——"

"Damned silly idea!"

"Corky my boy," said Ukridge gravely, "to a man
as up against it as I am no idea is silly that looks as
if it might work. Don't you think this will work?"

"Well, it might, of course," I admitted.

"Then I shall have a dash at it. I can rely on you
to do your part?"

"How am I supposed to know that your aunt is
ill?"

"Perfectly simple. They 'phoned from her house,
and you are the only person who knows where I'm
spending the evening."

"And will you swear that this is really all you want
me to do?"

"Absolutely all."

"No getting me there and letting me in for something foul?"

"My dear old man!"

"All right," I said. "I feel in my bones that something's going to go wrong, but I suppose I've got to
do it."

"Spoken like a true friend," said Ukridge.

At nine o'clock on the following evening I stood on
the steps of Balbriggan waiting for my ring at the
bell to be answered. Cats prowled furtively in the
purple dusk, and from behind a lighted window on the
ground floor of the house came the tinkle of a piano
and the sound of voices raised in one of the more
mournful types of hymn. I recognised Ukridge's

above the rest. He was expressing with a vigour
which nearly cracked the glass a desire to be as a
little child washed clean of sin, and it somehow seemed
to deepen my already substantial gloom. Long experience of Ukridge's ingenious schemes had given me
a fatalistic feeling with regard to them. With whatever fair prospects I started out to co-operate with
him on these occasions, I almost invariably found myself entangled sooner or later in some nightmare im-
broglio.

The door opened. A maid appeared.

"Is Mr. Ukridge here?"

"Yes, sir."

"Could I see him for a moment?"

I followed her into the drawing-room.

"Gentleman to see Mr. Ukridge, please," said the
maid, and left me to do my stuff.

I was aware of a peculiar feeling. It was a sort of
dry-mouthed panic, and I suddenly recognised it as the
same helpless stage-fright which I had experienced
years before on the occasion when, the old place presumably being short of talent, I had been picked on to
sing a solo at the annual concert at school. I gazed
upon the roomful of Prices, and words failed me.
Near the bookshelf against the wall was a stuffed sea-
gull of blackguardly aspect, suspended with out-
stretched wings by a piece of string. It had a gaping
gamboge beak and its eye was bright and sardonic.
I found myself gazing at it in a hypnotised manner. It
seemed to see through me at a glance.

It was Ukridge who came to the rescue. Incredibly

at his ease in this frightful room, he advanced to welcome me, resplendent in a morning-coat, patent-leather
shoes, and tie, all of which I recognised as my property.   As always when he looted my wardrobe, he
exuded wealth and respectability.

"Want to see me, laddie?"

His eye met mine meaningly, and I found speech.
We had rehearsed this little scene with a good deal of
care over the luncheon-table, and the dialogue began
to come back to me.   I was able to ignore the seagull
and proceed.

"I'm afraid I have serious news, old man," I said,
in a hushed voice.

"Serious news?" said Ukridge, trying to turn pale.

"Serious news!"

I had warned him during rehearsals that this was
going to sound uncommonly like a vaudeville cross-
talk act of the Argumentative College Chums type, but
he had ruled out the objection as far-fetched.   Nevertheless, that is just what it did sound like, and I found
myself blushing warmly.

"What is it?" demanded Ukridge, emotionally,
clutching me by the arm in a grip like the bite of a
horse.

"Ouch!" I cried.   "Your aunt!"

"My aunt?"

"They telephoned from the house just now," I proceeded, warming to my work, "to say that she had had
a relapse.   Her condition is very serious.   They want
you there at once.   Even now it may be too late."

"Water!" said Ukridge, staggering back and clawing at his waistcoat—or rather at my waistcoat, which I had foolishly omitted to lock up. "Water!"

It was well done. Even I, much as I wished that he would stop wrenching one of my best ties all out of shape, was obliged to admit that. I suppose it was his lifelong training in staggering under the blows of Fate that made him so convincing. The Price family seemed to be shaken to its foundations. There was no water in the room, but a horde of juvenile Prices immediately rushed off in quest of some, and meanwhile the rest of the family gathered about the stricken man, solicitous and sympathetic.

"My aunt! Ill!" moaned Ukridge.

"I shouldn't worry, o' man," said a voice at the door.

So sneering and altogether unpleasant was this voice that for a moment I almost thought that it must have been the sea-gull that had spoken. Then, turning, I perceived a young man in a blue flannel suit. A young man whom I had seen before. It was the peacemaker, the fellow who had soothed and led away the infuriated bloke to whom Ukridge owed a bit of money.

"I shouldn't worry," he said again, and looked malevolently upon Ukridge. His advent caused a sensation. Mr. Price, who had been kneading Ukridge's shoulder with a strong man's silent sympathy, towered as majestically as his five feet six would permit him.

"Mr. Finch," he said, "may I enquire what you are doing in my house?"

"All right, all right——"

"I thought I told you——"

"All right, all right," repeated Ernie Finch, who appeared to be a young man of character. "I've only come to expose an impostor."

"Impostor!"

"Him!" said young Mr. Finch, pointing a scornful finger at Ukridge.

I think Ukridge was about to speak, but he seemed to change his mind. As for me, I had edged out of the centre of things, and was looking on as inconspicuously as I could from behind a red plush sofa. I wished to dissociate myself entirely from the proceedings.

"Ernie Finch," said Mrs. Price, swelling, "what do you mean?"

The young man seemed in no way discouraged by the general atmosphere of hostility. He twirled his small moustache and smiled a frosty smile.

"I mean," he said, feeling in his pocket and producing an envelope, "that this fellow here hasn't got an aunt. Or, if he has, she isn't Miss Julia Ukridge, the well-known and wealthy novelist. I had my suspicions about this gentleman right from the first, I may as well tell you, and ever since he came to this house I've been going round making a few enquiries about him. The first thing I did was to write his aunt—the lady he says is his aunt—making out I wanted her nephew's address, me being an old school chum of his. Here's what she writes back—you can see it for yourselves if you want to: 'Miss Ukridge acknowledges receipt of Mr. Finch's letter, and in reply wishes to state that she has no nephew.' No nephew! That's plain enough, isn't it?" He raised a hand to

check comment. "And here's another thing," he proceeded. "That motor-car he's been swanking about
in. It doesn't belong to him at all. It belongs to a
man named Fillmore. I noted the number and made
investigations. This fellow's name isn't Ukridge at
all. It's Smallweed. He's a penniless imposter who's
been pulling all your legs from the moment he came
into the house; and if you let Mabel marry him you'll
be making the biggest bloomer of your lives!"

There was an awestruck silence. Price looked upon
Price in dumb consternation.

"I don't believe you," said the master of the house
at length, but he spoke without conviction.

"Then perhaps," retorted Ernie Finch, "you'll believe this gentleman. Come in, Mr. Grindlay."

Bearded, frock-coated, and sinister beyond words,
the creditor stalked into the room.

"You tell 'em," said Ernie Finch.

The creditor appeared more than willing. He fixed
Ukridge with a glittering eye, and his bosom heaved
with pent-up emotion.

"Sorry to intrude on a family on Sunday evening,"
he said, "but this young man told me I should find Mr.
Smallweed here, so I came along. I've been hunting
for him high and low for two years and more about
a matter of one pound two and threepence for goods
supplied."

"He owes you money?" faltered Mr. Price.

"He bilked me," said the creditor, precisely.

"Is this true?" said Mr. Price, turning to Ukridge.

Ukridge had risen and seemed to be wondering

whether it was possible to sidle unobserved from the room. At this question he halted, and a weak smile played about his lips.

"Well———" said Ukridge.

The head of the family pursued his examination no further. His mind appeared to be made up. He had weighed the evidence and reached a decision. His eyes flashed. He raised a hand and pointed to the door.

"Leave my house!" he thundered.

"Right-o!" said Ukridge, mildly.

"And never enter it again!"

"Right-o!" said Ukridge.

Mr. Price turned to his daughter.

"Mabel," he said, "this engagement of yours is broken. Broken, do you understand? I forbid you ever to see this scoundrel again. You hear me?"

"All right, pa," said Miss Price, speaking for the first and last time. She seemed to be of a docile and equable disposition. I fancied I caught a not-displeased glance on its way to Ernie Finch.

"And now, sir," cried Mr. Price, "go!"

"Right-o!" said Ukridge.

But here the creditor struck a business note.

"And what," he enquired, "about my one pound two and threepence?"

It seemed for a moment that matters were about to become difficult. But Ukridge, ever ready-witted, found the solution.

"Have you got one pound two and threepence on you, old man?" he said to me.

And with my usual bad luck I had.

We walked together down Peabody Road. Already Ukridge's momentary discomfiture had passed.

"It just shows, laddie," he said, exuberantly, "that one should never despair. However black the outlook, old horse, never, never despair. That scheme of mine might or might not have worked—one cannot tell. But, instead of having to go to all the bother of subterfuge, to which I always object, here we have a nice, clean-cut solution of the thing without any trouble at all." He mused happily for a moment. "I never thought," he said, "that the time would come when I would feel a gush of kindly feeling towards Ernie Finch; but, upon my Sam, laddie, if he were here now, I would embrace the fellow. Clasp him to my bosom, dash it!" He fell once more into a reverie. "Amazing, old horse," he proceeded, "how things work out. Many a time I've been on the very point of paying that blighter Grindlay his money, merely to be rid of the annoyance of having him always popping up, but every time something seemed to stop me. I can't tell you what it was—a sort of feeling. Almost as if one had a guardian angel at one's elbow guiding one. My gosh, just think where I would have been if I had yielded to the impulse. It was Grindlay blowing in that turned the scale. By Gad, Corky, my boy, this is the happiest moment of my life."

"It might be the happiest of mine," I said, churlishly, "if I thought I should ever see that one pound two and threepence again."

"Now, laddie, laddie," protested Ukridge, "these

are not the words of a friend. Don't mar a moment
of unalloyed gladness. Don't worry, you'll get your
money back.   A thousandfold!"

"When?"

"One of these days," said Ukridge, buoyantly.
"One of these days."

UKRIDGE ROUNDS A NASTY
CORNER

T HE late Sir Rupert Lakenheath, K.C.M.G.,C.B., M.V.O., was one of those men at whom their countries point with pride. Until his retirement on a pension in the year 1906, he had been governor of various insanitary outposts of the British Empire situated around the equator, and as such had won respect and esteem from all. A kindly editor of my acquaintance secured for me the job of assisting the widow of this great administrator to prepare his memoirs for publication; and on a certain summer afternoon I had just finished arraying myself suitably for my first call on her at her residence in Thurloe Square, South Kensington, when there was a knock at the door, and Bowles, my landlord, entered, bearing gifts.

These consisted of a bottle with a staring label and a large cardboard hat-box. I gazed at them blankly, for they held no message for me.

Bowles, in his ambassadorial manner, condescended to explain.

"Mr. Ukridge," he said, with the ring of paternal affection in his voice which always crept into it when speaking of that menace to civilisation, "called a moment ago, sir, and desired me to hand you these."

Having now approached the table on which he had placed the objects, I was enabled to solve the mystery of the bottle. It was one of those fat, bulging bottles, and it bore across its diaphragm in red letters the single word "PEPPO." Beneath this, in black letters, ran the legend, "It Bucks You Up." I had not seen Ukridge for more than two weeks, but at our last meeting, I remembered, he had spoken of some foul patent medicine of which he had somehow secured the agency. This, apparently, was it.

"But what's in the hat-box?" I asked.

"I could not say, sir," replied Bowles.

At this point the hat-box, which had hitherto not spoken, uttered a crisp, sailorly oath, and followed it up by singing the opening bars of "Annie Laurie." It then relapsed into its former moody silence.

A few doses of Peppo would, no doubt, have enabled me to endure this remarkable happening with fortitude and phlegm. Not having taken that specific, the thing had a devastating effect upon my nervous centres. I bounded back and upset a chair, while Bowles, his dignity laid aside, leaped silently towards the ceiling. It was the first time I had ever seen him lay off the mask, and even in that trying moment I could not help being gratified by the spectacle. It gave me one of those thrills that come once in a lifetime.

"For Gord's sake!" ejaculated Bowles.

"Have a nut," observed the hat-box, hospitably. "Have a nut."

Bowles's panic subsided.

"It's a bird, sir. A parrot!"

"What the deuce does Ukridge mean," I cried, becoming the outraged householder, "by cluttering up my rooms with his beastly parrots? I'd like that man to know——"

The mention of Ukridge's name seemed to act on Bowles like a soothing draught. He recovered his poise.

"I have no doubt, sir," he said, a touch of coldness in his voice that rebuked my outburst, "that Mr. Ukridge has good reasons for depositing the bird in our custody. I fancy he must wish you to take charge of it for him."

"He may wish it——" I was beginning, when my eye fell on the clock. If I did not want to alienate my employer by keeping her waiting, I must be on my way immediately.

"Put that hat-box in the other room, Bowles," I said. "And I suppose you had better give the bird something to eat."

"Very good, sir. You may leave the matter in my hands with complete confidence."

The drawing-room into which I was shown on arriving at Thurloe Square was filled with many mementoes of the late Sir Rupert's gubernatorial career. In addition the room contained a small and bewilderingly pretty girl in a blue dress, who smiled upon me pleasantly.

"My aunt will be down in a moment," she said, and for a few moments we exchanged commonplaces. Then the door opened and Lady Lakenheath appeared.

The widow of the administrator was tall, angular,

and thin, with a sun-tanned face of a cast so determined as to make it seem a tenable theory that in the years previous to 1906 she had done at least her share of the administrating. Her whole appearance was that of a woman designed by nature to instil law and order into the bosoms of boisterous cannibal kings. She surveyed me with an appraising glance, and then, as if reconciled to the fact that, poor specimen though I might be, I was probably as good as anything else that could be got for the money, received me into the fold by pressing the bell and ordering tea.

Tea had arrived, and I was trying to combine bright dialogue with the difficult feat of balancing my cup on the smallest saucer I had ever seen, when my hostess, happening to glance out of the window into the street below, uttered something midway between a sigh and a click of the tongue.

"Oh, dear! That extraordinary man again!"

The girl in the blue dress, who had declined tea and was sewing in a distant corner, bent a little closer over her work.

"Millie!" said the administratress, plaintively, as if desiring sympathy in her trouble.

"Yes, Aunt Elizabeth?"

"That man is calling again!"

There was a short but perceptible pause. A delicate pink appeared in the girl's cheeks.

"Yes, Aunt Elizabeth?" she said.

"Mr. Ukridge," announced the maid at the door.

It seemed to me that if this sort of thing was to continue, if existence was to become a mere series of

shocks and surprises, Peppo would have to be installed
as an essential factor in my life. I stared speechlessly
at Ukridge as he breezed in with the unmistakable air
of sunny confidence which a man shows on familiar
ground. Even if I had not had Lady Lakenheath's
words as evidence, his manner would have been enough
to tell me that he was a frequent visitor in her drawing-room; and how he had come to be on calling terms
with a lady so pre-eminently respectable it was beyond
me to imagine. I awoke from my stupor to find that
we were being introduced, and that Ukridge, for some
reason clear, no doubt, to his own tortuous mind but
inexplicable to me, was treating me as a complete
stranger. He nodded courteously but distantly, and I,
falling in with his unspoken wishes, nodded back.
Plainly relieved, he turned to Lady Lakenheath and
plunged forthwith into the talk of intimacy.

"I've got good news for you," he said. "News about
Leonard."

The alteration in our hostess's manner at these words
was remarkable. Her somewhat forbidding manner
softened in an instant to quite a tremulous fluttering.
Gone was the hauteur which had caused her but a
moment back to allude to him as "that extraordinary
man." She pressed tea upon him, and scones.

"Oh, Mr. Ukridge!" she cried.

"I don't want to rouse false hopes and all that sort
of thing, laddie—I mean, Lady Lakenheath, but upon
my Sam, I really believe I am on the track. I have
been making the most assiduous enquiries."

"How very kind of you!"

"No, no," said Ukridge, modestly.

"I have been so worried," said Lady Lakenheath, "that I have scarcely been able to rest."

"Too bad!"

"Last night I had a return of my wretched malaria."

At these words, as if he had been given a cue, Ukridge reached under his chair and produced from his hat, like some conjurer, a bottle that was own brother to the one he had left in my rooms. Even from where I sat I could read those magic words of cheer on its flaunting label.

"Then I've got the very stuff for you," he boomed. "This is what you want. Glowing reports on all sides. Two doses, and cripples fling away their crutches and join the Beauty Chorus."

"I am scarcely a cripple, Mr. Ukridge," said Lady Lakenheath, with a return of her earlier bleakness.

"No, no! Good heavens, no! But you can't go wrong by taking Peppo."

"Peppo?" said Lady Lakenheath, doubtfully.

"It bucks you up."

"You think it might do me good?" asked the sufferer, wavering. There was a glitter in her eye that betrayed the hypochondriac, the woman who will try anything once.

"Can't fail."

"Well, it is most kind and thoughtful of you to have brought it. What with worrying over Leonard——"

"I know, I know," murmured Ukridge, in a positively bedside manner.

"It seems so strange," said Lady Lakenheath, "that, after I had advertised in all the papers, someone did not find him."

"Perhaps someone did find him!" said Ukridge, darkly.

"You think he must have been stolen?"

"I am convinced of it. A beautiful parrot like Leonard, able to talk in six languages——"

"And sing," murmured Lady Lakenheath.

"—— *and* sing," added Ukridge, "is worth a lot of money. But don't you worry, old—er—don't you worry. If the investigations which I am conducting now are successful, you will have Leonard back safe and sound to-morrow."

"To-morrow?"

"Absolutely to-morrow. Now tell me all about your malaria."

I felt that the time had come for me to leave. It was not merely that the conversation had taken a purely medical turn and that I was practically excluded from it; what was really driving me away was the imperative necessity of getting out in the open somewhere and thinking. My brain was whirling. The world seemed to have become suddenly full of significant and disturbing parrots. I seized my hat and rose. My hostess was able to take only an absent-minded interest in my departure. The last thing I saw as the door closed was Ukridge's look of big-hearted tenderness as he leaned forward so as not to miss a syllable of his companion's clinical revelations. He was not actually patting Lady Lakenheath's hand and telling her to be a brave little woman, but short of that he appeared to be doing everything a man could do to show her that, rugged though his exterior might be, his heart was in the right place and aching for her troubles.

I walked back to my rooms. I walked slowly and pensively, bumping into lamp-posts and pedestrians. It was a relief, when I finally reached Ebury Street, to find Ukridge smoking on my sofa. I was resolved that before he left he should explain what this was all about, if I had to wrench the truth from him.

"Hallo, laddie!" he said. "Upon my Sam, Corky, old horse, did you ever in your puff hear of anything so astounding as our meeting like that? Hope you didn't mind my pretending not to know you. The fact is my position in that house—— What the dickens were you doing there, by the way?"

"I'm helping Lady Lakenheath prepare her husband's memoirs."

"Of course, yes. I remember hearing her say she was going to rope in someone. But what a dashed extraordinary thing it should be you! However, where was I? Oh, yes. My position in the house, Corky, is so delicate that I simply didn't dare risk entering into any entangling alliances. What I mean to say is, if we had rushed into each other's arms, and you had been established in the old lady's eyes as a friend of mine, and then one of these days you had happened to make a bloomer of some kind—as you well might, laddie—and got heaved into the street on your left ear —well, you see where I would be. I should be involved in your downfall. And I solemnly assure you, laddie, that my whole existence is staked on keeping in with that female. I *must* get her consent!"

"Her what?"

"Her consent. To the marriage."

"The marriage?"

Ukridge blew a cloud of smoke, and gazed through it sentimentally at the ceiling.

"Isn't she a perfect angel?" he breathed, softly.

"Do you mean Lady Lakenheath?" I asked, bewildered.

"Fool! No, Millie."

"Millie? The girl in blue?"

Ukridge sighed dreamily.

"She was wearing that blue dress when I first met her, Corky. And a hat with thingummies. It was on the Underground. I gave her my seat, and, as I hung over her, suspended by a strap, I fell in love absolutely in a flash. I give you my honest word, laddie, I fell in love with her for all eternity between Sloane Square and South Kensington stations. She got out at South Kensington. So did I. I followed her to the house, rang the bell, got the maid to show me in, and, once I was in, put up a yarn about being misdirected and coming to the wrong address and all that sort of thing. I think they thought I was looney or trying to sell life insurance or something, but I didn't mind that. A few days later I called, and after that I hung about, keeping an eye on their movements, met 'em everywhere they went, and bowed and passed a word and generally made my presence felt, and—

well, to cut a long story short, old horse, we're engaged.
I happened to find out that Millie was in the habit
of taking the dog for a run in Kensington Gardens
every morning at eleven, and after that things began
to move. It took a bit of doing, of course, getting
up so early, but I was on the spot every day and we
talked and bunged sticks for the dog, and—well, as
I say, we're engaged. She is the most amazing, wonderful girl, laddie, that you ever encountered in your
life."

I had listened to this recital dumbly. The thing was
too cataclysmal for my mind. It overwhelmed me.

"But——" I began.

"But," said Ukridge, "the news has yet to be broken
to the old lady, and I am striving with every nerve in
my body, with every fibre of my brain, old horse, to
get in right with her. That is why I brought her that
Peppo. Not much, you may say, but every little helps.
Shows zeal. Nothing like zeal. But, of course, what
I'm really relying on is the parrot. That's my ace
of trumps."

I passed a hand over my corrugated forehead.

"The parrot!" I said, feebly. "Explain about the
parrot." Ukridge eyed me with honest astonishment.

"Do you mean to tell me you haven't got on to
that? A man of your intelligence! Corky, you amaze
me. Why, I pinched it, of course. Or, rather, Millie
and I pinched it together. Millie—a girl in a million,
laddie!—put the bird in a string-bag one night when
her aunt was dining out and lowered it to me out
of the drawing-room window. And I've been keeping

it in the background till the moment was ripe for the
spectacular return. Wouldn't have done to take it
back at once. Bad strategy. Wiser to hold it in
reserve for a few days and show zeal and work up the
interest. Millie and I are building on the old lady's
being so supremely bucked at having the bird restored
to her that there will be nothing she won't be willing to
do for me."

"But what do you want to dump the thing in my
rooms for?" I demanded, reminded of my grievance.
"I never got such a shock as when that damned hat-box
began to back-chat at me."

"I am sorry, old man, but it had to be. I could
never tell that the old lady might not take it into
her head to come round to my rooms about something.
I'd thrown out—mistakenly, I realise now—an occasional suggestion about tea there some afternoon. So
I had to park the bird with you. I'll take it away
to-morrow."

"You'll take it away to-night!"

"Not to-night, old man," pleaded Ukridge. "First
thing to-morrow. You won't find it any trouble.
Just throw it a word or two every now and then and
give it a bit of bread dipped in tea or something, and
you won't have to worry about it at all. And I'll be
round by noon at the latest to take it away. May
Heaven reward you, laddie, for the way you have stood
by me this day!"

For a man like myself, who finds at least eight hours
of sleep essential if that schoolgirl complexion is to be
preserved, it was unfortunate that Léonard the parrot

should have proved to be a bird of high-strung temperament, easily upset. The experiences which he had
undergone since leaving home, had, I was to discover,
jarred his nervous system. He was reasonably tranquil during the hours preceding bedtime, and had
started his beauty-sleep before I myself turned in;
but at two in the morning something in the nature
of a nightmare must have attacked him, for I was
wrenched from slumber by the sound of a hoarse
soliloquy in what I took to be some native dialect.
This lasted without a break till two-fifteen, when he
made a noise like a steam-riveter for some moments;
after which, apparently soothed, he fell asleep again.
I dropped off at about three, and at three-thirty was
awakened by the strains of a deep-sea chanty. From
then on our periods of sleep never seemed to coincide.
It was a wearing night, and before I went out after
breakfast I left imperative instructions with Bowles
for Ukridge, on arrival, to be informed that, if anything went wrong with his plans for removing my
guest that day, the mortality statistics among parrots
would take an up-curve. Returning to my rooms in the
evening, I was pleased to see that this manifesto had
been taken to heart. The hat-box was gone, and
about six o'clock Ukridge appeared, so beaming and
effervescent that I understood what had happened before he spoke. "Corky my boy," he said, vehemently,
"this is the maddest, merriest day of all the glad New
Year, and you can quote me as saying so!"

"Lady Lakenheath has given her consent?"

"Not merely given it, but bestowed it blithely, jubilantly."

"It beats me," I said.

"What beats you?" demanded Ukridge, sensitive to the jarring note.

"Well, I don't want to cast any aspersions, but I should have thought the first thing she would have done would be to make searching enquiries about your financial position."

"My financial position? What's wrong with my financial position? I've got considerably over fifty quid in the bank, and I'm on the eve of making an enormous fortune out of this Peppo stuff."

"And that satisfies Lady Lakenheath?" I said, incredulously.

Ukridge hesitated for a moment.

"Well, to be absolutely frank, laddie," he admitted, "I have an idea that she rather supposes that in the matter of financing the venture my aunt will rally round and keep things going till I am on my feet."

"Your aunt! But your aunt has finally and definitely disowned you."

"Yes. To be perfectly accurate, she has. But the old lady doesn't know that. In fact, I rather made a point of keeping it from her. You see, I found it necessary, as things turned out, to play my aunt as my ace of trumps."

"You told me the parrot was your ace of trumps."

"I know I did. But these things slip up at the last moment. She seethed with gratitude about the bird, but when I seized the opportunity to ask her for her blessing I was shocked to see that she put her ears back and jibbed. Got that nasty steely look in her eyes and began to talk about clandestine meetings and things being kept from her. It was an occasion for the swiftest thinking, laddie. I got an inspiration. I played up my aunt. It worked like magic. It seems the old lady has long been an admirer of her novels, and has always wanted to meet her. She went down and out for the full count the moment I introduced my aunt into the conversation, and I have had no trouble with her since."

"Have you thought what is going to happen when they do meet? I can't see your aunt delivering a strik- ing testimonial to your merits."

"That's all right. The fact of the matter is, luck has stood by me in the most amazing way all through. It happens that my aunt is out of town. She's down at her cottage in Sussex finishing a novel, and on Saturday she sails for America on a lecturing tour."

"How did you find that out?"

"Another bit of luck. I ran into her new secretary, a bloke named Wassick, at the Savage smoker last Saturday. There's no chance of their meeting. When my aunt's finishing a novel, she won't read letters or telegrams, so it's no good the old lady trying to get a communication through to her. It's Wednesday now, she sails on Saturday, she will be away six months— why, damme, by the time she hears of the thing I shall be an old married man."

It had been arranged between my employer and myself during the preliminary negotiations that I

should give up my afternoons to the memoirs and that
the most convenient plan would be for me to present
myself at Thurloe Square daily at three o'clock. I
had just settled myself on the following day in the
ground-floor study when the girl Millie came in, carrying papers.

"My aunt asked me to give you these," she said.
"They are Uncle Rupert's letters home for the year
1889."

I looked at her with interest and something bordering on awe. This was the girl who had actually committed herself to the appalling task of going through
life as Mrs. Stanley Featherstonehaugh Ukridge—and,
what is more, seemed to like the prospect. Of such
stuff are heroines made.

"Thank you," I said, putting the papers on the
desk. "By the way, may I—I hope you will——
What I mean is, Ukridge told me all about it. I
hope you will be very happy."

Her face lit up. She really was the most delightful
girl to look at I ever met. I could not blame Ukridge
for falling in love with her.

"Thank you very much," she said. She sat in the
huge arm-chair, looking very small. "Stanley has
been telling me what friends you and he are. He is
devoted to you."

"Great chap!" I said heartily. I would have said
anything which I thought would please her. She
exercised a spell, this girl. "We were at school together."

"I know. He is always talking about it." She

looked at me with round eyes exactly like a Persian kitten's. "I suppose you will be his best man?" She bubbled with happy laughter. "At one time I was awfully afraid there wouldn't be any need for a best man. Do you think it was wrong of us to steal Aunt Elizabeth's parrot?"

"Wrong?" I said, stoutly. "Not a bit of it. What an idea!"

"She was terribly worried," argued the girl.

"Best thing in the world," I assured her. "Too much peace of mind leads to premature old age."

"All the same, I have never felt so wicked and ashamed of myself. And I know Stanley felt just like that, too."

"I bet he did!" I agreed, effusively. Such was the magic of this Dresden china child that even her preposterous suggestion that Ukridge possessed a conscience could not shake me.

"He's so wonderful and chivalrous and considerate."

"The very words I should have used myself!"

"Why, to show you what a beautiful nature he has, he's gone out now with my aunt to help her do her shopping."

"You don't say so!"

"Just to try to make it up to her, you see, for the anxiety we caused her."

"It's noble! That's what it is. Absolutely noble!"

"And if there's one thing in the world he loathes it is carrying parcels."

"The man," I exclaimed, with fanatical enthusiasm, "is a perfect Sir Galahad!"

"Isn't he? Why, only the other day——"

She was interrupted. Outside, the front door slammed. There came a pounding of large feet in the passage. The door of the study flew open, and Sir Galahad himself charged in, his arms full of parcels.

"Corky!" he began. Then, perceiving his future wife, who had risen from the chair in alarm, he gazed at her with a wild pity in his eyes, as one who has bad news to spring. "Millie, old girl," he said, feverishly, "we're in the soup!"

The girl clutched the table.

"Oh, Stanley, darling!"

"There is just one hope. It occurred to me as I was——"

"You don't mean that Aunt Elizabeth has changed her mind?"

"She hasn't yet. But," said Ukridge, grimly, "she's pretty soon going to, unless we move with the utmost despatch."

"But what has happened?"

Ukridge shed the parcels. The action seemed to make him calmer.

"We had just come out of Harrod's," he said, "and I was about to leg it home with these parcels, when she sprang it on me! Right out of a blue sky!"

"What, Stanley, dear? Sprang what?"

"This ghastly thing. This frightful news that she proposes to attend the dinner of the Pen and Ink Club on Friday night. I saw her talking to a pug-nosed female we met in the fruit, vegetable, birds, and pet dogs department, but I never guessed what they were talking about. She was inviting the old lady to that infernal dinner!"

"But, Stanley, why shouldn't Aunt Elizabeth go to the Pen and Ink Club dinner?"

"Because my aunt is coming up to town on Friday specially to speak at that dinner, and your aunt is going to make a point of introducing herself and having a long chat about me."

We gazed at one another silently. There was no disguising the gravity of the news. Like the coming together of two uncongenial chemicals, this meeting of aunt with aunt must inevitably produce an explosion. And in that explosion would perish the hopes and dreams of two loving hearts.

"Oh, Stanley! What can we do?"

If the question had been directed at me, I should have been hard put to it to answer; but Ukridge, that man of resource, though he might be down, was never out.

"There is just one scheme. It occurred to me as I was sprinting along the Brompton Road. Laddie," he proceeded, laying a heavy hand on my shoulder, "it involves your co-operation."

"Oh, how splendid!" cried Millie.

It was not quite the comment I would have made myself. She proceeded to explain.

"Mr. Corcoran is so clever. I'm sure, if it's anything that can be done, he will do it."

This ruled me out as a potential resister. Ukridge

I might have been able to withstand, but so potently had this girl's spell worked upon me that in her hands I was as wax.

Ukridge sat down on the desk, and spoke with a tenseness befitting the occasion.

"It's rummy in this life, laddie," he began in moralising vein, "how the rottenest times a fellow goes through may often do him a bit of good in the end. I don't suppose I have ever enjoyed any period of my existence less than those months I spent at my aunt's house in Wimbledon. But mark the sequel, old horse! It was while going through that ghastly experience that I gained a knowledge of her habits which is going to save us now. You remember Dora Mason?"

"Who is Dora Mason?" enquired Millie, quickly.

"A plain, elderly sort of female who used to be my aunt's secretary," replied Ukridge, with equal promptness.

Personally, I remembered Miss Mason as a rather unusually pretty and attractive girl, but I felt that it would be injudicious to say so. I contented myself with making a mental note to the effect that Ukridge, whatever his drawbacks as a husband, had at any rate that ready tact which is so helpful in the home.

"Miss Mason," he proceeded, speaking, I thought, in a manner a shade more careful and measured, "used to talk to me about her job from time to time. I was sorry for the poor thing, you understand, because hers was a grey life, and I made rather a point of trying to cheer her up now and then."

"How like you, dear!"

It was not I who spoke—it was Millie. She regarded her betrothed with shining and admiring eyes, and I could see that she was thinking that my description of him as a modern Galahad was altogether too tame.

"And one of the things she told me," continued Ukridge, "was that my aunt, though she's always speaking at these bally dinners, can't say a word unless she has her speech written for her and memorises it. Miss Mason swore solemnly to me that she had written every word my aunt had spoken in public in the last two years. You begin to get on to the scheme, laddie? The long and the short of it is that we must get hold of that speech she's going to deliver at the Pen and Ink Club binge. We must intercept it, old horse, before it can reach her. We shall thus spike her guns. Collar that speech, Corky, old man, before she can get her hooks on it, and you can take it from me that she'll find she has a headache on Friday night and can't appear."

There stole over me that sickening conviction that comes to those in peril that I was in for it.

"But it may be too late," I faltered, with a last feeble effort at self-preservation. "She may have the speech already."

"Not a chance. I know what she's like when she's finishing one of these beastly books. No distractions of any sort are permitted. Wassick, the secretary bloke, will have had instructions to send the thing to her by registered post to arrive Friday morning, so that she can study it in the train. Now, listen carefully, laddie, for I have thought this thing out to the last detail. My aunt is at her cottage at Market Deeping, in Sussex. I don't know how the trains go, but there's sure to be one that'll get me to Market Deeping to-night. Directly I arrive I shall send a wire to Wassick—signed 'Ukridge,' " said the schemer. "I have a perfect right to sign telegrams 'Ukridge,' " he added, virtuously, "in which I tell him to hand the speech over to a gentleman who will call for it, as arrangements have been made for him to take it down to the cottage. All you have to do is to call at my aunt's house, see Wassick—a splendid fellow, and just the sort of chump who won't suspect a thing—get the manuscript, and biff off. Once round the corner, you dump it in the nearest garbage-box, and all is well."

"Isn't he wonderful, Mr. Corcoran?" cried Millie.

"I can rely on you, Corky? You will not let me down over your end of the business?"

"You *will* do this for us, Mr. Corcoran, won't you?" pleaded Millie.

I gave one look at her. Her Persian kitten eyes beamed into mine—gaily, trustfully, confidently. I gulped.

"All right," I said, huskily.

A leaden premonition of impending doom weighed me down next morning as I got into the cab which was to take me to Heath House, Wimbledon Common. I tried to correct this shuddering panic, by telling myself that it was simply due to my recollection of what I had suffered at my previous visit to the place, but it refused to leave me. A black devil of apprehension sat on my shoulder all the way, and as I rang the front-door bell it seemed to me that this imp emitted a chuckle more sinister than any that had gone before. And suddenly as I waited there I understood.

No wonder the imp had chuckled! Like a flash I perceived where the fatal flaw in this enterprise lay. It was just like Ukridge, poor impetuous, woollen-headed ass, not to have spotted it; but that I myself should have overlooked it was bitter indeed. The simple fact which had escaped our joint attention was this—that, as I had visited the house before, the butler would recognise me. I might succeed in purloining the speech, but it would be reported to the Woman Up Top that the mysterious visitor who had called for the manuscript was none other than the loathly Mr. Corcoran of hideous memory—and what would happen then? Prosecution? Jail? Social ruin?

I was on the very point of retreating down the steps when the door was flung open, and there swept over me the most exquisite relief I have ever known.

It was a new butler who stood before me.

"Well?"

He did not actually speak the word, but he had a pair of those expressive, beetling eyebrows, and they said it for him. A most forbidding man, fully as grim and austere as his predecessor.

"I wish to see Mr. Wassick," I said firmly.

The butler's manners betrayed no cordiality, but he evidently saw that I was not to be trifled with. He led the way down that familiar hall, and presently I was in the drawing-room, being inspected once more by the six Pekingese, who, as on that other occasion, left their baskets, smelt me, registered disappointment, and made for their baskets again.

"What name shall I say, sir?"

I was not to be had like that.

"Mr. Wassick is expecting me," I replied, coldly.

"Very good, sir."

I strolled buoyantly about the room, inspecting this object and that. I hummed lightly. I spoke kindly to the Pekes.

"Hallo, you Pekes!" I said.

I sauntered over to the mantelpiece, over which was a mirror. I was gazing at myself and thinking that it was not such a bad sort of face—not handsome, perhaps, but with a sort of something about it—when of a sudden the mirror reflected something else.

That something was the figure of that popular novelist and well-known after-dinner speaker, Miss Julia Ukridge. "Good-morning," she said.

It is curious how often the gods who make sport of us poor humans defeat their own ends by overdoing the thing. Any contretemps less awful than this, however slightly less awful, would undoubtedly have left me as limp as a sheet of carbon paper, rattled and stammering, in prime condition to be made sport of. But as it was I found myself strangely cool. I had a subconscious feeling that there would be a reaction later, and that the next time I looked in a mirror I should find my hair strangely whitened, but for the moment I was unnaturally composed, and my brain buzzed like a circular-saw in an ice-box.

"How do you do?" I heard myself say. My voice seemed to come from a long distance, but it was steady and even pleasing in timbre.

"You wished to see me, Mr. Corcoran?"

"Yes."

"Then why," enquired Miss Ukridge, softly, "did you ask for my secretary?"

There was that same acid sub-tinkle in her voice which had been there at our previous battle in the same ring. But that odd alertness stood by me well.

"I understood that you were out of town," I said.

"Who told you that?"

"They were saying so at the Savage Club the other night." This seemed to hold her.

"Why did you wish to see me?" she asked, baffled by my ready intelligence.

"I hoped to get a few facts concerning your proposed lecture tour in America."

"How did you know that I was about to lecture in America?" I raised my eyebrows. This was childish.

"They were saying so at the Savage Club," I replied. Baffled again.

"I had an idea, Mr. Corcoran," she said, with a nasty gleam in her blue eyes, "that you might be the person alluded to in my nephew Stanley's telegram."

"Telegram?"

"Yes. I altered my plans and returned to London last night instead of waiting till this evening, and I had scarcely arrived when a telegram came, signed Ukridge, from the village where I had been staying. It instructed my secretary to hand over to a gentleman

who would call this morning the draft of the speech
which I am to deliver at the dinner of the Pen and
Ink Club. I assume the thing to have been some
obscure practical joke on the part of my nephew,
Stanley. And I also assumed, Mr. Corcoran, that you
must be the gentleman alluded to."

I could parry this sort of stuff all day.

"What an odd idea!" I said.

"You think it odd? Then why did you tell my
butler that my secretary was expecting you?"

It was the worst one yet, but I blocked it.

"The man must have misunderstood me. He
seemed," I added, loftily, "an unintelligent sort of
fellow."

Our eyes met in silent conflict for a brief instant,
but all was well. Julia Ukridge was a civilised woman,
and this handicapped her in the contest. For people
may say what they like about the artificialities of
modern civilisation and hold its hypocrisies up to
scorn, but there is no denying that it has one outstanding merit. Whatever its defects, civilisation pre-
vents a gently-bred lady of high standing in the literary
world from calling a man a liar and punching him on
the nose, however convinced she may be that he deserves it. Miss Ukridge's hands twitched, her lips
tightened, and her eyes gleamed bluely—but she restrained herself. She shrugged her shoulders.

"What do you wish to know about my lecture tour?"
she said.

It was the white flag.

Ukridge and I had arranged to dine together at

the Regent Grill Room that night and celebrate the
happy ending of his troubles. I was first at the tryst,
and my heart bled for my poor friend as I noted the
care-free way in which he ambled up the aisle to our
table. I broke the bad news as gently as I could, and
the man sagged like a filleted fish. It was not a cheery
meal. I extended myself as host, plying him with
rich foods and spirited young wines, but he would not
be comforted. The only remark he contributed to the
conversation, outside of scattered monosyllables, occurred as the waiter retired with the cigar-box.

"What's the time, Corky, old man?"

I looked at my watch.

"Just on half-past nine."

"About now," said Ukridge, dully, "my aunt is
starting to give the old lady an earful!"

Lady Lakenheath was never, even at the best of
times, what I should call a sparkling woman, but it
seemed to me, as I sat with her at tea on the following
afternoon, that her manner was more sombre than
usual. She had all the earmarks of a woman who has
had disturbing news. She looked, in fact, exactly like
a woman who has been told by the aunt of the man who
is endeavouring to marry into her respectable family
the true character of that individual.

It was not easy in the circumstances to keep the
ball rolling on the subject of the 'Mgomo-'Mgomos, but
I was struggling bravely, when the last thing happened
which I should have predicted.

"Mr. Ukridge," announced the maid.

That Ukridge should be here at all was astounding;

but that he should bustle in, as he did, with that same air of being the household pet which had marked his demeanour at our first meeting in this drawing-room, soared into the very empyrean of the inexplicable. So acutely was I affected by the spectacle of this man, whom I had left on the previous night a broken hulk, behaving with the ebullience of an honoured member of the family, that I did what I had been on the verge of doing every time I had partaken of Lady Laken-heath's hospitality—upset my tea.

"I wonder," said Ukridge, plunging into speech with the same old breezy abruptness, "if this stuff would be any good, Aunt Elizabeth."

I had got my cup balanced again as he started speaking, but at the sound of this affectionate address over it went again. Only a juggler of long experience could have manipulated Lady Lakenheath's miniature cups and saucers successfully under the stress of emotions such as I was experiencing.

"What is it, Stanley?" asked Lady Lakenheath with a flicker of interest.

They were bending their heads over a bottle which Ukridge had pulled out of his pocket.

"It's some new stuff, Aunt Elizabeth. Just put on the market. Said to be excellent for parrots. Might be worth trying."

"It is exceedingly thoughtful of you, Stanley, to have brought it," said Lady Lakenheath, warmly. "And I shall certainly try the effect of a dose if Leonard has another seizure. Fortunately, he seemed almost himself again this afternoon."

"Splendid!"

"My parrot," said Lady Lakenheath, including me in the conversation, "had a most peculiar attack last night. I cannot account for it. His health has always been so particularly good. I was dressing for dinner at the time, and so was not present at the outset of the seizure, but my niece, who was an eye-witness of what occurred, tells me he behaved in a most unusual way. Quite suddenly, it appears, he started to sing very excitedly; then, after awhile, he stopped in the middle of a bar and appeared to be suffering. My niece, who is a most warm-hearted girl, was naturally exceedingly alarmed. She ran to fetch me, and when I came down poor Leonard was leaning against the side of his cage in an attitude of complete exhaustion, and all he would say was, 'Have a nut!' He repeated this several times in a low voice, and then closed his eyes and tumbled off his perch. I was up half the night with him, but now he seems mercifully to have turned the corner. This afternoon he is almost his old bright self again, and has been talking in Swahili, always a sign that he is feeling cheerful."

I murmured my condolences and congratulations.

"It was particularly unfortunate," observed Ukridge, sympathetically, "that the thing should have happened last night, because it prevented Aunt Elizabeth going to the Pen and Ink Club dinner."

"What!" Fortunately I had set down my cup by this time.

"Yes," said Lady Lakenheath, regretfully. "And I had been so looking forward to meeting Stanley's

aunt there. Miss Julia Ukridge, the novelist. I have
been an admirer of hers for many years. But, with
Leonard in this terrible state, naturally I could not stir
from the house. His claims were paramount. I shall
have to wait till Miss Ukridge returns from America."

"Next April," murmured Ukridge, softly.

"I think, if you will excuse me now, Mr. Corcoran,
I will just run up and see how Leonard is."

The door closed.

"Laddie," said Ukridge, solemnly, "doesn't this just
show——"

I gazed at him accusingly.

"Did you poison that parrot?"

"Me? Poison the parrot? Of course I didn't poison
the parrot. The whole thing was due to an act of
mistaken kindness carried out in a spirit of the purest
altruism. And, as I was saying, doesn't it just show
that no little act of kindness, however trivial, is ever
wasted in the great scheme of things? One might have
supposed that when I brought the old lady that bottle
of Peppo the thing would have begun and ended there
with a few conventional words of thanks. But mark,
laddie, how all things work together for good. Millie,
who, between ourselves, is absolutely a girl in a million,
happened to think the bird was looking a bit off colour
last night, and with a kindly anxiety to do him a bit
of good, gave him a slice of bread soaked in Peppo.
Thought it might brace him up. Now, what they put
in that stuff, old man, I don't know, but the fact remains that the bird almost instantly became perfectly
pie-eyed. You have heard the old lady's account of the

affair, but, believe me, she doesn't know one half of it. Millie informs me that Leonard's behaviour had to be seen to be believed. When the old lady came down he was practically in a drunken stupor, and all to-day he has been suffering from a shocking head. If he's really sitting up and taking notice again, it simply means that he has worked off one of the finest hang-overs of the age. Let this be a lesson to you, laddie, never to let a day go by without its act of kindness. What's the time, old horse?"

"Getting on for five."

Ukridge seemed to muse for a moment, and a happy smile irradiated his face.

"About now," he said, complacently, "my aunt is out in the Channel somewhere. And I see by the morning paper that there is a nasty gale blowing up from the southeast!"

MEET MR. MULLINER

PRESENTING *Mr. Mulliner, angler, uncle, and raconteur extraordinary; also his nephew George, who stuttered into matrimony, his brother Wilfred who pronounced ffinch-ffarowmere with a capital F and practically turned his fiancée into a lobster; and a bevy of relatives who conduct themselves with precarious abandon.*

THE TRUTH ABOUT GEORGE

THE TRUTH ABOUT GEORGE

TWO men were sitting in the bar-parlour of the Angler's Rest as I entered it; and one of them, I gathered from his low, excited voice and wide gestures, was telling the other a story. I could hear nothing but an occasional "Biggest I ever saw in my life!" and "Fully as large as that!" but in such a place it was not difficult to imagine the rest; and when the second man, catching my eye, winked at me with a sort of humorous misery, I smiled sympathetically back at him.

The action had the effect of establishing a bond between us; and when the story-teller finished his tale and left, he came over to my table as if answering a formal invitation.

"Dreadful liars some men are," he said genially.

1

"Fishermen," I suggested, "are traditionally careless of the truth."

"He wasn't a fisherman," said my companion. "That was our local doctor. He was telling me about his latest case of dropsy. Besides"—he tapped me earnestly on the knee—"you must not fall into the popular error about fishermen. Tradition has maligned them. I am a fisherman myself, and I have never told a lie in my life."

I could well believe it. He was a short, stout, comfortable man of middle age, and the thing that struck me first about him was the extraordinary childlike candour of his eyes. They were large and round and honest. I would have bought oil stock from him without a tremor.

The door leading into the white dusty road opened, and a small man with rimless pince-nez and an anxious expression shot in like a rabbit and had consumed a gin and ginger-beer almost before we knew he was there. Having thus refreshed himself, he stood looking at us, seemingly ill at ease.

"N-n-n-n-n-n——" he said.

We looked at him inquiringly.

"N-n-n-n-n-n-ice d-d-d-d——"

His nerve appeared to fail him, and he vanished as abruptly as he had come.

"I think he was leading up to telling us that it was a nice day," hazarded my companion.

"It must be very embarrassing," I said "for a man with such a painful impediment in his speech to open conversation with strangers."

"Probably trying to cure himself. Like my nephew George. Have I ever told you about my nephew George?"

I reminded him that we had only just met, and that this was the first time I had learned that he had a nephew George.

"Young George Mulliner. My name is Mulliner. I will tell you about George's case —in many ways a rather remarkable one."

My nephew George (said Mr. Mulliner) was as nice a young fellow as you would ever wish to meet, but from childhood up he had been cursed with a terrible stammer. If he had had to earn his living, he would undoubtedly have found this affliction a great handicap, but fortunately his father had left him a comfortable income; and George spent a not unhappy life, residing in the village where he had been born and passing his days in the usual country sports and his evenings in doing cross-word puzzles. By the time he was thirty he knew more about Eli, the prophet, Ra, the Sun God, and the bird Emu than anybody else in the county except Susan Blake, the vicar's daughter, who had also taken up the solving of cross-word puzzles and was the first girl in Worcestershire to find out the meaning of "stearine" and "crepuscular."

It was his association with Miss Blake that first turned George's thoughts to a serious endeavour to cure himself of his stammer. Naturally, with this hobby in common, the young people saw a great deal of one another: for George was always looking in at the vicarage to ask her if she knew a word of seven letters meaning "appertaining to the profession of plumbing," and Susan was just as constant a caller at George's cosy little cottage—being frequently stumped, as girls will be, by words of eight letters signifying "largely used in the manufacture of poppet-valves." The consequence was that one evening, just after she had helped him out of a tight place with the word "disestablishmentarianism," the boy suddenly awoke to the truth and realised that she was all the world to him—or, as he put it to himself from force of habit, precious, beloved, darling, much-loved, highly esteemed or valued.

And yet, every time he tried to tell her so, he could get no farther than a sibilant gurgle which was no more practical use than a hiccup.

Something obviously had to be done, and George went to London to see a specialist.

"Yes?" said the specialist.

"I-I-I-I-I-I——" said George.

"You were saying——?"

"Woo-woo-woo-woo-woo-woo——"

"Sing it," said the specialist.

"S-s-s-s-s-s-s——?" said George, puzzled.

The specialist explained. He was a kindly man with moth-eaten whiskers and an eye like a meditative cod-fish.

"Many people," he said, "who are unable to articulate clearly in ordinary speech find themselves lucid and bell-like when they burst into song."

It seemed a good idea to George. He thought for a moment; then threw his head back, shut his eyes, and let it go in a musical baritone.

"I love a lassie, a bonny, bonny lassie," sang George. "She's as pure as the lily in the dell."

"No doubt," said the specialist, wincing a little.

"She's as sweet as the heather, the bonny purple heather—Susan, my Worcestershire bluebell."

"Ah!" said the specialist. "Sounds a nice girl. Is this she?" he asked, adjusting his glasses and peering at the photograph which George had extracted from the interior of the left side of his under-vest.

George nodded, and drew in breath.

"Yes, sir," he carolled, "that's my baby. No, sir, don't mean maybe. Yes, sir, that's my baby now. And, by the way, by the way, when I meet that preacher I shall say—'Yes, sir, that's my——'"

"Quite," said the specialist, hurriedly. He had a sensitive ear. "Quite, quite."

"If you knew Susie like I know Susie," George was beginning, but the other stopped him.

"Quite. Exactly. I shouldn't wonder. And now," said the specialist, "what precisely is the trouble? No," he added, hastily, as George inflated his lungs, "don't sing it. Write the particulars on this piece of paper."

George did so.

"H'm!" said the specialist, examining the screed. "You wish to woo, court, and become betrothed, engaged, affianced to this girl, but you find yourself unable, incapable, incompetent, impotent, and powerless. Every time you attempt it, your vocal cords fail, fall short, are insufficient, wanting, deficient. and go blooey."

George nodded.

"A not unusual case. I have had to deal with this sort of thing before. The effect of love on the vocal cords of even a normally eloquent subject is frequently deleterious. As regards the habitual stammerer, tests have shown that in ninety-seven point five six nine recurring of cases the divine passion reduces him to a condition where he sounds like a soda-water siphon trying to recite Gunga Din. There is only one cure."

"W-w-w-w-w——?" asked George.

"I will tell you. Stammering," proceeded the specialist, putting the tips of his fingers together and eyeing George benevolently, "is mainly mental and is caused by shyness, which is caused by the inferiority complex, which in its turn is caused by suppressed desires or introverted inhibitions or something. The advice I give to all young men who come in here behaving like soda-water siphons is to go out and make a point of speaking to at least three perfect strangers every day. Engage these strangers in conversation, persevering no matter how priceless a chump you may feel, and before many weeks are out you will find that the little daily dose has had its effect. Shyness will wear off, and with it the stammer."

And, having requested the young man—in a voice of the clearest timbre, free from all trace of impediment—to hand over a fee of five guineas, the specialist sent George out into the world.

The more George thought about the advice he had been given, the less he liked it. He shivered in the cab that took him to the station to catch the train back to East Wobsley. Like all shy young men, he had never hitherto looked upon himself as shy—preferring to attribute his distaste for the society of his fellows to some subtle rareness of soul. But now that the thing had been put squarely up to him, he was compelled to realise that in all essentials he was a perfect rabbit. The thought of accosting perfect strangers and forcing his conversation upon them sickened him.

But no Mulliner has ever shirked an unpleasant duty. As he reached the platform and strode along it to the train, his teeth were set, his eyes shone with an almost fanatical light of determination, and he intended before his journey was over to conduct three heart-to-heart chats if he had to sing every bar of them.

The compartment into which he had made

his way was empty at the moment, but just before the train started a very large, fierce-looking man got in. George would have preferred somebody a little less formidable for his first subject, but he braced himself and bent forward. And, as he did so, the man spoke.

"The wur-wur-wur-wur-weather," he said, "sus-sus-seems to be ter-ter-taking a tur-tur-turn for the ber-ber-better, der-doesn't it?"

George sank back as if he had been hit between the eyes. The train had moved out of the dimness of the station by now, and the sun was shining brightly on the speaker, illuminating his knobbly shoulders, his craggy jaw, and, above all, the shockingly choleric look in his eyes. To reply "Y-y-y-y-y-y-y-yes" to such a man would obviously be madness.

But to abstain from speech did not seem to be much better as a policy. George's silence appeared to arouse this man's worst passions. His face had turned purple and he glared painfully.

"I uk-uk-asked you a sus-sus-civil quk-quk-quk," he said, irascibly. "Are you d-d-d-d-deaf?"

All we Mulliners have been noted for our presence of mind. To open his mouth, point to his tonsils, and utter a strangled gurgle was with George the work of a moment.

The tension relaxed. The man's annoyance abated.

"D-d-d-dumb?" he said, commiseratingly. "I beg your p-p-p-p-pup. I t-t-trust I have not caused you p-p-p-p-pup. It m-must be tut-tut-tut-tut-tut not to be able to sus-sus-speak fuf-fuf-fuf-fuf-fluently."

He then buried himself in his paper, and George sank back in his corner, quivering in every limb.

To get to East Wobsley, as you doubtless know, you have to change at Ippleton and take the branch-line. By the time the train reached this junction, George's composure was somewhat restored. He deposited his belongings in a compartment of the East Wobsley train, which was waiting in a glued manner on the other side of the platform, and, finding that it would not start for some ten minutes, decided to pass the time by strolling up and down in the pleasant air.

It was a lovely afternoon. The sun was gilding the platform with its rays, and a gentle breeze blew from the west. A little brook ran tinkling at the side of the road; birds were singing in the hedgerows; and through the trees could be discerned dimly the noble façade of the County Lunatic Asylum. Soothed by his surroundings, George began to feel so refreshed that he regretted that in this wayside station there was no one present whom he could engage in talk.

It was at this moment that the distinguished-looking stranger entered the platform.

The newcomer was a man of imposing physique, simply dressed in pyjamas, brown boots, and a mackintosh. In his hand he carried a top-hat, and into this he was dipping his fingers, taking them out, and then waving them in a curious manner to right and left. He nodded so affably to George that the latter, though a little surprised at the other's costume, decided to speak. After all, he reflected, clothes do not make the man, and, judging from the other's smile, a warm heart appeared to beat beneath that orange-and-mauve striped pyjama jacket.

"N-n-n-n-nice weather," he said.

"Glad you like it," said the stranger. "I ordered it specially."

George was a little puzzled by this remark, but he persevered.

"M-might I ask wur-wur-what you are dud-doing?"

"Doing?"

"With that her-her-her-her-hat?"

"Oh, with this hat? I see what you mean. Just scattering largesse to the multitude," replied the stranger, dipping his fingers once more and waving them with a generous gesture. "Devil of a bore, but it's expected of a man in my position. The fact is," he said, linking his arm in George's and speaking in a confidential undertone, "I'm the Emperor of Abyssinia. That's my palace over there," he said, pointing through the trees. "Don't let it go any farther. It's not supposed to be generally known."

It was with a rather sickly smile that George now endeavoured to withdraw his arm from that of his companion, but the other would have none of this aloofness. He seemed to be in complete agreement with

Shakespeare's dictum that a friend, when found, should be grappled to you with hooks of steel. He held George in a vise-like grip and drew him into a recess of the platform. He looked about him, and seemed satisfied.

"We are alone at last," he said.

This fact had already impressed itself with sickening clearness on the young man. There are few spots in the civilised world more deserted than the platform of a small country station. The sun shone on the smooth asphalt, on the gleaming rails, and on the machine which, in exchange for a penny placed in the slot marked "Matches," would supply a package of wholesome butter-scotch—but on nothing else.

What George could have done with at the moment was a posse of police armed with stout clubs, and there was not even a dog in sight.

"I've been wanting to talk to you for a long time," said the stranger, genially.

"Huh-huh-have you?" said George.

"Yes. I want your opinion of human sacrifices."

George said he didn't like them.

"Why not?" asked the other, surprised.

George said it was hard to explain. He just didn't.

"Well, I think you're wrong," said the Emperor. "I know there's a school of thought growing up that holds your views, but I disapprove of it. I hate all this modern advanced thought. Human sacrifices have always been good enough for the Emperors of Abyssinia, and they're good enough for me. Kindly step in here, if you please."

He indicated the lamp-and-mop room, at which they had now arrived. It was a dark and sinister apartment, smelling strongly of oil and porters, and was probably the last place on earth in which George would have wished to be closeted with a man of such peculiar views. He shrank back.

"You go in first," he said.

"No larks," said the other, suspiciously.

"L-l-l-l-larks?"

"Yes. No pushing a fellow in and locking the door and squirting water at him through the window. I've had that happen to me before."

"Sus-certainly not."

"Right!" said the Emperor. "You're a gentleman and I'm a gentleman. Both gentlemen. Have you a knife, by the way? We shall need a knife."

"No. No knife."

"Ah, well," said the Emperor, "then we'll have to look about for something else. No doubt we shall manage somehow."

And with the debonair manner which so became him, he scattered another handful of largesse and walked into the lamproom.

It was not the fact that he had given his word as a gentleman that kept George from locking the door. There is probably no family on earth more nicely scrupulous as regards keeping its promises than the Mulliners, but I am compelled to admit that, had George been able to find the key, he would have locked the door without hesitation. Not being able to find the key, he had to be satisfied with banging it. This done, he leaped back and raced away down the platform. A confused noise within seemed to indicate that the Emperor had become involved with some lamps.

George made the best of the respite. Covering the ground at a high rate of speed, he flung himself into the train and took refuge under the seat.

There he remained, quaking. At one time he thought that his uncongenial acquaintance had got upon his track, for the door of the compartment opened and a cool wind blew in upon him. Then, glancing along the floor, he perceived feminine ankles. The relief was enormous, but even in his relief George, who was the soul of modesty, did not forget his manners. He closed his eyes.

A voice spoke.

"Porter!"

"Yes, ma'am?"

"What was all that disturbance as I came into the station?"

"Patient escaped from the asylum, ma'am."

"Good gracious!"

The voice would undoubtedly have spoken further, but at this moment the train began to move. There came the sound of a body descending upon a cushioned seat, and some little time later the rustling of a paper. The train gathered speed and jolted on.

George had never before travelled under the seat of a railway-carriage; and, though he belonged to the younger generation, which is supposed to be so avid of new experiences, he had no desire to do so now. He decided to emerge, and, if possible, to emerge with the minimum of ostentation. Little as he knew of women, he was aware that as a sex they are apt to be startled by the sight of men crawling out from under the seats of compartments. He began his manœuvres by poking out his head and surveying the terrain.

All was well. The woman, in her seat across the way, was engrossed in her paper. Moving in a series of noiseless wriggles, George extricated himself from his hiding-place and, with a twist which would have been impossible to a man not in the habit of doing Swedish exercises daily before breakfast, heaved himself into the corner seat. The woman continued reading her paper.

The events of the past quarter of an hour had tended rather to drive from George's mind the mission which he had undertaken on leaving the specialist's office. But now, having leisure for reflection, he realised that.

if he meant to complete his first day of the cure, he was allowing himself to run sadly behind schedule. Speak to three strangers, the specialist had told him, and up to the present he had spoken to only one. True, this one had been a pretty considerable stranger, and a less conscientious young man than George Mulliner might have considered himself justified in chalking him up on the score-board as one and a half or even two. But George had the dogged, honest Mulliner streak in him, and he refused to quibble.

He nerved himself for action, and cleared his throat.

"Ah-h'rm!" said George.

And, having opened the ball, he smiled a winning smile and waited for his companion to make the next move.

The move which his companion made was in an upwards direction, and measured from six to eight inches. She dropped her paper and regarded George with a pale-eyed horror. One pictures her a little in the position of Robinson Crusoe when he saw the footprint in the sand. She had been convinced that she was completely alone, and lo! out of space a voice had spoken to her. Her face worked, but she made no remark.

George, on his side, was also feeling a little ill at ease. Women always increased his natural shyness. He never knew what to say to them.

Then a happy thought struck him. He had just glanced at his watch and found the hour to be nearly four-thirty. Women, he knew, loved a drop of tea at about this time, and fortunately there was in his suitcase a full thermos-flask.

"Pardon me, but I wonder if you would care for a cup of tea?" was what he wanted to say, but, as so often happened with him when in the presence of the opposite sex, he could get no farther than a sort of sizzling sound like a cockroach calling to its young.

The woman continued to stare at him. Her eyes were now about the size of regulation standard golf-balls, and her breathing suggested the last stages of asthma. And it was at this point that George, struggling for speech, had one of those inspirations which frequently came to Mulliners. There flashed into his mind what the specialist had

told him about singing. Say it with music—
that was the thing to do.

He delayed no longer.

"Tea for two and two for tea and me for
you and you for me——"

He was shocked to observe his companion
turning Nile-green. He decided to make his
meaning clearer.

"I have a nice thermos. I have a full
thermos. Won't you share my thermos, too?
When skies are grey and you feel you are
blue, tea sends the sun smiling through. I
have a nice thermos. I have a full thermos.
May I pour out some for you?"

You will agree with me, I think, that no
invitation could have been more happily put,
but his companion was not responsive. With
one last agonised look at him, she closed her
eyes and sank back in her seat. Her lips
had now turned a curious grey-blue colour,
and they were moving feebly. She reminded
George, who, like myself, was a keen fisherman, of a newly-gaffed salmon.

George sat back in his corner, brooding.
Rack his brain as he might, he could think

of no topic which could be guaranteed to
interest, elevate, and amuse. He looked out
of the window with a sigh.

The train was now approaching the dear
old familiar East Wobsley country. He began
to recognise landmarks. A wave of sentiment
poured over George as he thought of Susan,
and he reached for the bag of buns which
he had bought at the refreshment room at
Ippleton. Sentiment always made him hungry.

He took his thermos out of the suit-case,
and, unscrewing the top, poured himself out
a cup of tea. Then, placing the thermos on
the seat, he drank.

He looked across at his companion. Her
eyes were still closed, and she uttered little
sighing noises. George was half inclined to
renew his offer of tea, but the only tune he
could remember was "Hard-Hearted Hannah,
the Vamp from Savannah," and it was
difficult to fit suitable words to it. He ate
his bun and gazed out at the familiar scenery.

Now, as you approach East Wobsley, the
train, I must mention, has to pass over some
points; and so violent is the sudden jerking
that strong men have been known to spill

their beer. George, forgetting this in his pre-occupation, had placed the thermos only a few inches from the edge of the seat. The result was that, as the train reached the points, the flask leaped like a live thing, dived to the floor, and exploded.

Even George was distinctly upset by the sudden sharpness of the report. His bun sprang from his hand and was dashed to fragments. He blinked thrice in rapid succession. His heart tried to jump out of his mouth and loosened a front tooth.

But on the woman opposite the effect of the untoward occurrence was still more marked. With a single piercing shriek, she rose from her seat straight into the air like a rocketing pheasant; and, having clutched the communication-cord, fell back again. Impressive as her previous leap had been, she excelled it now by several inches. I do not know what the existing record for the Sitting High-Jump is, but she undoubtedly lowered it; and if George had been a member of the Olympic Games Selection Committee, he would have signed this woman up immediately.

It is a curious thing that, in spite of the railway companies' sporting willingness to let their patrons have a tug at the extremely moderate price of five pounds a go, very few people have ever either pulled a communication-cord or seen one pulled. There is, thus, a widespread ignorance as to what precisely happens on such occasions.

The procedure, George tells me, is as follows: First there comes a grinding noise, as the brakes are applied. Then the train stops. And finally, from every point of the compass, a seething mob of interested onlookers begins to appear.

It was about a mile and a half from East Wobsley that the affair had taken place, and as far as the eye could reach the countryside was totally devoid of humanity. A moment before nothing had been visible but smiling cornfields and broad pasture-lands; but now from east, west, north, and south running figures began to appear. We must remember that George at the time was in a somewhat overwrought frame of mind, and his statements should therefore be accepted with caution; but he tells me that out of

the middle of a single empty meadow, entirely
devoid of cover, no fewer than twenty-seven
distinct rustics suddenly appeared, having
undoubtedly shot up through the ground.

The rails, which had been completely
unoccupied, were now thronged with so
dense a crowd of navvies that it seemed to
George absurd to pretend that there was any
unemployment in England. Every member
of the labouring classes throughout the country was so palpably present. Moreover, the
train, which at Ippleton had seemed sparsely
occupied, was disgorging passengers from
every door. It was the sort of mob-scene
which would have made David W. Griffith
scream with delight; and it looked, George
says, like Guest Night at the Royal Automobile Club. But, as I say, we must remember
that he was overwrought.

It is difficult to say what precisely would
have been the correct behaviour of your
polished man of the world in such a situation.
I think myself that a great deal of sang-froid
and address would be required even by the
most self-possessed in order to pass off such

a contretemps. To George, I may say at once, the crisis revealed itself immediately as one which he was totally incapable of handling. The one clear thought that stood out from the welter of his emotions was the reflection that it was advisable to remove himself, and to do so without delay. Drawing a deep breath, he shot swiftly off the mark.

All we Mulliners have been athletes; and George, when at the University, had been noted for his speed of foot. He ran now as he had never run before. His statement, however, that as he sprinted across the first field he distinctly saw a rabbit shoot an envious glance at him as he passed and shrug its shoulders hopelessly, I am inclined to discount. George, as I have said before, was a little over-excited.

Nevertheless, it is not to be questioned that he made good going. And he had need to, for after the first instant of surprise, which had enabled him to secure a lead, the whole nob was pouring across country after him; and dimly, as he ran, he could hear voices in the throng informally discussing the advisability of lynching him. Moreover, the field through which he was running, a moment before a bare expanse of green, was now black with figures, headed by a man with a beard who carried a pitchfork. George swerved sharply to the right, casting a swift glance over his shoulder at his pursuers. He disliked them all, but especially the man with the pitchfork.

It is impossible for one who was not an eye-witness to say how long the chase continued and how much ground was covered by the interested parties. I know the East Wobsley country well, and I have checked George's statements; and, if it is true that he travelled east as far as Little-Wigmarsh-in-the-Dell and as far west as Higgleford-cum-Wortlebury-beneath-the-Hill, he must undoubtedly have done a lot of running.

But a point which must not be forgotten is that, to a man not in a condition to observe closely, the village of Higgleford-cum-Wortle-bury-beneath-the-Hill might easily not have been   Higgleford-cum-Wortlebury-beneath-the-Hill at all, but another hamlet which in many respects closely resembles it. I need scarcely say that I allude to Lesser-Snods-bury-in-the-Vale.

Let us assume, therefore, that George, having touched Little-Wigmarsh-in-the-Dell, shot off at a tangent and reached Lesser-Snodsbury-in-the-Vale. This would be a considerable run. And, as he remembers flitting past Farmer Higgins's pigsty and the Dog and Duck at Pondlebury Parva and splashing through the brook Wipple at the point where it joins the River Wopple, we can safely assume that, wherever else he went, he got plenty of exercise.

But the pleasantest of functions must end, and, just as the setting sun was gilding the spire of the ivy-covered church of St. Barnabas the Resilient, where George as a child had sat so often, enlivening the tedium of the sermon by making faces at the choir-boys, a damp and bedraggled figure might have been observed crawling painfully along the High Street of East Wobsley in the direction of the cosy little cottage known to its builder as Chatsworth and to the village tradesmen as "Mulliner's."

It was George, home from the hunting-field.

Slowly George Mulliner made his way to the familiar door, and, passing through it, flung himself into his favourite chair. But a moment later a more imperious need than the desire to rest forced itself upon his attention. Rising stiffly, he tottered to the kitchen and mixed himself a revivifying whisky-and-soda. Then, refilling his glass, he returned to the sitting-room, to find that it was no longer empty. A slim, fair girl, tastefully attired in tailor-made tweeds, was leaning over the desk on which he kept his Dictionary of English Synonyms.

She looked up as he entered, startled.

"Why, Mr. Mulliner!" she exclaimed. "What has been happening? Your clothes are torn, rent, ragged, tattered, and your hair is all dishevelled, untrimmed, hanging loose or negligently, at loose ends!"

George smiled a wan smile.

"You are right," he said. "And, what is more, I am suffering from extreme fatigue, weariness, lassitude, exhaustion, prostration, and languor."

The girl gazed at him, a divine pity in her soft eyes.

"I'm so sorry," she murmured. "So very sorry, grieved, distressed, afflicted, pained, mortified, dejected, and upset."

George took her hand. Her sweet sympathy had effected the cure for which he had been seeking so long. Coming on top of the violent emotions through which he had been passing all day, it seemed to work on him like some healing spell, charm, or incantation. Suddenly, in a flash, he realised that he was no longer a stammerer. Had he wished at that moment to say, "Peter Piper picked a peck of pickled peppers," he could have done it without a second thought.

But he had better things to say than that.

"Miss Blake—Susan—Susie." He took her other hand in his. His voice rang out clear and unimpeded. It seemed to him incredible that he had ever yammered at this girl like an overheated steam-radiator. "It cannot have escaped your notice that I have long entertained towards you sentiments warmer and deeper than those of ordinary friendship. It is love, Susan, that has been animating my bosom. Love, first a tiny seed, has burgeoned in my heart till, blazing into flame, it has swept away on the crest of its wave my diffidence, my doubt, my fears, and my foreboding, and now, like the topmost topaz of some ancient tower, it cries to all the world in a voice of thunder: 'You are mine! My mate! Predestined to me since Time first began!' As the star guides the mariner when, battered by boiling billows, he hies him home to the haven of hope and happiness, so do you gleam upon me along life's rough road and seem to say, 'Have courage, George! I am here!' Susan, I am not an eloquent man—I cannot speak fluently as I could wish—but these simple words which you have just heard come from the heart, from the unspotted heart of an English gentleman. Susan, I love you. Will you be my wife, married woman, matron, spouse, help-meet, consort, partner or better half?"

"Oh, George!" said Susan. "Yes, yea, ay, aye! Decidedly, unquestionably, indubitably, incontrovertibly, and past all dispute!"

He folded her in his arms. And, as he did so, there came from the street outside—faintly, as from a distance—the sound of feet and voices. George leaped to the window. Rounding the corner, just by the Cow and Wheelbarrow public-house, licensed to sell ales, wines, and spirits, was the man with the pitchfork, and behind him followed a vast crowd.

"My darling," said George. "For purely personal and private reasons, into which I need not enter, I must now leave you. Will you join me later?"

"I will follow you to the ends of the earth," replied Susan, passionately.

"It will not be necessary," said George. "I am only going down to the coal-cellar. I shall spend the next half-hour or so there. If anybody calls and asks for me, perhaps you would not mind telling them that I am out."

"I will, I will," said Susan. "And, George, by the way. What I really came here for was to ask you if you knew a hyphenated word of nine letters, ending in k and signifying an implement employed in the pursuit of agriculture."

"Pitch-fork, sweetheart," said George.

"But you may take it from me, as one who knows, that agriculture isn't the only thing it is used in pursuit of."

And since that day (concluded Mr. Mulliner) George, believe me or believe me not, has not had the slightest trace of an impediment in his speech. He is now the chosen orator at all political rallies for miles around; and so offensively self-confident has his manner become that only last Friday he had his eye blacked by a hay-corn-and-feed merchant of the name of Stubbs. It just shows you, doesn't it?

A SLICE OF LIFE

A SLICE OF LIFE

THE conversation in the bar-parlour of the Anglers' Rest had drifted round to the subject of the Arts: and somebody asked if that film-serial, "The Vicissitudes of Vera," which they were showing down at the Bijou Dream, was worth seeing.

"It's very good," said Miss Postlethwaite, our courteous and efficient barmaid, who is a prominent first-nighter. "It's about this mad professor who gets this girl into his toils and tries to turn her into a lobster."

"Tries to turn her into a lobster?" echoed we, surprised.

"Yes, sir. Into *a* lobster. It seems he collected thousands and thousand of lobsters and mashed them up and boiled down the juice from their glands and was just going to inject it into this Vera Dalrymple's spinal column when Jack Frobisher broke into the house and stopped him."

"Why did he do that?"

"Because he didn't want the girl he loved to be turned into a lobster."

"What we mean," said we, "is why did the professor want to turn the girl into a lobster?"

"He had a grudge against her."

This seemed plausible, and we thought it over for a while. Then one of the company shook his head disapprovingly.

"I don't like stories like that," he said. "They aren't true to life."

"Pardon me, sir," said a voice. And we were aware of Mr. Mulliner in our midst.

"Excuse me interrupting what may be a private discussion," said Mr. Mulliner, "but I chanced to overhear the recent remarks, and you, sir, have opened up a subject on which I happen to hold strong views—to wit, the question of what is and what is not true to life. How can we, with our limited experience, answer that question? For all we know, at this very moment hundreds of young women all over the country may be in the process of being turned into lobsters. Forgive my warmth, but I have suffered a good deal from this sceptical attitude of mind which is so prevalent nowadays. I have even met people who refused to believe my story about my brother Wilfred, purely because it was a little out of the ordinary run of the average man's experience."

Considerably moved, Mr. Mulliner ordered a hot Scotch with a slice of lemon.

"What happened to your brother Wilfred? Was he turned into a lobster?"

"No," said Mr. Mulliner, fixing his honest blue eyes on the speaker, "he was not. It would be perfectly easy for me to pretend that he was turned into a lobster; but I have always made it a practice—and I always shall make it a practice—to speak nothing but the bare truth. My brother Wilfred simply had rather a curious adventure."

My brother Wilfred (said Mr. Mulliner) is the clever one of the family. Even as a boy he was always messing about with chemicals, and at the University he devoted his time entirely to research. The result was that while still quite a young man he had won an established reputation as the inventor of what are known to the trade as Mulliner's

Magic Marvels—a general term embracing the Raven Gipsy Face-Cream, the Snow of the Mountains Lotion, and many other preparations, some designed exclusively for the toilet, others of a curative nature, intended to alleviate the many ills to which the flesh is heir.

Naturally, he was a very busy man: and it is to this absorption in his work that I attribute the fact 'that, though—like all the Mulliners—a man of striking personal charm, he had reached his thirty-first. year without ever having been involved in an affair of the heart. I remember him telling me once that he simply had no time for girls.

But we all fall sooner or later, and these strong concentrated men harder than any. While taking a brief holiday one year at Cannes, he met a Miss Angela Purdue, who was staying at his hotel, and she bowled him over completely.

She was one of these jolly, outdoor girls; and Wilfred had told me that what attracted him first about her was her wholesome, sunburned complexion. In fact, he told Miss Purdue the same thing when, shortly after he had proposed and been accepted, she asked him in her girlish way what it was that had first made him begin to love her.

"It's such a pity," said Miss Purdue, "that sunburn fades so soon. I do wish I knew some way of keeping it."

Even in his moments of holiest emotion Wilfred never forgot that he was a business man.

"You should try Mulliner's Raven Gipsy Face-Cream," he said. "It comes in two sizes—the small (or half-crown) jar and the large jar at seven shillings and sixpence. The large jar contains three and a half times as much as the small jar. It is applied nightly with a small sponge before retiring to rest. Testimonials have been received from numerous members of the aristocracy and may be examined at the office by any bona-fide inquirer."

"Is it really good?"

"I invented it," said Wilfred, simply.

She looked at him adoringly.

"How clever you are! Any girl ought to be proud to marry you."

"Oh, well," said Wilfred, with a modest wave of his hand.

"All the same, my guardian is going to be terribly angry when I tell him we're engaged."

"Why?"

"I inherited the Purdue millions when my uncle died, you see, and my guardian has always wanted me to marry his son, Percy."

Wilfred kissed her fondly, and laughed a defiant laugh.

"Jer mong feesh der selar," he said lightly.

But, some days after his return to London, whither the girl had preceded him, he had occasion to recall her words. As he sat in his study, musing on a preparation to cure the pip in canaries, a card was brought to him.

"Sir Jasper ffinch-ffarrowmere, Bart.," he read. The name was strange to him.

"Show the gentleman in," he said. And presently there entered a very stout man with a broad pink face. It was a face whose natural expression should, Wilfred felt, have been jovial, but at the moment it was grave.

"Sir Jasper Finch-Farrowmere?" said Wilfred.

"ffinch-ffarrowmere," corrected the visitor, his sensitive ear detecting the capital letters.

"Ah, yes. You spell it with two small f's."

"Four small f's."

"And to what do I owe the honour——"

"I am Angela Purdue's guardian."

"How do you do? A whisky-and-soda?"

"I thank you, no. I am a total abstainer. I found that alcohol had a tendency to increase my weight, so I gave it up. I have also given up butter, potatoes, soups of all kinds, and—— However," he broke off, the fanatic gleam which comes into the eyes of all fat men who are describing their system of diet fading away, "this is not a social call, and I must not take up your time with idle talk. I have a message for you, Mr. Mulliner. From Angela."

"Bless her!" said Wilfred. "Sir Jasper, I love that girl with a fervour which increases daily."

"Is that so?" said the baronet. "Well, what I came to say was, it's all off."

"What?"

"All off. She sent me to say that she had thought it over and wanted to break the engagement."

Wilfred's eyes narrowed. He had not forgotten what Angela had said about this man wanting her to marry his son. He gazed piercingly at his visitor, no longer deceived by the superficial geniality of his appearance. He had read too many detective stories where the fat, jolly, red-faced man turns out a fiend in human shape to be a ready victim to appearances.

"Indeed?" he said, coldly. "I should prefer to have this information from Miss Purdue's own lips."

"She won't see you. But, anticipating this attitude on your part, I brought a letter from her. You recognise the writing?"

Wilfred took the letter. Certainly, the hand was Angela's, and the meaning of the words he read unmistakable. Nevertheless, as he handed the missive back, there was a hard smile on his face.

"There is such a thing as writing a letter under compulsion," he said.

The baronet's pink face turned mauve.

"What do you mean, sir?"

"What I say."

"Are you insinuating——"

"Yes, I am."

"Pooh, sir!"

"Pooh to you!" said Wilfred. "And, if you want to know what I think, you poor ffish, I believe your name is spelled with a capital F, like anybody else's."

Stung to the quick, the baronet turned on his heel and left the room without another word.

Although he had given up his life to chemical research, Wilfred Mulliner was no mere dreamer. He could be the man of action when necessity demanded. Scarcely had his visitor left when he was on his way to the Senior Test-Tubes, the famous chemists' club in St. James's. There, consulting Kelly's "County Families," he learnt that Sir Jasper's address was ffinch Hall in Yorkshire. He had found out all he wanted to know. It was at ffinch Hall, he decided, that Angela must now be immured.

For that she was being immured somewhere he had no doubt. That letter, he was positive, had been written by her under stress of threats. The writing was Angela's but he declined to believe that she was responsible

for the phraseology and sentiments. He remembered reading a story where the heroine
was forced into courses which she would not
otherwise have contemplated by the fact
that somebody was standing over her with
a flask of vitriol. Possibly this was what
that bounder of a baronet had done to Angela.

Considering this possibility, he did not
blame her for what she had said about him,
Wilfred, in the second paragraph of her note.
Nor did he reproach her for signing herself
"Yrs truly, A. Purdue." Naturally, when
baronets are threatening to pour vitriol down
her neck, a refined and sensitive young girl
cannot pick her words. This sort of thing
must of necessity interfere with the selection
of the *mot juste*.

That afternoon, Wilfred was in a train
on his way to Yorkshire. That evening, he
was in the ffinch Arms in the village of which
Sir Jasper was the squire. That night, he
was in the gardens of ffinch Hall, prowling
softly round the house, listening.

And presently, as he prowled, there came
to his ears from an upper window a sound

that made him stiffen like a statue and clench his hands till the knuckles stood out white under the strain.

It was the sound of a woman sobbing.

Wilfred spent a sleepless night, but by morning he had formed his plan of action. I will not weary you with a description of the slow and tedious steps by which he first made the acquaintance of Sir Jasper's valet, who was an habitué of the village inn, and then by careful stages won the man's confidence with friendly words and beer. Suffice it to say that, about a week later, Wilfred had induced this man with bribes to leave suddenly on the plea of an aunt's illness, supplying—so as to cause his employer no inconvenience—a cousin to take his place.

This cousin, as you will have guessed, was Wilfred himself. But a very different Wilfred from the dark-haired, clean-cut young scientist who had revolutionised the world of chemistry a few months before by proving that $H_2O + b3g4z7 - m9z8 = g6f5p3x$. Before leaving London on what he knew would be a dark and dangerous enterprise, Wilfred had

taken the precaution of calling in at a well-
known costumier's and buying a red wig.
He had also purchased a pair of blue spectacles: but for the *rôle* which he had now
undertaken these were, of course, useless.
A blue-spectacled valet could not but have
aroused suspicion in the most guileless baronet.
All that Wilfred did, therefore, in the way of
preparation, was to don the wig, shave off his
moustache, and treat his face to a light coating
of the Raven Gipsy Face-Cream. This done,
he set out for ffinch Hall.

Externally, ffinch Hall was one of those
gloomy, sombre country-houses which seem
to exist only for the purpose of having horrid
crimes committed in them. Even in his brief
visit to the grounds, Wilfred had noticed
fully half a dozen places which seemed incomplete without a cross indicating spot
where body was found by the police. It was the
sort of house where ravens croak in the front
garden just before the death of the heir, and
shrieks ring out from behind barred windows
in the night.

Nor was its interior more cheerful. And,
as for the personnel of the domestic staff,

that was less exhilarating than anything else about the place. It consisted of an aged cook who, as she bent over her cauldrons, looked like something out of a travelling company of "Macbeth," touring the smaller towns of the North, and Murgatroyd, the butler, a huge, sinister man with a cast in one eye and an evil light in the other.

Many men, under these conditions, would have been daunted. But not Wilfred Mulliner. Apart from the fact that, like all the Mulliners, he was as brave as a lion, he had come expecting something of this nature. He settled down to his duties and kept his eyes open, and before long his vigilance was rewarded.

One day, as he lurked about the dim-lit passage-ways, he saw Sir Jasper coming up the stairs with a laden tray in his hands. It contained a toast-rack, a half bot. of white wine, pepper, salt, veg., and in a covered dish something which Wilfred, sniffing cautiously, decided was a cutlet.

Lurking in the shadows, he followed the baronet to the top of the house. Sir Jasper paused at a door on the second floor. He knocked. The door opened, a hand was stretched forth, the tray vanished, the door closed, and the baronet moved away.

So did Wilfred. He had seen what he had wanted to see, discovered what he had wanted to discover. He returned to the servants' hall, and under the gloomy eyes of Murgatroyd began to shape his plans.

"Where you been?" demanded the butler, suspiciously.

"Oh, hither and thither," said Wilfred, with a well-assumed airiness.

Murgatroyd directed a menacing glance at him.

"You'd better stay where you belong," he said, in his thick, growling voice. "There's things in this house that don't want seeing."

"Ah!" agreed the cook, dropping an onion in the cauldron.

Wilfred could not repress a shudder.

But, even as he shuddered, he was conscious of a certain relief. At least, he reflected, they were not starving his darling. That cutlet had smelt uncommonly good: and, if the bill of fare was always maintained at this level, she had nothing to complain of in the catering.

But his relief was short-lived. What, after all, he asked himself, are cutlets to a girl who is imprisoned in a locked room of a sinister country-house and is being forced to marry a man she does not love? Practically nothing. When the heart is sick, cutlets merely alleviate, they do not cure. Fiercely Wilfred told himself that, come what might, few days should pass before he found the key to that locked door and bore away his love to freedom and happiness.

The only obstacle in the way of this scheme was that it was plainly going to be a matter of the greatest difficulty to find the key. That night, when his employer dined, Wilfred searched his room thoroughly. He found nothing. The key, he was forced to conclude, was kept on the baronet's person.

Then how to secure it?

It is not too much to say that Wilfred Mulliner was nonplussed. The brain which had electrified the world of Science by discovering that if you mixed a stiffish oxygen and potassium and added a splash of trinitrotoluol and a spot of old brandy you got something that could be sold in America as champagne at a hundred and fifty dollars the case, had to confess itself baffled.

To attempt to analyse the young man's emotions, as the next week dragged itself by, would be merely morbid. Life cannot, of course, be all sunshine: and in relating a story like this, which is a slice of life, one must pay as much attention to shade as to light: nevertheless, it would be tedious were I to describe to you in detail the soul-torments which afflicted Wilfred Mulliner as day followed day and no solution to the problem presented itself. You are all intelligent men, and you can picture to yourselves how a high-spirited young fellow, deeply in love, must have felt; knowing that the girl he loved was languishing in what practically amounted to a dungeon, though situated on an upper floor, and chafing at his inability to set her free.

His eyes became sunken. His cheek-bones stood out. He lost weight. And so noticeable was this change in his physique that Sir Jasper ffinch-ffarrowmere commented on it one evening in tones of unconcealed envy.

"How the devil, Straker," he said—for this was the pseudonym under which Wilfred was passing, "do you manage to keep so thin? Judging by the weekly books, you eat like a starving Esquimau, and yet you don't put on weight. Now I, in addition to knocking off butter and potatoes, have started drinking hot unsweetened lemon-juice each night before retiring: and yet, damme," he said —for, like all baronets, he was careless in his language, "I weighed myself this morning, and I was up another six ounces. What's the explanation?"

"Yes, Sir Jasper," said Wilfred, mechanically.

"What the devil do you mean, Yes, Sir Jasper?"

"No, Sir Jasper."

The baronet wheezed plaintively.

"I've been studying this matter closely," he said, "and it's one of the seven wonders of the world. Have you ever seen a fat valet? Of course not. Nor has anybody else. There is no such thing as a fat valet. And yet there is scarcely a moment during the day when a valet is not eating. He rises at six-thirty.

and at seven is having coffee and buttered toast. At eight, he breakfasts off porridge, cream, eggs, bacon, jam, bread, butter, more eggs, more bacon, more jam, more tea, and more butter, finishing up with a slice of cold ham and a sardine. At eleven o'clock he has his 'elevenses,' consisting of coffee, cream, more bread and more butter. At one, luncheon —a hearty meal, replete with every form of starchy food and lots of beer. If he can get at the port, he has port. At three, a snack. At four, another snack. At five, tea and buttered toast. At seven—dinner, probably with floury potatoes, and certainly with lots more beer. At nine, another snack. And at ten-thirty he retires to bed, taking with him a glass of milk and a plate of biscuits to keep himself from getting hungry in the night. And yet he remains as slender as a string-bean, while I, who have been dieting for years, tip the beam at two hundred and seventeen pounds, and am growing a third and supplementary chin. These are mysteries, Straker."

"Yes, Sir Jasper."

"Well, I'll tell you one thing," said the

baronet, "I'm getting down one of those indoor Turkish Bath cabinet-affairs from London; and if that doesn't do the trick, I give up the struggle."

The indoor Turkish Bath duly arrived and was unpacked; and it was some three nights later that Wilfred, brooding in the servants' hall, was aroused from his reverie by Murgatroyd.

"Here," said Murgatroyd, "wake up. Sir Jasper's calling you."

"Calling me what?" asked Wilfred, coming to himself with a start.

"Calling you very loud," growled the butler.

It was indeed so. From the upper regions of the house there was proceeding a series of sharp yelps, evidently those of a man in mortal stress. Wilfred was reluctant to interfere in any way if, as seemed probable, his employer was dying in agony; but he was a conscientious man, and it was his duty, while in this sinister house, to perform the work for which he was paid. He hurried up the stairs; and, entering Sir Jasper's bedroom, perceived the baronet's crimson face protruding from the top of the indoor Turkish Bath.

"So you've come at last!" cried Sir Jasper. "Look here, when you put me into this infernal contrivance just now, what did you do to the dashed thing?"

"Nothing beyond what was indicated in the printed pamphlet accompanying the machine, Sir Jasper. Following the instructions, I slid Rod A into Groove B, fastening with Catch C——"

"Well, you must have made a mess of it, somehow. The thing's stuck. I can't get out."

"You can't?" cried Wilfred.

"No. And the bally apparatus is getting considerably hotter than the hinges of the Inferno." I must apologise for Sir Jasper's language, but you know what baronets are. "I'm being cooked to a crisp."

A sudden flash of light seemed to blaze upon Wilfred Mulliner.

"I will release you, Sir Jasper——"

"Well, hurry up, then."

"On one condition." Wilfred fixed him with a piercing gaze. "First, I must have the key."

"There isn't a key, you idiot. It doesn't lock. It just clicks when you slide Gadget D into Thingummybob E."

"The key I require is that of the room in which you are holding Angela Purdue a prisoner."

"What the devil do you mean? Ouch!"

"I will tell you what I mean, Sir Jasper ffinch-ffarrowmere. I am Wilfred Mulliner!"

"Don't be an ass. Wilfred Mulliner has black hair. Yours is red. You must be thinking of someone else."

"This is a wig," said Wilfred. "By Clarkson." He shook a menacing finger at the baronet. "You little thought, Sir Jasper ffinch-ffarrowmere, when you embarked on this dastardly scheme, that Wilfred Mulliner was watching your every move. I guessed your plans from the start. And now is the moment when I checkmate them. Give me that key, you Fiend."

"ffiend," corrected Sir Jasper, automatically.

"I am going to release my darling, to take her away from this dreadful house, to marry her by special licence as soon as it can legally be done."

In spite of his sufferings, a ghastly laugh escaped Sir Jasper's lips.

"You are, are you!"

"I am."

"Yes, you are!"

"Give me the key."

"I haven't got it, you chump. It's in the door."

"Ha, ha!"

"It's no good saying 'Ha, ha!' It is in the door. On Angela's side of the door."

"A likely story! But I cannot stay here wasting time. If you will not give me the key, I shall go up and break in the door."

"Do!" Once more the baronet laughed like a tortured soul. "And see what she'll say."

Wilfred could make nothing of this last remark. He could, he thought, imagine very clearly what Angela would say. He could picture her sobbing on his chest, murmuring that she knew he would come, that she had never doubted him for an instant. He leapt for the door.

"Here! Hi! Aren't you going to let me out?"

"Presently," said Wilfred. "Keep cool." He raced up the stairs.

"Angela," he cried, pressing his lips against the panel. "Angela!"

"Who's that?" answered a well-remembered voice from within.

"It is I—Wilfred. I am going to burst open the door. Stand clear of the gates."

He drew back a few paces, and hurled himself at the woodwork. There was a grinding crash, as the lock gave. And Wilfred, staggering on, found himself in a room so dark that he could see nothing.

"Angela, where are you?"

"I'm here. And I'd like to know why you are, after that letter I wrote you. Some men," continued the strangely cold voice, "do not seem to know how to take a hint."

Wilfred staggered, and would have fallen had he not clutched at his forehead.

"That letter?" he stammered. "You surely didn't mean what you wrote in that letter?"

"I meant every word and I wish I had put in more."

"But—but—but—— But don't you love me, Angela?"

A hard, mocking laugh rang through the room.

"Love you? Love the man who recommended me to try Mulliner's Raven Gipsy Face-Cream!"

"What do you mean?"

"I will tell you what I mean. Wilfred Mulliner, look on your handiwork!"

The room became suddenly flooded with light. And there, standing with her hand on the switch, stood Angela—a queenly, lovely figure, in whose radiant beauty the sternest critic would have noted but one flaw—the fact that she was piebald.

Wilfred gazed at her with adoring eyes. Her face was partly brown and partly white, and on her snowy neck were patches of sepia that looked like the thumb-prints you find on the pages of books in the Free Library: but he thought her the most beautiful creature he had ever seen. He longed to fold her in his arms: and but for the fact that her eyes told him that she would undoubtedly land an upper-cut on him if he tried it he would have done so.

"Yes," she went on, "this is what you have made of me, Wilfred Mulliner—you and that awful stuff you call the Raven Gipsy

Face-Cream. This is the skin you loved to
touch! I took your advice and bought one
of the large jars at seven and six, and see
the result! Barely twenty-four hours after
the first application, I could have walked
into any circus and named my own terms as
the Spotted Princess of the Fiji Islands. I
fled here to my childhood home, to hide
myself. And the first thing that happened"
—her voice broke—"was that my favourite
hunter shied at me and tried to bite pieces
out of his manger: while Ponto, my little
dog, whom I have reared from a puppy,
caught one sight of my face and is now in
the hands of the vet. and unlikely to recover.
And it was you, Wilfred Mulliner, who
brought this curse upon me."

Many men would have wilted beneath
these searing words, but Wilfred Mulliner
merely smiled with infinite compassion and
understanding.

"It is quite all right," he said. "I should
have warned you, sweetheart, that this occasionally happens in cases where the skin is
exceptionally delicate and finely-textured. It

can be speedily remedied by an application of the Mulliner Snow of the Mountains Lotion, four shillings the medium-sized bottle."

"Wilfred! Is this true?"

"Perfectly true, dearest. And is this all that stands between us?"

"No!" shouted a voice of thunder.

Wilfred wheeled sharply. In the doorway stood Sir Jasper ffinch-ffarrowmere. He was swathed in a bath-towel, what was visible of his person being a bright crimson. Behind him, toying with a horse-whip, stood Murgatroyd, the butler.

"You didn't expect to see me, did you?"

"I certainly," replied Wilfred, severely, "did not expect to see you in a lady's presence in a costume like that."

"Never mind my costume." Sir Jasper turned.

"Murgatroyd, do your duty!"

The butler, scowling horribly, advanced into the room.

"Stop!" screamed Angela.

"I haven't begun yet, miss," said the butler, deferentially.

"You sha'n't touch Wilfred. I love him."

"What!" cried Sir Jasper. "After all that has happened?"

"Yes. He has explained everything."

A grim frown appeared on the baronet's vermilion face.

"I'll bet he hasn't explained why he left me to be cooked in that infernal Turkish Bath. I was beginning to throw out clouds of smoke when Murgatroyd, faithful fellow, heard my cries and came and released me."

"Though not my work," added the butler.

Wilfred eyed him steadily.

"If," he said, "you used Mulliner's Reduc-o, the recognised specific for obesity, whether in the tabloid form at three shillings the tin, or as a liquid at five and six the flask, you would have no need to stew in Turkish Baths. Mulliner's Reduc-o, which contains no injurious chemicals, but is compounded purely of health-giving herbs, is guaranteed to remove excess weight, steadily and without weakening after-effects, at the rate of two pounds a week. As used by the nobility."

The glare of hatred faded from the baronet's eyes.

"Is that a fact?" he whispered.

"It is."

"You guarantee it?"

"All the Mulliner preparations are fully guaranteed."

"My boy!" cried the baronet. He shook Wilfred by the hand. "Take her," he said, brokenly. "And with her my b-blessing."

A discreet cough sounded in the background.

"You haven't anything, by any chance, sir," asked Murgatroyd, "that's good for lumbago?"

"Mulliner's Ease-o will cure the most stubborn case in six days."

"Bless you, sir, bless you," sobbed Murgatroyd. "Where can I get it?"

"At all chemists."

"It catches me in the small of the back principally, sir."

"It need catch you no longer," said Wilfred.

There is little to add. Murgatroyd is now the most lissom butler in Yorkshire. Sir Jasper's weight is down under the fifteen stone and he is thinking of taking up hunting again. Wilfred and Angela are man and wife; and never, I am informed, have the wedding-bells of the old church at ffinch village rung out a blither peal than they did on that June morning when Angela, raising to her love a face on which the brown was as evenly distributed as on an antique walnut table, replied to the clergyman's question, "Wilt thou, Angela, take this Wilfred?" with a shy, "I will." They now have two bonny bairns—the small, or Percival, at a preparatory school in Sussex, and the large, or Ferdinand, at Eton.

Here Mr. Mulliner, having finished his hot Scotch, bade us farewell and took his departure.

A silence followed his exit. The company seemed plunged in deep thought. Then somebody rose.

"Well, good-night all," he said.

It seemed to sum up the situation.

MULLINER'S BUCK-U-UPPO

MULLINER'S BUCK—U—UPPO

THE village Choral Society had been giving a performance of Gilbert and Sullivan's "Sorcerer" in aid of the Church Organ Fund; and, as we sat in the window of the Anglers' Rest, smoking our pipes, the audience came streaming past us down the little street. Snatches of song floated to our ears, and Mr. Mulliner began to croon in unison.

"'Ah me! I was a pa-ale you-oung curate then!'" chanted Mr. Mulliner in the rather snuffling voice in which the amateur singer seems to find it necessary to render the old songs.

"Remarkable," he said, resuming his natural tones, "how fashions change, even in clergymen. There are very few pale young curates nowadays."

"True," I agreed. "Most of them are beefy young fellows who rowed for their colleges. I don't believe I have ever seen a pale young curate."

"You never met my nephew Augustine, I think?"

"Never."

"The description in the song would have fitted him perfectly. You will want to hear all about my nephew Augustine."

At the time of which I am speaking (said Mr. Mulliner) my nephew Augustine was a curate, and very young and extremely pale. As a boy he had completely outgrown his strength, and I rather think that at his Theological College some of the wilder spirits must have bullied him; for when he went to Lower Briskett-in-the-Midden to assist the vicar, the Rev. Stanley Brandon, in his cure of souls, he was as meek and mild a young man as you could meet in a day's journey. He had flaxen hair, weak blue eyes, and the general demeanour of a saintly but timid codfish. Precisely, in short, the sort of young curate who seems to have been so common in the 'eighties, or whenever it was that Gilbert wrote "The Sorcerer."

The personality of his immediate superior did little or nothing to help him to overcome his native diffidence. The Rev. Stanley Brandon was a huge and sinewy man of violent temper, whose red face and glittering eyes might well have intimidated the toughest curate. The Rev. Stanley had been a heavy-weight boxer at Cambridge, and I gather from Augustine that he seemed to be always on the point of introducing into debates on parish matters the methods which had made him so successful in the roped ring. I remember Augustine telling me that once, on the occasion when he had ventured to oppose the other's views in the matter of decorating the church for the Harvest Festival, he thought for a moment that the vicar was going to drop him with a right hook to the chin. It was some quite trivial point that had come up—a question as to whether the pumpkin would look better in the apse or the clerestory, if I recollect rightly—but for several seconds it seemed as if blood was about to be shed.

Such was the Rev. Stanley Brandon.

And yet it was to the daughter of this formidable man that Augustine Mulliner had permitted himself to lose his heart. Truly, Cupid makes heroes of us all.

Jane was a very nice girl, and just as fond of Augustine as he was of her. But, as each lacked the nerve to go to the girl's father and put him abreast of the position of affairs, they were forced to meet surreptitiously. This jarred upon Augustine, who, like all the Mulliners, loved the truth and hated any form of deception. And one evening, as they paced beside the laurels at the bottom of the vicarage garden, he rebelled.

"My dearest," said Augustine, "I can no longer brook this secrecy. I shall go into the house immediately and ask your father for your hand."

Jane paled and clung to his arm. She knew so well that it was not her hand but her father's foot which he would receive if he carried out this mad scheme.

"No, no, Augustine! You must not!"

"But, darling, it is the only straightforward course."

"But not to-night. I beg of you, not to-night."

"Why not?"

"Because father is in a very bad temper. He has just had a letter from the bishop, rebuking him for wearing too many orphreys on his chasuble, and it has upset him terribly. You see, he and the bishop were at school together, and father can never forget it. He said at dinner that if old Boko Bickerton thought he was going to order him about he would jolly well show him."

"And the bishop comes here to-morrow for the Confirmation services!" gasped Augustine.

"Yes. And I'm so afraid they will quarrel. It's such a pity father hasn't some other bishop over him. He always remembers that he once hit this one in the eye for pouring ink on his collar, and this lowers his respect for his spiritual authority. So you won't go in and tell him to-night, will you?"

"I will not," Augustine assured her with a slight shiver.

"And you will be sure to put your feet in hot mustard and water when you get home? The dew has made the grass so wet."

"I will indeed, dearest."

"You are not strong, you know."

"No, I am not strong."

"You ought to take some really good tonic."

"Perhaps I ought. Good-night, Jane."

"Good-night, Augustine."

The lovers parted. Jane slipped back into the vicarage, and Augustine made his way to his cosy rooms in the High Street. And the first thing he noticed on entering was a parcel on the table, and beside it a letter.

He opened it listlessly, his thoughts far away.

"*My dear Augustine.*"

He turned to the last page and glanced at the signature. The letter was from his Aunt Angela, the wife of my brother, Wilfred Mulliner. You may remember that I once told you the story of how these two came together. If so, you will recall that my brother Wilfred was the eminent chemical researcher who had invented, among other specifics, such world-famous preparations as Mulliner's Raven Gipsy Face-Cream and the Mulliner Snow of the Mountains Lotion. He and Augustine had never been particularly intimate, but between Augustine and his aunt there had always existed a warm friendship.

My dear Augustine (wrote Angela Mulliner),
I have been thinking so much about you lately, and I cannot forget that, when I saw you last, you seemed very fragile and deficient in vitamines. I do hope you take care of yourself.

I have been feeling for some time that you ought to take a tonic, and by a lucky chance Wilfred has just invented one which he tells me is the finest thing he has ever done. It is called Buck-U-Uppo, and acts directly on the red corpuscles. It is not yet on the market, but I have managed to smuggle a sample bottle from Wilfred's laboratory, and I want you to try it at once. I am sure it is just what you need.

Your affectionate aunt,
Angela Mulliner.

P. S.—You take a tablespoonful before going to bed, and another just before breakfast.

Augustine was not an unduly superstitious young man, but the coincidence of this tonic arriving so soon after Jane had told him that a tonic was what he needed affected him deeply. It seemed to him that this thing must have been meant. He shook the bottle, uncorked it, and, pouring out a liberal table-spoonful, shut his eyes and swallowed it.

The medicine, he was glad to find, was not unpleasant to the taste. It had a slightly pungent flavour, rather like old boot-soles beaten up in sherry. Having taken the dose, he read for a while in a book of theological essays, and then went to bed.

And as his feet slipped between the sheets, he was annoyed to find that Mrs. Wardle, his housekeeper, had once more forgotten his hot-water bottle.

"Oh, dash!" said Augustine.

He was thoroughly upset. He had told the woman over and over again that he suffered from cold feet and could not get to sleep unless the dogs were properly warmed up. He sprang out of bed and went to the head of the stairs.

"Mrs. Wardle!" he cried.

There was no reply.

"Mrs. Wardle!" bellowed Augustine in a voice that rattled the window-panes like a strong nor'-easter. Until to-night he had

always been very much afraid of his housekeeper and had both walked and talked softly
in her presence. But now he was conscious of
a strange new fortitude. His head was singing
a little, and he felt equal to a dozen Mrs.
Wardles.

Shuffling footsteps made themselves heard.

"Well, what is it now?" asked a querulous
voice.

Augustine snorted.

"I'll tell you what it is now," he roared.
"How many times have I told you always
to put a hot-water bottle in my bed? You've
forgotten it again, you old cloth-head!"

Mrs. Wardle peered up, astounded and
militant.

"Mr. Mulliner, I am not accustomed——"

"Shut up!" thundered Augustine. "What
I want from you is less back-chat and more
hot-water bottles. Bring it up at once, or I
leave to-morrow. Let me endeavour to get it
into your concrete skull that you aren't the
only person letting rooms in this village.
Any more lip and I walk straight round the
corner, where I'll be appreciated. Hot-water
bottle ho! And look slippy about it."

"Yes, Mr. Mulliner. Certainly, Mr. Mulliner. In one moment, Mr. Mulliner."

"Action! Action!" boomed Augustine. "Show some speed. Put a little snap into it."

"Yes, yes, most decidedly, Mr. Mulliner," replied the chastened voice from below.

An hour later, as he was dropping off to sleep, a thought crept into Augustine's mind. Had he not been a little brusque with Mrs. Wardle? Had there not been in his manner something a shade abrupt—almost rude? Yes, he decided regretfully, there had. He lit a candle and reached for the diary which lay on the table at his bedside.

He made an entry.

The meek shall inherit the earth. Am I sufficiently meek? I wonder. This evening, when reproaching Mrs. Wardle, my worthy housekeeper, for omitting to place a hot-water bottle in my bed, I spoke quite crossly. The provocation was severe, but still I was surely to blame for allowing my passions to run riot. Mem: Must guard agst this.

But when he woke next morning, different feelings prevailed. He took his ante-breakfast dose of Buck-U-Uppo: and looking at the entry in the diary, could scarcely believe that it was he who had written it. "Quite cross?" Of course he had been quite cross. Wouldn't anybody be quite cross who was for ever being persecuted by beetle-wits who forgot hot-water bottles?

Erasing the words with one strong dash of a thick-leaded pencil, he scribbled in the margin a hasty "Mashed potatoes! Served the old idiot right!" and went down to breakfast.

He felt most amazingly fit. Undoubtedly, in asserting that this tonic of his acted forcefully upon the red corpuscles, his Uncle Wilfred had been right. Until that moment Augustine had never supposed that he had any red corpuscles; but now, as he sat waiting for Mrs. Wardle to bring him his fried egg, he could feel them dancing about all over him. They seemed to be forming rowdy parties and sliding down his spine. His eyes sparkled, and from sheer joy of living he sang a few bars from the hymn for those of riper years at sea.

He was still singing when Mrs. Wardle entered with a dish.

"What's this?" demanded Augustine, eyeing it dangerously.

"A nice fried egg, sir."

"And what, pray, do you mean by nice? It may be an amiable egg. It may be a civil, well-meaning egg. But if you think it is fit for human consumption, adjust that impression. Go back to your kitchen, woman; select another; and remember this time that you are a cook, not an incinerating machine. Between an egg that is fried and an egg that is cremated there is a wide and substantial difference. This difference, if you wish to retain me as a lodger in these far too expensive rooms, you will endeavour to appreciate."

The glowing sense of well-being with which Augustine had begun the day did not diminish with the passage of time. It seemed, indeed, to increase. So full of effervescing energy did the young man feel that, departing from his usual custom of spending the morning crouched over the fire, he picked up his hat, stuck it at a rakish angle on his head, and sallied out for a healthy tramp across the fields.

It was while he was returning, flushed and rosy, that he observed a sight which is rare in the country districts of England—the spectacle of a bishop running. It is not often in a place like Lower Briskett-in-the-Midden that you see a bishop at all; and when you do he is either riding in a stately car or pacing at a dignified walk. This one was sprinting like a Derby winner, and Augustine paused to drink in the sight.

The bishop was a large, burly bishop, built for endurance rather than speed; but he was making excellent going. He flashed past Augustine in a whirl of flying gaiters: and then, proving himself thereby no mere specialist but a versatile all-round athlete, suddenly dived for a tree and climbed rapidly into its branches. His motive, Augustine readily divined, was to elude a rough, hairy dog which was toiling in his wake. The dog reached the tree a moment after his quarry had climbed it, and stood there, barking.

Augustine strolled up.

"Having a little trouble with the dumb friend, bish?" he asked, genially.

The bishop peered down from his eyrie.

"Young man," he said, "save me!"

"Right most indubitably ho!" replied Augustine. "Leave it to me."

Until to-day he had always been terrified of dogs, but now he did not hesitate. Almost quicker than words can tell, he picked up a stone, discharged it at the animal, and whooped cheerily as it got home with a thud. The dog, knowing when he had had enough, removed himself at some forty-five m.p.h.; and the bishop, descending cautiously, clasped Augustine's hand in his.

"My preserver!" said the bishop.

"Don't give it another thought," said Augustine, cheerily. "Always glad to do a pal a good turn. We clergymen must stick together."

"I thought he had me for a minute."

"Quite a nasty customer. Full of rude energy."

The bishop nodded.

"His eye was not dim, nor his natural force abated. Deuteronomy xxxiv. 7," he agreed. "I wonder if you can direct me to the vicarage? I fear I have come a little out of my way."

"I'll take you there."

"Thank you. Perhaps it would be as well if you did not come in. I have a serious matter to discuss with old Pieface—I mean, with the Rev. Stanley Brandon."

"I have a serious matter to discuss with his daughter. I'll just hang about the garden."

"You are a very excellent young man," said the bishop, as they walked along. "You are a curate, eh?"

"At present. But," said Augustine, tapping his companion on the chest, "just watch my smoke. That's all I ask you to do—just watch my smoke."

"I will. You should rise to great heights —to the very top of the tree."

"Like you did just now, eh? Ha, ha!"

"Ha, ha!" said the bishop. "You young rogue!"

He poked Augustine in the ribs.

"Ha, ha, ha!" said Augustine.

He slapped the bishop on the back.

"But all joking aside," said the bishop as they entered the vicarage grounds, "I really shall keep my eye on you and see that you receive the swift preferment which your talents and character deserve. I say to you, my dear young friend, speaking seriously and weighing my words, that the way you picked that dog off with that stone was the smoothest thing I ever saw. And I am a man who always tells the strict truth."

"Great is truth and mighty above all things. Esdras iv. 41," said Augustine.

He turned away and strolled towards the laurel bushes, which were his customary meeting-place with Jane. The bishop went on to the front door and rang the bell.

Although they had made no definite appointment, Augustine was surprised when the minutes passed and no Jane appeared. He did not know that she had been told off by her father to entertain the bishop's wife that morning, and show her the sights of Lower Briskett-in-the-Midden. He waited some quarter of an hour with growing impatience, and was about to leave when suddenly from the house there came to his ears the sound of voices raised angrily.

He stopped. The voices appeared to proceed

from a room on the ground floor facing the garden.

Running lightly over the turf, Augustine paused outside the window and listened. The window was open at the bottom, and he could hear quite distinctly.

The vicar was speaking in a voice that vibrated through the room.

"Is that so?" said the vicar.

"Yes, it is!" said the bishop.

"Ha, ha!"

"Ha, ha! to you, and see how you like it!" rejoined the bishop with spirit.

Augustine drew a step closer. It was plain that Jane's fears had been justified and that there was serious trouble afoot between these two old schoolfellows. He peeped in. The vicar, his hands behind his coat-tails, was striding up and down the carpet, while the bishop, his back to the fireplace, glared defiance at him from the hearth-rug.

"Who ever told you you were an authority on chasubles?" demanded the vicar.

"That's all right who told me," rejoined the bishop.

"I don't believe you know what a chasuble is."

"Is that so?"

"Well, what is it, then?"

"It's a circular cloak hanging from the shoulders, elaborately embroidered with a pattern and with orphreys. And you can argue as much as you like, young Pieface, but you can't get away from the fact that there are too many orphreys on yours. And what I'm telling you is that you've jolly well got to switch off a few of those orphreys or you'll get it in the neck."

The vicar's eyes glittered furiously.

"Is that so?" he said. "Well, I just won't, so there! And it's like your cheek coming here and trying to high-hat me. You seem to have forgotten that I knew you when you were an inky-faced kid at school, and that, if I liked, I could tell the world one or two things about you which would probably amuse it."

"My past is an open book."

"Is it?" The vicar laughed malevolently. "Who put the white mouse in the French master's desk?"

The bishop started.

"Who put jam in the dormitory prefect's bed?" he retorted.

"Who couldn't keep his collar clean?"

"Who used to wear a dickey?" The bishop's wonderful organ-like voice, whose softest whisper could be heard throughout a vast cathedral, rang out in tones of thunder. "Who was sick at the house supper?"

The vicar quivered from head to foot. His rubicund face turned a deeper crimson.

"You know jolly well," he said, in shaking accents, "that there was something wrong with the turkey. Might have upset any one."

"The only thing wrong with the turkey was that you ate too much of it. If you had paid as much attention to developing your soul as you did to developing your tummy, you might by now," said the bishop, "have risen to my own eminence."

"Oh, might I?"

"No, perhaps I am wrong. You never had the brain."

The vicar uttered another discordant laugh.

"Brain is good! We know all about your eminence, as you call it, and how you rose to that eminence."

"What do you mean?"

"You are a bishop. How you became one we will not inquire."

"What do you mean?"

"What I say. We will not inquire."

"Why don't you inquire?"

"Because," said the vicar, "it is better not!"

The bishop's self-control left him. His face contorted with fury, he took a step forward. And simultaneously Augustine sprang lightly into the room.

"Now, now, now!" said Augustine. "Now, now, now, now, now!"

The two men stood transfixed. They stared at the intruder dumbly.

"Come, come!" said Augustine.

The vicar was the first to recover. He glowered at Augustine.

"What do you mean by jumping through my window?" he thundered. "Are you a curate or a harlequin?"

Augustine met his gaze with an unfaltering eye.

"I am a curate," he replied, with a dignity that well became him. "And, as a curate,

I cannot stand by and see two superiors of the cloth, who are moreover old schoolfellows, forgetting themselves. It isn't right. Absolutely not right, my dear old superiors of the cloth."

The vicar bit his lip. The bishop bowed his head.

"Listen," proceeded Augustine, placing a hand on the shoulder of each. "I hate to see you two dear good chaps quarrelling like this."

"He started it," said the vicar sullenly.

"Never mind who started it." Augustine silenced the bishop with a curt gesture as he made to speak. "Be sensible, my dear fellows. Respect the decencies of debate. Exercise a little good-humoured give-and-take. You say," he went on, turning to the bishop, "that our good friend here has too many orphreys on his chasuble?"

"I do. And I stick to it."

"Yes, yes, yes. But what," said Augustine, soothingly, "are a few orphreys between friends? Reflect! You and our worthy vicar here were at school together. You are bound by the sacred ties of the old Alma Mater. With him you sported on the green. With him you shared a crib and threw inked darts in the hour supposed to be devoted to the study of French. Do these things mean nothing to you? Do these memories touch no chord?" He turned appealingly from one to the other. "Vicar! Bish!"

The vicar had moved away and was wiping his eyes. The bishop fumbled for a pocket-handkerchief. There was a silence.

"Sorry, Pieface," said the bishop, in a choking voice.

"Shouldn't have spoken as I did, Boko," mumbled the vicar.

"If you want to know what I think," said the bishop, "you are right in attributing your indisposition at the house supper to something wrong with the turkey. I recollect saying at the time that the bird should never have been served in such a condition."

"And when you put that white mouse in the French master's desk," said the vicar, "you performed one of the noblest services to humanity of which there is any record. They ought to have made you a bishop on the spot."

"Pieface!"

"Boko!"

The two men clasped hands.

"Splendid!" said Augustine. "Everything hotsy-totsy now?"

"Quite, quite," said the vicar.

"As far as I am concerned, completely hotsy-totsy," said the bishop. He turned to his old friend solicitously. "You will continue to wear all the orphreys you want—will you not, Pieface?"

"No, no. I see now that I was wrong. From now on, Boko, I abandon orphreys altogether."

"But, Pieface——"

"It's all right," the vicar assured him. "I can take them or leave them alone."

"Splendid fellow!" The bishop coughed to hide his emotion, and there was another silence. "I think, perhaps," he went on, after a pause, "I should be leaving you now, my dear chap, and going in search of my wife. She is with your daughter, I believe, somewhere in the village."

"They are coming up the drive now."

"Ah, yes, I see them. A charming girl, your daughter."

Augustine clapped him on the shoulder.

"Bish," he exclaimed, "you said a mouthful. She is the dearest, sweetest girl in the whole world. And I should be glad, vicar, if you would give your consent to our immediate union. I love Jane with a good man's fervour, and I am happy to inform you that my sentiments are returned. Assure us, therefore, of your approval, and I will go at once and have the banns put up."

The vicar leaped as though he had been stung. Like so many vicars, he had a poor opinion of curates, and he had always regarded Augustine as rather below than above the general norm or level of the despised class.

"What!" he cried.

"A most excellent idea," said the bishop, beaming. "A very happy notion, I call it."

"My daughter!" The vicar seemed dazed. "My daughter marry a curate!"

"You were a curate once yourself, Pieface."

"Yes, but not a curate like that."

"No!" said the bishop. "You were not. Nor was I. Better for us both had we been. This young man, I would have you know, is the most outstandingly excellent young

man I have ever encountered. Are you aware
that scarcely an hour ago he saved me with
the most consummate address from a large
shaggy dog with black spots and a kink in his
tail? I was sorely pressed, Pieface, when this
young man came up and, with a readiness of
resource and an accuracy of aim which it would
be impossible to over-praise, got that dog in
the short ribs with a rock and sent him flying."

The vicar seemed to be struggling with
some powerful emotion. His eyes had widened.

"A dog with black spots?"

"Very black spots. But no blacker, I fear,
than the heart they hid."

"And he really plugged him in the short
ribs?"

"As far as I could see, squarely in the short
ribs."

The vicar held out his hand.

"Mulliner," he said, "I was not aware
of this. In the light of the facts which have
just been drawn to my attention, I have no
hesitation in saying that my objections are
removed. I have had it in for that dog since
the second Sunday before Septuagesima, when
he pinned me by the ankle as I paced beside

the river composing a sermon on Certain Alarming Manifestations of the So-called Modern Spirit. Take Jane. I give my consent freely. And may she be as happy as any girl with such a husband ought to be."

A few more affecting words were exchanged, and then the bishop and Augustine left the house. The bishop was silent and thoughtful.

"I owe you a great deal, Mulliner," he said at length.

"Oh, I don't know," said Augustine. "Would you say that?"

"A very great deal. You saved me from a terrible disaster. Had you not leaped through that window at that precise juncture and intervened, I really believe I should have pasted my dear old friend Brandon in the eye. I was sorely exasperated."

"Our good vicar can be trying at times," agreed Augustine.

"My fist was already clenched, and I was just hauling off for the swing when you checked me. What the result would have been, had you not exhibited a tact and discretion beyond your years, I do not like to

think. I might have been unfrocked." He
shivered at the thought, though the weather
was mild. "I could never have shown my
face at the Athenæum again. But, tut, tut!"
went on the bishop, patting Augustine on the
shoulder, "let us not dwell on what might have
been. Speak to me of yourself. The vicar's
charming daughter—you really love her?"

"I do, indeed."

The bishop's face had grown grave.

"Think well, Mulliner," he said. "Marriage
is a serious affair. Do not plunge into it without
due reflection. I myself am a husband, and,
though singularly blessed in the possession
of a devoted helpmeet, cannot but feel sometimes that a man is better off as a bachelor.
Women, Mulliner, are odd."

"True," said Augustine.

' My own dear wife is the best of women.
And, as I never weary of saying, a good woman
is a wondrous creature, cleaving to the right
and the good under all change; lovely in youth-
ful comeliness, lovely all her life in comeliness
of heart. And yet——"

"And yet?" said Augustine.

The bishop mused for a moment. He

wriggled a little with an expression of pain, and scratched himself between the shoulder-blades.

"Well, I'll tell you," said the bishop. "It is a warm and pleasant day to-day, is it not?"

"Exceptionally clement," said Augustine.

"A fair, sunny day, made gracious by a temperate westerly breeze. And yet, Mulliner, if you will credit my statement, my wife insisted on my putting on my thick winter woollies this morning. Truly," sighed the bishop, "as a jewel of gold in a swine's snout, so is a fair woman which is without discretion. Proverbs xi. 21."

"Twenty-two," corrected Augustine.

"I should have said twenty-two. They are made of thick flannel, and I have an exceptionally sensitive skin. Oblige me, my dear fellow, by rubbing me in the small of the back with the ferrule of your stick. I think it will ease the irritation."

"But, my poor dear old bish," said Augustine, sympathetically, "this must not be."

The bishop shook his head ruefully.

"You would not speak so hardily, Mulliner,

if you knew my wife. There is no appeal from her decrees."

"Nonsense," cried Augustine, cheerily. He looked through the trees to where the lady bishopess, escorted by Jane, was examining a lobelia through her lorgnette with just the right bend of cordiality and condescension. "I'll fix that for you in a second."

The bishop clutched at his arm.

"My boy! What are you going to do?"

"I'm just going to have a word with your wife and put the matter up to her as a reasonable woman. Thick winter woollies on a day like this! Absurd!" said Augustine. "Preposterous! I never heard such rot."

The bishop gazed after him with a laden heart. Already he had come to love this young man like a son: and to see him charging so light-heartedly into the very jaws of destruction afflicted him with a deep and poignant sadness. He knew what his wife was like when even the highest in the land attempted to thwart her; and this brave lad was but a curate. In another moment she would be looking at him through her lorgnette: and England was littered with the shrivelled remains of curates at whom the lady bishopess had looked through her lorgnette. He had seen them wilt like salted slugs at the episcopal breakfast-table.

He held his breath. Augustine had reached the lady bishopess, and the lady bishopess was even now raising her lorgnette.

The bishop shut his eyes and turned away. And then—years afterwards, it seemed to him —a cheery voice hailed him: and, turning, he perceived Augustine bounding back through the trees.

"It's all right, bish," said Augustine.

"All—all right?" faltered the bishop.

"Yes. She says you can go and change into the thin cashmere."

The bishop reeled.

"But—but—but what did you say to her? What arguments did you employ?"

"Oh, I just pointed out what a warm day it was and jollied her along a bit——"

"Jollied her along a bit!"

"And she agreed in the most friendly and cordial manner. She has asked me to call at the Palace one of these days."

The bishop seized Augustine's hand.

"My boy," he said in a broken voice, "you shall do more than call at the Palace. You shall come and live at the Palace. Become my secretary, Mulliner, and name your own salary. If you intend to marry, you will require an increased stipend. Become my secretary, boy, and never leave my side. I have needed somebody like you for years."

It was late in the afternoon when Augustine returned to his rooms, for he had been invited to lunch at the vicarage and had been the life and soul of the cheery little party.

"A letter for you, sir," said Mrs. Wardle, obsequiously.

Augustine took the letter.

"I am sorry to say I shall be leaving you shortly, Mrs. Wardle."

"Oh, sir! If there's anything I can do——"

"Oh, it's not that. The fact is, the bishop has made me his secretary, and I shall have to shift my toothbrush and spats to the Palace, you see."

"Well, fancy that, sir! Why, you'll be a bishop yourself one of these days."

"Possibly," said Augustine. "Possibly. And now let me read this."

He opened the letter. A thoughtful frown appeared on his face as he read.

My dear Augustine,

I am writing in some haste to tell you that the impulsiveness of your aunt has led to a rather serious mistake.

She tells me that she dispatched to you yesterday by parcels post a sample bottle of my new Buck-U-Uppo, which she obtained without my knowledge from my laboratory. Had she mentioned what she was intending to do, I could have prevented a very unfortunate occurrence.

Mulliner's Buck-U-Uppo is of two grades or qualities—the A and the B. The A is a mild, but strengthening, tonic designed for human invalids. The B, on the other hand, is purely for circulation in the animal kingdom, and was invented to fill a long-felt want throughout our Indian possessions.

As you are doubtless aware, the favourite pastime of the Indian Maharajahs is the hunting of the tiger of the jungle from the backs of

*elephants; and it has happened frequently in the
past that hunts have been spoiled by the failure
of the elephant to see eye to eye with its owner in
the matter of what constitutes sport.*

*Too often elephants, on sighting the tiger,
have turned and galloped home: and it was
to correct this tendency on their part that I
invented Mulliner's Buck-U-Uppo "B." One
teaspoonful of the Buck-U-Uppo "B" administered in its morning bran-mash will cause the
most timid elephant to trumpet loudly and charge
the fiercest tiger without a qualm.*

*Abstain, therefore, from taking any of the
contents of the bottle you now possess,*

And believe me,

Your affectionate uncle,

Wilfred Mulliner.

Augustine remained for some time in deep
thought after perusing this communication.
Then, rising, he whistled a few bars of the
psalm appointed for the twenty-sixth of June
and left the room.

Half an hour later a telegraphic message
was speeding over the wires.

It ran as follows:—

Wilfred Mulliner,
     The Gables,
          Lesser Lossingham,
               Salop.

Letter received. Send immediately, C. O. D., three cases of the "B." "Blessed shall be thy basket and thy store." Deuteronomy xxviii. 5.

Augustine.

THE REVERENT WOOING
OF ARCHIBALD

The Reverent Wooing of Archibald

THE conversation in the bar-parlour of the Anglers' Rest, which always tends to get deepish towards closing time, had turned to the subject of the Modern Girl; and a Gin-and-Ginger-Ale sitting in the corner by the window remarked that it was strange how types die out.

"I can remember the days," said the Gin-and-Ginger-Ale, "when every other girl you met stood about six feet two in her dancing-shoes, and had as many curves as a Scenic Railway. Now they are all five foot nothing and you can't see them sideways. Why is this?"

The Draught Stout shook his head.

"Nobody can say. It's the same with dogs. One moment the world is full of pugs as far as the eye can reach; the next, not a pug in sight, only Pekes and Alsatians. Odd!"

The Small Bass and the Double-Whisky-and-

Splash admitted that these things were very mysterious, and supposed we should never know the reason for them. Probably we were not meant to know.

"I cannot agree with you, gentlemen," said Mr. Mulliner. He had been sipping his hot Scotch and lemon with a rather abstracted air: but now he sat up alertly, prepared to deliver judgment. "The reason for the disappearance of the dignified, queenly type of girl is surely obvious. It is Nature's method of ensuring the continuance of the species. A world full of the sort of young woman that Meredith used to put into his novels and du Maurier into his pictures in *Punch* would be a world full of permanent spinsters. The modern young man would never be able to summon up the nerve to propose to them."

"Something in that," assented the Draught Stout.

"I speak with authority on the point," said Mr. Mulliner, "because my nephew, Archibald, made me his confidant when he fell in love with Aurelia Cammarleigh. He worshipped that girl with a fervour which threatened to unseat his reason, such as it was: but the mere idea of asking her to be his wife gave him, he informed me, such a feeling of sick faintness that only by means of a very stiff brandy and soda, or some similar restorative, was he able to pull himself together on the occasions when he contemplated it. Had it not been for . . . But perhaps you would care to hear the story from the beginning?

People who enjoyed a merely superficial acquaintance with my nephew Archibald (said Mr. Mulliner) were accustomed to set him down as just an ordinary pinheaded young man. It was only when they came to know him better that they discovered their mistake. Then they realised that his pinheadedness, so far from being ordinary, was exceptional. Even at the Drones Club, where the average of intellect is not high, it was often said of Archibald that, had his brain been constructed of silk, he would have been hard put to it to find sufficient material to make a canary a pair of cami-knickers. He sauntered through life with a cheerful insouciance, and up to the age of twenty-five had only once been moved by anything in the nature of a really strong emotion —on the occasion when, in the heart of Bond Street and at the height of the London season,

he discovered that his man, Meadowes, had carelessly sent him out with odd spats on.

And then he met Aurelia Cammarleigh.

The first encounter between these two has
always seemed to me to bear an extraordinary
resemblance to the famous meeting between the
poet Dante and Beatrice Fortinari. Dante, if you
remember, exchanged no remarks with Beatrice
on that occasion. Nor did Archibald with Aurelia. Dante just goggled at the girl. So did
Archibald. Like Archibald, Dante loved at first
sight: and the poet's age at the time was, we are
told, nine—which was almost exactly the mental
age of Archibald Mulliner when he first set eyeglass on Aurelia Cammarleigh.

Only in the actual locale of the encounter do
the two cases cease to be parallel. Dante, the
story relates, was walking on the Ponte Vecchia,
while Archibald Mulliner was having a thoughtful cocktail in the window of the Drones Club,
looking out on Dover Street.

And he had just relaxed his lower jaw in order
to examine Dover Street more comfortably when
there swam into his line of vision something that
looked like a Greek goddess. She came out of a

shop opposite the club and stood on the pavement waiting for a taxi. And, as he saw her standing there, love at first sight seemed to go all over Archibald Mulliner like nettlerash.

It was strange that this should have been so, for she was not at all the sort of girl with whom Archibald had fallen in love at first sight in the past. I chanced, while in here the other day, to pick up a copy of one of the old yellowback novels of fifty years ago—the property, I believe, of Miss Postlethwaite, our courteous and erudite barmaid. It was entitled *Sir Ralph's Secret,* and its heroine, the Lady Elaine, was described as a superbly handsome girl, divinely tall, with a noble figure, the arched Montresor nose, haughty eyes beneath delicately pencilled brows, and that indefinable air of aristocratic aloofness which marks the daughter of a hundred Earls. And Aurelia Cammarleigh might have been this formidable creature's double.

Yet Archibald, sighting her, reeled as if the cocktail he had just consumed had been his tenth instead of his first.

"Golly!" said Archibald.

To save himself from falling, he had clutched at a passing fellow-member: and now, examin-

ing his catch, he saw that it was young Algy Wymondham-Wymondham. Just the fellow-member he would have preferred to clutch at, for
Algy was a man who went everywhere and knew
everybody and could doubtless give him the information he desired.

"Algy, old prune," said Archibald in a low,
throaty voice, "a moment of your valuable time,
if you don't mind."

He paused, for he had perceived the need for
caution. Algy was a notorious babbler, and it
would be the height of rashness to give him an
inkling of the passion which blazed within his
breast. With a strong effort, he donned the mask.
When he spoke again, it was with a deceiving
nonchalance.

"I was just wondering if you happened to know
who that girl is, across the street there. I suppose
you don't know what her name is in rough num-
bers? Seems to me I've met her somewhere or
something, or seen her, or something. Or something, if you know what I mean."

Algy followed his pointing finger and was in
time to observe Aurelia as she disappeared into
the cab.

"That girl?"

"Yes," said Archibald, yawning. "Who is she, if any?"

"Girl named Cammarleigh."

"Ah?" said Archibald, yawning again. "Then I haven't met her."

"Introduce you if you like. She's sure to be at Ascot. Look out for us there."

Archibald yawned for the third time.

"All right," he said, "I'll try to remember. Tell me about her. I mean, has she any fathers or mothers or any rot of that description?"

"Only an aunt. She lives with her in Park Street. She's potty."

Archilbald started, stung to the quick.

"Potty? That divine. . . . I mean, that rather attractive-looking girl?"

"Not Aurelia. The aunt. She thinks Bacon wrote Shakespeare."

"Thinks who wrote what?" asked Archibald, puzzled, for the names were strange to him.

"You must have heard of Shakespeare. He's well known. Fellow who used to write plays. Only Aurelia's aunt says he didn't. She maintains that a bloke called Bacon wrote them for him."

"Dashed decent of him," said Archibald, ap-

provingly. "Of course, he may have owed Shakespeare money."

"There's that, of course."

"What was the name again?"

"Bacon."

"Bacon," said Archibald, jotting it down on
his cuff. "Right."

Algy moved on, and Archibald, his soul bub-
bling within him like a welsh rabbit at the height
of its fever, sank into a chair and stared sight-
lessly at the ceiling. Then, rising, he went off to
the Burlington Arcade to buy socks.

The process of buying socks eased for awhile
the turmoil that ran riot in Archibald's veins.
But even socks with lavender clocks can only
alleviate: they do not cure. Returning to his
rooms, he found the anguish rather more overwhelming than ever. For at last he had leisure to
think: and thinking always hurt his head.

Algy's careless words had confirmed his worst
suspicions. A girl with an aunt who knew all
about Shakespeare and Bacon must of necessity
live in a mental atmosphere into which a lame-
brained bird like himself could scarcely hope to
soar. Even if he did meet her—even if she asked
him to call—even if in due time their relations

became positively cordial, what then? How could he aspire to such a goddess? What had he to offer her?

Money?

Plenty of that, yes, but what was money?

Socks?

Of these he had the finest collection in London, but socks are not everything.

A loving heart?

A fat lot of use that was.

No, a girl like Aurelia Cammarleigh would, he felt, demand from the man who aspired to her hand something in the nature of gifts, of accomplishments. He would have to be a man who Did Things.

And what, Archibald asked himself, could he do? Absolutely nothing except give an imitation of a hen laying an egg.

That he could do. At imitating a hen laying an egg he was admittedly a master. His fame in that one respect had spread all over the West End of London. "Others abide our question. Thou art free," was the verdict of London's gilded youth on Archibald Mulliner when considered purely in the light of a man who could imitate a hen laying an egg. "Mulliner," they said to one another, "may be a pretty minus quantity in many ways, but he can imitate a hen laying an egg."

And, so far from helping him, this one accomplishment of his would, reason told him, be a positive handicap. A girl like Aurelia Cammarleigh would simply be sickened by such coarse buffoonery. He blushed at the very thought of her ever learning that he was capable of sinking to such depths.

And so, when some weeks later he was introduced to her in the paddock at Ascot and she, gazing at him with what seemed to his sensitive mind contemptuous loathing, said:

"They tell me you give an imitation of a hen laying an egg, Mr. Mulliner."

He replied with extraordinary vehemence:

"It is a lie—a foul and contemptible lie which I shall track to its source and nail to the counter."

Brave words! But had they clicked? Had she believed him? He trusted so. But her haughty eyes were very penetrating. They seemd to pierce through to the depths of his soul and lay it bare for what it was—the soul of a hen-imitator.

However, she did ask him to call. With a sort of queenly, bored disdain and only after he had asked twice if he might—but she did it. And Archibald resolved that, no matter what the mental strain, he would show her that her first impression of him had been erroneous; that, trivial and vapid though he might seem, there were in his nature deeps whose existence she had not suspected.

For a young man who had been super-annuated from Eton and believed everything he read in the Racing Expert's column in the morning paper, Archibald, I am bound to admit, exhibited in this crisis a sagacity for which few of his intimates would have given him credit. It may be that love stimulates the mind, or it may be that when the moment comes Blood will tell. Archibald, you must remember, was, after all, a Mulliner: and now the old canny strain of the Mulliners came out in him.

"Meadowes, my man," he said to Meadowes, his man.

"Sir," said Meadowes.

"It appears," said Archibald, "that there is— or was—a cove of the name of Shakespeare. Also a second cove of the name of Bacon. Bacon wrote plays, it seems, and Shakespeare went and put his own name on the programme and copped the credit."

"Indeed, sir?"

"If true, not right, Meadowes."

"Far from it, sir."

"Very well, then. I wish to go into this matter carefully. Kindly pop out and get me a book or two bearing on the business."

He had planned his campaign with infinite cunning. He knew that, before anything could be done in the direction of winning the heart of Aurelia Cammarleigh, he must first establish himself solidly with the aunt. He must court the aunt, ingratiate himself with her—always, of course, making it clear from the start that she was not the one. And, if reading about Shakespeare and Bacon could do it, he would, he told himself, have her eating out of his hand in a week.

Meadowes returned with a parcel of forbidding-looking volumes, and Archibald put in a fortnight's intensive study. Then, discarding the monocle which had up till then been his constant companion, and substituting for it a pair of horn-rimmed spectacles which gave him something of the look of an earnest sheep, he set out for Park Street to pay his first call. And within five minutes of his arrival he had declined a cigarette on the plea that he was a non-smoker, and had managed to say some rather caustic things about the practice, so prevalent among his contemporaries, of drinking cocktails.

Life, said Archibald, toying with his teacup, was surely given to us for some better purpose than the destruction of our brains and digestions with alcohol. Bacon, for instance, never took a cocktail in his life, and look at him.

At this, the aunt, who up till now had plainly been regarding him as just another of those unfortunate incidents, sprang to life.

"You admire Bacon, Mr. Mulliner?" she asked eagerly.

And, reaching out an arm like the tentacle of an octopus, she drew him into a corner and talked about Cryptograms for forty-seven minutes by the drawing-room clock. In short, to sum the thing up, my nephew Archibald, at his initial meeting with the only relative of the girl he loved, went like a sirocco. A Mulliner is always a Mulliner. Apply the acid test, and he will meet it.

It was not long after this that he informed me that he had sown the good seed to such an extent that Aurelia's aunt had invited him to pay a long visit to her country house, Brawstead Towers, in Sussex.

He was seated at the Savoy bar when he told me this, rather feverishly putting himself outside a Scotch and soda: and I was perplexed to note that his face was drawn and his eyes haggard.

"But you do not seem happy, my boy," I said.

"I'm not happy."

"But surely this should be an occasion for rejoicing. Thrown together as you will be in the pleasant surroundings of a country house, you ought easily to find an opportunity of asking this girl to marry you."

"And a lot of good that will be," said Archibald moodily. "Even if I do get a chance I shan't be able to make any use of it. I wouldn't have the nerve. You don't seem to realize what it means being in love with a girl like Aurelia. When I look into those clear, soulful eyes, or see that perfect profile bobbing about on the horizon, a sense of my unworthiness seems to slosh me amidships like some blunt instrument. My tongue gets entangled with my front teeth, and all I can do is stand there feeling like a piece of Gorgonzola that has been condemned by the local sanitary inspector. I'm going to Brawstead Towers, yes, but I don't expect anything to come of it. I know exactly what's going to happen to me. I shall just buzz along through life, pining dumbly, and in the end slide into the tomb of a blasted, blighted bachelor. Another whisky, please, and jolly well make it a double."

Brawstead Towers, situated as it is in the pleasant Weald of Sussex, stands some fifty miles from London: and Archibald, taking the trip easily in his car, arrived there in time to dress comfortably for dinner. It was only when he reached the drawing-room at eight o'clock that he discovered that the younger members of the house-party had gone off in a body to dine and dance at a hospitable neighbour's, leaving him to waste the evening tie of a lifetime, to the com-position of which he had devoted no less than twenty-two minutes, on Aurelia's aunt.

Dinner in these circumstances could hardly hope to be an unmixedly exhilarating function. Among the things which helped to differentiate it from a Babylonian orgy was the fact that, in deference to his known prejudices, no wine was served to Archibald. And, lacking artificial stimulus, he found the aunt even harder to endure philosophically than ever.

Archibald had long since come to a definite decision that what this woman needed was a fluid ounce of weed-killer, scientifically administered. With a good deal of adroitness he contrived to head her off from her favourite topic during the meal: but after the coffee had been disposed of she threw off all restraint. Scooping him up and bearing him off into the recesses of the west wing, she wedged him into a corner of a settee and began to tell him all about the remarkable discovery which had been made by applying the Plain Cipher to Milton's well-known Epitaph on Shakespeare.

"The one beginning 'What needs my Shakespeare for his honoured bones?'" said the aunt.

"Oh, that one?" said Archibald.

"'What needs my Shakespeare for his honoured bones? The labour of an Age in piled stones? Or that his hallowed Reliques should be hid under a starry-pointing Pyramid?'" said the aunt.

Archibald, who was not good at riddles, said he didn't know.

"As in the Plays and Sonnets," said the aunt, "we substitute the name equivalents of the figure totals."

"We do what?"

"Substitute the name equivalents of the figure totals."

"The which?"

"The figure totals."

"All right," said Archibald. "Let it go. I daresay you know best."

The aunt inflated her lungs.

"These figure totals," she said, "are always taken out in the Plain Cipher, A equalling one to Z equals twenty-four. The names are counted in the same way. A capital letter with the figures indicates an occasional variation in the Name Count. For instance, A equals twenty-seven, B twenty-eight, until K equals ten is reached, when K, instead of ten, becomes one, and T instead of nineteen, is one, and R or Reverse, and so on, until A equals twenty-four is reached. The short or single Digit is not used here. Reading the Epitaph in the light of this Cipher, it becomes: What need Verulam for Shakespeare? Francis

Bacon England's King be hid under a W. Shakespeare? William Shakespeare. Fame, what needst Francis Tudor, King of England? Francis. Francis W. Shakespeare. For Francis thy William Shakespeare hath England's King took W. Shakespeare. Then thou our W. Shakespeare Francis Tudor bereaving Francis Bacon Francis Tudor such a tomb William Shakespeare.' "

The speech to which he had been listening was unusually lucid and simple for a Baconian, yet Archibald, his eye catching a battle-axe that hung on the wall, could not but stifle a wistful sigh. How simple it would have been, had he not been a Mulliner and a gentleman, to remove the weapon from its hook, spit on his hands, and haul off and dot this doddering old ruin one just above the imitation pearl necklace. Placing his twitching hands underneath him and sitting on them, he stayed where he was, until just as the clock on the mantelpiece chimed the hour of midnight, a merciful fit of hiccoughs on the part of his hostess enabled him to retire. As she reached the twenty-seventh "hic," his fingers found the door-handle and a moment later he was outside, streaking up the stairs.

The room they had given Archibald was at the end of a corridor, a pleasant, airy apartment with French windows opening upon a broad balcony. At any other time he would have found it agreeable to hop out onto this balcony and revel in the scents and sounds of the summer night, thinking the while long, lingering thoughts of Aurelia. But what with all that Francis Tudor Francis Bacon such a tomb William Shakespeare count seventeen drop one knit purl and set them up in the other alley stuff, not even thoughts of Aurelia could keep him from his bed.

Moodily tearing off his clothes and donning his pyjamas, Archibald Mulliner climbed in and instantaneously discovered that the bed was an apple-pie bed. When and how it had happened he did not know, but at a point during the day some loving hand had sewn up the sheets and put two hair-brushes and a branch of some prickly shrub between them.

Himself from earliest boyhood an adept at the construction of booby-traps, Archibald, had his frame of mind been sunnier, would doubtless have greeted this really extremely sound effort

with a cheery laugh. As it was, weighed down
with Verulams and Francis Tudors, he swore
for a while with considerable fervour: then, rip-
ping off the sheets and tossing the prickly shrub
wearily into a corner, crawled between the
blankets and was soon asleep.

His last waking thought was that if the aunt
hoped to catch him on the morrow, she would
have to be considerably quicker on her pins than
her physique indicated.

How long Archibald slept he could not have
said. He woke some hours later with a vague
feeling that a thunderstorm of unusual violence
had broken out in his immediate neighbourhood.
But this, he realized as the mists of slumber
cleared away, was an error. The noise which had
disturbed him was not thunder but the sound of
someone snoring. Snoring like the dickens. The
walls seemed to be vibrating like the deck of an
ocean liner.

Archibald Mulliner might have had a tough
evening with the aunt, but his spirit was not so
completely broken as to make him lie supinely
down beneath that snoring. The sound filled him,
as snoring fills every right-thinking man, with a

seething resentment and a passionate yearning for justice, and he climbed out of bed with the intention of taking the proper steps through the recognised channels. It is the custom nowadays to disparage the educational methods of the English public-school and to maintain that they are not practical and of a kind to fit the growing boy for the problems of after-life. But you do learn one thing at a public-school, and that is how to act when somebody starts snoring.

You jolly well grab a cake of soap and pop in and stuff it down the blighter's throat. And this Archibald proposed—God willing—to do. It was the work of but a moment with him to dash to the washstand and arm himself. Then he moved softly out through the French windows onto the balcony.

The snoring, he had ascertained, proceeded from the next room. Presumably this room also would have French windows: and presumably, as the night was warm, these would be open. It would be a simple task to oil in, insert the soap, and buzz back undetected.

It was a lovely night, but Archibald paid no attention to it. Clasping his cake of soap, he crept on and was pleased to discover, on arriving outside the snorer's room, that his surmise had been correct. The windows were open. Beyond them, screening the interior of the room, were heavy curtains. And he had just placed his hand upon these when from inside a voice spoke. At the same moment the light was turned on.

"Who's that?" said the voice.

And it was as if Brawstead Towers with all its stabling, outhouses and messuages had fallen on Archibald's head. A mist rose before his eyes. He gasped and tottered.

The voice was that of Aurelia Cammarleigh.

For an instant, for a single long, sickening instant, I am compelled to admit that Archibald's love, deep as the sea though it was, definitely wobbled. It had received a grievous blow. It was not simply the discovery that the girl he adored was a snorer that unmanned him: it was the thought that she could snore like that. There was something about those snores that had seemed to sin against his whole conception of womanly purity.

Then he recovered. Even though this girl's slumber was not, as the poet Milton so beautifully puts it, "airy light," but rather reminiscent of a lumber-camp when the wood-sawing is proceeding at its briskest, he loved her still.

He had just reached this conclusion when a second voice spoke inside the room.

"I say, Aurelia."

It was the voice of another girl. He perceived now that the question "Who's that?" had been addressed not to him but to this newcomer fumbling at the door-handle.

"I say, Aurelia," said the girl complainingly, "you've simply got to do something about that bally bulldog of yours. I can't possibly get to sleep with him snoring like that. He's making the plaster come down from the ceiling in my room."

"I'm sorry," said Aurelia. "I've got so used to it that I don't notice."

"Well, I do. Put a green-baize cloth over him or something."

Out on the moonlit balcony Archibald Mulliner stood shaking like a blancmange. Although he had contrived to maintain his great love practically intact when he had supposed the snores to proceed from the girl he worshipped, it had been tough going, and for an instant, as I have said, a very near thing. The relief that swept over him at the discovery that Aurelia could still justifiably remain on her pinnacle was so profound that it made him feel filleted. He seemed for a moment in a daze. Then he was brought out of the ether by hearing his name spoken.

"Did Archie Mulliner arrive to-night?" asked Aurelia's friend.

"I suppose so," said Aurelia. "He wired that he was motoring down."

"Just between us girls," said Aurelia's friend, "what do you think of that bird?"

To listen to a private conversation—especially a private conversation between two modern girls when you never know what may come next— is rightly considered an action incompatible with the claim to be a gentleman. I regret to say, therefore, that Archibald, ignoring the fact that he belonged to a family whose code is as high as that of any in the land, instead of creeping away to his room edged at this point a step closer to the curtains and stood there with his ears flapping. It might be an ignoble thing to eavesdrop, but it was apparent that Aurelia Cammarleigh was about to reveal her candid opinion of him: and the prospect of getting the true facts—

straight, as it were, from the horse's mouth—held him so fascinated that he could not move.

"Archie Mulliner?" said Aurelia meditatively.

"Yes. The betting at the Junior Lipstick is seven to two that you'll marry him."

"Why on earth?"

"Well, people have noticed he's always round at your place, and they seem to think it significant. Anyway, that's how the odds stood when I left London—seven to two."

"Get in on the short end," said Aurelia earnestly, "and you'll make a packet."

"Is that official?"

"Absolutely," said Aurelia.

Out in the moonlight, Archibald Mulliner uttered a low, bleak moan rather like the last bit of wind going out of a dying duck. True, he had always told himself that he hadn't a chance, but, however much a man may say that, he never in his heart really believes it. And now from an authoritative source he had learned that his romance was definitely blue round the edges. It was a shattering blow. He wondered dully how the trains ran to the Rocky Mountains. A spot of grizzly-bear shooting seemed indicated.

Inside the room, the other girl appeared perplexed.

"But you told me at Ascot," she said, "just after he had been introduced to you, that you rather thought you had at last met your ideal. When did the good thing begin to come unstuck?"

A silvery sigh came through the curtains.

"I did think so then," said Aurelia wistfully. "There was something about him. I liked the way his ears wiggled. And I had always heard he was such a perfectly genial, cheery, merry old soul. Algy Wymondham-Wymondham told me that his imitation of a hen laying an egg was alone enough to keep any reasonable girl happy through a long married life."

"Can he imitate a hen?"

"No. It was nothing but an idle rumour. I asked him, and he stoutly denied that he had ever done such a thing in his life. He was quite stuffy about it. I felt a little uneasy then, and the moment he started calling and hanging about the house I knew that my fears had been well-founded. The man is beyond question a flat tire and a wet smack."

"As bad as that?"

"I'm not exaggerating a bit. Where people

ever got the idea that Archie Mulliner is a bonhomous old bean beats me. He is the world's
worst monkey-wrench. He doesn't drink cocktails, he doesn't smoke cigarettes, and the thing he
seems to enjoy most in the world is to sit for hours
listening to the conversation of my aunt, who,
as you know, is pure goof from the soles of the
feet to the tortoiseshell comb and should long
ago have been renting a padded cell in Earls-
wood. Believe me, Muriel, if you can really get
seven to two, you are onto the best thing since
Buttercup won the Lincolnshire."

"You don't say!"

"I do say. Apart from anything else, he's got
a beastly habit of looking at me reverently. And
if you knew how sick I am of being looked at
reverently! They will do it, these lads. I suppose
it's because I'm rather an out-size and modelled
on the lines of Cleopatra."

"Tough!"

"You bet it's tough. A girl can't help her appearance. I may look as if my ideal man was the
hero of a Viennese operetta, but I don't feel that
way. What I want is some good sprightly sportsman who sets a neat booby-trap, and who'll rush
up and grab me in his arms and say to me, 'Au-

relia, old girl, you're the bee's roller-skates!' "

And Aurelia Cammarleigh emitted another sigh.

"Talking of booby-traps," said the other girl, "if Archie Mulliner has arrived he's in the next room, isn't he?"

"I suppose so. That's where he was to be. Why?"

"Because I made him an apple-pie bed."

"It was the right spirit," said Aurelia warmly. "I wish I'd thought of it myself."

"Too late now."

"Yes," said Aurelia. "But I'll tell you what I can and will do. You say you object to Lysander's snoring. Well, I'll go and pop him in at Archie Mulliner's window. That'll give him pause for thought."

"Splendid," agreed the girl Muriel. "Well, good night."

"Good night," said Aurelia.

There followed the sound of a door closing.

There was, as I have indicated, not much of my nephew Archibald's mind, but what there was of it was now in a whirl. He was stunned. Like every man who is abruptly called upon to revise his entire scheme of values, he felt as if he had been standing on top of the Eiffel Tower and some practical joker had suddenly drawn it away from under him. Tottering back to his room, he replaced the cake of soap in its dish and sat down on the bed to grapple with this amazing development.

Aurelia Cammarleigh had compared herself to Cleopatra. It is not too much to say that my nephew Archibald's emotions at this juncture were very similar to what Marc Antony's would have been had Egypt's queen risen from her throne at his entry and without a word of warning started to dance the Black Bottom.

He was roused from his thoughts by the sound of a light footstep on the balcony outside. At the same moment he heard a low woofly gruffle, the unmistakable note of a bulldog of regular habits who has been jerked out of his basket in the small hours and forced to take the night air.

She is coming, my own, my sweet!
Were it never so airy a tread,
My heart would hear her and beat,
Were it earth in an earthy bed,

whispered Archibald's soul, or words to that effect. He rose from his seat and paused for an instant, irresolute. Then inspiration descended on him. He knew what to do, and he did it.

Yes, gentlemen, in that supreme crisis of his life, with his whole fate hanging, as you might say, in the balance, Archibald Mulliner, showing for almost the first time in his career a well-nigh human intelligence, began to give his celebrated imitation of a hen laying an egg.

Archibald's imitation of a hen laying an egg was conceived on broad and sympathetic lines. Less violent than Salvini's *Othello,* it had in it something of the poignant wistfulness of Mrs. Siddons in the sleep-walking scene of *Macbeth.* The rendition started quietly, almost inaudibly, with a sort of soft, liquid crooning—the joyful yet half-incredulous murmur of a mother who can scarcely believe as yet that her union has really been blessed, and that it is indeed she who is responsible for that oval mixture of chalk and albumen which she sees lying beside her in the straw.

Then, gradually, conviction comes.

"It looks like an egg," one seems to hear her

say. "It feels like an egg. It's shaped like an egg. Damme, it *is* an egg!"

And at that, all doubting resolved, the crooning changes; takes on a firmer note; soars into the upper register; and finally swells into a maternal pæan of joy—a "Charawk-chawk-chawk-chawk" of such a calibre that few had ever been able to listen to it dry-eyed. Following which, it was Archibald's custom to run round the room, flapping the sides of his coat, and then, leaping onto a sofa or some convenient chair, to stand there with his arms at right angles, crowing himself purple in the face.

All these things he had done many a time for the idle entertainment of fellow-members in the smoking-room of the Drones, but never with the gusto, the *brio,* with which he performed them now. Essentially a modest man, like all the Mulliners, he was compelled, nevertheless, to recognise that to-night he was surpassing himself. Every artist knows when the authentic divine fire is within him, and an inner voice told Archibald Mulliner that he was at the top of his form and giving the performance of a lifetime. Love thrilled through every "Brt-t't-t't" that he uttered, animated each flap of his arms. Indeed, so deeply did Love drive in its spur that he tells me that, instead of the customary once, he actually made the circle of the room three times before coming to rest on top of the chest of drawers.

When at length he did so he glanced towards the window and saw that through the curtains the loveliest face in the world was peering. And in Aurelia Cammarleigh's glorious eyes there was a look he had never seen before, the sort of look Kreisler or somebody like that beholds in the eyes of the front row as he lowers his violin and brushes his forehead with the back of his hand. A look of worship.

There was a long silence. Then she spoke.

"Do it again!" she said.

And Archibald did it again. He did it four times and could, he tells me, if he had pleased, have taken a fifth encore or at any rate a couple of bows. And then, leaping lightly to the floor, he advanced towards her. He felt conquering, dominant. It was his hour. He reached out and clasped her in his arms.

"Aurelia, old girl," said Archibald Mulliner in a clear, firm voice, "you are the bee's roller-skates."

And at that she seemed to melt into his embrace. Her lovely face was raised to his.

"Archibald!" she whispered.

There was another throbbing silence, broken only by the beating of two hearts and the wheezing of the bulldog, who seemed to suffer a good deal in his bronchial tubes. Then Archibald released her.

"Well, that's that," he said. "Glad everything's all settled and hotsy-totsy. Gosh, I wish I had a cigarette. This is the sort of moment a bloke needs one."

She looked at him, surprised.

"But I thought you didn't smoke."

"Oh yes, I do."

"And do you drink as well?"

"Quite as well," said Archibald. "In fact, rather better. Oh, by the way."

"Yes?"

"There's just one other thing. Suppose that aunt of yours wants to come and visit us when we are settled down in our little nest, what, dearest, would be your reaction to the scheme of soaking her on the base of the skull with a stuffed eel-skin?"

"I should like it," said Aurelia warmly, "above all things."

"Twin souls," cried Archibald. "That's what we are, when you come right down to it. I suspected it all along, and now I know. Two jolly old twin souls." He embraced her ardently. "And now," he said, "let us pop downstairs and put this bulldog in the butler's pantry, where he will come upon him unexpectedly in the morning and doubtless get a shock which will do him as much good as a week at the seaside. Are you on?"

"I am," whispered Aurelia. "Oh, I am!"

And hand in hand they wandered out together onto the broad staircase.

THE ORDEAL OF OSBERT MULLINER

The Ordeal of Osbert Mulliner

THE unwonted gravity of Mr. Mulliner's demeanour had struck us all directly he entered the bar-parlour of the Anglers' Rest: and the silent, moody way in which he sipped his hot Scotch and lemon convinced us that something was wrong. We hastened to make sympathetic inquiries.

Our solicitude seemed to please him. He brightened a little.

"Well, gentlemen," he said, "I had not intended to intrude my private troubles on this happy gathering, but, if you must know, a young second cousin of mine has left his wife and is filing papers of divorce. It has upset me very much."

Miss Postlethwaite, our warm-hearted barmaid, who was polishing glasses, introduced a sort of bedside manner into her task.

"Some viper crept into his home?" she asked.

Mr. Mulliner shook his head.

"No," he said. "No vipers. The whole trouble appears to have been that, whenever my second cousin spoke to his wife, she would open her eyes to their fullest extent, put her head on one side like a canary, and say 'What?' He said he had stood it for eleven months and three days, which he believes to be a European record, and that the time had now come, in his opinion, to take steps."

Mr. Mulliner sighed.

"The fact of the matter is," he said, "marriage to-day is made much too simple for a man. He finds it so easy to go out and grab some sweet girl that when he has got her he does not value her. I am convinced that that is the real cause of this modern boom in divorce. What marriage needs, to make it a stable institution, is something in the nature of obstacles during the courtship period. I attribute the solid happiness of my nephew Osbert's union, to take but one instance, to the events which preceded it. If the thing had been a walk-over, he would have prized his wife far less highly."

"It took him a long time to teach her his true worth?" we asked.

"Love burgeoned slowly?" hazarded Miss Postlethwaite.

"On the contrary," said Mr. Mulliner, "she loved him at first sight. What made the wooing of Mabel Petherick-Soames so extraordinarily difficult for my nephew Osbert was not any coldness on her part, but the unfortunate mental attitude of J. Bashford Braddock. Does that name suggest anything to you, gentlemen?"

"No."

"You do not think that a man with such a name would be likely to be a toughish sort of egg?"

"He might be, now you mention it."

"He was. In Central Africa, where he spent a good deal of his time exploring, ostriches would bury their heads in the sand at Bashford Braddock's approach and even rhinoceroses, the most ferocious beasts in existence, frequently edged behind trees and hid till he had passed. And the moment he came into Osbert's life my nephew realized with a sickening clearness that those rhinoceroses had known their business."

Until the advent of this man Braddock (said Mr. Mulliner), Fortune seemed to have lavished her favours on my nephew Osbert in full and even overflowing measure. Handsome, like all the Mulliners, he possessed in addition to good looks the inestimable blessings of perfect health, a cheerful disposition and so much money that Income-Tax assessors screamed with joy when forwarding Schedule D to his address. And, on top of all this, he had fallen deeply in love with a most charming girl and rather fancied that his passion was reciprocated.

For several peaceful, happy weeks all went well. Osbert advanced without a set-back of any description through the various stages of calling, sending flowers, asking after her father's lumbago, and patting her mother's Pomeranian to the point where he was able, with the family's full approval, to invite the girl out alone to dinner and a theatre. And it was on this night of nights, when all should have been joy and happiness, that the Braddock menace took shape.

Until Bashford Braddock made his appearance, no sort of hitch had occurred to mar the perfect tranquillity of the evening's proceedings. The dinner had been excellent, the play entertaining. Twice during the third act Osbert had ventured to squeeze the girl's hand in a warm, though of course gentlemanly, manner: and it seemed to him that the pressure had been re-turned. It is not surprising, therefore, that by the time they were parting on the steps of her house he had reached the conclusion that he was onto a good thing which should be pushed along.

Putting his fortune to the test, to win or lose it all, Osbert Mulliner reached forward, clasped Mabel Petherick-Soames to his bosom, and gave her a kiss so ardent that in the silent night it sounded like somebody letting off a Mills bomb.

And scarcely had the echoes died away, when he became aware that there was standing at his elbow a tall, broad-shouldered man in evening dress and an opera hat.

There was a pause. The girl was the first to speak.

"Hullo, Bashy," she said, and there was annoyance in her voice. "Where on earth did you spring from? I thought you were exploring on the Congo or somewhere."

The man removed his opera hat, squashed it flat, popped it out again and spoke in a deep, rumbling voice.

"I returned from the Congo this morning. I have been dining with your father and mother.

They informed me that you had gone to the theatre with this gentleman."

"Mr. Mulliner. My cousin, Bashford Braddock."

"How do you do?" said Osbert.

There was another pause. Bashford Braddock removed his opera hat, squashed it flat, popped it out again and replaced it on his head. He seemed disappointed that he could not play a tune on it.

"Well, good night," said Mabel.

"Good night," said Osbert.

"Good night," said Bashford Braddock.

The door closed, and Osbert, looking from it to his companion, found that the other was staring at him with a peculiar expression in his eyes. They were hard, glittering eyes. Osbert did not like them.

"Mr. Mulliner," said Bashford Braddock.

"Hullo?" said Osbert.

"A word with you. I saw all."

"All?"

"All. Mr. Mulliner, you love that girl."

"I do."

"So do I."

"You do?"

"I do."

Osbert felt a little embarrassed. All he could think of to say was that it made them seem like one great big family.

"I have loved her since she was so high."

"How high?" asked Osbert, for the light was uncertain.

"About so high. And I have always sworn that if ever any man came between us; if ever any slinking, sneaking, pop-eyed, lop-eared son of a sea-cook attempted to rob me of that girl, I would . . ."

"Er—what?" asked Osbert.

Bashford Braddock laughed a short, metallic laugh.

"Did you ever hear what I did to the King of Mgumbo-Mgumbo?"

"I didn't even know there was a King of Mgumbo-Mgumbo."

"There isn't—now," said Bashford Braddock.

Osbert was conscious of a clammy, creeping sensation in the region of his spine.

"What did you do to him?"

"Don't ask."

"But I want to know."

"Far better not. You will find out quite soon

enough if you continue to hang round Mabel
Petherick-Soames. That is all, Mr. Mulliner."
Bashford Braddock looked up at the twinkling
stars. "What delightful weather we are having,"
he said. "There was just the same quiet hush and
peaceful starlight, I recollect, that time out in
the Ngobi desert when I strangled the jaguar."

Osbert's Adam's Apple slipped a cog.

"W—what jaguar?"

"Oh, you wouldn't know it. Just one of the
jaguars out there. I had a rather tricky five minutes of it at first, because my right arm was in a
sling and I could only use my left. Well, good
night, Mr. Mulliner, good night."

And Bashford Braddock, having removed his
opera hat, squashed it flat, popped it out again
and replaced it on his head, stalked off into the
darkness.

For several minutes after he had disappeared
Osbert Mulliner stood motionless, staring after
him with unseeing eyes. Then, tottering round
the corner, he made his way to his residence in
South Audley Street, and, contriving after three
false starts to unlock the front door, climbed the
stairs to his cosy library. There, having mixed

himself a strong brandy-and-soda, he sat down and gave himself up to meditation: and eventually, after one quick drink and another taken rather slower, was able to marshal his thoughts with a certain measure of coherence. And those thoughts, I regret to say, when marshalled, were of a nature which I shrink from revealing to you.

It is never pleasant, gentlemen, to have to display a relative in an unsympathetic light, but the truth is the truth and must be told. I am compelled, therefore, to confess that my nephew Osbert, forgetting that he was a Mulliner, writhed at this moment in an agony of craven fear.

It would be possible, of course, to find excuses for him. The thing had come upon him very suddenly, and even the stoutest are sometimes disconcerted by sudden peril. Then, again, his circumstances and upbringing had fitted him ill for such a crisis. A man who has been pampered by Fortune from birth becomes highly civilized: and the more highly civilized we are, the less adroitly do we cope with bounders of the Braddock type who seem to belong to an earlier and rougher age. Osbert Mulliner was simply unequal to the task of tackling cavemen.

Apart from some slight skill at contract bridge, the only thing he was really good at was collecting old jade: and what a help that would be, he felt as he mixed himself a third brandy-and-soda, in a personal combat with a man who appeared to think it only sporting to give jaguars a chance by fighting them one-handed.

He could see but one way out of the delicate situation in which he had been placed. To give Mabel Petherick-Soames up would break his heart, but it seemed to be a straight issue between that and his neck, and in this black hour the voting in favour of the neck was a positive land-slide. Trembling in every limb, my nephew Osbert went to the desk and began to compose a letter of farewell.

He was sorry, he wrote, that he would be unable to see Miss Petherick-Soames on the morrow, as they had planned, owing to his unfortunately being called away to Australia. He added that he was pleased to have made her acquaintance and that if, as seemed probable, they never saw each other again, he would always watch her future career with considerable interest.

Signing the letter "Yrs. truly, O. Mulliner,"

Osbert addressed the envelope and, taking it up the street to the post-office, dropped it in the box. Then he returned home and went to bed.

The telephone, ringing by his bedside, woke Osbert at an early hour next morning. He did not answer it. A glance at his watch had told him that the time was half-past eight, when the first delivery of letters is made in London. It seemed only too likely that Mabel, having just received and read his communication, was endeavouring to discuss the matter with him over the wire. He rose, bathed, shaved and dressed, and had just finished a sombre breakfast when the door opened and Parker, his man, announced Major-General Sir Masterman Petherick-Soames.

An icy finger seemed to travel slowly down Osbert's backbone. He cursed the preoccupation which had made him omit to instruct Parker to inform all callers that he was not at home. With some difficulty, for the bones seemed to have been removed from his legs, he rose to receive the tall, upright, grizzled and formidable old man who entered, and rallied himself to play the host.

"Good morning," he said. "Will you have a poached egg?"

"I will not have a poached egg," replied Sir Masterman. "Poached egg, indeed! Poached egg, forsooth! Ha! Tchal! Bah!"

He spoke with such curt brusqueness that a stranger, had one been present, might have supposed him to belong to some league or society for the suppression of poached eggs. Osbert, however, with his special knowledge of the facts, was able to interpret this brusqueness correctly and was not surprised when his visitor, gazing at him keenly with a pair of steely blue eyes which must have got him very much disliked in military circles, plunged at once into the subject of the letter.

"Mr. Mulliner, my niece Mabel has received a strange communication from you."

"Oh, she got it all right?" said Osbert, with an attempt at ease.

"It arrived this morning. You had omitted to stamp it. There was threepence to pay."

"Oh, I say, I'm fearfully sorry. I must . . ."

Major-General Sir Masterman Petherick-Soames waved down his apologies.

"It is not the monetary loss which has so distressed my niece, but the letter's contents. My niece is under the impression that last night she and you became engaged to be married, Mr. Mulliner."

Osbert coughed.

"Well—er—not exactly. Not altogether. Not, as it were . . . I mean . . . You see . . ."

"I see very clearly. You have been trifling with my niece's affections, Mr. Mulliner. And I have always sworn that if ever a man trifled with the affections of any of my nieces, I would . . ." He broke off and, taking a lump of sugar from the bowl, balanced it absently on the edge of a slice of toast. "Did you ever hear of a Captain Walkinshaw?"

"No."

"Captain J. G. Walkinshaw? Dark man with an eyeglass. Used to play the saxophone."

"No."

"Ah? I thought you might have met him. He trifled with the affections of my niece, Hester. I horsewhipped him on the steps of the Drones Club. Is the name Blenkinsop-Bustard familiar to you?"

"No."

"Rupert Blenkinsop-Bustard trifled with the affections of my niece Gertrude. He was one of the Somersetshire Blenkinsop-Bustards. Wore a fair moustache and kept pigeons. I horsewhipped him on the steps of the Junior Bird-Fanciers. By the way, Mr. Mulliner, what is your club?"

"The United Jade-Collectors," quavered Osbert.

"Has it steps?"

"I—I believe so."

"Good. Good." A dreamy look came into the General's eyes. "Well, the announcement of your engagement to my niece Mabel will appear in to-morrow's *Morning Post*. If it is contradicted . . . Well, good morning, Mr. Mulliner, good morning."

And, replacing in the dish the piece of bacon which he had been poising on a teaspoon, Major-General Sir Masterman Petherick-Soames left the room.

The meditation to which my nephew Osbert had given himself up on the previous night was as nothing to the meditation to which he gave himself up now. For fully an hour he must have sat, his head supported by his hands, frowning

despairingly at the remains of the marmalade
on the plate before him. Though, like all the
Mulliners, a clear thinker, he had to confess
himself completely non-plussed. The situation
had become so complicated that after awhile he
went up to the library and tried to work it out on
paper, letting X equal himself. But even this
brought no solution, and he was still pondering
deeply when Parker came up to announce lunch.

"Lunch?" said Osbert, amazed. "Is it lunch-
time already?"

"Yes, sir. And might I be permitted to offer my
respectful congratulations and good wishes, sir?"

"Eh?"

"On your engagement, sir. The General happened to mention to me as I let him out that a
marriage had been arranged and would shortly
take place between yourself and Miss Mabel
Petherick-Soames. It was fortunate that he did
so, as I was thus enabled to give the gentleman the
information he required."

"Gentleman?"

"A Mr. Bashford Braddock, sir. He rang up
about an hour after the General had left and said
he had been informed of your engagement and
wished to know if the news was well-founded. I

assured him that it was, and he said he would be calling to see you later. He was very anxious to know when you would be at home. He seemed a nice, friendly gentleman, sir."

Osbert rose as if the chair in which he sat had suddenly become incandescent.

"Parker!"

"Sir?"

"I am unexpectedly obliged to leave London, Parker. I don't know where I am going—probably the Zambesi or Greenland—but I shall be away a long time. I shall close the house and give the staff an indefinite holiday. They will receive three months' wages in advance, and at the end of that period will communicate with my lawyers, Messrs. Peabody, Thrupp, Thrupp, Thrupp, Thrupp and Peabody of Lincoln's Inn. Inform them of this."

"Very good, sir."

"And, Parker."

"Sir?"

"I am thinking of appearing shortly in some amateur theatricals. Kindly step round the corner and get me a false wig, a false nose, some false whiskers and a good stout pair of blue spectacles."

Osbert's plans when, after a cautious glance up and down the street, he left the house an hour later and directed a taxi-cab to take him to an obscure hotel in the wildest and least-known part of the Cromwell Road were of the vaguest. It was only when he reached that haven and had thoroughly wigged, nosed, whiskered and blue-spectacled himself that he began to formulate a definite plan of campaign. He spent the rest of the day in his room, and shortly before lunch next morning set out for the Second-Hand Clothing establishment of the Bros. Cohen, near Covent Garden, to purchase a complete traveller's outfit. It was his intention to board the boat sailing on the morrow for India and to potter awhile about the world, taking in *en route* Japan, South Africa, Peru, Mexico, China, Venezuela, the Fiji Islands and other beauty-spots.

All the Cohens seemed glad to see him when he arrived at the shop. They clustered about him in a body, as if guessing by instinct that here came one of those big orders. At this excellent emporium one may buy, in addition to second-hand clothing, practically anything that exists: and the difficulty—for the brothers are all thrustful salesmen—is to avoid doing so. At the end of five minutes, Osbert was mildly surprised to find himself in possession of a smoking-cap, three boxes of poker chips, some polo sticks, a fishing-rod, a concertina, a ukulele, and a bowl of gold-fish.

He clicked his tongue in annoyance. These men appeared to him to have got quite a wrong angle on the situation. They seemed to think that he proposed to make his travels one long round of pleasure. As clearly as he was able, he tried to tell them that in the few broken years that remained to him before a shark or jungle-fever put an end to his sorrows he would have little heart for polo, for poker, or for playing the concertina while watching the gambols of goldfish. They might just as well offer him, he said querulously, a cocked hat or a sewing-machine.

Instant activity prevailed among the brothers.

"Fetch the gentleman his sewing-machine, Isadore."

"And, while you're getting him the cocked hat, Lou," said Irving, "ask the customer in the shoe department if he'll be kind enough to step this way. You're in luck," he assured Osbert. "If you're going travelling in foreign parts, he's the very man to advise you. You've heard of Mr. Braddock?"

There was very little of Osbert's face visible behind his whiskers, but that little paled beneath its tan.

"Mr. B—b—b . . .?"

"That's right. Mr. Braddock, the explorer."

"Air!" said Osbert. "Give me air!"

He made rapidly for the door, and was about to charge through when it opened to admit a tall, distinguished-looking man of military appearance.

"Shop!" cried the newcomer in a clear, patrician voice, and Osbert reeled back against a pile of trousers. It was Major-General Sir Masterman Petherick-Soames.

A platoon of Cohens advanced upon him, Isadore hastily snatching up a fireman's helmet and Irving a microscope and a couple of jig-saw puzzles. The General waved them aside.

"Do you," he asked, "keep horsewhips?"

"Yes, sir. Plenty of horsewhips."

"I want a nice strong one with a medium sized handle and lots of spring," said Major-General Sir Masterman Petherick-Soames.

And at this moment Lou returned, followed by Bashford Braddock.

"Is this the gentleman?" said Bashford Braddock genially. "You're going abroad, sir, I understand. Delighted if I can be of any service."

"Bless my soul," said Major-General Sir Masterman Petherick-Soames. "Bashford? It's so confoundedly dark in here, I didn't recognize you."

"Switch on the light, Irving," said Isadore.

"No, don't," said Osbert. "My eyes are weak."

"If your eyes are weak you ought not to be going to the Tropics," said Bashford Braddock.

"This gentleman a friend of yours?" asked the General.

"Oh, no. I'm just going to help him to buy an outfit."

"The gentleman's already got a smoking-cap, poker chips, polo sticks, a fishing-rod, a concertina, a ukulele, a bowl of goldfish, a cocked hat and a sewing-machine," said Isadore.

"Ah?" said Bashford Braddock. "Then all he will require now is a sun helmet, a pair of puttees, and a pot of ointment for relieving alligator-bites."

With the rapid decision of an explorer who is buying things for which somebody else is going to pay, he completed the selection of Osbert's outfit.

"And what brings you here, Bashford?" asked the General.

"Me? Oh, I looked in to buy a pair of spiked boots. I want to trample on a snake."

"An odd coincidence. I came here to buy a horsewhip to horsewhip a snake."

"A bad week-end for snakes," said Bashford Braddock.

The General nodded gravely.

"Of course, my snake," he said, "may prove not to be a snake. In classifying him as a snake I may have misjudged him. In that case I shall not require this horsewhip. Still, they're always useful to have about the house."

"Undoubtedly. Lunch with me, General?"

"Delighted, my dear fellow."

"Goodbye, sir," said Bashford Braddock, giving Osbert a friendly nod. "Glad I was able to be of some use. When do you sail?"

"Gentleman's sailing to-morrow morning on the *Rajputana*," said Isadore.

"What!" cried Major-General Sir Masterman

Petherick-Soames. "Bless my soul! I didn't realize you were going to *India*. I was out there for
years and can give you all sorts of useful hints.
The old *Rajputana?* Why, I know the purser
well. I'll come and see you off and have a chat
with him. No doubt I shall be able to get you a
number of little extra attentions. No, no, my dear
fellow, don't thank me. I have a good deal on my
mind at the moment, and it will be a relief to do
somebody a kindness."

It seemed to Osbert, as he crawled back to the
shelter of his Cromwell Road bedroom, that Fate
was being altogether too rough with him. Obviously, if Sir Masterman Petherick-Soames intended to come down to the boat to see him off, it
would be madness to attempt to sail. On the deck
of a liner under the noon-day sun the General
must inevitably penetrate his disguise. His whole
scheme of escape must be cancelled and another
substituted. Osbert ordered two pots of black
coffee, tied a wet handkerchief round his forehead, and plunged once more into thought.

It has been frequently said of the Mulliners
that you may perplex but you cannot baffle them.
It was getting on for dinner-time before Osbert

finally decided upon a plan of action: but this plan, he perceived as he examined it, was far superior to the first one.

He had been wrong, he saw, in thinking of flying to foreign climes. For one who desired as fervently as he did never to see Major-General Sir Masterman Petherick-Soames again in this world, the only real refuge was a London suburb. Any momentary whim might lead Sir Masterman to pack a suitcase and take the next boat to the Far East, but nothing would ever cause him to take a tram for Dulwich, Cricklewood, Winchmore Hill, Brixton, Balham or Surbiton. In those trackless wastes Osbert would be safe.

Osbert decided to wait till late at night; then go back to his house in South Audley Street, pack his collection of old jade and a few other necessaries, and vanish into the unknown.

It was getting on for midnight when, creeping warily to the familiar steps, he inserted his latchkey in the familiar keyhole. He had feared that Bashford Braddock might be watching the house, but there were no signs of him. He slipped swiftly into the dark hall and closed the front door softly behind him.

It was at this moment that he became aware that from under the door of the dining-room at the other end of the hall there was stealing a thin stream of light.

For an instant, this evidence that the house was not, as he had supposed, unoccupied startled Osbert considerably. Then, recovering himself, he understood what must have happened. Parker, his man, instead of leaving as he had been told to do, was taking advantage of his employer's presumed absence from London to stay on and do some informal entertaining. Osbert, thoroughly incensed, hurried to the dining-room and felt that his suspicion had been confirmed. On the table were set out all the materials, except food and drink, of a cosy little supper for two. The absence of food and drink was accounted for, no doubt, by the fact that Parker and—Osbert saw only too good reason to fear—his lady-friend were down in the larder, fetching them.

Osbert boiled from his false wig to the soles of his feet with a passionate fury. So this was the sort of thing that went on the moment his back was turned, was it? There were heavy curtains hiding the window, and behind these he crept. It was his intention to permit the feast to begin and then, stepping forth like some avenging Nemesis, to confront his erring man-servant and put it across him in no uncertain manner. Bashford Braddock and Major-General Sir Masterman Petherick-Soames, with their towering stature and whipcord muscles, might intimidate him, but with a shrimp like Parker he felt that he could do himself justice. Osbert had been through much in the last forty-eight hours, and unpleasantness with a man who, like Parker, stood a mere five feet five in his socks appeared to him rather in the nature of a tonic.

He had not been waiting long when there came to his ears the sound of footsteps outside. He softly removed his wig, his nose, his whiskers and his blue spectacles. There must be no disguise to soften the shock when Parker found himself confronted. Then, peeping through the curtains, he prepared to spring.

Osbert did not spring. Instead, he shrank back like a more than ordinarily diffident tortoise into its shell, and tried to achieve the maximum of silence by breathing through his ears. For it was no Parker who had entered, no frivolous lady-friend, but a couple of plug-uglies of such outstanding physique that Bashford Braddock might have been the little brother of either of them.

Osbert stood petrified. He had never seen a burglar before, and he wished, now that he was seeing these, that it could have been arranged for him to do so through a telescope. At this close range, they gave him much the same feeling the prophet Daniel must have had on entering the lions' den, before his relations with the animals had been established on their subsequent basis of easy camaraderie. He was thankful that when the breath which he had been holding for some eighty seconds at length forced itself out in a loud gasp, the noise was drowned by the popping of a cork.

It was from a bottle of Osbert's best Bollinger that this cork had been removed. The marauders, he was able to see, were men who believed in doing themselves well. In these days when almost everybody is on some sort of diet it is rarely that one comes across the old-fashioned type of diner who does not worry about balanced meals and calories but just squares his shoulders and goes at it till his eyes bubble. Osbert's two guests plainly belonged to this nearly obsolete species.

They were drinking out of tankards and eating three varieties of meat simultaneously, as if no such thing as a high blood-pressure had ever been invented. A second pop announced the opening of another quart of champagne.

At the outset of the proceedings, there had been little or nothing in the way of supper-table conversation. But now, the first keen edge of his appetite satisfied by about three pounds of ham, beef and mutton, the burglar who sat nearest to Osbert was able to relax. He looked about him approvingly.

"Nice little crib, this, Ernest," he said.

"R!" replied his companion—a man of few words, and those somewhat impeded by cold potatoes and bread.

"Must have been some real swells in here one time and another."

"R!"

"Baronets and such, I wouldn't be surprised."

"R!" said the second burglar, helping himself to more champagne and mixing in a little port, sherry, Italian vermuth, old brandy and green Chartreuse to give it body.

The first burglar looked thoughtful.

"Talking of baronets," he said, "a thing I've

often wondered is—well, suppose you're having a dinner, see?"

"R!"

"As it might be in this very room."

"R!"

"Well, would a baronet's sister go in before the daughter of the younger son of a peer? I've often wondered about that."

The second burglar finished his champagne, port, sherry, Italian vermuth, old brandy and green Chartreuse, and mixed himself another.

"Go in?"

"Go in to dinner."

"If she was quicker on her feet, she would," said the second burglar. "She'd get to the door first. Stands to reason."

The first burglar raised his eyebrows.

"Ernest," he said coldly, "you talk like an uneducated son of a what-not. Haven't you never been taught nothing about the rules and manners of good Society?"

The second burglar flushed. It was plain that the rebuke had touched a tender spot. There was a strained silence. The first burglar resumed his meal. The second burglar watched him with a hostile eye. He had the air of a man who is waiting for his chance, and it was not long before he found it.

"Harold," he said.

"Well?" said the first burglar.

"Don't gollup your food, Harold," said the second burglar.

The first burglar stared. His eyes gleamed with sudden fury. His armour, like his companion's, had been pierced.

"Who's golluping his food?"

"You are."

"I am?"

"Yes, you."

"Who, me?"

"R!"

"Golluping my food?"

"R! Like a pig or something."

It was evident to Osbert, peeping warily through the curtains, that the generous fluids which these two men had been drinking so lavishly had begun to have their effect. They spoke thickly, and their eyes had become red and swollen.

"I may not know all about baronets' younger sisters," said the burglar Ernest, "but I don't gollup my food like pigs or something."

And, as if to drive home the reproach, he picked up the leg of mutton and began to gnaw it with an affected daintiness.

The next moment the battle had been joined. The spectacle of the other's priggish object-lesson was too much for the burglar Harold. He plainly resented tuition in the amenities from one on whom he had always looked as a social inferior. With a swift movement of the hand he grasped the bottle before him and bounced it smartly on his colleague's head.

Osbert Mulliner cowered behind the curtain. The sportsman in him whispered that he was missing something good, for ring-seats to view which many men would have paid large sums, but he could not nerve himself to look out. However, there was plenty of interest in the thing, even if you merely listened. The bumps and crashes seemed to indicate that the two principals were hitting one another with virtually everything in the room except the wall-paper and the large side-board. Now they appeared to be grappling on the floor, anon fighting at long range with bottles. Words and combinations of whose existence he had till then been unaware, floated to Osbert's ears: and more and more he asked himself, as the combat proceeded: What would the harvest be?

And then, with one titanic crash, the battle ceased as suddenly as it had begun.

It was some moments before Osbert Mulliner could bring himself to peep from behind the curtains. When he did so, he seemed to be gazing upon one of those Orgy scenes which have done so much to popularize the motion-pictures. Scenically, the thing was perfect. All that was needed to complete the resemblance was a few attractive-looking girls with hardly any clothes on.

He came out and gaped down at the ruins. The burglar Harold was lying with his head in the fireplace: the burglar Ernest was doubled up under the table: and it seemed to Osbert almost absurd to think that these were the same hearty fellows who had come into the room to take pot-luck so short a while before. Harold had the appearance of a man who has been passed through a wringer. Ernest gave the illusion of having recently become entangled in some powerful machinery. If, as was probable, they were known to the police, it would take a singularly keen-eyed constable to recognize them now.

The thought of the police reminded Osbert of his duty as a citizen. He went to the telephone and called up the nearest station and was informed that representatives of the Law would be round immediately to scoop up the remains. He went back to the dining-room to wait, but its atmosphere jarred upon him. He felt the need of fresh air: and, going to the front door, he opened it and stood upon the steps, breathing deeply.

And, as he stood there, a form loomed through the darkness and a heavy hand fell on his arm.

"Mr. Mulliner, I think? Mr. Mulliner, if I mistake not? Good evening, Mr. Mulliner," said the voice of Bashford Braddock. "A word with you, Mr. Mulliner."

Osbert returned his gaze without flinching. He was conscious of a strange, almost uncanny calm. The fact was that, everything in this world being relative, he was regarding Bashford Braddock at this moment as rather an undersized little pipsqueak, and wondering why he had ever worried about the man. To one who had come so recently from the society of Harold and Ernest, Bashford Braddock seemed like one of Singer's Midgets.

"Ah, Braddock?" said Osbert.

At this moment, with a grinding of brakes, a van stopped before the door and policemen began to emerge.

"Mr. Mulliner?" asked the sergeant.

Osbert greeted him affably.

"Come in," he said. "Come in. Go straight through. You will find them in the dining-room. I'm afraid I had to handle them a little roughly. You had better 'phone for a doctor."

"Bad are they?"

"A little the worse for wear."

"Well, they asked for it," said the sergeant.

"Exactly, Sergeant," said Osbert. *"Rem acŭ tetigisti."*

Bashford Braddock had been standing listening to this exchange of remarks with a somewhat perplexed air.

"What's all this?" he said.

Osbert came out of his thoughts with a start.

"You still here, my dear chap?"

"I am."

"Want to see me about anything, dear boy? Something on your mind?"

"I just want a quiet five minutes alone with you, Mr. Mulliner."

"Certainly, my dear old fellow," said Osbert. "Certainly, certainly, certainly. Just wait till these policemen have gone and I will be at your disposal. We have had a little burglary."

"Burg—," Bashford Braddock was beginning, when there came out onto the steps a couple of policemen. They were supporting the burglar Harold, and were followed by others assisting the burglar Ernest. The sergeant, coming last, shook his head at Osbert a little gravely.

"You ought to be careful, sir," he said. "I don't say these fellows didn't deserve all you gave them, but you want to watch yourself. One of these days . . ."

"Perhaps I did overdo it a little," admitted Osbert. "But I am rather apt to see red on these occasions. One's fighting blood, you know. Well, good night, Sergeant, good night. And now," he said, taking Bashford Braddock's arm in a genial grip, "what was it you wanted to talk to me about? Come into the house. We shall be all alone there. I gave the staff a holiday. There won't be a soul except ourselves."

Bashford Braddock released his arm. He

seemed embarrassed. His face, as the light of the street lamp shone upon it, was strangely pale.

"Did you——" He gulped a little. "Was that really you?"

"Really me? Oh, you mean those two fellows. Oh, yes, I found them in my dining-room, eating my food and drinking my wine as cool as you please, and naturally I set about them. But the sergeant was quite right. I *do* get too rough when I lose my temper. I must remember," he said, taking out his handkerchief and tying a knot in it, "to cure myself of that. The fact is, I sometimes don't know my own strength. But you haven't told me what it is you want to see me about?"

Bashford Braddock swallowed twice in quick succession. He edged past Osbert to the foot of the steps. He seemed oddly uneasy. His face had now taken on a greenish tinge.

"Oh, nothing, nothing."

"But, my dear fellow," protested Osbert, "it must have been something important to bring you round at this time of night."

Bashford Braddock gulped.

"Well, it was like this. I—er—saw the announcement of your engagement in the paper this morning, and I thought—— I—er—just thought I would look in and ask you what you would like for a wedding-present."

"My dear chap! Much too kind of you."

"So—er—so silly if I gave a fish-slice and found that everybody else had given fish-slices."

"That's true. Well, why not come inside and talk it over."

"No, I won't come in, thanks. I'd rather not come in. Perhaps you will write and let me know. *Poste Restante,* Bongo on the Congo, will find me. I am returning there immediately."

"Certainly," said Osbert. He looked down at his companion's feet. "My dear old lad, what on earth are you wearing those extraordinary boots for?"

"Corns," said Bashford Braddock.

"Why the spikes?"

"They relieve the pressure on the feet."

"I see, well, good night, Mr. Braddock."

"Good night, Mr. Mulliner."

"Good night," said Osbert.

"Good night," said Bashford Braddock.

UNPLEASANTNESS
AT BLUDLEIGH COURT

Unpleasantness at Bludleigh Court

THE poet who was spending the summer at the Anglers' Rest had just begun to read us his new sonnet-sequence when the door of the bar-parlour opened and there entered a young man in gaiters. He came quickly in and ordered beer. In one hand he was carrying a double-barrelled gun, in the other a posy of dead rabbits. These he dropped squashily to the floor: and the poet, stopping in mid-sentence, took one long, earnest look at the remains. Then, wincing painfully, he turned a light green and closed his eyes. It was not until the banging of the door announced the visitor's departure that he came to life again.

Mr. Mulliner regarded him sympathetically over his hot Scotch and lemon.

"You appear upset," he said.

"A little," admitted the poet. "A momentary malaise. It may be a purely personal prejudice, but I confess to preferring rabbits with rather more of their contents inside them."

"Many sensitive souls in your line of business hold similar views," Mr. Mulliner assured him. "My niece Charlotte did."

"It is my temperament," said the poet. "I dislike all dead things—particularly when, as in the case of the above rabbits, they have so obviously, so—shall I say?—blatantly made the Great Change. Give me," he went on, the greenish tinge fading from his face, "life and joy and beauty."

"Just what my niece Charlotte used to say."

"Oddly enough, that thought forms the theme of the second sonnet in my sequence—which, now that the young gentleman with the portable Morgue has left us, I will . . ."

"My niece Charlotte," said Mr. Mulliner, with quiet firmness, "was one of those gentle, dreamy, wistful girls who take what I have sometimes felt to be a mean advantage of having an ample private income to write Vignettes in Verse for the artistic weeklies. Charlotte's Vignettes in Verse had a wide vogue among the editors of London's higher-browed but less prosperous periodicals. Directly these frugal men realized that she was willing to supply unstinted

Vignettes gratis, for the mere pleasure of seeing herself in print, they were all over her. The consequence was that before long she had begun to move freely in the most refined literary circles: and one day, at a little luncheon at the Crushed Pansy (The Restaurant With A Soul), she found herself seated next to a godlike young man at the sight of whom something seemed to go off inside her like a spring."

"Talking of Spring . . ." said the poet.

"Cupid," proceeded Mr. Mulliner, "has always found the family to which I belong a ready mark for his bow. Our hearts are warm, our passions quick. It is not too much to say that my niece Charlotte was in love with this young man before she had finished spearing the first anchovy out of the hors-d'œuvres dish. He was intensely spiritual-looking, with a broad, white forehead and eyes that seemed to Charlotte not so much eyes as a couple of holes punched in the surface of a beautiful soul. He wrote, she learned, Pastels in Prose: and his name, if she had caught it correctly at the moment of their introduction, was Aubrey Trefusis.

Friendship ripens quickly at the Crushed Pansy. The *poulet rôti au cresson* had scarcely been distributed before the young man was telling Charlotte his hopes, his fears, and the story of his boyhood. And she was amazed to find that he sprang—not from a long line of artists but from an ordinary, conventional county family of the type that cares for nothing except hunting and shooting.

"You can readily imagine," he said, helping her to Brussels sprouts, "how intensely such an environment jarred upon my unfolding spirit. My family are greatly respected in the neighbourhood, but I personally have always looked upon them as a gang of blood-imbrued plug-uglies. My views on kindness to animals are rigid. My impulse, on encountering a rabbit, is to offer it lettuce. To my family, on the other hand, a rabbit seems incomplete without a deposit of small shot in it. My father, I believe, has cut off more assorted birds in their prime than any other man in the Midlands. A whole morning was spoiled for me last week by the sight of a photograph of him in the *Tatler*, looking rather severely at a dying duck. My elder brother Reginald spreads destruction in every branch of the animal kingdom. And my younger brother Wilfred is, I understand, working his way up to the larger fauna by killing sparrows with an air-gun. Spiritually, one might just as well live in Chicago as at Bludleigh Court."

"Bludleigh Court?" cried Charlotte.

"The moment I was twenty-one and came into a modest but sufficient inheritance, I left the place and went to London to lead the life literary. The family, of course, were appalled. My uncle Francis, I remember, tried to reason with me for hours. Uncle Francis, you see, used to be a famous big-game hunter. They tell me he has shot more gnus than any other man who ever went to Africa. In fact, until recently he virtually never stopped shooting gnus. Now, I hear, he has developed lumbago and is down at Bludleigh treating it with Riggs's Superfine Emulsion and sun-baths."

"But is Bludleigh Court your home?"

"That's right. Bludleigh Court, Lesser Bludleigh, near Goresby-on-the-Ouse, Bedfordshire."

"But Bludleigh Court belongs to Sir Alexander Bassinger."

"My name is really Bassinger. I adopted the pen-name of Trefusis to spare the family's feelings. But how do you come to know of the place?"

"I'm going down there next week for a visit.

My mother was an old friend of Lady Bassinger."

Aubrey was astonished. And, being, like all writers of Pastels in Prose, a neat phrase-maker, he said what a small world it is, after all.

"Well, well, well!" he said.

"From what you tell me," said Charlotte, "I'm afraid I shall not enjoy my visit. If there's one thing I loathe, it's anything connected with sport."

"Two minds with but a single thought," said Aubrey. "Look here, I'll tell you what. I haven't been near Bludleigh for years, but if you're going there, why, dash it, I'll come too—aye, even though it means meeting my uncle Francis."

"You will?"

"I certainly will. I don't consider it safe that a girl of your exquisite refinement and sensibility should be dumped down at an abattoir like Bludleigh Court without a kindred spirit to lend her moral stability."

"What do you mean?"

"I'll tell you." His voice was grave. "That house exercises a spell."

"A what?"

"A spell. A ghastly spell that saps the strongest humanitarian principles. Who knows what effect it might have upon you, should you go there without someone like me to stand by you and guide you in your hour of need?"

"What nonsense!"

"Well, all I can tell you is that once, when I was a boy, a high official of Our Dumb Brothers' League of Mercy arrived there latish on a Friday night, and at two-fifteen on the Saturday afternoon he was the life and soul of an informal party got up for the purpose of drawing one of the local badgers out of an upturned barrel."

Charlotte laughed merrily.

"The spell will not affect me," she said.

"Nor me, of course," said Aubrey. "But all the same, I would prefer to be by your side, if you don't mind."

"Mind, Mr. Bassinger!" breathed Charlotte softly, and was thrilled to note that at the words and the look with which she accompanied them this man to whom—for, as I say, we Mulliners are quick workers—she had already given her heart, quivered violently. It seemed to her that in those soulful eyes of his she had seen the love-light.

Bludleigh Court, when Charlotte reached it some days later, proved to be a noble old pile of Tudor architecture, situated in rolling parkland and flanked by pleasant gardens leading to a lake with a tree-fringed boathouse. Inside, it was comfortably furnished and decorated throughout with groves of glass cases containing the goggle-eyed remnants of birds and beasts assassinated at one time or another by Sir Alexander Bassinger and his son, Reginald. From every wall there peered down with an air of mild reproach selected portions of the gnus, moose, elks, zebus, antelopes, giraffes, mountain goats and wapiti which had had the misfortune to meet Colonel Sir Francis Pashley-Drake before lumbago spoiled him for the chase. The cemetery also included a few stuffed sparrows, which showed that little Wilfred was doing his bit.

The first two days of her visit Charlotte passed mostly in the society of Colonel Pashley-Drake, the uncle Francis to whom Aubrey had alluded. He seemed to have taken a paternal fancy to her: and, lithely though she dodged down back-stairs and passages, she generally found him breathing heavily at her side. He was a red-faced, almost circular man, with eyes like a prawn's, and he spoke to her freely of lumbago, gnus and Aubrey.

"So you're a friend of my young nephew?" he said, snorting twice in a rather unpleasant manner. It was plain that he disapproved of the pastel-artist. "Shouldn't see too much of him, if I were you. Not the sort of fellow I'd like any daughter of mine to get friendly with."

"You are quite wrong," said Charlotte warmly. "You have only to gaze into Mr. Bassinger's eyes to see that his morals are above reproach."

"I never gaze into his eyes," replied Colonel Pashley-Drake. "Don't like his eyes. Wouldn't gaze into them if you paid me. I maintain his whole outlook on life is morbid and unwholesome. I like a man to be a clean, strong, upstanding Englishman who can look his gnu in the face and put an ounce of lead in it."

"Life," said Charlotte coldly, "is not all gnus."

"You imply that there are also wapiti, moose, zebus and mountain goats?" said Sir Francis. "Well, maybe you're right. All the same, I'd give the fellow a wide berth, if I were you."

"So far from doing so," replied Charlotte proudly, "I am about to go for a stroll with him by the lake at this very moment."

And, turning away with a petulant toss of her

head, she moved off to meet Aubrey, who was hurrying towards her across the terrace.

"I am so glad you came, Mr. Bassinger," she said to him as they walked together in the direction of the lake. "I was beginning to find your uncle Francis a little excessive."

Aubrey nodded sympathetically. He had observed her in conversation with his relative and his heart had gone out to her.

"Two minutes of my uncle Francis," he said, "is considered by the best judges a good medium dose for an adult. So you find him trying, eh? I was wondering what impression my family had made on you."

Charlotte was silent for a moment.

"How relative everything is in this world," she said pensively. "When I first met your father, I thought I had never seen anybody more completely loathsome. Then I was introduced to your brother Reginald, and I realized that, after all, your father might have been considerably worse. And, just as I was thinking that Reginald was the furthest point possible, along came your uncle Francis, and Reginald's quiet charm seemed to leap out at me like a beacon on a dark night. Tell me," she said, "has no one ever thought of doing anything about your uncle Francis?"

Aubrey shook his head gently.

"It is pretty generally recognised now that he is beyond the reach of human science. The only thing to do seems to be to let him go on till he eventually runs down."

They sat together on a rustic bench overlooking the water. It was a lovely morning. The sun shone on the little wavelets which the sighing breeze drove gently to the shore. A dreamy stillness had fallen on the world, broken only by the distant sound of Sir Alexander Bassinger murdering magpies, of Reginald Bassinger encouraging dogs to eviscerate a rabbit, of Wilfred busy among the sparrows, and a monotonous droning noise from the upper terrace, which was Colonel Sir Francis Pashley-Drake telling Lady Bassinger what to do with the dead gnu.

Aubrey was the first to break the silence.

"How lovely the world is, Miss Mulliner."

"Yes, isn't it!"

"How softly the breeze caresses yonder water."

"Yes, doesn't it!"

"How fragrant a scent of wild flowers it has."

"Yes, hasn't it!"

They were silent again.

"On such a day," said Aubrey, "the mind seems to turn irresistibly to Love."

"Love?" said Charlotte, her heart beginning to flutter.

"Love," said Aubrey. "Tell me, Miss Mulliner, have you ever thought of Love?"

He took her hand. Her head was bent, and with the toe of her dainty shoe she toyed with a passing snail.

"Life, Miss Mulliner," said Aubrey, "is a Sahara through which we all must pass. We start at the Cairo of the cradle and we travel on to the—er—well, we go travelling on."

"Yes, don't we!" said Charlotte.

"Afar we can see the distant goal . . ."

"Yes, can't we!"

". . . and would fain reach it."

"Yes, wouldn't we!"

"But the way is rough and weary. We have to battle through the sand-storms of Destiny, face with what courage we may the howling simoons of Fate. And very unpleasant it all is. But sometimes in the Sahara of Life, if we are fortunate, we come upon the Oasis of Love. That oasis, when I had all but lost hope, I reached at one-fifteen on the afternoon of Tuesday, the twenty-second of last month. There comes a time in the life of every man when he sees Happiness beckoning to him and must grasp it. Miss Mulliner, I have something to ask you which I have been trying to ask ever since the day when we two first met. Miss Mulliner . . . Charlotte . . . Will you be my . . . Gosh! Look at that whacking great rat! Loo-loo-loo-loo-loo-loo-loo-loo!" said Aubrey, changing the subject.

Once, in her childhood, a sportive playmate had secretly withdrawn the chair on which Charlotte Mulliner was preparing to seat herself. Years had passed, but the recollection of the incident remained green in her memory. In frosty weather she could still feel the old wound. And now, as Aubrey Bassinger suddenly behaved in this remarkable manner, she experienced the same sensation again. It was as though something blunt and heavy had hit her on the head at the exact moment when she was slipping on a banana-skin.

She stared round-eyed at Aubrey. He had released her hand, sprung to his feet, and now, armed with her parasol, was beating furiously in the lush grass at the waterside. And every little while his mouth would open, his head would go back, and uncouth sounds would proceed from his slavering jaws.

"Yoicks! Yoicks! Yoicks!" cried Aubrey. And again,

"Tally-ho! Hard For'ard! Tally-ho!"

Presently the fever seemed to pass. He straightened himself and came back to where she stood.

"It must have got away into a hole or something," he said, removing a bead of perspiration from his forehead with the ferrule of the parasol. "The fact of the matter is, it's silly ever to go out in the country without a good dog. If only I'd had a nice, nippy terrier with me, I might have obtained some solid results. As it is, a fine rat— gone—just like that! Oh, well, that's Life, I suppose." He paused. "Let me see," he said. "Where was I?"

And then it was as though he waked from a trance. His flushed face paled.

"I say," he stammered, "I'm afraid you must think me most awfully rude."

"Pray do not mention it," said Charlotte coldly.

"Oh, but you must. Dashing off like that."

"Not at all."

"What I was going to say, when I was interrupted, was, will you be my wife?"

"Oh?"

"Yes."

"Well, I won't."

"You won't?"

"No. Never." Charlotte's voice was tense with a scorn which she did not attempt to conceal. "So this is what you were all the time, Mr. Bassinger—a secret sportsman!"

Aubrey quivered from head to foot.

"I'm not! I'm not! It was the hideous spell of this ghastly house that overcame me."

"Pah!"

"What did you say?"

"I said 'Pah'!"

"Why did you say 'Pah'?"

"Because," said Charlotte, with flashing eyes, "I do not believe you. Your story is thin and fishy."

"But it's the truth. It was as if some hypnotic influence had gripped me, forcing me to act against all my higher inclinations. Can't you understand? Would you condemn me for a moment's passing weakness? Do you think," he cried passionately, "that the real Aubrey Bassinger would raise a hand to touch a rat, save in the way of kindness? I love rats, I tell you—love them. I used to keep them as a boy. White ones with pink eyes."

Charlotte shook her head. Her face was cold and hard.

"Good-bye, Mr. Bassinger," she said. "From this instant we meet as strangers."

She turned and was gone. And Aubrey Bassinger, covering his face with his hands, sank on the bench, feeling like a sand-bagged leper.

The mind of Charlotte Mulliner, in the days which followed the painful scene which I have just described, was torn, as you may well imagine, with conflicting emotions. For a time, as was natural, anger predominated. But after a while sadness overcame indignation. She mourned for her lost happiness.

And yet, she asked herself, how else could she have acted? She had worshipped Aubrey Bassinger. She had set him upon a pedestal, looked up to him as a great white soul. She had supposed him one who lived, far above this world's coarseness and grime, on a rarefied plane of his own, thinking beautiful thoughts. Instead of which, it now appeared, he went about the place chasing rats with parasols. What could she have done but spurn him?

That there lurked in the atmosphere of Bludleigh Court a sinister influence that sapped the principles of the most humanitarian and sent them ravening to and fro, seeking for prey, she declined to believe. The theory was pure banana-oil. If such an influence was in operation at Bludleigh, why had it not affected her?

No, if Aubrey Bassinger chased rats with parasols, it could only mean that he was one of Nature's rat-chasers. And to such a one, cost what it might to refuse, she could never confide her heart

Few things are more embarrassing to a highly-strung girl than to be for any length of time in the same house with a man whose love she has been compelled to decline, and Charlotte would have given much to be able to leave Bludleigh Court. But there was, it seemed, to be a garden party on the following Tuesday, and Lady Bassinger had urged her so strongly to stay on for it that departure was out of the question.

To fill the leaden moments, she immersed herself in her work. She had a long-standing commission to supply the *Animal-Lovers Gazette* with a poem for its Christmas number, and to the task of writing this she proceeded to devote herself. And gradually the ecstasy of literary composition eased her pain.

The days crept by. Old Sir Alexander continued to maltreat magpies. Reginald and the local rabbits fought a never-ceasing battle, they striving to keep up the birth-rate, he to reduce it. Colonel Pashley-Drake maundered on about gnus he had met. And Aubrey dragged himself about the house, looking licked to a splinter. Eventually Tuesday came, and with it the garden party.

Lady Bassinger's annual garden party was one of the big events of the countryside. By four o'clock all that was bravest and fairest for miles around had assembled on the big lawn. But Charlotte, though she had stayed on specially to be present, was not one of the gay throng. At about the time when the first strawberry was being dipped in its cream, she was up in her room, staring with bewildered eyes at a letter which had arrived by the second post.

The *Animal-Lovers Gazette* had turned her poem down!

Yes, turned it down flat, in spite of the fact that it had been commissioned and that she was not asking a penny for it. Accompanying the rejected manuscript was a curt note from the editor, in which he said that he feared its tone might offend his readers.

Charlotte was stunned. She was not accustomed to having her efforts rejected. This one, moreover, had seemed to her so particularly good. A hard judge of her own work, she had said to herself, as she licked the envelope, that this time, if never before, she had delivered the goods.

She unfolded the manuscript and re-read it. It ran as follows:

GOOD GNUS
(*A Vignette in Verse*)

BY

CHARLOTTE MULLINER

When cares attack and life seems black,
How sweet it is to pot a yak,
   Or puncture hares and grizzly bears,
    And others I could mention:
But in my Animals' "Who's Who"
No name stands higher than the Gnu:
   And each new gnu that comes in view
    Receives my prompt attention.

When Afric's sun is sinking low,
And shadows wander to and fro,
    And everywhere there's in the air
        A hush that's deep and solemn;
Then is the time good men and true
With View Halloo pursue the gnu:
    (The safest spot to put your shot
        Is through the spinal column).

To take the creature by surprise
We must adopt some rude disguise,
    Although deceit is never sweet,
        And falsehoods don't attract us:
So, as with gun in hand you wait,
Remember to impersonate
    A tuft of grass, or mountain-pass,
        A kopje or a cactus.

A brief suspense, and then at last
The waiting's o'er, the vigil past:
    A careful aim. A spurt of flame.
        It's done. You've pulled the trigger,
And one more gnu, so fair and frail,
Has handed in its dinner-pail:
    (The females all are rather small,
        The males are somewhat bigger).

Charlotte laid the manuscript down, frowning. She chafed at the imbecility of editors. Less

than ever was she able to understand what anyone could find in it to cavil at. Tone likely to offend? What did the man mean about the tone being likely to offend? She had never heard such nonsense in her life. How could the tone possibly offend? It was unexceptionable. The whole poem breathed that clean, wholesome, healthy spirit of Sport which has made England what it is. And the thing was not only lyrically perfect, but educational as well. It told the young reader, anxious to shoot gnus but uncertain of the correct procedure, exactly what he wanted to know.

She bit her lip. Well, if this Animal-Lovers bird didn't know a red-hot contribution when he saw one, she would jolly well find somebody else who did—and quick, too. She . . .

At this moment, something occurred to distract her thoughts. Down on the terrace below, little Wilfred, complete with airgun, had come into her line of vision. The boy was creeping along in a quiet, purposeful manner, obviously intent on the chase: and it suddenly came over Charlotte Mulliner in a wave that here she had been in this house all this time and never once had thought of borrowing the child's weapon and having a plug at something with it.

The sky was blue. The sun was shining. All Nature seemed to call to her to come out and kill things.

She left the room and ran quickly down the stairs.

And what of Aubrey, meanwhile? Grief having slowed him up on his feet, he had been cornered by his mother and marched off to hand cucumber sandwiches at the garden party. After a brief spell of servitude, however, he had contrived to escape and was wandering on the terrace, musing mournfully, when he observed his brother Wilfred approaching. And at the same moment Charlotte Mulliner emerged from the house and came hurrying in their direction. In a flash, Aubrey perceived that here was a situation which, shrewdly handled, could be turned greatly to his advantage. Affecting to be unaware of Charlotte's approach, he stopped his brother and eyed the young thug sternly.

"Wilfred," he said, "where are you going with that gun?"

The boy appeared embarrassed.

"Just shooting."

Aubrey took the weapon from him and raised

his voice slightly. Out of the corner of his eye he had seen that Charlotte was now well within hearing.

"Shooting, eh?" he said. "Shooting? I see. And have you never been taught, wretched child, that you should be kind to the animals that crave your compassion? Has no one ever told you that he prayeth best who loveth best all things both great and small? For shame, Wilfred, for shame!"

Charlotte had come up, and was standing there, looking at them inquiringly.

"What's all this about?" she asked.

Aubrey started dramatically.

"Miss Mulliner! I was not aware that you were there. All this? Oh, nothing. I found this lad here on his way to shoot sparrows with his airgun, and I am taking the thing from him. It may seem to you a high-handed action on my part. You may consider me hyper-sensitive. You may ask, Why all this fuss about a few birds? But that is Aubrey Bassinger. Aubrey Bassinger will not lightly allow even the merest sparrow to be placed in jeopardy. Tut, Wilfred," he said. "Tut! Cannot you see now how wrong it is to shoot the poor sparrows?"

"But I wasn't going to shoot sparrows," said

the boy. "I was going to shoot Uncle Francis while he is having his sun-bath."

"It is also wrong," said Aubrey, after a slight hesitation, "to shoot Uncle Francis while he is having his sun-bath."

Charlotte Mulliner uttered an impatient exclamation. And Aubrey, looking at her, saw that her eyes were glittering with a strange light. She breathed quickly through her delicately-chiselled nose. She seemed feverish, and a medical man would have been concerned about her blood-pressure.

"Why?" she demanded vehemently. "Why is it wrong? Why shouldn't he shoot his Uncle Francis while he is having his sun-bath?"

Aubrey stood for a moment, pondering. Her razor-like feminine intelligence had cut cleanly to the core of the matter. After all, now that she put it like that, why not?

"Think how it would tickle him up."

"True," said Aubrey, nodding. "True."

"And his Uncle Francis is precisely the sort of man who ought to have been shot at with air-guns incessantly for the last thirty years. The moment I met him, I said to myself, 'That man ought to be shot at with airguns.'"

Aubrey nodded again. Her girlish enthusiasm had begun to infect him.

"There is much in what you say," he admitted.

"Where is he?" asked Charlotte, turning to the boy.

"On the roof of the boathouse."

Charlotte's face clouded.

"H'm!" she said. "That's awkward. How is one to get at him?"

"I remember Uncle Francis telling me once," said Aubrey, "that, when you went shooting tigers, you climbed a tree. There are plenty of trees by the boathouse."

"Admirable!"

For an instant there came to disturb Aubrey's hearty joy in the chase a brief, faint flicker of prudence.

"But . . . I say . . . Do you really think . . . Ought we . . . ?"

Charlotte's eyes flashed scornfully.

"Infirm of purpose," she said. "Give me the airgun!"

"I was only thinking . . ."

"Well?"

"I suppose you know he'll have practically nothing on?"

Charlotte Mulliner laughed lightly.

"He can't intimidate *me,*" she said. "Come! Let us be going."

Up on the roof of the boathouse, the beneficent ultra-violet rays of the afternoon sun pouring down on his globular surface, Colonel Sir Francis Pashley-Drake lay in that pleasant half-waking, half-dreaming state that accompanies this particular form of lumbago-treatment. His mind flitted lightly from one soothing subject to another. He thought of elks he had shot in Canada, of moufflon he had shot in the Grecian Archipelago, of giraffes he had shot in Nigeria. He was just on the point of thinking of a hippopotamus which he had shot in Egypt, when the train of his meditations was interrupted by a soft popping sound not far away. He smiled affectionately. So little Wilfred was out with his airgun, eh?

A thrill of quiet pride passed through Colonel Pashley-Drake. He had trained the lad well, he felt. With a garden party in progress, with all the opportunities it offered for quiet gorging, how many boys of Wilfred's age would have neglected their shooting to hang round the tea-table and stuff themselves with cakes. But this fine lad . . .

Ping! There it was again. The boy must be somewhere quite close at hand. He wished he could be at his side, giving him kindly advice. Wilfred, he felt, was a young fellow after his own heart. What destruction he would spread among the really worthwhile animals when he grew up and put aside childish things and exchanged his airgun for a Winchester repeater.

Sir Francis Pashley-Drake started. Two inches from where he lay a splinter of wood had sprung from the boathouse roof. He sat up, feeling a little less affectionate.

"Wilfred!"

There was no reply.

"Be careful, Wilfred, my boy. You nearly . . ."

A sharp, agonizing twinge caused him to break off abruptly. He sprang to his feet and began to address the surrounding landscape passionately in one of the lesser-known dialects of the Congo basin. He no longer thought of Wilfred with quiet pride. Few things so speedily modify an uncle's love as a nephew's airgun bullet in the fleshy part of the leg. Sir Francis Pashley-Drake's plans for this boy's future had undergone in one brief instant a complete change. He no longer desired to stand beside him through his formative years, teaching him the secrets of shikari. All he wanted to do was to get close enough to him to teach him with the flat of his right hand to be a bit more careful where he pointed his gun.

He was expressing a synopsis of these views in a mixture of Urdu and Cape Dutch, when the words were swept from his lips by the sight of a woman's face, peering from the branches of a near-by tree.

Colonel Pashley-Drake reeled where he stood. Like so many out-door men, he was the soul of modesty. Once, in Bechuanaland, he had left a native witch-dance in a marked manner because he considered the chief's third supplementary wife insufficiently clad. An acute consciousness of the sketchiness of his costume overcame him. He blushed brightly.

"My dear young lady . . ." he stammered.

He had got thus far when he perceived that the young woman was aiming at him something that looked remarkably like an airgun. Her tongue protruded thoughtfully from the corner of her mouth, she had closed one eye and with the other was squinting tensely along the barrel.

Colonel Sir Francis Pashley-Drake did not linger. In all England there was probably no man more enthusiastic about shooting: but the fascination of shooting as a sport depends almost wholly on whether you are at the right or wrong end of the gun. With an agility which no gnu, unless in the very pink of condition, could have surpassed, he sprang to the side of the roof and leaped off. There was a clump of reeds not far from the boathouse. He galloped across the turf and dived into them.

Charlotte descended from her tree. Her expression was petulant. Girls nowadays are spoiled, and only too readily become peevish when baulked of their pleasures.

"I had no idea he was so nippy," she said.

"A quick mover," agreed Aubrey. "I imagine he got that way from dodging rhinoceroses."

"Why can't they make these silly guns with two barrels? A single barrel doesn't give a girl a chance."

Nestling among the reeds, Colonel Sir Francis Pashley-Drake, in spite of the indignation natural to a man in his position, could not help feeling a certain complacency. The old woodcraft of the hunter had stood him, he felt, in good stead. Not many men, he told himself, would have had the initiative and swift intelligence to act so promptly in the face of peril.

He was aware of voices close by.

"What do we do now?" he heard Charlotte Mulliner say.

"We must think," said the voice of his nephew Aubrey.

"He's in there somewhere."

"Yes."

"I hate to see a fine head like that get away," said Charlotte, and her voice was still querulous. "Especially after I winged him. The very next poem I write is going to be an appeal to airgun manufacturers to use their intelligence, if they have any, and turn out a line with two barrels."

"I shall write a Pastel in Prose on the same subject," agreed Aubrey.

"Well, what shall we do?"

There was a short silence. An insect of unknown species crept up Colonel Pashley-Drake and bit him in the small of the back.

"I'll tell you what," said Aubrey. "I remember Uncle Francis mentioning to me once that when wounded zebus take cover by the reaches of the Lower Zambesi, the sportsman despatches a native assistant to set fire to . . ."

Sir Francis Pashley-Drake emitted a hollow groan. It was drowned by Charlotte's cry of delight.

"Why, of course! How clever you are, Mr. Bassinger."

"Oh, no," said Aubrey modestly.

"Have you matches?"

"I have a cigarette-lighter."

"Then would it be bothering you too much to go and set light to those reeds—about there would be a good place—and I'll wait here with the gun."

"I should be charmed."

"I hate to trouble you."

"No trouble, I assure you," said Aubrey. "A pleasure."

Three minutes later the revellers on the lawn were interested to observe a sight rare at the better class of English garden party. Out of a clump of laurel-bushes that bordered the smoothly mown turf there came charging a stout, pink gentleman of middle age who hopped from side to side as he ran. He was wearing a loin-cloth, and seemed in a hurry. They had just time to recognize in this newcomer their hostess's brother, Colonel Sir Francis Pashley-Drake, when he snatched a cloth from the nearest table, draped it round him, and with a quick leap took refuge behind the portly form of the Bishop of Stortford, who was talking to the local Master of Hounds about the difficulty he had in keeping his vicars off the incense.

Charlotte and Aubrey had paused in the shelter of the laurels. Aubrey, peering through this zareba, clicked his tongue regretfully.

"He's taken cover again," he said. "I'm afraid we shall find it difficult to dig him out of there. He's gone to earth behind a bishop."

Receiving no reply, he turned.

"Miss Mulliner!" he exclaimed. "Charlotte! What is the matter?"

A strange change had come over the girl's beautiful face since he had last gazed at it. The fire had died out of those lovely eyes, leaving them looking like those of a newly awakened somnambulist. She was pale, and the tip of her nose quivered.

"Where am I?" she murmured.

"Bludleigh Manor, Lesser Bludleigh, Goresby-on-the-Ouse, Bedfordshire. Telephone 28 Goresby," said Aubrey quickly.

"Have I been dreaming? Or did I really . . . Ah, yes, yes!" she moaned, shuddering violently. "It all comes back to me. I shot Sir Francis with the airgun!"

"You certainly did," said Aubrey, and would have gone on to comment with warm approbation on the skill she had shown, a skill which—in an untrained novice—had struck him as really remarkable. But he checked himself. "Surely," he said, "you are not letting the fact disturb you? It's the sort of thing that might have happened to anyone."

She interrupted him.

"How right you were, Mr. Bassinger, to warn me against the spell of Bludleigh. And how wrong I was to blame you for borrowing my parasol to chase a rat. Can you ever forgive me?"

"Charlotte!"

"Aubrey!"

"Charlotte!"

"Hush!" she said. "Listen."

On the lawn, Sir Francis Pashley-Drake was

telling his story to an enthralled audience. The sympathy of the meeting, it was only too plain, was entirely with him. This shooting of a sitting sun-bather had stirred the feelings of his hearers deeply. Indignant exclamations came faintly to the ears of the young couple in the laurels.

"Most irregular!"

"Not done!"

"Scarcely cricket!"

And then, from Sir Alexander Bassinger, a stern, "I shall require a full explanation."

Charlotte turned to Aubrey.

"What shall we do?"

"Well," said Aubrey, reflecting, "I don't think we had better just go and join the party and behave as if nothing had happened. The atmosphere doesn't seem right. What I would propose is that we take a short cut through the fields to the station, hook up with the five-fifty express at Goresby, go to London, have a bit of dinner, get married and . . ."

"Yes, yes," cried Charlotte. "Take me away from this awful house."

"To the ends of the world," said Aubrey fervently. He paused. "Look here," he said suddenly, "if you move over to where I'm standing, you get the old boy plumb spang against the sky-line. You wouldn't care for just one last . . ."

"No, no!"

"Merely a suggestion," said Aubrey. "Ah well, perhaps you're right. Then let's be shifting."

SOMETHING SQUISHY

Something Squishy

THERE had been a gap for a week or so in our little circle at the Anglers' Rest, and that gap the most serious that could have occurred. Mr. Mulliner's had been the vacant chair, and we had felt his absence acutely. Inquiry on his welcome return elicited the fact that he had been down in Hertfordshire, paying a visit to his cousin Lady Wickham, at her historic residence, Skeldings Hall. He had left her well, he informed us, but somewhat worried.

"About her daughter Roberta," said Mr. Mulliner.

"Delicate girl?" we asked sympathetically.

"Not at all. Physically, most robust. What is troubling my cousin is the fact that she does not get married."

A tactless Mild-and-Bitter, who was a newcomer to the bar-parlour and so should not have spoken at all, said that that was often the way with these plain girls. The modern young man, he said, valued mere looks too highly, and instead of being patient, and carrying on pluckily till he was able to penetrate the unsightly exterior to the good womanly heart within . . .

"My cousin's daughter Roberta," said Mr. Mulliner with some asperity, "is not plain. Like all the Mulliners on the female side, however distantly removed from the main branch, she is remarkably beautiful. And yet she does not get married."

"A mystery," we mused.

"One," said Mr. Mulliner, "that I have been able to solve. I was privileged to enjoy a good deal of Roberta's confidence during my visit, and I also met a young man named Algernon Crufts who appears to enjoy still more and also to be friendly with some of those of the male sex in whose society she has been moving lately. I am afraid that, like so many spirited girls of to-day, she is inclined to treat her suitors badly. They get discouraged, and I think with some excuse. There was young Attwater, for instance . . ."

Mr. Mulliner broke off and sipped his hot Scotch and lemon. He appeared to have fallen into a reverie. From time to time, as he paused in his sipping, a chuckle escaped him.

"Attwater?" we said.

"Yes, that was the name."

"What happened to him?"

"Oh, you wish to hear the story? Certainly, certainly, by all means."

He rapped gently on the table, eyed his re-charged glass with quiet satisfaction, and proceeded.

In the demeanour of Roland Moresby Attwater, that rising young essayist and literary critic, there appeared (said Mr. Mulliner) as he stood holding the door open to allow the ladies to leave his uncle Joseph's dining-room, no outward and visible sign of the irritation that seethed beneath his mud-stained shirt-front. Well-bred and highly civilized, he knew how to wear the mask. The lofty forehead that shone above his rimless pince-nez was smooth and unruffled, and if he bared his teeth it was only in a polite smile. Nevertheless, Roland Attwater was fed to the eyebrows.

In the first place, he hated these family dinners. In the second place, he had been longing all the evening for a chance to explain that muddy shirt, and everybody had treated it with a silent tact which was simply maddening. In the third place, he knew that his uncle Joseph was only waiting for the women to go to bring up once again the infuriating topic of Lucy.

After a preliminary fluttering, not unlike that of hens disturbed in a barnyard, the female members of the party rustled past him in single file —his aunt Emily; his aunt Emily's friend, Mrs. Hughes Higham; his aunt Emily's companion and secretary, Miss Partlett; and his aunt Emily's adopted daughter, Lucy. The last-named brought up the rear of the procession. She was a gentle-looking girl with spaniel eyes and freckles, and as she passed she gave Roland a swift, shy glance of admiration and gratitude. It was the sort of look Ariadne might have given Theseus immediately after his turn-up with the Minotaur: and a casual observer, not knowing the facts, would have supposed that, instead of merely opening a door for her, Roland had rescued her at considerable bodily risk from some frightful doom.

Roland closed the door and returned to the table. His uncle, having pushed port towards him, coughed significantly and opened fire.

"How did you think Lucy was looking to-night, Roland?"

The young man winced, but the fine courtly spirit which is such a characteristic of the younger members of the intelligentsia did not fail him. Instead of banging the speaker over the head with the decanter, he replied with quiet civility:

"Splendid."

"Nice girl."

"Very."

"Wonderful disposition."

"Quite."

"And so sensible."

"Precisely."

"Very different from these shingled, cigarette-smoking young women who infest the place nowadays."

"Decidedly."

"Had one of 'em up before me this morning," said Uncle Joseph, frowning austerely over his port. Sir Joseph Moresby was by profession a metropolitan magistrate. "Charged with speeding. That's their idea of life."

"Girls," argued Roland, "will be girls."

"Not while I'm sitting at Bosher Street police-court, they won't," said his uncle, with decision. "Unless they want to pay five-pound fines and have their licenses endorsed." He sipped thoughtfully. "Look here, Roland," he said, as one struck by a novel idea, "why the devil don't you marry Lucy?"

"Well, Uncle——"

"You've got a bit of money, she's got a bit of money. Ideal. Besides, you want somebody to look after you."

"Do you suggest," inquired Roland, his eyebrows rising coldly, "that I am incapable of looking after myself?"

"Yes, I do. Why, dammit, you can't even dress for dinner, apparently, without getting mud all over your shirt-front."

Roland's cue had been long in coming, but it had arrived at a very acceptable moment.

"If you really want to know how that mud came to be on my shirt-front, Uncle Joseph," he said, with quiet dignity, "I got it saving a man's life."

"Eh? What? How?"

"A man slipped on the pavement as I was passing through Grosvenor Square on my way here. It was raining, you know, and I——"

"You walked here?"

"Yes. And just as I reached the corner of Duke Street——"

"Walked here in the rain? There you are! Lucy would never let you do a foolish thing like that."

"It began to rain after I had started."

"Lucy would never have let you start."

"Are you interested in my story, Uncle," said Roland, stiffly, "or shall we go upstairs?"

"Eh? My dear boy, of course, of course. Most interested. Want to hear the whole thing from beginning to end. You say it was raining and this fellow slipped off the pavement. And then I suppose a car or a taxi or something came along suddenly and you pulled him out of danger. Yes, go on, my boy."

"How do you mean, go on?" said Roland, morosely. He felt like a public speaker whose chairman has appropriated the cream of his speech and inserted it in his own introductory remarks. "That's all there is."

"Well, who was the man? Did he ask you for your name and address?"

"He did."

"Good! A young fellow once did something

very similar to what you did, and the man turned out to be a millionaire and left him his entire fortune. I remember reading about it."

"In the *Family Herald,* no doubt?"

"Did your man look like a millionaire?"

"He did not. He looked like what he actually was—the proprietor of a small bird-and-snake shop in the Seven Dials."

"Oh!" said Sir Joseph, a trifle dashed. "Well, I must tell Lucy about this," he said, brightening. "She will be tremendously excited. Just the sort of thing to appeal to a warm-hearted girl like her. Look here, Roland, why don't you marry Lucy?"

Roland came to a swift decision. It had not been his intention to lay bare his secret dreams to this pertinacious old blighter, but there seemed no other way of stopping him. He drained a glass of port and spoke crisply.

"Uncle Joseph, I love somebody else."

"Eh? What's that? Who?"

"This is, of course, strictly between ourselves."

"Of course."

"Her name is Wickham. I expect you know the family? The Hertfordshire Wickhams."

"Hertfordshire Wickhams!" Sir Joseph

snorted with extraordinary violence. "Bosher Street Wickhams, you mean. If it's Roberta Wickham, a red-headed hussy who ought to be smacked and sent to bed without her supper, that's the girl I fined this morning."

"You fined her!" gasped Roland.

"Five pounds," said his uncle, complacently. "Wish I could have given her five years. Menace to the public safety. How on earth did you get to know a girl like that?"

"I met her at a dance. I happened to mention that I was a critic of some small standing, and she told me that her mother wrote novels. I chanced to receive one of Lady Wickham's books for review shortly afterwards, and the—er—favourable tone of my notice apparently gave her some pleasure." Roland's voice trembled slightly, and he blushed. Only he knew what it had cost him to write eulogistically of that terrible book. "She has invited me down to Skeldings, their place in Hertfordshire, for the week end to-morrow."

"Send her a telegram."

"Saying what?"

"That you can't go."

"But I am going." It is a pretty tough thing

if a man of letters who has sold his critical soul is not to receive the reward of his crime. "I wouldn't miss it for anything."

"Don't you be a fool, my boy," said Sir Joseph. "I've known you all your life—know you better than you know yourself—and I tell you it's sheer insanity for a man like you to dream of marrying a girl like that. Forty miles an hour she was going, right down the middle of Piccadilly. The constable proved it up to the hilt. You're a quiet, sensible fellow, and you ought to marry a quiet, sensible girl. You're what I call a rabbit."

"A rabbit!"

"There is no stigma attached to being a rabbit," said Sir Joseph, pacifically. "Every man with a grain of sense is one. It simply means that you prefer a normal, wholesome life to gadding about like a—like a non-rabbit. You're going out of your class, my boy. You're trying to change your zoological species, and it can't be done. Half the divorces to-day are due to the fact that rabbits won't believe they're rabbits till it's too late. It is the peculiar nature of the rabbit——"

"I think we had better join the ladies, Uncle Joseph," said Roland, frostily. "Aunt Emily will be wondering what has become of us."

In spite of the innate modesty of all heroes, it was with something closely resembling chagrin that Roland discovered, on going to his club in the morning, that the Press of London was unanimously silent on the subject of his last night's exploit. Not that one expected anything in the nature of publicity, of course, or even desired it. Still, if there had happened to be some small paragraph under some such title as "Gallant Behaviour of an Author" or "Critical Moment for a Critic," it would have done no harm to the sale of that little book of thoughtful essays which Blenkinsop's had just put on the market.

And the fellow had seemed so touchingly grateful at the time.

Pawing at Roland's chest with muddy hands he had told him that he would never forget this moment as long as he lived. And he had not bothered even to go and call at a newspaper office.

Well, well! He swallowed his disappointment and a light lunch and returned to his flat, where he found Bryce, his man-servant, completing the packing of his suit-case.

"Packing?" said Roland. "That's right. Did those socks arrive?"

"Yes, sir."

"Good!" said Roland. They were some rather special gents' half-hose from the Burlington Arcade, subtly passionate, and he was hoping much from them. He wandered to a table, and became aware that on it lay a large cardboard box. "Hullo, what's this?"

"A man left it a short while ago, sir. A somewhat shabbily-dressed person. The note accompanying it is on the mantelpiece, sir."

Roland went to the mantelpiece; and, having inspected the dirty envelope for a moment with fastidious distaste, opened it in a gingerly manner.

"The box appears to me, sir," continued Bryce, "to contain something alive. It seemed to me that I received the impression of something squirming."

"Good Lord!" exclaimed Roland, staring at the letter.

"Sir?"

"It's a snake. That fool has sent me a snake. Of all the——"

A hearty ringing at the front-door bell interrupted him. Bryce, rising from the suit-case, vanished silently. Roland continued to regard the unwelcome gift with a peevish frown.

"Miss Wickham, sir," said Bryce at the door.

The visitor, who walked springily into the room, was a girl of remarkable beauty. She resembled a particularly good-looking schoolboy who had dressed up in his sister's clothes.

"Ah!" she said, cocking a bright eye at the suit-case. "I'm glad you're bustling about. We ought to be starting soon. I'm going to drive you down in the two-seater." She began a restless tour of the room. "Hullo!" she said, arriving at the box. "What might this be?" She shook it experimentally. "I say! There's something squishy inside!"

"Yes, it's——"

"Roland," said Miss Wickham, having conducted further experiments, "immediate investigation is called for. Inside this box there is most certainly some living organism. When you shake it it definitely squishes."

"It's all right. It's only a snake."

"Snake!"

"Perfectly harmless," he hastened to assure her. "The fool expressly states that. Not that it matters, because I'm going to send it straight back, unopened."

Miss Wickham squeaked with pleased excitement.

"Who's been sending you snakes?"

Roland coughed diffidently.

"I happened to—er—save a man's life last night. I was coming along at the corner of Duke Street——"

"Now, isn't that an extraordinary thing?" said Miss Wickham, meditatively. "Here have I lived all these years and never thought of getting a snake!"

"——when a man——"

"The one thing every young girl should have."

"——slipped off the pavement——"

"There are the most tremendous possibilities in a snake. The diner-out's best friend. Pop it on the table after the soup and be Society's pet."

Roland, though nothing, of course, could shake his great love, was conscious of a passing feeling of annoyance.

"I'll tell Bryce to take the thing back to the man," he said, abandoning his story as a total loss.

"Take it back?" said Miss Wickham, amazed. "But, Roland, what frightful waste! Why, there are moments in life when knowing where to lay your hand on a snake means more than words can tell." She started. "Golly! Didn't you once say that old Sir Joseph What's-his-name—the beak, you know—was your uncle? He fined me five of the best yesterday for absolutely crawling along Piccadilly. He needs a sharp lesson. He must be taught that he can't go about the place persecuting the innocent like that. I'll tell you what. Ask him to lunch here and hide the thing in his napkin! That'll make him think a bit!"

"No, no!" cried Roland, shuddering strongly.

"Roland! For my sake!"

"No, no, really!"

"And you said dozens of times that you would do anything in the world for me!" She mused. "Well, at least let me tie a string to it and dangle it out of the window in front of the next old lady that comes along."

"No, no, please! I must send it back to the man."

Miss Wickham's discontent was plain, but she seemed to accept defeat.

"Oh, all right if you're going to refuse me every little thing! But let me tell you, my lad, that you're throwing away the laugh of a life-time. Wantonly and callously chucking it away

Where is Bryce? Gone to earth in the kitchen, I suppose. I'll go and give him the thing while you strap the suit-case. We ought to be starting, or we sha'n't get there by tea-time."

"Let me do it."

"No, I'll do it."

"You mustn't trouble."

"No trouble," said Miss Wickham, amiably.

In this world, as has been pointed out in various ways by a great many sages and philosophers, it is wiser for the man who shrinks from being disappointed not to look forward too keenly to moments that promise pleasure. Roland Attwater, who had anticipated considerable enjoyment from his drive down to Skeldings Hall, soon discovered, when the car had threaded its way through the London traffic and was out in the open country, that the conditions were not right for enjoyment. Miss Wickham did not appear to share the modern girl's distaste for her home. She plainly wanted to get there as quickly as possible. It seemed to Roland that from the time they left High Barnet to the moment when with a grinding of brakes they drew up at the door of Skeldings Hall the two-seater had only touched Hertfordshire at odd spots.

Yet, as they alighted, Roberta Wickham voiced a certain dissatisfaction with her work.

"Forty-three minutes," she said, frowning at her watch. "I can do better than that."

"Can you?" gulped Roland. "Can you, indeed?"

"Well, we're in time for tea, anyhow. Come in and meet the mater. Forgotten Sports of the Past—Number Three, Meeting the Mater."

Roland met the mater. The phrase, however, is too mild and inexpressive and does not give a true picture of the facts. He not merely met the mater; he was engulfed and swallowed up by the mater. Lady Wickham, that popular novelist ("Strikes a singularly fresh note."—R. Moresby Attwater in the *New Examiner*), was delighted to see her guest. Welcoming Roland to her side, she proceeded to strike so many singularly fresh notes that he was unable to tear himself away till it was time to dress for dinner. She was still talking with unimpaired volubility on the subject of her books, of which Roland had been kind enough to write so appreciatively, when the gong went.

"Is it as late as that?" she said, surprised, releasing Roland, who had thought it later. "We shall have to go on with our little talk after dinner. You know your room? No? Oh, well, Claude will show you. Claude, will you take Mr. Attwater up with you? His room is at the end of your corridor. By the way, you don't know each other, do you? Sir Claude Lynn—Mr. Attwater."

The two men bowed; but in Roland's bow there was not that heartiness which we like to see in our friends when we introduce them to fellow-guests. A considerable part of the agony which he had been enduring for the last two hours had been caused not so much by Lady Wickham's eloquence, though that had afflicted him sorely, as by the spectacle of this man Lynn, whoever he might be, monopolizing the society of Bobbie Wickham in a distant corner. There had been to him something intolerably possessive about the back of Sir Claude's neck as he bent toward Miss Wickham. It was the neck of a man who is being much more intimate and devotional than a jealous rival cares about.

The close-up which he now received of this person did nothing to allay Roland's apprehension. The man was handsome, sickeningly handsome, with just that dark, dignified, clean-cut handsomeness which attracts impressionable girls. It was, indeed, his dignity that so oppressed Roland now. There was that about Sir Claude Lynn's calm and supercilious eye that made a fellow feel he belonged to entirely the wrong set in London and that his trousers were bagging at the knees.

"A most delightful man," whispered Lady Wickham, as Sir Claude moved away to open the door for Bobbie. "Between ourselves, the original of Captain Mauleverer, D.S.O., in my *Blood Will Tell*. Very old family, ever so much money. Plays polo splendidly. And tennis. And golf. A superb shot. Member for East Bittlesham, and I hear on all sides that he may be in the Cabinet any day."

"Indeed?" said Roland, coldly.

It seemed to Lady Wickham, as she sat with him in her study after dinner—she had stated authoritatively that he would much prefer a quiet chat in that shrine of literature to any shallow revelry that might be going on elsewhere—that Roland was a trifle distrait. Nobody could have worked harder to entertain him than she. She read him the first seven chapters of the new novel on which she was engaged, and told him in gratifying detail the plot of the rest of it, but somehow all did not seem well. The young man, she noticed, had developed a habit of plucking at his hair; and once he gave a sharp, gulping cry which startled her. Lady Wickham began to feel disappointed in Roland, and was not sorry when he excused himself.

"I wonder," he said, in a rather overwrought sort of way, "if you would mind if I just went and had a word with Miss Wickham? I—I—there's something I wanted to ask her."

"Certainly," said Lady Wickham, without warmth. "You will probably find her in the billiard-room. She said something about having a game with Claude. Sir Claude is wonderful at billiards. Almost like a professional."

Bobbie was not in the billiard-room, but Sir Claude was, practising dignified cannons which never failed to come off. At Roland's entrance he looked up like an inquiring statue.

"Miss Wickham?" he said. "She left half an hour ago. I think she went to bed."

He surveyed Roland's flushed dishevelment for a moment with a touch of disapproval, then resumed his cannons. Roland, though he had that on his mind concerning which he desired Miss Wickham's counsel and sympathy, felt that it would have to stand over till the morning. Meanwhile, lest his hostess should pop out of the study and recapture him, he decided to go to bed himself.

He had just reached the passage where his haven lay, when a door which had apparently been standing ajar opened and Bobbie appeared, draped in a sea-green négligée of such a calibre that Roland's heart leaped convulsively and he clutched at the wall for support.

"Oh, there you are," she said, a little petulantly. "What a time you've been!"

"Your mother was——"

"Yes, I suppose she would be," said Miss Wickham, understandingly. "Well, I only wanted to tell you about Sidney."

"Sidney? Do you mean Claude?"

"No. Sidney. The snake. I was in your room just after dinner, to see if you had everything you wanted, and I noticed the box on your dressing table."

"I've been trying to get hold of you all the evening to ask you what to do about that," said

Roland, feverishly. "I was most awfully upset when I saw the beastly thing. How Bryce came to be such an idiot as to put it in the car——"

"He must have misunderstood me," said Bobbie, with a clear and childlike light shining in her hazel eyes. "I suppose he thought I said, 'Put this in the back' instead of 'Take this back.' But what I wanted to say was that it's all right."

"All right?"

"Yes. That's why I've been waiting up to see you. I thought that, when you went to your room and found the box open, you might be a bit worried."

"The box open!"

"Yes. But it's all right. It was I who opened it."

"Oh, but I say—you—you oughtn't to have done that. The snake may be roaming about all over the house."

"Oh, no, it's all right. I know where it is."

"That's good."

"Yes, it's all right. I put it in Claude's bed."

Roland Attwater clutched at his hair as violently as if he had been listening to chapter six of Lady Wickham's new novel.

"You—you—you—what?"

"I put it in Claude's bed."

Roland uttered a little whinnying sound, like a very old horse a very long way away.

"Put it in Claude's bed!"

"Put it in Claude's bed."

"But—but—but why?"

"Why not?" asked Miss Wickham, reasonably.

"But—oh, my heavens!"

"Something on your mind?" inquired Miss Wickham, solicitously.

"It will give him an awful fright."

"Jolly good for him. I was reading an article in the evening paper about it. Did you know that fear increases the secretory activity of the thyroid, suprarenal, and pituitary glands? Well, it does. Bucks you up, you know. Regular tonic. It'll be like a day at the seaside for old Claude when he puts his bare foot on Sidney. Well, I must be turning in. Got that schoolgirl complexion to think about. Good night."

For some minutes after he had tottered to his room, Roland sat on the edge of the bed in deep meditation. At one time it seemed as if his reverie was going to take a pleasant turn. This was when the thought presented itself to him that he must

have overestimated the power of Sir Claude's
fascination. A girl could not, he felt, have fallen
very deeply under a man's spell if she started
filling his bed with snakes the moment she left
him.

For an instant, as he toyed with this heartening reflection, something remotely resembling
a smile played about Roland's sensitive mouth.
Then another thought came to wipe the smile
away—the realization that, while the broad general principle of putting snakes in Sir Claude's
bed was entirely admirable, the flaw in the present situation lay in the fact that this particular
snake could be so easily traced to its source. The
butler, or whoever had taken his luggage upstairs, would be sure to remember carrying up a
mysterious box. Probably it had squished as he
carried it and was already the subject of comment in the servants' hall. Discovery was practically certain.

Roland rose jerkily from his bed. There was
only one thing to be done, and he must do it immediately. He must go to Sir Claude's room
and retrieve his lost pet. He crept to the door and
listened carefully. No sound came to disturb the

stillness of the house. He stole out into the corridor.

It was at this precise moment that Sir Claude Lynn, surfeited with cannons, put on his coat, replaced his cue in the rack, and came out of the billiard-room.

If there is one thing in this world that should be done quickly or not at all, it is the removal of one's personal snake from the bed of a comparative stranger. Yet Roland, brooding over the snowy coverlet, hesitated. All his life he had had a horror of crawling and slippery things. At his private school, while other boys had fondled frogs and achieved terms of intimacy with slowworms, he had not been able to bring himself even to keep white mice. The thought of plunging his hand between those sheets and groping for an object of such recognized squishiness as Sidney appalled him. And, even as he hesitated, there came from the corridor outside the sound of advancing footsteps.

Roland was not by nature a resourceful young man, but even a child would have known what to do in this crisis. There was a large cupboard on the other side of the room, and its door had been left invitingly open. In the rapidity with which he bolted into this his uncle Joseph would no doubt have seen further convincing evidence of his rabbit-hood. He reached it and burrowed behind a mass of hanging clothes just as Sir Claude entered the room.

It was some small comfort to Roland—and at the moment he needed what comfort he could get, however small—to find that there was plenty of space in the cupboard. And what was even better, seeing that he had had no time to close the door, it was generously filled with coats, overcoats, raincoats, and trousers. Sir Claude Lynn was evidently a man who believed in taking an extensive wardrobe with him on country-house visits; and, while he deplored the dandyism which this implied, Roland would not have had it otherwise. Nestling in the undergrowth, he peered out between a raincoat and a pair of golfing knickerbockers. A strange silence had fallen, and he was curious to know what his host was doing with himself.

At first he could not sight him; but, shifting slightly to the left, he brought him into focus, and discovered that in the interval that had passed Sir Claude had removed nearly all his clothes and was now standing before the open window, doing exercises.

It was not prudery that caused this spectacle to give Roland a sharp shock. What made him start so convulsively was the man's horrifying aspect as revealed in the nude. Downstairs, in the conventional dinner-costume of the well-dressed man, Sir Claude Lynn had seemed robust and soldierly, but nothing in his appearance then had prepared Roland for the ghastly physique which he exhibited now. He seemed twice his previous size as if the removal of constricting garments had caused him to bulge in every direction. When he inflated his chest, it looked like a barrel. And, though Roland in the circumstances would have preferred any other simile, there was only one thing to which his rippling muscles could be compared. They were like snakes, and nothing but snakes. They heaved and twisted beneath his skin just as Sidney was presumably even now heaving and twisting beneath the sheets.

If ever there was a man, in short, in whose bedroom one would rather not have been concealed in circumstances which might only too easily lead to a physical encounter, that man was Sir Claude Lynn; and Roland, seeing him, winced away with a shudder so violent that a coat-hanger which had been trembling on the edge of its peg fell with a disintegrating clatter.

There was a moment of complete silence: then the trousers behind which he cowered were snatched away, and a huge hand, groping like the tentacle of some dreadful marine monster, seized him painfully by the hair and started pulling.

"Ouch!" said Roland, and came out like a winkle at the end of a pin.

A modesty which Roland, who was modest himself, should have been the first to applaud had led the other to clothe himself hastily for this interview in a suit of pyjamas of a stupefying mauve. In all his life Roland had never seen such a colour-scheme; and in some curious way the brilliance of them seemed to complete his confusion. The result was that, instead of plunging at once into apologies and explanations, he remained staring with fallen jaw; and his expression, taken in conjunction with the fact that his hair, rumpled by the coats, appeared to be standing on end, supplied Sir Claude with a theory which seemed to cover the case. He remembered that Roland had had much the same cock-eyed look when he had come into the billiard-room. He recalled that immediately after dinner Roland had disappeared and had not joined the rest of the party in the drawing-room. Obviously the fellow must have been drinking like a fish in some secret part of the house for hours.

"Get out!" he said curtly, taking Roland by the arm with a look of disgust and leading him sternly to the door. An abstemious man himself, Sir Claude Lynn had a correct horror of excess in others. "Go and sleep it off. I suppose you can find your way to your room? It's the one at the end of the corridor, as you seem to have forgotten."

"But listen——"

"I cannot understand how a man of any decent upbringing can make such a beast of himself."

"Do listen!"

"Don't shout like that," snapped Sir Claude, severely. "Good heavens, man, do you want to wake the whole house? If you dare to open your mouth again, I'll break you into little bits."

Roland found himself out in the passage, staring at a closed door. Even as he stared it opened sharply, and the upper half of the mauve-clad Sir Claude popped out.

"No drunken singing in the corridor, mind!" said Sir Claude, sternly, and disappeared.

It was a little difficult to know what to do. Sir Claude had counselled slumber, but the suggestion was scarcely a practical one. On the other hand there seemed nothing to be gained by hanging about in the passage. With slow and lingering steps Roland moved towards his room, and had just reached it when the silence of the night was rent by a shattering scream; and the next moment there shot through the door he had left a large body. And, as Roland gazed dumbly, a voice was raised in deafening appeal.

"Shot-gun!" vociferated Sir Claude. "Help! Shot-gun! Bring a shot-gun, somebody!"

There was not the smallest room for doubt that the secretory activity of his thyroid, suprarenal, and pituitary glands had been increased to an almost painful extent.

It is only in the most modern and lively country houses that this sort of thing can happen without attracting attention. So quickly did the corridor fill that it seemed to Roland as if dressing-gowned figures had shot up through the carpet.

Among those present he noticed Lady Wickham
in blue, her daughter Roberta in green, three
male guests in bath-robes, the under-housemaid
in curl-papers, and Simmons, the butler, completely and correctly clad in full afternoon costume. They were all asking what was the matter,
but, as Lady Wickham's penetrating voice o'er-
topped the rest, it was to her that Sir Claude
turned to tell his story.

"A snake?" said Lady Wickham, interested.

"A snake."

"In your bed?"

"In my bed."

"Most unusual," said Lady Wickham, with
a touch of displeasure.

Sir Claude's rolling eye wandering along the
corridor, picked out Roland as he shrank among
the shadows. He pointed at him with such swift
suddenness that his hostess only saved herself
from a nasty blow by means of some shifty foot-
work.

"That's the man!" he cried.

Lady Wickham, already ruffled, showed signs
of peevishness.

"My dear Claude," she said, with a certain
asperity, "do come to some definite decision. A

moment ago you said there was a snake in your room; now you say it was a man. Besides, can't you see that that is Mr. Attwater? What would he be doing in your room?"

"I'm telling you what he was doing. He was putting that infernal snake in my bed. I found him there."

"Found him there? In your bed?"

"In my cupboard. Hiding. I hauled him out."

All eyes were turned upon Roland. His own he turned with a look of wistful entreaty upon Roberta Wickham. A cavalier of the nicest gallantry, nothing, of course, would induce him to betray the girl; but surely she would appreciate that the moment had come for her to step forward and clear a good man's name with a full explanation.

He had been too sanguine. A pretty astonishment lit up Miss Wickham's lovely eyes. But her equally lovely mouth did not open.

"But Mr. Attwater has no snakes," argued Lady Wickham. "He is a well-known man-of-letters. Well-known men-of-letters," she said, stating a pretty generally recognized fact, "do not take snakes with them when they go on visits."

A new voice joined in the discussion.

"Begging your pardon, your ladyship."

It was the voice of Simmons, grave and respectful.

"Begging your pardon, your ladyship, it is my belief that Mr. Attwater did have a serpent in his possession. Thomas, who conveyed his baggage to his room, mentioned a cardboard box that seemed to contain something alive."

From the expression of the eyes that once more raked him in his retirement, it was plain that the assembled company were of the opinion that it was Roland's turn to speak. But speech was beyond him. He had been backing slowly for some little time, and now, as he backed another step, the handle of his bedroom door insinuated itself into the small of his back. It was almost as if the thing were hinting to him that refuge lay beyond.

He did not resist the kindly suggestion. With one quick, emotional movement he turned, plunged into his room, and slammed the door behind him.

From the corridor without came the sound of voices in debate. He was unable to distinguish words, but the general trend of them was clear. Then silence fell.

Roland sat on his bed, staring before him. He was roused from his trance by a tap on the door.

"Who's that?" he cried, bounding up. His eye was wild. He was prepared to sell his life dearly.

"It is I, sir. Simmons."

"What do you want?"

The door opened a few inches. Through the gap there came a hand. In the hand was a silver salver. On the salver lay something squishy that writhed and wriggled.

"Your serpent, sir," said the voice of Simmons.

It was the opinion of Roland Attwater that he was now entitled to the remainder of the night in peace. The hostile forces outside must now, he felt, have fired their last shot. He sat on his bed, thinking deeply, if incoherently. From time to time the clock on the stables struck the quarters, but he did not move. And then into the silence it seemed to him that some sound intruded —a small tapping sound that might have been the first tentative efforts of a very young woodpecker just starting out in business for itself. It was only after this small noise had continued for some moments that he recognized it for what it was. Somebody was knocking softly on his door.

There are moods in which even the mildest man will turn to bay, and there gleamed in Roland Attwater's eyes as he strode to the door and flung it open a baleful light. And such was his militant condition that, even when he glared out and beheld Roberta Wickham, still in that green négligée, the light did not fade away. He regarded her malevolently.

"I thought I'd better come and have a word with you," whispered Miss Wickham.

"Indeed?" said Roland.

"I wanted to explain."

"Explain!"

"Well," said Miss Wickham, "you may not think there's any explanation due to you, but I really feel there is. Oh, yes, I do. You see, it was this way. Claude had asked me to marry him."

"And so you put a snake in his bed? Of course! Quite natural!"

"Well, you see, he was so frightfully perfect and immaculate and dignified and—oh, well, you've seen him for yourself, so you know what I mean. He was too darned overpowering—that's what I'm driving at—and it seemed to me that if I could only see him really human and undignified just once—I might—well, you see what I mean?"

"And the experiment, I take it, was successful?"

Miss Wickham wriggled her small toes inside her slippers.

"It depends which way you look at it. I'm not going to marry him, if that's what you mean."

"I should have thought," said Roland, coldly, "that Sir Claude behaved in a manner sufficiently —shall I say human?—to satisfy even you."

Miss Wickham giggled reminiscently.

"He did leap, didn't he? But it's all off, just the same."

"Might I ask why?"

"Those pyjamas," said Miss Wickham, firmly. "The moment I caught a glimpse of them, I said to myself, 'No wedding bells for me!' No! I've seen too much of life to be optimistic about a man who wears mauve pyjamas." She plunged for a space into maiden meditation. When she spoke again, it was on another aspect of the affair. "I'm afraid mother is rather cross with you, Roland."

"You surprise me!"

"Never mind. You can slate her next novel."

"I intend to," said Roland, grimly, remembering what he had suffered in the study from chapters one to seven of it.

"But meanwhile I don't think you had better meet her again just yet. Do you know, I really think the best plan would be for you to go away to-night without saying good-bye. There is a very good milk-train which gets you into London at six-forty-five."

"When does it start?"

"At three-fifteen."

"I'll take it," said Roland.

There was a pause. Roberta Wickham drew a step closer.

"Roland," she said, softly, "you were a dear not to give me away. I do appreciate it so much."

"Not at all!"

"There would have been an awful row. I expect mother would have taken away my car."

"Ghastly!"

"I want to see you again quite soon, Roland. I'm coming up to London next week. Will you give me lunch? And then we might go and sit in Kensington Gardens or somewhere where it's quiet."

Roland eyed her fixedly.

"I'll drop you a line," he said.

Sir Joseph Moresby was an early breakfaster. The hands of the clock pointed to five minutes past eight as he entered his dining-room with a jaunty and hopeful step. There were, his senses told him, kidneys and bacon beyond that door. To his surprise he found that there was also his nephew Roland. The young man was pacing the carpet restlessly. He had a rumpled look, as if he had slept poorly, and his eyes were pink about the rims.

"Roland!" exclaimed Sir Joseph. "Good gracious! What are you doing here? Didn't you go to Skeldings after all?"

"Yes, I went," said Roland, in a strange, tone-less voice.

"Then what——?"

"Uncle Joseph," said Roland, "you remember what we were talking about at dinner? Do you really think Lucy would have me if I asked her to marry me?"

"What! My dear boy, she's been in love with you for years."

"Is she up yet?"

"No. She doesn't breakfast till nine."

"I'll wait."

Sir Joseph grasped his hand.

"Roland, my boy——" he began.

But there was that on Roland's mind that made him unwilling to listen to set speeches.

"Uncle Joseph," he said, "do you mind if I join you for a bite of breakfast?"

"My dear boy, of course——"

"Then I wish you would ask them to be frying two or three eggs and another rasher or so. While I'm waiting I'll be starting on a few kidneys."

It was ten minutes past nine when Sir Joseph happened to go into the morning-room. He had supposed it empty, but he perceived that the large armchair by the window was occupied by his nephew Roland. He was leaning back with the air of one whom the world is treating well. On the floor beside him sat Lucy, her eyes fixed adoringly on the young man's face.

"Yes, yes," she was saying. "How wonderful! Do go on, darling."

Sir Joseph tiptoed out, unnoticed. Roland was speaking as he softly closed the door.

"Well," Sir Joseph heard him say, "it was raining, you know, and just as I reached the corner of Duke Street——"

LEAVE IT TO PSMITH

—and, at last—Psmith!

CONTENTS

LEAVE IT TO PSMITH

CHAPTER I

DARK PLOTTINGS AT BLANDINGS CASTLE

§ 1

AT the open window of the great library of Blandings
Castle, drooping like a wet sock, as was his habit
when he had nothing to prop his spine against, the Earl of
Emsworth, that amiable and boneheaded peer, stood gazing out over his domain.

It was a lovely morning, and the air was fragrant with
gentle summer scents. Yet in his lordship's pale blue
eyes there was a look of melancholy. His brow was furrowed, his mouth peevish. And this was all the more
strange in that he was normally as happy as only a fluffy-
minded man with excellent health and a large income
can be. A writer, describing Blandings Castle in a magazine article, had once said: "Tiny mosses have grown in
the cavities of the stones, until, viewed near at hand, the
place seems shaggy with vegetation." It would not have
been a bad description of the proprietor. Fifty-odd years
of serene and unruffled placidity had given Lord Emsworth
a curiously moss-covered look. Very few things had the
power to disturb him. Even his younger son, the Hon.
Freddie Threepwood, could only do it occasionally.

Yet now he was sad. And—not to make a mystery of

it any longer—the reason of his sorrow was the fact that he had mislaid his glasses and without them was as blind, to use his own neat simile, as a bat. He was keenly aware of the sunshine that poured down on his gardens, and was yearning to pop out and potter among the flowers he loved. But no man, pop he never so wisely, can hope to potter with any good result if the world is a mere blur.

The door behind him opened, and Beach the butler entered, a dignified procession of one.

"Who's that?" inquired Lord Emsworth, spinning on his axis.

"It is I, your lordship—Beach."

"Have you found them?"

"Not yet, your lordship," sighed the butler.

"You can't have looked."

"I have searched assiduously, your lordship, but without avail. Thomas and Charles also announce non-success. Stokes has not yet made his report."

"Ah!"

"I am re-despatching Thomas and Charles to your lordship's bedroom," said the Master of the Hunt. "I trust that their efforts will be rewarded."

Beach withdrew, and Lord Emsworth turned to the window again. The scene that spread itself beneath him —though he was unfortunately not able to see it—was a singularly beautiful one, for the castle, which is one of the oldest inhabited houses in England, stands upon a knoll of rising ground at the southern end of the celebrated Vale of Blandings in the county of Shropshire. Away in the blue distance wooded hills ran down to where the Severn gleamed like an unsheathed sword; while up from the river rolling park-land, mounting and dipping,

surged in a green wave almost to the castle walls, breaking
on the terraces in a many-coloured flurry of flowers as it
reached the spot where the province of Angus McAllister, his lordship's head gardener, began. The day being
June the thirtieth, which is the very high-tide time of
summer flowers, the immediate neighbourhood of the castle was ablaze with roses, pinks, pansies, carnations, hollyhocks, columbines, larkspurs, London pride, Canterbury
bells, and a multitude of other choice blooms of which
only Angus could have told you the names. A conscientious man was Angus; and in spite of being a good deal
hampered by Lord Emsworth's amateur assistance, he
showed excellent results in his department. In his beds
there was much at which to point with pride, little to view
with concern.

Scarcely had Beach removed himself when Lord
Emsworth was called upon to turn again. The door had
opened for the second time, and a young man in a beau-
tifully-cut suit of grey flannel was standing in the doorway. He had a long and vacant face topped by shining
hair brushed back and heavily brilliantined after the pre-
vailing mode, and he was standing on one leg. For
Freddie Threepwood was seldom completely at his ease
in his parent's presence.

"Hallo, guv'nor."

"Well, Frederick?"

It would be paltering with the truth to say that Lord
Emsworth's greeting was a warm one. It lacked the note
of true affection. A few weeks before he had had to pay
a matter of five hundred pounds to settle certain racing
debts for his offspring; and, while this had not actually
dealt an irretrievable blow at his bank account, it had

undeniably tended to diminish Freddie's charm in his
eyes.

"Hear you've lost your glasses, guv'nor."

"That is so."

"Nuisance, what?"

"Undeniably."

"Ought to have a spare pair."

"I have broken my spare pair."

"Tough luck! And lost the other?"

"And, as you say, lost the other."

"Have you looked for the bally things?"

"I have."

"Must be somewhere, I mean."

"Quite possibly."

"Where," asked Freddie, warming to his work, "did
you see them last?"

"Go away!" said Lord Emsworth, on whom his
child's conversation had begun to exercise an oppressive
effect.

"Eh?"

"Go away!"

"Go away?"

"Yes, go away!"

"Right ho!"

The door closed. His lordship returned to the window
once more.

He had been standing there some few minutes when
one of those miracles occurred which happen in libraries.
Without sound or warning a section of books started to
move away from the parent body and, swinging out in
a solid chunk into the room, showed a glimpse of a small,
study-like apartment. A young man in spectacles came

noiselessly through and the books returned to their place.

The contrast between Lord Emsworth and the new-comer, as they stood there, was striking, almost dramatic. Lord Emsworth was so acutely spectacle-less; Rupert Baxter, his secretary, so pronouncedly spectacled. It was his spectacles that struck you first as you saw the man. They gleamed efficiently at you. If you had a guilty conscience, they pierced you through and through; and even if your conscience was one hundred per cent. pure you could not ignore them. "Here," you said to yourself, "is an efficient young man in spectacles."

In describing Rupert Baxter as efficient, you did not over-estimate him. He was essentially that. Technically but a salaried subordinate, he had become by degrees, owing to the limp amiability of his employer, the real master of the house. He was the Brains of Blandings, the man at the switch, the person in charge, and the pilot, so to speak, who weathered the storm. Lord Emsworth left everything to Baxter, only asking to be allowed to potter in peace; and Baxter, more than equal to the task, shouldered it without wincing.

Having got within range, Baxter coughed; and Lord Emsworth, recognising the sound, wheeled round with a faint flicker of hope. It might be that even this apparently insoluble problem of the missing pince-nez would yield before the other's efficiency.

"Baxter, my dear fellow, I've lost my glasses. My glasses. I have mislaid them. I cannot think where they can have gone to. You haven't seen them anywhere by any chance?"

"Yes, Lord Emsworth," replied the secretary, quietly equal to the crisis. "They are hanging down your back."

"Down my back? Why, bless my soul!" His lordship
tested the statement and found it—like all Baxter's statements—accurate. "Why, bless my soul, so they are! Do
you know, Baxter, I really believe I must be growing
absent-minded." He hauled in the slack, secured the
pince-nez, adjusted them beamingly. His irritability had
vanished like the dew off one of his roses. "Thank you,
Baxter, thank you. You are invaluable."

And with a radiant smile Lord Emsworth made buoyantly for the door, en route for God's air and the society
of McAllister. The movement drew from Baxter another cough—a sharp, peremptory cough this time; and
his lordship paused, reluctantly, like a dog whistled back
from the chase. A cloud fell over the sunniness of his
mood. Admirable as Baxter was in so many respects, he
had a tendency to worry him at times; and something told
Lord Emsworth that he was going to worry him now.

"The car will be at the door," said Baxter with quiet
firmness, "at two sharp."

"Car? What car?"

"The car to take you to the station."

"Station? What station?"

Rupert Baxter preserved his calm. There were times
when he found his employer a little trying, but he never
showed it.

"You have perhaps forgotten, Lord Emsworth, that you
arranged with Lady Constance to go to London this afternoon."

"Go to London!" gasped Lord Emsworth, appalled.
"In weather like this? With a thousand things to attend
to in the garden? What a perfectly preposterous notion!
Why should I go to London? I hate London."

"You arranged with Lady Constance that you would give Mr. McTodd lunch to-morrow at your club."

"Who the devil is Mr. McTodd?"

"The well-known Canadian poet."

"Never heard of him."

"Lady Constance has long been a great admirer of his work. She wrote inviting him, should he ever come to England, to pay a visit to Blandings. He is now in London and is to come down to-morrow for two weeks. Lady Constance's suggestion was that, as a compliment to Mr. McTodd's eminence in the world of literature, you should meet him in London and bring him back here yourself."

Lord Emsworth remembered now. He also remembered that this positively infernal scheme had not been his sister Constance's in the first place. It was Baxter who had made the suggestion, and Constance had approved. He made use of the recovered pince-nez to glower through them at his secretary; and not for the first time in recent months was aware of a feeling that this fellow Baxter was becoming a dashed infliction. Baxter was getting above himself, throwing his weight about, making himself a confounded nuisance. He wished he could get rid of the man. But where could he find an adequate successor? That was the trouble. With all his drawbacks, Baxter *was* efficient. Nevertheless, for a moment Lord Emsworth toyed with the pleasant dream of dismissing him. And it is possible, such was his exasperation, that he might on this occasion have done something practical in that direction, had not the library door at this moment opened for the third time, to admit yet another intruder —at the sight of whom his lordship's militant mood faded weakly.

"Oh—hallo, Connie!" he said, guiltily, like a small boy caught in the jam cupboard. Somehow his sister always had this effect upon him.

Of all those who had entered the library that morning the new arrival was the best worth looking at. Lord Emsworth was tall and lean and scraggy; Rupert Baxter thick-set and handicapped by that vaguely grubby appearance which is presented by swarthy young men of bad complexion; and even Beach, though dignified, and Freddie, though slim, would never have got far in a beauty competition. But Lady Constance Keeble really took the eye. She was a strikingly handsome woman in the middle forties. She had a fair, broad brow, teeth of a perfect even whiteness, and the carriage of an empress. Her eyes were large and grey, and gentle—and incidentally misleading, for gentle was hardly the adjective which anybody who knew her would have applied to Lady Constance. Though genial enough when she got her way, on the rare occasions when people attempted to thwart her she was apt to comport herself in a manner reminiscent of Cleopatra on one of the latter's bad mornings.

"I hope I am not disturbing you," said Lady Constance with a bright smile. "I just came in to tell you to be sure not to forget, Clarence, that you are going to London this afternoon to meet Mr. McTodd."

"I was just telling Lord Emsworth," said Baxter, "that the car would be at the door at two."

"Thank you, Mr. Baxter. Of course I might have known that you would not forget. You are so wonderfully capable. I don't know what in the world we would do without you."

The Efficient Baxter bowed. But, though gratified, he was not overwhelmed by the tribute. The same thought had often occurred to him independently.

"If you will excuse me," he said, "I have one or two things to attend to . . ."

"Certainly, Mr. Baxter."

The Efficient One withdrew through the door in the bookshelf. He realised that his employer was in fractious mood, but knew that he was leaving him in capable hands.

Lord Emsworth turned from the window, out of which he had been gazing with a plaintive detachment.

"Look here, Connie," he grumbled feebly. "You know I hate literary fellows. It's bad enough having them in the house, but when it comes to going to London to fetch 'em . . ."

He shuffled morosely. It was a perpetual grievance of his, this practice of his sister's of collecting literary celebrities and dumping them down in the home for indeterminate visits. You never knew when she was going to spring another on you. Already since the beginning of the year he had suffered from a round dozen of the species at brief intervals; and at this very moment his life was being poisoned by the fact that Blandings was sheltering a certain Miss Aileen Peavey, the mere thought of whom was enough to turn the sunshine off as with a tap.

"Can't stand literary fellows," proceeded his lordship. "Never could. And, by Jove, literary females are worse. Miss Peavey . . ." Here words temporarily failed the owner of Blandings. "Miss Peavey . . ." he resumed after an eloquent pause. "Who *is* Miss Peavey?"

"My dear Clarence," replied Lady Constance tolerantly,

for the fine morning had made her mild and amiable, "if you do not know that Aileen is one of the leading poetesses of the younger school, you must be very ignorant."

"I don't mean that. I know she writes poetry. I mean who *is* she? You suddenly produced her here like a rabbit out of a hat," said his lordship, in a tone of strong resentment. "Where did you find her?"

"I first made Aileen's acquaintance on an Atlantic liner when Joe and I were coming back from our trip round the world. She was very kind to me when I was feeling the motion of the vessel. . . . If you mean what is her family, I think Aileen told me once that she was connected with the Rutlandshire Peaveys."

"Never heard of them!" snapped Lord Emsworth. "And, if they're anything like Miss Peavey, God help Rutlandshire!"

Tranquil as Lady Constance's mood was this morning, an ominous stoniness came into her grey eyes at these words, and there is little doubt that in another instant she would have discharged at her mutinous brother one of those shattering come-backs for which she had been celebrated in the family from nursery days onward; but at this juncture the Efficient Baxter appeared again through the bookshelf.

"Excuse me," said Baxter, securing attention with a flash of his spectacles. "I forgot to mention, Lord Emsworth, that, to suit everybody's convenience, I have arranged that Miss Halliday shall call to see you at your club to-morrow after lunch."

"Good Lord, Baxter!" The harassed peer started as if he had been bitten in the leg. "Who's Miss Halliday? Not another literary female?"

"Miss Halliday is the young lady who is coming to Blandings to catalogue the library."

"Catalogue the library ? What does it want cataloguing for ?"

"It has not been done since the year 1885."

"Well, and look how splendidly we've got along without it," said Lord Emsworth acutely.

"Don't be so ridiculous, Clarence," said Lady Constance, annoyed. "The catalogue of a great library like this must be brought up to date." She moved to the door. "I do wish you would try to wake up and take an interest in things. If it wasn't for Mr. Baxter, I don't know what would happen."

And with a beaming glance of approval at her ally she left the room. Baxter, coldly austere, returned to the subject under discussion.

"I have written to Miss Halliday suggesting two-thirty as a suitable hour for the interview."

"But look here . . ."

"You will wish to see her before definitely confirming the engagement."

"Yes, but look here, I wish you wouldn't go tying me up with all these appointments."

"I thought that as you were going to London to meet Mr. McTodd . . ."

"But I'm not going to London to meet Mr. McTodd," cried Lord Emsworth with weak fury. "It's out of the question. I can't possibly leave Blandings. The weather may break at any moment. I don't want to miss a day of it."

"The arrangements are all made."

"Send the fellow a wire . . . 'unavoidably detained.' "

"I could not take the responsibility for such a course myself," said Baxter coldly. "But possibly if you were to make the suggestion to Lady Constance . . ."

"Oh, dash it!" said Lord Emsworth unhappily, at once realising the impossibility of the scheme. "Oh, well, if I've got to go, I've got to go," he said after a gloomy pause. "But to leave my garden and stew in London at this time of the year . . ."

There seemed nothing further to say on the subject. He took off his glasses, polished them, put them on again, and shuffled to the door. After all, he reflected, even though the car was coming for him at two, at least he had the morning, and he proposed to make the most of it. But his first careless rapture at the prospect of pottering among his flowers was dimmed, and would not be recaptured. He did not entertain any project so mad as the idea of defying his sister Constance, but he felt extremely bitter about the whole affair. Confound Constance! . . . Dash Baxter! . . . Miss Peavey . . .

The door closed behind Lord Emsworth.

§ 2

Lady Constance meanwhile, proceeding downstairs, had reached the big hall, when the door of the smoking-room opened and a head popped out. A round, grizzled head with a healthy pink face attached to it.

"Connie!" said the head.

Lady Constance halted.

"Yes, Joe?"

"Come in here a minute," said the head. "Want to speak to you."

Lady Constance went into the smoking-room. It was large and cosily book-lined, and its window looked out on to an Italian garden. A wide fire-place occupied nearly the whole of one side of it, and in front of this, his legs spread to an invisible blaze, Mr. Joseph Keeble had already taken his stand. His manner was bluff, but an acute observer might have detected embarrassment in it.

"What is it, Joe?" asked Lady Constance, and smiled pleasantly at her husband. When, two years previously, she had married this elderly widower, of whom the world knew nothing beyond the fact that he had amassed a large fortune in South African diamond mines, there had not been wanting cynics to set the match down as one of convenience, a purely business arrangement by which Mr. Keeble exchanged his money for Lady Constance's social position. Such was not the case. It had been a genuine marriage of affection on both sides. Mr. Keeble worshipped his wife, and she was devoted to him, though never foolishly indulgent. They were a happy and united couple.

Mr. Keeble cleared his throat. He seemed to find some difficulty in speaking. And when he spoke it was not on the subject which he had intended to open, but on one which had already been worn out in previous conversations.

"Connie, I've been thinking about that necklace again."

Lady Constance laughed.

"Oh, don't be silly, Joe. You haven't called me into this stuffy room on a lovely morning like this to talk about that for the hundredth time."

"Well, you know, there's no sense in taking risks."

"Don't be absurd. What risks can there be?"

"There was a burglary over at Winstone Court, not ten miles from here, only a day or two ago."

"Don't be so fussy, Joe."

"That necklace cost nearly twenty thousand pounds," said Mr. Keeble, in the reverent voice in which men of business traditions speak of large sums.

"I know."

"It ought to be in the bank."

"Once and for all, Joe," said Lady Constance, losing her amiability and becoming suddenly imperious and Cleopatrine, "I will *not* keep that necklace in a bank. What on earth is the use of having a beautiful necklace if it is lying in the strong-room of a bank all the time? There is the County Ball coming on, and the Bachelors' Ball after that, and . . . well, I *need* it. I will send the thing to the bank when we pass through London on our way to Scotland, but not till then. And I do wish you would stop worrying me about it."

There was a silence. Mr. Keeble was regretting now that his unfortunate poltroonery had stopped him from tackling in a straightforward and manly fashion the really important matter which was weighing on his mind; for he perceived that his remarks about the necklace, eminently sensible though they were, had marred the genial mood in which his wife had begun this interview. It was going to be more difficult now than ever to approach the main issue. Still, ruffled though she might be, the thing had to be done: for it involved a matter of finance, and in matters of finance Mr. Keeble was no longer a free agent. He and Lady Constance had a mutual banking account, and it was she who supervised the spending of it. This was an arrangement, subsequently regretted by Mr. Kee ble, which had been come to in the early days of the honeymoon, when men are apt to do foolish things.

Mr. Keeble coughed. Not the sharp, efficient cough which we have heard Rupert Baxter uttering in the library, but a feeble, strangled thing like the bleat of a diffident sheep.

"Connie," he said. "Er—Connie."

And at the words a sort of cold film seemed to come over Lady Constance's eyes: for some sixth sense told her what subject it was that was now about to be introduced.

"Connie, I—er—had a letter from Phyllis this morning."

Lady Constance said nothing. Her eyes gleamed for an instant, then became frozen again. Her intuition had not deceived her.

Into the married life of this happy couple only one shadow had intruded itself up to the present. But unfortunately it was a shadow of considerable proportions, a kind of super-shadow; and its effect had been chilling. It was Phyllis, Mr. Keeble's step-daughter, who had caused it—by the simple process of jilting the rich and suitable young man whom Lady Constance had attached to her (rather in the manner of a conjurer forcing a card upon his victim) and running off and marrying a far from rich and quite unsuitable person of whom all that seemed to be known was that his name was Jackson. Mr. Keeble, whose simple creed was that Phyllis could do no wrong, had been prepared to accept the situation philosophically; but his wife's wrath had been deep and enduring. So much so that the mere mentioning of the girl's name must be accounted to him for a brave deed, Lady Constance having specifically stated that she never wished to hear it again.

Keenly alive to this prejudice of hers, Mr. Keeble stopped after making his announcement, and had to rattle his keys in his pocket in order to acquire the necessary courage to continue. He was not looking at his wife, but he knew just how forbidding her expression must be. This task of his was no easy, congenial task for a pleasant summer morning.

"She says in her letter," proceeded Mr. Keeble, his eyes on the carpet and his cheeks a deeper pink, "that young Jackson has got the chance of buying a big farm . . . in Lincolnshire, I think she said . . . if he can raise three thousand pounds."

He paused and stole a glance at his wife. It was as he had feared. She had congealed. Like some spell, the name Jackson had apparently turned her to marble. It was like the Pygmalion and Galatea business working the wrong way round. She was presumably breathing, but there was no sign of it.

"So I was just thinking," said Mr. Keeble, producing another *obbligato* on the keys, "it just crossed my mind . . . it isn't as if the thing were a speculation . . . the place is apparently coining money . . . present owner only selling because he wants to go abroad . . . it occurred to me . . . and they would pay good interest on the loan . . ."

"What loan?" inquired the statue icily, coming to life.

"Well, what I was thinking . . . just a suggestion, you know . . . what struck me was that if you were willing we might . . . good investment, you know, and nowadays it's deuced hard to find good investments. . . . I was thinking that we might lend them the money."

He stopped. But he had got the thing out and felt happier. He rattled his keys again, and rubbed the back of his head against the mantelpiece. The friction seemed to give him confidence.

"We had better settle this thing once and for all, Joe," said Lady Constance. "As you know, when we were married, I was ready to do everything for Phyllis. I was prepared to be a mother to her. I gave her every chance, took her everywhere. And what happened?"

"Yes, I know. But . . ."

"She became engaged to a man with plenty of money . . ."

"Shocking young ass," interjected Mr. Keeble, perking up for a moment at the recollection of the late lamented, whom he had never liked. "And a rip, what's more. I've heard stories."

"Nonsense! If you are going to believe all the gossip you hear about people, nobody would be safe. He was a delightful young man and he would have made Phyllis perfectly happy. Instead of marrying him, she chose to go off with this—Jackson." Lady Constance's voice quivered. Greater scorn could hardly have been packed into two syllables. "After what has happened, I certainly intend to have nothing more to do with her. I shall not lend them a penny, so please do not let us continue this discussion any longer. I hope I am not an unjust woman, but I must say that I consider, after the way Phyllis behaved . . ."

The sudden opening of the door caused her to break off.

Lord Emsworth, mould-stained and wearing a deplorable old jacket, pottered into the room. He peered benevolently at his sister and his brother-in-law, but seemed unaware that he was interrupting a conversation.

" 'Gardening As A Fine Art,' " he murmured. "Connie, have you seen a book called 'Gardening As A Fine Art'? I was reading it in here last night. 'Gardening As A Fine Art.' That is the title. Now, where can it have got to?" His dreamy eye flitted to and fro. "I want to show it to McAllister. There is a passage in it that directly refutes his anarchistic views on . . ."

"It is probably on one of the shelves," said Lady Constance shortly.

"On one of the shelves?" said Lord Emsworth, obviously impressed by this bright suggestion. "Why, of course, to be sure."

Mr. Keeble was rattling his keys moodily. A mutinous expression was on his pink face. These moments of rebellion did not come to him very often, for he loved his wife with a dog-like affection and had grown accustomed to being ruled by her, but now resentment filled him. She was unreasonable, he considered. She ought to have realised how strongly he felt about poor little Phyllis. It was too infernally cold-blooded to abandon the poor child like an old shoe simply because . . ."

"Are you going?" he asked, observing his wife moving to the door.

"Yes. I am going into the garden," said Lady Constance. "Why? Was there anything else you wanted to talk to me about?"

"No," said Mr. Keeble despondently. "Oh, no."

Lady Constance left the room, and a deep masculine

silence fell. Mr. Keeble rubbed the back of his head meditatively against the mantelpiece, and Lord Emsworth
scratched among the book-shelves.

"Clarence!" said Mr. Keeble suddenly. An idea—one
might almost say an inspiration—had come to him.

"Eh?" responded his lordship absently. He had found
his book and was turning its pages, absorbed.

"Clarence, can you . . ."

"Angus McAllister," observed Lord Emsworth bitterly,
"is an obstinate, stiff-necked son of Belial. The writer of
this book distinctly states in so many words . . ."

"Clarence, can you lend me three thousand pounds on
good security and keep it dark from Connie?"

Lord Emsworth blinked.

"Keep something dark from Connie?" He raised his
eyes from his book in order to peer at this visionary with a
gentle pity. "My dear fellow, it can't be done."

"She would never know. I will tell you just why I
want this money . . ."

"Money?" Lord Emsworth's eye had become vacant
again. He was reading once more. "Money? Money,
my dear fellow? Money? Money? What money? If
I have said once," declared Lord Emsworth, "that Angus
McAllister is all wrong on the subject of hollyhocks, I've
said it a hundred times."

"Let me explain. This three thousand pounds . . ."

"My dear fellow, no. No, no. It was like you," said
his lordship with a vague heartiness, "it was like you—
good and generous—to make this offer, but I have ample,
thank you, ample. I don't *need* three thousand pounds."

"You don't understand. I . . ."

"No, no. No, no. But I am very much obliged, all the

same. It was kind of you, my dear fellow, to give me the opportunity. Very kind. Very, very, very kind," proceeded his lordship, trailing to the door and reading as he went. "Oh, very, very, very . . ."

The door closed behind him.

"Oh, *damn!*" said Mr. Keeble.

He sank into a chair in a state of profound dejection. He thought of the letter he would have to write to Phyllis. Poor little Phyllis . . . he would have to tell her that what she asked could not be managed. And why, thought Mr. Keeble sourly, as he rose from his seat and went to the writing-table, could it not be managed? Simply because he was a weak-kneed, spineless creature who was afraid of a pair of grey eyes that had a tendency to freeze.

"My dear Phyllis," he wrote.

Here he stopped. How on earth was he to put it? What a letter to have to write! Mr. Keeble placed his head between his hands and groaned aloud.

"Hallo, Uncle Joe!"

The letter-writer, turning sharply, was aware—without pleasure—of his nephew Frederick, standing beside his chair. He eyed him resentfully, for he was not only exasperated but startled. He had not heard the door open. It was as if the smooth-haired youth had popped up out of a trap.

"Came in through the window," explained the Hon. Freddie. "I say, Uncle Joe."

"Well, what is it?"

"I say, Uncle Joe," said Freddie, "can you lend me a thousand quid?"

Mr. Keeble uttered a yelp like a pinched Pomeranian.

§ 3

As Mr. Keeble, red-eyed and overwrought, rose slowly from his chair and began to swell in ominous silence, his nephew raised his hand appealingly. It began to occur to the Hon. Freddie that he had perhaps not led up to his request with the maximum of smooth tact.

"Half a jiffy!" he entreated. "I say, don't go in off the deep end for just a second. I can explain."

Mr. Keeble's feelings expressed themselves in a loud snort.

"Explain!"

"Well, I can. Whole trouble was, I started at the wrong end. Shouldn't have sprung it on you like that. The fact is, Uncle Joe, I've got a scheme. I give you my word that, if you'll only put off having apoplexy for about three minutes," said Freddie, scanning his fermenting relative with some anxiety, "I can shove you on to a good thing. Honestly I can. And all I say is, if this scheme I'm talking about is worth a thousand quid to you, will you slip it across? I'm game to spill it and leave it to your honesty to cash up if the thing looks good to you."

"A thousand pounds!"

"Nice round sum," urged Freddie ingratiatingly.

"Why," demanded Mr. Keeble, now somewhat recovered, "do you want a thousand pounds?"

"Well, who doesn't, if it comes to that?" said Freddie. "But I don't mind telling you my special reason for wanting it at just this moment, if you'll swear to keep it under your hat as far as the guv'nor is concerned."

"If you mean that you wish me not to repeat to your father anything you may tell me in confidence, naturally I should not dream of doing such a thing."

Freddie looked puzzled. His was no lightning brain.

"Can't quite work that out," he confessed. "Do you mean you will tell him or you won't?"

"I will not tell him."

"Good old Uncle Joe!" said Freddie, relieved. "A topper! I've always said so. Well, look here, you know all the trouble there's been about my dropping a bit on the races lately?"

"I do."

"Between ourselves, I dropped about five hundred of the best. And I just want to ask you one simple question. *Why* did I drop it?"

"Because you were an infernal young ass."

"Well, yes," agreed Freddie, having considered the point, "you might put it that way, of course. But why was I an ass?"

"Good God!" exclaimed the exasperated Mr. Keeble. "Am I a psycho-analyst?"

"I mean to say, if you come right down to it, I lost all that stuff simply because I was on the wrong side of the fence. It's a mug's game betting on horses. The only way to make money is to be a bookie, and that's what I'm going to do if you'll part with that thousand. Pal of mine, who was up at Oxford with me, is in a bookie's office, and they're game to take me in too if I can put up a thousand quid. Only I must let them know quick, because the offer's not going to be open for ever. You've no notion what a deuce of a lot of competition there is for that sort of job."

Mr. Keeble, who had been endeavouring with some energy to get a word in during this harangue, now contrived to speak.

"And do you seriously suppose that I would . . . But what's the use of wasting time talking? I have no means of laying my hands on the sum you mention. If I had," said Mr. Keeble wistfully. 'If I had . . ." And his eye strayed to the letter on the desk, the letter which had got as far as "My dear Phyllis" and stuck there.

Freddie gazed upon him with cordial sympathy.

"Oh, I know how you're situated, Uncle Joe, and I'm dashed sorry for you. I mean, Aunt Constance and all that."

"What!" Irksome as Mr. Keeble sometimes found the peculiar condition of his financial arrangements, he had always had the consolation of supposing that they were a secret between his wife and himself. "What do you mean?"

"Well, I know that Aunt Constance keeps an eye on the doubloons and checks the outgoings pretty narrowly. And I think it's a dashed shame that she won't unbuckle to help poor old Phyllis. A girl," said Freddie, "I always liked. Bally shame! Why the dickens shouldn't she marry that fellow Jackson? I mean, love's love," said Freddie, who felt strongly on this point.

Mr. Keeble was making curious gulping noises.

"Perhaps I ought to explain," said Freddie, "that I was having a quiet after-breakfast smoke outside the window there and heard the whole thing. I mean, you and Aunt Constance going to the mat about poor old Phyllis and you trying to bite the guv'nor's ear and so forth."

Mr. Keeble bubbled for awhile.

"You—you listened!" he managed to ejaculate at length.

"And dashed lucky for you," said Freddie with a cordiality unimpaired by the frankly unfriendly stare under which a nicer-minded youth would have withered; "dashed lucky for you that I did. Because I've got a scheme."

Mr. Keeble's estimate of his young relative's sagacity was not a high one, and it is doubtful whether, had the latter caught him in a less despondent mood, he would have wasted time in inquiring into the details of this scheme, the mention of which had been playing in and out of Freddie's conversation like a will-o'-the-wisp. But such was his reduced state at the moment that a reluctant gleam of hope crept into his troubled eye.

"A scheme? Do you mean a scheme to help me out of—out of my difficulty?"

"Absolutely! You want the best seats, we have 'em. I mean," Freddie went on in interpretation of these peculiar words, "you want three thousand quid, and I can show you how to get it."

"Then kindly do so," said Mr. Keeble; and, having opened the door, peered cautiously out, and closed it again, he crossed the room and shut the window.

"Makes it a bit fuggy, but perhaps you're right," said Freddie, eyeing these manœuvres. "Well, it's like this, Uncle Joe. You remember what you were saying to Aunt Constance about some bird being apt to sneak up and pinch her necklace?"

"I do."

"Well, why not?"

"What do you mean?"

"I mean, why don't you?"

Mr. Keeble regarded his nephew with unconcealed astonishment. He had been prepared for imbecility, but
this exceeded his expectations.

"Steal my wife's necklace!"

"That's it. Frightfully quick you are, getting on to an
idea. Pinch Aunt Connie's necklace. For, mark you,"
continued Freddie, so far forgetting the respect due from
a nephew as to tap his uncle sharply on the chest, "if a
husband pinches anything from a wife, it isn't stealing.
That's law. I found that out from a movie I saw in
town."

The Hon. Freddie was a great student of the movies.
He could tell a super-film from a super-super-film at a
glance, and what he did not know about erring wives and
licentious clubmen could have been written in a sub-title.

"Are you insane?" growled Mr. Keeble.

"It wouldn't be hard for you to get hold of it. And
once you'd got it everybody would be happy. I mean, all
you'd have to do would be to draw a cheque to pay for
another one for Aunt Connie—which would make her perfectly chirpy, as well as putting you one up, if you follow
me. Then you would have the other necklace, the pinched
one, to play about with. See what I mean? You could
sell it privily and by stealth, ship Phyllis her three thousand, push across my thousand, and what was left over
would be a nice little private account for you to tuck away
somewhere where Aunt Connie wouldn't know anything
about it. And a dashed useful thing," said Freddie, "to
have up your sleeve in case of emergencies."

"Are you . . .?"

Mr. Keeble was on the point of repeating his previous
remark when suddenly there came the realisation that,

despite all preconceived opinions, the young man was anything but insane. The scheme, at which he had been prepared to scoff, was so brilliant, yet simple, that it seemed
almost incredible that its sponsor could have worked it out
for himself.

"Not my own," said Freddie modestly, as if in answer
to the thought. "Saw much the same thing in a movie
once. Only there the fellow, if I remember, wanted to do
down an insurance company, and it wasn't a necklace that
he pinched but bonds. Still, the principle's the same.
Well, how do we go, Uncle Joe? How about it? Is that
worth a thousand quid or not?"

Even though he had seen in person to the closing of the
door and the window, Mr. Keeble could not refrain from
a conspirator-like glance about him. They had been speaking with lowered voices, but now words came from him
in an almost inaudible whisper.

"Could it really be done? Is it feasible?"

"Feasible? Why, dash it, what the dickens is there to
stop you? You could do it in a second. And the beauty
of the whole thing is that, if you were copped, nobody
could say a word, because husband pinching from wife
isn't stealing. Law."

The statement that in the circumstances indicated nobody could say a word seemed to Mr. Keeble so at vari-
ance with the facts that he was compelled to challenge it.

"Your aunt would have a good deal to say," he observed ruefully.

"Eh? Oh, yes, I see what you mean. Well, you would
have to risk that. After all, the chances would be dead
against her finding out."

"But she might."

"Oh, well, if you put it like that, I suppose she might."

"Freddie, my boy," said Mr. Keeble weakly, "I daren't do it!"

The vision of his thousand pounds slipping from his grasp so wrought upon Freddie that he expressed himself in a manner far from fitting in one of his years towards an older man.

"Oh, I say, don't be such a rabbit!"

Mr. Keeble shook his head.

"No," he repeated, "I daren't."

It might have seemed that the negotiations had reached a deadlock, but Freddie, with a thousand pounds in sight, was in far too stimulated a condition to permit so tame an ending to such a promising plot. As he stood there, chafing at his uncle's pusillanimity, an idea was vouchsafed to him.

"By Jove! I'll tell you what!" he cried.

"Not so loud!" moaned the apprehensive Mr. Keeble. "Not so loud!"

"I'll tell you what," repeated Freddie in a hoarse whisper. "How would it be if I did the pinching?"

"What!"

"How would it . . ."

"Would you?" Hope, which had vanished from Mr. Keeble's face, came flooding back. "My boy, would you really?"

"For a thousand quid you bet I would."

Mr. Keeble clutched at his young relative's hand and gripped it feverishly.

"Freddie," he said, "the moment you place that necklace in my hands, I will give you not a thousand but two thousand pounds."

"Uncle Joe," said Freddie with equal intensity, "it's a bet!"

Mr. Keeble mopped at his forehead.

"You think you can manage it?"

"Manage it?" Freddie laughed a light laugh. "Just watch me!"

Mr. Keeble grasped his hand again with the utmost warmth.

"I must go out and get some air," he said. "I'm all upset. May I really leave this matter to you, Freddie?"

"Rather!"

"Good! Then to-night I will write to Phyllis and say that I may be able to do what she wishes."

"Don't say 'may,'" cried Freddie buoyantly. "The word is 'will.' Bally will! What ho!"

§ 4

Exhilaration is a heady drug; but, like other drugs, it has the disadvantage that its stimulating effects seldom last for very long. For perhaps ten minutes after his uncle had left him, Freddie Threepwood lay back in his chair in a sort of ecstasy. He felt strong, vigorous, alert. Then by degrees, like a chilling wind, doubt began to creep upon him—faintly at first, then more and more insistently, till by the end of a quarter of an hour he was in a state of pronounced self-mistrust. Or, to put it with less elegance, he was suffering from an exceedingly severe attack of cold feet.

The more he contemplated the venture which he had undertaken, the less alluring did it appear to him. His was not a keen imagination, but even he could shape with

a gruesome clearness a vision of the frightful bust-up that
would ensue should he be detected stealing his Aunt Constance's diamond necklace. Common decency would in
such an event seal his lips as regarded his Uncle Joseph's
share in the matter. And even if—as might conceivably
happen—common decency failed at the crisis, reason told
him that his Uncle Joseph would infallibly disclaim any
knowledge of or connection with the rash act. And then
where would he be? In the soup, undoubtedly. For
Freddie could not conceal it from himself that there was
nothing in his previous record to make it seem inconceiva-
ble to his nearest and dearest that he should steal the
jewellery of a female relative for purely personal ends.
The verdict in the event of detection would be one of uncompromising condemnation.

And yet he hated the idea of meekly allowing that two
thousand pounds to escape from his clutch . . .

A young man's cross-roads.

.   .   .   .

The agony of spirit into which these meditations cast
him had brought him up with a bound from the comfortable depths of his arm-chair and had set him prowling
restlessly about the room. His wanderings led him at
this point to collide somewhat painfully with the long
table on which Beach the butler, a tidy soul, was in the
habit of arranging in a neat row the daily papers, weekly
papers, and magazines which found their way into the
castle. The shock had the effect of rousing him from his
stupor, and in an absent way he clutched the nearest daily
paper, which happened to be the *Morning Globe,* and returned to his chair in the hope of quieting his nerves
with a perusal of the racing intelligence. For, though far

removed now from any practical share in the doings of the racing world, he still took a faint melancholy interest in ascertaining what Captain Curb, the Head Lad, Little Brighteyes, and the rest of the newspaper experts fancied for the day's big event. He lit a cigarette and unfolded the journal.

The next moment, instead of passing directly, as was his usual practice, to the last page, which was devoted to sport, he was gazing with a strange dry feeling in his throat at a certain advertisement on page one.

It was a well-displayed advertisement, and one that had caught the eye of many other readers of the paper that morning. It was worded to attract attention, and it had achieved its object. But where others who read it had merely smiled and marvelled idly how anybody could spend good money putting nonsense like this in the paper, to Freddie its import was wholly serious. It read to him like the Real Thing. His motion-picture-trained mind accepted this advertisement at its face-value.

It ran as follows:—

LEAVE IT TO PSMITH!
Psmith Will Help You
Psmith Is Ready for Anything
DO YOU WANT
Some One To Manage Your Affairs?
Some One To Handle Your Business?
Some One To Take the Dog for a Run?
Some One To Assassinate Your Aunt?
PSMITH WILL DO IT
CRIME NOT OBJECTED TO
Whatever Job You Have To Offer

(Provided It Has Nothing To Do with Fish)
LEAVE IT TO PSMITH!
Address Applications To "R. Psmith, Box 365"
LEAVE IT TO PSMITH!

Freddie laid the paper down with a deep intake of breath. He picked it up again, and read the advertisement a second time. Yes, it sounded good.

More, it had something of the quality of a direct answer to prayer. Very vividly now Freddie realised that what he had been wishing for was a partner to share the perils of this enterprise which he had so rashly undertaken. In fact, not so much to share them as to take them off his shoulders altogether. And such a partner he was now in a position to command. Uncle Joe was going to give him two thousand if he brought the thing off. This advertisement fellow would probably be charmed to come in for a few hundred . . .

.   .   .   .

Two minutes later, Freddie was at the writing-desk, scribbling a letter. From time to time he glanced furtively over his shoulder at the door. But the house was still. No footsteps came to interrupt him at his task.

§ 5

Freddie went out into the garden. He had not wandered far when from somewhere close at hand there was borne to him on the breeze a remark in a high voice about Scottish obstinacy, which could only have proceeded from one source. He quickened his steps.

"Hallo, guv'nor."

"Well, Frederick?"

Freddie shuffled.

"I say, guv'nor, do you think I might go up to town with you this afternoon?"

"What!"

"Fact is, I ought to see my dentist. Haven't been to him for a deuce of a time."

"I cannot see the necessity for you to visit a London dentist. There is an excellent man in Shrewsbury, and you know I have the strongest objection to your going to London."

"Well, you see, this fellow understands my snappers. Always been to him, I mean to say. Anybody who knows anything about these things will tell you greatest mistake go buzzing about to different dentists."

Already Lord Emsworth's attention was wandering back to the waiting McAllister.

"Oh, very well, very well."

"Thanks awfully, guv'nor."

"But on one thing I insist, Frederick. I cannot have you loafing about London the whole day. You must catch the twelve-fifty train back."

"Right ho. That'll be all right, guv'nor."

"Now, listen to reason, McAllister," said his lordship. "That is all I ask you to do—listen to reason . . ."

CHAPTER II

§ 1

AT about the hour when Lord Emsworth's train, whirling him and his son Freddie to London, had reached
the half-way point in its journey, a very tall, very thin,
very solemn young man, gleaming in a speckless top hat
and a morning-coat of irreproachable fit, mounted the steps
of Number Eighteen, Wallingford Street, West Kensington, and rang the front-door bell. This done, he removed
the hat; and having touched his forehead lightly with a
silk handkerchief, for the afternoon sun was warm, gazed
about him with a grave distaste.

"A scaly neighbourhood!" he murmured.

The young man's judgment was one at which few
people with an eye for beauty would have cavilled. When
the great revolution against London's ugliness really starts
and yelling hordes of artists and architects, maddened
beyond endurance, finally take the law into their own
hands and rage through the city burning and destroying,
Wallingford Street, West Kensington, will surely not
escape the torch. Long since it must have been marked
down for destruction. For, though it possesses certain
merits of a low practical kind, being inexpensive in the
matter of rents and handy for the busses and the Underground, it is a peculiarly beastly little street. Situated in
the middle of one of those districts where London breaks

43

out into a sort of eczema of red brick, it consists of two parallel rows of semi-detached villas, all exactly alike, each guarded by a ragged evergreen hedge, each with coloured glass of an extremely regrettable nature let into the panels of the front door; and sensitive young impressionists from the artists' colony up Holland Park way may sometimes be seen stumbling through it with hands over their eyes, muttering between clenched teeth "How long? How long?"

A small maid-of-all-work appeared in answer to the bell, and stood transfixed as the visitor, producing a monocle, placed it in his right eye and inspected her through it.

"A warm afternoon," he said cordially.

"Yes, sir."

"But pleasant," urged the young man. "Tell me, is Mrs. Jackson at home?"

"No, sir."

"Not at home?"

"No, sir."

The young man sighed.

"Ah well," he said, "we must always remember that these disappointments are sent to us for some good purpose. No doubt they make us more spiritual. Will you inform her that I called? The name is Psmith. P-smith."

"Peasmith, sir?"

"No, no. P-s-m-i-t-h. I should explain to you that I started life without the initial letter, and my father always clung ruggedly to the plain Smith. But it seemed to me that there were so many Smiths in the world that a little variety might well be introduced. Smythe I look on as a cowardly evasion, nor do I approve of the too prevalent custom of tacking another name on in front by means of a hyphen. So I decided to adopt the Psmith. The p, I should add for your guidance, is silent, as in phthisis, psychic, and ptarmigan. You follow me?"

"Y-yes, sir."

"You don't think," he said anxiously, "that I did wrong in pursuing this course?"

"N-no, sir."

"Splendid!" said the young man, flicking a speck of dust from his coat-sleeve. "Splendid! Splendid!"

And with a courteous bow he descended the steps and made his way down the street. The little maid, having followed him with bulging eyes till he was out of sight, closed the door and returned to her kitchen.

Psmith strolled meditatively on. The genial warmth of the afternoon soothed him. He hummed lightly—only stopping when, as he reached the end of the street, a young man of his own age, rounding the corner rapidly, almost ran into him.

"Sorry," said the young man. "Hallo, Smith."

Psmith gazed upon him with benevolent affection.

"Comrade Jackson," he said, "this is well met. The one man of all others whom I would have wished to encounter. We will pop off somewhere, Comrade Jackson, should your engagements permit, and restore our tissues with a cup of tea. I had hoped to touch the Jackson family for some slight refreshment, but I was informed that your wife was out."

Mike Jackson laughed.

"Phyllis isn't out. She . . ."

"Not out? Then," said Psmith, pained, "there has been dirty work done this day. For I was turned from the door. It would not be exaggerating to say that I was given the bird. Is this the boasted Jackson hospitality?"

"Phyllis is giving a tea to some of her old school pals," explained Mike. "She told the maid to say she wasn't at home to anybody else. I'm not allowed in myself."

"Enough, Comrade Jackson!" said Psmith agreeably. "Say no more. If you yourself have been booted out in spite of all the loving, honouring, and obeying your wife promised at the altar, who am I to complain? And possibly, one can console oneself by reflecting, we are well out of it. These gatherings of old girls'-school chums are not the sort of function your man of affairs wants to get lugged into. Capital company as we are, Comrade Jackson, we should doubtless have been extremely in the way. I suppose the conversation would have dealt exclusively with reminiscences of the dear old school, of tales of surreptitious cocoa-drinking in the dormitories and what the deportment mistress said when Angela was found chewing tobacco in the shrubbery. Yes, I fancy we have not missed a lot. . . . By the way, I don't think much of the new home. True, I only saw it from the outside, but . . . no, I don't think much of it."

"Best we can afford."

"And who," said Psmith, "am I to taunt my boyhood friend with his honest poverty? Especially as I myself am standing on the very brink of destitution."

"You?"

"I in person. That low moaning sound you hear is the wolf bivouacked outside my door."

"But I thought your uncle gave you rather a good salary."

"So he did. But my uncle and I are about to part company. From now on he, so to speak, will take the high road and I'll take the low road. I dine with him to-night, and over the nuts and wine, I shall hand him the bad news that I propose to resign my position in the firm. I have no doubt that he supposed he was doing me a good turn by starting me in his fish business, but even what little experience I have had of it has convinced me that it is not my proper sphere. The whisper flies round the clubs, 'Psmith has not found his niche!'

"I am not," said Psmith, "an unreasonable man. I realise that humanity must be supplied with fish. I am not averse to a bit of fish myself. But to be professionally connected with a firm that handles the material in the raw is not my idea of a large life-work. Remind me to tell you some time what it feels like to sling yourself out of bed at four a.m. and go down to toil in Billingsgate Market. No, there is money in fish—my uncle has made a pot of it—but what I feel is that there must be other walks in life for a bright young man. I chuck it to-night."

"What are you going to do, then?"

"That, Comrade Jackson, is more or less on the knees of the gods. To-morrow morning I think I will stroll round to an employment agency and see how the market for bright young men stands. Do you know a good one?"

"Phyllis always goes to Miss Clarkson's in Shaftesbury Avenue. But . . ."

"Miss Clarkson's in Shaftesbury Avenue. I will make a note of it . . . Meanwhile, I wonder if you saw the *Morning Globe* to-day?"

"No. Why?"

"I had an advertisement in it, in which I expressed myself as willing—indeed, eager—to tackle any undertaking that had nothing to do with fish. I am confidently expecting shoals of replies. I look forward to winnowing the heap and selecting the most desirable."

"Pretty hard to get a job these days," said Mike doubtfully.

"Not if you have something superlatively good to offer."

"What have you got to offer?"

"My services," said Psmith with faint reproach.

"What as?"

"As anything. I made no restrictions. Would you care to take a look at my manifesto? I have a copy in my pocket."

Psmith produced from inside his immaculate waistcoat a folded clipping.

"I should welcome your opinion of it, Comrade Jackson. I have frequently said that for sturdy common sense you stand alone. Your judgment should be invaluable."

The advertisement, which some hours earlier had so electrified the Hon. Freddie Threepwood in the smoking-room at Blandings Castle, seemed to affect Mike, whose mind was of the stolid and serious type, somewhat differently. He finished his perusal and stared speechlessly.

"Neat, don't you think?" said Psmith. "Covers the ground adequately? I think so, I think so."

"Do you mean to say you're going to put drivel like that in the paper?" asked Mike.

"I *have* put it in the paper. As I told you, it appeared this morning. By this time to-morrow I shall no doubt have finished sorting out the first batch of replies."

Mike's emotion took him back to the phraseology of school days.

"You *are* an ass!"

Psmith restored the clipping to his waistcoat pocket.

"You wound me, Comrade Jackson," he said. "I had expected a broader outlook from you. In fact, I rather supposed that you would have rushed round instantly to the offices of the journal and shoved in a similar advertisement yourself. But nothing that you can say can damp my buoyant spirit. The cry goes round Kensington (and district) 'Psmith is off!' In what direction the cry omits to state: but that information the future will supply. And now, Comrade Jackson, let us trickle into yonder tea-shop and drink success to the venture in a cup of the steaming. I had a particularly hard morning to-day among the white-bait, and I need refreshment."

§ 2

After Psmith had withdrawn his spectacular person from it, there was an interval of perhaps twenty minutes before anything else occurred to brighten the drabness of Wallingford Street. The lethargy of afternoon held the thoroughfare in its grip. Occasionally a tradesman's cart would rattle round the corner, and from time to time cats appeared, stalking purposefully among the evergreens. But at ten minutes to five a girl ran up the steps of Number Eighteen and rang the bell.

She was a girl of medium height, very straight and slim; and her fair hair, her cheerful smile, and the boyish suppleness of her body all contributed to a general effect of valiant gaiety, a sort of golden sunniness—ac-

centuated by the fact that, like all girls who looked to
Paris for inspiration in their dress that season, she was
wearing black.

The small maid appeared again.

"Is Mrs. Jackson at home?" said the girl. "I think
she's expecting me. Miss Halliday."

"Yes, miss."

A door at the end of the narrow hall had opened.

"Is that you, Eve?"

"Hallo, Phyl, darling."

Phyllis Jackson fluttered down the passage like a rose-
leaf on the wind, and hurled herself into Eve's arms. She
was small and fragile, with great brown eyes under a
cloud of dark hair. She had a wistful look, and most
people who knew her wanted to pet her. Eve had always
petted her, from their first days at school together.

"Am I late or early?" asked Eve.

"You're the first, but we won't wait. Jane, will you
bring tea into the drawing-room."

"Yes'm."

"And, remember, I don't want to see any one for the
rest of the afternoon. If anybody calls, tell them I'm
not at home. Except Miss Clarkson and Mrs. McTodd,
of course."

"Yes'm."

"Who is Mrs. McTodd?" inquired Eve. "Is that
Cynthia?"

"Yes. Didn't you know she had married Ralston Mc-
Todd, the Canadian poet? You knew she went out to
Canada?"

"I knew that, yes. But I hadn't heard that she was
married. Funny how out of touch one gets with girls

who were one's best friends at school. Do you realise it's nearly two years since I saw you?"

"I know. Isn't it awful! I got your address from Elsa Wentworth two or three days ago, and then Clarkie told me that Cynthia was over here on a visit with her husband, so I thought how jolly it would be to have a regular reunion. We three were such friends in the old days. . . . You remember Clarkie, of course? Miss Clarkson, who used to be English mistress at Wayland House."

"Yes, of course. Where did you run into her?"

"Oh, I see a lot of her. She runs a Domestic Employment Agency in Shaftesbury Avenue now, and I have to go there about once a fortnight to get a new maid. She supplied Jane."

"Is Cynthia's husband coming with her this afternoon?"

"No. I wanted it to be simply us four. Do you know him? But of course you don't. This is his first visit to England."

"I know his poetry. He's quite a celebrity. Cynthia's lucky."

They had made their way into the drawing-room, a gruesome little apartment full of all those antimacassars, wax flowers, and china dogs inseparable from the cheaper type of London furnished house. Eve, though the exterior of Number Eighteen should have prepared her for all this, was unable to check a slight shudder as she caught the eye of the least prepossessing of the dogs, goggling at her from the mantelpiece.

"Don't look at them," recommended Phyllis, following her gaze. "I try not to. We've only just moved in here.

so I haven't had time to make the place nice. Here's tea. All right, Jane, put it down there. Tea, Eve?"

Eve sat down. She was puzzled and curious. She threw her mind back to the days at school and remembered the Phyllis of that epoch as almost indecently opulent. A millionaire stepfather there had been then, she recollected. What had become of him now, that he should allow Phyllis to stay in surroundings like this? Eve scented a mystery, and in her customary straightforward way went to the heart of it.

"Tell me all about yourself," she said, having achieved as much comfort as the peculiar structure of her chair would permit. "And remember that I haven't seen you for two years, so don't leave anything out."

"It's so difficult to know where to start."

"Well, you signed your letter 'Phyllis Jackson.' Start with the mysterious Jackson. Where does he come in? The last I heard about you was an announcement in the *Morning Post* that you were engaged to—I've forgotten the name, but I'm certain it wasn't Jackson."

"Rollo Mountford."

"Was it? Well, what has become of Rollo? You seem to have mislaid him. Did you break off the engagement?"

"Well, it—sort of broke itself off. I mean, you see, I went and married Mike."

"Eloped with him, do you mean?"

"Yes."

"Good heavens!"

"I'm awfully ashamed about that, Eve. I suppose I treated Rollo awfully badly."

"Never mind. A man with a name like that was made for suffering."

"I never really cared for him. He had horrid swimmy eyes . . ."

"I understand. So you eloped with your Mike. Tell me about him. Who is he? What does he do?"

"Well, at present he's master at a school. But he doesn't like it. He wants to get back to the country again. When I met him, he was agent on a place in the country belonging to some people named Smith. Mike had been at school and Cambridge with the son. They were very rich then and had a big estate. It was the next place to the Edgelows. I had gone to stay with Mary Edgelow— I don't know if you remember her at school? I met Mike first at a dance, and then I met him out riding, and then— well, after that we used to meet every day. And we fell in love right from the start and we went and got married. Oh, Eve, I wish you could have seen our darling little house. It was all over ivy and roses, and we had horses and dogs and . . ."

Phyllis' narrative broke off with a gulp. Eve looked at her sympathetically. All her life she herself had been joyously impecunious, but it had never seemed to matter. She was strong and adventurous, and revelled in the perpetual excitement of trying to make both ends meet. But Phyllis was one of those sweet porcelain girls whom the roughnesses of life bruise instead of stimulating. She needed comfort and pleasant surroundings. Eve looked morosely at the china dog, which leered back at her with an insufferable good-fellowship.

"We had hardly got married," resumed Phyllis, blinking, "when poor Mr. Smith died and the whole place was broken up. He must have been speculating or something, I suppose, because he hardly left any money, and the estate had to be sold. And the people who bought it—they were coal people from Wolverhampton—had a nephew for whom they wanted the agent job, so Mike had to go. So here we are."

Eve put the question which she had been waiting to ask ever since she had entered the house.

"But what about your stepfather? Surely, when we were at school, you had a rich stepfather in the background. Has he lost his money, too?"

"No."

"Well, why doesn't he help you, then?"

"He would, I know, if he was left to himself. But it's Aunt Constance."

"What's Aunt Constance? And who *is* Aunt Constance?"

"Well, I call her that, but she's really my stepmother—sort of. I suppose she's really my step-stepmother. My stepfather married again two years ago. It was Aunt Constance who was so furious when I married Mike. She wanted me to marry Rollo. She has never forgiven me, and she won't let my stepfather do anything to help us."

"But the man must be a worm!" said Eve indignantly. "Why doesn't he insist? You always used to tell me how fond he was of you."

"He isn't a worm, Eve. He's a dear. It's just that he has let her boss him. She's rather a terror, you know. She can be quite nice, and they're awfully fond of each other, but she is as hard as nails sometimes." Phyllis broke off. The front door had opened, and there were footsteps in the hall. "Here's Clarkie. I hope she has brought Cynthia with her. She was to pick her up on her way. Don't talk about what I've been telling you in front of her, Eve, there's an angel."

"Why not?"

"She's so motherly about it. It's sweet of her, but . . ."

Eve understood.

"All right. Later on."

The door opened to admit Miss Clarkson.

The adjective which Phyllis had applied to her late schoolmistress was obviously well chosen. Miss Clarkson exuded motherliness. She was large, wholesome, and soft, and she swooped on Eve like a hen on its chicker almost before the door had closed.

"Eve! How nice to see you after all this time! My dear, you're looking perfectly lovely! And *so* prosperous. What a beautiful hat!"

"I've been envying it ever since you came, Eve," said Phyllis. "Where did you get it?"

"Madeleine Sœurs, in Regent Street."

Miss Clarkson, having acquired and stirred a cup of tea, started to improve the occasion. Eve had always been a favourite of hers at school. She beamed affectionately upon her.

"Now doesn't this show—what I always used to say to you in the dear old days, Eve—that one must never despair, however black the outlook may seem? I remember you at school, dear, as poor as a church mouse, and with no prospects, none whatever. And yet here you are— rich . . ."

Eve laughed. She got up and kissed Miss Clarkson. She regretted that she was compelled to strike a jarring note, but it had to be done.

"I'm awfully sorry, Clarkie dear," she said, "but I'm afraid I've misled you. I'm just as broke as I ever was. In fact, when Phyllis told me you were running an Employment Agency, I made a note to come and see you and ask if you had some attractive billet to dispose of. Governess to a thoroughly angelic child would do. Or isn't there some nice cosy author or something who wants his letters answered and his press-clippings pasted in an album?"

"Oh, my dear!" Miss Clarkson was deeply concerned. "I did hope . . . That hat . . . !"

"The hat's the whole trouble. Of course I had no business even to think of it, but I saw it in the shop-window and coveted it for days, and finally fell. And then, you see, I had to live up to it—buy shoes, and a dress to match. I tell you it was a perfect orgy, and I'm thoroughly ashamed of myself now. Too late, as usual."

"Oh, dear! You always were such a wild, impetuous child, even at school. I remember how often I used to speak to you about it."

"Well, when it was all over and I was sane again, I found I had only a few pounds left, not nearly enough to see me through till the relief expedition arrived. So I thought it over and decided to invest my little all."

"I hope you chose something safe?"

"It ought to have been. The *Sporting Express* called it 'To-day's Safety Bet.' It was Bounding Willie for the two-thirty race at Sandown last Wednesday."

"Oh, dear!"

"That's what I said when poor old Willie came in sixth. But it's no good worrying, is it? What it means is that I simply must find something to do that will carry me through till I get my next quarter's allowance. And that won't be till September. . . . But don't let's talk business here. I'll come round to your office, Clarkie, to-morrow. . . . Where's Cynthia? Didn't you bring her?"

"Yes, I thought you were going to pick Cynthia up on your way, Clarkie," said Phyllis.

If Eve's information as to her financial affairs had caused Miss Clarkson to mourn, the mention of Cynthia plunged her into the very depths of woe. Her mouth quivered and a tear stole down her cheek. Eve and Phyllis exchanged bewildered glances.

"I say," said Eve after a moment's pause and a silence broken only by a smothered sob from their late instructress, "we aren't being very cheerful, are we, considering that this is supposed to be a joyous reunion? Is anything wrong with Cynthia?"

So poignant was Miss Clarkson's anguish that Phyllis, in a flutter of alarm, rose and left the room swiftly in search of the only remedy that suggested itself to her— her smelling salts.

"Poor dear Cynthia!" moaned Miss Clarkson.

"Why, what's the matter with her?" asked Eve. She was not callous to Miss Clarkson's grief, but she could not help the tiniest of smiles. In a flash she had been transported to her school-days, when the other's habit of extracting the utmost tragedy out of the slimmest material had been a source of ever-fresh amusement to her. Not for an instant did she expect to hear any worse news of her old friend than that she was in bed with a cold or had twisted her ankle.

"She's married, you know," said Miss Clarkson.

"Well. I see no harm in that, Clarkie. If a few more

Safety Bets go wrong, I shall probably have to rush out and marry some one myself. Some nice, rich, indulgent man who will spoil me."

"Oh, Eve, my dear," pleaded Miss Clarkson, bleating with alarm, "do please be careful whom you marry. I never hear of one of my girls marrying without feeling that the worst may happen and that, all unknowing, she may be stepping over a grim precipice!"

"You don't *tell* them that, do you? Because I should think it would rather cast a damper on the wedding festivities. Has Cynthia gone stepping over grim precipices? I was just saying to Phyllis that I envied her, marrying a celebrity like Ralston McTodd."

Miss Clarkson gulped.

"The man must be a *fiend!*" she said brokenly. "I have just left poor dear Cynthia in floods of tears at the Cadogan Hotel—she has a very nice quiet room on the fourth floor, though the carpet does not harmonise with the wall-paper. . . . She was broken-hearted, poor child. I did what I could to console her, but it was useless. She always was so highly strung. I must be getting back to her very soon. I only came on here because I did not want to disappoint you two dear girls . . ."

"Why?" said Eve with quiet intensity. She knew from experience that Miss Clarkson, unless firmly checked, would pirouette round and round the point for minutes without ever touching it.

"Why?" echoed Miss Clarkson, blinking as if the word was something solid that had struck her unexpectedly.

"Why was Cynthia in floods of tears?"

"But I'm telling you, my dear. That man has left her!"

"Left her!"

"They had a quarrel, and he walked straight out of the hotel. That was the day before yesterday, and he has not been back since. This afternoon the cutest note came from him to say that he never intended to return. He had secretly and in a most underhand way arranged for his luggage to be removed from the hotel to a District Messenger office, and from there he has taken it no one knows where. He has completely disappeared."

Eve stared. She had not been prepared for news of this momentous order.

"But what did they quarrel about?"

"Cynthia, poor child, was too overwrought to tell me!"

Eve clenched her teeth.

"The beast! . . . Poor old Cynthia. . . . Shall I come round with you?"

"No, my dear, better let me look after her alone. I will tell her to write and let you know when she can see you. I must be going, Phyllis dear," she said, as her hostess re-entered, bearing a small bottle.

"But you've only just come!" said Phyllis, surprised.

"Poor old Cynthia's husband has left her," explained Eve briefly. "And Clarkie's going back to look after her. She's in a pretty bad way, it seems."

"Oh, no!"

"Yes, indeed. And I really must be going at once," said Miss Clarkson.

Eve waited in the drawing-room till the front door banged and Phyllis came back to her. Phyllis was more wistful than ever. She had been looking forward to this tea-party, and it had not been the happy occasion she had anticipated. The two girls sat in silence for a moment.

"What brutes some men are!" said Eve at length.

"Mike," said Phyllis dreamily, "is an angel."

Eve welcomed the unspoken invitation to return to a more agreeable topic. She felt very deeply for the stricken Cynthia, but she hated aimless talk, and nothing could have been more aimless than for her and Phyllis to sit there exchanging lamentations concerning a tragedy of which neither knew more than the bare outlines. Phyllis had her tragedy, too, and it was one where Eve saw the possibility of doing something practical and helpful. She was a girl of action, and was glad to be able to attack a living issue.

"Yes, let's go on talking about you and Mike," she said. "At present I can't understand the position at all. When Clarkie came in, you were just telling me about your step-father and why he wouldn't help you. And I thought you made out a very poor case for him. Tell me some more. I've forgotten his name, by the way."

"Keeble."

"Oh? Well, I think you ought to write and tell him how hard up you are. He may be under the impression that you are still living in luxury and don't need any help. After all, he can't know unless you tell him. And I should ask him straight out to come to the rescue. It isn't as if it was your Mike's fault that you're broke. He married you on the strength of a very good position which looked like a permanency, and lost it through no fault of his own. I should write to him, Phyl. Pitch it strong."

"I have. I wrote to-day. Mike's just been offered a wonderful opportunity. A sort of farm place in Lincoln-shire. You know. Cows and things. Just what he would like and just what he would do awfully well. And we only need three thousand pounds to get it. . . . But I'm afraid nothing will come of it."

"Because of Aunt Constance, you mean?"

"Yes."

"You must *make* something come of it." Eve's chin went up. She looked like a Goddess of Determination. "If I were you, I'd haunt their doorstep till they had to give you the money to get rid of you. The idea of anybody doing that absurd driving-into-the-snow business in these days! Why *shouldn't* you marry the man you were in love with? If I were you, I'd go and chain myself to their railings and howl like a dog till they rushed out with cheque-books just to get some peace. Do they live in London?"

"They are down in Shropshire at present at a place called Blandings Castle."

Eve started.

"Blandings Castle? Good gracious!"

"Aunt Constance is Lord Emsworth's sister."

"But this is the most extraordinary thing. I'm going to Blandings myself in a few days."

"No!"

"They've engaged me to catalogue the castle library."

"But, Eve, were you only joking when you asked Clarkie to find you something to do? She took you quite seriously."

"No, I wasn't joking. There's a drawback to my going to Blandings. I suppose you know the place pretty well?"

"I've often stayed there. It's beautiful."

"Then you know Lord Emsworth's second son, Freddie Threepwood?"

"Of course."

"Well, he's the drawback. He wants to marry me, and I certainly don't want to marry him. And what I've been wondering is whether a nice easy job like that, which would tide me over beautifully till September, is attractive enough to make up for the nuisance of having to be always squelching poor Freddie. I ought to have thought of it right at the beginning, of course, when he wrote and told me to apply for the position, but I was so delighted at the idea of regular work that it didn't occur to me. Then I began to wonder. He's such a persevering young man. He proposes early and often."

"Where did you meet Freddie?"

"At a theatre party. About two months ago. He was living in London then, but he suddenly disappeared and I had a heart-broken letter from him, saying that he had been running up debts and things and his father had snatched him away to live at Blandings, which apparently is Freddie's idea of the Inferno. The world seems full of hard-hearted relatives."

"Oh, Lord Emsworth isn't really hard-hearted. You will love him. He's so dreamy and absent-minded. He potters about the garden all the time. I don't think you'll like Aunt Constance much. But I suppose you won't see a great deal of her."

"Whom *shall* I see much of—except Freddie, of course?"

"Mr. Baxter, Lord Emsworth's secretary, I expect. I don't like him at all. He's a sort of spectacled cave-man."

"He doesn't sound attractive. But you say the place is nice?"

"It's gorgeous. I should go, if I were you, Eve."

"Well, I had intended not to. But now you've told me

about Mr. Keeble and Aunt Constance, I've changed my mind. I'll have to look in at Clarkie's office to-morrow and tell her I'm fixed up and shan't need her help. I'm going to take your sad case in hand, darling. I shall go to Blandings, and I will dog your stepfather's footsteps. . . . Well, I must be going. Come and see me to the front door, or I'll be losing my way in the miles of stately corridors. . . . I suppose I mayn't smash that china dog before I go? Oh, well, I just thought I'd ask."

Out in the hall the little maid-of-all-work bobbed up and intercepted them.

"I forgot to tell you, mum, a gentleman called. I told him you was out."

"Quite right, Jane."

"Said his name was Smith, 'm."

Phyllis gave a cry of dismay.

"Oh, no! What a shame! I particularly wanted you to meet him, Eve. I wish I'd known."

"Smith?" said Eve. "The name seems familiar. Why were you so anxious for me to meet him?"

"He's Mike's best friend. Mike worships him. He's the son of the Mr. Smith I was telling you about—the one Mike was at school and Cambridge with. He's a perfect darling, Eve, and you would love him. He's just your sort. I do wish we had known. And now you're going to Blandings for goodness knows how long, and you won't be able to see him."

"What a pity," said Eve, politely uninterested.

"I'm so sorry for him."

"Why?"

"He's in the fish business."

"Ugh!"

"Well, he hates it, poor dear. But he was left stranded like all the rest of us after the crash, and he was put into the business by an uncle who is a sort of fish magnate."

"Well, why does he stay there, if he dislikes it so much?" said Eve with indignation. The helpless type of man was her pet aversion. "I hate a man who's got no enterprise."

"I don't think you could call him unenterprising. He never struck me like that. . . . You simply must meet him when you come back to London."

"All right," said Eve indifferently. "Just as you like. I might put business in his way. I'm very fond of fish."

CHAPTER III

EVE BORROWS AN UMBRELLA

WHAT strikes the visitor to London most forcibly, as he enters the heart of that city's fashionable shopping district, is the almost entire absence of ostentation in the shop-windows, the studied avoidance of garish display. About the front of the premises of Messrs. Thorpe & Briscoe, for instance, who sell coal in Dover Street, there is as a rule nothing whatever to attract fascinated attention. You might give the place a glance as you passed, but you would certainly not pause and stand staring at it as at the Sistine Chapel or the Taj Mahal. Yet at ten-thirty on the morning after Eve Halliday had taken tea with her friend Phyllis Jackson in West Kensington, Psmith, lounging gracefully in the smoking-room window of the Drones Club, which is immediately opposite the Thorpe & Briscoe establishment, had been gazing at it fixedly for a full five minutes. One would have said that the spectacle enthralled him. He seemed unable to take his eyes off it.

There is always a reason for the most apparently inexplicable happenings. It is the practice of Thorpe (or Briscoe) during the months of summer to run out an awning over the shop. A quiet, genteel awning, of course, nothing to offend the eye—but an awning which offers a quite adequate protection against those sudden showers which are such a delightfully piquant feature of the English summer: one of which had just begun to sprinkle the West End of London with a good deal of heartiness and vigour. And under this awning, peering plaintively out at the rain, Eve Halliday, on her way to the Ada Clarkson Employment Bureau, had taken refuge. It was she who had so enchained Psmith's interest. It was his considered opinion that she improved the Thorpe & Briscoe frontage by about ninety-five per cent.

Pleased and gratified as Psmith was to have something nice to look at out of the smoking-room window, he was also somewhat puzzled. This girl seemed to him to radiate an atmosphere of wealth. Starting at farthest south and proceeding northward, she began in a gleam of patent-leather shoes. Fawn stockings, obviously expensive, led up to a black crêpe frock. And then, just as the eye was beginning to feel that there could be nothing more, it was stunned by a supreme hat of soft, dull satin with a black bird of Paradise feather falling down over the left shoulder. Even to the masculine eye, which is notoriously to seek in these matters, a whale of a hat. And yet this sumptuously upholstered young woman had been marooned by a shower of rain beneath the awning of Messrs. Thorpe & Briscoe. Why, Psmith asked himself, was this? Even, he argued, if Charles the chauffeur had been given the day off or was driving her father the millionaire to the City to attend to his vast interests, she could surely afford a cab-fare? We, who are familiar with the state of Eve's finances, can understand her inability to take cabs, but Psmith was frankly perplexed.

Being, however, both ready-witted and chivalrous, he perceived that this was no time for idle speculation. His not to reason why; his obvious duty was to take steps to

assist Beauty in distress. He left the window of the
smoking-room, and, having made his way with a smooth
dignity to the club's cloak-room, proceeded to submit a row
of umbrellas to a close inspection. He was not easy to
satisfy. Two which he went so far as to pull out of the
rack he returned with a shake of the head. Quite good
umbrellas, but not fit for this special service. At length,
however, he found a beauty, and a gentle smile flickered
across his solemn face. He put up his monocle and gazed
searchingly at this umbrella. It seemed to answer every
test. He was well pleased with it.

"Whose," he inquired of the attendant, "is this?"

"Belongs to the Honourable Mr. Walderwick, sir."

"Ah!" said Psmith tolerantly.

He tucked the umbrella under his arm and went out.

.   .   .   .

Meanwhile Eve Halliday, lightening up the sombre austerity of Messrs. Thorpe & Briscoe's shop-front, continued
to think hard thoughts of the English climate and to inspect the sky in the hope of detecting a spot of blue. She
was engaged in this cheerless occupation when at her side
a voice spoke.

"Excuse me!"

A hatless young man was standing beside her, holding
an umbrella. He was a striking-looking young man, very
tall, very thin, and very well dressed. In his right eye
there was a monocle, and through this he looked down at
her with a grave friendliness. He said nothing further,
but, taking her fingers, clasped them round the handle of
the umbrella, which he had obligingly opened, and then
with a courteous bow proceeded to dash with long strides
across the road, disappearing through the doorway of a

gloomy building which, from the number of men who had gone in and out during her vigil, she had set down as a club of some sort.

A good many surprising things had happened to Eve since first she had come to live in London, but nothing quite so surprising as this. For several minutes she stood where she was without moving, staring round-eyed at the building opposite. The episode was, however, apparently ended. The young man did not reappear. He did not even show himself at the window. The club had swallowed him up. And eventually Eve, deciding that this was not the sort of day on which to refuse umbrellas even if they dropped inexplicably from heaven, stepped out from under the awning, laughing helplessly, and started to resume her interrupted journey to Miss Clarkson's.

.   .   .   .

The offices of the Ada Clarkson International Employment Bureau ("Promptitude—Courtesy—Intelligence") are at the top of Shaftesbury Avenue, a little way past the Palace Theatre. Eve, closing the umbrella, which had prevented even a spot of rain falling on her hat, climbed the short stair leading to the door and tapped on the window marked "Enquiries."

"Can I see Miss Clarkson?"

"What name, please?" responded Enquiries promptly and with intelligent courtesy.

"Miss Halliday."

Brief interlude, involving business with speaking-tube.

"Will you go into the private office, please," said Enquiries a moment later, in a voice which now added respect to the other advertised qualities, for she had had time to observe and digest the hat.

Eve passed in through the general waiting-room with its magazine-covered table, and tapped at the door beyond marked "Private."

"Eve, dear!" exclaimed Miss Clarkson the moment she had entered, "I don't know how to tell you, but I have been looking through my books and I have nothing, simply nothing. There is not a single place that you could possibly take. What *is* to be done?"

"That's all right, Clarkie."

"But . . ."

"I didn't come to talk business. I came to ask after Cynthia. How is she?"

Miss Clarkson sighed.

"Poor child, she is still in a dreadful state, and no wonder. No news at all from her husband. He has simply deserted her."

"Poor darling! Can't I see her?"

"Not at present. I have persuaded her to go down to Brighton for a day or two. I think the sea air will pick her up. So much better than mooning about in a London hotel. She is leaving on the eleven o'clock train. I gave her your love, and she was most grateful that you should have remembered your old friendship and be sorry for her in her affliction?"

"Well, I can write to her. Where is she staying?"

"I don't know her Brighton address, but no doubt the Cadogan Hotel would forward letters. I think she would be glad to hear from you, dear."

Eve looked sadly at the framed testimonials which decorated the wall. She was not often melancholy, but it was such a beast of a day and all her friends seemed to be having such a bad time.

"Oh, Clarkie," she said, "what a lot of trouble there is in the world!"

"Yes, yes!" sighed Miss Clarkson, a specialist on this subject.

"All the horses you back finish sixth and all the girls you like best come croppers. Poor little Phyllis! weren't you sorry for her?"

"But her husband, surely, is most devoted?"

"Yes, but she's frightfully hard up, and you remember how opulent she used to be at school. Of course, it must sound funny hearing me pitying people for having no money. But somehow other people's hard-upness always seems so much worse than mine. Especially poor old Phyl's, because she really isn't fit to stand it. I've been used to being absolutely broke all my life. Poor dear father always seemed to be writing an article against time, with creditors scratching earnestly at the door." Eve laughed, but her eyes were misty. "He was a brick, wasn't he? I mean, sending me to a first-class school like Wayland House when he often hadn't enough money to buy tobacco, poor angel. I expect he wasn't always up to time with fees, was he?"

"Well, my dear, of course I was only an assistant mistress at Wayland House and had nothing to do with the financial side, but I did hear sometimes . . ."

"Poor darling father! Do you know, one of my earliest recollections—I couldn't have been more than ten—is of a ring at the front-door bell and father diving like a seal under the sofa and poking his head out and imploring me in a hoarse voice to hold the fort. I went to the door and found an indignant man with a blue paper. I prattled so prettily and innocently that he not only went away quite contentedly but actually patted me on the head and gave me a penny. And when the door had shut father crawled out from under the sofa and gave me twopence, making threepence in all—a good morning's work. I bought father a diamond ring with it at a shop down the street, I remember. At least I thought it was a diamond. They may have swindled me, for I was very young."

"You have had a hard life, my dear."

"Yes, but hasn't it been a lark! I've loved every minute of it. Besides, you can't call me really one of the submerged tenth. Uncle Thomas left me a hundred and fifty pounds a year, and mercifully I'm not allowed to touch the capital. If only there were no hats or safety bets in the world, I should be smugly opulent. . . . But I mustn't keep you any longer, Clarkie dear. I expect the waiting-room is full of dukes who want cooks and cooks who want dukes, all fidgeting and wondering how much longer you're going to keep them. Good-bye, darling."

And, having kissed Miss Clarkson fondly and straightened her hat, which the other's motherly embrace had disarranged, Eve left the room.

CHAPTER IV

MEANWHILE, at the Drones Club, a rather painful scene had been taking place. Psmith, regaining the shelter of the building, had made his way to the wash-room, where, having studied his features with interest for a moment in the mirror, he smoothed his hair, which the rain had somewhat disordered, and brushed his clothes with extreme care. He then went to the cloak-room for his hat. The attendant regarded him as he entered with the air of one whose mind is not wholly at rest.

"Mr. Walderwick was in here a moment ago, sir," said the attendant.

"Yes?" said Psmith, mildly interested. "An energetic, bustling soul, Comrade Walderwick. Always somewhere. Now here, now there."

"Asking about his umbrella, he was," pursued the attendant with a touch of coldness.

"Indeed? Asking about his umbrellla, eh?"

"Made a great fuss about it, sir, he did."

"And rightly," said Psmith with approval. "The good man loves his umbrella."

"Of course I had to tell him that you had took it, sir."

"I would not have it otherwise," assented Psmith heartily. "I like this spirit of candour. There must be no reservations, no subterfuges between you and Comrade Walderwick. Let all be open and above-board."

"He seemed very put out, sir. He went off to find you."

72

"I am always glad of a chat with Comrade Walderwick," said Psmith. "Always."

He left the cloak-room and made for the hall, where he desired the porter to procure him a cab. This having drawn up in front of the club, he descended the steps and was about to enter it, when there was a hoarse cry in his rear, and through the front door there came bounding a pinkly indignant youth, who called loudly:

"Here! Hi! Smith! Dash it!"

Psmith climbed into the cab and gazed benevolently out at the new-comer.

"Ah, Comrade Walderwick!" he said. "What have we on our mind?"

"Where's my umbrella?" demanded the pink one. "The cloak-room waiter says you took my umbrella. I mean, a joke's a joke, but that was a dashed good umbrella."

"It was, indeed," Psmith agreed cordially. "It may be of interest to you to know that I selected it as the only possible one from among a number of competitors. I fear this club is becoming very mixed, Comrade Walderwick. You with your pure mind would hardly believe the rottenness of some of the umbrellas I inspected in the cloak-room."

"Where is it?"

"The cloak-room? You turn to the left as you go in at the main entrance and . . ."

"My umbrella, dash it! Where's my umbrella?"

"Ah, there," said Psmith, and there was a touch of manly regret in his voice, "you have me. I gave it to a young lady in the street. Where she is at the present moment I could not say."

The pink youth tottered slightly.

"You gave my umbrella to a girl?"

"A very loose way of describing her. You would not speak of her in that light fashion if you had seen her. Comrade Walderwick, she was wonderful! I am a plain, blunt, rugged man, above the softer emotions as a general thing, but I frankly confess that she stirred a chord in me which is not often stirred. She thrilled my battered old heart, Comrade Walderwick. There is no other word. Thrilled it!"

"But, dash it! . . ."

Psmith reached out a long arm and laid his hand paternally on the other's shoulder.

"Be brave, Comrade Walderwick!" he said. "Face this thing like a man! I am sorry to have been the means of depriving you of an excellent umbrella, but as you will readily understand I had no alternative. It was raining. She was over there, crouched despairingly beneath the awning of that shop. She wanted to be elsewhere, but the moisture lay in wait to damage her hat. What could I do? What could any man worthy of the name do but go down to the cloak-room and pinch the best umbrella in sight and take it to her? Yours was easily the best. There was absolutely no comparison. I gave it to her, and she has gone off with it, happy once more. This explanation," said Psmith, "will, I am sure, sensibly diminish your natural chagrin. You have lost your umbrella, Comrade Walderwick, but in what a cause! In what a cause, Comrade Walderwick! You are now entitled to rank with Sir Philip Sidney and Sir Walter Raleigh. The latter is perhaps the closer historical parallel. He spread his cloak to keep a queen from wetting her feet. You—by proxy—

yielded up your umbrella to save a girl's hat.   Posterity
will be proud of you, Comrade Walderwick.   I shall be
vastly surprised if you do not go down in legend and
song.   Children in ages to come will cluster about their
grandfather's knees, saying, 'Tell us how the great Walderwick lost his umbrella, grandpapa!'   And he will tell them,
and they will rise from the recital better, deeper, broader
children. . . .   But now, as I see the driver has started his
meter, I fear I must conclude this little chat—which I,
for one, have heartily enjoyed.   Drive on," he said, leaning out of the window.   "I want to go to Ada Clarkson's
International Employment Bureau in Shaftesbury Avenue."

The cab moved off.   The Hon. Hugo Walderwick, after
one passionate glance in its wake, realised that he was
getting wet and went back into the club.

.   .   .   .

Arriving at the address named, Smith paid his cab and,
having mounted the stairs, delicately knuckled the ground-
glass window of Enquiries.

"My dear Miss Clarkson," he began in an affable voice,
the instant the window had shot up, "if you can spare me
a few moments of your valuable time . . ."

"Miss Clarkson's engaged."

Psmith scrutinised her gravely through his monocle.

"Aren't *you* Miss Clarkson?"

Enquiries said she was not.

"Then," said Psmith, "there has been a misunderstanding, for which," he added cordially, "I am to blame.   Perhaps I could see her anon?   You will find me in the waiting-room when required."

He went into the waiting-room, and, having picked up

a magazine from the table, settled down to read a story in *The Girl's Pet*—the January number of the year 1919, for Employment Agencies, like dentists, prefer their literature of a matured vintage. He was absorbed in this when Eve came out of the private office.

CHAPTER V

PSMITH rose courteously as she entered.

"My dear Miss Clarkson," he said, "if you can spare me a moment of your valuable time . . ."

"Good gracious!" said Eve. "How extraordinary!"

"A singular coincidence," agreed Psmith.

"You never gave me time to thank you for the umbrella," said Eve reproachfully. "You must have thought me awfully rude. But you took my breath away."

"My dear Miss Clarkson, please do not . . ."

"Why do you keep calling me that?"

"Aren't *you* Miss Clarkson either?"

"Of course I'm not."

"Then," said Psmith, "I must start my quest all over again. These constant checks are trying to an ardent spirit. Perhaps you are a young bride come to engage her first cook?"

"No. I'm not married."

"Good!"

Eve found his relieved thankfulness a little embarrassing. In the momentary pause which followed his remark, Enquiries entered alertly.

"Miss Clarkson will see you now, sir."

"Leave us," said Psmith with a wave of his hand. "We would be alone."

Enquiries stared; then, awed by his manner and general appearance of magnificence, withdrew.

"I suppose really," said Eve, toying with the umbrella, "I ought to give this back to you." She glanced at the dripping window. "But it *is* raining rather hard, isn't it?"

"Like the dickens," assented Psmith.

"Then would you mind very much if I kept it till this evening?"

"Please do."

"Thanks ever so much. I will send it back to you to-night if you will give me the name and address."

Psmith waved his hand deprecatingly.

"No, no. If it is of any use to you, I hope that you will look on it as a present."

"A present!"

"A gift," explained Psmith.

"But I really can't go about accepting expensive umbrellas from people. Where shall I send it?"

"If you insist, you may send it to the Hon. Hugo Walderwick, Drones Club, Dover Street. But it really isn't necessary."

"I won't forget. And thank you very much, Mr. Walderwick."

"Why do you call me that?"

"Well, you said . . ."

"Ah, I see. A slight confusion of ideas. No, I am not Mr. Walderwick. And between ourselves I should hate to be. His is a very C3 intelligence. Comrade Walderwick is merely the man to whom the umbrella belongs."

Eve's eyes opened wide.

"Do you mean to say you gave me somebody else's umbrella?"

"I had unfortunately omitted to bring my own out with me this morning."

"I never heard of such a thing!"

"Merely practical Socialism. Other people are content to talk about the Redistribution of Property. I go out and do it."

"But won't he be awfully angry when he finds out it has gone?"

"He *has* found out. And it was pretty to see his delight. I explained the circumstances, and he was charmed to have been of service to you."

The door opened again, and this time it was Miss Clarkson in person who entered. She had found Enquiries' statement over the speaking-tube rambling and unsatisfactory, and had come to investigate for herself the reason why the machinery of the office was being held up.

"Oh, I must go," said Eve, as she saw her. "I'm interrupting your business."

"I'm so glad you're still here, dear," said Miss Clarkson. "I have just been looking over my files, and I see that there *is* one vacancy. For a nurse," said Miss Clarkson with a touch of the apologetic in her voice.

"Oh, no, that's all right," said Eve. "I don't really need anything. But thanks ever so much for bothering."

She smiled affectionately upon the proprietress, bestowed another smile upon Psmith as he opened the door for her, and went out. Psmith turned away from the door with a thoughtful look upon his face.

"Is that young lady a nurse?" he asked.

"Do you want a nurse?" inquired Miss Clarkson, at once the woman of business.

"I want that nurse," said Psmith with conviction.

"She is a delightful girl," said Miss Clarkson with enthusiasm. "There is no one in whom I would feel more confidence in recommending to a position. She is a Miss Halliday, the daughter of a very clever but erratic writer, who died some years ago. I can speak with particular knowledge of Miss Halliday, for I was for many years an assistant mistress at Wayland House, where she was at school. She is a charming, warm-hearted, impulsive girl. . . . But you will hardly want to hear all this."

"On the contrary," said Psmith, "I could listen for hours. You have stumbled upon my favourite subject."

Miss Clarkson eyed him a little doubtfully, and decided that it would be best to reintroduce the business theme.

"Perhaps, when you say you are looking for a nurse, you mean you need a hospital nurse ?"

"My friends have sometimes suggested it."

"Miss Halliday's greatest experience has, of course, been as a governess."

"A governess is just as good," said Psmith agreeably.

Miss Clarkson began to be conscious of a sensation of being out of her depth.

"How old are your children, sir ?" she asked.

"I fear," said Psmith, "you are peeping into Volume Two. This romance has only just started."

"I am afraid," said Miss Clarkson, now completely fogged, "I do not quite understand. What exactly are you looking for ?"

Psmith flicked a speck of fluff from his coat-sleeve.

"A job," he said.

"A job!" echoed Miss Clarkson, her voice breaking in an amazed squeak.

Psmith raised his eyebrows

"You seem surprised. Isn't this a job emporium?"

"This *is* an Employment Bureau," admitted Miss Clarkson.

"I knew it, I knew it," said Psmith. "Something seemed to tell me. Possibly it was the legend 'Employment Bureau' over the door. And those framed testimonials would convince the most sceptical. Yes, Miss Clarkson, I want a job, and I feel somehow that you are the woman to find it for me. I have inserted an advertisement in the papers, expressing my readiness to undertake any form of employment, but I have since begun to wonder if after all this will lead to wealth and fame. At any rate, it is wise to attack the great world from another angle as well, so I come to you."

"But you must excuse me if I remark that this application of yours strikes me as most extraordinary."

"Why? I am young, active, and extremely broke."

"But your—er—your clothes . . ."

Psmith squinted, not without complacency, down a faultlessly fitting waistcoat, and flicked another speck of dust off his sleeve.

"You consider me well dressed?" he said. "You find me natty? Well, well, perhaps you are right, perhaps you are right. But consider, Miss Clarkson. If one expects to find employment in these days of strenuous competition, one must be neatly and decently clad. Employers look askance at a baggy trouser-leg. A zippy waistcoat is more to them than an honest heart. This beautiful crease was obtained with the aid of the mattress upon which I tossed feverishly last night in my attic room."

"I can't take you seriously."

"Oh, don't say that, please."

"You really want me to find you work?"

"I prefer the term 'employment.' "

Miss Clarkson produced a notebook.

"If you are really not making this application just as a joke . . ."

"I assure you, no. My entire capital consists, in specie, of about ten pounds."

"Then perhaps you will tell me your name."

"Ah! Things are beginning to move. The name is Psmith. P-smith. The p is silent."

"Psmith?"

"Psmith."

Miss Clarkson brooded over this for a moment in almost pained silence, then recovered her slipping grip of affairs.

"I think," she said, "you had better give me a few particulars about yourself."

"There is nothing I should like better," responded Psmith warmly. "I am always ready—I may say eager—to tell people the story of my life, but in this rushing age I get little encouragement. Let us start at the beginning. My infancy. When I was but a babe, my eldest sister was bribed with sixpence an hour by my nurse to keep an eye on me and see that I did not raise Cain. At the end of the first day she struck for a shilling, and got it. We now pass to my boyhood. At an early age I was sent to Eton, everybody predicting a bright career for me. Those were happy days, Miss Clarkson. A merry, laughing lad with curly hair and a sunny smile, it is not too much to say that I was the pet of the place. The old cloisters. . . . But I am boring you. I can see it in your eye."

"No, no," protested Miss Clarkson. "But what I meant was . . . I thought you might have had some experience in some particular line of . . . In fact, what sort of work . . . ?"

"Employment."

"What sort of employment do you require?"

"Broadly speaking," said Psmith, "any reasonably salaried position that has nothing to do with fish."

"Fish!" quavered Miss Clarkson, slipping again. "Why fish?"

"Because, Miss Clarkson, the fish trade was until this morning my walk in life, and my soul has sickened of it."

"You are in the *fish* trade?" squeaked Miss Clarkson, with an amazed glance at the knife-like crease in his trousers.

"These are not my working clothes," said Psmith, following and interpreting her glance. "Yes, owing to a financial upheaval in my branch of the family, I was until this morning at the beck and call of an uncle who unfortunately happens to be a Mackerel Monarch or a Sardine Sultan, or whatever these merchant princes are called who rule the fish market. He insisted on my going into the business to learn it from the bottom up, thinking, no doubt, that I would follow in his footsteps and eventually work my way to the position of a Whitebait Wizard. Alas! he was too sanguine. It was not to be," said Psmith solemnly, fixing an owl-like gaze on Miss Clarkson through his eyeglass.

"No?" said Miss Clarkson.

"No. Last night I was obliged to inform him that I proposed to sever my connection with the firm for ever. I may say at once that there ensued something in the nature of a family earthquake. Hard words," sighed Psmith. "Black looks. Unseemly wrangle. And the upshot of it all was that my uncle washed his hands of me and drove me forth into the great world. Hence my anxiety to find employment. My uncle has definitely withdrawn his countenance from me, Miss Clarkson."

"Dear, dear!" murmured the proprietress sympathetically.

"Yes. He is a hard man, and he judges his fellows solely by their devotion to fish. I never in my life met a man so wrapped up in a subject. For years he has been practically a monomaniac on the subject of fish. So much so that he actually looks like one. It is as if he had taken one of those auto-suggestion courses and had kept saying to himself, 'Every day, in every way, I grow more and more like a fish.' His closest friends can hardly tell now whether he more nearly resembles a halibut or a cod. . . . But I am boring you again with this family gossip?"

He eyed Miss Clarkson with such a sudden and penetrating glance that she started nervously.

"No, no," she exclaimed.

"You relieve my apprehensions. I am only too well aware that, when fairly launched on the topic of fish, I am more than apt to weary my audience. I cannot understand this enthusiasm for fish. My uncle used to talk about an unusually large catch of pilchards in Cornwall in much the same awed way as a right-minded curate would talk about the spiritual excellence of his bishop. To me, Miss Clarkson, from the very start, the fish business was what I can only describe as a wash-out. It nauseated my finer feelings. It got right in amongst my fibres. I had to rise and partake of a simple breakfast at about four in the morning, after which I would make my way to Gillingsgate Market and stand for some hours knee-deep in dead fish of every description. A jolly life for a cat, no doubt, but a bit too thick for a Shropshire Psmith. Mine, Miss Clarkson, is a refined and poetic nature. I like to be surrounded by joy and life, and I know nothing more joyless and deader than a dead fish. Multiply that dead fish by a million, and you have an environment which only a Dante could contemplate with equanimity. My uncle used to tell me that the way to ascertain whether a fish was fresh was to peer into its eyes. Could I spend the springtime of life staring into the eyes of dead fish? No!" He rose. "Well, I will not detain you any longer. Thank you for the unfailing courtesy and attention with which you have listened to me. You can understand now why my talents are on the market and why I am compelled to state specifically that no employment can be considered which has anything to do with fish. I am convinced that you will shortly have something particularly good to offer me."

"I don't know that I can say that, Mr. Psmith."

"The p is silent, as in pshrimp," he reminded her. "Oh, by the way," he said, pausing at the door, "there is one other thing before I go. While I was waiting for you to be disengaged, I chanced on an instalment of a serial story in *The Girl's Pet* for January, 1919. My search for the remaining issues proved fruitless. The title was 'Her Honour At Stake,' by Jane Emmeline Moss. You don't happen to know how it all came out in the end, do you? Did Lord Eustace ever learn that, when he found Clarice in Sir Jasper's rooms at midnight, she had only gone there to recover some compromising letters for a girl friend?

You don't know? I feared as much. Well, good morning, Miss Clarkson, good morning. I leave my future in your hands with a light heart."

"I will do my best for you, of course."

"And what," said Psmith cordially, "could be better than Miss Clarkson's best?"

He closed the door gently behind him, and went out. Struck by a kindly thought, he tapped upon Enquiries' window, and beamed benevolently as her bobbed head shot into view.

"They tell me," he said, "that Aspidistra is much fancied for the four o'clock race at Birmingham this afternoon. I give the information without prejudice, for what it is worth. Good day!"

CHAPTER VI

LORD EMSWORTH MEETS A POET

§ 1

THE rain had stopped when Psmith stepped out into the street, and the sun was shining again in that half blustering, half apologetic manner which it affects on its reappearance after a summer shower. The pavements glistened cheerfully, and the air had a welcome freshness. Pausing at the corner, he pondered for a moment as to the best method of passing the hour and twenty minutes which must elapse before he could reasonably think of lunching. The fact that the offices of the *Morning Globe* were within easy strolling distance decided him to go thither and see if the first post had brought anything in the shape of answers to his advertisements. And his energy was rewarded a few minutes later when Box 365 on being opened yielded up quite a little budget of literary matter. No fewer than seven letters in all. A nice bag.

What, however, had appeared at first sight evidence of a pleasing ebullition of enterprise on the part of the news-paper-reading public turned out on closer inspection, when he had retired to a corner where he could concentrate in peace, a hollow delusion. Enterprising in a sense though the communications were—and they certainly showed the writers as men of considerable ginger and business push—to Psmith they came as a disappointment. He had expected better things. These letters were not at all what he had paid good money to receive. They missed the point altogether. The right spirit, it seemed to him, was entirely absent.

The first envelope, attractive though it looked from the outside, being of an expensive brand of stationery and gaily adorned with a somewhat startling crest merely contained a pleasantly-worded offer from a Mr. Alistair Mac-Dougall to advance him any sum from ten to fifty thousand pounds on his note of hand only. The second revealed a similar proposal from another Scot named Colin MacDonald. While in the third Mr. Ian Campbell was prepared to go as high as one hundred thousand. All three philanthropists had but one stipulation to make—they would have no dealings with minors. Youth, with all its glorious traditions, did not seem to appeal to them. But they cordially urged Psmith, in the event of his having celebrated his twenty-first birthday, to come round to the office and take the stuff away in a sack.

Keeping his head well in the midst of this shower of riches, Psmith dropped the three letters with a sigh into the waste-paper basket, and opened the next in order. This was a bulky envelope, and its contents consisted of a printed brochure entitled, "This Night Shall Thy Soul Be Required Of Thee"—while, by a curious and appropriate coincidence, Number Five proved to be a circular from an energetic firm of coffin-makers offering to bury him for eight pounds ten. Number Six, also printed, was a manifesto from one Howard Hill, of Newmarket, recommending him to apply without delay for "Hill's Three-Horse Special," without which ("Who," demanded Mr. Hill in large type, "gave you Wibbly-Wob for the Jubilee

Cup?")—no sportsman could hope to accomplish the un-
doing of the bookmakers.

Although by doing so he convicted himself of that very
lack of enterprise which he had been deploring in the
great public, Psmith placed this communication with the
others in the waste-paper baskets. There now remained
only Number Seven, and a slight flicker of hope returned
to him when he perceived that this envelope was addressed
by hand and not in typescript. He opened it.

Beyond a doubt he had kept the pick of the bunch to
the last. Here was something that made up for all those
other disappointments. Written in a scrawly and apparently agitated hand, the letter ran as follows:

> *"If R. Psmith will meet the writer in the lobby of the
> Piccadilly Palace Hotel at twelve sharp, Friday, July 1,
> business may result if business meant and terms reason-
> able. R. Psmith will wear a pink chrysanthemum in his
> buttonhole, and will say to the writer, 'There will be
> rain in Northumberland to-morrow,' to which the writer
> will reply, 'Good for the crops.' Kindly be punctual."*

A pleased smile played about Psmith's solemn face as
he read this communication for the second time. It was
much more the sort of thing for which he had been hoping.
Although his closest friend, Mike Jackson, was a young
man of complete ordinariness, Psmith's tastes when he
sought companionship lay as a rule in the direction of the
bizarre. He preferred his humanity eccentric. And "the
writer," to judge him by this specimen of his correspondence, appeared to be eccentric enough for the most exacting
taste. Whether this promising person turned out to be

a ribald jester or an earnest crank, Psmith felt no doubt whatever as to the advisability of following the matter up. Whichever he might be, his society ought to afford entertainment during the interval before lunch. Psmith glanced at his watch. The hour was a quarter to twelve. He would be able to secure the necessary chrysanthemum and reach the Piccadilly Palace Hotel by twelve sharp, thus achieving the businesslike punctuality on which the unknown writer seemed to set such store.

.   .   .   .

It was not until he had entered a florist's shop on the way to the tryst that it was borne in upon him that the adventure was going to have its drawbacks. The first of these was the chrysanthemum. Preoccupied with the rest of the communication, Psmith, when he had read the letter, had not given much thought to the decoration which it would be necessary for him to wear; and it was only when, in reply to his demand for a chrysanthemum, the florist came forward, almost hidden, like the army at Dunsinane, behind what looked like a small shrubbery, that he realised what he, a correct and fastidious dresser, was up against.

"Is that a chrysanthemum?"

"Yes, sir. Pink chrysanthemum."

"One?"

"Yes, sir. One pink chrysanthemum."

Psmith regarded the repellent object with disfavour through his eyeglass. Then, having placed it in his buttonhole, he proceeded on his way, feeling like some wild thing peering through the undergrowth. The distressing shrub completely spoiled his walk.

Arrived at the hotel and standing in the lobby, he perceived the existence of further complications. The lobby was in its usual state of congestion, it being a recognised meeting-place for those who did not find it convenient to go as far east as that traditional rendezvous of Londoners, the spot under the clock at Charing Cross Station; and "the writer," while giving instructions as to how Psmith should ornament his exterior, had carelessly omitted to mention how he himself was to be recognised. A rollicking, slap-dash conspirator, was Psmith's opinion.

It seemed best to take up a position as nearly as possible in the centre of the lobby and stand there until "the writer," lured by the chrysanthemum, should come forward and start something. This he accordingly did, but when at the end of ten minutes nothing had happened beyond a series of collisions with perhaps a dozen hurrying visitors to the hotel, he decided on a more active course. A young man of sporting appearance had been standing beside him for the last five minutes, and ever and anon this young man had glanced with some impatience at his watch. He was plainly waiting for some one, so Psmith tried the formula on him.

"There will be rain," said Psmith, "in Northumberland to-morrow."

The young man looked at him, not without interest, certainly, but without that gleam of intelligence in his eye which Psmith had hoped to see.

"What?" he replied.

"There will be rain in Northumberland to-morrow."

"Thanks, Zadkiel," said the young man. "Deuced gratifying, I'm sure. I suppose you couldn't predict the winner of the Goodwood Cup as well?"

He then withdrew rapidly to intercept a young woman

in a large hat who had just come through the swing doors. Psmith was forced to the conclusion that this was not his man. He was sorry on the whole, for he had seemed a pleasant fellow.

As Psmith had taken up a stationary position and the population of the lobby was for the most part in a state of flux, he was finding himself next to some one new all the time; and now he decided to accost the individual whom the reshuffle had just brought elbow to elbow with him. This was a jovial-looking soul with a flowered waist-coat, a white hat, and a mottled face. Just the man who might have written that letter.

The effect upon this person of Psmith's meteorological remark was instantaneous. A light of the utmost friend-liness shone in his beautifully-shaven face as he turned. He seized Psmith's hand and gripped it with a delightful heartiness. He had the air of a man who has found a friend, and what is more, an old friend. He had a sort of journeys-end-in-lovers'-meeting look.

"My dear old chap!" he cried. "I've been waiting for you to speak for the last five minutes. Knew we'd met before somewhere, but couldn't place you. Face familiar as the dickens, of course. Well, well, well! And how are they all?"

"Who?" said Psmith courteously.

"Why, the boys, my dear chap."

"Oh, the boys?"

"The dear old boys," said the other, specifying more exactly. He slapped Psmith on the shoulder. "What times those were, eh?"

"Which?" said Psmith.

"The times we all used to have together."

"Oh, *those?*" said Psmith.

Something of discouragement seemed to creep over the other's exuberance, as a cloud creeps over the summer sky. But he persevered.

"Fancy meeting you again like this!"

"It is a small world," agreed Psmith.

"I'd ask you to come and have a drink," said the jovial one, with the slight increase of tensity which comes to a man who approaches the core of a business deal, "but the fact is my ass of a man sent me out this morning without a penny. Forgot to give me my note-case. Damn' careless! I'll have to sack the fellow."

"Annoying, certainly," said Psmith.

"I wish I could have stood you a drink," said the other wistfully.

"Of all sad words of tongue or pen, the saddest are these, 'It might have been,' " sighed Psmith.

"I'll tell you what," said the jovial one, inspired. "Lend me a fiver, my dear old boy. That's the best way out of the difficulty. I can send it round to your hotel or wherever you are this evening when I get home."

A sweet, sad smile played over Psmith's face.

"Leave me, comrade!" he murmured.

"Eh?"

"Pass along, old friend, pass along."

Resignation displaced joviality in the other's countenance.

"Nothing doing?" he inquired.

"Nothing."

"Well, there was no harm in trying," argued the other.

"None whatever."

"You see," said the now far less jovial man confidentially, "you look such a perfect mug with that eyeglass that it tempts a chap."

"I can quite understand how it must!"

"No offence."

"Assuredly not."

The white hat disappeared through the swing doors, and Psmith returned to his quest. He engaged the attention of a middle-aged man in a snuff-coloured suit who had just come within hail.

"There will be rain in Northumberland to-morrow," he said.

The man peered at him inquiringly.

"Hey?" he said.

Psmith repeated his observation.

"Huh?" said the man.

Psmith was beginning to lose the unruffled calm which made him such an impressive figure to the public eye. He had not taken into consideration the possibility that the object of his search might be deaf. It undoubtedly added to the embarrassment of the pursuit. He was moving away, when a hand fell on his sleeve.

Psmith turned. The hand which still grasped his sleeve belonged to an elegantly dressed young man of somewhat nervous and feverish appearance. During his recent vigil Psmith had noticed this young man standing not far away, and had had half a mind to include him in the platoon of new friends he was making that morning.

"I say," said this young man in a tense whisper, "did I hear you say that there would be rain in Northumberland to-morrow?"

"If," said Psmith, "you were anywhere within the

radius of a dozen yards while I was chatting with the recent deaf adder, I think it is possible that you did."

"Good for the crops," said the young man. "Come over
here where we can talk quietly."

§ 2

"So you're R. Psmith?" said the young man, when they
had made their way to a remote corner of the lobby, apart
from the throng.

"The same."

"I say, dash it, you're frightfully late, you know. I
told you to be here at twelve sharp. It's nearly twelve
past."

"You wrong me," said Psmith. "I arrived here precisely at twelve. Since when, I have been standing like
Patience on a monument. . . ."

"Like what?"

"Let it go," said Psmith. "It is not important."

"I asked you to wear a pink chrysanthemum. So I
could recognise you, you know."

"I *am* wearing a pink chrysanthemum. I should have
imagined that that was a fact that the most casual could
hardly have overlooked."

"That thing?" The other gazed disparagingly at the
floral decoration. "I thought it was some kind of cab-
bage. I meant one of those little what-d'you-may-call-its
that people do wear in their button-holes."

"Carnation, possibly?"

"Carnation! That's right."

Psmith removed the chrysanthemum and dropped it behind his chair. He looked at his companion reproachfully.

"If you had studied botany at school, comrade," he said, "much misery might have been averted. I cannot begin to tell you the spiritual agony I suffered, trailing through the metropolis behind that shrub."

Whatever decent sympathy and remorse the other might have shown at these words was swept away in the shock resultant on a glance at his watch. Not for an instant during this brief return of his to London had Freddie Threepwood been unmindful of his father's stern injunction to him to catch the twelve-fifty train back to Market Blandings. If he missed it, there would be the deuce of a lot of unpleasantness, and unpleasantness in the home was the one thing Freddie wanted to avoid nowadays; for, like a prudent convict in a prison, he hoped by exemplary behaviour to get his sentencce of imprisonment at Blandings Castle reduced for good conduct.

"Good Lord! I've only got about five minutes. Got to talk quick. . . . About this thing. This business. That advertisement of yours."

"Ah, yes. My advertisement. It interested you?"

"Was it on the level?"

"Assuredly. We Psmiths do not deceive."

Freddie looked at him doubtfully.

"You know, you aren't a bit like I expected you'd be."

"In what respect," inquired Psmith, "do I fall short of the ideal?"

"It isn't so much falling short. It's—oh, I don't know . . . Well, yes, if you want to know, I thought you'd be a tougher specimen altogether. I got the impression from your advertisement that you were down and out and ready for anything, and you look as if you were on your way to a garden-party at Buckingham Palace."

"Ah!" said Psmith, enlightened. "It is my costume that is causing these doubts in your mind. This is the second time this morning that such a misunderstanding has occurred. Have no misgivings. These trousers may sit well, but, if they do, it is because the pockets are empty."

"Are you really broke?"

"As broke as the Ten Commandments."

"I'm hanged if I can believe it."

"Suppose I brush my hat the wrong way for a moment?" said Psmith obligingly. "Would that help?"

His companion remained silent for a few moments. In spite of the fact that he was in so great a hurry and that every minute that passed brought nearer the moment when he would be compelled to tear himself away and make a dash for Paddington Station, Freddie was finding it dif-ficult to open the subject he had come there to discuss.

"Look here," he said at length, "I shall have to trust you, dash it."

"You could pursue no better course."

"It's like this. I'm trying to raise a thousand quid . . ."

"I regret that I cannot offer to advance it to you my-self. I have, indeed, already been compelled to decline to lend a gentleman who claimed to be an old friend of mine so small a sum as a fiver. But there is a dear, obliging soul of the name of Alistair MacDougall who . . ."

"Good Lord? You don't think I'm trying to touch you?"

"That impression did flit through my mind."

"Oh, dash it, no. No, but—well, as I was saying, I'm frightfully keen to get hold of a thousand quid."

"So am I," said Psmith. "Two minds with but a single thought. How do *you* propose to start about it? For my part, I must freely confess that I haven't a notion. I am stumped. The cry goes round the chancelleries, 'Psmith is baffled!'"

"I say, old thing," said Freddie plaintively, "you couldn't talk a bit less, could you? I've only got about two minutes."

"I beg your pardon. Proceed."

"It's so dashed difficult to know how to begin the thing. I mean, it's all a bit complicated till you get the hang of it. . . . Look here, you said in your advertisement that you had no objection to crime."

Psmith considered the point.

"Within reason—and if undetected—I see no objection to two-pennorth of crime."

"Well, look here . . . look here . . . Well, look here," said Freddie, "will you steal my aunt's diamond necklace?"

Psmith placed his monocle in his eye and bent gravely toward his companion.

"Steal your aunt's necklace?" he said indulgently.

"Yes."

"You do not think she might consider it a liberty from one to whom she has never been introduced?"

What Freddie might have replied to this pertinent question will never be known, for at this moment, looking nervously at his watch for the twentieth time, he observed that the hands had passed the half-hour and were well on their way to twenty-five minutes to one. He bounded up with a cry.

"I must go!   I shall miss that damned train!"

"And meanwhile . . .?" said Psmith.

The familiar phrase—the words "And meanwhile" had occurred at least once in every film Freddie had ever seen —had the effect of wrenching the latter's mind back to the subject in hand for a moment.   Freddie was not a clear-thinking young man, but even he could see that he had left the negotiations suspended at a very satisfactory point. Nevertheless, he had to catch that twelve-fifty.

"Write and tell me what you think about it," panted Freddie, skimming through the lobby like a swallow.

"You have unfortunately omitted to leave a name and address," Psmith pointed out, following him at an easy jog-trot.

In spite of his hurry, a prudence born of much movie-seeing restrained Freddie from supplying the information asked for.   Give away your name and address and you never knew what might happen.

"I'll write to you," he cried, racing for a cab.

"I shall count the minutes," said Psmith courteously.

"Drive like blazes!" said Freddie to the chauffeur.

"Where?" inquired the man, not unreasonably.

"Eh? Oh, Paddington."

The cab whirled off, and Psmith, pleasantly conscious of a morning not ill-spent, gazed after it pensively for a moment.   Then, with the feeling that the authorities of Colney Hatch or some kindred establishment had been extraordinarily negligent, he permitted his mind to turn with genial anticipation in the direction of lunch.   For, though he had celebrated his first day of emancipation from Billingsgate Fish Market by rising late and break-

fasting later, he had become aware by now of that not
unpleasant emptiness which is the silent luncheon-gong of
the soul.

§ 3

The minor problem now presented itself of where to
lunch; and with scarcely a moment's consideration he dismissed those large, noisy, and bustling restaurants which
lie near Piccadilly Circus. After a morning spent with
Eve Halliday and the young man who was going about the
place asking people to steal his aunt's necklace, it was
imperative that he select some place where he could sit
and think quietly. Any food of which he partook must
be consumed in calm, even cloistral surroundings, unpol-
luted by the presence of a first violin who tied himself
into knots and an orchestra in whose lexicon there was no
such word as *piano*. One of his clubs seemed indicated.

In the days of his prosperity, Psmith's father, an enthusiastic clubman, had enrolled his son's name on the list
of several institutions: and now, although the lean years
had arrived, he was still a member of six, and would
continue to be a member till the beginning of the new year
and the consequent call for fresh subscriptions. These
clubs ranged from the Drones, frankly frivolous, to the
Senior Conservative, solidly worthy. Almost immediately
Psmith decided that for such a mood as was upon him
at the moment, the latter might have been specially constructed.

Anybody familiar with the interior of the Senior Conservative Club would have applauded his choice. In the
whole of London no better haven could have been found

by one desirous of staying his interior with excellently-
cooked food while passing his soul under a leisurely examination.   They fed you well at the Drones, too, no
doubt: but there Youth held carnival, and the thoughtful
man, examining his soul, was apt at any moment to have
his meditations broken in upon by a chunk of bread, dex-
terously thrown by some bright spirit at an adjoining
table.   No horror of that description could possibly occur
at the Senior Conservative.   The Senior Conservative has
six thousand one hundred and eleven members.   Some of
the six thousand one hundred and eleven are more respectable than the others, but they are all respectable—
whether they be numbered among the oldest inhabitants
like the Earl of Emsworth, who joined as a country member in 1888, or are among the recent creations of the last
election of candidates.   They are bald, reverend men,
who look as if they are on their way to the City to preside
at directors' meetings or have dropped in after conferring
with the Prime Minister at Downing Street as to the prospects at the coming by-election in the Little Wabsley
Division.

   With the quiet dignity which atoned for his lack in
years in this stronghold of mellow worth, Psmith mounted
the steps, passed through the doors which were obligingly
flung open for him by two uniformed dignitaries, and
made his way to the coffee-room.   Here, having selected
a table in the middle of the room and ordered a simple and
appetising lunch, he gave himself up to thoughts of Eve
Halliday.   As he had confessed to his young friend Mr.
Walderwick, she had made a powerful impression upon
him.   He was tearing himself from his day-dreams in
order to wrestle with a mutton chop, when a foreign body

shot into his orbit and blundered heavily against the table. Looking up, he perceived a long, thin, elderly gentleman of pleasantly vague aspect, who immediately began to apologise.

"My dear sir, I am extremely sorry. I trust I have caused no damage."

"None whatever," replied Psmith courteously.

"The fact is, I have mislaid my glasses. Blind as a bat without them. Can't see where I'm going."

A gloomy-looking young man with long and disordered hair, who stood at the elderly gentleman's elbow, coughed suggestively. He was shuffling restlessly, and appeared to be anxious to close the episode and move on. A young man, evidently, of highly-strung temperament. He had a sullen air.

The elderly gentleman started vaguely at the sound of the cough.

"Eh?" he said, as if in answer to some spoken remark. "Oh, yes, quite so, quite so, my dear fellow. Mustn't stop here chatting, eh? Had to apologise, though. Nearly upset this gentleman's table. Can't see where I'm going without my glasses. Blind as a bat. Eh? What? Quite so, quite so."

He ambled off, doddering cheerfully, while his companion still preserved his look of sulky aloofness. Psmith gazed after them with interest.

"Can you tell me," he asked of the waiter, who was rallying round with the potatoes, "who that was?"

The waiter followed his glance.

"Don't know who the young gentleman is, sir. Guest here, I fancy. The old gentleman is the Earl of Emsworth. Lives in the country and doesn't often come to

the club. Very absent-minded gentleman, they tell me.
Potatoes, sir?"

"Thank you," said Psmith.

The waiter drifted away, and returned.

"I have been looking at the guest book, sir. The name
of the gentleman lunching with Lord Emsworth is Mr.
Ralston McTodd."

"Thank you very much. I am sorry you had the
trouble."

"No trouble, sir."

Psmith resumed his meal.

§ 4

The sullen demeanour of the young man who had accompanied Lord Emsworth through the coffee-room ac-
curately reflected the emotions which were vexing his
troubled soul. Ralston McTodd, the powerful young
singer of Saskatoon ("Plumbs the depths of human emotion and strikes a new note"—*Montreal Star.* "Very
readable"—*Ipsilanti Herald*), had not enjoyed his lunch.
The pleasing sense of importance induced by the fact that
for the first time in his life he was hob-nobbing with a
genuine earl had given way after ten minutes of his host's
society to a mingled despair and irritation which had
grown steadily deeper as the meal proceeded. It is not
too much to say that by the time the fish course arrived it
would have been a relief to Mr. McTodd's feelings if he
could have taken up the butter-dish and banged it down,
butter and all, on his lordship's bald head.

A temperamental young man was Ralston McTodd. He
liked to be the centre of the picture, to do the talking, to

air his views, to be listened to respectfully and with interest by a submissive audience. At the meal which had just concluded none of these reasonable demands had been permitted to him. From the very beginning, Lord Emsworth had collared the conversation and held it with a gentle, beating persistency against all assaults. Five times had Mr. McTodd almost succeeded in launching one of his best epigrams, only to see it swept away on the tossing flood of a lecture on hollyhocks. At the sixth attempt he had managed to get it out, complete and sparkling, and the old ass opposite him had taken it in his stride like a hurdle and gone galloping off about the mental and moral defects of a creature named Angus McAllister, who appeared to be his head gardener or something of the kind. The luncheon, though he was a hearty feeder and as a rule appreciative of good cooking, had turned to ashes in Mr. McTodd's mouth, and it was a soured and chafing Singer of Saskatoon who dropped scowlingly into an armchair by the window of the lower smoking-room a few moments later. We introduce Ralston McTodd to the reader, in short, at a moment when he is very near the breaking-point. A little more provocation, and goodness knows what he may not do. For the time being, he is merely leaning back in his chair and scowling. He has a faint hope, however, that a cigar may bring some sort of relief, and he is waiting for one to be ordered for him.

The Earl of Emsworth did not see the scowl. He had not really seen Mr. McTodd at all from the moment of his arrival at the club, when somebody, who sounded like the head porter, had informed him that a gentleman was waiting to see him and had led him up to a shapeless blur which had introduced itself as his expected guest. The loss of his glasses had had its usual effect on Lord Emsworth, making the world a misty place in which indefinite objects swam dimly like fish in muddy water. Not that this mattered much, seeing that he was in London, for in London there was never anything worth looking at. Beyond a vague feeling that it would be more comfortable on the whole if he had his glasses—a feeling just strong enough to have made him send off a messenger boy to his hotel to hunt for them—Lord Emsworth had not allowed lack of vision to interfere with his enjoyment of the proceedings.

And, unlike Mr. McTodd, he had been enjoying himself very much. A good listener, this young man, he felt. Very soothing, the way he had constituted himself a willing audience, never interrupting or thrusting himself forward, as is so often the deplorable tendency of the modern young man. Lord Emsworth was bound to admit that, much as he had disliked the idea of going to London to pick up this poet or whatever he was, the thing had turned out better than he had expected. He liked Mr. McTodd's silent but obvious interest in flowers, his tacit but warm-hearted sympathy in the matter of Angus McAllister. He was glad he was coming to Blandings. It would be agreeable to conduct him personally through the gardens, to introduce him to Angus McAllister and allow him to plumb for himself the black abyss of that outcast's mental processes.

Meanwhile, he had forgotten all about ordering that cigar . . .

"In large gardens where ample space permits," said Lord Emsworth, dropping cosily into his chair and taking up the conversation at the point where it had been broken off, "nothing is more desirable than that there should be some places, or one at least, of quiet greenery alone, without any flowers whatever. I see that you agree with me."

Mr. McTodd had not agreed with him. The grunt which Lord Emsworth had taken for an exclamation of rapturous adhesion to his sentiments had been merely a sort of bubble of sound rising from the tortured depths of Mr. McTodd's suffering soul—the cry, as the poet beautifully puts it, "of some strong smoker in his agony." The desire to smoke had now gripped Mr. McTodd's very vitals; but, as some lingering remains of the social sense kept him from asking point-blank for the cigar for which he yearned, he sought in his mind for a way of approaching the subject obliquely.

"In no other way," proceeded Lord Emsworth, "can the brilliancy of flowers be so keenly enjoyed as by . . ."

"Talking of flowers," said Mr. McTodd, "it is a fact, I believe, that tobacco smoke is good for roses."

". . . as by pacing for a time," said Lord Emsworth, "in some cool, green alley, and then passing on to the flowery places. It is partly, no doubt, the unconscious working out of some optical law, the explanation of which in everyday language is that the eye . . ."

"Some people say that smoking is bad for the eyes. I don't agree with them," said Mr. McTodd warmly.

". . . being, as it were, saturated with the green colour, is the more attuned to receive the others, especially the reds. It was probably some such consideration that influenced the designers of the many old gardens of England in devoting so much attention to the cult of the yew tree. When you come to Blandings, my dear fellow, I will show you our celebrated yew alley. And, when you see it, you will agree that I was right in taking the stand I did against Angus McAllister's pernicious views."

"I was lunching in a club yesterday," said Mr. McTodd, with the splendid McTodd doggedness, "where they had no matches on the tables in the smoking-room. Only spills. It made it very inconvenient . . ."

"Angus McAllister," said Lord Emsworth, "is a professional gardener. I need say no more. You know as well as I do, my dear fellow, what professional gardeners are like when it is a question of moss . . ."

"What it meant was that, when you wanted to light your after-luncheon cigar, you had to get up and go to a gas-burner on a bracket at the other end of the room . . ."

"Moss, for some obscure reason, appears to infuriate them. It rouses their basest passions. Nature intended a yew alley to be carpeted with a mossy growth. The mossy path in the yew alley at Blandings is in true relation for colour to the trees and grassy edges; yet will you credit it that that soulless disgrace to Scotland actually wished to grub it all up and have a rolled gravel path staring up from beneath those immemorial trees! I have already told you how I was compelled to give in to him in the matter of the hollyhocks—head gardeners of any ability at all are rare in these days and one has to make concessions—but this was too much. I was perfectly friendly and civil about it. 'Certainly, McAllister,' I said, 'you may have your gravel path if you wish it. I make but one proviso, that you construct it over my dead body. Only when I am weltering in my blood on the threshold of that yew alley shall you disturb one inch of my beautiful moss. Try to remember, McAllister,' I said. still quite cordially, 'that you are not laying out a recreation-ground in a Glasgow suburb—you are proposing to make an eye-sore of what is possibly the most beautiful nook in one of the finest and oldest gardens in the United Kingdom.' He made some repulsive Scotch noise at the back of his throat, and there the matter rests. . . . Let me, my dear fellow," said Lord Emsworth, writhing down into the depths of his chair like an aristocratic snake until his spine rested snugly against the leather, "let me describe for you the Yew Alley at Blandings. Entering from the west . . ."

Mr. McTodd gave up the struggle and sank back, filled with black and deleterious thoughts, into a tobaccoless hell. The smoking-room was full now, and on all sides fragrant blue clouds arose from the little groups of serious thinkers who were discussing what Gladstone had said in '78. Mr. McTodd, as he watched them, had something of the emotions of the Peri excluded from Paradise. So reduced was he by this time that he would have accepted gratefully the meanest straight-cut cigarette in place of the Corona of his dreams. But even this poor substitute for smoking was denied him.

Lord Emsworth droned on. Having approached from the west, he was now well inside the yew alley.

"Many of the yews, no doubt, have taken forms other than those that were originally designed. Some are like turned chessmen; some might be taken for adaptations of human figures, for one can trace here and there a hat-covered head or a spreading petticoat. Some rise in solid blocks with rounded roof and stemless mushroom finial. These have for the most part arched recesses, forming arbours. One of the tallest . . . Eh? What?"

Lord Emsworth blinked vaguely at the waiter who had sidled up. A moment before he had been a hundred odd miles away, and it was not easy to adjust his mind immediately to the fact that he was in the smoking-room of the Senior Conservative Club.

"Eh? What?"

"A messenger boy has just arrived with these, your lordship."

Lord Emsworth peered in a dazed and woolly manner at the proffered spectacle-case. Intelligence returned to him.

"Oh, thank you. Thank you very much. My glasses. Capital! Thank you, thank you, thank you."

He removed the glasses from their case and placed them on his nose: and instantly the world sprang into being before his eyes, sharp and well-defined. It was like coming out of a fog.

"Dear me!" he said in a self-congratulatory voice.

Then abruptly he sat up, transfixed. The lower smoking-room at the Senior Conservative Club is on the street level, and Lord Emsworth's chair faced the large window. Through this, as he raised his now spectacled face, he perceived for the first time that among the row of shops on the opposite side of the road was a jaunty new florist's. It had not been there at his last visit to the metropolis, and he stared at it raptly, as a small boy would stare at a saucer of ice-cream if such a thing had suddenly descended from heaven immediately in front of him. And, like a small boy in such a situation, he had eyes for nothing else. He did not look at his guest. Indeed, in the ecstasy of his discovery, he had completely forgotten that he had a guest.

Any flower shop, however small, was a magnet to the Earl of Emsworth. And this was a particularly spacious and arresting flower shop. Its window was gay with summer blooms. And Lord Emsworth, slowly rising from his chair, "pointed" like a dog that sees a pheasant.

"Bless my soul!" he murmured.

If the reader has followed with the closeness which it deserves the extremely entertaining conversation of his lordship recorded in the last few paragraphs, he will have noted a reference to hollyhocks. Lord Emsworth had ventilated the hollyhock question at some little length while seated at the luncheon table. But, as we had not the good fortune to be present at that enjoyable meal, a brief résumé of the situation must now be given and the intelligent public allowed to judge between his lordship and the uncompromising McAllister.

Briefly, the position was this. Many head gardeners are apt to favour in the hollyhock forms that one cannot but think have for their aim an ideal that is a false and unworthy one. Angus McAllister, clinging to the head-gardeneresque standard of beauty and correct form, would not sanction the wide outer petal. The flower, so Angus held, must be very tight and very round, like the uniform of a major-general. Lord Emsworth, on the other hand, considered this view narrow, and claimed the liberty to try for the very highest and truest beauty in hollyhocks. The loosely-folded inner petals of the hollyhock, he considered, invited a wonderful play and brilliancy of colour; while the wide outer petal, with its slightly waved surface and gently frilled edge . . . well, anyway, Lord Emsworth liked his hollyhocks floppy and Angus McAllister liked them tight, and bitter warfare had resulted, in which, as we have seen, his lordship had been compelled to give way. He had been brooding on this defeat ever since, and in the florist opposite he saw a possible sympathiser, a potential ally, an intelligent chum with whom he could get together and thoroughly damn Angus McAllister's Glaswegian obstinacy.

You would not have suspected Lord Emsworth, from a causal glance, of having within him the ability to move rapidly; but it is a fact that he was out of the smoking-room and skimming down the front steps of the club before Mr. McTodd's jaw, which had fallen at the spectacle of his host bounding out of his horizon of vision like a jack-rabbit, had time to hitch itself up again. A moment later, Mr. McTodd, happening to direct his gaze out of the window, saw him whiz across the road and vanish into the florist's shop.

It was at this juncture that Psmith, having finished his lunch, came downstairs to enjoy a quiet cup of coffee. The room was rather crowded, and the chair which Lord Emsworth had vacated offered a wide invitation. He made his way to it.

"Is this chair occupied?" he inquired politely. So politely that Mr. McTodd's reply sounded by contrast even more violent than it might otherwise have done.

"No, it isn't!" snapped Mr. McTodd.

Psmith seated himself. He was feeling agreeably disposed to conversation.

"Lord Emsworth has left you then?" he said.

"Is he a friend of yours?" inquired Mr. McTodd in a voice that suggested that he was perfectly willing to accept a proxy as a target for his wrath.

"I know him by sight. Nothing more."

"Blast him!" muttered Mr. McTodd with indescribable virulence.

Psmith eyed him inquiringly.

"Correct me if I am wrong," he said, "but I seem to detect in your manner a certain half-veiled annoyance. Is anything the matter?"

Mr. McTodd barked bitterly.

"Oh, no. Nothing's the matter. Nothing whatever, except that that old beaver—"—here he wronged Lord Emsworth, who, whatever his faults, was not a bearded man—"that old beaver invited me to lunch, talked all the time about his infernal flowers, never let me get a word in edgeways, hadn't the common civility to offer me a cigar, and now has gone off without a word of apology and buried himself in that shop over the way. I've never been so insulted in my life!" raved Mr. McTodd.

"Scarcely the perfect host," admitted Psmith.

"And if he thinks," said Mr. McTodd, rising, "that I'm going to go and stay with him at his beastly castle after this, he's mistaken. I'm supposed to go down there with him this evening. And perhaps the old fossil thinks I will! After this!" A horrid laugh rolled up from Mr. McTodd's interior. "Likely! I see myself! After being insulted like this . . . Would *you?*" he demanded.

Psmith gave the matter thought.

"I am inclined to think no."

"And so am I damned well inclined to think no!" cried Mr. McTodd. "I'm going away now, this very minute. And if that old total loss ever comes back, you can tell him he's seen the last of me."

And Ralston McTodd, his blood boiling with justifiable indignation and pique to a degree dangerous on such a warm day, stalked off towards the door with a hard, set face. Through the door he stalked to the cloak-room for his hat and cane; then, his lips moving silently, he stalked through the hall, stalked down the steps, and passed from the scene, stalking furiously round the corner in quest of a tobacconist's. At the moment of his disappearance, the Earl of Emsworth had just begun to give the sympathetic florist a limpid character-sketch of Angus McAllister.

.   .   .   .

Psmith shook his head sadly. These clashings of human temperament were very lamentable. They disturbed the after-luncheon repose of the man of sensibility. He ordered coffee, and endeavoured to forget the painful scene by thinking of Eve Halliday.

§ 5

The florist who had settled down to ply his trade opposite the Senior Conservative Club was a delightful fellow, thoroughly sound on the hollyhock question and so informative in the matter of delphiniums, achilleas, coreopsis, eryngiums, geums, lupines, bergamot and early phloxes that Lord Emsworth gave himself up wholeheartedly to the feast of reason and the flow of soul; and it was only some fifteen minutes later that he remembered that he had left a guest languishing in the lower smoking-room and that this guest might be thinking him a trifle remiss in the observance of the sacred duties of hospitality.

"Bless my soul, yes!" said his lordship, coming out from under the influence with a start.

Even then he could not bring himself to dash abruptly from the shop. Twice he reached the door and twice pottered back to sniff at flowers and say something he had forgotten to mention about the Stronger Growing Clematis. Finally, however, with one last, longing, lingering look behind, he tore himself away and trotted back across the road.

Arrived in the lower smoking-room, he stood in the doorway for a moment, peering. The place had been a blur to him when he had left it, but he remembered that he had been sitting in the middle window and, as there were only two seats by the window, that tall, dark young man in one of them must be the guest he had deserted. That he could be a changeling never occurred to Lord Emsworth. So pleasantly had the time passed in the shop across the way that he had the impression that he had only been gone a couple of minutes or so. He made his way to where the young man sat. A vague idea came into his head that the other had grown a bit in his absence, but it passed.

"My dear fellow," he said genially, as he slid into the other chair, "I really must apologise."

It was plain to Psmith that the other was under a mis-apprehension, and a really nice-minded young man would no doubt have put the matter right at once. The fact that it never for a single instant occurred to Psmith to do so was due, no doubt, to some innate defect in his character. He was essentially a young man who took life as it came, and the more inconsequently it came the better he liked it. Presently, he reflected, it would become necessary for him to make some excuse and steal quietly out of the other's life; but meanwhile the situation seemed to him to present entertaining possibilities.

"Not at all," he replied graciously. "Not at all."

"I was afraid for a moment," said Lord Emsworth, "that you might—quite naturally—be offended."

"Absurd!"

"Shouldn't have left you like that. Shocking bad manners. But, my dear fellow, I simply had to pop across the street."

"Most decidedly," said Psmith. "Always pop across streets. It is the secret of a happy and successful life."

Lord Emsworth looked at him a little perplexedly, and wondered if he had caught the last remark correctly. But his mind had never been designed for the purpose of dwelling closely on problems for any length of time, and he let it go.

"Beautiful roses that man has," he observed. "Really an extraordinarily fine display."

"Indeed?" said Psmith.

"Nothing to touch mine, though. I wish, my dear fellow, you could have been down at Blandings at the beginning of the month. My roses were at their best then. It's too bad you weren't there to see them."

"The fault no doubt was mine," said Psmith.

"Of course you weren't in England then."

"Ah! That explains it."

"Still, I shall have plenty of flowers to show you when you are at Blandings, I expect," said Lord Emsworth, at last showing a host-like disposition to give his guest a belated innings, "I expect you'll write one of your poems about my gardens, eh?"

Psmith was conscious of a feeling of distinct gratification. Weeks of toil among the herrings of Billingsgate had left him with a sort of haunting fear that even in private life there clung to him the miasma of the fish market. Yet here was a perfectly unprejudiced observer looking squarely at him and mistaking him for a poet— showing that in spite of all he had gone through there must still be something notably spiritual and unfishy about his outward appearance.

"Very possibly," he said, "very possibly."

"I suppose you get ideas for your poetry from all sorts of things," said Lord Emsworth, nobly resisting the temptation to collar the conversation again. He was feeling extremely friendly towards this poet fellow. It was deuced civil of him not to be put out and huffy at being left alone in the smoking-room.

"From practically everything," said Psmith, "except fish."

"Fish?"

"I have never written a poem about fish."

"No?" said Lord Emsworth, again feeling that a pin had worked loose in the machinery of the conversation.

"I was once offered a princely sum," went on Psmith, now floating happily along on the tide of his native exuberance, "to write a ballad for the *Fishmonger's Gazette* entitled, 'Herbert the Turbot.' But I was firm. I declined."

"Indeed?" said Lord Emsworth.

"One has one's self-respect," said Psmith.

"Oh, decidedly," said Lord Emsworth.

"It was painful, of course. The editor broke down completely when he realised that my refusal was final. However, I sent him on with a letter of introduction to John Drinkwater, who, I believe, turned him out quite a good little effort on the theme."

At this moment, when Lord Emsworth was feeling a trifle dizzy, and Psmith, on whom conversation always acted as a mental stimulus, was on the point of plunging even deeper into the agreeable depths of light persiflage, a waiter approached.

"A lady to see you, your lordship."

"Eh? Ah, yes, of course, of course. I was expecting her. It is a Miss —— what is the name? Holliday? Halliday. It is a Miss Halliday," he said in explanation to Psmith, "who is coming down to Blandings to catalogue the library. My secretary, Baxter, told her to call here and see me. If you will excuse me for a moment, my dear fellow?"

"Certainly."

As Lord Emsworth disappeared, it occurred to Psmith that the moment had arrived for him to get his hat and steal softly out of the other's life for ever. Only so could confusion and embarrassing explanations be avoided. And it was Psmith's guiding rule in life always to avoid explanations. It might, he felt, cause Lord Emsworth a momentary pang when he returned to the smoking-room and found that he was a poet short, but what is that in these modern days when poets are so plentiful that it is almost impossible to fling a brick in any public place without damaging some stern young singer. Psmith's view of the matter was that, if Lord Emsworth was bent on associating with poets, there was bound to be another one along in a minute. He was on the point, therefore, of rising, when the laziness induced by a good lunch decided him to remain in his comfortable chair for a few minutes longer. He was in one of those moods of rare tranquillity which it is rash to break.

He lit another cigarette, and his thoughts, as they had done after the departure of Mr. McTodd, turned dreamily in the direction of the girl he had met at Miss Clarkson's Employment Bureau. He mused upon her with a gentle melancholy. Sad, he felt, that two obviously kindred spirits like himself and her should meet in the whirl of London life, only to separate again—presumably for ever —simply because the etiquette governing those who are created male and female forbids a man to cement a chance acquaintanceship by ascertaining the lady's name and address, asking her to lunch, and swearing eternal friendship. He sighed as he gazed thoughtfully out of the lower smoking-room window. As he had indicated in his conversation with Mr. Walderwick, those blue eyes and that cheerful, friendly face had made a deep impression on him. Who was she? Where did she live? And was he ever to see her again?

He was. Even as he asked himself the question, two figures came down the steps of the club, and paused. One was Lord Emsworth, without his hat. The other—and Psmith's usually orderly heart gave a spasmodic bound at the sight of her—was the very girl who was occupying his thoughts. There she stood, as blue-eyed, as fair-haired, as indescribably jolly and charming as ever.

Psmith rose from his chair with a vehemence almost equal to that recently displayed by Mr. McTodd. It was his intention to add himself immediately to the group. He raced across the room in a manner that drew censorious glances from the local greybeards, many of whom had half a mind to write to the committee about it.

But when he reached the open air the pavement at the foot of the club steps was empty. The girl was just van-

ishing round the corner into the Strand, and of Lord
Emsworth there was no sign whatever.

By this time, however, Psmith had acquired a useful
working knowledge of his lordship's habits, and he knew
where to look. He crossed the street and headed for the
florist's shop.

"Ah, my dear fellow," said his lordship amiably, suspending his conversation with the proprietor on the subject of delphiniums, "must you be off? Don't forget that
our train leaves Paddington at five sharp. You take your
ticket for Market Blandings."

Psmith had come into the shop merely with the intention of asking his lordship if he happened to know Miss
Halliday's address, but these words opened out such a
vista of attractive possibilities that he had abandoned this
tame programme immediately. He remembered now that
among Mr. McTodd's remarks on things in general had
been one to the effect that he had received an invitation
to visit Blandings Castle—of which invitation he did not
propose to avail himself; and he argued that if he had
acted as substitute for Mr. McTodd at the club, he might
well continue the kindly work by officiating for him at
Blandings. Looking at the matter altruistically, he woul l
prevent his kind host much disappointment by taking th s
course; and, looking at it from a more personal view-
point, only by going to Blandings could he renew his
acquaintance with this girl. Psmith had never been on?
of those who hang back diffidently when Adventure call .
and he did not hang back now.

"At five sharp," he said. "I will be there."

"Capital, my dear fellow," said his lordship.

"Does Miss Halliday travel with us?"

"Eh? No, she is coming down in a day or two."

"I shall look forward to meeting her," said Psmith.

He turned to the door, and Lord Emsworth with a farewell beam resumed his conversation with the florist.

CHAPTER VII

§ 1

THE five o'clock train, having given itself a spasmodic jerk, began to move slowly out of Paddington Station. The platform past which it was gliding was crowded with a number of the fauna always to be seen at railway stations at such moments, but in their ranks there was no sign of Mr. Ralston McTodd: and Psmith, as he sat opposite Lord Emsworth in a corner seat of a first-class compartment, felt that genial glow of satisfaction which comes to the man who has successfully taken a chance. Until now, he had been half afraid that McTodd, having changed his mind, might suddenly appear with bag and baggage—an event which must necessarily have caused confusion and discomfort. His mind was now tranquil. Concerning the future he declined to worry. It would, no doubt, contain its little difficulties, but he was prepared to meet them in the right spirit; and his only trouble in the world now was the difficulty he was experiencing in avoiding his lordship's legs, which showed a disposition to pervade the compartment like the tentacles of an octopus. Lord Emsworth rather ran to leg, and his practice of reclining when at ease on the base of his spine was causing him to straddle, like Apollyon in Pilgrim's Progress, "right across the way." It became manifest that in a journey lasting several hours his society was likely to

121

prove irksome. For the time being, however, he endured it, and listened with polite attention to his host's remarks on the subject of the Blandings gardens. Lord Emsworth, in a train moving in the direction of home, was behaving like a horse heading for his stable. He snorted eagerly, and spoke at length and with emotion of roses and herbaceous borders.

"It will be dark, I suppose, by the time we arrive," he said regretfully, "but the first thing to-morrow, my dear fellow, I must take you round and show you my gardens."

"I shall look forward to it keenly," said Psmith. "They are, I can readily imagine, distinctly oojah-cum-spiff."

"I beg your pardon?" said Lord Emsworth with a start.

"Not at all," said Psmith graciously.

"Er—what did you say?" asked his lordship after a slight pause.

"I was saying that, from all reports, you must have a very nifty display of garden-produce at your rural seat."

"Oh, yes. Oh, most," said his lordship, looking puzzled. He examined Psmith across the compartment with something of the peering curiosity which he would have bestowed upon a new and unclassified shrub. "Most extraordinary!" he murmured. "I trust, my dear fellow, you will not think me personal, but, do you know, nobody would imagine that you were a poet. You don't look like a poet, and, dash it, you don't talk like a poet."

"How should a poet talk?"

"Well . . ." Lord Emsworth considered the point. "Well, Miss Peavey . . . But of course you don't know Miss Peavey . . . Miss Peavey is a poetess, and she waylaid me the other morning while I was having a most important conference with McAllister on the subject of bulbs and asked me if I didn't think that it was fairies' teardrops that made the dew. Did you ever hear such dashed nonsense?"

"Evidently an aggravated case. Is Miss Peavey staying at the castle?"

"My dear fellow, you couldn't shift her with blasting-powder. Really this craze of my sister Constance for filling the house with these infernal literary people is getting on my nerves. I can't stand these poets and what not. Never could."

"We must always remember, however," said Psmith gravely, "that poets are also God's creatures."

"Good heavens!" exclaimed his lordship, aghast. "I had forgotten that you were one. What will you think of me, my dear fellow! But, of course, as I said a moment ago, you are different. I admit that when Constance told me that she had invited you to the house I was not cheered, but, now that I have had the pleasure of meeting you . . ."

The conversation had worked round to the very point to which Psmith had been wishing to direct it. He was keenly desirous of finding out why Mr. McTodd had been invited to Blandings and—a still more vital matter—of ascertaining whether, on his arrival there as Mr. McTodd's understudy, he was going to meet people who knew the poet by sight. On this latter point, it seemed to him, hung the question of whether he was about to enjoy a delightful visit to a historic country house in the society of Eve Halliday—or leave the train at the next stop and omit to return to it.

"It was extremely kind of Lady Constance," he hazarded, "to invite a perfect stranger to Blandings."

"Oh, she's always doing that sort of thing," said his lordship. "It didn't matter to her that she'd never seen you in her life. She had read your books, you know, and liked them: and when she heard that you were coming to England, she wrote to you."

"I see," said Psmith, relieved.

"Of course, it is all right as it has turned out," said Lord Emsworth handsomely. "As I say, you're different. And how you came to write that . . . that . . ."

"Bilge?" suggested Psmith.

"The very word I was about to employ, my dear fellow . . . No, no, I don't mean that . . . I—I . . . Capital stuff, no doubt, capital stuff . . . but . . ."

"I understand."

"Constance tried to make me read the things, but I couldn't. I fell asleep over them."

"I hope you rested well."

"I—er—the fact is, I suppose they were beyond me. I couldn't see any sense in the things."

"If you would care to have another pop at them," said Psmith agreeably, "I have a complete set in my bag."

"No, no, my dear fellow, thank you very much, thank you a thousand times. I—er—find that reading in the train tries my eyes."

"Ah! You would prefer that I read them aloud?"

"No, no." A look of hunted alarm came into his lordship's speaking countenance at the suggestion. "As a matter of fact, I generally take a short nap at the beginning of a railway journey. I find it refreshing and—er—in short, refreshing. You will excuse me?"

"If you think you can get to sleep all right without the aid of my poems, certainly."

"You won't think me rude?"

"Not at all, not at all. By the way, am I likely to meet any old friends at Blandings?"

"Eh? Oh, no. There will be nobody but ourselves. Except my sister and Miss Peavey, of course. You said you had not met Miss Peavey, I think?"

"I have not had that pleasure. I am, of course, looking forward to it with the utmost keenness."

Lord Emsworth eyed him for a moment, astonished: then concluded the conversation by closing his eyes defensively. Psmith was left to his reflections, which a few minutes later were interrupted by a smart kick on the shin, as Lord Emsworth, a jumpy sleeper, began to throw his long legs about. Psmith moved to the other end of the seat, and, taking his bag down from the rack, extracted a slim volume bound in squashy mauve. After gazing at this in an unfriendly manner for a moment, he opened it at random and began to read. His first move on leaving Lord Emsworth at the florist's had been to spend a portion of his slender capital on the works of Ralston McTodd in order not to be taken at a disadvantage in the event of questions about them at Blandings: but he speedily realised, as he dipped into the poems, that anything in the nature of a prolonged study of them was likely to spoil his little holiday. They were not light summer reading.

"Across the pale parabola of Joy . . ."

A gurgling snort from the other end of the compartment abruptly detached his mind from its struggle with this mystic line. He perceived that his host had slipped even further down on to his spine and was now lying with open mouth in an attitude suggestive of dislocation. And as he looked, there was a whistling sound, and another snore proceeded from the back of his lordship's throat.

Psmith rose and took his book of poems out into the corridor with the purpose of roaming along the train until he should find an empty compartment in which to read in peace.

With the two adjoining compartments he had no luck. One was occupied by an elderly man with a retriever, while the presence of a baby in the other ruled it out of consideration. The third, however, looked more promising. It was not actually empty, but there was only one occupant, and he was asleep. He was lying back in the far corner with a large silk handkerchief draped over his face and his feet propped up on the seat opposite. His society did not seem likely to act as a bar to the study of Mr. McTodd's masterpieces. Psmith sat down and resumed his reading.

"Across the pale parabola of Joy . . ."

Psmith knitted his brow. It was just the sort of line which was likely to have puzzled his patroness, Lady Constance, and he anticipated that she would come to him directly he arrived and ask for an explanation. It would obviously be a poor start for his visit to confess that he had no theory as to its meaning himself. He tried it again.

"Across the pale parabola of Joy . . ."

A sound like two or three pigs feeding rather noisily in the middle of a thunderstorm interrupted his meditations. Psmith laid his book down and gazed in a pained way across the compartment. There came to him a sense of being unfairly put upon, as towards the end of his troubles it might have come upon Job. This, he felt, was too much. He was being harried.

The man in the corner went on snoring.

. . . .

There is always a way. Almost immediately Psmith saw what Napoleon would have done in this crisis. On the seat beside the sleeper was lying a compact little suit-case with hard, sharp edges. Rising softly, Psmith edged along the compartment and secured this. Then, having balanced it carefully on the rack above the sleeper's stomach, he returned to his seat to await developments.

These were not long in coming. The train, now flying at its best speed through open country, was shaking itself at intervals in a vigorous way as it raced along. A few seconds later it apparently passed over some points, and shivered briskly down its whole length. The suit-case wobbled insecurely, hesitated, and fell chunkily in the exact middle of its owner's waistcoat. There was a smothered gulp beneath the handkerchief. The sleeper sat up with a jerk. The handkerchief fell off. And there was revealed to Psmith's interested gaze the face of the Hon. Freddie Threepwood.

§ 2

"Goo!" observed Freddie. He removed the bag from his midriff and began to massage the stricken spot. Then suddenly perceiving that he was not alone he looked up and saw Psmith.

"Goo!" said Freddie, and sat staring wildly.

Nobody is more alive than we are to the fact that the dialogue of Frederick Threepwood, recorded above, is not bright. Nevertheless, those were his opening remarks, and the excuse must be that he had passed through a trying time and had just received two shocks, one after the other. From the first of these, the physical impact of the suit-case, he was recovering; but the second had simply paralysed him. When, the mists of sleep having cleared away, he saw sitting but a few feet away from him on the train that was carrying him home the very man with whom he had plotted in the lobby of the Piccadilly Palace Hotel, a cold fear gripped Freddie's very vitals.

Freddie's troubles had begun when he just missed the twelve-fifty train. This disaster had perturbed him greatly, for he could not forget his father's stern injunctions on the subject. But what had really upset him was the fact that he had come within an ace of missing the five o'clock train as well. He had spent the afternoon in a motion-picture palace, and the fascination of the film had caused him to lose all sense of time, so that only the slow fade-out on the embrace and the words "The End" reminded him to look at his watch. A mad rush had got him to Paddington just as the five o'clock express was leaving the station. Exhausted, he had fallen into a troubled sleep, from which he had been aroused by a violent blow in the waistcoat and the nightmare vision of Psmith in the seat across the compartment. One cannot wonder in these circumstances that Freddie did not immediately soar to the heights of eloquence.

The picture which the Hon. Frederick Threepwood had selected for his patronage that afternoon was the well-known super-super-film, "Fangs of the Past," featuring Bertha Blevitch and Maurice Heddlestone—which, as everybody knows, is all about blackmail. Green-walled by primeval hills, bathed in the golden sunshine of peace and happiness, the village of Honeydean slumbered in the clear morning air. But off the train from the city stepped A Stranger—(The Stranger—Maxwell Bannister). He inquired of a passing rustic—(The Passing Rustic—Claude Hepworth)—the way to the great house where Myrtle Dale, the Lady Bountiful of the village . . . well, anyway, it is all about blackmail, and it had affected Freddie profoundly. It still coloured his imagination, and the conclusion to which he came the moment he saw Psmith was that the latter had shadowed him and was following him home with the purpose of extracting hush-money.

While he was still gurgling wordlessly, Psmith opened the conversation.

"A delightful and unexpected pleasure, comrade. I thought you had left the metropolis some hours since."

As Freddie sat looking like a cornered dormouse a voice from the corridor spoke.

"Ah, there you are, my dear fellow!"

Lord Emsworth was beaming in the doorway. His slumbers, like those of Freddie, had not lasted long. He had been aroused only a few minutes after Psmith's departure by the arrival of the retriever from the next compartment, which, bored by the society of its owner, had strolled off on a tour of investigation and, finding next door an old acquaintance in the person of his lordship, had jumped on the seat and licked his face with such hearty good will that further sleep was out of the question. Being awake, Lord Emsworth, as always when he was awake, had begun to potter.

When he saw Freddie his amiability suffered a shock.

"Frederick! I thought I told you to be sure to return on the twelve-fifty train!"

"Missed it, guv'nor," mumbled Freddie thickly. "Not my fault."

"H'mph!" His father seemed about to pursue the subject, but the fact that a stranger and one who was his guest was present apparently decided him to avoid anything in the shape of family wrangles. He peered from Freddie to Psmith and back again. "Do you two know each other?" he said.

"Not yet," said Psmith. "We only met a moment ago."

"My son Frederick," said Lord Emsworth, rather in the voice with which he would have called attention to the presence of a slug among his flowers. "Frederick, this is Mr. McTodd, the poet, who is coming to stay at Blandings."

Freddie started, and his mouth opened. But, meeting Psmith's friendly gaze, he closed the orifice again without speaking. He licked his lips in an overwrought way.

"You'll find me next door, if you want me," said Lord Emsworth to Psmith. "Just discovered that George Willard, very old friend of mine, is in there. Never saw him get on the train. His dog came into my compartment and licked my face. One of my neighbours. A remarkable rose-grower. As you are so interested in flowers, I will take you over to his place some time. Why don't you join us now?"

"I would prefer, if you do not mind," said Psmith, "to remain here for the moment and foster what I feel sure is about to develop into a great and lasting friendship. I am convinced that your son and I will have much to talk about together."

"Very well, my dear fellow. We will meet at dinner in the restaurant-car."

Lord Emsworth pottered off, and Psmith rose and closed the door. He returned to his seat to find Freddie regarding him with a tortured expression in his rather prominent eyes. Freddie's brain had had more exercise in the last few minutes than in years of his normal life, and he was feeling the strain.

"I say, what?" he observed feebly.

"If there is anything," said Psmith kindly, "that I can do to clear up any little difficulty that is perplexing you, call on me. What is biting you?"

Freddie swallowed convulsively.

"I say, he said your name was McTodd!"

"Precisely."

"But you said it was Psmith."

"It is."

"Then why did father call you McTodd?"

"He thinks I am. It is a harmless error, and I see no reason why it should be discouraged."

"But why does he think you're McTodd?"

"It is a long story, which you may find tedious. But, if you really wish to hear it . . ."

Nothing could have exceeded the raptness of Freddie's attention as he listened to the tale of the encounter with Lord Emsworth at the Senior Conservative Club.

"Do you mean to say," he demanded at its conclusion,

"that you're coming to Blandings pretending to be this poet blighter?"

"That is the scheme."

"But why?"

"I have my reasons, Comrade—what is the name? Threepwood? I thank you. You will pardon me, Comrade Threepwood, if I do not go into them. And now," said Psmith, "to resume our very interesting chat which was unfortunately cut short this morning, why do you want me to steal your aunt's necklace?"

Freddie jumped. For the moment, so tensely had the fact of his companion's audacity chained his interest, he had actually forgotten about the necklace.

"Great Scott!" he exclaimed. "Why, of course!"

"You still have not made it quite clear."

"It fits splendidly."

"The necklace?"

"I mean to say, the great difficulty would have been to find a way of getting you into the house, and here you are, coming there as this poet bird. Topping!"

"If," said Psmith, regarding him patiently through his eyeglass, "I do not seem to be immediately infected by your joyous enthusiasm, put it down to the fact that I haven't the remotest idea what you're talking about. Could you give me a pointer or two? What, for instance, assuming that I agreed to steal your aunt's necklace, would you expect me to do with it, when and if stolen?"

"Why, hand it over to me."

"I see. And what would you do with it?"

"Hand it over to my uncle."

"And whom would he hand it over to?"

"Look here," said Freddie, "I might as well start at the beginning."

"An excellent idea."

The speed at which the train was now proceeding had begun to render conversation in anything but stentorian tones somewhat difficulty. Freddie accordingly bent forward till his mouth almost touched Psmith's ear.

"You see, it's like this. My uncle, old Joe Keeble . . ."

"Keeble?" said Psmith. "Why," he murmured meditatively, "is that name familiar?"

"Don't interrupt, old lad," pleaded Freddie.

"I stand corrected."

"Uncle Joe has a stepdaughter—Phyllis her name is—and some time ago she popped off and married a cove called Jackson . . ."

Psmith did not interrupt the narrative again, but as it proceeded his look of interest deepened. And at the conclusion he patted his companion encouragingly on the shoulder.

"The proceeds, then, of this jewel-robbery, if it comes off," he said, "will go to establish the Jackson home on a firm footing? Am I right in thinking that?"

"Absolutely."

"There is no danger—you will pardon the suggestion—of you clinging like glue to the swag and using it to maintain yourself in the position to which you are accustomed?"

"Absolutely not. Uncle Joe is giving me—er—giving me a bit for myself. Just a small bit, you understand. This is the scheme. You sneak the necklace and hand it over to me. I push the necklace over to Uncle Joe, who hides it somewhere for the moment. There is the dickens of a fuss, and Uncle Joe comes out strong by telling Aunt Constance that he'll buy her another necklace, just as good. Then he takes the stones out of the necklace, has them reset, and gives them to Aunt Constance. Looks like a new necklace, if you see what I mean. Then he draws a cheque for twenty thousand quid, which Aunt Constance naturally thinks is for the new necklace, and he shoves the money somewhere as a little private account. He gives Phyllis her money, and everybody's happy. Aunt Constance has got her necklace, Phyllis has got her money, and all that's happened is that Aunt Constance's and Uncle Joe's combined bank balance has had a bit of a hole knocked in it. See?"

"I see. It is a little difficult to follow all the necklaces. I seemed to count about seventeen of them while you were talking, but I suppose I was wrong. Yes, I see, Comrade Threepwood, and I may say at once that you can rely on my co-operation."

"You'll do it?"

"I will."

"Of course," said Freddie awkwardly, "I'll see that you get a bit all right. I mean . . ."

Psmith waved his hand deprecatingly.

"My dear Comrade Threepwood, let us not become sordid on this glad occasion. As far as I am concerned, there will be no charge."

"What! But look here . . ."

"Any assistance I can give will be offered in a purely amateur spirit. I would have mentioned before, only I was reluctant to interrupt you, that Comrade Jackson is my boyhood chum, and that Phyllis, his wife, injects into my life the few beams of sunshine that illumine its dreary round. I have long desired to do something to ameliorate their lot, and now that the chance has come I am delighted. It is true that I am not a man of affluence—my bank-manager, I am told, winces in a rather painful manner whenever my name is mentioned—but I am not so reduced that I must charge a fee for performing, on behalf of a pal, a simple act of courtesy like pinching a twenty thousand pound necklace."

"Good Lord! Fancy that!"

"Fancy what, Comrade Threepwood?"

"Fancy your knowing Phyllis and her husband."

"It is odd, no doubt. But true. Many a whack at the cold beef have I had on Sunday evenings under their roof, and I am much obliged to you for putting in my way this opportunity of repaying their hospitality. Thank you!"

"Oh, that's all right," said Freddie, somewhat bewildered by this eloquence.

"Even if the little enterprise meets with disaster, the reflection that I did my best for the young couple will be a great consolation to me when I am serving my bit of time in Wormwood Scrubbs. It will cheer me up. The jailers will cluster outside the door to listen to me singing in my cell. My pet rat, as he creeps out to share the crumbs of my breakfast, will wonder why I whistle as I pick the morning's oakum. I shall join in the hymns on Sundays in a way that will electrify the chaplain. That is to say, if anything goes wrong and I am what I believe is technically termed 'copped.' I say 'if,'" said Psmith, gazing solemnly at his companion. "But I do not intend to be copped. I have never gone in largely for crime

hitherto), but something tells me I shall be rather good at
it. I look forward confidently to making a nice, clean
job of the thing. And now, Comrade Threepwood, I must
ask you to excuse me while I get the half-nelson on this
rather poisonous poetry of good old McTodd's. From
the cursory glance I have taken at it, the stuff doesn't
seem to mean anything. I think the boy's *non compos*.
You don't happen to understand the expression 'Across
the pale parabola of Joy,' do you? . . . I feared as much.
Well, pip-pip for the present, Comrade Threepwood. I
shall now ask you to retire into your corner and amuse
yourself for awhile as you best can. I must concentrate,
concentrate."

And Psmith, having put his feet up on the opposite seat
and reopened the mauve volume, began to read. Freddie,
his mind still in a whirl, looked out of the window at the
passing scenery in a mood which was a nice blend of ela-
tion and apprehension.

§ 3

Although the hands of the station clock pointed to several minutes past nine, it was still apparently early
evening when the train drew up at the platform of Market
Blandings and discharged its distinguished passengers.
The sun, taken in as usual by the never-failing practical
joke of the Daylight Saving Act, had only just set, and
a golden afterglow lingered on the fields as the car which
had met the train purred over the two miles of country
road that separated the little town from the castle. As
they passed in between the great stone gate-posts and shot
up the winding drive, the soft murmur of the engines

seemed to deepen rather than break the soothing stillness.
The air was fragrant with indescribable English scents.
Somewhere in the distance sheep-bells tinkled; rabbits,
waggling white tails, bolted across the path; and once a
herd of agitated deer made a brief appearance among the
trees. The only thing that disturbed the magic hush was
the fluting voice of Lord Emsworth, on whom the spectacle of his beloved property had acted as an immediate
stimulant. Unlike his son Freddie, who sat silent in his
corner wrestling with his hopes and fears, Lord Emsworth
had plunged into a perfect Niagara of speech the moment
the car entered the park. In a high tenor voice, and with
wide, excited gestures, he pointed out to Psmith oaks with
a history and rhododendrons with a past: his conversation
as they drew near the castle and came in sight of the
flower-beds taking on an almost lyrical note and becoming
a sort of anthem of gladness, through which, like some
theme in the minor, ran a series of opprobrious observations on the subject of Angus McAllister.

Beach, the butler, solicitously scooping them out of the
car at the front door, announced that her ladyship and
Miss Peavey were taking their after-dinner coffee in the
arbour by the bowling-green; and presently Psmith, conducted by his lordship, found himself shaking hands with
a strikingly handsome woman in whom, though her manner was friendliness itself, he could detect a marked suggestion of the formidable. Æsthetically, he admired Lady
Constance's appearance, but he could not conceal from
himself that in the peculiar circumstances he would have
preferred something rather more fragile and drooping.
Lady Constance conveyed the impression that anybody
who had the choice between stealing anything from her and

stirring up a nest of hornets with a short walking-stick would do well to choose the hornets.

"How do you do, Mr. McTodd?" said Lady Constance with great amiability. "I am so glad you were able to come after all."

Psmith wondered what she meant by "after all," but there were so many things about his present situation calculated to tax the mind that he had no desire to probe slight verbal ambiguities. He shook her hand and replied that it was very kind of her to say so.

"We are quite a small party at present," continued Lady Constance, "but we are expecting a number of people quite soon. For the moment Aileen and you are our only guests. Oh, I am sorry, I should have . . . Miss Peavey, Mr. McTodd."

The slim and willowy female who during this brief conversation had been waiting in an attitude of suspended animation, gazing at Psmith with large, wistful eyes, stepped forward. She clasped Psmith's hand in hers, held it, and in a low, soft voice, like thick cream made audible, uttered one reverent word.

"Maître!"

"I beg your pardon?" said Psmith. A young man capable of bearing himself with calm and dignity in most circumstances, however trying, he found his poise wobbling under the impact of Miss Aileen Peavey.

Miss Peavey often had this effect on the less soulful type of man, especially in the mornings, when such men are not at their strongest and best. When she came into the breakfast-room of a country house, brave men who had been up a bit late the night before quailed and tried to hide behind newspapers. She was the sort of woman who tells a man who is propping his eyes open with his fingers and endeavouring to correct a headache with strong tea, that she was up at six watching the dew fade off the grass, and didn't he think that those wisps of morning mist were the elves' bridal-veils. She had large, fine, melancholy eyes, and was apt to droop dreamily.

"Master!" said Miss Peavey, obligingly translating.

There did not seem to be any immediate come-back to a remark like this, so Psmith contented himself with beaming genially at her through his monocle: and Miss Peavey came to bat again.

"How wonderful that you were able to come—after all!"

Again this "after all" motive creeping into the theme. . . .

"You know Miss Peavey's work, of course?" said Lady Constance, smiling pleasantly on her two celebrities.

"Who does not?" said Psmith courteously.

"Oh *do* you?" said Miss Peavey, gratification causing her slender body to perform a sort of ladylike shimmy down its whole length. "I scarcely hoped that you would know my name. My Canadian sales have not been large."

"Quite large enough," said Psmith. "I mean, of course," he added with a paternal smile, "that, while your delicate art may not have a universal appeal in a young country, it is intensely appreciated by a small and select body of the intelligentsia."

And if that was not the stuff to give them, he reflected with not a little complacency, he was dashed.

"Your own wonderful poems," replied Miss Peavey, "are, of course, known the whole world over. Oh, Mr. McTodd, you can hardly appreciate how I feel, meeting you. It is like the realisation of some golden dream of childhood. It is like . . ."

Here the Hon. Freddie Threepwood remarked suddenly that he was going to pop into the house for a whisky and soda. As he had not previously spoken, his observation had something of the effect of a voice from the tomb. The daylight was ebbing fast now, and in the shadows he had contrived to pass out of sight as well as out of mind. Miss Peavey started like an abruptly awakened somnambulist, and Psmith was at least able to release his hand, which he had begun to look on as gone beyond his control for ever. Until this fortunate interruption there had seemed no reason why Miss Peavey should not have continued to hold it till bedtime.

Freddie's departure had the effect of breaking a spell. Lord Emsworth, who had been standing perfectly still with vacant eyes, like a dog listening to a noise a long way off, came to life with a jerk.

"I'm going to have a look at my flowers," he announced.

"Don't be silly, Clarence," said his sister. "It's much too dark to see flowers."

"I could smell 'em," retorted his lordship argumentatively.

It seemed as if the party must break up, for already his lordship had begun to potter off, when a new-comer arrived to solidify it again.

"Ah, Baxter, my dear fellow," said Lord Emsworth. "Here we are, you see."

"Mr. Baxter," said Lady Constance, "I want you to meet Mr. McTodd."

"Mr. McTodd!" said the new arrival, on a note of surprise.

"Yes, he found himself able to come after all."

"Ah!" said the Efficient Baxter.

It occurred to Psmith as a passing thought, to which he gave no more than a momentary attention, that this spectacled and capable-looking man was gazing at him, as they shook hands, with a curious intensity. But possibly, he reflected, this was merely a species of optical illusion due to the other's spectacles. Baxter, staring through his spectacles, often gave people the impression of possessing an eye that could pierce six inches of Harvey-ised steel and stick out on the other side. Having registered in his consciousness the fact that he had been stared at keenly by this stranger, Psmith thought no more of the matter.

In thus lightly dismissing the Baxterian stare, Psmith had acted injudiciously. He should have examined it more closely and made an effort to analyse it, for it was by no means without its message. It was a stare of suspicion. Vague suspicion as yet, but nevertheless suspicion. Rupert Baxter was one of those men whose chief characteristic is a disposition to suspect their fellows. He did not suspect them of this or that definite crime: he simply suspected them. He had not yet definitely accused Psmith in his mind of any specific tort or malfeasance. He merely had a nebulous feeling that he would bear watching.

Miss Peavey now fluttered again into the centre of things. On the arrival of Baxter she had withdrawn for a moment into the background, but she was not the woman to stay there long. She came forward holding out a small oblong book, which, with a languishing firmness, she pressed into Psmith's hands.

"Could I persuade you, Mr. McTodd," said Miss Peavey pleadingly, "to write some little thought in my autograph-book and sign it? I have a fountain-pen."

Light flooded the arbour. The Efficient Baxter, who knew where everything was, had found and pressed the switch. He did this not so much to oblige Miss Peavey as to enable him to obtain a clearer view of the visitor. With each minute that passed the Efficient Baxter was finding himself more and more doubtful in his mind about this visitor.

"There!" said Miss Peavey, welcoming the illumination.

Psmith tapped his chin thoughtfully with the fountain-pen. He felt that he should have foreseen this emergency earlier. If ever there was a woman who was bound to have an autograph-book, that woman was Miss Peavey.

"Just some little thought . . ."

Psmith hesitated no longer. In a firm hand he wrote the words "Across the pale parabola of Joy . . ." added an unfaltering "Ralston McTodd," and handed the book back.

"How strange," sighed Miss Peavey.

"May I look?" said Baxter, moving quickly to her side.

"How strange!" repeated Miss Peavey. "To think that you should have chosen that line! There are several of your more mystic passages that I meant to ask you to explain, but particularly 'Across the pale parabola of Joy' . . ."

"You find it difficult to understand?"

"A little, I confess."

"Well, well," said Psmith indulgently, "perhaps I did put a bit of top-spin on that one."

"I beg your pardon?"

"I say, perhaps it is a little obscure. We must have a long chat about it—later on."

"Why not now?" demanded the Efficient Baxter, flashing his spectacles.

"I am rather tired," said Psmith with gentle reproach, "after my journey. Fatigued. We artists . . ."

"Of course," said Miss Peavey, with an indignant glance at the secretary. "Mr. Baxter does not understand the sensitive poetic temperament."

"A bit unspiritual, eh?" said Psmith tolerantly. "A trifle earthy? So I thought, so I thought. One of these strong, hard men of affairs, I shouldn't wonder."

"Shall we go and find Lord Emsworth, Mr. McTodd?" said Miss Peavey, dismissing the fermenting Baxter with a scornful look. "He wandered off just now. I suppose he is among his flowers. Flowers are very beautiful by night."

"Indeed, yes," said Psmith. "And also by day. When I am surrounded by flowers, a sort of divine peace floods over me, and the rough, harsh world seems far away. I feel soothed, tranquil. I sometimes think, Miss Peavey, that flowers must be the souls of little children who have died in their innocence."

"What a beautiful thought, Mr. McTodd!" exclaimed Miss Peavey rapturously.

"Yes," agreed Psmith. "Don't pinch it. It's copyright."

The darkness swallowed them up. Lady Constance turned to the Efficient Baxter, who was brooding with furrowed brow.

"Charming, is he not?"

"I beg your pardon?"

"I said I thought Mr. McTodd was charming."

"Oh, quite."

"Completely unspoiled."

"Oh, decidedly."

"I am so glad that he was able to come after all. That telegram he sent this afternoon cancelling his visit seemed so curt and final."

"So I thought it."

"Almost as if he had taken offence at something and decided to have nothing to do with us."

"Quite."

Lady Constance shivered delicately. A cool breeze had sprung up. She drew her wrap more closely about her shapely shoulders, and began to walk to the house. Baxter did not accompany her. The moment she had gone he switched off the light and sat down, chin in hand. That massive brain was working hard.

CHAPTER VIII

§ 1

"MISS HALLIDAY," announced the Efficient Baxter, removing another letter from its envelope and submitting it to a swift, keen scrutiny, "arrives at about three to-day. She is catching the twelve-fifty train."

He placed the letter on the pile beside his plate; and, having decapitated an egg, peered sharply into its interior as if hoping to surprise guilty secrets. For it was the breakfast hour, and the members of the house party, scattered up and down the long table, were fortifying their tissues against another day. An agreeable scent of bacon floated over the scene like a benediction.

Lord Emsworth looked up from the seed catalogue in which he was immersed. For some time past his enjoyment of the meal had been marred by a vague sense of something missing, and now he knew what it was.

"Coffee!" he said, not violently, but in the voice of a good man oppressed. "I want coffee. Why have I no coffee? Constance, my dear, I should have coffee. Why have I none?"

"I'm sure I gave you some," said Lady Constance, brightly presiding over the beverages at the other end of the table.

"Then where is it?" demanded his lordship clinchingly.

Baxter—almost regretfully, it seemed—gave the egg a

clean bill of health, and turned in his able way to cope
with this domestic problem.

"Your coffee is behind the catalogue you are reading,
Lord Emsworth. You propped the catalogue against your
cup."

"Did I? Did I? Why, so I did! Bless my soul!"
His lordship, relieved, took an invigorating sip. "What
were you saying just then, my dear fellow?"

"I have had a letter from Miss Halliday," said Baxter.
"She writes that she is catching the twelve-fifty train at
Paddington, which means that she should arrive at Market
Blandings at about three."

"Who," asked Miss Peavey, in a low, thrilling voice,
ceasing for a moment to peck at her plate of kedgeree, "is
Miss Halliday?"

"The exact question I was about to ask myself," said
Lord Emsworth. "Baxter, my dear fellow, who is Miss
Halliday?"

Baxter, with a stifled sigh, was about to refresh his employer's memory, when Psmith anticipated him. Psmith
had been consuming toast and marmalade with his customary languid grace and up till now had firmly checked
all attempts to engage him in conversation.

"Miss Halliday," he said, "is a very old and valued
friend of mine. We two have, so to speak, pulled the
gowans fine. I had been hoping to hear that she had been
sighted on the horizon."

The effect of these words on two of the company was
somewhat remarkable. Baxter, hearing them, gave such
a violent start that he spilled half the contents of his cup:
and Freddie, who had been flitting like a butterfly among
the dishes on the sideboard and had just decided to help

himself to scrambled eggs, deposited a liberal spoonful on the carpet, where it was found and salvaged a moment later by Lady Constance's spaniel.

Psmith did not observe these phenomena, for he had returned to his toast and marmalade. He thus missed encountering perhaps the keenest glance that had ever come through Rupert Baxter's spectacles. It was not a protracted glance, but while it lasted it was like the ray from an oxyacetylene blowpipe.

"A friend of yours?" said Lord Emsworth. "Indeed? Of course, Baxter, I remember now. Miss Halliday is the young lady who is coming to catalogue the library."

"What a delightful task!" cooed Miss Peavey. "To live among the stored-up thoughts of dead and gone genius!"

"You had better go down and meet her, my dear fellow," said Lord Emsworth. "At the station, you know," he continued, clarifying his meaning. "She will be glad to see you."

"I was about to suggest it myself," said Psmith.

"Though why the library needs cataloguing," said his lordship, returning to a problem which still vexed his soul when he had leisure to give a thought to it, "I can't . . . However . . ."

He finished his coffee and rose from the table. A stray shaft of sunlight had fallen provocatively on his bald head, and sunshine always made him restive.

"Are you going to your flowers, Lord Emsworth?" asked Miss Peavey.

"Eh? What? Yes. Oh, yes. Going to have a look at those lobelias."

"I will accompany you, if I may," said Psmith.

"Eh? Why, certainly, certainly."

"I have always held," said Psmith, "that there is no finer tonic than a good look at a lobelia immediately after breakfast. Doctors, I believe, recommend it."

"Oh, I say," said Freddie hastily, as he reached the door, "can I have a couple of words with you a bit later on?"

"A thousand if you wish it," said Psmith. "You will find me somewhere out there in the great open spaces where men are men."

He included the entire company in a benevolent smile, and left the room.

"How charming he is!" sighed Miss Peavey. "Don't you think so, Mr. Baxter?"

The Efficient Baxter seemed for a moment to find some difficulty in replying.

"Oh, very," he said, but not heartily.

"And such a *soul!* It shines on that wonderful brow of his, doesn't it?"

"He has a good forehead," said Lady Constance. "But I wish he wouldn't wear his hair so short. Somehow it makes him seem unlike a poet."

Freddie, alarmed, swallowed a mouthful of scrambled egg.

"Oh, he's a poet all right," he said hastily.

"Well, really, Freddie," said Lady Constance, piqued, "I think we hardly need *you* to tell us that."

"No, no, of course. But what I mean is, in spite of his wearing his hair short, you know."

"I ventured to speak to him of that yesterday," said Miss Peavey, "and he said he rather expected to be wearing it even shorter very soon."

"Freddie!" cried Lady Constance with asperity. "What *are* you doing?"

A brown lake of tea was filling the portion of the table-cloth immediately opposite the Hon. Frederick Threepwood. Like the Efficient Baxter a few minutes before, sudden emotion had caused him to upset his cup.

§ 2

The scrutiny of his lordship's lobelias had palled upon Psmith at a fairly early stage in the proceedings, and he was sitting on the terrace wall enjoying a meditative cigarette when Freddie found him.

"Ah, Comrade Threepwood," said Psmith, "welcome to Blandings Castle! You said something about wishing to have speech with me, if I remember rightly?"

The Hon. Freddie shot a nervous glance about him, and seated himself on the wall.

"I say," he said, "I wish you wouldn't say things like that."

"Like what, Comrade Threepwood?"

"What you said to the Peavey woman."

"I recollect having a refreshing chat with Miss Peavey yesterday afternoon," said Psmith, "but I cannot recall saying anything calculated to bring the blush of shame to the cheek of modesty. What observation of mine was it that meets with your censure?"

"Why, that stuff about expecting to wear your hair shorter. If you're going to go about saying that sort of thing—well, dash it, you might just as well give the whole bally show away at once and have done with it."

Psmith nodded gravely.

"Your generous heat, Comrade Threepwood, is not unjustified. It was undoubtedly an error of judgment. If I have a fault—which I am not prepared to admit—it is a perhaps ungentlemanly desire to pull that curious female's leg. A stronger man than myself might well find it hard to battle against the temptation. However, now that you have called it to my notice, it shall not occur again. In future I will moderate the persiflage. Cheer up, therefore, Comrade Threepwood, and let us see that merry smile of yours, of which I hear such good reports."

The appeal failed to alleviate Freddie's gloom. He smote morosely at a fly which had settled on his furrowed brow.

"I'm getting as jumpy as a cat," he said.

"Fight against this unmanly weakness," urged Psmith. "As far as I can see, everything is going along nicely."

"I'm not so sure. I believe that blighter Baxter suspects something."

"What do you think he suspects?"

"Why, that there's something fishy about you."

Psmith winced.

"I would be infinitely obliged to you, Comrade Threepwood, if you would not use that particular adjective. It awakens old memories, all very painful. But let us go more deeply into this matter, for you interest me strangely. Why do you think that cheery old Baxter, a delightful personality if ever I met one, suspects me?"

"It's the way he looks at you."

"I know what you mean, but I attribute no importance to it. As far as I have been able to ascertain during my brief visit, he looks at everybody and everything in precisely the same way. Only last night at dinner I observed him glaring with keen mistrust at about as blameless and innocent a plate of clear soup as was ever dished up. He then proceeded to shovel it down with quite undisguised relish. So possibly you are all wrong about his motive for looking at me like that. It may be admiration."

"Well, I don't like it."

"Nor, from an æsthetic point of view, do I. But we must bear these things manfully. We must remind ourselves that it is Baxter's misfortune rather than his fault that he looks like a dyspeptic lizard."

Freddie was not to be consoled. His gloom deepened.

"And it isn't only Baxter."

"What else is on your mind?"

"The whole atmosphere of the place is getting rummy, if you know what I mean." He bent towards Psmith and whispered pallidly. "I say, I believe that new house-maid is a detective!"

Psmith eyed him patiently.

"Which new housemaid, Comrade Threepwood? Brooding, as I do, pretty tensely all the time on deep and wonderful subjects, I have little leisure to keep tab on the domestic staff. *Is* there a new housemaid?"

"Yes. Susan, her name is."

"Susan? Susan? That sounds all right. Just the name a real housemaid would have."

"Did you ever," demanded Freddie earnestly, "see a real housemaid sweep under a bureau?"

"Does she?"

"Caught her at it in my room this morning."

"But isn't it a trifle far-fetched to imagine that she is a detective? Why should she be a detective?"

"Well, I've seen such a dashed lot of films where the

housemaid or the parlourmaid or what not were detec-
tives. Makes a fellow uneasy."

"Fortunately," said Psmith, "there is no necessity to
remain in a state of doubt. I can give you an unfailing
method by means of which you may discover if she is
what she would have us believe her."

"What's that?"

"Kiss her."

"Kiss her!"

"Precisely. Go to her and say, 'Susan, you're a very
pretty girl . . .'"

"But she isn't."

"We will assume, for purposes of argument, that she
is. Go to her and say, 'Susan, you are a very pretty girl.
What would you do if I were to kiss you?' If she is a
detective, she will reply, 'How dare you, sir!' or, possibly,
more simply, 'Sir!' Whereas if she is the genuine housemaid I believe her to be and only sweeps under bureaux
out of pure zeal, she will giggle and remark, 'Oh, don't
be silly, sir!' You appreciate the distinction?"

"How do you know?"

"My grandmother told me, Comrade Threepwood. My
advice to you, if the state of doubt you are in is affecting
your enjoyment of life, is to put the matter to the test at
the earliest convenient opportunity."

"I'll think it over," said Freddie dubiously.

Silence fell upon him for a space, and Psmith was well
content to have it so. He had no specific need of Freddie's prattle to help him enjoy the pleasant sunshine and
the scent of Angus McAllister's innumerable flowers.
Presently, however, his companion was off again. But
now there was a different note in his voice. Alarm

seemed to have given place to something which appeared to be embarrassment. He coughed several times, and his neatly-shod feet, writhing in self-conscious circles, scraped against the wall.

"I say!"

"You have our ear once more, Comrade Threepwood," said Psmith politely.

"I say, what I really came out here to talk about was something else. I say, are you really a pal of Miss Halliday's?"

"Assuredly. Why?"

"I say!" A rosy blush mantled the Hon. Freddie's young cheek. "I say, I wish you would put in a word for me, then."

"Put in a word for you?"

Freddie gulped.

"I love her, dash it!"

"A noble emotion," said Psmith courteously. "When did you feel it coming on?"

"I've been in love with her for months. But she won't look at me."

"That, of course," agreed Smith, "must be a disadvantage. Yes, I should imagine that that would stick the gaff into the course of true love to no small extent."

"I mean, won't take me seriously, and all that. Laughs at me, don't you know, when I propose. What would you do?"

"I should stop proposing," said Psmith, having given the matter thought.

"But I can't."

"Tut, tut!" said Psmith severely. "And, in case the expression is new to you, what I mean is 'Pooh, pooh!'

Just say to yourself, 'From now on I will not start proposing until after lunch.' That done, it will be an easy step to do no proposing during the afternoon. And by degrees you will find that you can give it up altogether. Once you have conquered the impulse for the after-breakfast proposal, the rest will be easy. The first one of the day is always the hardest to drop."

"I believe she thinks me a mere butterfly," said Freddie, who had not been listening to this most valuable homily.

Psmith slid down from the wall and stretched himself.

"Why," he said, "are butterflies so often described as 'mere'? I have heard them so called a hundred times, and I cannot understand the reason. . . . Well, it would, no doubt, be both interesting and improving to go into the problem, but at this point, Comrade Threepwood, I leave you. I would brood."

"Yes, but, I say, will you?"

"Will I what?"

"Put in a word for me?"

"If," said Psmith, "the subject crops up in the course of the chit-chat, I shall be delighted to spread myself with no little vim on the theme of your fine qualities."

He melted away into the shrubbery, just in time to avoid Miss Peavey, who broke in on Freddie's meditations a moment later and kept him company till lunch.

§ 3

The twelve-fifty train drew up with a grinding of brakes at the platform of Market Blandings, and Psmith, who had been whiling away the time of waiting by squandering money which he could ill afford on the slot-machine which supplied butter-scotch, turned and submitted it to a grave scrutiny. Eve Halliday got out of a third-class compartment.

"Welcome to our village, Miss Halliday," said Psmith, advancing.

Eve regarded him with frank astonishment.

"What are you doing here?" she asked.

"Lord Emsworth was kind enough to suggest that, as we were such old friends, I should come down in the car and meet you."

"Are we old friends?"

"Surely. Have you forgotten all those happy days in London?"

"There was only one."

"True. But think how many meetings we crammed into it."

"Are you staying at the castle?"

"Yes. And what is more, I am the life and soul of the party. Have you anything in the shape of luggage?"

"I nearly always take luggage when I am going to stay a month or so in the country. It's at the back somewhere."

"I will look after it. You will find the car outside. If you care to go and sit in it, I will join you in a moment. And, lest the time hangs heavy on your hands, take this. Butter-scotch. Delicious, and, so I understand, wholesome. I bought it specially for you."

A few minutes later, having arranged for the trunk to be taken to the castle, Psmith emerged from the station and found Eve drinking in the beauties of the town of Market Blandings.

"What a delightful old place," she said as they drove off. "I almost wish I lived here."

"During the brief period of my stay at the castle," said Psmith, "the same thought has occurred to me. It is the sort of place where one feels that one could gladly settle down into a peaceful retirement and grow a honey-coloured beard." He looked at her with solemn admiration. "Women are wonderful," he said.

"And why, Mr. Bones, are women wonderful?" asked Eve.

"I was thinking at the moment of your appearance. You have just stepped off the train after a four-hour journey, and you are as fresh and blooming as—if I may coin a simile—a rose. How do you do it? When I arrived I was deep in alluvial deposits, and have only just managed to scrape them off."

"When did you arrive?"

"On the evening of the day on which I met you."

"But it's so extraordinary. That you should be here, I mean. I was wondering if I should ever see you again." Eve coloured a little, and went on rather hurriedly. "I mean, it seems so strange that we should always be meeting like this."

"Fate, probably," said Psmith. "I hope it isn't going to spoil your visit?"

"Oh, no."

"I could have done with a trifle more emphasis on the last word," said Psmith gently. "Forgive me for criticising your methods of voice production, but surely you can see how much better it would have sounded spoken thus: 'Oh, *no!*'"

Eve laughed.

"Very well, then," she said. "Oh, *no!*"

"Much better," said Psmith. "Much better."

He began to see that it was going to be difficult to introduce a eulogy of the Hon. Freddie Threepwood into this conversation.

"I'm very glad you're here," said Eve, resuming the talk after a slight pause. "Because, as a matter of fact, I'm feeling just the least bit nervous."

"Nervous? Why?"

"This is my first visit to a place of this size." The car had turned in at the big stone gates, and they were bowling smoothly up the winding drive. Through an avenue of trees to the right the great bulk of the castle had just appeared, grey and imposing against the sky. The afternoon sun glittered on the lake beyond it. "Is everything very stately?"

"Not at all. We are very homely folk, we of Blandings Castle. We go about, simple and unaffected, dropping gracious words all over the place. Lord Emsworth didn't overawe you, did he?"

"Oh, he's a dear. And, of course, I know Freddie quite well."

Psmith nodded. If she knew Freddie quite well, there was naturally no need to talk about him. He did not talk about him, therefore.

"Have you known Lord Emsworth long?" asked Eve.

"I met him for the first time the day I met you."

"Good gracious!" Eve stared. "And he invited you to the castle?"

Psmith smoothed his waistcoat.

"Strange, I agree. One can only account for it, can one not, by supposing that I radiate some extraordinary attraction. Have you noticed it?"

"No!"

"No?" said Psmith, surprised. "Ah, well," he went on tolerantly, "no doubt it will flash upon you quite unexpectedly sooner or later. Like a thunderbolt or something."

"I think you're terribly conceited."

"Not at all," said Psmith. "Conceited? No, no. Success has not spoiled me."

"Have you had any success?"

"None whatever." The car stopped. "We get down here," said Psmith, opening the door.

"Here? Why?"

"Because, if we go up to the house, you will infallibly be pounced on and set to work by one Baxter—a delightful fellow, but a whale for toil. I propose to conduct you on a tour round the grounds, and then we will go for a row on the lake. You will enjoy that."

"You seem to have mapped out my future for me."

"I have," said Psmith with emphasis, and in the monocled eye that met hers Eve detected so beaming a glance of esteem and admiration that she retreated warily into herself and endeavoured to be frigid.

"I'm afraid I haven't time to wander about the grounds," she said aloofly. "I must be going and seeing Mr. Baxter."

"Baxter," said Psmith, "is not one of the natural beauties of the place. Time enough to see him when you are compelled to . . . We are now in the southern pleasaunce or the west home-park or something. Note the refined way the deer are cropping the grass. All the ground on which we are now standing is of historic interest. Oliver Cromwell went through here in 1550. The record has since been lowered."

"I haven't time . . ."

"Leaving the pleasaunce on our left, we proceed to the northern messuage. The dandelions were imported from Egypt by the ninth Earl."

"Well, anyhow," said Eve mutinously, "I won't come on the lake."

"You will enjoy the lake," said Psmith. "The newts are of the famous old Blandings strain. They were introduced, together with the water-beetles, in the reign of Queen Elizabeth. Lord Emsworth, of course, holds manorial rights over the mosquito-swatting."

Eve was a girl of high and haughty spirit, and as such strongly resented being appropriated and having her movements directed by one who, in spite of his specious claims, was almost a stranger. But somehow she found her companion's placid assumption of authority hard to resist. Almost meekly she accompanied him through meadow and shrubbery, over velvet lawns and past gleaming flower-beds, and her indignation evaporated as her eyes absorbed the beauty of it all. She gave a little sigh. If Market Blandings had seemed a place in which one might dwell happily, Blandings Castle was a paradise.

"Before us now," said Psmith, "lies the celebrated Yew Alley, so called from the yews which hem it in. Speaking in my capacity of guide to the estate, I may say that when we have turned this next corner you will see a most remarkable sight."

And they did. Before them, as they passed in under the

boughs of an aged tree lay a green vista, faintly dappled with stray shafts of sunshine. In the middle of this vista the Hon. Frederick Threepwood was embracing a young woman in the dress of a housemaid.

§ 4

Psmith was the first of the little group to recover from the shock of this unexpected encounter, the Hon. Freddie the last. That unfortunate youth, meeting Eve's astonished eye as he raised his head, froze where he stood and remained with his mouth open until she had disappeared, which she did a few moments later, led away by Psmith, who, as he went, directed at his young friend a look in which surprise, pain, and reproof were so nicely blended that it would have been hard to say which predominated. All that a spectator could have said with certainty was that Psmith's finer feelings had suffered a severe blow.

"A painful scene," he remarked to Eve, as he drew her away in the direction of the house. "But we must always strive to be charitable. He may have been taking a fly out of her eye, or teaching her jiu-jitsu."

He looked at her searchingly.

"You seem less revolted," he said, "than one might have expected. This argues a sweet, shall we say, angelic disposition and confirms my already high opinion of you."

"Thank you."

"Not at all. Mark you," said Psmith, "I don't think that this sort of thing is a hobby of Comrade Threepwood's. He probably has many other ways of passing his spare time. Remember that before you pass judgment upon him. Also—Young Blood, and all that sort of thing."

"I haven't any intention of passing judgment upon him. It doesn't interest me what Mr. Threepwood does, either in his spare time or out of it."

"His interest in you, on the other hand, is vast. I forgot to tell you before, but he loves you. He asked me to mention it if the conversation happened to veer round in that direction."

"I know he does," said Eve ruefully.

"And does the fact stir no chord in you?"

"I think he's a nuisance."

"That," said Psmith cordially, "is the right spirit. I like to see it. Very well, then, we will discard the topic of Freddie, and I will try to find others that may interest, elevate, and amuse you. We are now approaching the main buildings. I am no expert in architecture, so cannot tell you all I could wish about the façade, but you can see there *is* a façade, and in my opinion—for what it is worth —a jolly good one. We approach by a sweeping gravel walk."

"I am going in to report to Mr. Baxter," said Eve with decision. "It's too absurd. I mustn't spend my time strolling about the grounds. I must see Mr. Baxter at once.

Psmith inclined his head courteously.

"Nothing easier. That big, open window there is the library. Doubtless Comrade Baxter is somewhere inside, toiling away among the archives."

"Yes, but I can't announce myself by shouting to him."

"Assuredly not," said Psmith. "No need for that at all. Leave it to me." He stooped and picked up a large flower-pot which stood under the terrace wall, and before Eve could intervene had tossed it lightly through the open window. A muffled thud, followed by a sharp exclamation from within, caused a faint smile of gratification to illumine his solemn countenance. "He *is* in. I thought he would be. Ah, Baxter," he said graciously, as the upper half of a body surmounted by a spectacled face framed itself suddenly in the window, "a pleasant, sunny afternoon. How is everything?"

The Efficient Baxter struggled for utterance.

"You look like the Blessed Damozel gazing down from the gold bar of Heaven," said Psmith genially. "Baxter, I want to introduce you to Miss Halliday. She arrived safely after a somewhat fatiguing journey. You will like Miss Halliday. If I had a library, I could not wish for a more courteous, obliging, and capable cataloguist."

This striking and unsolicited testimonial made no appeal to the Efficient Baxter. His mind seemed occupied with other matters.

"Did you throw that flower-pot?" he demanded coldly.

"You will no doubt," said Psmith, "wish on some later occasion to have a nice long talk with Miss Halliday in order to give her an outline of her duties. I have been showing her the grounds and am about to take her for a row on the lake. But after that she will—and I know I may speak for Miss Halliday in this matter—be entirely at your disposal."

"Did you throw that flower-pot?"

"I look forward confidently to the pleasantest of associations between you and Miss Halliday. You will find her," said Psmith warmly, "a willing assistant, a tireless worker."

"Did you . . . ?"

"But now," said Psmith, "I must be tearing myself away. In order to impress Miss Halliday, I put on my best suit when I went to meet her. For a row upon the lake something simpler in pale flannel is indicated. I shall only be a few minutes," he said to Eve. "Would you mind meeting me at the boat-house?"

"I am not coming on the lake with you."

"At the boat-house in—say—six and a quarter minutes," said Psmith with a gentle smile, and pranced into the house like a long-legged mustang.

Eve remained where she stood, struggling between laughter and embarrassment. The Efficient Baxter was still leaning wrathfully out of the library window, and it began to seem a little difficult to carry on an ordinary conversation. The problem of what she was to say in order to continue the scene in an agreeable manner was solved by the arrival of Lord Emsworth, who pottered out from the bushes with a rake in his hand. He stood eyeing Eve for a moment, then memory seemed to wake. Eve's appearance was easier to remember, possibly, than some of the things which his lordship was wont to forget. He came forward beamingly.

"Ah, there you are, Miss . . . Dear me, I'm really afraid I have forgotten your name. My memory is excellent as a rule, but I cannot remember names . . . Miss Halliday! Of course, of course. Baxter, my dear fellow," he proceeded, sighting the watcher at the window, "this is Miss Halliday."

"Mr. McTodd," said the Efficient One sourly, "has already introduced me to Miss Halliday."

"Has he? Deuced civil of him, deuced civil of him.

But where *is* he?" inquired his lordship, scanning the surrounding scenery with a vague eye.

"He went into the house. After," said Baxter in a cold voice, "throwing a flower-pot at me."

"Doing what?"

"He threw a flower-pot at me," said Baxter, and vanished moodily.

Lord Emsworth stared at the open window, then turned to Eve for enlightenment.

"*Why* did Baxter throw a flower-pot at McTodd?" he said. "And," he went on, ventilating an even deeper question, "where the deuce did he get a flower-pot? There are no flower-pots in the library."

Eve, on her side, was also seeking information.

"Did you say his name was McTodd, Lord Emsworth?"

"No, no. Baxter. That was Baxter, my secretary."

"No, I mean the one who met me at the station."

"Baxter did not meet you at the station. The man who met you at the station," said Lord Emsworth, speaking slowly, for women are so apt to get things muddled, "was McTodd. He's staying here. Constance asked him, and I'm bound to say when I first heard of it I was not any too well pleased. I don't like poets as a rule. But this fellow's so different from the other poets I've met. Different altogether. And," said Lord Emsworth with not a little heat, "I strongly object to Baxter throwing flower-pots at him, I won't *have* Baxter throwing flower-pots at my guests," he said firmly; for Lord Emsworth, though occasionally a little vague, was keenly alive to the ancient traditions of his family regarding hospitality.

"Is Mr. McTodd a poet?" said Eve, her heart beating.

"Eh? Oh yes, yes. There seems to be no doubt about

that. A Canadian poet. Apparently they have poets out there. And," demanded his lordship, ever a fair-minded man, "why not? A remarkably growing country. I was there in the year '98. Or was it," he added, thoughtfully passing a muddy hand over his chin and leaving a rich brown stain, " '99? I forget. My memory isn't good for dates . . . If you will excuse me, Miss—Miss Halliday, of course—if you will excuse me, I must be leaving you. I have to see McAllister, my head gardener. An obstinate man. A Scotchman. If you go into the house, my sister Constance will give you a cup of tea. I don't know what the time is, but I suppose there will be tea soon. Never take it myself."

"Mr. McTodd asked me to go for a row on the lake."

"On the lake, eh? On the *lake?*" said his lordship, as if this was the last place in the neighbourhood where he would have expected to hear of people proposing to row. Then he brightened. "Of course, yes, on the lake. I think you will like the lake. I take a dip there myself every morning before breakfast. I find it good for the health and appetite. I plunge in and swim perhaps fifty yards, and then return." Lord Emsworth suspended the gossip from the training-camp in order to look at his watch. "Dear me," he said, "I must be going. McAllister has been waiting fully ten minutes. Good-bye, then, for the present, Miss—er—good-bye."

And Lord Emsworth ambled off, on his face that look of tense concentration which it always wore when interviews with Angus McAllister were in prospect—the look which stern warriors wear when about to meet a foeman worthy of their steel.

§ 5

There was a cold expression in Eve's eyes as she made her way slowly to the boat-house. The information which she had just received had come as a shock, and she was trying to adjust her mind to it. When Miss Clarkson had told her of the unhappy conclusion to her old school friend's marriage to Ralston McTodd, she had immediately, without knowing anything of the facts, arrayed herself loyally on Cynthia's side and condemned the unknown McTodd uncompromisingly and without hesitation. It was many years since she had seen Cynthia, and their friendship might almost have been said to have lapsed; but Eve's affection, when she had once given it, was a durable thing, capable of surviving long separation. She had loved Cynthia at school, and she could feel nothing but animosity towards any one who had treated her badly. She eyed the glittering water of the lake from under lowered brows, and prepared to be frigid and hostile when the villain of the piece should arrive. It was only when she heard footsteps behind her and turned to perceive Psmith hurrying up, radiant in gleaming flannel, that it occurred to her for the first time that there might have been faults on both sides. She had not known Psmith long, it was true, but already his personality had made a somewhat deep impression on her, and she was loath to believe that he could be the callous scoundrel of her imagination. She decided to suspend judgment until they should be out in mid-water and in a position to discuss the matter without interruption.

"I am a little late," said Psmith, as he came up. "I was detained by our young friend Freddie. He came into

my room and started talking about himself at the very
moment when I was tying my tie and needed every ounce
of concentration for that delicate task. The recent painful
episode appeared to be weighing on his mind to some
extent." He helped Eve into the boat and started to row.
"I consoled him as best I could by telling him that it
would probably have made you think all the more highly
of him. I ventured the suggestion that girls worship the
strong, rough, dashing type of man. And, after I had
done my best to convince him that he was a strong, rough,
dashing man, I came away. By now, of course, he may
have had a relapse into despair; so, if you happen to see
a body bobbing about in the water as we row along, it will
probably be Freddie's."

"Never mind about Freddie."

"I don't if you don't," said Psmith agreeably. "Very
well, then, if we see a body, we will ignore it." He rowed
on a few strokes. "Correct me if I am wrong," he said,
resting on his oars and leaning forward, "but you appear
to be brooding about something. If you will give me a
clue, I will endeavour to assist you to grapple with any
little problem which is troubling you. What is the matter?"

Eve, questioned thus directly, found it difficult to open
the subject. She hesitated a moment, and let the water
ripple through her fingers.

"I have only just found out your name, Mr. McTodd,"
she said at length.

Psmith nodded.

"It is always thus," he said. "Passing through this
life, we meet a fellow-mortal, chat awhile, and part; and
the last thing we think of doing is to ask him in a manly

and direct way what his label is. There is something oddly furtive and shamefaced in one's attitude towards people's names. It is as if we shrank from probing some hideous secret. We say to ourselves, 'This pleasant stranger may be a Snooks or a Buggins. Better not inquire.' But in my case . . ."

"It was a great shock to me."

"Now there," said Psmith, "I cannot follow you. I wouldn't call McTodd a bad name, as names go. Don't you think there is a sort of Highland strength about it? It sounds to me like something out of 'The Lady of the Lake' or 'The Lay of the Last Minstrel.' 'The stag at eve had drunk its fill adoon the glen beyint the hill, and welcomed with a friendly nod old Scotland's pride, young Laird McTodd.' You don't think it has a sort of wild romantic ring?"

"I ought to tell you, Mr. McTodd," said Eve, "that I was at school with Cynthia."

Psmith was not a young man who often found himself at a loss, but this remark gave him a bewildered feeling such as comes in dreams. It was plain to him that this delightful girl thought she had said something serious, even impressive; but for the moment it did not seem to him to make sense. He sparred warily for time.

"Indeed? With Cynthia? That must have been jolly."

The harmless observation appeared to have the worst effect upon his companion. The frown came back to her face.

"Oh, don't speak in that flippant, sneering way," she said. "It's so cheap."

Psmith, having nothing to say, remained silent, and the boat drifted on. Eve's face was delicately pink, for she was feeling extraordinarily embarrassed. There was something in the solemn gaze of the man before her which made it difficult for her to go on. But, with the stout-heartedness which was one of her characteristics, she stuck to her task.

"After all," she said, "however you may feel about her now, you must have been fond of poor Cynthia at one time, or I don't see why you should have married her."

Psmith, for want of conversation, had begun rowing again. The start he gave at these remarkable words caused him to skim the surface of the water with the left oar in such a manner as to send a liberal pint into Eve's lap. He started forward with apologies.

"Oh, never mind about that," said Eve impatiently. "It doesn't matter. . . . Mr. McTodd," she said, and there was a note of gentleness in her voice, "I do wish you would tell me what the trouble was."

Psmith stared at the floor of the boat in silence. He was wrestling with a feeling of injury. True, he had not during their brief conversation at the Senior Conservative Club specifically inquired of Mr. McTodd whether he was a bachelor, but somehow he felt that the man should have dropped some hint as to his married state. True, again, Mr. McTodd had not asked him to impersonate him at Blandings Castle. And yet, undeniably, he felt that he had a grievance. Psmith's was an orderly mind. He had proposed to continue the pleasant relations which had begun between Eve and himself, seeing to it that every day they became a little pleasanter, until eventually, in due season, they should reach the point where it would become possible to lay heart and hand at her feet. For there was no doubt in his mind that in a world congested

to overflowing with girls Eve Halliday stood entirely
alone. And now this infernal Cynthia had risen from
nowhere to stand between them. Even a young man as
liberally endowed with calm assurance as he was might
find it awkward to conduct his wooing with such a handicap as a wife in the background.

Eve misinterpreted his silence.

"I suppose you are thinking that it is no business of
mine?"

Psmith came out of his thoughts with a start.

"No, no. Not at all."

"You see, I'm devoted to Cynthia—and I like you."

She smiled for the first time. Her embarrassment was
passing.

"That is the whole point," she said. "I do like you.
And I'm quite sure that if you were really the sort of
man I thought you when I first heard about all this, I
shouldn't. The friend who told me about you and Cynthia made it seem as if the whole fault had been yours.
I got the impression that you had been very unkind to
Cynthia. I thought you must be a brute. And when
Lord Emsworth told me who you were, my first impulse
was to hate you. I think if you had come along just
then I should have been rather horrid to you. But you
were late, and that gave me time to think it over. And
then I remembered how nice you had been to me and I
felt somehow that—that you must really be quite nice,
and it occurred to me that there might be some explanation. And I thought that—perhaps—if you would let me
interfere in your private affairs—and if things hadn't
gone too far—I might do something to help—try to bring
you together, you know."

She broke off, a little confused, for now that the words were out she was conscious of a return of her former shyness. Even though she was an old friend of Cynthia's, there did seem something insufferably officious in this meddling. And when she saw the look of pain on her companion's face, she regretted that she had spoken. Naturally, she thought, he was offended.

In supposing that Psmith was offended she was mistaken. Internally he was glowing with a renewed admiration for all those beautiful qualities in her which he had detected, before they had ever met, at several yards' range across the street from the window of the Drones Club smoking-room. His look of pain was due to the fact that, naving now had time to grapple with the problem, he had decided to dispose of this Cynthia once and for all. He proposed to eliminate her for ever from his life. And the elimination of even such a comparative stranger seemed to him to call for a pained look. So he assumed one.

"That," he said gravely, "would, I fear, be impossible. It is like you to suggest it, and I cannot tell you how much I appreciate the kindness which has made you interest yourself in my troubles, but it is too late for any reconciliation. Cynthia and I are divorced."

For a moment the temptation had come to him to kill the woman off with some wasting sickness, but this he resisted as tending towards possible future complications. He was resolved, however, that there should be no question of bringing them together again.

He was disturbed to find Eve staring at him in amazement.

"Divorced? But how can you be divorced? It's only

a few days since you and she were in London together."

Psmith ceased to wonder that Mr. McTodd had had trouble with his wife. The woman was a perfect pest.

"I used the term in a spiritual rather than a legal sense," he replied. "True, there has been no actual decree, but we are separated beyond hope of reunion." He saw the distress in Eve's eyes and hurried on. "There are things," he said, "which it is impossible for a man to overlook, however broad-minded he may be. Love, Miss Halliday, is a delicate plant. It needs tending, nursing, assiduous fostering. This cannot be done by throwing the breakfast bacon at a husband's head."

"What!" Eve's astonishment was such that the word came out in a startled squeak.

"*In* the dish," said Psmith sadly.

Eve's blue eyes opened wide.

"*Cynthia* did that!"

"On more than one occasion. Her temper in the mornings was terrible. I have known her lift the cat over two chairs and a settee with a single kick. And all because there were no mushrooms."

"But—but I can't believe it!"

"Come over to Canada," said Psmith, "and I will show you the cat."

"Cynthia did that!—Cynthia—why, she was always the gentlest little creature."

"At school, you mean?"

"Yes."

"That," said Psmith, "would, I suppose, be before she had taken to drink."

"Taken to drink!"

Psmith was feeling happier. A passing thought did come to him that all this was perhaps a trifle rough on the absent Cynthia, but he mastered the unmanly weakness. It was necessary that Cynthia should suffer in the good cause. Already he had begun to detect in Eve's eyes the faint dawnings of an angelic pity, and pity is recognised by all the best authorities as one of the most valuable emotions which your wooer can awaken.

"Drink!" Eve repeated, with a little shudder.

"We lived in one of the dry provinces of Canada, and, as so often happens, that started the trouble. From the moment when she installed a private still her downfall was swift. I have seen her, under the influence of home-brew, rage through the house like a devastating cyclone . . . I hate speaking like this of one who was your friend," said Psmith, in a low, vibrating voice. "I would not tell these things to any one but you. The world, of course, supposes that the entire blame for the collapse of our home was mine. I took care that it should be so. The opinion of the world matters little to me. But with you it is different. I should not like you to think badly of me, Miss Halliday. I do not make friends easily—I am a lonely man—but somehow it has seemed to me since we met that you and I might be friends."

Eve stretched her hand out impulsively.

"Why, of course!"

Psmith took her hand and held it far longer than was strictly speaking necessary.

"Thank you," he said. "Thank you."

He turned the nose of the boat to the shore, and rowed slowly back.

"I have suffered," said Psmith gravely, as he helped her ashore. "But, if you will be my friend, I think that I may forget."

They walked in silence up the winding path to the castle.

§ 6

To Psmith five minutes later, as he sat in his room smoking a cigarette and looking dreamily out at the distant hills, there entered the Hon. Frederick Threepwood, who, having closed the door behind him, tottered to the bed and uttered a deep and discordant groan. Psmith, his mind thus rudely wrenched from pleasant meditations, turned and regarded the gloomy youth with disfavour.

"At any other time, Comrade Threepwood," he said politely but with firmness, "certainly. But not now. I am not in the vein."

"What?" said the Hon. Freddie vacantly.

"I say that at any other time I shall be delighted to listen to your farmyard imitations, but not now. At the moment I am deep in thoughts of my own, and I may say frankly that I regard you as more or less of an excrescence. I want solitude, solitude. I am in a beautiful reverie, and your presence jars upon me somewhat profoundly."

The Hon. Freddie ruined the symmetry of his hair by passing his fingers feverishly through it.

"Don't *talk* so much! I never met a fellow like you for talking." Having rumpled his hair to the left, he went through it again and rumpled it to the right. "I say, do you know what? You've jolly well got to clear out of here quick!" He got up from the bed, and approached the window. Having done which, he bent towards Psmith and whispered in his ear. "The game's up!"

Psmith withdrew his ear with a touch of hauteur, but he looked at his companion with a little more interest. He had feared, when he saw Freddie stagger in with such melodramatic despair and emit so hollow a groan, that the topic on which he wished to converse was the already exhausted one of his broken heart. It now began to appear that weightier matters were on his mind.

"I fail to understand you, Comrade Threepwood," he said. "The last time I had the privilege of conversing with you, you informed me that Susan, or whatever her name is, merely giggled and told you not to be silly when you embraced her. In other words, she is *not* a detective. What has happened since then to get you all worked up?"

"Baxter!"

"What has Baxter been doing?"

"Only giving the whole bally show away to me, that's all," said Freddie feverishly. He clutched Psmith's arm violently, causing that exquisite to utter a slight moan and smooth out the wrinkles thus created in his sleeve. "Listen! I've just been talking to the blighter. I was passing the library just now, when he popped out of the door and hauled me in. And, dash it, he hadn't been talking two seconds before I realised that he has seen through the whole dam' thing practically from the moment you got here. Though he doesn't seem to know that I've anything to do with it, thank goodness."

"I should imagine not, if he makes you his confidant. Why did he do that, by the way? What made him select you as the recipient of his secrets?"

"As far as I can make out, his idea was to form a gang,

if you know what I mean. He said a lot of stuff about him and me being the only two able-bodied young men in the place, and we ought to be prepared to tackle you if you started anything."

"I see. And now tell me how our delightful friend ever happened to begin suspecting that I was not all I seemed to be. I had been flattering myself that I had put the little deception over with complete success."

"Well, in the first place, dash it, that dam' fellow McTodd—the real one, you know—sent a telegram saying that he wasn't coming. So it seemed rummy to Baxter bang from the start when you blew in all merry and bright."

"Ah! That was what they all meant by saying they were glad I had come 'after all.' A phrase which at the moment, I confess, rather mystified me."

"And then you went and wrote in the Peavey female's autograph-book."

"In what way was that a false move?"

"Why, that was the biggest bloomer on record, as it has turned out," said Freddie vehemently. "Baxter apparently keeps every letter that comes to the place on a file, and he'd skewered McTodd's original letter with the rest. I mean, the one he wrote accepting the invitation to come here. And Baxter compared his handwriting with what you wrote in the Peavey's album, and, of course, they weren't a dam' bit alike. And that put the lid on it."

Psmith lit another cigarette and drew at it thoughtfully. He realised that he had made a tactical error in underestimating the antagonism of the Efficient One.

"Does he seem to have any idea why I have come to the castle?" he asked.

"Any idea ? Why, dash it, the very first thing he said to me was that you must have come to sneak Aunt Connie's necklace."

"In that case, why has he made no move till to-day ? I should have supposed that he would long since have denounced me before as large an audience as he could assemble. Why this reticence on the part of genial old Baxter ?"

A crimson flush of chivalrous indignation spread itself over Freddie's face.

"He told me that, too."

"There seem to have been no reserves between Comrade Baxter and yourself. And very healthy, too, this spirit of confidence. What was his reason for abstaining from loosing the bomb ?"

"He said he was pretty sure you wouldn't try to do anything on your own. He thought you would wait till your accomplice arrived. And, damn him," cried Freddie heatedly, "do you know who he's got the infernal gall to think is your accomplice ? Miss Halliday. Dash him !"

Psmith smoked in thoughtful silence.

"Well, of course, now that this has happened," said Freddie, "I suppose it's no good thinking of going on with the thing. You'd better pop off, what ? If I were you, I'd leg it to-day and have your luggage sent on after you."

Psmith threw away his cigarette and stretched himself. During the last few moments he had been thinking with some tenseness.

"Comrade Threepwood," he said reprovingly, "you suggest a cowardly and weak-minded action. I admit that the outlook would be distinctly rosier if no such person as Baxter were on the premises, but nevertheless the thing must be seen through to a finish. At least we have this advantage over our spectacled friend, that we know he suspects me and he doesn't know we know. I think that with a little resource and ingenuity we may yet win through." He turned to the window and looked out. "Sad," he sighed, "that these idyllic surroundings should have become oppressed with a cloud of sinister menace. One thinks one sees a faun popping about in the under growth, and on looking more closely perceives that it i. in reality a detective with a notebook. What one fanciec was the piping of Pan turns out to be a police-whistle summoning assistance. Still, we must bear these things without wincing. They are our cross. What you have told me will render me, if possible, warier and more snake-like than ever, but my purpose remains firm. The cry goes round the castle battlements 'Psmith intends to keep the old flag flying!' So charge off and soothe your quivering ganglions with a couple of aspirins, Comrade Threepwood, and leave me to my thoughts. All will doubt-less come right in the future."

CHAPTER IX

PSMITH ENGAGES A VALET

§ 1

FROM out of the scented shade of the big cedar on the lawn in front of the castle Psmith looked at the flower-beds, jaunty and gleaming in the afternoon sun; then he looked back at Eve, incredulity in every feature.

"I must have misunderstood you. Surely," he said in a voice vibrant with reproach, "you do not seriously intend to *work* in weather like this?"

"I must. I've got a conscience. They aren't paying me a handsome salary—a fairly handsome salary—to sit about in deck-chairs."

"But you only came yesterday."

"Well, I ought to have worked yesterday."

"It seems to me," said Psmith, "the nearest thing to slavery that I have ever struck. I had hoped, seeing that everybody had gone off and left us alone, that we were going to spend a happy and instructive afternoon together under the shade of this noble tree, talking of this and that. Is it not to be?"

"No, it is not. It's lucky you're not the one who's supposed to be cataloguing this library. It would never get finished."

"And why, as your employer would say, should it? He has expressed the opinion several times in my hearing

179

that the library has jogged along quite comfortably for a great number of years without being catalogued. Why shouldn't it go on like that indefinitely?"

"It's no good trying to tempt me. There's nothing I should like better than to loaf here for hours and hours, but what would Mr. Baxter say when he got back and found out?"

"It is becoming increasingly clear to me each day that I stay in this place," said Psmith moodily, "that Comrade Baxter is little short of a blister on the community. Tell me, how do you get on with him?"

"I don't like him much."

"Nor do I. It is on these communities of taste that life-long attachments are built. Sit down and let us exchange confidences on the subject of Baxter."

Eve laughed.

"I won't. You're simply trying to lure me into staying out here and neglecting my duty. I really must be off now. You have no idea what a lot of work there is to be done."

"You are entirely spoiling my afternoon."

"No, I'm not. You've got a book. What is it?"

Psmith picked up the brightly-jacketed volume and glanced at it.

"*The Man With The Missing Toe.* Comrade Threepwood lent it to me. He has a vast store of this type of narrative. I expect he will be wanting you to catalogue his library next."

"Well, it looks interesting."

"Ah, but what does it *teach?* How long do you propose to shut yourself up in that evil-smelling library?"

"An hour or so."

"Then I shall rely on your society at the end of that period. We might go for another saunter on the lake."

"All right. I'll come and find you when I've finished."

Psmith watched her disappear into the house, then seated himself once more in the long chair under the cedar. A sense of loneliness oppressed him. He gave one look at *The Man With The Missing Toe,* and, having rejected the entertainment it offered, gave himself up to meditation.

Blandings Castle dozed in the midsummer heat like a Palace of Sleep. There had been an exodus of its inmates shortly after lunch, when Lord Emsworth, Lady Constance, Mr. Keeble, Miss Peavey, and the Efficient Baxter had left for the neighbouring town of Bridgeford in the big car, with the Hon. Freddie puffing in its wake in a natty two-seater. Psmith, who had been invited to accompany them, had declined on the plea that he wished to write a poem. He felt but a tepid interest in the afternoon's programme, which was to consist of the unveiling by his lordship of the recently completed memorial to the late Hartley Reddish, Esq., J.P., for so many years Member of Parliament for the Bridgeford and Shifley Division of Shropshire. Not even the prospect of hearing Lord Emsworth—clad, not without vain protest and weak grumbling, in a silk hat, morning coat, and sponge-bag trousers—deliver a speech, had been sufficient to lure him from the castle grounds.

But at the moment when he had uttered his refusal, thereby incurring the ill-concealed envy both of Lord Emsworth and his son Freddie, the latter also an unwilling celebrant, he had supposed that his solitude would be shared by Eve. This deplorable conscientiousness of hers, this morbid craving for work, had left him at a loose end. The time and the place were both above criticism, but, as so often happens in this life of ours, he had been let down by the girl.

But, though he chafed for awhile, it was not long before the dreamy peace of the afternoon began to exercise a soothing effect upon him. With the exception of the bees that worked with their usual misguided energy among the flowers and an occasional butterfly which flitted past in the sunshine, all nature seemed to be taking a siesta. Somewhere out of sight a lawn-mower had begun to emphasise the stillness with its musical whir. A telegraph-boy on a red bicycle passed up the drive to the front door, and seemed to have some difficulty in establishing communication with the domestic staff—from which Psmith deduced that Beach, the butler, like a good opportunist, was taking advantage of the absence of authority to enjoy a nap in some distant lair of his own. Eventually a parlour-maid appeared, accepted the telegram and, apparently, a rebuke from the boy, and the bicycle passed out of sight, leaving silence and peace once more.

The noblest minds are not proof against atmospheric conditions of this kind. Psmith's eyes closed, opened, closed again. And presently his regular breathing, varied by an occasional snore, was added to the rest of the small sounds of the summer afternoon.

The shadow of the cedar was appreciably longer when he awoke with that sudden start which generally terminates sleep in a garden-chair. A glance at his watch told him that it was close on five o'clock, a fact which was confirmed a moment later by the arrival of the parlour maid who had answered the summons of the telegraph boy. She appeared to be the sole survivor of the little world that had its centre in the servants' hall. A sort of female Casabianca.

"I have put your tea in the hall, sir."

"You could have performed no nobler or more charitable task," Psmith assured her; and, having corrected a certain stiffness of limb by means of massage, went in. It occurred to him that Eve, assiduous worker though she was, might have knocked off in order to keep him company.

The hope proved vain A single cup stood bleakly on the tray. Either Eve was superior to the feminine passion for tea or she was having hers up in the library. Filled with something of the sadness which he had felt at the sight of the toiling bees, Psmith embarked on his solitary meal, wondering sorrowfully at the perverseness which made girls work when there was no one to watch them.

It was very agreeable here in the coolness of the hall. The great door of the castle was open, and through it he had a view of lawns bathed in a thirst-provoking sunlight. Through the green-baize door to his left, which led to the servants' quarters, an occasional sharp giggle gave evidence of the presence of humanity, but apart from that he might have been alone in the world. Once again he fell into a dreamy meditation, and there is little reason to doubt that he would shortly have disgraced himself by falling asleep for the second time in a single afternoon, when he was restored to alertness by the sudden appearance of a foreign body in the open doorway. Against the background of golden light a black figure had abruptly manifested itself.

The sharp pang of apprehension which ran through Psmith's consciousness like an electric shock, causing him to stiffen like some wild creature surprised in the woods, was due to the momentary belief that the new-comer was the local vicar, of whose conversational powers he had had experience on the second day of his visit. Another glance showed him that he had been too pessimistic. This was not the vicar. It was some one whom he had never seen before—a slim and graceful young man with a dark, intelligent face, who stood blinking in the subdued light of the hall with eyes not yet accustomed to the absence of strong sunshine. Greatly relieved, Psmith rose and approached him.

"Hallo!" said the new-comer. "I didn't see you. It's quite dark in here after outside."

"The light is pleasantly dim," agreed Psmith.

"Is Lord Emsworth anywhere about?"

"I fear not. He has legged it, accompanied by the entire household, to superintend the unveiling of a memorial at Bridgeford to—if my memory serves me rightly—the late Hartley Reddish, Esq., J.P., M.P. Is there anything I can do?"

"Well, I've come to stay, you know."

"Indeed?"

"Lady Constance invited me to pay a visit as soon as I reached England."

"Ah! Then you have come from foreign parts?"

"Canada."

Psmith started slightly. This, he perceived, was going to complicate matters. The last thing he desired was the addition to the Blandings circle of one familiar with Canada. Nothing would militate against his peace of mind more than the society of a man who would want to exchange with him views on that growing country.

"Oh, Canada?" he said.

"I wired," proceeded the other, "but I suppose it came after everybody had left. Ah, that must be my telegram on that table over there. I walked up from the station." He was rambling idly about the hall after the fashion of one breaking new ground. He paused at an occasional table, the one where, when taking after-dinner coffee, Miss Peavey was wont to sit. He picked up a book, and uttered a gratified laugh. "One of my little things," he said.

"One of what?" said Psmith.

"This book. *Songs of Squalor.* I wrote it."

"You wrote it!"

"Yes. My name's McTodd. Ralston McTodd. I expect you have heard them speak of me?"

§ 2

The mind of a man who has undertaken a mission as delicate as Psmith's at Blandings Castle is necessarily alert. Ever since he had stepped into the five o'clock train at Paddington, when his adventure might have been said formally to have started, Psmith had walked warily, like one in a jungle on whom sudden and unexpected things might pounce out at any moment. This calm announcement from the slim young man, therefore, though it undoubtedly startled him, did not deprive him of his faculties. On the contrary, it quickened them. His first action was to step nimbly to the table on which the telegram lay awaiting the return of Lord Emsworth, his second was to slip the envelope into his pocket. It was imperative that telegrams signed McTodd should not lie about loose while he was enjoying the hospitality of the castle.

This done, he confronted the young man.

"Come, come!" he said with quiet severity.

He was extremely grateful to a kindly Providence which had arranged that this interview should take place at a time when nobody but himself was in the house.

"You say that you are Ralston McTodd, the author of these poems?"

"Yes, I do."

"Then what," said Psmith incisively, "is a pale parabola of Joy?"

"Er—what?" said the new-comer in an enfeebled voice. There was manifest in his demeanour now a marked nervousness.

"And here is another," said Psmith. " 'The——' Wait a minute, I'll get it soon. Yes. 'The sibilant, scented silence that shimmered where we sat.' Could you oblige me with a diagram of that one?"

"I—I—— What are you talking about?"

Psmith stretched out a long arm and patted him almost affectionately on the shoulder.

"It's lucky you met me before you had to face the others," he said. "I fear that you undertook this little venture without thoroughly equipping yourself. They would have detected your imposture in the first minute."

"What do you mean—imposture? I don't know what you're talking about."

Psmith waggled his forefinger at him reproachfully.

"My dear Comrade, I may as well tell you at once that the genuine McTodd is an old and dear friend of mine. I had a long and entertaining conversation with him only a few days ago. So that, I think we may confidently assert, is that. Or am I wrong?"

"Oh, hell!" said the young man. And, flopping bonelessly into a chair, he mopped his forehead in undisguised and abject collapse.

Silence reigned for awhile.

"What," inquired the visitor, raising a damp face that shone pallidly in the dim light, "are you going to do about it?"

"Nothing, Comrade—by the way, what is your name?"

"Cootes."

"Nothing, Comrade Cootes. Nothing whatever. You are free to leg it hence whenever you feel disposed. In fact, the sooner you do so, the better I shall be pleased."

"Say! That's darned good of you."

"Not at all, not at all."

"You're an ace——"

"Oh, hush!" interrupted Psmith modestly. "But before you go tell me one or two things. I take it that your object in coming here was to have a pop at Lady Constance's necklace?"

"Yes."

"I thought as much. And what made you suppose that the real McTodd would not be here when you arrived?"

"Oh, that was all right. I travelled over with that guy McTodd on the boat, and saw a good deal of him when we got to London. He was full of how he'd been invited here, and I got it out of him that no one here knew him by sight. And then one afternoon I met him in the Strand, all worked up. Madder than a hornet. Said he'd been insulted and wouldn't come down to this place if they came and begged him on their bended knees. I couldn't make out what it was all about, but apparently he had met Lord Emsworth and hadn't been treated right. He told me he was going straight off to Paris."

"And did he?"

"Sure. I saw him off myself at Charing Cross. That's why it seemed such a cinch coming here instead of him. It's just my darned luck that the first man I run into is a friend of his. How was I to know that he had any friends this side? He told me he'd never been in England before."

"In this life, Comrade Cootes," said Psmith, "we must always distinguish between the Unlikely and the Impossible. It was unlikely, as you say, that you would meet any friend of McTodd's in this out-of-the-way spot; and you rashly ordered your movements on the assumption that it was impossible. With what result? The cry goes round the Underworld, 'Poor old Cootes has made a bloomer!'"

"You needn't rub it in."

"I am only doing so for your good. It is my earnest hope that you will lay this lesson to heart and profit by it. Who knows that it may not be the turning-point in your career? Years hence, when you are a white-haired and opulent man of leisure, having retired from the crook business with a comfortable fortune, you may look back on your experience of to-day and realise that it was the means of starting you on the road to Success. You will lay stress on it when you are interviewed for the *Weekly Burglar* on 'How I Began' . . . But, talking of starting on roads, I think that perhaps it would be as well if you now had a dash at the one leading to the railway-station. The ‸ousehold may be returning at any moment now."

"That's right," agreed the visitor.

"I think so," said Psmith. "I think so. You will be happier when you are away from here. Once outside the castle precincts, a great weight will roll off your mind. A little fresh air will put the roses in your cheeks. You know your way out?"

He shepherded the young man to the door and with a cordial push started him on his way. Then with long strides he ran upstairs to the library to find Eve.

.   .   .   .

At about the same moment, on the platform of Market Blandings station, Miss Aileen Peavey was alighting from the train which had left Bridgeford some half an hour earlier. A headache, the fruit of standing about in the hot sun, had caused her to forgo the pleasure of hearing Lord Emsworth deliver his speech: and she had slipped back on a convenient train with the intention of lying down and resting. Finding, on reaching Market Blandings, that her head was much better, and the heat of the afternoon being now over, she started to walk to the castle, greatly refreshed by a cool breeze which had sprung up from the west. She left the town at almost the exact time when the disconsolate Mr. Cootes was passing out of the big gate at the end of the castle drive.

§ 3

The grey melancholy which accompanied Mr. Cootes like a diligent spectre as he began his walk back to the town of Market Blandings, and which not even the delightful evening could dispel, was due primarily, of course, to that sickening sense of defeat which afflicts a man whose high hopes have been wrecked at the very instant when success has seemed in sight. Once or twice in the life of every man there falls to his lot something which can only be described as a soft snap, and it had seemed to Mr. Cootes that this venture of his to Blandings Castle came into that category. He had, like most members of his profession, had his ups and downs in the past, but at last, he told himself, the goddess Fortune had handed him something on a plate with watercress round it. Once established in the castle, there would have been a hundred opportunities of achieving the capture of Lady Constance's necklace: and it had looked as though all he had to do was to walk in, announce himself, and be treated as the honoured guest. As he slouched moodily between the dusty hedges that fringed the road to Market Blandings, Edward Cootes tasted the bitterness that only those know whose plans have been upset by the hundredth chance.

But this was not all. In addition to the sadness of frustrated hope, he was also experiencing the anguish of troubled memories. Not only was the Present torturing him, but the Past had come to life and jumped out and bitten him. A sorrow's crown of sorrow is remembering happier things, and this was what Edward Cootes was doing now. It is at moments like this that a man needs a woman's tender care, and Mr. Cootes had lost the only woman in whom he could have confided his grief, the only woman who would have understood and sympathised.

We have been introduced to Mr. Cootes at a point in his career when he was practising upon dry land; but that was not his chosen environment. Until a few months back his business had lain upon deep waters. The salt scent of the sea was in his blood. To put it more exactly, he had been by profession a card-sharper on the Atlantic liners; and it was during this period that he had loved and lost. For three years and more he had worked in perfect harmony with the lady who, though she adopted a variety of names for purposes of travel, was known to her immediate circle as Smooth Lizzie. He had been the practitioner, she the decoy, and theirs had been one of those ideal business partnerships which one so seldom meets with in a world of cynicism and mistrust. Comradeship had ripened into something deeper and more sacred, and it was all settled between them that when they next touched New York, Mr. Cootes, if still at liberty, should proceed to the City Hall for a marriage-license; when they had quarrelled—quarrelled irrevocably over one of those trifling points over which lovers do quarrel. Some absurd dispute as to the proper division of the quite meagre sum obtained from a cattle millionaire on their last voyage had marred their golden dreams. One word had led to another. The lady, after woman's habit, had the last of the series, and even Mr. Cootes was forced to admit that it was a pippin. She had spoken it on the pier at New York, and then passed out of his life. And with her had gone all his luck. It was as if her going had brought a curse upon him. On the very next trip he had had an unfortunate misunderstanding with an irritable gentleman from the Middle West, who, piqued at what he considered—not unreasonably—the undue proportion of kings and aces in the hands which Mr. Cootes had been dealing himself, expressed his displeasure by biting off the first joint of the other's right index finger—thus putting an abrupt end to a brilliant career. For it was on this finger that Mr. Cootes principally relied for the almost magical effects which he was wont to produce with a pack of cards after a little quiet shuffling.

With an aching sense of what might have been he thought now of his lost Lizzie. Regretfully he admitted to himself that she had always been the brains of the firm. A certain manual dexterity he had no doubt possessed, but it was ever Lizzie who had been responsible for the finer work. If they had still been partners, he really believed that she could have discovered some way of getting round the obstacles which had reared themselves now between himself and the necklace of Lady Constance Keeble. It was in a humble and contrite spirit that Edward Cootes proceeded on his way to Market Blandings.

.   .   .   .

Miss Peavey, meanwhile, who, it will be remembered, was moving slowly along the road from the Market Blandings end, was finding her walk both restful and enjoyable. There were moments, it has to be recorded, when the society of her hostess and her hostess' relations was something of a strain to Miss Peavey; and she was glad to be alone. Her headache had disappeared, and she revelled in the quiet evening hush. About now, if she had not had the sense to detach herself from the castle platoon, she would, she reflected, be listening to Lord Emsworth's speech on the subject of the late Hartley Reddish, J.P., M.P.: a topic which even the noblest of orators might have failed to render really gripping. And what she knew of her host gave her little confidence in his powers of oratory.

Yes, she was well out of it. The gentle breeze played soothingly upon her face. Her delicately modelled nostrils drank in gratefully the scent from the hedgerows.

Somewhere out of sight a thrush was singing. And so moved was Miss Peavey by the peace and sweetness of it all that she, too, began to sing.

Had those who enjoyed the privilege of her acquaintance at Blandings Castle been informed that Miss Peavey was about to sing, they would doubtless have considered themselves on firm ground if called upon to make a conjecture as to the type of song which she would select. Something quaint, dreamy, a little wistful . . . that would have been the universal guess . . . some old-world ballad, possibily . . .

What Miss Peavey actually sang—in a soft, meditative voice like that of a linnet waking to greet a new dawn—was that curious composition known as "The Beale Street Blues."

As she reached the last line, she broke off abruptly. She was, she perceived, no longer alone. Down the road toward her, walking pensively like one with a secret sorrow, a man was approaching; and for an instant, as she turned the corner, something in his appearance seemed to catch her by the throat and her breath came sharply.

"Gee!" said Miss Peavey.

She was herself again the next moment. A chance resemblance had misled her. She could not see the man's face, for his head was bent, but how was it possible . . .

And then, when he was quite close, he raised his head, and the county of Shropshire, as far as it was visible to her amazed eyes, executed a sudden and eccentric dance. Trees bobbed up and down, hedgerows shimmied like a Broadway chorus; and from out of the midst of the whirling country-side a voice spoke.

"Liz!"

"Eddie!" ejaculated Miss Peavey faintly, and sat down in a heap on a grassy bank.

§ 4

"Well, for goodness' sake!" said Miss Peavey.

Shropshire had become static once more. She stared at him, wide-eyed.

"Can you tie it!" said Miss Peavey.

She ran her gaze over him once again from head to foot.

"Well, if this ain't the cat's whiskers!" said Miss Peavey. And with this final pronouncement she rose from her bank, somewhat restored, and addressed herself to the task of picking up old threads.

"Wherever," she inquired, "did you spring from, Ed?"

There was nothing but affection in her voice. Her gaze was that of a mother contemplating her long-lost child. The past was past and a new era had begun. In the past she had been compelled to describe this man as a hunk of cheese and to express the opinion that his crookedness was such as to enable him to hide at will behind a spiral staircase; but now, in the joy of this unexpected reunion, all these harsh views were forgotten. This was Eddie Cootes, her old side-kick, come back to her after many days, and only now was it borne in upon her what a gap in her life his going had made. She flung herself into his arms with a glad cry.

Mr. Cootes, who had not been expecting this demonstration of esteem, staggered a trifle at the impact, but recovered himself sufficiently to return the embrace, with something of his ancient warmth. He was delighted at this

cordiality, but also surprised. The memory of the lady's
parting words on the occasion of their last meeting was
still green, and he had not realised how quickly women
forget and forgive, and how a sensitive girl, stirred by
some fancied injury, may address a man as a pie-faced
plugugly and yet retain in her inmost heart all the old
love and affection. He kissed Miss Peavey fondly.

"Liz," he said with fervour, "you're prettier than
ever."

"Now you behave," responded Miss Peavey coyly.

The arrival of a baaing flock of sheep, escorted by a
priggish dog and followed by a couple of the local peasantry, caused an intermission in these tender exchanges;
and by the time the procession had moved off down the
road they were in a more suitable frame of mind to converse quietly and in a practical spirit, to compare notes,
and to fill up the blanks.

"Wherever," inquired Miss Peavey again, "did you
spring from, Ed? You could of knocked me down with a
feather when I saw you coming along the road. I couldn't
have believed it was you, this far from the ocean. What
are you doing inland like this? Taking a vacation, or
aren't you working the boats any more?"

"No, Liz," said Mr. Cootes sadly. "I've had to give
that up."

And he exhibited the hiatus where an important section
of his finger had been and told his painful tale. His
companion's sympathy was balm to his wounded soul.

"The risks of the profession, of course," said Mr. Cootes
moodily, removing the exhibit in order to place his arm
about her slender waist. "Still, it's done me in. I tried
once or twice, but I couldn't seem to make the cards behave

no more, so I quit. Ah, Liz," said Mr. Cootes with feeling, "you can take it from me that I've had no luck since you left me. Regular hoodoo there's been on me. If I'd walked under a ladder on a Friday to smash a mirror over the dome of a black cat I couldn't have had it tougher."

"You poor boy!"

Mr. Cootes nodded sombrely.

"Tough," he agreed, "but there it is. Only this afternoon my jinx gummed the game for me and threw a spanner into the prettiest little scenario you ever thought of . . . But let's not talk about my troubles. What are you doing now, Liz?"

"Me? Oh, I'm living near here."

Mr. Cootes started.

"Not married?" he exclaimed in alarm.

"No!" cried Miss Peavey with vehemence, and shot a tender glance up at his face. "And I guess you know why, Ed."

"You don't mean . . . you hadn't forgotten me?"

"As if I could ever forget you, Eddie! There's only one tintype on *my* mantelpiece."

"But it struck me . . . it sort of occurred to me as a passing thought that, when we saw each other last, you were a mite peeved with your Eddie . . ."

It was the first allusion either of them had made to the past unpleasantness, and it caused a faint blush to dye Miss Peavey's soft cheek.

"Oh, shucks!" she said. "I'd forgotten all about that next day. I was good and mad at the time, I'll allow, but if only you'd called me up next morning, Ed . . ."

There was a silence, as they mused on what might have been.

"What are you doing, living here?" asked Mr. Cootes after a pregnant pause. "Have you retired?"

"No, *sir*. I'm sitting in at a game with real worthwhile stakes. But, darn it," said Miss Peavey regretfully, "I'm wondering if it isn't too big for me to put through alone. Oh, Eddie, if only there was some way you and me could work it together like in the old days."

"What is it?"

"Diamonds, Eddie. A necklace. I've only had one look at it so far, but that was enough. Some of the best ice I've saw in years, Ed. Worth every cent of a hundred thousand berries."

The coincidence drew from Mr. Cootes a sharp exclamation.

"A necklace!"

"Listen, Ed, while I slip you the low-down. And, say, if you knew the relief it was to me talking good United States again! Like taking off a pair of tight shoes. I'm doing the high-toned stuff for the moment. Soulful. *You* remember, like I used to pull once or twice in the old days. Just after you and me had that little spat of ours I thought I'd take another trip in the old *Atlantic*—force of habit or something, I guess. Anyway, I sailed, and we weren't two days out from New York when I made the biggest kind of a hit with the dame this necklace belongs to. Seemed to take a shine to me right away . . ."

"I don't blame her!" murmured Mr. Cootes devotedly.

"Now don't you interrupt," said Miss Peavey, administering a gratified slap. "Where was I? Oh yes. This here now Lady Constance Keeble I'm telling you about . . ."

"What!"

"What's the matter now?"

"Lady Constance Keeble?"

"That's the name. She's Lord Emsworth's sister, who lives at a big place up the road. Blandings Castle it's called. She didn't seem like she was able to let me out of her sight, and I've been with her off and on ever since we landed. I'm visiting at the castle now."

A deep sigh, like the groan of some great spirit in travail, forced itself from between Mr. Cootes's lips.

"Well, wouldn't that jar you!" he demanded of circumambient space. "Of all the lucky ones! getting into the place like that, with the band playing and a red carpet laid down for you to walk on! Gee, if you fell down a well, Liz, you'd come up with the bucket. You're a human horseshoe, that's what you are. Say, listen. Lemme-tell-ya-sumf'n. Do you know what *I've* been doing this afternoon? Only trying to edge into the dam' place myself and getting the air two minutes after I was past the front door."

"What! *You*, Ed?"

"Sure. You're not the only one that's heard of that collection of ice."

"Oh, Ed!" Bitter disappointment rang in Miss Peavey's voice. "If only you could have worked it! Me and you partners again! It hurts to think of it. What was the stuff you pulled to get you in?"

Mr. Cootes so far forgot himself in his agony of spirit as to expectorate disgustedly at a passing frog. And even in this trivial enterprise failure dogged him. He missed the frog, which withdrew into the grass with a cold look of disapproval.

"Me?" said Mr. Cootes. "I thought I'd got it smooth.

I'd chummed up with a fellow who had been invited down to the place and had thought it over and decided not to go, so I said to myself, What's the matter with going there instead of him? A gink called McTodd this was, a poet, and none of the folks had ever set eyes on him, except the old man, who's too short-sighted to see any one, so . . ."

Miss Peavey interrupted.

"You don't mean to tell me, Ed Cootes, that you thought you could get into the castle by pretending to be Ralston McTodd?"

"Sure I did. Why not? It didn't seem like there was anything to it. A cinch, that's what it looked like. And the first guy I meet in the joint is a mutt who knows this McTodd well. We had a couple of words, and I beat it. I know when I'm not wanted."

"But, Ed! Ed! What do you mean? Ralston Mc-Todd is at the castle now, this very moment."

"How's that?"

"Sure. Been there coupla days and more. Long, thin bird with an eyeglass."

Mr. Cootes's mind was in a whirl. He could make nothing of this matter.

"Nothing like it! McTodd's not so darned tall or so thin, if it comes to that. And he didn't wear no eyeglass all the time I was with him. This . . ." He broke off sharply. "My gosh! I wonder!" he cried. "Liz! How many men are there in the joint right now?"

"Only four besides Lord Emsworth. There's a big party coming down for the County Ball, but that's all there is at present. There's Lord Emsworth's son, Freddie . . ."

"What does he look like?"

"Sort of a dude with blond hair slicked back. Then there's Mr. Keeble. He's short with a red face."

"And?"

"And Baxter. He's Lord Emsworth's secretary. Wears spectacles."

"And that's the lot?"

"That's all there is, not counting this here now McTodd and the help."

Mr. Cootes brought his hand down with a resounding report on his leg. The mildly pleasant look which had been a feature of his appearance during his interview with Psmith had vanished now, its place taken by one of an extremely sinister malevolence.

"And I let him shoo me out as if I was a stray pup!" he muttered through clenched teeth. "Of all the bunk games!"

"What *are* you talking about, Ed?"

"And I thanked him! *Thanked* him!" moaned Edward Cootes, writhing at the memory. "I thanked him for letting me go!"

"Eddie Cootes, whatever are you . . .?"

"Listen, Liz." Mr. Cootes mastered his emotion with a strong effort. "I blew into that joint and met this fellow with the eyeglass, and he told me he knew McTodd well and that I wasn't him. And, from what you tell me, this must be the very guy that's passing himself off as McTodd! Don't you see? This baby must have started working on the same lines I did. Got to know McTodd, found he wasn't coming to the castle, and came down instead of him, same as me. Only he got there first, damn him! Wouldn't that give you a pain in the neck!"

Amazement held Miss Peavey dumb for an instant. Then she spoke.

"The big stiff!" said Miss Peavey.

Mr. Cootes, regardless of a lady's presence, went even further in his censure.

"I had a feeling from the first that there was something not on the level about that guy!" said Miss Peavey. "Gee! He must be after that necklace too."

"Sure he's after the necklace," said Mr. Cootes impatiently. "What did you think he'd come down for? A change of air?"

"But, Ed! Say! Are you going to let him get away with it?"

"Am *I* going to let him get away with it!" said Mr. Cootes, annoyed by the foolish question. "Wake me up in the night and ask me!"

"But what are you going to do?"

"Do!" said Mr. Cootes. "Do! I'll tell you what I'm going to . . ." He paused, and the stern resolve that shone in his face seemed to flicker. "Say, what the hell *am* I going to do?" he went on somewhat weakly.

"You won't get anything by putting the folks wise that he's a fake. That would be the finish of him, but it wouldn't get *you* anywhere."

"No," said Mr. Cootes.

"Wait a minute while I think," said Miss Peavey.

There was a pause. Miss Peavey sat with knit brows.

"How would it be . . . ?" ventured Mr. Cootes.

"Cheese it!" said Miss Peavey.

Mr. Cootes cheesed it. The minutes ticked on.

"I've got it," said Miss Peavey. "This guy's ace-high with Lady Constance. You've got to get him alone right away and tell him he's got to get you invited to the place as a friend of his."

"I knew you'd think of something, Liz," said Mr. Cootes, almost humbly. "You always were a wonder like that. How am I to get him alone?"

"I can fix that. I'll ask him to come for a stroll with me. He's not what you'd call crazy about me, but he can't very well duck if I keep after him. We'll go down the drive. You'll be in the bushes—I'll show you the place. Then I'll send him to fetch me a wrap or something, and while I walk on he'll come back past where you're hiding, and you jump out at him."

"Liz," said Mr. Cootes, lost in admiration, "when it comes to doping out a scheme, you're the snake's eyebrows!"

"But what are you going to do if he just turns you down?"

Mr. Cootes uttered a bleak laugh, and from the recesses of his costume produced a neat little revolver.

"*He* won't turn me down!" he said.

§ 5

"Fancy!" said Miss Peavey. "If I had not had a headache and come back early, we should never have had this little chat!"

She gazed up at Psmith in her gentle, wistful way as they started together down the broad gravel drive. A timid, soulful little thing she looked.

"No," said Psmith.

It was not a gushing reply, but he was not feeling at

his sunniest. The idea that Miss Peavey might return from Bridgeford in advance of the main body had not occurred to him. As he would have said himself, he had confused the Unlikely with the Impossible. And the result had been that she had caught him beyond hope of retreat as he sat in his garden-chair and thought of Eve Halliday, who on their return from the lake had been seized with a fresh spasm of conscience and had gone back to the library to put in another hour's work before dinner. To decline Miss Peavey's invitation to accompany her down the drive in order to see if there were any signs of those who had been doing honour to the late Hartley Reddish, M.P., had been out of the question. But Psmith, though he went, went without pleasure. Every moment he spent in her society tended to confirm him more and more in the opinion that Miss Peavey was the curse of the species.

"And I have been so longing," continued his companion, "to have a nice, long talk. All these days I have felt that I haven't been able to get as *near* you as I should wish."

"Well, of course, with the others always about . . ."

"I meant in a spiritual sense, of course."

"I see."

"I wanted so much to discuss your wonderful poetry with you. You haven't so much as *mentioned* your work since you came here. *Have* you!"

"Ah, but, you see, I am trying to keep my mind off it."

"Really? Why?"

"My medical adviser warned me that I had been concentrating a trifle too much. He offered me the choice, in fact, between a complete rest and the loony-bin."

"The *what*, Mr. McTodd?"

"The lunatic asylum, he meant. These medical men express themselves oddly."

"But surely, then, you ought not to *dream* of trying to compose if it is as bad as that? And you told Lord Emsworth that you wished to stay at home this afternoon to write a poem."

Her glance showed nothing but tender solicitude, but inwardly Miss Peavey was telling herself that *that* would hold him for a while.

"True," said Psmith, "true. But you know what Art is. An inexorable mistress. The inspiration came, and I felt that I must take the risk. But it has left me weak, weak."

"You BIG STIFF!" said Miss Peavey. But not aloud. They walked on a few steps.

"In fact," said Psmith, with another inspiration. "I'm not sure I ought not to be going back and resting now."

Miss Peavey eyed a clump of bushes some dozen yards farther down the drive. They were quivering slightly, as though they sheltered some alien body; and Miss Peavey, whose temper was apt to be impatient, registered a resolve to tell Edward Cootes that, if he couldn't hide behind a bush without dancing about like a cat on hot bricks, he had better give up his profession and take to selling jellied eels. In which, it may be mentioned, she wronged her old friend. He had been as still as a statue until a moment before, when a large and excitable beetle had fallen down the space between his collar and his neck, an experience which might well have tried the subtlest woodsman.

"Oh, please don't go in yet," said Miss Peavey. "It is such a lovely evening. Hark to the music of the breeze in the tree-tops. So soothing. Like a far-away harp. I wonder if it is whispering secrets to the birds."

Psmith forbore to follow her into this region of speculation, and they walked past the bushes in silence.

Some little distance farther on, however, Miss Peavey seemed to relent.

"You *are* looking tired, Mr. McTodd," she said anxiously. "I am afraid you really have been overtaxing your strength. Perhaps after all you had better go back and lie down."

"You think so?"

"I am sure of it. I will just stroll on to the gates and see if the car is in sight."

"I feel that I am deserting you."

"Oh, please!" said Miss Peavey deprecatingly.

With something of the feelings of a long-sentence convict unexpectedly released immediately on his arrival in jail, Psmith retraced his steps. Glancing over his shoulder, he saw that Miss Peavey had disappeared round a bend in the drive; and he paused to light a cigarette. He had just thrown away the match and was walking on, well content with life, when a voice behind him said "Hey!" and the well-remembered form of Mr. Edward Cootes stepped out of the bushes.

"See this?" said Mr. Cootes, exhibiting his revolver.

"I do indeed, Comrade Cootes," replied Psmith. "And, if it is not an untimely question, what is the idea?"

"That," said Mr. Cootes, "is just in case you try any funny business." And, replacing the weapon in a handy pocket, he proceeded to slap vigorously at the region between his shoulder blades. He also wriggled with not a little animation.

Psmith watched these manœuvres gravely.

"You did not stop me at the pistol's point merely to watch you go through your Swedish exercises?" he said.

Mr. Cootes paused for an instant.

"Got a beetle or something down my back," he explained curtly.

"Ah? Then, as you will naturally wish to be alone in such a sad moment, I will be bidding you a cordial good evening and strolling on."

"No, you don't!"

"Don't I?" said Psmith resignedly. "Perhaps you are right, perhaps you are right." Mr. Cootes replaced the revolver once more. "I take it, then, Comrade Cootes, that you would have speech with me. Carry on, old friend, and get it off your diaphragm. What seems to be on your mind?"

A lucky blow appeared to have stunned Mr. Cootes's beetle, and he was able to give his full attention to the matter in hand. He stared at Psmith with considerable distaste.

"I'm on to you, Bill!" he said.

"My name is not Bill," said Psmith.

"No," snapped Mr. Cootes, his annoyance by this time very manifest. "And it's not McTodd."

Psmith looked at his companion thoughtfully. This was an unforeseen complication, and for the moment he would readily have admitted that he saw no way of over-coming it. That the other was in no genial frame of mind towards him the expression on his face would have showed, even if his actions had not been sufficient indication of the fact. Mr. Cootes, having disposed of his beetle and being now at leisure to concentrate his whole attention on Psmith, was eyeing that immaculate young man with a dislike which he did not attempt to conceal.

"Shall we be strolling on?" suggested Psmith. "Walking may assist thought. At the moment I am free to confess that you have opened up a subject which causes me some perplexity. I think, Comrade Cootes, having given the position of affairs a careful examination, that we may say that the next move is with you. What do you propose to do about it?"

"I'd like," said Mr. Cootes with asperity, "to beat your block off."

"No doubt. But . . ."

"I'd like to knock you for a goal!"

Psmith discouraged these Utopian dreams with a deprecating wave of the hand.

"I can readily understand it," he said courteously. "But, to keep within the sphere of practical politics, what is the actual move which you contemplate? You could expose me, no doubt, to my host, but I cannot see how that would profit you."

"I know that. But you can remember I've got that up my sleeve in case you try any funny business."

"You persist in harping on that possibility, Comrade Cootes. The idea seems to be an obsession with you. I can assure you that I contemplate no such thing. What, to return to the point, do you intend to do?"

They had reached the broad expanse opposite the front door, where the drive, from being a river, spread out into a lake of gravel. Psmith stopped.

"You've got to get me into this joint," said Mr. Cootes.

"I feared that that was what you were about to suggest. In my peculiar position I have naturally no choice but to endeavour to carry out your wishes. Any attempt not to do so would, I imagine, infallibly strike so keen a critic as yourself as 'funny business.' But how can I get you into what you breezily describe as 'this joint'?"

"You can say I'm a friend of yours and ask them to invite me."

Psmith shook his head gently.

"Not one of your brightest suggestions, Comrade Cootes. Tactfully refraining from stressing the point that an instant lowering of my prestige would inevitably ensue should it be supposed that you were a friend of mine, I will merely mention that, being myself merely a guest in this stately home of England, I can hardly go about inviting my chums here for indefinite visits. No, we must find another way. . . . You're sure you want to stay? Quite so, quite so, I merely asked. . . . Now, let us think."

Through the belt of rhododendrons which jutted out from one side of the castle a portly form at this point made itself visible, moving high and disposedly in the direction of the back premises. It was Beach, the butler, returning from the pleasant ramble in which he had indulged himself on the departure of his employer and the rest of the party. Revived by some gracious hours in the open air, Beach was returning to duty. And with the sight of him there came to Psmith a neat solution of the problem confronting him.

"Oh, Beach," he called.

"Sir?" responded a fruity voice. There was a brief pause while the butler navigated into the open. He removed the straw hat which he had donned for his excursion, and enfolded Psmith in a pop-eyed but not unkindly gaze. A thoughtful critic of country-house humanity, he had long since decided that he approved of Psmith. Since Lady Constance had first begun to offer the hospitality of the castle to the literary and artistic world, he had been profoundly shocked by some of the rare and curious specimens who had nodded their disordered locks and flaunted their ill-cut evening clothes at the dinner-table over which he presided; and Psmith had come as a pleasant surprise.

"Sorry to trouble you, Beach."

"Not at all, sir."

"This," said Psmith, indicating Mr. Cootes, who was viewing the scene with a wary and suspicious eye, an eye obviously alert for any signs of funny business, "is my man. My valet, you know. He has just arrived from town. I had to leave him behind to attend the bedside of a sick aunt. Your aunt was better when you came away, Cootes?" he inquired graciously

Mr. Cootes correctly interpreted this question as a feeler with regard to his views on this new development, and decided to accept the situation. True, he had hoped to enter the castle in a slightly higher capacity than that of a gentleman's personal gentleman, but he was an old campaigner. Once in, as he put it to himself with admirable common sense, he would be in.

"Yes, sir," he replied.

"Capital," said Psmith. "Capital. Then will you look after Cootes, Beach."

"Very good, sir," said the butler in a voice of cordial approval. The only point he had found to cavil at in Psmith had been removed; for it had hitherto pained him a little that a gentleman with so nice a taste in clothes as that dignified guest should have embarked on a visit to such a place as Blandings Castle without a personal attendant. Now all was explained and, as far as Beach was concerned, forgiven. He proceeded to escort Mr. Cootes to the rear. They disappeared behind the rhododendrons.

They had hardly gone when a sudden thought came to Psmith as he sat once more in the coolness of the hall. He pressed the bell. Strange, he reflected, how one overlooked these obvious things. That was how generals lost battles.

"Sir?" said Beach, appearing through the green baize door.

"Sorry to trouble you again, Beach."

"Not at all, sir."

"I hope you will make Cootes comfortable. I think you will like him. His, when you get to know him, is a very winning personality."

"He seems a nice young fellow, sir."

"Oh, by the way, Beach. You might ask him if he brought my revolver from town with him."

"Yes, sir," said Beach, who would have scorned to betray emotion if it had been a Lewis gun.

"I think I saw it sticking out of his pocket. You might bring it to me, will you?"

"Very good, sir."

Beach retired, to return a moment later. On the silver salver which he carried the lethal weapon was duly reposing.

"Your revolver, sir," said Beach.

"Thank you," said Psmith.

§ 6

For some moments after the butler had withdrawn in his stately pigeon-toed way through the green baize door, Psmith lay back in his chair with the feeling that something attempted, something done, had earned a night's repose. He was not so sanguine as to suppose that he had actually checkmated an adversary of Mr. Cootes's strenuousness by the simple act of removing a revolver from his possession; but there was no denying the fact that the feel of the thing in his pocket engendered a certain cosy satisfaction. The little he had seen of Mr. Cootes had been enough to convince him that the other was a man who was far better off without an automatic pistol. There was an impulsiveness about his character which did not go well with the possession of fire-arms.

Psmith's meditations had taken him thus far when they were interrupted by an imperative voice.

"Hey!"

Only one person of Psmith's acquaintance was in the habit of opening his remarks in this manner. It was consequently no surprise to him to find Mr. Edward Cootes standing at his elbow.

"Hey!"

"All right, Comrade Cootes," said Psmith with a touch of austerity, "I heard you the first time. And may I remind you that this habit of yours of popping out from unexpected places and saying 'Hey!' is one which should be overcome. Valets are supposed to wait till rung for. At least, I think so. I must confess that until this moment I have never had a valet."

"And you wouldn't have one now if I could help it," responded Mr. Cootes.

Psmith raised his eyebrows.

"Why," he inquired, surprised, "this peevishness? Don't you like being a valet?"

"No, I don't."

"You astonish me. I should have thought you would have gone singing about the house. Have you considered that the tenancy of such a position throws you into the constant society of Comrade Beach, than whom it would be difficult to imagine a more delightful companion?"

"Old stiff!" said Mr. Cootes sourly. "If there's one thing that makes me tired, it's a guy that talks about his darned stomach all the time."

"I beg your pardon?"

"The Beach gook," explained Mr. Cootes, "has got something wrong with the lining of his stomach, and if I hadn't made my getaway he'd be talking about it yet."

"If you fail to find entertainment and uplift in first-hand information about Comrade Beach's stomach, you must indeed be hard to please. I am to take it, then, that you came snorting out here, interrupting my daydreams, merely in order to seek my sympathy?"

Mr. Cootes gazed upon him with a smouldering eye.

"I came to tell you I suppose you think you're darned smart."

"And very nice of you, too," said Psmith, touched. "A pretty compliment, for which I am not ungrateful."

"You got that gun away from me mighty smoothly, didn't you?"

"Since you mention it, yes."

"And now I suppose you think you're going to slip in

ahead of me and get away with that necklace? Well, say, listen, lemme tell you it'll take some one better than a half-baked string-bean like you to put one over on me."

"I seem," said Psmith, pained, "to detect a certain animus creeping into your tone. Surely we can be trade rivals without this spirit of hostility. My attitude towards you is one of kindly tolerance."

"Even if you get it, where do you think you're going to hide it? And, believe me, it'll take some hiding. Say, lemme tell you something. I'm your valet, ain't I? Well, then, I can come into your room and be tidying up whenever I darn please, can't I? Sure I can. I'll tell the world I can do just that little thing. And you take it from me, Bill . . ."

"You persist in the delusion that my name is William . . ."

"You take it from me, Bill, that if ever that necklace disappears and it isn't me that's done the disappearing, you'll find me tidying up in a way that'll make you dizzy. I'll go through that room of yours with a fine-tooth comb. So chew on that, will you?"

And Edward Cootes, moving sombrely across the hall, made a sinister exit. The mood of cool reflection was still to come, when he would realise that, in his desire to administer what he would have described as a hot one, he had acted a little rashly in putting his enemy on his guard. All he was thinking now was that his brief sketch of the position of affairs would have the effect of diminishing Psmith's complacency a trifle. He had, he flattered himself, slipped over something that could be classed as a jolt.

Nor was he unjustified in this view. The aspect of the matter on which he had touched was one that had not previously presented itself to Psmith: and, musing on it as he resettled himself in his chair, he could see that it afforded food for thought. As regarded the disposal of the necklace, should it ever come into his possession, he had formed no definite plan. He had assumed that he would conceal it somewhere until the first excitement of the chase slackened, and it was only now that he realised the difficulty of finding a suitable hiding-place outside his bedroom. Yes, it was certainly a matter on which, as Mr. Cootes had suggested, he would do well to chew. For ten minutes, accordingly, he did so. And—it being practically impossible to keep a good man down—at the end of that period he was rewarded with an idea. He rose from his chair and pressed the bell.

"Ah, Beach," he said affably, as the green baize door swung open, "I must apologise once more for troubling you. I keep ringing, don't I?"

"No trouble at all, sir," responded the butler paternally. "But if you were ringing to summon your personal attendant, I fear he is not immediately available. He left me somewhat abruptly a few moments ago. I was not aware that you would be requiring his services until the dressing-gong sounded, or I would have detained him."

"Never mind. It was you I wished to see. Beach," said Psmith, "I am concerned about you. I learn from my man that the lining of your stomach is not all it should be."

"That is true, sir," replied Beach, an excited gleam coming into his dull eyes. He shivered slightly, as might a war-horse at the sound of the bugle. "I do have trouble with the lining of my stomach."

"Every stomach has a silver lining."

"Sir?"

"I said, tell me all about it."

"Well, really, sir . . ." said Beach wistfully.

"To please me," urged Psmith.

"Well, sir, it is extremely kind of you to take an interest. It generally starts with a dull shooting pain on the right side of the abdomen from twenty minutes to half an hour after the conclusion of a meal. The symptoms . . ."

There was nothing but courteous sympathy in Psmith's gaze as he listened to what sounded like an eyewitness's account of the San Francisco earthquake, but inwardly he was wishing that his companion could see his way to making it a bit briefer and snappier. However, all things come to an end. Even the weariest river winds somewhere to the sea. With a moving period, the butler finally concluded his narrative.

"Parks' Pepsinine," said Psmith promptly.

"Sir?"

"That's what you want. Parks' Pepsinine. It would set you right in no time."

"I will make a note of the name, sir. The specific has not come to my notice until now. And, if I may say so," added Beach, with a glassy but adoring look at his benefactor, "I should like to express my gratitude for your kindness."

"Not at all, Beach, not at all. Oh, Beach," he said, as the other started to manœuvre towards the door, "I've just remembered. There was something else I wanted to talk to you about."

"Yes, sir?"

"I thought it might be as well to speak to you about it

before approaching Lady Constance. The fact is, Beach, I am feeling cramped."

"Indeed, sir? I forgot to mention that one of the symptoms from which I suffer is a sharp cramp."

"Too bad. But let us, if you do not mind, shelve for the moment the subject of your interior organism and its ailments. When I say I am feeling cramped, I mean spiritually. Have you ever written poetry, Beach?"

"No, sir."

"Ah! Then it may be a little difficult for you to understand my feelings. My trouble is this. Out in Canada, Beach, I grew accustomed to doing my work in the most solitary surroundings. You remember that passage in my *Songs of Squalor* which begins 'Across the pale parabola of Joy . . .'?"

"I fear, sir . . ."

"You missed it? Tough luck. Try to get hold of it some time. It's a bird. Well, that passage was written in a lonely hut on the banks of the Saskatchewan, miles away from human habitation. I am like that, Beach. I need the stimulus of the great open spaces. When I am surrounded by my fellows, inspiration slackens and dies. You know how it is when there are people about. Just as you are starting in to write a nifty, some one comes and sits down on the desk and begins talking about himself. Every time you get going nicely, in barges some alien influence and the Muse goes blooey. You see what I mean?"

"Yes, sir," said Beach, gaping slightly.

"Well, that is why for a man like me existence in Blandings Castle has its drawbacks. I have got to get a place where I can be alone, Beach—alone with my dreams and visions. Some little eyrie perched on the cliffs of Time. . . . In other words, do you know of an empty cottage somewhere on the estate where I could betake myself when in the mood and swing a nib without any possibility of being interrupted?"

"A little cottage, sir?"

"A little cottage. With honeysuckle over the door, and Old Mister Moon climbing up above the trees. A cottage, Beach, where I can meditate, where I can turn the key in the door and bid the world go by. Now that the castle is going to be full of all these people who are coming for the County Ball, it is imperative that I wangle such a haven. Otherwise, a considerable slab of priceless poetry will be lost to humanity for ever."

"You desire," said Beach, feeling his way cautiously, "a small cottage where you can write poetry, sir?"

"You follow me like a leopard. Do you know of such a one?"

"There is an unoccupied gamekeeper's cottage in the west wood, sir, but it is an extremely humble place."

"Be it never so humble, it will do for me. Do you think Lady Constance would be offended if I were to ask for the loan of it for a few days?"

"I fancy that her ladyship would receive the request with equanimity, sir. She is used to . . . She is not unaccustomed . . . Well, I can only say, sir, that there was a literary gentleman visiting the castle last summer who expressed a desire to take sun-baths in the garden each morning before breakfast. In the nood, sir. And, beyond instructing me to warn the maids, her ladyship placed no obstacle in the way of the fulfilment of his wishes. So . . ."

"So a modest request like mine isn't likely to cause a heart-attack? Admirable! You don't know what it means to me to feel that I shall soon have a little refuge of my own, to which I can retreat and be in solitude."

"I can imagine that it must be extremely gratifying, sir."

"Then I will put the motion before the Board directly Lady Constance returns."

"Very good, sir."

"I should like to splash it on the record once more, Beach, that I am much obliged to you for your sympathy and advice in this matter. I knew you would not fail me."

"Not at all, sir. I am only too glad to have been able to be of assistance."

"Oh, and, Beach . . ."

"Sir?"

"Just one other thing. Will you be seeing Cootes, my valet, again shortly?"

"Quite shortly, sir, I should imagine."

"Then would you mind just prodding him smartly in the lower ribs . . ."

"Sir?" cried Beach, startled out of his butlerian calm. He swallowed a little convulsively. For eighteen months and more, ever since Lady Constance Keeble had first begun to cast her fly and hook over the murky water of the artistic world and jerk its denizens on to the pile carpets of Blandings Castle, Beach had had his fill of eccentricity. But until this moment he had hoped that Psmith was going to prove an agreeable change from the stream of literary lunatics which had been coming and going all that weary time. And lo! Psmith's name led all the rest.

Even the man who had come for a week in April and had wanted to eat jam with his fish paled in comparison.

"Prod him in the ribs, sir?" he quavered.

"Prod him in the ribs," said Psmith firmly. "And at the same time whisper in his ear the word 'Aha!'"

Beach licked his dry lips.

"Aha, sir?"

"Aha! And say it came from me."

"Very good, sir. The matter shall be attended to," said Beach. And with a muffled sound that was half a sigh, half a death-rattle, he tottered through the green-baize loor.

CHAPTER X

§ 1

BREAKFAST was over, and the guests of Blandings had scattered to their morning occupations. Some were writing letters, some were in the billiard-room: some had gone to the stables, some to the links: Lady Constance was interviewing the housekeeper, Lord Emsworth harrying head-gardener McAllister among the flower-beds: and in the Yew Alley, the dappled sunlight falling upon her graceful head, Miss Peavey walked pensively up and down.

She was alone. It is a sad but indisputable fact that in this imperfect world Genius is too often condemned to walk alone—if the earthier members of the community see it coming and have time to duck. Not one of the horde of visitors who had arrived overnight for the County Ball had shown any disposition whatever to court Miss Peavey's society.

One regrets this. Except for that slight bias towards dishonesty which led her to steal everything she could lay her hands on that was not nailed down, Aileen Peavey's was an admirable character; and, oddly enough, it was the noble side of her nature to which these coarse-fibred critics objected. Of Miss Peavey, the purloiner of other people's goods, they knew nothing; the woman they were dodging was Miss Peavey, the poetess. And it may be

220

mentioned that, however much she might unbend in the presence of a congenial friend like Mr. Edward Cootes, she was a perfectly genuine poetess. Those six volumes under her name in the British Museum catalogue were her own genuine and unaided work: and, though she had been compelled to pay for the production of the first of the series, the other five had been brought out at her publisher's own risk, and had even made a little money.

Miss Peavey, however, was not sorry to be alone: for she had that on her mind which called for solitary thinking. The matter engaging her attention was the problem of what on earth had happened to Mr. Edward Cootes. Two days had passed since he had left her to go and force Psmith at the pistol's point to introduce him into the castle: and since that moment he had vanished completely. Miss Peavey could not understand it.

His non-appearance was all the more galling in that her superb brain had just completed in every detail a scheme for the seizure of Lady Constance Keeble's diamond necklace; and to the success of this plot his aid was an indispensable adjunct. She was in the position of a general who comes from his tent with a plan of battle all mapped out, and finds that his army has strolled off somewhere and left him. Little wonder that, as she paced the Yew Alley, there was a frown on Miss Peavey's fair forehead.

The Yew Alley, as Lord Emsworth had indicated in his extremely interesting lecture to Mr. Ralston McTodd at the Senior Conservative Club, contained among other noteworthy features certain yews which rose in solid blocks with rounded roof and stemless mushroom finials, the majority possessing arched recesses, forming arbours. As

Miss Peavey was passing one of these, a voice suddenly addressed her.

"Hey!"

Miss Peavey started violently.

"Any one about?"

A damp face with twigs sticking to it was protruding from a near-by yew. It rolled its eyes in an ineffectual effort to see round the corner.

Miss Peavey drew nearer, breathing heavily. The question as to the whereabouts of her wandering boy was solved; but the abruptness of his return had caused her to bite her tongue; and joy, as she confronted him, was blended with other emotions.

"You dish-faced gazooni!" she exclaimed heatedly, her voice trembling with a sense of ill-usage, "where do you get that stuff, hiding in trees, and barking a girl's head off?"

"Sorry, Liz. I . . ."

"And where," proceeded Miss Peavey, ventilating another grievance, "have you been all this darned time? Gosh-dingit, you leave me a coupla days back saying you're going to stick up this bozo that calls himself Mc-Todd with a gat and make him get you into the house, and that's the last I see of you. What's the big idea?"

"It's all right, Liz. He did get me into the house. I'm his valet. That's why I couldn't get at you before. The way the help has to keep itself to itself in this joint, we might as well have been in different counties. If I hadn't happened to see you snooping off by yourself this morning . . ."

Miss Peavey's keen mind grasped the position of affairs.

"All right, all right," she interrupted, ever impatient

of long speeches from others. "I understand. Well, this is good, Ed. It couldn't have worked out better. I've got a scheme all doped out, and now you're here we can get busy."

"A scheme?"

"A pippin," assented Miss Peavey.

"It'll need to be," said Mr. Cootes, on whom the events of the last few days had caused pessimism to set its seal. "I tell you that McTodd gook is smooth. He somehow," said Mr. Cootes prudently, for he feared harsh criticisms from his lady-love should he reveal the whole truth, "he somehow got wise to the notion that, as I was his valet, I could go and snoop round in his room, where he'd be wanting to hide the stuff if he ever got it, and now he's gone and got them to let him have a kind of shack in the woods."

"H'm!" said Miss Peavey. "Well," she resumed after a thoughtful pause, "I'm not worrying about him. Let him go and roost in the woods all he wants to. I've got a scheme all ready, and it's gilt-edged. And, unless you ball up your end of it, Ed, it can't fail to drag home the gravy."

"Am I in it?"

"You bet you're in it. I can't work it without you. That's what's been making me so darned mad when you didn't show up all this time."

"Spill it, Liz," said Mr. Cootes, humbly. As always in the presence of this dynamic woman, he was suffering from an inferiority complex. From the very start of their combined activities she had been the brains of the firm, he merely the instrument to carry into effect the plans she dictated.

Miss Peavey glanced swiftly up and down the Yew Alley. It was still the same peaceful, lonely spot. She turned to Mr. Cootes again and spoke with brisk decision.

"Now, listen, Ed, and get this straight, because maybe I shan't have another chance of talking to you."

"I'm listening," said Mr. Cootes obsequiously.

"Well, to begin with, now that the house is full, Her Nibs is wearing that necklace every night. And you can take it from me, Ed, that you want to put on your smoked glasses before you look at it. It's a lalapaloosa."

"As good as that?"

"Ask me! You don't know the half of it."

"Where does she keep it, Liz? Have you found that out?" asked Mr. Cootes, a gleam of optimism playing across his sad face for an instant.

"No, I haven't. And I don't want to. I've not go. time to waste monkeying about with safes and maybe having the whole bunch pile on the back of my neck. I believe in getting things easy. Well, to-night this bimbo that calls himself McTodd is going to give a reading of his poems in the big drawing-room. You know where that is?"

"I can find out."

"And you better had find out," said Miss Peavey vehemently. "And before to-night at that. Well, there you are. Do you begin to get wise?"

Mr. Cootes, his head protruding unhappily from the yew tree, would have given much to have been able to make the demanded claim to wisdom, for he knew of old the store his alert partner set upon quickness of intellect. He was compelled, however, to disturb the branches by shaking his head.

"You always were pretty dumb," said Miss Peavey with scorn. "I'll say that you've got good solid qualities, Ed—from the neck up. Why, I'm going to sit behind Lady Constance while that goof is shooting his fool head off, and I'm going to reach out and grab that necklace off of her. See?"

"But, Liz"—Mr. Cootes diffidently summoned up courage to point out what appeared to him to be a flaw in the scheme—"if you start any strong-arm work in front of everybody like the way you say, won't they . . .?"

"No, they won't. And I'll tell you why they won't. They aren't going to see me do it, because when I do it it's going to be good and dark in that room. And it's going to be dark because you'll be somewheres out at the back of the house, wherever they keep the main electric-light works, turning the switch as hard as you can go. See? That's your end of it, and pretty soft for you at that. All you have to do is to find out where the thing is and what you have to do to it to put out all the lights in the joint. I guess I can trust you not to bungle that?"

"Liz," said Mr. Cootes, and there was reverence in his voice, "you can do just that little thing. But what . . .?"

"All right, I know what you're going to say. What happens after that, and how do I get away with the stuff? Well, the window'll be open and I'll just get to it and fling the necklace out. See? There'll be a big fuss going on in the room on account of the darkness and all that, and while everybody's cutting up and what-the-helling, you'll pick up your dogs and run round as quick as you can make it and pouch the thing. I guess it won't be hard for you to locate it. The window's just over the terrace, all smooth turf, and it isn't real dark nights now, and you ought to have plenty of time to hunt around before they can get the lights going again. . . . Well, what do you think of it?"

There was a brief silence.

"Liz," said Mr. Cootes at length.

"Is it or is it not," demanded Miss Peavey, "a ball of fire?"

"Liz," said Mr. Cootes, and his voice was husky with such awe as some young officer of Napoleon's staff might have felt on hearing the details of the latest plan of campaign, "Liz, I've said it before, and I'll say it again. When it comes to the smooth stuff, old girl, you're the oyster's eye-tooth!"

And, reaching out an arm from the recesses of the yew, he took Miss Peavey's hand in his and gave it a tender squeeze. A dreamy look came into the poetess's fine eyes, and she giggled a little. Dumb-bell though he was, she loved this man.

§ 2

"Mr. Baxter!"

"Yes, Miss Halliday?"

The Brains of Blandings looked abstractedly up from his desk. It was only some half-hour since luncheon had finished, but already he was in the library surrounded by large books like a sea-beast among rocks. Most of his time was spent in the library when the castle was full of guests, for his lofty mind was ill-attuned to the frivolous babblings of Society butterflies.

"I wonder if you could spare me this afternoon?" said Eve.

Baxter directed the glare of his spectacles upon her inquisitorially.

"The whole afternoon?"

"If you don't mind. You see, I had a letter by the second post from a great friend of mine, saying that she will be in Market Blandings this afternoon and asking me to meet her there. I must see her, Mr. Baxter, *please*. You've no notion how important it is."

Eve's manner was excited, and her eyes as they met Baxter's sparkled in a fashion that might have disturbed a man made of less stern stuff. If it had been the Hon. Freddie Threepwood, for instance, who had been gazing into their blue depths, that impulsive youth would have tied himself into knots and yapped like a dog. Baxter, the superman, felt no urge towards any such display. He reviewed her request calmly and judicially, and decided that it was a reasonable one.

"Very well, Miss Halliday."

"Thank you ever so much. I'll make up for it by working twice as hard to-morrow."

Eve flitted to the door, pausing there to bestow a grateful smile upon him before going out; and Baxter returned to his reading. For a moment he was conscious of a feeling of regret that this quite attractive and uniformly respectful girl should be the partner in crime of a man of whom he disapproved even more than he disapproved of most malefactors. Then he crushed down the weak emotion and was himself again.

Eve trotted downstairs, humming happily to herself. She had expected a longer and more strenuous struggle before she obtained her order of release, and told herself that, despite a manner which seldom deviated from the forbidding, Baxter was really quite nice. In short, it seemed to her that nothing could possibly occur to mar the joyfulness of this admirable afternoon; and it was only when a voice hailed her as she was going through the hall a few minutes later that she realised that she was mistaken. The voice, which trembled throatily, was that of the Hon. Freddie; and her first look at him told Eve, an expert diagnostician, that he was going to propose to her again.

"Well, Freddie?" said Eve resignedly.

The Hon. Frederick Threepwood was a young man who was used to hearing people say, "Well, Freddie?" resignedly when he appeared. His father said it; his Aunt Constance said it; all his other aunts and uncles said it. Widely differing personalities in every other respect, they all said, "Well, Freddie?" resignedly directly they caught sight of him. Eve's words, therefore, and the tone in which they were spoken, did not damp him as they might have damped another. His only feeling was one of solemn gladness at the thought that at last he had managed to get her alone for half a minute.

The fact that this was the first time he had been able to get her alone since her arrival at the castle had caused Freddie a good deal of sorrow. Bad luck was what he attributed it to, thereby giving the object of his affections less credit than was her due for a masterly policy of evasion. He sidled up, looking like a well-dressed sheep.

"Going anywhere?" he inquired.

"Yes. I'm going to Market Blandings. Isn't it a lovely afternoon? I suppose you are busy all the time now that the house is full? Good-bye," said Eve.

"Eh?" said Freddie, blinking.

"Good-bye. I must be hurrying."

"Where did you say you were going?"

"Market Blandings."

"I'll come with you."

"No, I want to be alone. I've got to meet some one there."

"Come with you as far as the gates," said Freddie, the human limpet.

The afternoon sun seemed to Eve to be shining a little less brightly as they started down the drive. She was a kind-hearted girl, and it irked her to have to be continually acting as a black frost in Freddie's garden of dreams. There appeared, however, to be but two ways out of the thing: either she must accept him or he must stop proposing. The first of these alternatives she resolutely declined to consider, and, as far as was ascertainable from his actions, Freddie declined just as resolutely to consider the second. The result was that solitary interviews between them were seldom wholly free from embarrassing developments.

They walked for a while in silence. Then:

"You're dashed hard on a fellow," said Freddie.

"How's your putting coming on?" asked Eve.

"Eh?"

"Your putting. You told me you had so much trouble with it."

She was not looking at him, for she had developed a habit of not looking at him on these occasions; but she assumed that the odd sound which greeted her remark was a hollow, mirthless laugh.

"My putting!"

"Well, you told me yourself it's the most important part of golf."

"Golf! Do you think I have time to worry about golf these days?"

"Oh, how splendid, Freddie! Are you really doing some work of some kind? It's quite time, you know. Think how pleased your father will be."

"I say," said Freddie, "I do think you might marry a chap."

"I suppose I shall some day," said Eve, "if I meet the right one."

"No, no!" said Freddie despairingly. She was not usually so dense as this. He had always looked on her as a dashed clever girl. "I mean *me.*"

Eve sighed. She had hoped to avert the inevitable.

"Oh, Freddie!" she exclaimed, exasperated. She was still sorry for him, but she could not help being irritated. It was such a splendid afternoon and she had been feeling so happy. And now he had spoiled everything. It always took her at least half an hour to get over the nervous strain of refusing his proposals.

"I love you, dash it!" said Freddie.

"Well, do stop loving me," said Eve. "I'm an awful girl, really. I'd make you miserable."

"Happiest man in the world," corrected Freddie devoutly.

"I've got a frightful temper."

"You're an angel."

Eve's exasperation increased. She always had a curious fear that one of these days, if he went on proposing, she might say "Yes" by mistake. She wished that there

was some way known to science of stopping him once and
for all. And in her desperation she thought of a line of
argument which she had not yet employed.

"It's so absurd, Freddie," she said. "Really, it is.
Apart from the fact that I don't want to marry you, how
can you marry any one—any one, I mean, who hasn't
plenty of money?"

"Wouldn't dream of marrying for money."

"No, of course not, but . . ."

"Cupid," said Freddie woodenly, "pines and sickens in
a gilded cage."

Eve had not expected to be surprised by anything her
companion might say, it being her experience that he
possessed a vocabulary of about forty-three words and a
sum-total of ideas that hardly ran into two figures; but
this poetic remark took her back.

"What!"

Freddie repeated the observation. When it had been
flashed on the screen as a spoken sub-title in the six-reel
wonder film, "Love or Mammon" (Beatrice Comely and
Brian Fraser), he had approved and made a note of it.

"Oh!" said Eve, and was silent. As Miss Peavey would
have put it, it held her for a while. "What I meant,"
she went on after a moment, "was that you can't possibly
marry a girl without money unless you've some money of
your own."

"I say, dash it!" A strange note of jubilation had
come into the wooer's voice. "I say, is that really all that
stands between us? Because . . ."

"No, it isn't!"

"Because, look here, I'm going to have quite a good
deal of money at any moment. It's more or less of a

secret, you know—in fact a pretty deadish secret—so keep it dark, but Uncle Joe is going to give me a couple of thousand quid. He promised me. Two thousand of the crispest. Absolutely!"

"Uncle Joe?"

"*You* know. Old Keeble. He's going to give me a couple of thousand quid, and then I'm going to buy a partnership in a bookie's business and simply coin money. Stands to reason, I mean. You can't help making your bally fortune. Look at all the mugs who are losing money all the time at the races. It's the bookies that get the stuff. A pal of mine who was up at Oxford with me is in a bookie's office, and they're going to let me in if I . . ."

The momentous nature of his information had caused Eve to deviate now from her policy of keeping her eyes off Freddie when in emotional vein. And, if she had desired to check his lecture on finance, she could have chosen no better method than to look at him; for, meeting her gaze, Freddie immediately lost the thread of his discourse and stood yammering. A direct hit from Eve's eyes always affected him in this way.

"Mr. Keeble is going to give you two thousand pounds!"

A wave of mortification swept over Eve. If there was one thing on which she prided herself, it was the belief that she was a loyal friend, a staunch pal; and now for the first time she found herself facing the unpleasant truth that she had been neglecting Phyllis Jackson's interests in the most abominable way ever since she had come to Blandings. She had definitely promised Phyllis that she would tackle this stepfather of hers and shame him with burning words into yielding up the three thousand pounds which Phyllis needed so desperately for her Lincolnshire farm. And what had she done? Nothing.

Eve was honest to the core, even in her dealings with herself. A less conscientious girl might have argued that she had had no opportunity of a private interview with Mr. Keeble. She scorned to soothe herself with this specious plea. If she had given her mind to it she could have brought about a dozen private interviews, and she knew it. No. She had allowed the pleasant persistence of Psmith to take up her time, and Phyllis and her troubles had been thrust into the background. She confessed, despising herself, that she had hardly given Phyllis a thought.

And all the while this Mr. Keeble had been in a position to scatter largess, thousands of pounds of it, to undeserving people like Freddie. Why, a word from her about Phyllis would have . . .

"Two thousand pounds?" she repeated dizzily. "Mr. Keeble!"

"Absolutely!" cried Freddie radiantly. The first shock of looking into her eyes had passed, and he was now revelling in that occupation.

"What for?"

Freddie's rapt gaze flickered. Love, he perceived, had nearly caused him to be indiscreet.

"Oh, I don't know," he mumbled. "He's just giving it me, you know, don't you know."

"Did you simply go to him and ask him for it?"

"Well—er—well, yes. That was about the strength of it."

"And he didn't object?"

"No. He seemed rather pleased."

"Pleased!" Eve found breathing difficult. She was feeling rather like a man who suddenly discovers that the hole in his back yard which he has been passing nonchalantly for months is a goldmine. If the operation of extracting money from Mr. Keeble was not only easy but also agreeable to the victim . . . She became aware of a sudden imperative need for Freddie's absence. She wanted to think this thing over.

"Well, then," said Freddie, "coming back to it, will you?"

"What?" said Eve, distrait.

"Marry me, you know. What I mean to say is, I worship the very ground you walk on, and all that sort of rot . . . I mean, and all that. And now that you realise that I'm going to get this couple of thousand . . . and the bookie's business . . . and what not, I mean to say . . ."

"Freddie," said Eve tensely, expressing her harassed nerves in a voice that came hotly through clenched teeth, "go away!"

"Eh?"

"I don't want to marry you, and I'm sick of having to keep on telling you so. Will you please go away and leave me alone?" She stopped. Her sense of fairness told her that she was working off on her hapless suitor venom which should have been expended on herself. "I'm sorry, Freddie," she said, softening; "I didn't mean to be such a beast as that. I know you're awfully fond of me, but really, really I can't marry you. You don't want to marry a girl who doesn't love you, do you?"

"Yes, I do," said Freddie stoutly. "If it's you, I

mean. Love is a tiny seed that coldness can wither, but
if tended and nurtured in the fostering warmth of an
honest heart . . ."

"But, Freddie."

"Blossoms into a flower," concluded Freddie rapidly.
"What I mean to say is, love would come after marriage."

"Nonsense!"

"Well, that's the way it happened in 'A Society
Mating.'"

"Freddie," said Eve, "I really don't want to talk any
more. Will you be a dear and just go away? I've got
a lot of thinking to do."

"Oh, thinking?" said Freddie, impressed. "Right
ho!"

"Thank you so much."

"Oh—er—not at all. Well, pip-pip."

"Good-bye."

"See you later, what?"

"Of course, of course."

"Fine! Well, toodle-oo!"

And the Hon. Freddie, not ill-pleased—for it seemed
to him that at long last he detected signs of melting in
the party of the second part—swivelled round on his
long legs and started for home.

§ 3

The little town of Market Blandings was a peaceful
sight as it slept in the sun. For the first time since
Freddie had left her, Eve became conscious of a certain
tranquillity as she entered the old grey High Street,
which was the centre of the place's life and thought.

Market Blandings had a comforting air of having been exactly the same for centuries. Troubles might vex the generations it housed, but they did not worry that lichened church with its sturdy four-square tower, nor those red-roofed shops, nor the age-old inns whose second stories bulged so comfortably out over the pavements. As Eve walked in slow meditation towards the "Emsworth Arms," the intensely respectable hostelry which was her objective, archways met her gaze, opening with a picturesque unexpectedness to show heartening glimpses of ancient nooks all cool and green. There was about the High Street of Market Blandings a suggestion of a slumbering cathedral close. Nothing was modern in it except the moving-picture house—and even that called itself an Electric Theatre, and was ivy-covered and surmounted by stone gables.

On second thoughts, that statement is too sweeping. There was one other modern building in the High Street —Jno. Banks, Hairdresser, to wit, and Eve was just coming abreast of Mr. Banks's emporium now.

In any ordinary surroundings these premises would have been a tolerably attractive sight, but in Market Blandings they were almost an eyesore; and Eve, finding herself at the door, was jarred out of her reverie as if she had heard a false note in a solemn anthem. She was on the point of hurrying past, when the door opened and a short, solid figure came out. And at the sight of this short, solid figure Eve stopped abruptly.

It was with the object of getting his grizzled locks clipped in preparation for the County Ball that Joseph Keeble had come to Mr. Banks's shop as soon as he had finished lunch. As he emerged now into the High Street

he was wondering why he had permitted Mr. Banks to
finish off the job with a heliotrope-scented hair-wash. It
seemed to Mr. Keeble that the air was heavy with heliotrope, and it came to him suddenly that heliotrope was
a scent which he always found particularly objectionable.

Ordinarily Joseph Keeble was accustomed to show an
iron front to hairdressers who tried to inflict lotions
upon him; and the reason his vigilance had relaxed
under the ministrations of Jno. Banks was that the
second post, which arrived at the castle at the luncheon
hour, had brought him a plaintive letter from his step-
daughter Phyllis—the second he had had from her since
the one which had caused him to tackle his masterful
wife in the smoking-room. Immediately after the conclusion of his business deal with the Hon. Freddie, he
had written to Phyllis in a vein of optimism rendered
glowing by Freddie's promises, assuring her that at any
moment he would be in a position to send her the three
thousand pounds which she required to clinch the purchase of that dream-farm in Lincolnshire. To this she
had replied with thanks. And after that there had been
a lapse of days and still he had not made good. Phyllis
was becoming worried, and said so in six closely-written
pages.

Mr. Keeble, as he sat in the barber's chair going over
this letter in his mind, had groaned in spirit, while Jno.
Banks with gleaming eyes did practically what he liked
with the heliotrope bottle. Not for the first time since
the formation of their partnership, Joseph Keeble was
tormented with doubts as to this wisdom in entrusting
a commission so delicate as the purloining of his wife's
diamond necklace to one of his nephew Freddie's known

feebleness of intellect.   Here, he told himself unhappily, was a job of work which would have tested the combined abilities of a syndicate consisting of Charles Peace and the James Brothers, and he had put it in the hands of a young man who in all his life had only once shown genuine inspiration and initiative—on the occasion when he had parted his hair in the middle at a time when all the other members of the Bachelors' Club were brushing it straight back.   The more Mr. Keeble thought of Freddie's chances, the slimmer they appeared.   By the time Jno. Banks had released him from the spotted apron he was thoroughly pessimistic, and as he passed out of the door, "so perfumed that the winds were love-sick with him," his estimate of his colleague's abilities was reduced to a point where he began to doubt whether the stealing of a mere milk-can was not beyond his scope. So deeply immersed was he in these gloomy thoughts that Eve had to call his name twice before he came out of them.

"Miss Halliday?" he said apologetically.   "I beg your pardon.   I was thinking."

Eve, though they had hardly exchanged a word since her arrival at the castle, had taken a liking to Mr. Keeble; and she felt in consequence none of the embarrassment which might have handicapped her in the discussion of an extremely delicate matter with another man.   By nature direct and straightforward, she came to the point at once.

"Can you spare me a moment or two, Mr. Keeble?" she said.   She glanced at the clock on the church tower and saw that she had ample time before her own appointment.   "I want to talk to you about Phyllis."

Mr. Keeble jerked his head back in astonishment, and the world became noisome with heliotrope. It was as if the Voice of Conscience had suddenly addressed him.

"Phyllis!" he gasped, and the letter crackled in his breast-pocket.

"Your stepdaughter Phyllis."

"Do you know her?"

"She was my best friend at school. I had tea with her just before I came to the castle."

"Extraordinary!" said Mr. Keeble.

A customer in quest of a shave thrust himself between them and went into the shop. They moved away a few paces.

"Of course if you say it is not of my business . . ."

"My dear young lady . . ."

"Well, it *is* my business, because she's my friend," said Eve firmly. "Mr. Keeble, Phyllis told me she had written to you about buying that farm. Why don't you help her?"

The afternoon was warm, but not warm enough to account for the moistness of Mr. Keeble's brow. He drew out a large handkerchief and mopped his forehead. A hunted look was in his eyes. The hand which was not occupied with the handkerchief had sought his pocket and was busy rattling keys.

"I want to help her. I would do anything in the world to help her."

"Then why don't you?"

"I—I am curiously situated."

"Yes, Phyllis told me something about that. I can see that it is a difficult position for you. But, Mr. Keeble, surely, surely if you can manage to give Freddie

Threepwood two thousand pounds to start a bookmaker's business . . ."

Her words were cut short by a strangled cry from her companion. Sheer panic was in his eyes now, and in his heart an overwhelming regret that he had ever been fool enough to dabble in crime in the company of a mere animated talking-machine like his nephew Freddie. This girl knew! And if she knew, how many others knew? The young imbecile had probably babbled his hideous secret into the ears of every human being in the place who would listen to him.

"He told you!" he stammered. "He t-told you!"

"Yes. Just now."

"Gosh!" muttered Mr. Keeble brokenly.

Eve stared at him in surprise. She could not understand this emotion. The handkerchief, after a busy session, was lowered now, and he was looking at her imploringly.

"You haven't told any one?" he croaked hoarsely.

"Of course not. I said I had only heard of it just now."

"You wouldn't tell any one?"

"Why should I?"

Mr. Keeble's breath, which had seemed to him for a moment gone for ever, began to return timidly. Relief for a space held him dumb. What nonsense, he reflected, these newspapers and people talked about the modern girl. It was this very broad-mindedness of hers, to which they objected so absurdly, that made her a creature of such charm. She might behave in certain ways in a fashion that would have shocked her grandmother, but how comforting it was to find her calm and

unmoved in the contemplation of another's crime.   His
heart warmed to Eve.

"You're wonderful!" he said.

"What do you mean?"

"Of course," argued Mr. Keeble, "it isn't really
stealing."

"What!"

"I shall buy my wife another necklace."

"You will—what?"

"So everything will be all right.   Constance will be
perfectly happy, and Phyllis will have her money,
and . . ."

Something in Eve's astonished gaze seemed to smite
Mr. Keeble.

"Don't you *know?*" he broke off.

"Know?   Know what?"

Mr. Keeble perceived that he had wronged Freddie.
The young ass had been a fool even to mention the money
to this girl, but he had at least, it seemed, stopped short
of disclosing the entire plot.   An oyster-like reserve
came upon him.

"Nothing, nothing," he said hastily.   "Forget what
I was going to say.   Well, I must be going, I must be
going."

Eve clutched wildly at his retreating sleeve.   Unin-
telligible though his words had been, one sentence had
come home to her, the one about Phyllis having her
money.   It was no time for half-measures.   She grabbed
him.

"Mr. Keeble," she cried urgently.   "I don't know
what you mean, but you were just going to say something which sounded . . . Mr. Keeble, do trust me.   I'm

Phyllis's best friend, and if you've thought out any way of helping her I wish you would tell me . . . You must tell me. I might be able to help . . ."

Mr. Keeble, as she began her broken speech, had been endeavouring with deprecatory tugs to disengage his coat from her grasp. But now he ceased to struggle. Those doubts of Freddie's efficiency, which had troubled him in Jno. Banks's chair, still lingered. His opinion that Freddie was but a broken reed had not changed. Indeed, it had grown. He looked at Eve. He looked at her searchingly. Into her pleading eyes he directed a stare that sought to probe her soul, and saw there honesty, sympathy, and—better still—intelligence. He might have stood and gazed into Freddie's fishy eyes for weeks without discovering a tithe of such intelligence. His mind was made up. This girl was an ally. A girl of dash and vigour. A girl worth a thousand Freddies—not, however, reflected Mr. Keeble, that that was saying much. He hesitated no longer.

"It's like this," said Mr. Keeble.

§ 4

The information, authoritatively conveyed to him during breakfast by Lady Constance, that he was scheduled that night to read select passages from Ralston McTodd's *Songs of Squalor* to the entire house-party assembled in the big drawing-room, had come as a complete surprise to Psmith, and to his fellow-guests—such of them as were young and of the soulless sex—as a shock from which they found it hard to rally. True, they had before now gathered in a vague sort of way that he was one of those literary fellows, but so normal and engaging had they found his whole manner and appearance that it had never occurred to them that he concealed anything up his sleeve as lethal as *Songs of Squalor*. Among these members of the younger set the consensus of opinion was that it was a bit thick, and that at such a price even the lavish hospitality of Blandings was scarcely worth having. Only those who had visited the castle before during the era of her ladyship's flirtation with Art could have been described as resigned. These stout hearts argued that while this latest blister was probably going to be pretty bad, he could hardly be worse than the chappie who had lectured on Theosophy last November, and must almost of necessity be better than the bird who during the Shiffley race-week had attempted in a two-hour discourse to convert them to vegetarianism.

Psmith himself regarded the coming ordeal with equanimity. He was not one of those whom the prospect of speaking in public afflicts with nervous horror. He liked the sound of his own voice, and night, when it came, found him calmly cheerful. He listened contentedly to the murmur of the drawing-room filling up as he strolled on the star-lit terrace, smoking a last cigarette before duty called him elsewhere. And when, some few yards away, seated on the terrace wall gazing out into the velvet darkness, he perceived Eve Halliday, his sense of well-being became acute.

All day he had been conscious of a growing desire for another of those cosy chats with Eve which had done so much to make life agreeable for him during his stay at Blandings. Her prejudice—which he deplored—in favour of doing a certain amount of work to justify her salary, had kept him during the morning away from the little room off the library where she was wont to sit cataloguing books; and when he had gone there after lunch he had found it empty. As he approached her now, he was thinking pleasantly of all those delightful walks, those excellent driftings on the lake, and those cheery conversations which had gone to cement his con' viction that of all possible girls she was the only possible one. It seemed to him that in addition to being beau tiful she brought out all that was best in him of intellect and soul. That is to say, she let him talk oftener and longer than any girl he had ever known.

It struck him as a little curious that she made no move to greet him. She remained apparently unaware of his approach. And yet the summer night was not of such density as to hide him from view—and, even if she could not see him, she must undoubtedly have heard him; for only a moment before he had tripped with some violence over a large flower-pot, one of a row of sixteen which Angus McAllister, doubtless for some good pur pose, had placed in the fairway that afternoon.

"A pleasant night," he said, seating himself gracefully beside her on the wall.

She turned her head for a brief instant, and, having turned it, looked away again.

"Yes," she said.

Her manner was not effusive, but Psmith persevered.

"The stars," he proceeded, indicating them with a kindly yet not patronising wave of the hand. "Bright, twinkling, and—if I may say so—rather neatly arranged. When I was a mere lad, some one whose name I cannot recollect taught me which was Orion. Also Mars, Venus, and Jupiter. This thoroughly useless chunk of knowledge has, I am happy to say, long since passed from my mind. However, I am in a position to state that that wiggly thing up there a little to the right is King Charles's Wain."

"Yes?"

"Yes, indeed, I assure you." It struck Psmith that Astronomy was not gripping his audience, so he tried Travel. "I hear," he said, "you went to Market Blandings this afternoon."

"Yes."

"An attractive settlement."

"Yes."

There was a pause. Psmith removed his monocle and polished it thoughtfully. The summer night seemed to him to have taken on a touch of chill.

"What I like about the English rural districts," he went on, "is that when the authorities have finished building a place they stop. Somewhere about the reign of Henry the Eighth, I imagine that the master-mason gave the final house a pat with his trowel and said, 'Well, boys, that's Market Blandings.' To which his assistants no doubt assented with many a hearty 'Grammercy!' and 'I'fackins!' these being expletives to which they were much addicted. And they went away and left it, and nobody has touched it since. And I, for one, thoroughly approve. I think it makes the place soothing. Don't you?"

"Yes."

As far as the darkness would permit, Psmith subjected Eve to an inquiring glance through his monocle. This was a strange new mood in which he had found her. Hitherto, though she had always endeared herself to him by permitting him the major portion of the dialogue, they had usually split conversations on at least a seventy-five-twenty-five basis. And though it gratified Psmith to be allowed to deliver a monologue when talking with most people, he found Eve more companionable when in a slightly chattier vein.

"Are you coming in to hear me read?" he asked.

"No."

It was a change from "Yes," but that was the best that could be said of it. A good deal of discouragement was always required to damp Psmith, but he could not help feeling a slight diminution of buoyancy. However, he kept on trying.

"You show your usual sterling good sense," he said approvingly. "A scalier method of passing the scented summer night could hardly be hit upon." He abandoned the topic of the reading. It did not grip. That was manifest. It lacked appeal. "I went to Market Blandings this afternoon, too," he said. "Comrade Baxter informed me that you had gone thither, so I went after you. Not being able to find you, I turned in for half an hour at the local moving-picture palace. They were showing Episode Eleven of a serial. It concluded with the heroine, kidnapped by Indians, stretched on the sacrificial altar with the high-priest making passes at her with a knife. The hero meanwhile had started to climb a rather nasty precipice on his way to the rescue. The final picture was a close-up of his fingers slipping slowly off a rock. Episode Twelve next week."

Eve looked out into the night without speaking.

"I'm afraid it won't end happily," said Psmith with a sigh. "I think he'll save her."

Eve turned on him with a menacing abruptness.

"Shall I tell you why I went to Market Blandings this afternoon?" she said.

"Do," said Psmith cordially. "It is not for me to criticise, but as a matter of fact I was rather wondering when you were going to begin telling me all about your adventures. I have been monopolising the conversation."

"I went to meet Cynthia."

Psmith's monocle fell out of his eye and swung jerkily on its cord. He was not easily disconcerted, but this unexpected piece of information, coming on top of her peculiar manner, undoubtedly jarred him. He foresaw difficulties, and once again found himself thinking hard thoughts of this confounded female who kept bobbing up when least expected. How simple life would have been, he mused wistfully, had Ralston McTodd only had the good sense to remain a bachelor.

"Oh, Cynthia?" he said.

"Yes, Cynthia," said Eve. The inconvenient Mrs. McTodd possessed a Christian name admirably adapted for being hissed between clenched teeth, and Eve hissed it in this fashion now. It became evident to Psmith that the dear girl was in a condition of hardly suppressed fury and that trouble was coming his way. He braced himself to meet it.

"Directly after we had that talk on the lake, the day I arrived," continued Eve tersely, "I wrote to Cynthia, telling her to come here at once and meet me at the 'Emsworth Arms' . . ."

"In the High Street," said Psmith. "I know it. Good beer."

"What!"

"I said they sell good beer . . ."

"Never mind about the beer," cried Eve.

"No, no. I merely mentioned it in passing."

"At lunch to-day I got a letter from her saying that she would be there this afternoon. So I hurried off. I wanted"—Eve laughed a hollow, mirthless laugh of a calibre which even the Hon. Freddie Threepwood would have found beyond his powers, and he was a specialist—"I wanted to try to bring you two together. I thought that if I could see her and have a talk with her that you might become reconciled."

Psmith, though obsessed with a disquieting feeling that he was fighting in the last ditch, pulled himself together sufficiently to pat her hand as it lay beside him on the wall like some white and fragile flower.

"That was like you," he murmured. "That was an act worthy of your great heart. But I fear that the rift between Cynthia and myself has reached such dimensions . . ."

Eve drew her hand away. She swung round, and the battery of her indignant gaze raked him furiously.

"I saw Cynthia," she said, "and she told me that her husband was in Paris."

"Now, how in the world," said Psmith, struggling bravely but with a growing sense that they were coming over the plate a bit too fast for him, "how in the world did she get an idea like that?"

"Do you really want to know?"

"I do, indeed."

"Then I'll tell you. She got the idea because she had had a letter from him, begging her to join him there. She had just finished telling me this, when I caught sight of you from the inn window, walking along the High Street. I pointed you out to Cynthia, and she said she had never seen you before in her life."

"Women soon forget," sighed Psmith.

"The only excuse I can find for you," stormed Eve in a vibrant undertone necessitated by the fact that somebody had just emerged from the castle door and they no longer had the terrace to themselves, "is that you're mad. When I think of all you said to me about poor Cynthia on the lake that afternoon, when I think of all the sympathy I wasted on you . . ."

"Not wasted," corrected Psmith firmly. "It was by no means wasted. It made me love you—if possible—even more."

Eve had supposed that she had embarked on a tirade which would last until she had worked off her indignation and felt composed again, but this extraordinary remark scattered the thread of her harangue so hopelessly that all she could do was to stare at him in amazed silence.

"Womanly intuition," proceeded Psmith gravely, "will have told you long ere this that I love you with a fervour which with my poor vocabulary I cannot hope to express. True, as you are about to say, we have known each other but a short time, as time is measured. But what of that?"

Eve raised her eyebrows. Her voice was cold and hostile.

"After what has happened," she said, "I suppose I

ought not to be surprised at finding you capable of anything, but—are you really choosing this moment to—
to propose to me?"

"To employ a favourite word of your own—yes."

"And you expect me to take you seriously?"

"Assuredly not. I look upon the present disclosure
purely as a sighting shot. You may regard it, if you
will, as a kind of formal proclamation. I wish simply
to go on record as an aspirant to your hand. I want
you, if you will be so good, to make a note of my words
and give them a thought from time to time. As Comrade
Cootes—a young friend of mine whom you have not yet
met—would say, 'Chew on them.'"

"I . . ."

"It is possible," continued Psmith, "that black moments will come to you—for they come to all of us, even
the sunniest—when you will find yourself saying, 'Nobody loves me!' On such occasions I should like you
to add, 'No, I am wrong. There *is* somebody who loves
me.' At first, it may be, that reflection will bring but
scant balm. Gradually, however, as the days go by and
we are constantly together and my nature unfolds itself
before you like the petals of some timid flower beneath
the rays of the sun . . ."

Eve's eyes opened wider. She had supposed herself
incapable of further astonishment, but she saw that she
had been mistaken.

"You surely aren't dreaming of staying on here *now?*"
she gasped.

"Most decidedly. Why not?"

"But—but what is to prevent me telling everybody
that you are not Mr. McTodd?"

"Your sweet, generous nature," said Psmith. "Your big heart. Your angelic forbearance."

"Oh!"

"Considering that I only came here as McTodd—and if you had seen him you would realise that he is not a person for whom the man of sensibility and refinement would lightly allow himself to be mistaken—I say considering that I only took on the job of understudy so as to get to the castle and be near you, I hardly think that you will be able to bring yourself to get me slung out. You must try to understand what happened. When Lord Emsworth started chatting with me under the impression that I was Comrade McTodd, I encouraged the mistake purely with the kindly intention of putting him at his ease. Even when he informed me that he was expecting me to come down to Blandings with him on the five o'clock train, it never occurred to me to do so. It was only when I saw you talking to him in the street and he revealed the fact that you were about to enjoy his hospitality that I decided that there was no other course open to the man of spirit. Consider! Twice that day you had passed out of my life—may I say taking the sunshine with you?—and I began to fear you might pass out of it for ever. So, loath though I was to commit the solecism of planting myself in this happy home under false pretences, I could see no other way. And here I am!"

"You *must* be mad!"

"Well, as I was saying, the days will go by, you will have ample opportunity of studying my personality, and it is quite possible that in due season the love of an honest heart may impress you as worth having. I may add that I have loved you since the moment when I saw you sheltering from the rain under that awning in Dover Street, and I recall saying as much to Comrade Walderwick when he was chatting with me some short time later on the subject of his umbrella. I do not press you for an answer now . . ."

"I should hope not!"

"I merely say, 'Think it over.' It is nothing to cause you mental distress. Other men love you. Freddie Threepwood loves you. Just add me to the list. That is all I ask. Muse on me from time to time. Reflect that I may be an acquired taste. You probably did not like olives the first time you tasted them. Now you probably do. Give me the same chance you would an olive. Consider, also, how little you actually have against me. What, indeed, does it amount to, when you come to examine it narrowly? All you have against me is the fact that I am not Ralston McTodd. Think how comparatively few people *are* Ralston McTodd. Let your meditations proceed along these lines and . . ."

He broke off, for at this moment the individual who had come out of the front door a short while back loomed beside them, and the glint of starlight on glass revealed him as the Efficient Baxter.

"Everybody is waiting, Mr. McTodd," said the Efficient Baxter. He spoke the name, as always, with a certain sardonic emphasis.

"Of course," said Psmith affably, "of course, I was forgetting. I will get to work at once. You are quite sure you do not wish to hear a scuttleful of modern poetry, Miss Halliday?"

"Quite sure."

"And yet even now, so our genial friend here informs us, a bevy of youth and beauty is crowding the drawing-room, agog for the treat. Well, well! It is these strange clashings of personal taste which constitute what we call Life. I think I will write a poem about it some day. Come, Comrade Baxter, let us be up and doing. I must not disappoint my public."

For some moments after the two had left her—Baxter silent and chilly, Psmith, all debonair chumminess, kneading the other's arm and pointing out as they went objects of interest by the wayside—Eve remained on the terrace wall, thinking. She was laughing now, but behind her amusement there was another feeling, and one that perplexed her. A good many men had proposed to her in the course of her career, but none of them had ever left her with this odd feeling of exhilaration. Psmith was different from any other man who had come her way, and difference was a quality which Eve esteemed. . . .

She had just reached the conclusion that life for whatever girl might eventually decide to risk it in Psmith's company would never be dull, when strange doings in her immediate neighbourhood roused her from her meditations.

The thing happened as she rose from her seat on the wall and started to cross the terrace on her way to the front door. She had stopped for an instant beneath the huge open window of the drawing-room to listen to what was going on inside. Faintly, with something of the quality of a far-off phonograph, the sound of Psmith reading came to her; and even at this distance there was a composed blandness about his voice which brought a smile to her lips.

And then, with a startling abruptness, the lighted window was dark. And she was aware that all the lighted windows on that side of the castle had suddenly become dark. The lamp that shone over the great door ceased to shine. And above the hubbub of voices in the drawing-room she heard Psmith's patient drawl.

"Ladies and gentlemen, I think the lights have gone out."

The night air was rent by a single piercing scream. Something flashed like a shooting star and fell at her feet; and, stooping, Eve found in her hands Lady Constance Keeble's diamond necklace.

§ 5

To be prepared is everything in this life. Ever since her talk with Mr. Joseph Keeble in the High Street of Market Blandings that afternoon Eve's mind had been flitting nimbly from one scheme to another, all designed to end in this very act of seizing the necklace in her hands and each rendered impracticable by some annoying flaw. And now that Fate in its impulsive way had achieved for her what she had begun to feel she could never accomplish for herself, she wasted no time in bewildered inaction. The miracle found her ready for it.

For an instant she debated with herself the chances of a dash through the darkened hall up the stairs to her room. But the lights might go on again, and she might meet some one. Memories of sensational novels read in the past told her that on occasions such as this people were detained and searched. . . .

Suddenly, as she stood there, she found the way. Close

beside her, lying on its side, was the flower-pot which Psmith had overturned as he came to join her on the terrace wall. It might have defects as a cache, but at that moment she could perceive none. Most flower-pots are alike, but this was a particularly easily-remembered flower-pot: for in its journeying from the potting shed to the terrace it had acquired on its side a splash of white paint. She would be able to distinguish it from its fellows when, late that night, she crept out to retrieve the spoil. And surely nobody would ever think of suspecting . . .

She plunged her fingers into the soft mould, and straightened herself, breathing quickly. It was not an ideal piece of work, but it would serve.

She rubbed her fingers on the turf, put the flower-pot back in the row with the others, and then, like a flying white phantom, darted across the terrace and into the house. And so with beating heart, groping her way, to the bathroom to wash her hands.

The twenty-thousand-pound flower-pot looked placidly up at the winking stars.

§ 6

It was perhaps two minutes later that Mr. Cootes, sprinting lustily, rounded the corner of the house and burst on to the terrace. Late as usual.

CHAPTER XI

ALMOST ENTIRELY ABOUT FLOWER-POTS

§ 1

THE Efficient Baxter prowled feverishly up and down the yielding carpet of the big drawing-room. His eyes gleamed behind their spectacles, his dome-like brow was corrugated. Except for himself, the room was empty. As far as the scene of the disaster was concerned, the tumult and the shouting had died. It was going on vigorously in practically every other part of the house, but in the drawing-room there was stillness, if not peace.

Baxter paused, came to a decision, went to the wall and pressed the bell.

"Thomas," he said, when that footman presented himself a few moments later.

"Sir?"

"Send Susan to me."

"Susan, sir?"

"Yes, Susan," snapped the Efficient One, who had always a short way with the domestic staff. "Susan, Susan, Susan. . . . The new parlourmaid."

"Oh, yes, sir. Very good, sir."

Thomas withdrew, outwardly all grave respectfulness, inwardly piqued, as was his wont, at the airy manner in which the secretary flung his orders about at the castle. The domestic staff at Blandings lived in a perpetual state of smouldering discontent under Baxter's rule.

"Susan," said Thomas, when he arrived in the lower regions, "you're to go up to the drawing-room. Nosey Park wants you."

The pleasant-faced young woman whom he addressed laid down her knitting.

"Who?" she asked.

"Mister Blooming Baxter. When you've been here a little longer you'll know that he's the feller that owns the place. How he got it I don't know. Found it," said Thomas satirically, "in his Christmas stocking, I expect. Anyhow, you're to go up."

Thomas's fellow-footman, Stokes, a serious-looking man with a bald forehead, shook that forehead solemnly.

"Something's the matter," he asserted. "You can't tell me that wasn't a scream we heard when them lights was out. Or," he added weightily, for he was a man who looked at every side of a question, "a shriek. It was a shriek or scream. I said so at the time. 'There,' I said, 'listen!' I said. 'That's somebody screaming,' I said. 'Or shrieking.' Something's up."

"Well, Baxter hasn't been murdered, worse luck," said Thomas. "He's up there screaming or shrieking for Susan. 'Send Susan to me!'" proceeded Thomas, giving an always popular imitation. "'Susan, Susan, Susan.' So you'd best go, my girl, and see what he wants."

"Very well."

"And, Susan," said Thomas, a tender note creeping into his voice, for already, brief as had been her sojourn at Blandings, he had found the new parlourmaid making a deep impression on him, "if it's a row of any kind . . ."

"Or description," interjected Stokes.

"Or description," continued Thomas, accepting the

word, "if 'e's 'arsh with you for some reason or other you come right back to me and sob out your troubles on my chest, see? Lay your little 'ead on my shoulder and tell me all about it."

The new parlourmaid, primly declining to reply to this alluring invitation, started on her journey upstairs; and Thomas, with a not unmanly sigh, resumed his interrupted game of halfpenny nap with colleague Stokes.

.   .   .   .

The Efficient Baxter had gone to the open window and was gazing out into the night when Susan entered the drawing-room.

"You wished to see me, Mr. Baxter?"

The secretary spun round. So softly had she opened the door, and so noiselessly had she moved when inside the room, that it was not until she spoke that he had become aware of her arrival. It was a characteristic of this girl Susan that she was always apt to be among those present some time before the latter became cognisant of the fact.

"Oh, good evening, Miss Simmons. You came in very quietly."

"Habit," said the parlourmaid.

"You gave me quite a start."

"I'm sorry. What was it," she asked, dismissing in a positively unfeeling manner the subject of her companion's jarred nerves, "that you wished to see me about?"

"Shut that door."

"I have. I always shut doors."

"Please sit down."

"No, thank you, Mr. Baxter. It might look odd if any one should come in."

"Of course. You think of everything."

"I always do."

Baxter stood for a moment, frowning.

"Miss Simmons," he said, "when I thought it expe dient to install a private detective in this house, I insisted on Wragge's sending you. We had worked to gether before . . ."

"Sixteenth of December, 1918, to January twelve, 1919, when you were secretary to Mr. Horace Jevons, the American millionaire," said Miss Simmons, as promptly as if he had touched a spring. It was her hobby to remember dates with precision.

"Exactly. I insisted upon your being sent because I knew from experience that you were reliable. At that time I looked on your presence here merely as a precautionary measure. Now, I am sorry to say . . ."

"Did some one steal Lady Constance's necklace tonight?"

"Yes!"

"When the lights went out just now?"

"Exactly."

"Well, why couldn't you say so at once? Good gracious, man, you don't have to break the thing gently to me."

The Efficient Baxter, though he strongly objected to being addressed as "man," decided to overlook the solecism.

"The lights suddenly went out," he said. "There was a certain amount of laughter and confusion. Then a piercing shriek . . ."

"I heard it."

"And immediately after Lady Constance's voice cry-ing that her jewels had been snatched from her neck "

"Then what happened?"

"Still greater confusion, which lasted until one of the maids arrived with a candle. Eventually the lights went on again, but of the necklace there was no sign whatever."

"Well? Were you expecting the thief to wear it as a watch-chain or hang it from his teeth?"

Baxter was finding his companion's manner more trying every minute, but he preserved his calm.

"Naturally the doors were barred and a complete search instituted. And extremely embarrassing it was. With the single exception of the scoundrel who has been palming himself off as McTodd, all those present were well-known members of Society."

"Well-known members of Society might not object to getting hold of a twenty-thousand pound necklace. But still, with the McTodd fellow there, you oughtn't to have had far to look. What had he to say about it?"

"He was among the first to empty his pockets."

"Well, then, he must have hidden the thing somewhere."

"Not in this room. I have searched assiduously."

"H'm."

There was a silence.

"It is baffling," said Baxter, "baffling."

"It is nothing of the kind," replied Miss Simmons tartly. "This wasn't a one-man job. How could it have been? I should be inclined to call it a three-man job. One to switch off the lights, one to snatch the necklace, and one to—was that window open all the time? I thought so—and one to pick up the necklace when the second fellow threw it out on to the terrace."

"Terrace!"

The word shot from Baxter's lips with explosive force. Miss Simmons looked at him curiously.

"Thought of something?"

"Miss Simmons," said the Efficient One impressively, "everybody was assembled in here waiting for the reading to begin, but the pseudo-McTodd was nowhere to be found. I discovered him eventually on the terrace in close talk with the Halliday girl."

"His partner," said Miss Simmons, nodding. "We thought so all along. And let me add my little bit. "There's a fellow down in the servants' hall that calls himself a valet, and I'll bet he didn't know what a valet was till he came here. I thought he was a crook the moment I set eyes on him. I can tell 'em in the dark. Now, do you know whose valet he is? This McTodd fellow's!"

Baxter bounded to and fro like a caged tiger.

"And with my own ears," he cried excitedly, "I heard the Halliday girl refuse to come to the drawing-room to listen to the reading. She was out on the terrace throughout the whole affair. Miss Simmons, we must act! We must act!"

"Yes, but not like idiots," replied the detective frostily.

"What do you mean?"

"Well, you can't charge out, as you looked as if you wanted to just then, and denounce these crooks where they sit. We've got to go carefully."

"But meanwhile they will smuggle the necklace away!"

"They won't smuggle any necklace away, not while I'm around. Suspicion's no good. We've made out a nice little case against the three of them, but it's no use unless we catch them with the goods. The first thing we have to do is to find out where they've hidden the stuff. And that'll take patience. I'll start by searching that girl's room. Then I'll search the valet fellow's room. And if the stuff isn't there it'll mean they've hidden it out in the open somewhere."

"But this McTodd fellow. This fellow who poses as McTodd. He may have it all the while."

"No. I'll search his room, too, but the stuff won't be there. He's the fellow who's going to get it in the end, because he's got that place out in the woods to hide it in. But they wouldn't have had time to slip it to him yet. That necklace is somewhere right here. And if," said Miss Simmons with grim facetiousness, "they can hide it from me, they may keep it as a birthday present."

§ 2

How wonderful, if we pause to examine it, is Nature's inexorable law of compensation. Instead of wasting time in envy of our mental superiors, we would do well to reflect that these gifts of theirs which excite our wistful jealousy are ever attended by corresponding penalties. To take an example that lies to hand, it was the very fact that he possessed a brain like a buzz-saw that rendered the Efficient Baxter a bad sleeper. Just as he would be dropping off, bing! would go that brain of his, melting the mists of sleep like snow in a furnace.

This was so even when life was running calmly for

him and without excitement. To-night, his mind, bearing the load it did, firmly declined even to consider the question of slumber. The hour of two, chiming from the clock over the stables, found him as wide awake as ever he was at high noon.

Lying in bed in the darkness, he reviewed the situation as far as he had the data. Shortly before he retired, Miss Simmons had made her report about the bedrooms. Though subjected to the severest scrutiny, neither Psmith's boudoir nor Cootes's attic nor Eve's little nook on the third floor had yielded up treasure of any description. And this, Miss Simmons held, confirmed her original view that the necklace must be lying concealed in what might almost be called a public spot—on some window-ledge, maybe, or somewhere in the hall. . . .

Baxter lay considering this theory. It did appear to be the only tenable one; but it offended him by giving the search a frivolous suggestion of being some sort of round game like Hunt the Slipper or Find the Thimble. As a child he had held austerely aloof from these silly pastimes, and he resented being compelled to play them now. Still . . .

He sat up, thinking. He had heard a noise.

. . . .

The attitude of the majority of people towards noises in the night is one of cautious non-interference. But Rupert Baxter was made of sterner stuff. The sound had seemed to come from downstairs somewhere—perhaps from that very hall where, according to Miss Simmons, the stolen necklace might even now be lying hid. Whatever it was, it must certainly not be ignored. He reached for the spectacles which lay ever ready to his hand on the table beside him; then climbed out of bed, and, having put on a pair of slippers and opened the door, crept forth into the darkness. As far as he could ascertain by holding his breath and straining his ears, all was still from cellar to roof; but nevertheless he was not satisfied. He continued to listen. His room was on the second floor, one of a series that ran along a balcony overlooking the hall; and he stood, leaning over the balcony rail, a silent statue of Vigilance.

. . . .

The noise which had acted so electrically upon the Efficient Baxter had been a particularly noisy noise; and only the intervening distance and the fact that his door was closed had prevented it sounding to him like an explosion. It had been caused by the crashing downfall of a small table containing a vase, a jar of potpourri, an Indian sandalwood box of curious workmanship, and a cabinet-size photograph of the Earl of Emsworth's eldest son, Lord Bosham; and the table had fallen because Eve, *en route* across the hall in quest of her precious flower-pot, had collided with it while making for the front door. Of all indoor sports—and Eve, as she stood pallidly among the ruins, would have been the first to endorse this dictum—the one which offers the minimum of pleasure to the participant is that of roaming in pitch darkness through the hall of a country-house. Easily navigable in the daytime, these places become at night mere traps for the unwary.

Eve paused breathlessly. So terrific had the noise sounded to her guilty ears that every moment she was expecting doors to open all over the castle, belching forth shouting men with pistols. But as nothing happened, courage returned to her, and she resumed her journey. She found the great door, ran her fingers along its surface, and drew the chain. The shooting back of the bolts occupied but another instant, and then she was out on the terrace running her hardest towards the row of flower-pots.

Up on his balcony, meanwhile, the Efficient Baxter was stopping, looking, and listening. The looking brought no results, for all below was black as pitch; but the listening proved more fruitful. Faintly from down in the well of the hall there floated up to him a peculiar sound like something rustling in the darkness. Had he reached the balcony a moment earlier, he would have heard the rattle of the chain and the click of the bolts; but these noises had occurred just before he came out of his room. Now all that was audible was this rustling.

He could not analyse the sound, but the fact that there was any sound at all in such a place at such an hour increased his suspicions that dark doings were toward which would pay for investigation. With stealthy steps he crept to the head of the stairs and descended.

One uses the verb "descend" advisedly, for what is required is some word suggesting instantaneous activity. About Baxter's progress from the second floor to the first there was nothing halting or hesitating. He, so to speak, did it now. Planting his foot firmly on a golf-ball which the Hon. Freddie Threepwood, who had been practising putting in the corridor before retiring to bed, had left in his casual fashion just where the steps began, he took the entire staircase in one majestic, volplaning sweep. There were eleven stairs in all separating his landing from the landing below. and the only ones he hit were the third and tenth. He came to rest with a squattering thud on the lower landing, and for a moment or two the fever of the chase left him.

The fact that many writers in their time have commented at some length on the mysterious manner in which Fate is apt to perform its work must not deter us now from a brief survey of this latest manifestation of its ingenious methods. Had not his interview with Eve that afternoon so stimulated the Hon. Freddie as to revive in him a faint yet definite desire to putt, there would have been no golf-ball waiting for Baxter on the stairs. And had he been permitted to negotiate the stairs in a less impetuous manner, Baxter would not at this juncture have switched on the light.

It had not been his original intention to illuminate the theatre of action, but after that Lucifer-like descent from the second floor to the first he was taking no more chances. "Safety First" was Baxter's slogan. As soon, therefore, as he had shaken off a dazed sensation of mental and moral collapse, akin to that which comes to the man who steps on the teeth of a rake and is smitten on the forehead by the handle, he rose with infinite caution to his feet and, feeling his way down by the banisters, groped for the switch and pressed it. And so it came about that Eve, heading for home with her precious flower-pot in her arms, was stopped when at the very door by a sudden warning flood of light. Another instant, and she would have been across the threshold of disaster.

For a moment paralysis gripped her. The light had affected her like some one shouting loudly and unexpectedly in her ear. Her heart gave one convulsive bound, and she stood frozen. Then, filled with a blind desire for flight, she dashed like a hunted rabbit into the friendly shelter of a clump of bushes.

. . . .

Baxter stood blinking. Gradually his eyes adjusted themselves to the light, and immediately they had done so he was seized by a fresh frenzy of zeal. Now that all things were made visible to him he could see that that faint rustling sound had been caused by a curtain flapping in the breeze, and that the breeze which made the curtain flap was coming in through the open front door.

Baxter wasted no time in abstract thought. He acted swiftly and with decision. Straightening his spectacles on his nose, he girded up his pyjamas and galloped out into the night.

. . . .

The smooth terrace slept under the stars. To a more poetic man than Baxter it would have seemed to wear that faintly reproachful air which a garden always assumes when invaded at unseemly hours by people who ought to be in bed. Baxter, never fanciful, was blind to this. He was thinking, thinking. That shaking-up on the stairs had churned into activity the very depths of his brain and he was at the fever-point of his reasoning powers. A thought had come like a full-blown rose, flushing his brow. Miss Simmons, arguing plausibly, had suggested that the stolen necklace might be concealed in the hall. Baxter, inspired, fancied not. Whoever it was that had been at work in the hall just now had been making for the garden. It was not the desire to escape which had led him—or her—to open the front door, for the opening had been done before he, Baxter, had come out on to the balcony—otherwise he must have heard the shooting of the bolts. No. The enemy's objective had been the garden. In other words, the terrace. And why? Because somewhere on the terrace was the stolen necklace.

Standing there in the starlight, the Efficient Baxter endeavoured to reconstruct the scene, and did so with remarkable accuracy. He saw the jewels flashing down. He saw them picked up. But there he stopped. Try as he might, he could not see them hidden. And yet that they had been hidden—and that within a few feet of where he was now standing—he felt convinced.

He moved from his position near the door and began to roam restlessly. His slippered feet padded over the soft turf.

. . . .

Eve peered out from her clump of bushes. It was not easy to see any great distance, but Fate, her friend, was still with her. There had been a moment that night when Baxter, disrobing for bed, had wavered absently between his brown and his lemon-coloured pyjamas, little recking of what hung upon the choice. Fate had directed his hand to the lemon-coloured, and he had put them on; with the result that he shone now in the dim light like the white plume of Navarre. Eve could follow his movements perfectly, and, when he was far enough away from his base to make the enterprise prudent, she slipped out and raced for home and safety. Baxter at the moment was leaning on the terrace wall, thinking, thinking, thinking.

It was possibly the cool air, playing about his bare ankles, that at last chilled the secretary's dashing mood and brought the disquieting thought that he was doing something distinctly dangerous in remaining out here in the open like this. A gang of thieves are ugly customers, likely to stick at little when a valuable necklace is at stake, and it came to the Efficient Baxter that in his light pyjamas he must be offering a tempting mark for any marauder lurking—say in those bushes. And at the thought, the summer night, though pleasantly mild, grew suddenly chilly. With an almost convulsive rapidity he turned to re-enter the house. Zeal was well enough, but it was silly to be rash. He covered the last few yards of his journey at a rare burst of speed.

It was at this point that he discovered that the lights in the hall had been switched off and that the front door was closed and bolted.

§ 3

It is the opinion of most thoughtful students of life that happiness in this world depends chiefly on the ability to take things as they come. An instance of one who may be said to have perfected this attitude is to be found in the writings of a certain eminent Arabian author who tells of a traveller who, sinking to sleep one afternoon upon a patch of turf containing an acorn, discovered when he woke that the warmth of his body had caused the acorn to germinate and that he was now some sixty feet above the ground in the upper branches of a massive oak. Unable to descend, he faced the situation equably. "I cannot," he observed, "adapt circumstances

to my will: therefore I shall adapt my will to circumstances. I decide to remain here." Which he did.

Rupert Baxter, as he stood before the barred door of
Blandings Castle, was very far from imitating this admirable philosopher. To find oneself locked out of a
country-house at half-past two in the morning in lemon-
coloured pyjamas can never be an unmixedly agreeable
experience, and Baxter was a man less fitted by nature
to endure it with equanimity than most men. His was
a fiery and an arrogant soul, and he seethed in furious
rebellion against the intolerable position into which Fate
had manœuvred him. He even went so far as to give
the front door a petulant kick. Finding, however, that
this hurt his toes and accomplished no useful end, he
addressed himself to the task of ascertaining whethei
there was any way of getting in—short of banging the
knocker and rousing the house, a line of action which
did not commend itself to him. He made a practice of
avoiding as far as possible the ribald type of young man
of which the castle was now full, and he had no desire
to meet them at this hour in his present costume. He
left the front door and proceeded to make a circuit of
the castle walls; and his spirits sank even lower. In
the Middle Ages, during that stormy period of England's
history when walls were built six feet thick and a window was not so much a window as a handy place for
pouring molten lead on the heads of visitors, Blandings
had been an impregnable fortress. But in all its career
it can seldom have looked more of a fortress to any one
than it did now to the Efficient Baxter.

One of the disadvantages of being a man of action,
impervious to the softer emotions, is that in moments

of trial the beauties of Nature are powerless to soothe
the anguished heart. Had Baxter been of a dreamy and
poetic temperament he might now have been drawing
all sorts of balm from the loveliness of his surroundings.
The air was full of the scent of growing things; strange,
shy creatures came and went about him as he walked;
down in the woods a nightingale had begun to sing; and
there was something grandly majestic in the huge bulk
of the castle as it towered against the sky. But Baxter
had temporarily lost his sense of smell; he feared and
disliked the strange, shy creatures; the nightingale left
him cold; and the only thought the towering castle inspired in him was that it looked as if a fellow would
need half a ton of dynamite to get into it.

Baxter paused. He was back now near the spot from
which he had started, having completed two laps without finding any solution of his difficulties. The idea in
his mind had been to stand under somebody's window
and attract the sleeper's attention with soft, significant
whistles. But the first whistle he emitted had sounded
to him in the stillness of early morn so like a steam
siren that thereafter he had merely uttered timid, mouse-
like sounds which the breezes had carried away the moment they crept out. He proposed now to halt for a while
and rest his lips before making another attempt. He
proceeded to the terrace wall and sat down. The clock
over the stables struck three.

To the restless type of thinker like Rupert Baxter,
the act of sitting down is nearly always the signal for
the brain to begin working with even more than its
customary energy. The relaxed body seems to invite
thought. And Baxter, having suspended for the moment

his physical activities—and glad to do so, for his slippers hurt him—gave himself up to tense speculation as to the hiding-place of Lady Constance Keeble's necklace. From the spot where he now sat he was probably, he reflected, actually in a position to see that hiding-place—if only, when he saw it, he were able to recognise it for what it was. Somewhere out here—in yonder bushes or in some unsuspected hole in yonder tree—the jewels must have been placed. Or . . .

Something seemed to go off inside Baxter like a touched spring. One moment, he was sitting limply, keenly conscious of a blister on the sole of his left foot; the next, regardless of the blister, he was off the wall and racing madly along the terrace in a flurry of flying slippers. Inspiration had come to him.

Day dawns early in the summer months, and already a sort of unhealthy pallor had begun to manifest itself in the sky. It was still far from light, but objects hitherto hidden in the gloom had begun to take on uncertain shape. And among these there had come into the line of Baxter's vision a row of fifteen flower-pots.

There they stood, side by side, round and inviting, each with a geranium in its bed of mould. Fifteen flower-pots. There had originally been sixteen, but Baxter knew nothing of that. All he knew was that he was on the trail.

The quest for buried treasure is one which right through the ages has exercised an irresistible spell over humanity. Confronted with a spot where buried treasure may lurk, men do not stand upon the order of their digging; they go at it with both hands. No solicitude for his employer's geraniums came to hamper Rupert Baxter's researches. To grasp the first flower-pot and tilt out its contents was

with him the work of a moment. He scrabbled his fingers
through the little pile of mould . . .

Nothing.

A second geranium lay broken on the ground . . .

Nothing.

A third . . .

. . . .

The Efficient Baxter straightened himself painfully.
He was unused to stooping, and his back ached. But
physical discomfort was forgotten in the agony of hope
frustrated. As he stood there, wiping his forehead with an
earth-stained hand, fifteen geranium corpses gazed up at
him in the growing light, it seemed with reproach. But
Baxter felt no remorse. He included all geraniums, all
thieves, and most of the human race in one comprehensive
black hatred.

All that Rupert Baxter wanted in this world now was
bed. The clock over the stables had just struck four, and
he was aware of an overpowering fatigue. Somehow or
other, if he had to dig through the walls with his bare
hands, he must get into the house. He dragged himself
painfully from the scene of carnage and blinked up at the
row of silent windows above him. He was past whistling
now. He stooped for a pebble, and tossed it up at the
nearest window.

Nothing happened. Whoever was sleeping up there
continued to sleep. The sky had turned pink, birds were
twittering in the ivy, other birds had begun to sing in the
bushes. All Nature, in short, was waking—except the
unseen sluggard up in that room.

He threw another pebble . . .

It seemed to Rupert Baxter that he had been standing there throwing pebbles through a nightmare eternity. The whole universe had now become concentrated in his efforts to rouse that log-like sleeper; and for a brief instant fatigue left him, driven away by a sort of Berserk fury. And there floated into his mind, as if from some previous existence, a memory of somebody once standing near where he was standing now and throwing a flower-pot in at a window at some one. Who it was that had thrown the thing at whom, he could not at the moment recall; but the outstanding point on which his mind focused itself was the fact that the man had had the right idea. This was no time for pebbles. Pebbles were feeble and inadequate. With one voice the birds, the breezes, the grasshoppers, the whole chorus of Nature waking to another day seemed to shout at him, "Say it with flower-pots!"

§ 4

The ability to sleep soundly and deeply is the prerogative, as has been pointed out earlier in this straightforward narrative of the simple home-life of the English upper classes, of those who do not think quickly. The Earl of Emsworth, who had not thought quickly since the occasion in the summer of 1874 when he had heard his father's footsteps approaching the stable-loft in which he, a lad of fifteen, sat smoking his first cigar, was an excellent sleeper. He started early and finished late. It was his gentle boast that for more than twenty years he had never missed his full eight hours. Generally he managed to get something nearer ten.

But then, as a rule, people did not fling flower-pots through his window at four in the morning.

Even under this unusual handicap, however, he struggled bravely to preserve his record. The first of Baxter's missiles, falling on a settee, produced no change in his regular breathing. The second, which struck the carpet, caused him to stir. It was the third, colliding sharply with his humped back, that definitely woke him. He sat up in bed and stared at the thing.

In the first moment of his waking, relief was, oddly enough, his chief emotion. The blow had roused him from a disquieting dream in which he had been arguing with Angus McAllister about early spring bulbs, and McAllister, worsted verbally, had hit him in the ribs with a spud. Even in his dream Lord Emsworth had been perplexed as to what his next move ought to be; and when he found himself awake and in his bedroom he was at first merely thankful that the necessity for making a decision had at any rate been postponed. Angus McAllister might on some future occasion smite him with a spud, but he had not done it yet.

There followed a period of vague bewilderment. He looked at the flower-pot. It held no message for him. He had not put it there. He never took flower-pots to bed. Once, as a child, he had taken a dead pet rabbit, but never a flower-pot. The whole affair was completely inscrutable; and his lordship, unable to solve the mystery, was on the point of taking the statesmanlike course of going to sleep again, when something large and solid whizzed through the open window and crashed against the wall, where it broke, but not into such small fragments that he could not perceive that in its prime it, too, had been a flower-pot. And at this moment his eyes fell on the carpet and then on the settee; and the affair passed still farther into the realm of the inexplicable. The Hon. Freddie Threepwood, who had a poor singing-voice but was a game trier, had been annoying his father of late by crooning a ballad ending in the words:

> *"It is not raining rain at all:*
> *It's raining vi-o-lets."*

It seemed to Lord Emsworth now that matters had gone a step farther. It was raining flower-pots.

The customary attitude of the Earl of Emsworth towards all mundane affairs was one of vague detachment; but this phenomenon was so remarkable that he found himself stirred to quite a little flutter of excitement and interest. His brain still refused to cope with the problem of why anybody should be throwing flower-pots into his room at this hour—or, indeed, at any hour; but it seemed a good idea to go and ascertain who this peculiar person was.

He put on his glasses and hopped out of bed and trotted to the window. And it was while he was on his way there that memory stirred in him, as some minutes ago it had stirred in the Efficient Baxter. He recalled that odd episode of a few days back, when that delightful girl, Miss What's-her-name, had informed him that his secretary had been throwing flower-pots at that poet fellow, McTodd. He had been annoyed, he remembered, that Baxter should so far have forgotten himself. Now, he found himself more frightened than annoyed. Just as

every dog is permitted one bite without having its sanity
questioned, so, if you consider it in a broad-minded way,
may every man be allowed to throw one flower-pot. But
let the thing become a habit, and we look askance. This
strange hobby of his appeared to be growing on Baxter
like a drug, and Lord Emsworth did not like it at all. He
had never before suspected his secretary of an unbalanced
mind, but now he mused, as he tiptoed cautiously to the
window, that the Baxter sort of man, the energetic restless
type, was just the kind that does go off his head. Just
some such calamity as this, his lordship felt, he might have
foreseen. Day in, day out, Rupert Baxter had been exer-
cising his brain ever since he had come to the castle—and
now he had gone and sprained it. Lord Emsworth peeped
timidly out from behind a curtain.

His worst fears were realised. It was Baxter, sure
enough; and a towsled, wild-eyed Baxter incredibly clad in
lemon-coloured pyjamas.

. . . .

Lord Emsworth stepped back from the window. He
had seen sufficient. The pyjamas had in some curious way
set the coping-stone on his dismay, and he was now in a
condition approximating to panic. That Baxter should
be so irresistibly impelled by his strange mania as actually
to omit to attire himself decently before going out on one
of these flower-pot-hurling expeditions of his seemed to
make it all so sad and hopeless. The dreamy peer was no
poltroon, but he was past his first youth, and it came to
him very forcibly that the interviewing and pacifying of
secretaries who ran amok was young man's work. He
stole across the room and opened the door. It was his
purpose to put this matter into the hands of an agent.

And so it came about that Psmith was aroused some few minutes later from slumber by a touch on the arm and sat up to find his host's pale face peering at him in the weird light of early morning.

"My dear fellow," quavered Lord Emsworth.

Psmith, like Baxter, was a light sleeper; and it was only a moment before he was wide awake and exerting himself to do the courtesies.

"Good morning," he said pleasantly. "Will you take a seat?"

"I am extremely sorry to be obliged to wake you, my dear fellow," said his lordship, "but the fact of the matter is, my secretary, Baxter, has gone off his head."

"Much?" inquired Psmith, interested.

"He is out in the garden in his pyjamas, throwing flower-pots through my window."

"Flower-pots?"

"Flower-pots!"

"Oh, flower-pots!" said Psmith, frowning thoughtfully, as if he had expected it would be something else. "And what steps are you proposing to take? That is to say," he went on, "unless you wish him to continue throwing flower-pots."

"My dear fellow . . . !"

"Some people like it," explained Psmith. "But you do not? Quite so, quite so. I understand perfectly. We all have our likes and dislikes. Well, what would you suggest?"

"I was hoping that you might consent to go down—er—having possibly armed yourself with a good stout stick—and induce him to desist and return to bed."

"A sound suggestion in which I can see no flaw," said Psmith approvingly. "If you will make yourself at home in here—pardon me for issuing invitations to you in your own house—I will see what can be done. I have always found Comrade Baxter a reasonable man, ready to welcome suggestions from outside sources, and I have no doubt that we shall easily be able to reach some arrangement."

He got out of bed, and, having put on his slippers, and his monocle, paused before the mirror to brush his hair.

"For," he explained, "one must be natty when entering the presence of a Baxter."

He went to the closet and took from among a number of hats a neat Homburg. Then, having selected from a bowl of flowers on the mantelpiece a simple white rose, he pinned it in the coat of his pyjama-suit and announced himself ready.

§ 5

The sudden freshet of vicious energy which had spurred the Efficient Baxter on to his recent exhibition of marksmanship had not lasted. Lethargy was creeping back on him even as he stooped to pick up the flower-pot which had found its billet on Lord Emsworth's spine. And, as he stood there after hurling that final missile, he had realised that that was his last shot. If that produced no results, he was finished.

And, as far as he could gather, it had produced no results whatever. No head had popped inquiringly out of the window. No sound of anybody stirring had reached his ears. The place was as still as if he had been throwing marshmallows. A weary sigh escaped from Baxter's lips. And a moment later he was reclining on the ground with his head propped against the terrace wall, a beaten man.

His eyes closed. Sleep, which he had been denying to himself for so long, would be denied no more. When Psmith arrived, daintily swinging the Hon. Freddie Threepwood's niblick like a clouded cane, he had just begun to snore.

.   .   .   .

Psmith was a kindly soul. He did not like Rupert Baxter, but that was no reason why he should allow him to continue lying on turf wet with the morning dew, thus courting lumbago and sciatica. He prodded Baxter in the stomach with the niblick, and the secretary sat up, blinking. And with returning consciousness came a burning sense of grievance.

"Well, you've been long enough," he growled. Then, as he rubbed his red-rimmed eyes and was able to see more clearly, he perceived who it was that had come to his rescue. The spectacle of Psmith of all people beaming benignly down at him was an added offence. "Oh, it's you?" he said morosely.

"I in person," said Psmith genially. "Awake, beloved! Awake, for morning in the bowl of night has flung the stone that puts the stars to flight; and lo! the hunter of the East has caught the Sultan's turret in a noose of light. The Sultan himself," he added, "you will find behind yonder window, speculating idly on your motives for bunging flower-pots at him. Why, if I may venture the question, *did* you?"

Baxter was in no confiding mood. Without replying,

he rose to his feet and started to trudge wearily along the terrace to the front door. Psmith fell into step beside him.

"If I were you," said Psmith, "and I offer the suggestion in the most cordial spirit of goodwill, I would use every effort to prevent this passion for flinging flower-pots from growing upon me. I know you will say that you can take it or leave it alone; that just one more pot won't hurt you; but can you stop at one? Isn't it just that first insidious flower-pot that does all the mischief? Be a man, Comrade Baxter!" He laid his hand appealingly on the secretary's shoulder. "The next time the craving comes on you, fight it. Fight it! Are you, the heir of the ages, going to become a slave to a habit? Tush! You know and I know that there is better stuff in you than that. Use your will-power, man, use your will-power."

Whatever reply Baxter might have intended to make to this powerful harangue—and his attitude as he turned on his companion suggested that he had much to say— was checked by a voice from above.

"Baxter! My dear fellow!"

The Earl of Emsworth, having observed the secretary's awakening from the safe observation-post of Psmith's bedroom, and having noted that he seemed to be exhibiting no signs of violence, had decided to make his presence known. His panic had passed, and he wanted to go into first causes.

Baxter gazed wanly up at the window.

"I can explain everything, Lord Emsworth."

"What?" said his lordship, leaning farther out.

"I can explain everything," bellowed Baxter.

"It turns out after all," said Psmith pleasantly, "to be

very simple. He was practising for the Jerking the Geranium event at the next Olympic Games."

Lord Emsworth adjusted his glasses.

"Your face is dirty," he said, peering down at his dishevelled secretary. "Baxter, my dear fellow, your face is dirty."

"I was digging," replied Baxter sullenly.

"What?"

"Digging!"

"The terrier complex," explained Psmith. "What," he asked kindly, turning to his companion, "were you digging for? Forgive me if the question seems an impertinent one, but we are naturally curious."

Baxter hesitated.

"What were you digging for?" asked Lord Emsworth.

"You see," said Psmith. *"He* wants to know."

Not for the first time since they had become associated, a mad feeling of irritation at his employer's woolly persistence flared up in Rupert Baxter's bosom. The old ass was always pottering about asking questions. Fury and want of sleep combined to dull the secretary's normal prudence. Dimly he realised that he was imparting to Psmith, the scoundrel who he was convinced was the ringleader of last night's outrage, valuable information; but anything was better than to have to stand here shouting up at Lord Emsworth. He wanted to get it over and go to bed.

"I thought Lady Constance's necklace was in one of the flower-pots," he shrilled.

"What?"

The secretary's powers of endurance gave out. This

maddening inquisition, coming on top of the restless night he had had, was too much for him. With a low moan he made one agonised leap for the front door and passed through it to where beyond these voices there was peace.

Psmith, deprived thus abruptly of his stimulating society, remained for some moments standing near the front door, drinking in with grave approval the fresh scents of the summer morning. It was many years since he had been up and about as early as this, and he had forgotten how delightful the first beginnings of a July day can be. Unlike Baxter, on whose self-centred soul these things had been lost, he revelled in the soft breezes, the singing birds, the growing pinkness of the eastern sky. He awoke at length from his reverie to find that Lord Emsworth had toddled down and was tapping him on the arm.

"*What* did he say?" inquired his lordship. He was feeling like a man who has been cut off in the midst of an absorbing telephone conversation.

"Say?" said Psmith. "Oh, Comrade Baxter? Now, let me think. What *did* he say?"

"Something about something being in a flower-pot," prompted his lordship.

"Ah, yes. He said he thought that Lady Constance's necklace was in one of the flower-pots."

"What!"

Lord Emsworth, it should be mentioned, was not completely in touch with recent happenings in his home. His habit of going early to bed had caused him to miss the sensational events in the drawing-room: and, as he was a sound sleeper, the subsequent screams—or, as Stokes the footman would have said, shrieks—had not disturbed him.

He stared at Psmith, aghast. For a while the apparent placidity of Baxter had lulled his first suspicions, but now they returned with renewed force.

"Baxter thought my sister's necklace was in a flower-pot?" he gasped.

"So I understood him to say."

'But why should my sister keep her necklace in a flower-pot?"

"Ah, there you take me into deep waters."

"The man's mad," cried Lord Emsworth, his last doubts removed. "Stark, staring mad! I thought so before, and now I'm convinced of it."

His lordship was no novice in the symptoms of insanity. Several of his best friends were residing in those palatial establishments set in pleasant parks and surrounded by high walls with broken bottles on them, to which the wealthy and aristocratic are wont to retire when the strain of modern life becomes too great. And one of his uncles by marriage, who believed that he was a loaf of bread, had made his first public statement on the matter in the smoking-room of this very castle. What Lord Emsworth did not know about lunatics was not worth knowing.

"I must get rid of him," he said. And at the thought the fair morning seemed to Lord Emsworth to take on a sudden new beauty. Many a time had he toyed wistfully with the idea of dismissing his efficient but tyrannical secretary, but never before had that sickeningly competent young man given him any reasonable cause to act. Hitherto, moreover, he had feared his sister's wrath should he take the plunge. But now . . . Surely even Connie, pig-headed as she was, could not blame him for dispensing with the services of a secretary who thought he kept her necklaces in flower-pots, and went out into the garden in the early dawn to hurl them at his bedroom window.

His demeanour took on a sudden buoyancy. He hummed a gay air.

"Get rid of him," he murmured, rolling the blessed words round his tongue. He patted Psmith genially on the shoulder. "Well, my dear fellow," he said, "I suppose we had better be getting back to bed and seeing if we can't get a little sleep."

Psmith gave a little start. He had been somewhat deeply immersed in thought.

"Do not," he said courteously, "let me keep you from the hay if you wish to retire. To me——you know what we poets are——this lovely morning has brought inspiration. I think I will push off to my little nook in the woods, and write a poem about something."

He accompanied his host up the silent stairs, and they parted with mutual good will at their respective doors. Psmith, having cleared his brain with a hurried cold bath, began to dress.

As a rule, the donning of his clothes was a solemn ceremony over which he dwelt lovingly; but this morning he abandoned his customary leisurely habit. He climbed into his trousers with animation, and lingered but a moment over the tying of his tie. He was convinced that there was that before him which would pay for haste.

Nothing in this world is sadder than the frequency with which we suspect our fellows without just cause. In the happenings of the night before, Psmith had seen the hand of Edward Cootes. Edward Cootes, he considered, had been indulging in what—in another—he would certainly have described as funny business. Like Miss Simmons,

Psmith had quickly arrived at the conclusion that the necklace had been thrown out of the drawing-room window by one of those who made up the audience at his reading: and it was his firm belief that it had been picked up and hidden by Mr. Cootes. He had been trying to think ever since where that persevering man could have concealed it, and Baxter had provided the clue. But Psmith saw clearer than Baxter. The secretary, having disembowelled fifteen flower-pots and found nothing, had abandoned his theory. Psmith went further, and suspected the existence of a sixteenth. And he proposed as soon as he was dressed to sally downstairs in search of it.

He put on his shoes and left the room, buttoning his waistcoat as he went.

§ 6

The hands of the clock over the stables were pointing to half-past five when Eve Halliday, tiptoeing furtively, made another descent of the stairs. Her feelings as she went were very different from those which had caused her to jump at every sound when she had started on this same journey three hours earlier. Then, she had been a prowler in the darkness and, as such, a fitting object of suspicion: now, if she happened to run into anybody, she was merely a girl, who, unable to sleep, had risen early to take a stroll in the garden. It was a distinction that made all the difference.

Moreover, it covered the facts. She had not been able to sleep—except for an hour when she had dozed off in a chair by her window; and she certainly proposed to take a stroll in the garden. It was her intention to recover the necklace from the place where she had deposited it, and bury it somewhere where no one could possibly find it. There it could lie until she had a chance of meeting and talking to Mr. Keeble, and ascertaining what was the next step he wished taken.

Two reasons had led Eve, after making her panic dash back into the house after lurking in the bushes while Baxter patrolled the terrace, to leave her precious flower-pot on the sill of the window beside the front door. She had read in stories of sensation that for purposes of concealment the most open place is the best place: and, secondly, the nearer the front door she put the flower-pot, the less distance would she have to carry it when the time came for its removal. In the present excited condition of the household, with every guest an amateur detective, the spectacle of a girl tripping downstairs with a flower-pot in her arms would excite remark.

Eve felt exhilarated. She was not used to getting only one hour's sleep in the course of a night, but excitement and the reflection that she had played a difficult game and won it against odds bore her up so strongly that she was not conscious of fatigue: and so uplifted did she feel that as she reached the landing above the hall she abandoned her cautious mode of progress and ran down the remaining stairs. She had the sensation of being in the last few yards of a winning race.

.   .   .   .

The hall was quite light now. Every object in it was plainly visible. There was the huge dinner-gong: there was the long leather settee: there was the table which she had upset in the darkness. And there was the sill of the window by the front door. But the flower-pot which had been on it was gone.

CHAPTER XII

MORE ON THE FLOWER-POT THEME

IN any community in which a sensational crime has re cently been committed, the feelings of the individuals who go to make up that community must of necessity vary somewhat sharply according to the degree in which the personal fortunes of each are affected by the outrage. Vivid in their own way as may be the emotions of one who sees a fellow-citizen sandbagged in a quiet street, they differ in kind from those experienced by the victim himself. And so, though the theft of Lady Constance Keeble's diamond necklace had stirred Blandings Castle to its depths, it had not affected all those present in quite the same way. It left the house-party divided into two distinct schools of thought—the one finding in the occurrence material for gloom and despondency, the other deriving from it nothing but joyful excitement.

To this latter section belonged those free young spirits who had chafed at the prospect of being herded into the drawing-room on the eventful night to listen to Psmith's reading of *Songs of Squalor*. It made them tremble now to think of what they would have missed, had Lady Constance's vigilance relaxed sufficiently to enable them to execute the quiet sneak for the billiard-room of which even at the eleventh hour they had thought so wistfully. As far as the Reggies, Berties, Claudes, and Archies at that moment enjoying Lord Emsworth's hospitality were concerned the thing was top-hole, priceless, and indisputably what the doctor ordered.   They spent a great deal of their time going from one country-house to another, and as a rule found the routine a little monotonous.   A happening like that of the previous night gave a splendid zip to rural life.   And when they reflected that, right on top of this binge, there was coming the County Ball, it seemed to them that God was in His heaven and all right with the world.   They stuck cigarettes in long holders, and collected in groups, chattering like starlings.

The gloomy brigade, those with hearts bowed down, listened to their effervescent babbling with wan distaste. These last were a small body numerically, but very select. Lady Constance might have been described as their head and patroness.   Morning foun' her still in a state bordering on collapse.   After breakfast, however, which she took in her room, and which was sweetened by an interview with Mr. Joseph Keeble, her husband, she brightened considerably.   Mr. Keeble, thought Lady Constance, behaved magnificently.   She had always loved him dearly, but never so much as when, abstaining from the slightest reproach of her obstinacy in refusing to allow the jewels to be placed in the bank, he spaciously informed her that he would buy her another necklace, just as good and costing every penny as much as the old one.   It was at this point that Lady Constance almost seceded from the ranks of gloom.   She kissed Mr. Keeble gratefully, and attacked with something approaching animation the boiled egg at which she had been pecking when he came in.

But a few minutes later the average of despair was restored by the enrolment of Mr. Keeble in the ranks of the despondent.   He had gladsomely assumed overnight that one of his agents, either Eve or Freddie, had been responsible for the disappearance of the necklace. The fact that Freddie, interviewed by stealth in his room, gapingly disclaimed any share in the matter had not damped him. He had never expected results from Freddie. But when, after leaving Lady Constance, he encountered Eve and was given a short outline of history, beginning with her acquisition of the necklace, and ending—like a modern novel—on the sombre note of her finding the flower-pot gone, he too sat down and mourned as deeply as any one.

Passing with a brief mention over Freddie, whose morose bearing was the subject of considerable comment among the younger set; over Lord Emsworth, who woke at twelve o'clock disgusted to find that he had missed several hours among his beloved flower-beds; and over the Efficient Baxter, who was roused from sleep at twelve-fifteen by Thomas the footman knocking on his door in order to hand him a note from his employer enclosing a cheque, and dispensing with his services; we come to Miss Peavey.

At twenty minutes past eleven on this morning when so much was happening to so many people, Miss Peavey stood in the Yew Alley gazing belligerently at the stemless mushroom finial of a tree about half-way between the entrance and the point where the alley merged into the west wood. She appeared to be soliloquising. For, though words were proceeding from her with considerable rapidity, there seemed to be no one in sight to whom they were being addressed. Only an exceptionally keen observer would have noted a slight significant quivering among the tree's tightly-woven branches.

"You poor bone-headed fish," the poetess was saying with that strained tenseness which results from the churning up of a generous and emotional nature, "isn't there anything in this world you can do without tumbling over your feet and making a mess of it? All I ask of you is to stroll under a window and pick up a few jewels, and now you come and tell me . . ."

"But, Liz!" said the tree plaintively.

"I do all the difficult part of the job. All that there was left for you to handle was something a child of three could have done on its ear. And now . . ."

"But, Liz! I'm telling you I couldn't find the stuff. I was down there all right, but I couldn't find it."

"You couldn't find it!" Miss Peavey pawed restlessly at the soft turf with a shapely shoe. "You're the sort of dumb Isaac that couldn't find a bass-drum in a telephone-booth. You didn't *look*."

"I did look. Honest, I did."

"Well, the stuff was there. I threw it down the moment the lights went out."

"Somebody must have got there first, and swiped it."

"Who could have got there first? Everybody was up in the room where I was.

"Am I sure? Am I . . ." The poetess's voice trailed off. She was staring down the Yew Alley at a couple who had just entered. She hissed a warning in a sharp undertone. "Hsst! Cheese it, Ed. There's some one coming."

The two intruders who had caused Miss Peavey to suspend her remarks to her erring lieutenant were of opposite sexes—a tall girl with fair hair, and a taller young man irreproachably clad in white flannels who beamed down at his companion through a single eyeglass. Miss Peavey gazed at them searchingly as they approached. A sudden thought had come to her at the sight of them. Mistrusting Psmith as she had done ever since Mr. Cootes had unmasked him for the impostor that he was, the fact that they were so often together had led her to extend her suspicion to Eve. It might, of course, be nothing but a casual friendship, begun here at the castle; but Miss Peavey had always felt that Eve would bear watching. And now, seeing them together again this morning, it had suddenly come to her that she did not recall having observed Eve among the gathering in the drawing-room last night. True, there had been many people present, but Eve's appearance was striking, and she was sure that she would have noticed her, if she had been there. And, if she had not been there, why should she not have been on the terrace? Somebody had been on the terrace last night, that was certain. For all her censorious attitude in their recent conversation, Miss Peavey had not really in her heart believed that even a dumb-bell like Eddie Cootes would not have found the necklace if it had been lying under the window on his arrival.

"Oh, good morning, Mr. McTodd," she cooed. "I'm feeling *so* upset about this terrible affair. Aren't *you,* Miss Halliday?"

"Yes," said Eve, and she had never said a more truthful word.

Psmith, for his part, was in more debonair and cheerful mood even than was his wont. He had examined the position of affairs and found life good. He was particularly pleased with the fact that he had persuaded Eve to stroll with him this morning and inspect his cottage in the woods. Buoyant as was his temperament, he had been half afraid that last night's interview on the terrace might have had disastrous effects on their intimacy. He was now feeling full of kindliness and goodwill towards all mankind—even Miss Peavey; and he bestowed on the poetess a dazzling smile.

"We must always," he said, "endeavour to look on the bright side. It was a pity, no doubt, that my reading last night had to be stopped at a cost of about twenty thousand pounds to the Keeble coffers, but let us not forget that but for that timely interruption I should have gone on for about another hour. I am like that. My friends have frequently told me that when once I start talking it requires something in the nature of a cataclysm to stop me. But, of course, there are drawbacks to everything, and last night's rannygazoo perhaps shook your nervous system to some extent ?"

"I was dreadfully frightened," said Miss Peavey. She turned to Eve with a delicate shiver. "Weren't *you*, Miss Halliday ?"

"I wasn't there," said Eve absently.

"Miss Halliday," explained Psmith, "has had in the last few days some little experience of myself as orator, and with her usual good sense decided not to go out of her way to get more of me than was absolutely necessary. I was perhaps a trifle wounded at the moment, but on thinking it over came to the conclusion that she was perfectly justified in her attitude. I endeavour always in my conversation to instruct, elevate, and entertain, but there is no gainsaying the fact that a purist might consider enough of my chit-chat to be sufficient. Such, at any rate, was Miss Halliday's view, and I honour her for it. But here I am, rambling on again just when I can see that you wish to be alone. We will leave you, therefore, to muse. No doubt we have been interrupting a train of thought

which would have resulted but for my arrival in a rondel
or a ballade or some other poetic morceau. Come, Miss
Halliday. A weird and repellent female," he said to Eve,
as they drew out of hearing, "created for some purpose
which I cannot fathom. Everything in this world, I like
to think, is placed here for some useful end: but why the
authorities unleashed Miss Peavey on us is beyond me.
It is not too much to say that she gives me a pain in the
gizzard."

Miss Peavey, unaware of these harsh views, had watched
them out of sight, and now she turned excitedly to the
tree which sheltered her ally.

"Ed!"

"Hello?" replied the muffled voice of Mr. Cootes.

"Did you hear?"

"No."

"Oh, my heavens!" cried his overwrought partner.
"He's gone deaf now! That girl—you didn't hear what
she was saying? She said that she wasn't in the drawing-
room when those lights went out. Ed, she was down below
on the terrace, that's where she was, picking up the stuff.
And if it isn't hidden somewheres in that McTodd's shack
down there in the woods I'll eat my Sunday rubbers."

Eve, with Psmith prattling amiably at her side, pursued
her way through the wood. She was wondering why she
had come. She ought, she felt, to have been very cold
and distant to this young man after what had occurred
between them last night. But somehow it was difficult to
be cold and distant with Psmith. He cheered her stricken
soul. By the time they reached the little clearing and
came in sight of the squat, shed-like building with its
funny windows and stained door, her spirits, always mer-

curial, had risen to a point where she found herself almost able to forget her troubles.

"What a horrible-looking place!" she exclaimed. "Whatever did you want it for?"

"Purely as a nook," said Psmith, taking out his key. "You know how the man of sensibility and refinement needs a nook. In this rushing age it is imperative that the thinker shall have a place, however humble, where he can be alone."

"But you aren't a thinker."

"You wrong me. For the last few days I have been doing some extremely brisk thinking. And the strain has taken its toll. The fierce whirl of life at Blandings is wearing me away. There are dark circles under my eyes and I see floating spots." He opened the door. "Well, here we are. Will you pop in for a moment?"

Eve went in. The single sitting-room of the cottage certainly bore out the promise of the exterior. It contained a table with a red cloth, a chair, three stuffed birds in a glass case on the wall, and a small horsehair sofa. A depressing musty scent pervaded the place, as if a cheese had recently died there in painful circumstances. Eve gave a little shiver of distaste.

"I understand your silent criticism," said Psmith. "You are saying to yourself that plain living and high thinking is evidently the ideal of the gamekeepers on the Blandings estate. They are strong, rugged men who care little for the refinements of interior decoration. But shall we blame them? If I had to spend most of the day and night chivvying poachers and keeping an eye on the local rabbits, I imagine that in my off-hours practically anything with a roof would satisfy me. It was in the hope that you might be able to offer some hints and suggestions for small improvements here and there that I invited you to inspect my little place. There is no doubt that it wants doing up a bit, by a woman's gentle hand. Will you take a look round and give out a few ideas? The wall-paper is, I fear, a fixture, but in every other direction consider yourself untrammelled."

Eve looked about her.

"Well," she began dubiously, "I don't think . . ."

She stopped abruptly, tingling all over. A second glance had shown her something which her first careless inspection had overlooked. Half hidden by a ragged curtain, there stood on the window-sill a large flower-pot containing a geranium. And across the surface of the flower-pot was a broad splash of white paint.

"You were saying . . . ?" said Psmith courteously.

Eve did not reply. She hardly heard him. Her mind was in a confused whirl. A monstrous suspicion was forming itself in her brain.

"You are admiring the shrub?" said Psmith. "I found it lying about up at the castle this morning and pinched it. I thought it would add a touch of colour to the place."

Eve, looking at him keenly as his gaze shifted to the flower-pot, told herself that her suspicion had been absurd. Surely this blandness could not be a cloak for guilt.

"Where did you find it?"

"By one of the windows in the hall, more or less wasting its sweetness. I am bound to say I am a little disappointed in the thing. I had a sort of idea it would turn the old homestead into a floral bower, but it doesn't seem to."

"It's a beautiful geranium."

"There," said Psmith, "I cannot agree with you. It seems to me to have the glanders or something."

"It only wants watering."

"And unfortunately this cosy little place appears to possess no water supply. I take it that the late proprietor when in residence used to trudge to the back door of the castle and fetch what he needed in a bucket. If this moribund plant fancies that I am going to spend my time racing to and fro with refreshments, it is vastly mistaken. To-morrow it goes into the dustbin."

Eve shut her eyes. She was awed by a sense of having arrived at a supreme moment. She had the sensations of a gambler who risks all on a single throw.

"What a shame!" she said, and her voice, though she tried to control it, shook. "You had better give it to me. I'll take care of it. It's just what I want for my room."

"Pray take it," said Psmith. "It isn't mine, but pray take it. And very encouraging it is, let me add, that you should be accepting gifts from me in this hearty fashion; for it is well known that there is no surer sign of the dawning of the divine emotion—love," he explained, "than this willingness to receive presents from the hands of the adorer. I make progress, I make progress."

"You don't do anything of the kind," said Eve. Her eyes were sparkling and her heart sang within her. In the revulsion of feeling which had come to her on finding her suspicions unfounded she was aware of a warm friendliness towards this absurd young man.

"Pardon me," said Psmith firmly. "I am quoting an established authority—Auntie Belle of *Home Gossip*."

"I must be going," said Eve. She took the flower-pot and hugged it to her. "I've got work to do."

"Work, work, always work!" sighed Psmith. "The curse of the age. Well, I will escort you back to your cell."

"No, you won't," said Eve. "I mean, thank you for your polite offer, but I want to be alone."

"Alone?" Psmith looked at her, astonished. "When you have the chance of being with *me?* This is a strange attitude."

"Good-bye," said Eve. "Thank you for being so hospitable and lavish. I'll try to find some cushions and muslin and stuff to brighten up this place."

"Your presence does that adequately," said Psmith, accompanying her to the door. "By the way, returning to the subject we were discussing last night, I forgot to mention, when asking you to marry me, that I can do cardtricks."

"Really?"

"And also a passable imitation of a cat calling to her young. Has this no weight with you? Think! These things come in very handy in the long winter evenings."

"But I shan't be there when you are imitating cats in the long winter evenings."

"I think you are wrong. As I visualise my little home, I can see you there very clearly, sitting before the fire. Your maid has put you into something loose. The light of the flickering flames reflects itself in your lovely eyes. You are pleasantly tired after an afternoon's shopping, but not so tired as to be unable to select a card—*any* card —from the pack which I offer . . ."

"Good-bye," said Eve.

"If it must be so—good-bye. For the present. I shall see you anon?"

"I expect so."

"Good! I will count the minutes."

.   .   .   .

Eve walked rapidly away. As she snuggled the flower-pot under her arm she was feeling like a child about to open its Christmas stocking. Before she had gone far, a shout stopped her and she perceived Psmith galloping gracefully in her wake.

"Can you spare me a moment?" said Psmith.

"Certainly."

"I should have added that I can also recite 'Gunga-Din.' Will you think that over?"

"I will."

"Thank you," said Psmith. "Thank you. I have a feeling that it may just turn the scale."

He raised his hat ambassadorially and galloped away again.

.   .   .   .

Eve found herself unable to wait any longer. Psmith was out of sight now, and the wood was very still and empty. Birds twittered in the branches, and the sun made little pools of gold upon the ground. She cast a swift glance about her and crouched down in the shelter of a tree.

The birds stopped singing. The sun no longer shone. The wood had become cold and sinister. For Eve, with a heart of lead, was staring blankly at a little pile of mould at her feet; mould which she had sifted again and again in a frenzied, fruitless effort to find a necklace which was not there.

The empty flower-pot seemed to leer up at her in mockery.

CHAPTER XIII

§ 1

BLANDINGS CASTLE was astir from roof to hall.
Lights blazed, voices shouted, bells rang. All over
the huge building there prevailed a vast activity like that
of a barracks on the eve of the regiment's departure for
abroad. Dinner was over, and the Expeditionary Force
was making its final preparations before starting off in
many motor-cars for the County Ball at Shifley. In the
bedrooms on every floor, Reggies, doubtful at the last moment about their white ties, were feverishly arranging
new ones; Berties brushed their already glistening hair;
and Claudes shouted to Archies along the passages insulting inquiries as to whether they had been sneaking their
handkerchiefs. Valets skimmed like swallows up and
down corridors, maids fluttered in and out of rooms in aid
of Beauty in distress. The noise penetrated into every
nook and corner of the house. It vexed the Efficient Baxter, going through his papers in the library preparatory to
leaving Blandings on the morrow for ever. It disturbed
Lord Emsworth, who stoutly declining to go within ten
miles of the County Ball, had retired to his room with a
book on Herbaceous Borders. It troubled the peace of
Beach the butler, refreshing himself after his activities
around the dinner table with a glass of sound port in the
housekeeper's room. The only person in the place who
paid no attention to it was Eve Halliday.

Eve was too furious to pay attention to anything but her deleterious thoughts. As she walked on the terrace, to which she had fled in quest of solitude, her teeth were set and her blue eyes glowed belligerently. As Miss Peavey would have put it in one of her colloquial moods, she was mad clear through. For Eve was a girl of spirit, and there is nothing your girl of spirit so keenly resents as being made a fool of, whether it be by Fate or by a fellow human creature. Eve was in the uncomfortable position of having had this indignity put upon her by both. But, while as far as Fate was concerned she merely smouldered rebelliously, her animosity towards Psmith was vivid in the extreme.

A hot wave of humiliation made her writhe as she remembered the infantile guilelessness with which she had accepted the preposterous story he had told her in explanation of his presence at Blandings in another man's name. He had been playing with her all the time—fooling her—and, most unforgivable crime of all, he had dared to pretend that he was fond of her and—Eve's face burned again—to make her—almost—fond of him. How he must have laughed . . .

Well, she was not beaten yet. Her chin went up and she began to walk quicker. He was clever, but she would be cleverer. The game was not over . . .

"Hallo!"

A white waistcoat was gleaming at her side. Polished shoes shuffled on the turf. Light hair, brushed and brilliantined to the last possible pitch of perfection, shone in the light of the stars. The Hon. Freddie Threepwood was in her midst.

"Well, Freddie?" said Eve resignedly.

"I say," said Freddie in a voice in which self-pity fought with commiseration for her. "Beastly shame you aren't coming to the Lop."

"I don't mind."

"But I do, dash it! The thing won't be anything without you. A bally wash-out. And I've been trying out some new steps with the Victrola."

"Well, there will be plenty of other girls there for you to step on."

"I don't *want* other girls, dash them. I want you."

"That's very nice of you," said Eve. The first truculence of her manner had softened. She reminded herself, as she had so often been obliged to remind herself before, that Freddie meant well. "But it can't be helped. I'm only an employée here, not a guest. I'm not invited."

"I know," said Freddie. "And that's what makes it so dashed sickening. It's like that picture I saw once, 'A Modern Cinderella.' Only there the girl nipped off to the dance—disguised, you know—and had a most topping time. I wish life was a bit more like the movies."

"Well, it was enough like the movies last night when . . . Oh!"

Eve stopped. Her heart gave a sudden jump. Somehow the presence of Freddie was so inextricably associated in her mind with limp proposals of marriage that she had completely forgotten that there was another and a more dashing side to his nature, that side which Mr. Keeble had revealed to her at their meeting in Market Blandings on the previous afternoon. She looked at him with new eyes.

"Anything up?" said Freddie.

Eve took him excitedly by the sleeve and drew him

farther away from the house. Not that there was any
need to do so, for the bustle within continued unabated.

"Freddie," she whispered, "listen! I met Mr. Keeble
yesterday after I had left you, and he told me all about
how you and he had planned to steal Lady Constance's
necklace."

"Good Lord!" cried Freddie, and leaped like a
stranded fish.

"And I've got an idea," said Eve.

She had, and it was one which had only in this instant
come to her. Until now, though she had tilted her chin
bravely and assured herself that the game was not over
and that she was not yet beaten, a small discouraging
voice had whispered to her all the while that this was mere
bravado. What, the voice had asked, are you going to do?
And she had not been able to answer it. But now, with
Freddie as an ally, she could act.

Told you all about it?" Freddie was muttering pallidly. He had never had a very high opinion of his Uncle
Joseph's mentality, but he had supposed him capable of
keeping a thing like that to himself. He was, indeed,
thinking of Mr. Keeble almost the identical thoughts which
Mr. Keeble in the first moments of his interview with Eve
in Market Blandings had thought of him. And these reflections brought much the same qualms which they had
brought to the elder conspirator. Once these things got
talked about, mused Freddie agitatedly, you never knew
where they would stop. Before his mental eye there swam
a painful picture of his Aunt Constance, informed of the
plot, tackling him and demanding the return of her necklace. "Told you all about it?" he bleated, and, like Mr.
Keeble, mopped his brow.

"It's all right," said Eve impatiently. "It's quite all right. He asked me to steal the necklace, too."

"You?" said Freddie, gaping.

"Yes."

"My Gosh!" cried Freddie, electrified. "Then was it you who got the thing last night?"

"Yes, it was. But . . ."

For a moment Freddie had to wrestle with something that was almost a sordid envy. Then better feelings prevailed. He quivered with manly generosity. He gave Eve's hand a tender pat. It was too dark for her to see it, but he was registering renunciation.

"Little girl," he murmured, "there's no one I'd rather got that thousand quid than you. If I couldn't have it myself, I mean to say. Little girl . . ."

"Oh, be quiet!" cried Eve. "I wasn't doing it for any thousand pounds. I didn't want Mr. Keeble to give me money . . ."

"You didn't want him to give you money!" repeated Freddie wonderingly.

"I just wanted to help Phyllis. She's my friend."

"Pals, pardner, pals! Pals till hell freezes!" cried Freddie, deeply moved.

"What are you talking about?"

"Sorry. That was a sub-title from a thing called 'Prairie Nell,' you know. Just happened to cross my mind. It was in the second reel where the two fellows are . . ."

"Yes, yes; never mind."

"Thought I'd mention it."

"Tell me . . ."

"It seemed to fit in."

"Do *stop,* Freddie!"

"Right-ho!"

"Tell me," resumed Eve, "is Mr. McTodd going to the ball?"

"Eh? Why, yes, I suppose so."

"Then, listen. You know that little cottage your father has let him have?"

"Little cottage?"

"Yes. In the wood past the Yew Alley."

"Little cottage? I never heard of any little cottage."

"Well, he's got one," said Eve. "And as soon as everybody has gone to the ball you and I are going to burgle it."

"What!"

"Burgle it!"

"Burgle it?"

"Yes, *burgle* it!"

Freddie gulped.

"Look here, old thing," he said plaintively. "This is a bit beyond me. It doesn't seem to me to make sense."

Eve forced herself to be patient. After all, she reflected, perhaps she had been approaching the matter a little rapidly. The desire to beat Freddie violently over the head passed, and she began to speak slowly and, as far as she could manage it, in words of one syllable.

"I can make it quite clear if you will listen and not say a word till I've done. This man who calls himself McTodd is not Mr. McTodd at all. He is a thief who got into the place by saying that he was McTodd. He stole the jewels from me last night and hid them in his cottage."

"But, I say!"

"Don't interrupt. I know he has them there, so when he has gone to the ball and the coast is clear you and I will go and search till we find them."

"But, I say!"

Eve crushed down her impatience once more.

"Well?"

"Do you really think this cove has got the necklace?"

"I know he has."

"Well, then, it's jolly well the best thing that could possibly have happened, because I got him here to pinch it for Uncle Joseph."

"What!"

"Absolutely. You see, I began to have a doubt or two as to whether I was quite equal to the contract, so I roped in this bird by way of a gang."

"You got him here? You mean you sent for him and arranged that he should pass himself off as Mr. Mc-Todd?"

"Well, no, not exactly that. He was coming here as McTodd anyway, as far as I can gather. But I'd talked it over with him, you know, before that and asked him to pinch the necklace."

"Then you know him quite well? He is a friend of yours?"

"I wouldn't say that exactly. But he said he was a great pal of Phyllis and her husband."

"Did he tell you that?"

"Absolutely!"

"When?"

"In the train."

"I mean, was it before or after you had told him why you wanted the necklace stolen?"

"Eh? Let me think. After."

"You're sure?"

"Yes."

"Tell me exactly what happened," said Eve. "I can't understand it at all at present."

Freddie marshalled his thoughts.

"Well, let's see. Well, to start with, I told Uncle Joe I would pinch the necklace and slip it to him, and he said if I did he'd give me a thousand quid. As a matter of fact, he made it two thousand, and very decent of him, I thought it. Is that straight?"

"Yes."

"Then I sort of got cold feet. Began to wonder, don't you know, if I hadn't bitten off rather more than I could chew."

"Yes."

"And then I saw this advertisement in the paper."

"Advertisement? What advertisement?"

"There was an advertisement in the paper saying if anybody wanted anything done simply apply to this chap. So I wrote him a letter and went up and had a talk with him in the lobby of the Piccadilly Palace. Only, unfortunately, I'd promised the guv'nor I'd catch the twelve-fifty home, so I had to dash off in the middle. Must have thought me rather an ass, it's sometimes occurred to me since. I mean, practically all I said was, 'Will you pinch my aunt's necklace?' and then buzzed off to catch the train. Never thought I'd see the man again, but when I got into the five o'clock train—I missed the twelve-fifty—there he was, as large as life, and the guv'nor suddenly trickled in from another compartment and introduced him to me as McTodd the poet. Then the guv'nor legged it, and this

chap told me he wasn't really McTodd, only pretending
to be McTodd."

"Didn't that strike you as strange?"

"Yes, rather rummy."

"Did you ask him why he was doing such an extraordinary thing?"

"Oh, yes. But he wouldn't tell me. And then he asked
me why I wanted him to pinch Aunt Connie's necklace,
and it suddenly occurred to me that everything was working rather smoothly—I mean, him being on his way to the
castle like that. Right on the spot, don't you know. So
I told him all about Phyllis, and it was then that he said
that he had been a pal of hers and her husband's for years.
So we fixed it up that he was to get the necklace and hand
it over. I must say I was rather drawn to the chappie.
He said he didn't want any money for swiping the thing."

Eve laughed bitterly.

"Why should he, when he was going to get twenty thousand pounds' worth of diamonds and keep them? Oh,
Freddie, I should have thought that even you would have
seen through him. You go to this perfect stranger and tell
him that there is a valuable necklace waiting here to be
stolen, you find him on his way to steal it, and you trust
him implicitly just because he tells you he knows Phyllis
—whom he had never heard of in his life till you mentioned her. Freddie, really!"

The Hon. Freddie scratched his beautifully shaven chin.

"Well, when you put it like that," he said, "I must own
it does sound a bit off. But he seemed such a dashed
matey sort of bird. Cheery and all that. I liked the
feller."

"What nonsense!"

"Well, but you liked him, too. I mean to say, you were about with him a goodish lot."

"I hate him!" said Eve angrily. "I wish I had never seen him. And if I let him get away with that necklace and cheat poor little Phyllis out of her money, I'll— I'll . . ."

She raised a grimly determined chin to the stars. Freddie watched her admiringly.

"I say, you know, you are a wonderful girl," he said.

"He *shan't* get away with it, if I have to pull the place down."

"When you chuck your head up like that you remind me a bit of What's-her-name, the Famous Players star— you know, girl who was in 'Wed to a Satyr.' Only," added Freddie hurriedly, "she isn't half so pretty. I say, I was rather looking forward to that County Ball, but now this has happened I don't mind missing it a bit. I mean, it seems to draw us closer together somehow, if you follow me. I say, honestly, all kidding aside, don't you think that love might some day awaken in . . ."

"We shall want a lamp, of course," said Eve.

"Eh?"

"A lamp—to see with when we are in the cottage. Can you get one?"

Freddie reluctantly perceived that the moment for sentiment had not arrived.

"A lamp? Oh, yes, of course. Rather."

"Better get two," said Eve. "And meet me here about half an hour after everybody has gone to the ball."

§ 2

The tiny sitting-room of Psmith's haven of rest in the
woods had never reached a high standard of decorative-
ness even in its best days; but as Eve paused from her
labours and looked at it in the light of her lamp about an
hour after her conversation with Freddie on the terrace,
it presented a picture of desolation which would have
startled the plain-living game-keeper to whom it had once
been a home.   Even Freddie, though normally an un-
observant youth, seemed awed by the ruin he had helped
to create.

"Golly!" he observed.   "I say, we've rather mucked the
place up a bit!"

It was no over-statement.   Eve had come to the cottage
to search, and she had searched thoroughly.   The torn
carpet lay in an untidy heap against the wall.   The table
was overturned.   Boards had been wrenched from the
floor, bricks from the chimney-place.   The horsehair sofa
was in ribbons, and the one small cushion in the room lay
limply in a corner, its stuffing distributed north, south, east
and west.   There was soot everywhere—on the walls, on
the floor, on the fireplace, and on Freddie.   A brace of
dead bats, the further result of the latter's groping in a
chimney which had not been swept for seven months, re-
posed in the fender.   The sitting-room had never been
luxurious; it was now not even cosy.

Eve did not reply.   She was struggling with what she
was fair-minded enough to see was an entirely unjust
fever of irritation, with her courteous and obliging assistant as its object.   It was wrong, she knew, to feel like
th's.   That she should be furious at her failure to find the

jewels was excusable, but she had no possible right to be furious with Freddie. It was not his fault that soot had poured from the chimney in lieu of diamonds. If he had asked for a necklace and been given a dead bat, he was surely more to be pitied than censured. Yet Eve, eyeing his grimy face, would have given very much to have been able to scream loudly and throw something at him. The fact was, the Hon. Freddie belonged to that unfortunate type of humanity which automatically gets blamed for everything in moments of stress.

"Well, the bally thing isn't here," said Freddie. He spoke thickly, as a man will whose mouth is covered with soot.

"I know it isn't," said Eve. "But this isn't the only room in the house."

"Think he might have hidden the stuff upstairs?"

"Or downstairs."

Freddie shook his head, dislodging a portion of a third bat.

"Must be upstairs, if it's anywhere. Mean to say, there isn't any downstairs."

"There's the cellar," said Eve. "Take your lamp and go and have a look."

For the first time in the proceedings a spirit of dis-affection seemed to manifest itself in the bosom of her assistant. Up till this moment Freddie had taken his orders placidly and executed them with promptness and civility. Even when the first shower of soot had driven him choking from the fire-place, his manly spirit had not been crushed; he had merely uttered a startled, "Oh, I say!" and returned gallantly to the attack. But now he obviously hesitated.

"Go on," said Eve impatiently.

"Yes, but, I say, you know . . ."

"What's the matter?"

"I don't think the chap would be likely to hide a neck-lace in the cellar. I vote we give it a miss and try up-stairs."

"Don't be silly, Freddie. He may have hidden it any-where."

"Well, to be absolutely honest, I'd much rather not go into any bally cellar, if it's all the same to you."

"Whyever not?"

"Beetles. Always had a horror of beetles. Ever since I was a kid."

Eve bit her lip. She was feeling, as Miss Peavey had so often felt when associated in some delicate undertaking with Edward Cootes, that exasperating sense of man's inadequacy which comes to high-spirited girls at moments such as these. To achieve the end for which she had started out that night she would have waded waist-high through a sea of beetles. But, divining with that sixth sense which tells women when the male has been pushed just so far and can be pushed no farther, that Freddie, wax though he might be in her hands in any other circum-stances, was on this one point adamant, she made no further effort to bend him to her will.

"All right," she said. "I'll go down into the cellar. You go and look upstairs."

"No, I say. Sure you don't mind?"

Eve took up her lamp and left the craven.

.   .   .   .

For a girl of iron resolution and unswerving purpose,

Eve's inspection of the cellar was decidedly cursory. A distinct feeling of relief came over her as she stood at the top of the steps and saw by the light of the lamp how small and bare it was. For, impervious as she might be to the intimidation of beetles, her armour still contained a chink. She was terribly afraid of rats. And even when the rays of the lamp disclosed no scuttling horrors, she still lingered for a moment before descending. You never knew with rats. They pretended not to be there just to lure you on, and then came out and whizzed about your ankles. However, the memory of her scorn for Freddie's pusillanimity forced her on, and she went down.

The word "cellar" is an elastic one. It can be applied equally to the acres of bottle-fringed vaults which lie beneath a great pile like Blandings Castle and to a hole in the ground like the one in which she now found herself. This cellar was easily searched. She stamped on its stone flags with an ear strained to detect any note of hollowness, but none came. She moved the lamp so that it shone into every corner, but there was not even a crack in which a diamond necklace could have been concealed. Satisfied that the place contained nothing but a little coal-dust and a smell of damp decay, Eve passed thankfully out.

The law of elimination was doing its remorseless work. It had ruled out the cellar, the kitchen, and the living-room—that is to say, the whole of the lower of the two floors which made up the cottage. There now remained only the rooms upstairs. There were probably not more than two, and Freddie must already have searched one of these. The quest seemed to be nearing its end. As Eve made for the narrow staircase that led to the second floor, the lamp shook in her hand and cast weird shadows. Now that success was in sight, the strain was beginning to affect her nerves.

It was to nerves that in the first instant of hearing it she attributed what sounded like a soft cough in the sitting-room, a few feet from where she stood. Then a chill feeling of dismay gripped her. It could only, she thought, be Freddie, returned from his search; and if Freddie had returned from his search already, what could it mean except that those upstairs rooms, on which she had counted so confidently, had proved as empty as the others? Freddie was not one of your restrained, unemotional men. If he had found the necklace he would have been downstairs in two bounds, shouting. His silence was ominous. She opened the door and went quickly in.

"Freddie," she began, and broke off with a gasp.

It was not Freddie who had coughed. It was Psmith. He was seated on the remains of the horsehair sofa, toying with an automatic pistol and gravely surveying through his monocle the ruins of a home.

§ 3

"Good evening," said Psmith.

It was not for a philosopher like himself to display astonishment. He was, however, undeniably feeling it. When, a few minutes before, he had encountered Freddie in this same room, he had received a distinct shock; but a rough theory which would account for Freddie's presence in his home-from-home he had been able to work out He groped in vain for one which would explain Eve.

Mere surprise, however, was never enough to prevent Psmith talking. He began at once.

"It was nice of you," he said, rising courteously, "to look in. Won't you sit down? On the sofa, perhaps? Or would you prefer a brick?"

Eve was not yet equal to speech. She had been so firmly convinced that he was ten miles away at Shifley that his presence here in the sitting-room of the cottage had something of the breath-taking quality of a miracle. The explanation, if she could have known it, was simple. Two excellent reasons had kept Psmith from gracing the County Ball with his dignified support. In the first place, as Shifley was only four miles from the village where he had spent most of his life, he had regarded it as probable, if not certain, that he would have encountered there old friends to whom it would have been both tedious and embarrassing to explain why he had changed his name to McTodd. And secondly, though he had not actually anticipated a nocturnal raid on his little nook, he had thought it well to be on the premises that evening in case Mr. Edward Cootes should have been getting ideas into his head. As soon, therefore, as the castle had emptied itself and the wheels of the last car had passed away down the drive, he had pocketed Mr. Cootes' revolver and proceeded to the cottage.

Eve recovered her self-possession. She was not a girl given to collapse in moments of crisis. The first shock of amazement had passed; a humiliating feeling of extreme foolishness, which came directly after, had also passed; she was now grimly ready for battle.

"Where is Mr. Threepwood?" she asked.

"Upstairs. I have put him in storage for a while. Do not worry about Comrade Threepwood. He has lots to think about. He is under the impression that if he stirs out he will be instantly shot."

"Oh? Well, I want to put this lamp down. Will you please pick up that table?"

"By all means. But—I am a novice in these matters—ought I not first to say 'Hands up!' or something?"

"Will you please pick up that table?"

"A friend of mine—one Cootes—you must meet him some time—generally remarks 'Hey!' in a sharp, arresting voice on these occasions. Personally I consider the expression too abrupt. Still, he has had great experience . . ."

"Will you please pick up that table?"

"Most certainly. I take it, then, that you would prefer to dispense with the usual formalities. In that case, I will park this revolver on the mantelpiece while we chat. I have taken a curious dislike to the thing. It makes me feel like Dangerous Dan McGrew."

Eve put down the lamp, and there was silence for a moment. Psmith looked about him thoughtfully. He picked up one of the dead bats and covered it with his handkerchief.

"Somebody's mother," he murmured reverently.

Eve sat down on the sofa.

"Mr. . . ." She stopped. "I can't call you Mr. McTodd. Will you please tell me your name?"

"Ronald," said Psmith. "Ronald Eustace."

"I suppose you have a surname?" snapped Eve. "Or an alias?"

Psmith eyed her with a pained expression.

'I may be hyper-sensitive," he said, "but that last re-mark sounded to me like a dirty dig. You seem to imply that I am some sort of a criminal."

Eve laughed shortly.

"I'm sorry if I hurt your feelings. There's not much sense in pretending now, is there? What is your name?"

"Psmith. The p is silent."

"Well, Mr. Smith, I imagine you understand why I am here?"

"I took it for granted that you had come to fulfil your kindly promise of doing the place up a bit. Will you be wounded if I say frankly that I preferred it the way it was before? All this may be the last word in ultra-modern interior decoration, but I suppose I am old-fash-ioned. The whisper flies round Shropshire and adjoining counties, 'Psmith is hide-bound. He is not attuned to up-to-date methods.' Honestly, don't you think you have rather unduly stressed the bizarre note? This soot . . . these dead bats . . ."

"I have come to get that necklace."

"Ah! The necklace!"

"I'm going to get it, too."

Psmith shook his head gently.

"There," he said, "if you will pardon me, I take issue with you. There is nobody to whom I would rather give that necklace than you, but there are special circumstances connected with it which render such an action impossible. I fancy, Miss Halliday, that you have been misled by your young friend upstairs. No; let me speak," he said, raising a hand. "You know what a treat it is to me. The way I envisage the matter is thus. I still cannot un-derstand as completely as I could wish how you come to be mixed up in the affair, but it is plain that in some way or other Comrade Threepwood has enlisted your services, and I regret to be obliged to inform you that the motives animating him in this quest are not pure. To put it crisply, he is engaged in what Comrade Cootes, to whom I alluded just now, would call 'funny business.' "

"I . . ."

"Pardon me," said Psmith. "If you will be patient for a few minutes more, I shall have finished and shall then be delighted to lend an attentive ear to any remarks you may wish to make. As it occurs to me—indeed, you hinted as much yourself just now—that my own position in this little matter has an appearance which to the uninitiated might seem tolerably rummy, I had better explain how I come to be guarding a diamond necklace which does not belong to me. I rely on your womanly discretion to let the thing go no further."

"Will you please . . ."

"In one moment. The facts are as follows. Our mutual friend Mr. Keeble, Miss Halliday, has a step-daughter who is married to one Comrade Jackson who, if he had no other claim to fame, would go ringing down through history for this reason, that he and I were at school together and that he is my best friend. We two have sported on the green—ooh, a lot of times. Well, owing to one thing and another, the Jackson family is rather badly up against it at the present . . ."

Eve jumped up angrily.

"I don't believe a word of it," she cried. "What is the use of trying to fool me like this? You had never heard of Phyllis before Freddie spoke about her in the train . . ."

"Believe me . . ."

"I won't. Freddie got you down here to help him steal that necklace and give it to Mr. Keeble so that he could help Phyllis, and now you've got it and are trying to keep it for yourself."

Psmith started slightly. His monocle fell from its place.

"Is *everybody* in this little plot! Are you also one of Comrade Keeble's corps of assistants?"

"Mr. Keeble asked me to try to get the necklace for him."

Psmith replaced his monocle thoughtfully.

"This," he said, "opens up a new line of thought. Can it be that I have been wronging Comrade Threepwood all this time? I must confess that, when I found him here just now standing like Marius among the ruins of Carthage (the allusion is a classical one, and the fruit of an expensive education), I jumped—I may say, sprang— to the conclusion that he was endeavouring to double-cross both myself and the boss by getting hold of the necklace with a view to retaining it for his own benefit. It never occurred to me that he might be crediting me with the same sinful guile."

Eve ran to him and clutched his arm.

"Mr. Smith, is this really true? Are you really a friend of Phyllis?"

"She looks on me as a grandfather. Are *you* a friend of hers?"

"We were at school together."

"This," said Psmith cordially, "is one of the most gratifying moments of my life. It makes us all seem like one great big family."

"But I never heard Phyllis speak about you."

"Strange!" said Psmith. "Strange. Surely she was not ashamed of her humble friend?"

"Her what?"

"I must explain," said Psmith, "that until recently I was earning a difficult livelihood by slinging fish about in Billingsgate Market. It is possible that some snobbish strain in Comrade Jackson's bride, which I confess I had not suspected, kept her from admitting that she was accustomed to hob-nob with one in the fish business."

"Good gracious!" cried Eve.

"I beg your pardon?"

"Smith . . . Fish business . . . Why, it was you who called at Phyllis's house while I was there. Just before I came down here. I remember Phyllis saying how sorry she was that we had not met. She said you were just my sort of . . . I mean, she said she wanted me to meet you."

"This," said Psmith, "is becoming more and more gratifying every moment. It seems to me that you and I were made for each other. I am your best friend's best friend and we both have a taste for stealing other people's jewellery. I cannot see how you can very well resist the conclusion that we are twin-souls."

"Don't be silly."

"We shall get into that series of 'Husbands and Wives Who Work Together.' "

"Where is the necklace?"

Psmith sighed.

"The business note. Always the business note. Can't we keep all that till later?"

"No. We can't."

"Ah, well!"

Psmith crossed the room, and took down from the wall the case of stuffed birds.

"The one place," said Eve, with mortification, "where we didn't think of looking!"

Psmith opened the case and removed the centre bird, a depressed-looking fowl with glass eyes which stared with a haunting pathos. He felt in its interior and pulled ou' something that glittered and sparkled in the lamp-light.

"Oh?"

Eve ran her fingers almost lovingly through the jewels as they lay before her on the little table.

"Aren't they beautiful!"

"Distinctly. I think I may say that of all the jewels I have ever stolen . . ."

"HEY!"

Eve let the necklace fall with a cry. Psmith spun round. In the doorway stood Mr. Edward Cootes, pointing a pistol.

§ 4

"Hands up!" said Mr. Cootes with the uncouth curtness of one who has not had the advantages of a refined home and a nice upbringing. He advanced warily, preceded by the revolver. It was a dainty, miniature weapon, such as might have been the property of some gentle lady. Mr. Cootes had, in fact, borrowed it from Miss Peavey, who at this juncture entered the room in a black and silver dinner-dress surmounted by a Rose du Barri wrap, her spiritual face glowing softly in the subdued light.

" 'Attaboy, Ed," observed Miss Peavey crisply.

She swooped on the table and gathered up the necklace. Mr. Cootes, though probably gratified by the tribute, made no acknowledgment of it, but continued to direct an austere gaze at Eve and Psmith.

"No funny business," he advised.

"I would be the last person," said Psmith agreeably, "to advocate anything of the sort. This," he said to Eve, "is Comrade Cootes, of whom you have heard so much."

Eve was staring, bewildered, at the poetess, who, satisfied with the manner in which the preliminaries had been conducted, had begun looking about her with idle curiosity.

"Miss Peavey!" cried Eve. Of all the events of this eventful night the appearance of Lady Constance's emotional friend in the rôle of criminal was the most disconcerting. "Miss *Peavey!*"

"Hallo?" responded that lady agreeably.

"I . . . I . . ."

"What, I think, Miss Halliday is trying to say," cut in Psmith, "is that she is finding it a little difficult to adjust her mind to the present development. I, too, must confess myself somewhat at a loss. I knew, of course, that Comrade Cootes had—shall I say an acquisitive streak in him, but you I had always supposed to be one hundred per cent. soul—and snowy white at that."

"Yeah?" said Miss Peavey, but faintly interested.

"I imagined that you were a poetess."

"So I am a poetess," retorted Miss Peavey hotly. "Just you start in joshing my poems and see how quick I'll bean you with a brick. Well, Ed, no sense in sticking around here. Let's go."

"We'll have to tie these birds up," said Mr. Cootes.

"Otherwise we'll have them squealing before I can make a getaway."

"Ed," said Miss Peavey with the scorn which her colleague so often excited in her, "try to remember sometimes that that thing balanced on your collar is a head, not a hubbard squash. And be careful what you're doing with that gat! Waving it about like it was a bouquet or something. How are they going to squeal? They can't say a thing without telling every one they snitched the stuff first."

"That's right," admitted Mr. Cootes.

"Well, then, don't come butting in."

The silence into which this rebuke plunged Mr. Cootes gave Psmith the opportunity to resume speech. An opportunity of which he was glad, for, while he had nothing of definitely vital import to say, he was optimist enough to feel that his only hope of recovering the necklace was to keep the conversation going on the chance of something turning up. Affable though his manner was, he had never lost sight of the fact that one leap would take him across the space of floor separating him from Mr. Cootes. At present, that small but effective revolver precluded anything in the nature of leaps, however short, but if in the near future anything occurred to divert his adversary's vigilance even momentarily. . . . He pursued a policy of watchful waiting, and in the meantime started to talk again.

"If, before you go," he said, "you can spare us a moment of your valuable time, I should be glad of a few words. And, first, may I say that I cordially agree with your condemnation of Comrade Cootes's recent suggestion. The man is an ass."

"Say," cried Mr. Cootes, coming to life again, "that'll be about all from you. If there wasn't ladies present, I'd bust you one."

"Ed," said Miss Peavey with quiet authority, "shut your trap!"

Mr. Cootes subsided once more. Psmith gazed at him through his monocle, interested.

"Pardon me," he said, "but—if it is not a rude question—are you two married?"

"Eh?"

"You seemed to me to talk to him like a wife. Am I addressing Mrs. Cootes?"

"You will be if you stick around a while."

"A thousand congratulations to Comrade Cootes. Not quite so many to you, possibly, but fully that number of good wishes." He moved towards the poetess with extended hand. "I am thinking of getting married myself shortly."

"Keep those hands up," said Mr. Cootes.

"Surely," said Psmith reproachfully, "these conventions need not be observed among friends? You will find the only revolver I have ever possessed over there on the mantelpiece. Go and look at it."

"Yes, and have you jumping on my back the moment I took my eyes off you!"

"There is a suspicious vein in your nature, Comrade Cootes," sighed Psmith, "which I do not like to see. Fight against it." He turned to Miss Peavey once more. "To resume a pleasanter topic, you will let me know where to send the plated fish-slice, won't you?"

"Huh?" said the lady.

"I was hoping," proceeded Psmith, "if you do not think

it a liberty on the part of one who has known you but a short time, to be allowed to send you a small wedding-present in due season. And one of these days, perhaps, when I too am married, you and Comrade Cootes will come and visit us in our little home. You will receive a hearty, unaffected welcome. You must not be offended if, just before you say good-bye, we count the spoons."

One would scarcely have supposed Miss Peavey a sensitive woman, yet at this remark an ominous frown clouded her white forehead. Her careless amiability seemed to wane. She raked Psmith with a glittering eye.

"You're talking a dam' lot," she observed coldly.

"An old failing of mine," said Psmith apologetically, "and one concerning which there have been numerous complaints. I see now that I have been boring you, and I hope that you will allow me to express. . . ."

He broke off abruptly, not because he had reached the end of his remarks, but because at this moment there came from above their heads a sudden sharp cracking sound, and almost simultaneously a shower of plaster fell from the ceiling, followed by the startling appearance of a long, shapely leg, which remained waggling in space. And from somewhere out of sight there filtered down a sharp and agonised oath.

Time and neglect had done their work with the flooring of the room in which Psmith had bestowed the Hon. Freddie Threepwood, and, creeping cautiously about in the dark, he had had the misfortune to go through.

But, as so often happens in this life, the misfortune of one is the good fortune of another. Badly as the accident had shaken Freddie, from the point of view of Psmith it was almost ideal. The sudden appearance of a human leg through the ceiling at a moment of nervous tension is enough to unman the stoutest-hearted, and Edward Cootes made no attempt to conceal his perturbation. Leaping a clear six inches from the floor, he jerked up his head and quite unintentionally pulled the trigger of his revolver. A bullet ripped through the plaster.

The leg disappeared. Not for an instant since he had been shut in that upper room had Freddie Threepwood ceased to be mindful of Psmith's parting statement that he would be shot if he tried to escape, and Mr. Cootes' bullet seemed to him a dramatic fulfilment of that promise. Wrenching his leg with painful energy out of the abyss, he proceeded to execute a backward spring which took him to the far wall—at which point, as it was impossible to get any farther away from the centre of events, he was compelled to halt his retreat. Having rolled himself up into as small a ball as he could manage, he sat where he was, trying not to breathe. His momentary intention of explaining through the hole that the entire thing had been a regrettable accident, he prudently abandoned. Unintelligent though he had often proved himself in other crises of his life, he had the sagacity now to realise that the neighbourhood of the hole was unhealthy and should be avoided. So, preserving a complete and unbroken silence, he crouched there in the darkness, only asking to be left alone.

And it seemed, as the moments slipped by, that this modest wish was to be gratified. Noises and the sound of voices came up to him from the room below, but no more bullets. It would be paltering with the truth to say that this put him completely at his ease, but still it was something. Freddie's pulse began to return to the normal.

Mr. Cootes', on the other hand, was beating with a dangerous quickness. Swift and objectionable things had been happening to Edward Cootes in that lower room. His first impression was that the rift in the plaster above him had been instantly followed by the collapse of the entire ceiling, but this was a mistaken idea. All that had occurred was that Psmith, finding Mr. Cootes' eye and pistol functioning in another direction, had sprung forward, snatched up a chair, hit the unfortunate man over the head with it, relieved him of his pistol, leaped to the mantelpiece, removed the revolver which lay there, and now, holding both weapons in an attitude of menace, was regarding him censoriously through a gleaming eyeglass.

"No funny business, Comrade Cootes," said Psmith.

Mr. Cootes picked himself up painfully. His head was singing. He looked at the revolvers, blinked, opened his mouth and shut it again. He was oppressed with a sense of defeat. Nature had not built him for a man of violence. Peaceful manipulation of a pack of cards in the smoke-room of an Atlantic liner was a thing he understood and enjoyed: rough-and-tumble encounters were alien to him and distasteful. As far as Mr. Cootes was concerned, the war was over.

But Miss Peavey was a woman of spirit. Her hat was still in the ring. She clutched the necklace in a grasp of steel, and her fine eyes glared defiance.

"You think yourself smart, don't you?" she said.

Psmith eyed her commiseratingly. Her valorous attitude appealed to him. Nevertheless, business was business.

"I am afraid," he said regretfully, "that I must trouble you to hand over that necklace."

"Try and get it," said Miss Peavey.

Psmith looked hurt.

"I am a child in these matters," he said, "but I had always gathered that on these occasions the wishes of the man behind the gun were automatically respected."

"I'll call your bluff," said Miss Peavey firmly. "I'm going to walk straight out of here with this collection of ice right now, and I'll bet you won't have the nerve to start any shooting. Shoot a woman? Not you!"

Psmith nodded gravely.

"Your knowledge of psychology is absolutely correct. Your trust in my sense of chivalry rests on solid ground. But," he proceeded, cheering up, "I fancy that I see a way out of the difficulty. An idea has been vouchsafed to me. I shall shoot—not you, but Comrade Cootes. This will dispose of all unpleasantness. If you attempt to edge out through that door I shall immediately proceed to plug Comrade Cootes in the leg. At least, I shall try. I am a poor shot and may hit him in some more vital spot, but at least he will have the consolation of knowing that I did my best and meant well."

"Hey!" cried Mr. Cootes. And never, in a life liberally embellished with this favourite ejaculation of his, had he uttered it more feelingly. He shot a feverish glance at Miss Peavey; an' reading in her face indecision rather than that instant acquiescence which he had hoped to see, cast off his customary attitude of respectful humility and asserted himself. He was no cave-man, but this was one occasion when he meant to have his own way. With an agonised bound he reached Miss Peavey's side, wrenched the necklace from her grasp and flung it into the enemy's camp. Eve stooped and picked it up.

"I thank you," said Psmith with a brief bow in her direction.

Miss Peavey breathed heavily. Her strong hands clenched and unclenched. Between her parted lips her teeth showed in a thin white line. Suddenly she swallowed quickly, as if draining a glass of unpalatable medicine.

"Well," she said in a low, even voice, "that seems to be about all. Guess we'll be going. Come along, Ed, pick up the Henries."

"Coming, Liz," replied Mr. Cootes humbly.

They passed together into the night.

§ 5

Silence followed their departure. Eve, weak with the reaction from the complex emotions which she had undergone since her arrival at the cottage, sat on the battered sofa, her chin resting in her hands. She looked at Psmith, who, humming a light air, was delicately piling with the toe of his shoe a funeral mound over the second of the dead bats.

"So that's that!" she said.

Psmith looked up with a bright and friendly smile.

"You have a very happy gift of phrase," he said. "That, as you sensibly say, is that."

Eve was silent for awhile. Psmith completed the obsequies and stepped back with the air of a man who has done what he can for a fallen friend.

"Fancy Miss Peavey being a thief!" said Eve. She was somehow feeling a disinclination to allow the conversation to die down, and yet she had an idea that, unless

it was permitted to die down, it might become embarrass
ingly intimate. Subconsciously, she was endeavouring to
analyse her views on this long, calm person who had so
recently added himself to the list of those who claimed to
look upon her with affection.

"I confess it came as something of a shock to me also,"
said Psmith. "In fact, the revelation that there was this
other, deeper side to her nature materially altered the
opinion I had formed of her. I found myself warming to
Miss Peavey. Something that was akin to respect began to
stir within me. Indeed, I almost wish that we had not
been compelled to deprive her of the jewels."

" 'We'?" said Eve. "I'm afraid I didn't do much."

"Your attitude was exactly right," Psmith assured her.
"You afforded just the moral support which a man needs
in such a crisis."

Silence fell once more. Eve returned to her thoughts.
And then, with a suddenness which surprised her, she
found that she had made up her mind

"So you're going to be married?" she said.

Psmith polished his monocle thoughtfully.

"I think so," he said. "I think so. What do *you*
think?"

Eve regarded him steadfastly. Then she gave a little
laugh.

"Yes," she said, "I think so, too." She paused. "Shall
I tell you something?"

"You could tell me nothing more wonderful than that."

"When I met Cynthia in Market Blandings, she told
me what the trouble was which made her husband leave
her. What do you suppose it was?"

"From my brief acquaintance with Comrade McTodd,

I would hazard the guess that he tried to stab her with the bread-knife. He struck me as a murderous-looking specimen."

"They had some people to dinner, and there was chicken, and Cynthia gave all the giblets to the guests, and her husband bounded out of his seat with a wild cry, and, shouting 'You *know* I love those things better than anything in the world!' rushed from the house, never to return!"

"Precisely how I would have wished him to rush, had I been Mrs. McTodd."

"Cynthia told me that he had rushed from the house, never to return, six times since they were married."

"May I mention—in passing—" said Psmith, "that I do not like chicken giblets?"

"Cynthia advised me," proceeded Eve, "if ever I married, to marry some one eccentric. She said it was such fun . . . Well, I don't suppose I am ever likely to meet any one more eccentric than you, am I?"

"I think you would be unwise to wait on the chance."

"The only thing is . . .," said Eve reflectively. " 'Mrs. Smith' . . . It doesn't *sound* much, does it?"

Psmith beamed encouragingly.

"We must look into the future," he said. "We must remember that I am only at the beginning of what I am convinced is to be a singularly illustrious career. 'Lady Psmith' is better . . . 'Baroness Psmith' better still . . . And—who knows?—'The Duchess of Psmith' . . ."

"Well, anyhow," said Eve, "you were wonderful just now, simply wonderful. The way you made one spring . . ."

"Your words," said Psmith, "are music to my ears, but

we must not forget that the foundations of the success of the manœuvre were laid by Comrade Threepwood. Had it not been for the timely incursion of his leg . . ."

"Good gracious!" cried Eve. "Freddie! I had forgotten all about him!"

"The right spirit," said Psmith. "Quite the right spirit."

"We must go and let him out."

"Just as you say. And then he can come with us on the stroll I was about to propose that we should take through the woods. It is a lovely night, and what could be jollier than to have Comrade Threepwood prattling at our side? I will go and let him out at once."

"No, don't bother," said Eve.

CHAPTER XIV

THE golden stillness of a perfect summer morning brooded over Blandings Castle and its adjacent pleasure-grounds. From a sky of unbroken blue the sun poured down its heartening rays on all those roses, pinks, pansies, carnations, hollyhocks, columbines, larkspurs, London pride and Canterbury bells which made the gardens so rarely beautiful. Flannelled youths and maidens in white serge sported in the shade; gay cries arose from the tennis-courts behind the shrubbery; and birds, bees, and butterflies went about their business with a new energy and zip. In short, the casual observer, assuming that he was addicted to trite phrases, would have said that happiness reigned supreme.

But happiness, even on the finest mornings, is seldom universal. The strolling youths and maidens were happy; the tennis-players were happy; the birds, bees, and butterflies were happy. Eve, walking in pleasant meditation on the terrace, was happy. Freddie Threepwood was happy as he lounged in the smoking-room and gloated over the information, received from Psmith in the small hours, that his thousand pounds was safe. Mr. Keeble, writing to Phyllis to inform her that she might clinch the purchase of the Lincolnshire farm, was happy. Even Head-gardener Angus McAllister was as happy as a Scotsman can ever be. But Lord Emsworth, drooping out of the library window, felt only a nervous irritation more in keeping with the blizzards of winter than with the only fine July that England had known in the last ten years.

We have seen his lordship in a similar attitude and a like frame of mind on a previous occasion; but then his melancholy had been due to the loss of his glasses. This morning these were perched firmly on his nose and he saw all things clearly. What was causing his gloom now was that fact that some ten minutes earlier his sister Constance had trapped him in the library, full of jarring rebuke on the subject of the dismissal of Rupert Baxter, the world's most efficient secretary. It was to avoid her compelling eye that Lord Emsworth had turned to the window. And what he saw from that window thrust him even deeper into the abyss of gloom. The sun, the birds, the bees, the butterflies, and the flowers called to him to come out and have the time of his life, but he just lacked the nerve to make a dash for it.

"I think you must be mad," said Lady Constance bitterly, resuming her remarks and starting at the point where she had begun before.

"Baxter's mad," retorted his lordship, also re-treading old ground.

"You are too absurd!"

"He threw flower-pots at me."

"Do please stop talking about those flower-pots. Mr. Baxter has explained the whole thing to me, and surely even you can see that his behaviour was perfectly excusable."

"I don't like the fellow," cried Lord Emsworth, once more retreating to his last line of trenches—the one line from which all Lady Constance's eloquence had been unable to dislodge him.

There was a silence, as there had been a short while before when the discussion had reached this same point.

"You will be helpless without him," said Lady Constance.

"Nothing of the kind," said his lordship.

"You know you will. Where will you ever get another secretary capable of looking after everything like Mr. Baxter? You know you are a perfect child, and unless you have some one whom you can trust to manage your affairs I cannot see what will happen."

Lord Emsworth made no reply. He merely gazed wanly from the window.

"Chaos," moaned Lady Constance.

His lordship remained mute, but now there was a gleam of something approaching pleasure in his pale eyes; for at this moment a car rounded the corner of the house from the direction of the stables and stood purring at the door. There was a trunk on the car and a suit-case. And almost simultaneously the Efficient Baxter entered the library, clothed and spatted for travel.

"I have come to say good-bye, Lady Constance," said Baxter coldly and precisely, flashing at his late employer through his spectacles a look of stern reproach. "The car which is taking me to the station is at the door."

"Oh, Mr. Baxter." Lady Constance, strong woman though she was, fluttered with distress. "Oh, Mr. Baxter."

"Good-bye." He gripped her hand in brief farewell and directed his spectacles for another tense instant upon the sagging figure at the window. "Good-bye, Lord Emsworth."

"Eh? What? Oh! Ah, yes. Good-bye, my dear

fel——, I mean, good-bye. I—er—hope you will have a pleasant journey."

"Thank you," said Baxter.

"But, Mr. Baxter," said Lady Constance.

"Lord Emsworth," said the ex-secretary icily, "I am no longer in your employment . . ."

"But, Mr. Baxter," moaned Lady Constance, "surely . . . even now . . . misunderstanding . . . talk it all over quietly . . ."

Lord Emsworth started violently.

"Here!" he protested, in much the same manner as that in which the recent Mr. Cootes had been wont to say "Hey!"

"I fear it is too late," said Baxter, to his infinite relief, "to talk things over. My arrangements are already made and cannot be altered. Ever since I came here to work for Lord Emsworth, my former employer—an American millionaire named Jevons—has been making me flattering offers to return to him. Until now a mistaken sense of loyalty has kept me from accepting these offers, but this morning I telegraphed to Mr. Jevons to say that I was at liberty and could join him at once. It is too late now to cancel this promise."

"Quite, quite, oh, certainly, quite, mustn't dream of it, my dear fellow. No, no, no, indeed no," said Lord Emsworth with an effervescent cordiality which struck both his hearers as in the most dubious taste.

Baxter merely stiffened haughtily, but Lady Constance was so poignantly affected by the words and the joyous tone in which they were uttered that she could endure her brother's loathly society no longer. Shaking Baxter's hand once more and gazing stonily for a moment at the worm by the window, she left the room.

For some seconds after she had gone, there was silence —a silence which Lord Emsworth found embarrassing. He turned to the window again and took in with one wistful glance the roses, the pinks, the pansies, the carnations, the hollyhocks, the columbines, the larkspurs, the London pride and the Canterbury bells. And then suddenly there came to him the realisation that with Lady Constance gone there no longer existed any reason why he should stay cooped up in this stuffy library on the finest morning that had ever been sent to gladden the heart of man. He shivered ecstatically from the top of his bald head to the soles of his roomy shoes, and, bounding gleefully from the window, started to amble across the room.

"Lord Emsworth!"

His lordship halted. His was a one-track mind, capable of accommodating only one thought at a time—if that, and he had almost forgotten that Baxter was still there. He eyed his late secretary peevishly.

"Yes, yes? Is there anything . . .?"

"I should like to speak to you for a moment."

"I have a most important conference with Mc-Allister . . ."

"I will not detain you long. Lord Emsworth, I am no longer in your employment, but I think it my duty to say before I go . . ."

"No, no, my dear fellow, I quite understand. Quite, quite, quite. Constance has been going over all that. I know what you are trying to say. That matter of the flower-pots. Please do not apologise. It is quite all right.

I was startled at the time, I own, but no doubt you had excellent motives. Let us forget the whole affair."

Baxter ground an impatient heel into the carpet.

"I had no intention of referring to the matter to which you allude," he said. "I merely wished . . ."

"Yes, yes, of course." A vagrant breeze floated in at the window, languid with summer scents, and Lord Emsworth, sniffing, shuffled restlessly. "Of course, of course, of course. Some other time, eh? Yes, yes, that will be capital. Capital, capital, cap——"

The Efficient Baxter uttered a sound that was partly a cry, partly a snort. Its quality was so arresting that Lord Emsworth paused, his fingers on the door-handle, and peered back at him, startled.

"Very well," said Baxter shortly. "Pray do not let me keep you. If you are not interested in the fact that Blandings Castle is sheltering a criminal . . ."

It was not easy to divert Lord Emsworth when in quest of Angus McAllister, but this remark succeeded in doing so. He let go of the door-handle and came back a step or two into the room. "Sheltering a criminal?"

"Yes." Baxter glanced at his watch. "I must go now or I shall miss my train," he said curtly. "I was merely going to tell you that this fellow who calls himself Ralston McTodd is not Ralston McTodd at all."

"Not Ralston McTodd?" repeated his lordship blankly. "But——" He suddenly perceived a flaw in the argument. "But he *said* he was," he pointed out cleverly. "Yes, I remember distinctly. He said he was McTodd."

"He is an impostor. And I imagine that if you investigate you will find that it is he and his accomplices who stole Lady Constance's necklace."

"But, my dear fellow . . ."

Baxter walked briskly to the door.

"You need not take my word for it," he said. "What I say can easily be proved. Get this so-called McTodd to write his name on a piece of paper and then compare it with the signature to the letter which the real McTodd wrote when accepting Lady Constance's invitation to the castle. You will find it filed away in the drawer of that desk there."

Lord Emsworth adjusted his glasses and stared at the desk as if he expected it to do a conjuring-trick.

"I will leave you to take what steps you please," said Baxter. "Now that I am no longer in your employment, the thing does not concern me one way or another. But I thought you might be glad to hear the facts."

"Oh, I *am!*" responded his lordship, still peering vaguely. "Oh, I *am!* Oh, yes, yes, yes. Oh, yes, yes . . ."

"Good-bye."

"But, Baxter . . ."

Lord Emsworth trotted out on to the landing, but Baxter had got off to a good start and was almost out of sight round the bend of the stairs.

"But, my dear fellow . . ." bleated his lordship plaintively over the banisters.

From below, out on the drive, came the sound of an automobile getting into gear and moving off, than which no sound is more final. The great door of the castle closed with a soft but significant bang—as doors close when handled by an untipped butler. Lord Emsworth returned to the library to wrestle with his problem unaided.

He was greatly disturbed. Apart from the fact that

he disliked criminals and impostors as a class, it was a shock to him to learn that the particular criminal and impostor then in residence at Blandings was the man for whom, brief as had been the duration of their acquaintance, he had conceived a warm affection. He was fond of Psmith. Psmith soothed him. If he had had to choose any member of his immediate circle for the rôle of criminal and impostor, he would have chosen Psmith last.

He went to the window again and looked out. There was the sunshine, there were the birds, there were the hollyhocks, carnations, and Canterbury bells, all present and correct; but now they failed to cheer him. He was wondering dismally what on earth he was going to do. What *did* one do with criminals and impostors? Had 'em arrested, he supposed. But he shrank from the thought of arresting Psmith. It seemed so deuced unfriendly.

He was still meditating gloomily when a voice spoke behind him.

"Good morning. I am looking for Miss Halliday. You have not seen her by any chance? Ah, there she is down there on the terrace."

Lord Emsworth was aware of Psmith beside him at the window, waving cordially to Eve, who waved back.

"I thought possibly," continued Psmith, "that Miss Halliday would be in her little room yonder"—he indicated the dummy book-shelves through which he had entered. "But I am glad to see that the morning is so fine that she has given toil the miss-in-baulk. It is the right spirit," said Psmith. "I like to see it."

Lord Emsworth peered at him nervously through his glasses. His embarrassment and his distaste for the task that lay before him increased as he scanned his companion in vain for those signs of villainy which all well-regulated criminals and impostors ought to exhibit to the eye of discernment.

"I am surprised to find you indoors," said Psmith, "on so glorious a morning. I should have supposed that you would have been down there among the shrubs, taking a good sniff at a hollyhock or something."

Lord Emsworth braced himself for the ordeal.

"Er, my dear fellow . . . that is to say . . ." He paused. Psmith was regarding him almost lovingly through his monocle, and it was becoming increasingly difficult to warm up to the work of denouncing him.

"You were observing . . . ?" said Psmith.

Lord Emsworth uttered curious buzzing noises.

"I have just parted from Baxter," he said at length, deciding to approach the subject in more roundabout fashion.

"Indeed?" said Psmith courteously.

"Yes. Baxter has gone."

"For ever?"

"Er—yes."

"Splendid!" said Psmith. "Splendid, splendid."

Lord Emsworth removed his glasses, twiddled them on their cord, and replaced them on his nose.

"He made . . . He—er—the fact is, he made . . . Before he went Baxter made a most remarkable statement . . . a charge . . . Well, in short, he made a very strange statement about you."

Psmith nodded gravely.

"I had been expecting something of the kind," he said. "He said, no doubt, that I was not really Ralston Mc Todd?"

His lordship's mouth opened feebly.

"Er—yes," he said.

"I've been meaning to tell you about that," said Psmith amiably. "It is quite true. I am not Ralston McTodd."

"You—you admit it!"

"I am proud of it."

Lord Emsworth drew himself up. He endeavoured to assume the attitude of stern censure which came so naturally to him in interviews with his son Frederick. But he met Psmith's eye and sagged again. Beneath the solemn friendliness of Psmith's gaze hauteur was impossible.

"Then what the deuce are you doing here under his name?" he asked, placing his finger in statesmanlike fashion on the very nub of the problem. "I mean to say," he went on, making his meaning clearer, "if you aren't McTodd, why did you come here saying you were McTodd?"

Psmith nodded slowly.

"The point is well taken," he said. "I was expecting you to ask that question. Primarily—I want no thanks, but primarily I did it to save you embarrassment."

"Save me embarrassment?"

"Precisely. When I came into the smoking-room of our mutual club that afternoon when you had been entertaining Comrade McTodd at lunch, I found him on the point of passing out of your life for ever. It seems that he had taken umbrage to some slight extent because you had buzzed off to chat with the florist across the way instead of remaining with him. And, after we had exchanged a pleasant word or two, he legged it, leaving you short one modern poet. On your return I stepped into the breach to save you from the inconvenience of having to return here without a McTodd of any description. No one, of course, could have been more alive than myself to the fact that I was merely a poor substitute, a sort of synthetic McTodd, but still I considered that I was better than nothing, so I came along."

His lordship digested this explanation in silence. Then he seized on a significant point.

"Are you a member of the Senior Conservative Club?"

"Most certainly."

"Why, then, dash it," cried his lordship, paying to that august stronghold of respectability as striking a tribute as it had ever received, "if you're a member of the Senior Conservative, you can't be a criminal. Baxter's an ass!"

"Exactly."

"Baxter would have it that you had stolen my sister's necklace."

"I can assure you that I have not got Lady Constance's necklace."

"Of course not, of course not, my dear fellow. I'm only telling you what that idiot Baxter said. Thank goodness I've got rid of the fellow." A cloud passed over his now sunny face. "Though, confound it, Connie was right about one thing." He relapsed into a somewhat moody silence.

"Yes?" said Psmith.

"Eh?" said his lordship.

"You were saying that Lady Constance had been right about one thing."

"Oh, yes. She was saying that I should have a hard time finding another secretary as capable as Baxter."

Psmith permitted himself to bestow an encouraging pat on his host's shoulder.

"You have touched on a matter," he said, "which I had intended to broach to you at some convenient moment when you were at leisure. If you would care to accept my services, they are at your disposal."

"Eh?"

"The fact is," said Psmith, "I am shortly about to be married, and it is more or less imperative that I connect with some job which will ensure a moderate competence. Why should I not become your secretary?"

"You want to be my secretary?"

"You have unravelled my meaning exactly."

"But I've never had a married secretary."

"I think that you would find a steady married man an improvement on these wild, flower-pot-throwing bachelors. If it would help to influence your decision, I may say that my bride-to-be is Miss Halliday, probably the finest library-cataloguist in the United Kingdom."

"Eh? Miss Halliday? That girl down there?"

"No other," said Psmith, waving fondly at Eve as she passed underneath the window. "In fact, the same."

"But I like her," said Lord Emsworth, as if stating an insuperable objection.

"Excellent."

"She's a nice girl."

"I quite agree with you."

"Do you think you could really look after things here like Baxter?"

"I am convinced of it."

"Then, my dear fellow—well, really I must say . . . I must say . . . well, I mean, why shouldn't you?"

"Precisely," said Psmith. "You have put in a nutshell the very thing I have been trying to express."

"But have you had any experience as a secretary?"

"I must admit that I have not. You see, until recently I was more or less one of the idle rich. I toiled not, neither did I—except once, after a bump-supper at Cambridge—spin. My name, perhaps I ought to reveal to you, is Psmith—the p is silent—and until very recently I lived in affluence not far from the village of Much Middlefold in this county. My name is probably unfamiliar to you, but you may have heard of the house which was for many years the Psmith head-quarters—Corfby Hall."

Lord Emsworth jerked his glasses off his nose.

"Corfby Hall! Are you the son of the Smith who used to own Corfby Hall? Why, bless my soul, I knew your father well."

"Really?"

"Yes. That is to say, I never met him."

"No?"

"But I won the first prize for roses at the Shrewsbury Flower Show the year he won the prize for tulips."

"It seems to draw us very close together," said Psmith.

"Why, my dear boy," cried Lord Emsworth jubilantly. "if you are really looking for a position of some kind and would care to be my secretary, nothing could suit me better. Nothing, nothing, nothing. Why, bless my soul . . ."

"I am extremely obliged," said Psmith. "And I shall endeavour to give satisfaction. And surely, if a mere Baxter could hold down the job, it should be well within the scope of a Shropshire Psmith. I think so, I think so. . . . And now, if you will excuse me, I think I will go down and tell the glad news to the little woman, if I may so describe her."

    .   .   .   .

Psmith made his way down the broad staircase at an even better pace than that recently achieved by the departing Baxter, for he rightly considered each moment of this excellent day wasted that was not spent in the company of Eve. He crooned blithely to himself as he passed through the hall, only pausing when, as he passed the door of the smoking-room, the Hon. Freddie Threepwood suddenly emerged.

"Oh, I say!" said Freddie. "Just the fellow I wanted to see. I was going off to look for you."

Freddie's tone was cordiality itself. As far as Freddie was concerned, all that had passed between them in the cottage in the west wood last night was forgiven and forgotten.

"Say on, Comrade Threepwood," replied Psmith; "and, if I may offer the suggestion, make it snappy, for I would be elsewhere. I have man's work before me."

"Come over here." Freddie drew him into a far corner of the hall and lowered his voice to a whisper. "I say, it's all right, you know."

"Excellent!" said Psmith. "Splendid! This is great news. What is all right?"

"I've just seen Uncle Joe. He's going to cough up the money he promised me."

"I congratulate you."

"So now I shall be able to get into that bookie's business and make a pile. And, I say, you remember my telling you about Miss Halliday?"

"What was that?"

"Why, that I loved her, I mean, and all that."

"Ah, yes."

"Well, look here, between ourselves," said Freddie earnestly, "the whole trouble all along has been that she thought I hadn't any money to get married on. She didn't actually say so in so many words, but you know how it is with women—you can read between the lines, if you know what I mean. So now everything's going to be all right. I shall simply go to her and say, 'Well, what about it?' and—well, and so on, don't you know?"

Psmith considered the point gravely.

"I see your reasoning, Comrade Threepwood," he said. "I can detect but one flaw in it."

"Flaw? What flaw?"

"The fact that Miss Halliday is going to marry *me*."

The Hon. Freddie's jaw dropped. His prominent eyes became more prawn-like.

"What!"

Psmith patted his shoulder commiseratingly.

"Be a man, Comrade Threepwood, and bite the bullet. These things will happen to the best of us. Some day you will be thankful that this has occurred. Purged in the holocaust of a mighty love, you will wander out into the sunset, a finer, broader man. . . . And now I must reluctantly tear myself away. I have an important appointment." He patted his shoulder once more. "If you would care to be a page at the wedding, Comrade Threepwood, I can honestly say that there is no one whom I would rather have in that capacity."

And with a stately gesture of farewell, Psmith passed out on to the terrace to join Eve.

THE END